RELUCTANT CONFEDERATES

Fred W. Morrison Series in Southern Studies

Reluctant Confederates

UPPER SOUTH UNIONISTS IN THE SECESSION CRISIS

DANIEL W. CROFTS

The University of North Carolina Press
Chapel Hill and London

The paper in this book meets the guidelines for permanence and durability of the Committee on Production Guidelines for Book Longevity of the Council on Library Resources.

02 01 00 99 98 7 6 5 4 3

Library of Congress Cataloging-in-Publication Data

Crofts, Daniel W.

Reluctant Confederates: upper South unionists in the secession crisis / by Daniel W. Crofts.

p. cm.—(Fred W. Morrison series in Southern studies)

Bibliography: p.

Includes index.

ISBN 0-8078-1809-7 (cloth: alk. paper) — ISBN 0-8078-4430-6 (pbk.: alk. paper)

1. Secession. 2. United States—Politics and government—Civil War, 1861–1865. I. Title. II. Series.

E459.C92 1989 88-6927
973.7—dc19 CIP

Portions of this work appeared earlier in somewhat different form and are reproduced here with permission of the publisher, as follows:

"A Reluctant Unionist: John A. Gilmer and Lincoln's Cabinet," *Civil War History* 24 (Sept. 1978): 225–49. By permission of Kent State University Press.

"James E. Harvey and the Secession Crisis," *Pennsylvania Magazine of History and Biography* 103 (Apr. 1979): 177–95. By permission of the *Pennsylvania Magazine of History and Biography*.

"Secession Winter: William Henry Seward and the Decision for War," *New York History* 45 (July 1984): 229–56. By permission of the New York State Historical Association.

"The Union Party of 1861 and the Secession Crisis," *Perspectives in American History* 11 (1977–78): 327–76. By permission of *Perspectives in American History*.

For John T. Crofts and

Mary-Blanche Crofts

CONTENTS

TABLES

FIGURES

MAPS

ILLUSTRATIONS

PREFACE

THIS book sets into context a central but often overlooked aspect of the immediate pre–Civil War period: Abraham Lincoln's election as president did not unite the South in support of secession. Instead, events during the winter of 1860–61 split the South more deeply than ever before.[1] Seven deep South states from South Carolina west to Texas left the Union and began to establish an independent government, the Confederate States of America. But in eight of the fifteen slave states, including four that ultimately fought on the southern side, popular majorities emphatically opposed secession. Only when forced in April to choose sides in a war between North and South did Virginia, North Carolina, Tennessee, and Arkansas align with the Confederacy.

The focus of this book is on the three populous and pivotal states of Virginia, North Carolina, and Tennessee. These states contained almost half the white population of the area that became the Confederacy and an even larger share of the resources the South needed to fight a war. Their production of food and livestock, and especially their industrial output, dwarfed that of the original seceding states. Had the Confederacy not ultimately included these three states, its claim to independence would have been far less impressive, as would its ability to make good on that claim.

Our understanding of secession draws primarily on the experience of the lower South or cotton states, which abruptly left the Union after Lincoln's election. From such a perspective, the decision to wage the war for southern independence appears inevitable and even reasonable.[2] It cuts against the grain of much modern scholarship to emphasize that southerners disagreed on so fundamental a matter as secession.

And yet they did. Consider, for example, what a puzzled Alabamian wrote to a North Carolina friend in January 1861: "Our people are calmly and fully determined never to submit to Lincoln's administration, or to any Compromise with the Northern States," William M. Clark observed. "The people themselves in their primary meetings required from the candidates a solemn promise that they would agree to *no* compromise whatever. Their instructions are to separate immediately, form a Southern confederacy as soon as possible, and if the border states don't come in, to legislate against their slave interest so as to force them in, or place them as it were between two fires. . . . Never have I seen people more calmly determined. The old and young, rich and poor seem willing to die in defense of their principles."[3]

Clark then posed the critical question: "Can you explain to me why there should be such a different state of feeling in your state from what I have above described. Is it not strange, when the border states suffer so much more from Northern fanaticism, from actual loss in their property, and these same states equally interested in slavery, that a feeling of antagonism to the North, should be so much stronger [in the Gulf States]. I cannot understand it. It cannot be that we have more excitable and demagogue politicians to lead the people, because I know the people in this state have been far ahead of the politicians."

Upper South Unionists considered the behavior of the lower South similarly incomprehensible. Former Tennessee Governor William B. Campbell thought the cotton states had no legitimate complaints about the federal government. He tried to persuade an Alabama cousin that secession was "unwise and impolitic," liable to speed "the ruin and overthrow of negro slavery" and to jeopardize "the freedom and liberty of the white man." Like many upper South Unionists, Campbell condemned irresponsible politicians for stampeding people in the deep South and creating "estrangement" between the upper and lower South. He warned that Tennessee and Kentucky would never be "dragged into a rebellion that their whole population utterly disapproved."[4]

To anticipate themes that will be developed below, especially in Chapters 6 and 7, this study concludes that one must take into account both slaveholding and previous patterns of party allegiance to understand why the upper and lower South took such different stances during the months after Lincoln's election. High-slaveowning areas across the South generally displayed more support for secession, and slaveowning was more concentrated in the lower than the upper South. Deep South secessionists also benefited from virtually unchallenged statewide Democratic majorities. The party's radical Southern Rights wing planted seeds of poisonous suspicion that suddenly sprouted in late 1860, creating popular attitudes such as those described by William M. Clark. Closer two-party competition in the upper South, however, gave Whiggish opponents of secession a substantial nucleus from which to build. Antisecessionists there, using a new "Union party" label, could thus overwhelm the initial secessionist challenge.

THREE waves of change, each successively larger than the other, washed over and fundamentally reshaped political contours in Virginia, North Carolina, and Tennessee during the brief six-month interval between November 1860 and April 1861. Promoters of secession tried to spur the upper South to follow the example of the lower South. At first it appeared they might succeed. Those favoring secession were active, ardent, and outspoken after Lincoln's election. They had a program to confront northern menace and insult. And, not least among their assets, they had leverage in the Democratic party, which maintained a modest majority in all three states. Many Democrats, especially the officeholding elite, either supported secession overtly or allowed disunionists to lead. For perhaps two months, secession strength grew, creating a wave that surged formidably as it crested in late December and early January. In parts of "lower Virginia" and the Democratic plantation counties of North Carolina, the initial secessionist wave looked irresistible.

But in the upper South—unlike the lower South—the first wave did not dislodge any state from the Union. Instead, the push for secession created an explicitly antisecession countermobilization. Upper South Unionists organized, campaigned, and deeply stirred popular feeling, especially in nonplantation areas. They generated a second wave, greater than the first, that appeared to sweep away the popular underpinnings of secession in February 1861. Voters in all three states decisively rejected southern independence. To be sure, Unionists usually attached conditions to their allegiance, pledging to resist federal "coercion" of the seceding states. They nevertheless expected that secessionists would reconsider their rash action, thereby allowing peaceful restoration of the Union.

The Unionist coalition in the upper South was composed primarily of Whigs, often simply called "Opposition" by the late 1850s, after the collapse of their national party. The survival of competitive Opposition parties in the upper South, in contrast to the experience of the lower South during the 1850s, provided institutional barriers against secession. In nonplantation areas of the upper South, substantial increments of Union Democrats and previous nonvoters also voted against secession. Many other Democrats, uneasy about secession and about alliance with Whiggish Unionists, did not vote at all, thereby further depressing prosecession vote totals.

The action of the upper South stunned secessionists, as one famous example will illustrate. Edmund Ruffin, the elderly prophet of southern nationalism, fled from his native Virginia to South Carolina in early March 1861. He arrived just before Lincoln's inauguration, to avoid living "even for an hour" in a country with a Republican president. Ruffin had reason to feel frustrated as he traveled south. Lincoln's election had not united the South, as Ruffin had hoped. On

February 4, 1861, the very day that representatives from the seven seceding states met in Montgomery, Alabama, to organize the Confederate States of America, Ruffin's home state delivered a crippling blow against upper South secession. Strongly affirming their hopes for peaceful restoration of the Union, Virginia voters rejected most prosecession candidates for the state convention. More than two out of three of those voting also specified that any convention action be made subject to popular referendum, a provision secessionists bitterly opposed. Just before leaving Virginia, Ruffin visited the convention, by then in session in Richmond. "The majority of this Convention is more basely submissive than I had supposed possible," he fumed.[5]

The ability of Unionists to prevent the upper South from seceding gave legitimacy to the efforts of conciliatory Republicans, headed by the incoming secretary of state, William H. Seward. He tried to persuade President Lincoln that a noncoercive "hands-off" policy toward the seceded states would maintain the dominance of Unionists in the upper South and lead eventually to peaceful restoration of the Union. During March and early April, upper South Unionists believed Lincoln had agreed to the conciliatory plan.

Lincoln's proclamation calling for seventy-five thousand troops on April 15, in effect asking the upper South to fight the lower South, stirred the third and greatest wave. It immediately engulfed upper South Unionism. The three states studied here seceded in a frenzy of patriotic enthusiasm. Only in northwestern Virginia and East Tennessee did an unconditionally Unionist leadership and electorate resist the majority current. Elsewhere, original secessionists rolled out the red carpet for new converts. Believing they had been betrayed by the Lincoln administration, countless thousands who had earlier rejected secession embraced the cause of southern independence. Original and converted secessionists joined hands to defend southern honor and constitutional principles against what they perceived as corrupt, tyrannical oppression. They believed themselves fighting for the same cause as the patriots of 1776. So it was that Edmund Ruffin could return in triumph to Richmond on April 23. By then, a common resolve to resist "northern domination" had undermined Virginia's earlier Unionism, and the "submissive" convention had voted for secession. "There has been a complete and wonderful change here since I left," Ruffin exulted.[6]

This book concentrates on the second wave and the interval during which people did not know the third and biggest wave would strike. Of course we know the third was coming. Our hindsight thereby distorts our ability to comprehend the past. The Unionists were perceptive but not omniscient. Though anxious, they hoped the storm had passed. It had not. The third wave proved so overwhelming that it all but obliterated the new patterns left by the second. The significance of the second, indeed its very existence, has therefore often been overlooked. The task of this book is to correct that oversight.

SOME of the material covered in the following pages may appear familiar. The roles of Lincoln, Seward, and the Republican party in the secession crisis have received close scholarly scrutiny.[7] And there are able monographs about the secession crisis in all three states covered here. Indeed, books by Henry T. Shanks, Joseph Carlyle Sitterson, and Mary Emily Robertson Campbell will remain the most thorough accounts of developments within Virginia, North Carolina, and Tennessee, respectively, during the secession crisis.[8]

Never before, however, has anyone attempted to combine an analysis of the upper South in late 1860 and early 1861 with an analysis of the Republican party's response to upper South Unionism. Such an approach reveals major aspects of the secession crisis that have heretofore been neglected or misinterpreted. Indeed, secession created a triangular struggle between the North, the deep South, and the upper South. This study of the upper South provides a fresh angle of vision from which to view the entire crisis. By so doing, one may learn more not only about the upper South, but also about the North and the deep South, and about the basis for their mutual estrangement.

Those who consider North and South utterly distinct and antagonistic by the late antebellum period will find in this book an unmistakable challenge. The evidence presented here shows that many northerners and southerners believed that sectional differences were negotiable and looked forward to peaceful perpetuation of the Union. Upper South Unionists, the particular focus of this study, often embraced northern values. They expected the upper South's economy to develop increasing resemblance to the North's rather than to the deep South's. To be sure, the outbreak of war in April galvanized irreconcilable nationalisms North and South, inducing a defiant sense of southern separateness. But until that fateful juncture, the upper South spurned secession. Moderates both North and South outnumbered the antagonistic minorities in each section who fed on each other, gradually eroding the center. An undoubted majority of Americans preferred that the center hold and expected it to do so. Widespread surprise and astonishment thus greeted its sudden collapse in mid-April 1861.

Throughout this study, the term "Unionists" will be used to designate those who opposed secession in Virginia, North Carolina, and Tennessee in January and February 1861. The introductory section to Chapter 5 will differentiate between several varieties of Unionists, but the general label is nevertheless useful and appropriate. The great question confronting the upper South in early 1861 was whether to follow the lower South in seceding. Those opposed became, perforce, "Unionists." (Secessionist preferred to call their opponents "submissionists.") Allegiances formed during January and February persisted, with few exceptions, until mid-April. Unionists generally remained Unionists until confronted by Lincoln's proclamation. We may therefore identify and study "upper South Unionists in the secession crisis."

The upper South included eight states, but in this study the term will typically be used to designate Virginia, North Carolina, and Tennessee. Why have I not given equal coverage to all eight states? As already suggested, my concern has been to understand the pivotal states of the upper South that eventually seceded. Their location, manpower, and resources determined that the Confederacy would have a fighting chance. I can well imagine a book like my own focused on Maryland, Kentucky, and Missouri, the principal nonseceding slave states. That topic too should prove well suited for comparative study.[9]

Despite my own focus on the seceding states of the upper South, I have made substantial use of Union sources from several nonseceding states, primarily Maryland and Kentucky. Maryland Congressman Henry Winter Davis and Kentucky Senator John J. Crittenden played key roles in formulating Unionist strategy. Their public pronouncements and private papers, along with newspapers such as the *Louisville Journal* and the *Baltimore American*, will be cited freely whenever they can strengthen the narrative.

If the entire upper South lay beyond the scope of this study, it may yet be asked why I have not included Arkansas, the only other state besides Virginia, North Carolina, and Tennessee to secede after the events of mid-April. To that question, I offer several answers. Arkansas was a remote frontier region, with such a different and basically noncompetitive party system as to discourage comparison with the states on which my energy has been invested. Its relatively small population and trans-Mississippi location likewise made it a far smaller prize in the struggle for allegiances following Lincoln's election. So I have not done justice to Arkansas. Nicely timed to compensate for my willful oversight is the first book-length study of secession in Arkansas, by James M. Woods.[10] He finds that secession triggered an unprecedented polarization between high-slaveowning and low-slaveowning regions in Arkansas, just as in the states east of the Mississippi studied here. Even though Arkansas lacked a tradition of close two-party competition, it included sufficient nonslaveowning yeoman migrants from Tennessee and other parts of the upper South to give upcountry antisecessionists a narrow advantage—until the calamitous events of mid-April.

At a few points I have made use of deep South sources. Upper South Unionism was so much more robust and assertive than its feeble lower South counterpart that the two should not generally be considered together. But an occasional comment in early winter by Georgia's Alexander H. Stephens, for example, helped me to explain a viewpoint that he then shared with upper South Unionists.

IT is appropriate here to preview briefly the structure of the book. The Prologue and the first three chapters set the stage by introducing principal characters, by analyzing political institutions in the late antebellum upper South, and by examining the response of sectional moderates there to the deepening crisis of the late 1850s and 1860.

Starting with Chapter 4, which capsules the growth of secession sentiment in the upper South during the two months following Lincoln's election, the narrative focuses on events between November 1860 and April 1861. Chapters 5 through 9 explore in detail the response of upper South Unionists to the secession crisis during the months before Lincoln took office. After a consideration in Chapter 5 of Unionist thought, Chapter 6 recounts the principal Unionist achievement—blocking secession in the upper South in early 1861. Chapter 7 shows that popular opposition to secession triggered the greatest realignment of political loyalties in a generation, creating new "Union parties" across the upper South. (The Appendixes provide an explanation of statistical techniques used in Chapter 7 and an assessment of how other historians have applied such techniques to study secession.) Chapter 8 considers developments on the national stage, as Unionists worked in Congress and the so-called Peace Conference to secure a compromise on the vexing symbolic issue of slavery in the territories. The response of the Republican party to southern Unionism—at once enthusiastic and suspicious, and for the most part disinclined to offer the concessions Unionists wanted—is traced in Chapter 9.

The remainder of the book examines the critical first six weeks of Lincoln's presidency. Chapter 10 shows why Unionists believed during March and early April that the new president would seek reunion through a "hands-off" policy, thereby allowing them to consolidate power in the upper South. Chapter 11 explains why Lincoln decided instead that war offered the only hope for restoring the Union. Chapters 12 and 13 dissect the extraordinary final phase of the crisis. Lincoln's proclamation calling for seventy-five thousand troops, which forced the upper South to choose sides in a war, undermined the Unionist coalition and provoked the indignant secession of Virginia, North Carolina, and Tennessee. The Epilogue examines the wreckage of southern Unionism and muses about possible alternative outcomes. A bibliographical essay, of interest to those planning further reading or research on these topics, may be found at the end of the book.

Reluctant Confederates originated in early 1974 with a chance purchase of David M. Potter's *Lincoln and His Party in the Secession Crisis*, a young southerner's masterful effort to unravel perhaps the most complex snarl in American political history. By depicting Lincoln and Seward as responsible moderates who sought peace, Potter rejected the historical apologetics of his home region. What piqued the curiosity of the young northerner reading *Lincoln and His Party* was Potter's evidence that Seward had enlisted southern allies in the ill-fated search for peace. Who were these men? Why did some southerners stand aloof from the runaway fear and resentment that gripped their region in 1860–61, even going so far as to collaborate secretly with the Black Republican enemy? Here, surely, lay an intriguing tale.

In the spring of 1974, when first beginning to resurrect the lost world of southern Unionism, I experienced a deepening sense of personal involvement with the topic. Day after day, I retreated to a quiet upstairs room of the Sterling Library at Yale, reading old books in some of which the pages had never been cut. That summer, I initiated the first of many research expeditions to find unpublished sources. I found myself fascinated by the concatenation of powerful themes suggested by the history of southern Unionism. Here were men who correctly recognized that secession would boomerang—that it meant war and that war would destroy the very society secession was risked to protect. Yet even though the Unionists had a perceptive understanding of the sectional crisis, and even though they tried manfully to act on that understanding, they failed utterly. They suffered instead the excruciating fate of having been able to glimpse the future yet having been unable to make constructive use of their clairvoyance.

As I made the acquaintance of leading Unionists such as George W. Summers, John B. Baldwin, John A. Gilmer, and Robert Hatton, I inevitably began to look at the sectional crisis through their eyes. That conferred certain advantages because they saw things that too many other Americans had not seen, but it also deprived me for a time of the critical distance a historian must have. Confident that the Union could be restored without war, the Unionists reacted with bewildered outrage when Lincoln decided to pursue a very different policy. I needed to understand why the Unionists felt as they did, but I also needed to educate myself more fully about the entire situation. That has taken time. At long last, I am ready to tell the story of the Unionists, to evaluate their perceptions of the sectional crisis, and to explain what they considered inexplicable—Lincoln's refusal to follow their plan for peaceful restoration of the Union.

ACKNOWLEDGMENTS

DURING this book's incubation, I have accumulated many debts. Even if the practitioner of the historical craft ultimately struggles alone, he or she draws essential support from fellow strugglers and other interested parties.

I know that I would never have begun this work had it not been for encouragement from my mentors, Stephen G. Kurtz, then of Wabash College, and C. Vann Woodward, of Yale University. Both have been more than generous to me. I hope that both will see this book as a tangible repayment of a long overdue obligation. I wish especially to thank Steve Kurtz for stirring my interest in historical study and Vann Woodward for supporting my decision to tackle a new subject rather than to revise for publication the dissertation I earlier completed under his direction.

C. Peter Ripley, Lawrence N. Powell, and Marc W. Kruman played crucial roles in giving me an audience and providing wise counsel as this work began to take shape in 1974 and 1975. Gavin Wright and Frank A. Cassell have traded ideas with me since we were much younger. All five of these friends have established by example a demanding standard.

The statistical portions of my analysis could not have been developed without the assistance of Janet Vavra of the Inter-University Consortium of Political and Social Research, Richard Jensen and his staff at the summer 1980 Newberry Library Seminar on Quantitative History, Judith Rowe and her staff in the Social Science division of the Princeton University Computer Center, and Amy Zambrowski of the New Jersey Educational Computer Network.

Several specialists read and commented on part or all of the manuscript. I am obliged to William J. Cooper, Jr., William L. Barney, Dale Baum, John C. Inscoe, Clark Carney, Lee Benson, Thomas E. Jeffrey, and William T. Auman. Michael F. Holt and Craig M. Simpson wrote extensive assessments of the preliminary manuscript. Neither will be fully satisfied with the results here, but both have provided uniquely valuable assistance. Paul D. Escott ably scrutinized the final version.

Fellowships from the National Endowment for the Humanities enabled me to begin research in 1974–75 and to complete a first draft of the manuscript in 1982–83. These two academic years freed from teaching responsibilities were essential to the success of this enterprise.

Trenton State College has provided me with timely financial assistance, reduced teaching loads, interlibrary loans, free computer time, and free access to the marvelous IBM-5520 word processing system. In addition, the college aided publication of this work through a generous grant. Particular thanks must go to Wade C. Curry, Anthony J. DiGiorgio, Virginia C. Forcina, Carol Y. Miklovis, Geraldine J. Bresler, and Kathleen M. Walker. Several Trenton State students, notably Debra J. Levy, provided constructive criticisms of the manuscript. My department chairman, John P. Karras, has done a great deal to make this book a reality.

The University of North Carolina Press undertook the herculean challenge of extracting a book from my bulky manuscript. Lewis Bateman, Ron Maner, and Trudie Calvert have shared responsibility for initiating this fledgling author into the mysteries of their craft. A subvention from the Fred W. Morrison Fund helped to underwrite publication of this volume.

Benjamin R. LeFever, a sophomore at George School, used a Macintosh computer to draw the maps.

Librarians and archivists too numerous to mention extended to me every courtesy and made itinerant research an experience I have grown to enjoy. The bibliographical essay lists the repositories I have consulted.

The editors of *Perspectives in American History*, *Civil War History*, *Pennsylvania Magazine of History and Biography*, and *New York History* have graciously allowed me to incorporate material that originally appeared in somewhat different form in their journals.

My parents, John T. Crofts and Mary-Blanche Crofts, both read drafts of the manuscript with painstaking care and an eye for infelicities. For this and for so much else, they have more than earned my affectionate dedication. I am saddened that my mother did not live to see the book in print. Her precise handwriting in the margins of the copy from which I prepared my final revisions brought back many happy memories.

Ties of kinship and family, so important in the antebellum South, are very much a part of my life too. Each of the following persons connects me to a larger whole: Amy J. Crofts, Harriet Crofts Nathan, Neil Nathan, Thomas J. Crofts, Patricia M. Crofts, Verna I. Crofts, Pauline R. Agnew, Charles J. Moore, Joan W. Moore, William F. Maxfield, Anne B. Maxfield, William H. Maxfield, Susan P. Maxfield, Alice W. Maxfield, Nelson E. Camp, Elizabeth Maxfield-Miller, Edward R. Potts, and Grace L. Potts.

Why has it taken more than a decade to research and write my book? These happy golden years, to use Laura Ingalls Wilder's lovely phrase, have offered the grandest diversions. No excuses for procrastination will be offered here. The ladies of the family (and the rabbits) know that I have not always been the diligent scholar, but I hope they know me the better for it. Elizabeth M. Crofts has cheerfully tolerated me and my boxes of notes and the way I have converted one room after another of our home into a study or library. Busy with the demands of her own career, Betsy has sustained this undertaking to the fullest. Anita V. Crofts and Sarah B. Crofts, who in 1974 each enjoyed riding in the child's seat on the back of my bicycle, are today resplendent young women. During that same lapse of time, they assure me, I have crossed the frontier between young adulthood and middle age. My example will remind them that historians mature at an unimaginably glacial pace.

D. W. C.
Southampton, Pennsylvania
May 17, 1988

RELUCTANT CONFEDERATES

Statue of Robert Hatton, which stands in the town square of Lebanon, Tennessee (photograph by Bill Cook of the Lebanon Democrat*)*

PROLOGUE

DRIVE east from Nashville on Interstate 40 through Tennessee's rolling Cumberland Valley and you soon reach Lebanon, a quiet agricultural county seat. A short detour from the expressway brings you into town. Rectangular brick commercial buildings dating from the late nineteenth century, each several stories high, surround the town square (an incongruous Burger King has recently intruded on one corner). At the center of the square stands a Confederate monument: the statue of a tall, thin, bearded young rebel brigadier wearing a large hat. Boldly lettered at the base of the statue is the simple designation: "GEN'L HATTON."

The story behind the statue is encompassed in this book. Not that the reader should expect a biography of Robert Hatton. That task has already attracted several able writers, whose work has been of much value in the preparation of this study.[1] Rather, Robert Hatton so well symbolizes the major themes of this book that a brief review of his public career will make an illustrative prologue.

In mid-April 1861, when Hatton became a Confederate officer, he had just finished his first term in the U.S. House of Representatives. There he had been a leading southern Unionist. He and his allies had struggled to confine secession to the deep South and to promote peaceful reunion. They failed, of course. And having failed, they then had to decide their ultimate loyalty. Although some of his closest friends sided with the Union, Hatton nevertheless became a Confederate, as did a large majority of upper South Unionists. He organized the Seventh Tennessee Volunteer Infantry Regiment (CSA) and was promoted to brigade command in May 1862 when the Army of the Potomac under George B. McClellan surrounded Richmond. One week later, at Seven Pines, Hatton was killed instantly while leading his troops across an open field against well-positioned federal forces.

Hatton's home, the "pretty country town" of Lebanon, stands at the center of Wilson County. Situated primarily within the fertile Cumberland River basin that attracted the first surge of white settlers to Tennessee, Wilson County's eastern flanks rise to become part of Middle Tennessee's highland rim. Its per capita wealth of $6,626 and slave population of 30.5 percent in 1860 placed it considerably above the average for Tennessee counties, albeit far below comparable figures for the deep South cotton belt. A comfortable and prosperous corner of the Old South, Wilson County achieved special eminence as a generator of Whig talent. Former governor and U.S. Senator James C. Jones originally came from the county; former governor and Mexican War hero William B. Campbell moved to Lebanon as a young man; state supreme court justice Robert L. Caruthers, a former congressman and future governor, also lived in town. A "very cultivated society of old Whig families" thus dominated Lebanon. They nurtured a second generation of able Whig lawyer-politicians who became prominent during the 1850s. Jordan Stokes, Speaker of the Tennessee House in 1851 at the age of thirty-three before it came under Democratic control, remained prominent in the state legislature. His brother William B. Stokes, who lived in adjoining DeKalb County, won election to the U.S. House in 1859 from what the legislature had intended as a Democratic seat.[2]

Robert Hatton, the new congressman elected from the Wilson district in 1859, achieved that distinction under unusual circumstances. His victory displaced Charles Ready, an "aristocratic old Whig," whose strong Southern Rights stance diminished his support within the party. Attempting to win reelection as a Democrat, Ready lost decisively to Hatton. In how many other districts North or South, by the late 1850s, did a moderate displace an incumbent sectional advocate? Nor did Ready's successor share the core values that several historians have recently identified as characteristically southern. Deeply religious and opposed to any use of alcohol, Hatton stood outside the "culture of honor." The letters the freshman congressman sent to his wife, disdainfully describing the glitter, egotistical display, and drinking habits of Washington society, show that he prized self-control and restraint as much as any Yankee reformer.[3]

Hatton, even if not typical, had impressive political abilities. He achieved statewide recognition in 1857 by rallying the Whigs under the American party banner in an uphill race for governor. When the Whig-derived Opposition party rebounded in 1859 to carry seven of the state's ten congressional seats, the thirty-two-year-old Hatton stood as one of the most promising young politicians from the upper South. His first speech to the House in January 1860 "commanded attention," one northern observer noted. Hatton's voice was "musical and full." His gestures and oratorical technique suggested deliberate preparation, and he overcame interruptions with "force and determination." Hatton, slender and "rather tall," made a striking appearance. He had "a large head and a long face, made longer by a profusion of orange chin beard," a high forehead, blue eyes set wide apart, high cheekbones, and "a great quantity of thick brown hair, rather inclined to curl, but hardly having length sufficient to indulge its propensity."[4]

Robert Hatton (Tennessee State Library and Archives)

In more tranquil times Hatton could have looked forward to a bright political future. But all plans for the future were thrown into doubt by the astonishing events that followed Abraham Lincoln's election as president in November 1860. As the deep South rushed to establish a separate government, Tennessee and the states of the upper South faced a terrible dilemma. Torn by divergent regional and national loyalties, and positioned uncomfortably (and symbolically) between the estranged states of the North and the deep South, the upper South groped to find some peaceful resolution to the crisis not of its own making.

The network of prominent Whigs from Lebanon played leading roles in arresting the secession movement in Tennessee and trying to devise a compromise basis for reunion. State senator Jordan Stokes, a militant antisecessionist, led the legislative fight to ensure that Tennessee voters could forbid holding a state convention or approve any action decided upon by a convention, should one be held. Robert Caruthers, of the Tennessee Supreme Court, was appointed by the legislature to the state delegation at the Peace Conference in Washington, D.C., where he strongly supported the adoption of a Union-saving compromise.[5]

The Wilson County political leader best positioned to exert leverage at the federal level was the U.S. congressman, Robert Hatton. He had quickly emerged as a rising star among the southern Opposition, the bloc of twenty-three former Whigs who worked tirelessly during the secession winter to promote peaceful reunion. Hatton became very depressed after reaching Washington in December. He found that the states of the deep South were certain to leave the Union but that Republicans were "blind" to the danger and indisposed to take any action to avert it. He feared that civil war was "inevitable." New Year's Day dawned "bright" and "cheerful," but Hatton thought "the sky is dark, politically—dark as midnight." In early January, he served on the ad hoc "border state committee" that devised a compromise plan of settlement, but few Republicans would accept it. Nor did news from home provide any reassurance. As late as January 15, Hatton could write: "All my letters from Tennessee indicate that the feeling for secession is growing, daily and rapidly. I fear it will sweep the state."[6]

By the end of January, however, Hatton became slightly more hopeful. "The prospect of an adjustment," he thought, was "brightening," even though doubt still hung "like a dark pall over us." He and other southern Unionists busily dispatched countless thousands of Union speeches to the upper South, trying to stem the secession tide. In early February, he made a polished oration in the House, calling on Republicans to offer concessions that would allay southern fears and strengthen southern Unionists. Hatton condemned the instigators of secession in the deep South as "crazy enthusiasts," whose "reckless disregard" of the interests of the upper South made them "*practically* our enemies, as truly as the most unprincipled fanatics of the North." He feared that his speech would "not be well received at home" because it was "too strongly for the Union, to suit just now."[7]

Isolated in Washington, where the polarization between secessionists and hard-line Republicans dominated the political horizon, Hatton had lost touch with the mood of the Tennessee electorate. A strong resurgence of Unionism had taken place. His home county, reflecting its Whig proclivities, displayed emphatic Union tendencies. A convention in Lebanon on January 21 nominated former governor Campbell and state senator Stokes as delegates to the state convention. They campaigned vigorously, opposing both secession and the holding of a convention. Campbell also wrote letters to stir up Union strength in adjacent areas. He received assurances that Whigs were "sound to the core on the Union question" and certain to carry "a crushing-killing majority" for Union nominees. Tennessee voters on February 9 delivered a stern verdict against secession. Union candidates drew over 75 percent of all votes cast. A smaller but still decisive majority opposed even allowing a convention to meet. Whigs provided the backbone of Union support, but significant numbers of Democrats and former nonvoters, especially from nonplantation areas, joined to repudiate secession. Wilson County witnessed an enormous Union landslide, in which Stokes and Campbell outpolled their opponents more than ten to one. Wilson voters also opposed calling a convention by a thumping margin, 2,565 to 462.[8]

The news of the result in his home state and county delighted Hatton. "Excited and alarmed friends" had predicted that his congressional district would favor a convention and warned that a runaway convention might drive through a secession ordinance without referring it to the people. Suddenly that threat lifted. Hatton sent a joyful note to Campbell. "The consternation and dismay of the conspirators here, on the reception of the news of our election was the subject of universal observation and remark," he noted. "The swords of the wicked and reckless revolutionists" had been "turned upon their own breasts."[9]

Hatton returned home from Washington in early March. Abraham Lincoln took office, but Tennessee and the upper South remained in the Union. Reports indicated that Lincoln would adopt a peaceful policy and avoid an armed clash with the seceding states. Late in March, Hatton noted: "All is quiet here. Secession is making no headway. Can't for the present. Trust it never may." On Court Day, April 1, he made a long speech to the county convention of the recently formed Union party. Scornful of secession and hopeful that the Union could be peacefully reunited, he offered to run for another term in Congress. Hatton won renomination at this meeting and at similar ones held in other counties in the district. A newspaper in the next county reported it "the universal desire of the Unionists" that Hatton "again represent them in Congress."[10]

Hatton's ideas suited his Unionist constituents, but college students from the deep South attending Cumberland University in Lebanon took strong exception to his condemnation of secession. Although Hatton was a distinguished Cumberland alumnus, some of the students hissed during his Court Day speech, whereupon he "rebuked them in a most withering manner." That night a group of perhaps twenty persons, mostly students, roused Hatton and his family from sleep by beating on tin pans and buckets, blowing horns, and whooping in a "savage-like" manner. The congressman came out into the night armed with a pistol and told the demonstrators to listen to him or disperse. When the clamor continued, he fired a shot into the air. His fire was reportedly answered, but nobody was injured. Members of the crowd headed to the town square, where they intended to burn an effigy of Hatton. Apparently prevented from completing their ritual there, the demonstrators retreated back to the college to dispatch the effigy. The troubles in Lebanon on April 1 reflected the growing estrangement between secessionists and Unionists and between the lower and upper South. The students had given dramatic expression to a point of view that accurately reflected the crystallizing national sentiments of the deep South. But they won few friends in Lebanon. According to the *Lebanon Herald*, the mob action was "universally pronounced here by men of all parties as disgraceful."[11]

Most people in Wilson County remained loyal Unionists until receiving word about Lincoln's proclamation calling for seventy-five thousand troops, shortly after the fall of Fort Sumter. That changed everything. The proclamation came as an "awful shock" to southern Unionists in the Wilson County area, who grimly concluded that "Lincoln must be crazed." Two months later, the same voters who had pronounced so strongly for the Union in February endorsed secession, 2,644 to 353.[12]

Hatton had already indicated that he would resist any effort to hold the Union together by armed force. Called upon to speak after the proclamation arrived, he is alleged to have replied: "Now is the time for action; the time for speaking has passed."[13] Act he did. Within barely a year, as a Confederate brigadier general, he lay dead on the battlefield outside Richmond. His death, at the age of thirty-five, marked the ironic end to a tragically shortened life. The commemorative statue later erected in Lebanon, in the same town square where the pro-Confederate students tried to burn his effigy, honors a genuine Confederate hero. That same person, however, achieved his greatest political distinction by trying to thwart what he considered the reckless and suicidal movement to create the southern Confederacy.

1

UNIONIST PROFILES

Most literate Americans know that the Union disintegrated and civil war began in 1861. Far fewer know much about the desperate eleventh-hour effort to preserve the Union and prevent war. Hindsight suggests, of course, that the two objectives were contradictory—that the Union could have been preserved only by violent means, that disunion was an inevitable concomitant of peace.

But hindsight also distorts. During the first several months of 1861, saving the Union rather than preparing for war appeared the only rational course to many both North and South. Nowhere in the nation did Union-saving enjoy greater mass support than in the slave states of the upper South. There, in state after state in early 1861, voters spurned secession. Political leaders who identified too closely with the revolution in the deep South suddenly fell from public favor. Their constituencies instead demanded intensified efforts to enact compromise legislation and preserve the peace.

Reluctant Confederates will study the ideas and behavior of voters in the upper South as the secession dilemma unfolded, it will examine the response of political leaders there to the agenda endorsed by the electorate, and it will consider the daunting obstacles that frustrated the cause of peaceable reunion. The severity of the impasse can hardly be exaggerated. Secession, rooted in conflicting ideologies and fueled by widespread fear and hysteria, probably never could have been resolved through legislated compromise. So, with hindsight, we see it.

Many at the time, however, saw it otherwise. Southern Unionists acted on the hope that responsible moderates could somehow prevail. Their hope, if not their specific remedies, claimed broad support in the North. The secession crisis cannot be properly understood without examining what southern Unionists thought was happening, what they tried to do, and how the leaders of the Republican party responded to their efforts.

Several individuals deserve introduction before proceeding further. The three most notable northern politicians of the era—Abraham Lincoln, Stephen A. Douglas, and William H. Seward—each profoundly influenced the history of southern Unionism, as did Massachusetts Congressman Charles Francis Adams. Southern Unionists already prominent or destined to become so included Kentucky Senator John J. Crittenden, former Tennessee senator and 1860 presidential candidate John Bell, and Tennessee Senator Andrew Johnson, the future president. Two highly visible newspaper editors and postwar Republican governors, Tennessee's William G. Brownlow and North Carolina's William W. Holden, built mass support for the Union cause during the secession crisis.

Several other southern Unionists appeared in early 1861 to have bright futures, though none was yet widely known outside his home state. George W. Summers and John B. Baldwin vaulted from political retirement (an occupational hazard for Virginia Whigs) to dominate the Virginia convention. So, too, a group of Opposition or former Whig congressmen from the upper South, notably Tennessee's Robert Hatton and Emerson Etheridge and North Carolina's John A. Gilmer, found themselves in unaccustomed prominence during the secession crisis.

ANY examination of southern Unionism must assess a pivotal episode in the career of Abraham Lincoln. Within weeks after the presidential election on November 6, 1860, he faced a grave challenge. Growing numbers of southerners preferred to disrupt the Union rather than "submit" to his victory. Lincoln tried to explain that he intended to treat them fairly, to leave them alone, and "in no way" to interfere with slavery. He also tried to calm southern resentments, hoping to counter the idea that northerners held southerners in ill regard. "You are as good as we," he avowed, "there is no difference between us, other than the difference of circumstances."[1] But his reassurances failed to arrest the secession movement. Lincoln thus took office facing what he himself described as "a task before me greater than that which rested upon Washington."[2] Soon he had to make the most difficult decisions of his life.

Lincoln's decision-making process remains an enigma. The most widely read studies of Lincoln and the Republican party during the secession crisis offer startlingly different interpretations.[3] Uncertainty persists about why Lincoln opposed the compromise measures sought by southern Unionists and why he instead risked a military confrontation with secessionists at Fort Sumter. By analyzing Lincoln's inability to find common ground with those southerners who shared his hope of peacefully restoring the Union, this study offers a fresh perspective from which to reexamine his handling of the entire crisis.

Every American since the Civil War has had a clear mental image of the tall, sinewy sixteenth president with the unforgettably expressive face. But until 1860, Lincoln was less well known than his great Illinois rival, Stephen A. Douglas. For a generation the two had done battle, and Douglas gained a national reputation long before Lincoln. Indeed, Lincoln could never have risen to power had he not been paired against the only real mass leader of the northern Democracy.

Physically Lincoln and Douglas were a study in opposites. The Napoleonic Douglas stood only five feet four inches tall, so that Lincoln towered over him. Douglas had a disproportionately large head, broad shoulders, and powerful torso mounted incongruously on stubby legs. Though often described as a scrappy prize-fighter, he was in no sense a comical figure. The quick-witted, energetic, and resourceful Douglas, a tireless stump campaigner who instinctively knew how to build rapport with an audience, had a winning manner and an instinct for leadership. In an age of political oratory, many considered him the most formidable speaker in the U.S. Senate. His skills in the cloakrooms and behind the scenes were likewise of a high order.[4]

The long rivalry between Lincoln and Douglas, sharpened by the famous 1858 debates in Illinois, culminated in 1860 when both won presidential nominations. But whereas Lincoln's Republican party stood united and confident of victory, Douglas had the misfortune to lead a party too prosouthern to maintain its original strength in the North, yet insufficiently prosouthern to satisfy the party's extreme wing in the deep South. Douglas, breaking precedent by taking his case directly to the voters, could not overcome his many handicaps. He lost the North to Lincoln, while in the South he ran far behind John Bell and John C. Breckinridge, the nominees, respectively, of the southern Whigs and the breakaway southern Democrats.

The secession crisis following the 1860 election found Douglas trying to do for the Union what he had been unable to do for his own party. He and Kentucky Senator John J. Crittenden spearheaded efforts to enact a Union-saving compromise, but to no avail. Disappointment and exhaustion felled the "Little Giant." His death at the young age of forty-eight, less than two months after the start of the war, abruptly ended the career of the most national northern leader of his generation and symbolized the destruction of the old Union.

Lincoln in 1860 was also a less familiar figure than William H. Seward of upstate New York. Seward, the governor of New York from 1839 to 1843, had stood in the national spotlight even longer than Douglas. Both had served in the U.S. Senate since the late 1840s and had repeatedly clashed there. Widely judged the most talented antislavery politician, Seward moved deftly from the Whig to the

Abraham Lincoln in 1860 (ambrotype by Preston Butler, Springfield, Illinois; Illinois State Historical Library)

Stephen A. Douglas in the late 1850s (Illinois State Historical Library)

Republican party. In 1859, when he appeared poised to capture the presidency, Seward traveled to Europe and was treated as a virtual head of state. Lincoln thus eclipsed two eminent competitors by winning both the Republican nomination and the election.

Seward, eight years Lincoln's senior, stood almost a head shorter. A "slight, wiry man of scarcely medium height," Seward gained distinction for reasons other than physical appearance or oratorical genius. His strengths included a keen mind, a facility for effective written expression, and a warmth and charm that dominated small gatherings. No other political leader of the era combined Seward's ability to maintain the confidence of those who saw politics as a matter of principle and those, such as his alter ego Thurlow Weed, who made political organization and management a professional undertaking. Seward's pronouncements about a "higher law" than the Constitution and about the "irrepressible conflict" between slave and free labor stirred the antislavery constituencies of New England and the upper North, thereby securing for him an undeserved reputation as a sectional extremist.[5]

The secession crisis confronted Seward with the starkest challenge of his political career. Though displaced as party leader by Lincoln and deeply distrusted in the South, Seward threw himself into the struggle to save the Union. He reached out to southern Unionists such as Virginia's George W. Summers and North Carolina's John A. Gilmer while most others in his party stood passive on the sidelines. Both Douglas and Seward responded to the crisis with an earnestness and sense of responsibility that befit their stature, but neither could prevent the situation from degenerating into war.

Yet another prominent northerner played a significant role in the events to be chronicled below. Charles Francis Adams, the son and grandson of presidents, was finishing his first term in Congress at the time of the secession crisis. Adams, however, was neither young nor a political newcomer. After becoming deeply involved in Massachusetts politics as a "Conscience Whig" during the 1840s, he had run for vice-president on the Free Soil ticket in 1848. He thus brought to the Republican party an illustrious family legacy and a valuable symbolic link. His father, John Quincy Adams, had devoted the last years of his life to making antislavery a political force.

Charles Francis Adams was "reserved and austere" with little "natural charm or personal magnetism." Photos taken during his middle years capture an expressionless face that conveys no hint of warmth or humor. His voluminous diary suggests that he was shy and introverted, even though hungering for the public acknowledgment that his father likewise craved. He has been characterized as "pri-

William H. Seward, ca. 1850 (daguerreotype by J. H. Whitehurst; Chicago Historical Society)

Charles Francis Adams (U.S. Department of the Interior, National Park Service, Adams National Historic Site, Quincy, Massachusetts)

John J. Crittenden, ca. 1855 (daguerreotype; Chicago Historical Society)

marily a moralist," for whom "the calculations and bargains of the realistic world were always repugnant."[6]

During the secession crisis Adams astonished his more radical friends by following the lead of the conciliatory Seward, who had exceptionally close ties to the Adams family. Adams's eloquent speech in Congress on January 31, 1861, attempted to reassure southerners about northern intentions. His own diary and the writings during the secession crisis of his audacious twenty-two-year-old son, Henry Adams, who served that winter as his father's private secretary, offer many valuable glimpses of the struggle to find a way to save the Union. Henry Adams, already wielding the pen that would later earn him fame, displayed a keen grasp of the tangled situation. His letters and anonymous newspaper articles, together with an essay entitled "The Great Secession Winter," are essential sources.[7]

THE elder statesman among southern Unionists was John J. Crittenden of Kentucky. Born in 1786, fully a generation before Lincoln, Crittenden was at the end of a long and eventful political career. No southern Unionist had greater national stature than the retiring Kentucky senator. His proposed compromise of the sectional crisis became the most widely discussed attempt to save the Union during the winter of 1860–61.

A slender man of slightly more than average height with a lock of hair that tended to fall over his high, broad forehead, Crittenden won early distinction for eloquence and political skills. Following three terms as Speaker of the Kentucky legislature, he won a brief term in the U.S. Senate in 1817 at the age of thirty-one. He returned to the Senate in 1835 after having established himself as one of the most able lawyer-politicians in the state. Originally a lieutenant of Henry Clay, Crittenden eventually emerged as a power in his own right. He served as U.S. attorney general under both William Henry Harrison and Millard Fillmore, and his name was mentioned frequently as a possible presidential candidate during the late 1840s and 1850s.[8]

During his last years in the Senate, Crittenden stood almost alone. The disintegration of the Whig party left him with few political allies. Unwilling to support repeal of the Missouri Compromise, he opposed the Kansas-Nebraska Act. Again in 1858 he broke with most southerners on the Lecompton issue, claiming that the effort to get Kansas admitted to the Union as a slave state ignored the wishes of people living in that troubled territory. Crittenden shrugged off complaints that his stance regarding Kansas allied him with the Republican party of the North.

John Bell (engraving by J. C. Buttre from a photograph by Mathew B. Brady; Tennessee State Library and Archives)

When the outbreak of war doomed Crittenden's celebrated campaign to save the Union, he followed Kentucky by moving from anguished neutrality to qualified support for restoration of the old Union "as it was." Crittenden's home state and his own family remained cruelly divided: sons of his became officers in both the Union and Confederate armies. Like his ally Stephen A. Douglas, Crittenden did not long outlive the disintegration of the old Union.

John Bell of Tennessee had a career with many parallels to Crittenden's. Both were prominent Whig lawyer-politicians from the old upper Southwest who had been in the public eye for many decades. Born in 1796, Bell first won a congressional seat in 1827 after having earlier served in the legislature. Though originally a supporter of Andrew Jackson, he gained election as Speaker of the House with the support of anti-Jacksonians in 1834 and became a leader in the emerging Whig party. Like Crittenden, Bell briefly sat in William Henry Harrison's ill-fated cabinet in 1841. In 1847 he began the first of two terms in the U.S. Senate.[9]

Bell was respected but not loved. Once judged an "accomplished and effective debater" with an "exceptional command of language," Bell became less animated as he aged. Even his friends considered the elder Bell "cold and reserved." Possibly the wealth he acquired through a second marriage contributed to his aloofness: Bell and his wife commanded one of the largest family fortunes in the antebellum South through ownership of coal mines, ironworks, and a large slave labor force. Several who knew him thought Bell lacked the qualities necessary for a popular leader.[10]

Bell's career in the Senate coincided with growing sectional polarization. Though fearful of "losing standing in the South," he opposed both the Kansas-Nebraska Act and the Lecompton constitution. Bell and Crittenden thus won plaudits in the North for their "nationality." A strong showing by Tennessee's Whiggish "Opposition" in 1859, which won seven of ten seats in the U.S. House, suggested that a candidate such as Bell or Crittenden might attract moderates both North and South. When the septuagenarian Crittenden graciously stepped aside, former Whigs in the Constitutional Union party nominated Bell for president. Bell did carry three states: his and Crittenden's home states of Kentucky and Tennessee, plus Virginia. But hopes that Bell could emerge as the victor in an election decided by the House collapsed when Lincoln swept the North and won the election outright.[11]

Bell remained a pronounced Unionist during the secession crisis. Though less visible than Crittenden because he no longer sat in Congress, Bell nevertheless cautioned against secession in public letters

Andrew Johnson (photograph by Mathew B. Brady; Library of Congress)

and speeches and tried to calm southern anxieties. He conferred directly with Lincoln during the week before the March 4 inauguration. Only after the April 15 proclamation did the disillusioned Bell belatedly cast his lot with the Confederacy. Bell's critics claim that he could have "paralyzed" the secession movement and confined it to the seven states of the deep South had he decided differently, but his defenders counter that nobody had the personal influence to stem the secession tide in Middle and West Tennessee. Had Bell tried to do so he would have been "brushed aside or crushed."[12]

No southern Unionist reached such a portentous personal and political crossroads during the months after Lincoln's election as Andrew Johnson, the man destined to succeed Lincoln after the 1865 assassination. Johnson, who had represented Tennessee in the U.S. Senate since 1857 after having earlier served as congressman and governor, first achieved national prominence because of his uncompromising opposition to secession.

Many leaders of Johnson's generation had humble origins, but his were notably unpromising. Hired out as an apprentice by his penniless mother after his father had died, the unlettered Johnson ran away and established himself as a tailor in Greeneville, an East Tennessee county seat. There he worked his way up to middle-class respectability, aided by a young wife who taught him to read and write. Johnson apparently saw politics as a way to secure status and dignity. He became the outspokenly self-conscious "plebeian" who gloried in his rise from poverty and proclaimed a special bond between himself and other ordinary men. Yet his political posturing bespoke a deep ambivalence. Some surmised that Johnson was "really ashamed of having been a working man." Certainly he suffered from "the many taunts, the jeers," and the "gotten-up and intended slights to me and mine" directed at him by better-bred rivals.[13]

Photographs of Johnson usually captured a stern, determined expression. Square-jawed and beardless, with dark hair that curled behind his neck, the muscular Johnson stood slightly above medium height. He became a gifted stump speaker, ideally suited for a political environment in which many voters sooner heeded the oral than the printed word. He may have appeared a rough provincial in the halls of Congress, but his slashing assaults on a parasitic "aristocracy" won him an appreciative audience at home. Johnson also cultivated a common touch, as when he would order up treats for the citizenry when out campaigning. He was reported "perfectly indifferent to the *quality*" of what he drank and able to enjoy "the meanest whiskey" (the fifteen-cent-a-gallon variety) "hot and fresh from the still, with fusil oil on it."[14]

Johnson, who had never before strayed from the southern Democratic consensus, emerged as the most visible and controversial southern Unionist in Congress during the secession crisis. Avowing unconditional support for the Union, Johnson appeared more determined to condemn the secession conspirators of the deep South than to plead for a Union-saving compromise. Johnson's party affiliation added to his notoriety: he was by far the most prominent Democrat among the southern Unionists, who drew the bulk of their support from the Whiggish Opposition. After the war broke out, Johnson became the only senator from a seceding state who stayed loyal to the Union. He thereby maintained his political base in East Tennessee and won great acclaim throughout the North.

William G. Brownlow, the other notable unconditional Unionist from East Tennessee, had a career deeply intertwined with Johnson's. Bitter antagonists for twenty years, the two suddenly found themselves drawn together during the secession crisis. In Brownlow's eyes, Johnson had long been "a contemptible political prostitute," an "unprincipled knave," and a "disgrace to patriotic Tennessee." Johnson reciprocated in kind, labeling the Whig politico and newspaper editor a "vile miscreant," a "brute in human form," and a hypocritical liar.[15] Their relentless assaults on each other gave partisan differences in East Tennessee an almost pathological ferocity. The "Fighting Parson" challenged Johnson to "the bitterest race of his Congressional career" in 1845 and persistently ridiculed "Andy" in the columns of his newspaper.[16]

Brownlow like Johnson had struggled against the odds. An orphan and carpenter's apprentice, he spent ten years as a Methodist circuit rider before venturing into the newspaper business. The six-foot-tall Brownlow, erect but not heavy-set, had a rounded, clean-shaven face and long, dark hair combed back from his forehead. He enjoyed the rough and tumble of stump speaking, claiming to have had during his prime as strong a voice as anyone in East Tennessee. Brownlow's stock in trade, whether in print or in person, was vitriolic denunciation, so he was "constantly involved in altercations." A rival editor once shot Brownlow in the leg during a street fight. Another time, when hit from behind with a club, he suffered a skull fracture and remained unconscious for weeks. But Brownlow had many devoted friends who considered him "warm hearted and genial." His newspaper, *Brownlow's Knoxville Whig*, was "tremendously popular." Many readers apparently relished the "spicy and biting views" of an editor who gloried in controversy. Its circulation of twelve thousand, larger than any other journal in the state, gave Brownlow formidable political leverage.[17]

William G. Brownlow (engraving by R. Whitechurch; Tennessee State Library and Archives)

William W. Holden (engraving by E. G. Williams; Division of Archives and History, North Carolina State Department of Cultural Resources)

In November and December 1860 Brownlow and the Union Whigs from Knoxville undertook to block the "wild stampede toward secession." They stirred the "friends of the Union" from the outlying countryside, who surged into town "with dark and ominous determination depicted on their countenances." At a memorable five-hour public meeting on December 8, in a courthouse building so jammed that many people could not fit inside, Brownlow and the unconditional Unionists adopted resolutions denouncing secession. The meeting, details of which were soon broadcast across East Tennessee in the *Whig*, "encouraged and emboldened" the political leaders of the region to take an unqualified stand in favor of the Union. Ten days later, Brownlow's nemesis Andrew Johnson delivered the most important speech of his career. Brownlow put twenty years of acrimony behind him to stand with his old rival. "*Johnson is right*," Brownlow vowed, "*and I will defend him to the last*."[18] The reconciliation lasted as long as the Union issue was paramount and both confronted "rebels." During the postwar era, however, Brownlow as governor and U.S. senator allied with Andrew Johnson's critics in the Republican party, and he and the president once again attacked each other with hammer and tongs.

William W. Holden, North Carolina newspaper publisher and politician, had a life with many parallels to Brownlow's. Holden, however, gained prominence as a Democrat. The *North Carolina Standard*, which he edited after 1843 in the state capital, Raleigh, remained his party's statewide newspaper of record throughout the late antebellum period. Holden combined a vigorous prose style with relentless sarcasm and invective. He masterminded the Democratic revival of the late 1840s and 1850s, devising techniques to build party strength among nonslaveowners in the mountainous west while maintaining the party base in wealthy eastern plantation areas.

Holden, born illegitimately in 1818, apprenticed in the newspaper business at a young age. He raised anxieties similar to those stirred by Johnson and Brownlow in Tennessee. Hierarchies based on birth, family, and education were even more strongly rooted in longer-settled North Carolina, and Holden would always be considered an outsider by many. Holden's thick dark hair receded to expose a broad forehead by his middle years, and he then wore a full beard shaved only on the upper lip. Photographs capture an intense expression through narrowed eyelids.[19]

In 1858 the gentlemen of the Democratic party thwarted Holden's efforts to run for governor or U.S. senator. The snub embittered the sensitive editor. He believed that his services to the party entitled him to advancement, and he not unjustly considered himself a victim of class prejudice. Two years later, during the secession crisis, when Democratic leaders overwhelmingly took a Southern Rights stance, Holden broke with his party and became the most vehement antisecessionist in the state. Though his Unionism would falter after the war began, Holden led the wartime "peace movement" that many North Carolina Confederates considered treasonous. He, like Brownlow, became a postwar governor of his state under embattled circumstances. Both personified the scalawag element in the southern Republican party of Reconstruction.

WHEN most prominent Virginia Democrats took a quasi-secessionist Southern Rights position in early 1861, voters in the Old Dominion elected a large majority of Union Whigs and Douglas Democrats to the state convention ordered by the legislature. Two individuals, George W. Summers of Charleston and John B. Baldwin of Staunton, emerged as leaders of the Union bloc at the convention. Alert and quick-witted on the convention floor, Summers and Baldwin also worked effectively behind closed doors to devise a policy that would keep conditional and unconditional Unionists united.

Summers, the elder of the two, had moved with his family from Fairfax County outside Washington, D.C., to the Kanawha Valley in 1813, when he was nine years old. He followed his older brother Lewis into the legal profession and built a "large and lucrative" practice. Summers had "natural gifts as an orator." His voice was "rich and resonant" and his language "full, flowing, and forceful." His gift for appealing to a jury made him an "irresistable power in a court trial." A "stoutly built" man of medium height, with a full white beard and an aristocratic demeanor, Summers had a "commanding presence." His "firm and uncompromising expression" suggested a determined personality, possessed of the requisite "genius and talent" to distinguish himself in both law and public life.[20]

Summers first won a seat in the House of Delegates in 1830. He supported gradual emancipation during the historic legislative debates of 1831–32 following the Nat Turner insurrection. During the 1840s he served two terms in Congress as a national Whig. He gained recognition as the "ablest man" at the state Constitutional Convention of 1850–51, where he championed western interests and engineered the key compromise agreement on apportionment. Under the new constitution voters for the first time had the opportunity to elect their governor. Summers, the Whig candidate for that office in 1851, ran a creditable if losing race, plagued by accusations that he was unsound on the slave issue. After winning election as a judge in 1852, his political role diminished.[21]

The secession crisis returned Summers to center stage. Chosen by the legislature as a delegate to the Peace Conference in Washington, D.C., he consulted secretly with William H. Seward. Summers may have recognized in the New Yorker a kindred spirit. Close to the same age and sharing a Whig background, both were regarded by their peers as politicians of unusual talent. The two were, however,

George W. Summers (printed reproduction of a photograph; West Virginia Department of Culture and History)

products of very different political environments. Seward vaulted to national prominence in part because he lived in the right state. He and the master political organizer Thurlow Weed built a strong Whig party and then shepherded most of its constituency to the Republican party, aided by Seward's special ability to appeal to voters who opposed slavery and excessive southern power. Summers, by contrast, found his early emancipationism an albatross as Virginia politics moved in an explicitly proslavery direction. So, too, southern Whigs had far less success than their northern counterparts in seeking new party affiliations during the 1850s. Though Summers's home base in Charleston had Whiggish loyalties, Democrats outnumbered Whigs elsewhere in the fast-growing northwest. Until 1861 the Whig party and its successors appeared fated to remain a permanent minority in Virginia politics.

Summers, elected overwhelmingly to represent Kanawha County at the state convention, became the floor leader among the Unionists as soon as he returned from Washington. During March and early April 1861, he and Seward communicated surreptitiously through go-betweens. Hopes for peace and sectional reconciliation depended substantially on their furtive alliance. When these hopes suddenly collapsed, Summers cut himself off completely from public life. His destiny lay with the old Union, and he supported neither Confederate Virginia nor the new Unionist state of West Virginia that soon included his home in Charleston.

John B. Baldwin of Staunton, a fast-growing urban center in the Shenandoah Valley, was born to comfortable circumstances in 1820. He pursued a legal career after studying at the University of Virginia and soon demonstrated remarkable skills in public debate. Upon winning a seat in the House of Delegates, he gave "ample assurance of future eminence."[22] Baldwin, however, also demonstrated a Burkean readiness to trust his own political judgment even when it ran contrary to the wishes of his constituents. At a time when sentiment west of the Blue Ridge was almost unanimous for reapportioning the legislature on the basis of white population, rather than on a "mixed" formula including persons and property, Baldwin sided with the east in favor of the traditional "mixed basis." Defeated in seeking reelection to the legislature, he pursued a very successful legal practice and did not again seek elective office until 1861.

Baldwin, a man of "imposing physique and blunt manners," grew portly in his middle years. He had penetrating eyes, a full beard, and graying hair worn in the fashionably long style of the era.[23] A popular orator during Whig election campaigns, he was held in especially high regard in eastern Virginia, where his stance on representation

John B. Baldwin (Virginia State Library)

was deemed courageous. The secession crisis returned him to public life. He and two other Unionists won overwhelming victories to represent Augusta County in the Virginia convention. There Baldwin immediately became part of the small core of Union leaders who dominated the convention. As did Summers, Baldwin frequently participated in floor debate. He also delivered one of the most celebrated Union orations, a prodigious three-day effort.

The most controversial and significant episode in Baldwin's life, discussed in detail in Chapter 11 below, occurred in early April, when he was dispatched by Summers and other Union leaders to meet privately with President Lincoln in Washington. The enigmatic secret interview between Baldwin and Lincoln, held in a private room of the White House just as the president was readying the fateful expedition to resupply Fort Sumter, afforded southern Unionists one last chance to urge Lincoln to pursue a different course. Never, Baldwin recalled, did he "make a speech on behalf of a client in jeopardy of his life, with such earnest solemnity and endeavor."[24]

When the war broke out, Baldwin volunteered for Confederate service and gained appointment as colonel of an infantry regiment. He later sat in the Confederate Congress and became a power in postwar Virginia politics. Speaker of the House in the so-called "Baldwin legislature" of 1865–67, he played an instrumental role in keeping Virginia under Conservative rule after implementation of the Reconstruction Acts.[25]

DEMOCRATS controlled the governorships and legislatures of most states in the late antebellum upper South, including the three with which this study is particularly concerned. Legislative majorities conferred the power to select U.S. senators. Despite the Unionism of Andrew Johnson and Virginia Governor John Letcher (the latter until April 15), most prominent upper South Democrats had become quasi-secessionists by early 1861. All of the following were so regarded by Unionists: Virginia Senators Robert M. T. Hunter and James M. Mason, North Carolina Senators Thomas Bragg and Thomas L. Clingman, Tennessee Senator A. O. P. Nicholson, North Carolina Governor John W. Ellis, and Tennessee Governor Isham G. Harris.

Under the circumstances, Opposition congressmen from the upper South gravitated to leadership of the Union cause. Only retiring Kentucky Senator John J. Crittenden represented the Opposition in the upper house, but twenty former Whigs from the five states of Maryland, Kentucky, Virginia, North Carolina, and Tennessee held seats in the House of Representatives. Several individuals among this group deserve special mention here.

Henry Winter Davis, the wealthy, eloquent, and charismatic congressman from Baltimore, Maryland, had qualifications to lead the southern Opposition in the House. He and his wife entertained in a "most elegant style," and Davis impressed one newcomer to Washington as "the greatest man in Congress." He, however, had moved so close to the Republican party, with which he would soon affiliate, as to call his southern loyalties into question. His tie-breaking vote, the only one so cast from a slave state, allowed Republicans to elect New Jersey's William Pennington as Speaker of the House in early 1860. Davis, hopeful of strengthening ties between the southern Opposition and the Republican party, welcomed Lincoln's November victory. Davis played a significant role in the secession crisis but not as a spokesman for the southern Opposition.[26]

No state had a larger Opposition delegation in the Thirty-sixth Congress than Tennessee. Winning narrow victories in several closely contested races in 1859, former Whigs gained seven of that state's ten House seats. During the secession crisis all were firm Unionists, though their loyalties diverged widely when the war broke out. Two unconditional Unionists, Horace Maynard from East Tennessee and William B. Stokes from Middle Tennessee, embraced the Union war effort. Stokes raised a Union cavalry regiment, and both he and Maynard eventually joined the Republican party. Two other unconditional Unionists, Thomas A. R. Nelson of East Tennessee and Emerson Etheridge of West Tennessee, became estranged from the Union cause. Nelson, captured by a Confederate patrol in late 1861, won his freedom by muting his earlier Unionism. Etheridge, an outspoken Unionist during the first year and a half of the war, bitterly criticized the Lincoln administration after it made emancipation a war aim. Three others, Reese Brabson of East Tennessee, John M. Quarles of Middle Tennessee, and the man we have already met in the Prologue, Robert Hatton, renounced their Unionism as soon as the war started.

Of this group the most prominent and influential was Hatton's closest friend in Congress, Emerson Etheridge. "If he was a woman," Hatton explained to his wife, "you would be certain we were dead in love with each other." Hatton, new to Washington in 1859, found the veteran Etheridge a valuable friend and adviser: "We eat together, walk to and from the Capitol together, sit in the House together, room by each other, are alike in politics, in religion, and our feelings and sympathies." Both stubbornly shunned the alcoholic lubricants of Washington life. Etheridge, a widower with a small daughter, had large hazel eyes, a "well developed broad forehead," straight brown hair that curled over his ears, and a dense beard. He had a "fine mellow voice" and spoke with "a good deal of emphasis."[27]

Etheridge, seven years Hatton's senior, was born in 1819. He served a term in the state legislature in the 1840s and won election to Congress from the district on the west bank of the Tennessee River in both 1853 and 1855. Etheridge lost a close election in 1857 but won the seat back by an even narrower margin in 1859. The intensely competitive environment of his Ninth Congressional District made him a relentless partisan. One of the very few southerners to vote against the Kansas-Nebraska Act in 1854, and the only southerner to support an 1857 House resolution condemning the repeal of the Missouri Compromise as "unwise and unjust," Etheridge was constantly taunted by Democratic newspaper editors as a "Southern Black Republican" ready to sell out the South. Etheridge in turn spurned instructions from the Democratic majority in the legislature, saying that they hated him politically and that the feeling was mutual. The furor testified both to Etheridge's stature and to his independence. Whigs lionized Etheridge as courageous, intelligent, and a "true patriot of the Clay and Webster school," and candid opponents grudgingly acknowledged him to be "a man of talent and ability."[28]

During the secession crisis and the first months of the war, Etheridge stirred more controversy in Tennessee than anyone other than Andrew Johnson. He ridiculed the idea that Republicans intended to interfere with slavery and denounced secessionists for "persistent misrepresentation" and false accusations. More boldly than most antisecessionists, Etheridge proclaimed unconditional support for the Union.[29]

By March Etheridge and Johnson formed an alliance to lead the nascent Union party of Tennessee, thereby gaining control over the distribution of federal patronage under the Lincoln administration. Southern Rights supporters indignantly lambasted both men. One critic insisted that Etheridge had fallen into "the depths of disgrace and infamy," appealing only to the "ignorant and blind lick-spittles" rather than to "the slaveholding and enlightened portion of the people." Etheridge continued to campaign for the Union even after the war started. Facing mobs that killed one of his intended listeners and wounded several others, he bitterly condemned secession. The chairman of the state Democratic committee curtly announced: "If Etheridge speaks *for* the South, we have no reply. If against it, our only answer to him and his backers must be cold steel and bullets."[30]

Etheridge survived. His home county and two others in his district

Emerson Etheridge (photograph by Mathew B. Brady; Tennessee State Library and Archives)

voted against secession in the June 1861 referendum, although Unionism collapsed almost everywhere else in Middle and West Tennessee. He returned to Washington in an anomalous position. His state had left the Union, and it had decided to elect representatives to the Confederate Congress rather than to Washington. The spunky Etheridge, who gained many admirers in the first wartime Congress, won appointment as clerk of the House. When federal armies regained control over parts of Middle and West Tennessee early in 1862, he worked to rebuild Union support and to recruit soldiers for the federal armies. But when Lincoln announced emancipation, Etheridge regarded it as "treachery to the Union men of the South." He thereafter sided with Lincoln's opponents in Congress. During Reconstruction Etheridge found himself allied with his old Democratic enemies. He was the unsuccessful Conservative opponent to Brownlow in the race for governor in 1867.[31]

North Carolina had four Opposition congressmen during the secession crisis. Zebulon B. Vance, then a young freshman member from Asheville, would soon become a Confederate general and the wartime governor of his state. His postwar political career included a long tenure as one of the most durable Redeemer Democrats in the U.S. Senate.

In 1861, however, Vance was overshadowed by John A. Gilmer of Greensboro, the leading member of the southern Opposition in the House of Representatives. No southern Unionist during the secession crisis faced so excruciating a dilemma as Gilmer. At the behest of William H. Seward and Thurlow Weed, President-elect Lincoln invited Gilmer to serve in his cabinet. A full discussion of the secret cabinet offer must be deferred to Chapter 9; it may simply be stated here that it confronted the reluctant North Carolinian with a uniquely vexing responsibility.

Gilmer's stature resulted in part from the simple fact that people liked him. A man of medium height, with a "strong compact form and powerful muscular development," he had "a full round face," dark, thick hair, and long sideburns. His "deep-set and laughing dark eyes" beamed with "intelligence, energy, and kindness." He always conveyed "an atmosphere of hope, confidence and cheerfulness." By his middle years the farm boy who grew up wearing homespun had established himself as one of the best lawyers in the North Carolina piedmont and had built an extensive and profitable business. Gilmer, however, remained loyal "to the friends of his youth." Fame and wealth never impaired his instinctive rapport with a broad cross-section of humanity. He was neither the grasping parvenu, driven to "tower above" the class to which he had been born, nor

John A. Gilmer (engraving; Division of Archives and History, North Carolina State Department of Cultural Resources)

the self-designated antiaristocrat such as Andrew Johnson, who compulsively proclaimed the virtue of his humble origins. Gilmer also treated his slaves almost as if they were free.[32]

Gilmer first won election to the state legislature in 1846 and soon moved up to the state senate. Not until 1857, at the age of fifty-two, did he seek a seat in Congress. But once in Washington he quickly emerged as spokesman for the southern Opposition. Nominated by his party for Speaker of the House, he held an important committee chairmanship in 1860.

An appealing manner remained a key to Gilmer's success. In the dark days of the secession winter, he deeply moved many of his listeners when pleading for Congress to enact a Union-saving compromise. "Long before the close Mr. Gilmer's emotions were so powerful that his voice failed," one reporter wrote, "and when he sat down there was scarcely an eye in the house not filled with tears." Gilmer's "honest appeal of a great heart" won praise as the "most effective" speech of the session. Sympathetic Republicans said afterward "that some compromise must be made to keep John A. Gilmer from being carried down by the secession tide."[33]

Gilmer had a remarkable ability to turn potential rivals into friends. The magnetic Henry Winter Davis, the most polished member of the southern Opposition, repeatedly promoted Gilmer. Davis, branded as an apostate to the South because he considered Republicans better allies than southern Democrats, would not in any case have been the right candidate for the Opposition to put forward as House Speaker. So he made no sacrifice in orchestrating Opposition efforts to win the post for Gilmer. But Davis, who would have been far more receptive to a cabinet offer than the North Carolinian, nevertheless advised Lincoln to choose Gilmer. He was "a man of great personal popularity and ability," Davis explained, and his appointment would be the best way to hold the slave states of the upper South in the Union.[34]

Davis, Seward, and Lincoln thus all saw John A. Gilmer as the southerner best suited to help reverse the secession movement. On the merits of the issue, Gilmer had no reservation: he believed secessionists deranged and regarded their cause as suicidal madness. Yet he would not accept the appointment to Lincoln's cabinet. After the war started he sided with his state and eventually served in the Confederate Senate. To understand Gilmer is to understand the paradox of southern Unionism.[35]

2

POLITICAL PARTIES IN THE LATE ANTEBELLUM UPPER SOUTH

TO comprehend what happened in the upper South during the secession crisis, one must first examine the political parties of the late antebellum period. Most voters looked first to these parties for guidance when they found themselves caught between the efforts of the deep South to establish a separate government and the refusal of the North to countenance southern independence. Their reflex was both instinctive and predictable. The parties had acquired a near monopoly power during the preceding quarter-century to define public policy choices. Even though secession by the deep South raised new issues and threatened unprecedented dangers, most voters in the upper South viewed the crisis through partisan lenses.

Political parties flourished in Virginia, North Carolina, and Tennessee during the 1840s and 1850s. Andrew Jackson's Democratic heirs regularly did battle with the Whigs and, after the mid-1850s, with several Whig successor parties (American, Opposition, Constitutional Union) that remained more formidable in the upper South than in any other part of the country. Voters' loyalties, which first crystallized there during the 1830s, corresponded imperfectly, at best, to the sharp regional cleavages in all three states or to the divisions between planter and yeoman terrain. Instead, political parties in the upper South diminished potential sources of internal friction. By comparing the function of national political parties between the 1830s and the 1850s with the function of parties in Virginia, North Carolina, and Tennessee, it becomes possible to recognize the integrating role of upper South partisanship.

VIRGINIA, North Carolina, and Tennessee each contained fertile lowland areas dominated by plantation slavery and less accessible upland areas that depended on white rather than slave labor. Maps 2-1 through 2-6, which identify the major regions of each state and the extent of slaveowning in each county, will enable the reader to visualize salient patterns.

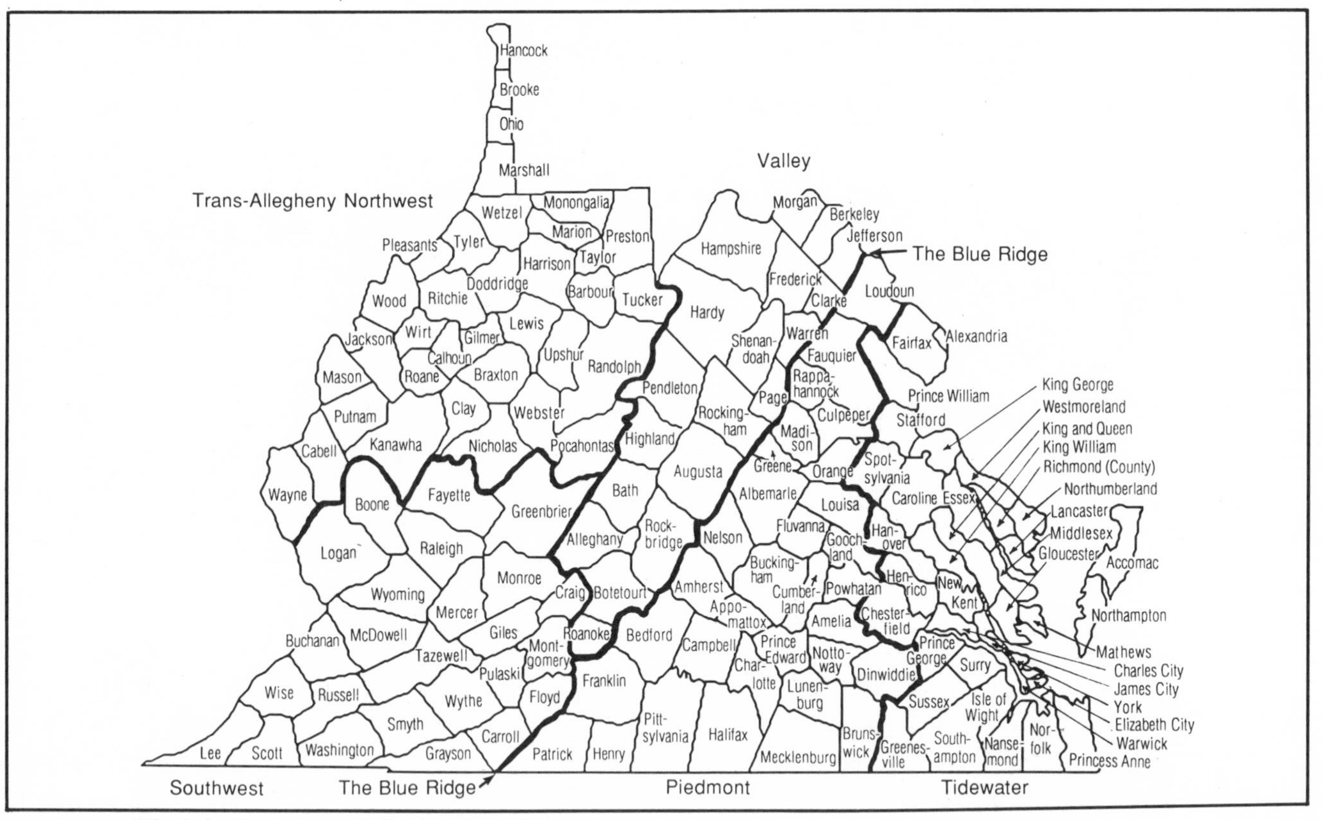

MAP 2-1. *Virginia Counties and Regions in 1860*

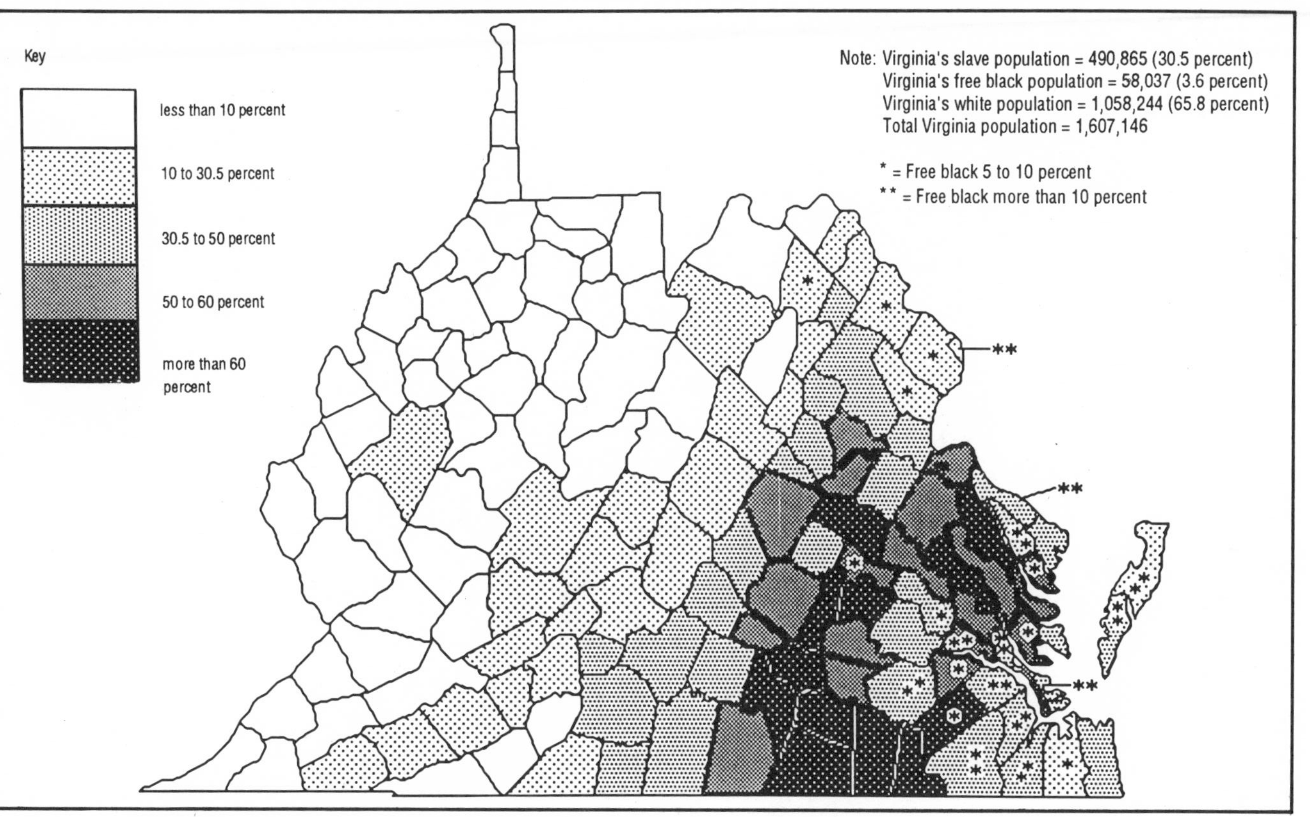

MAP 2-2. *Percentage of Slaves in Virginia's Population, by County, 1860 Census*

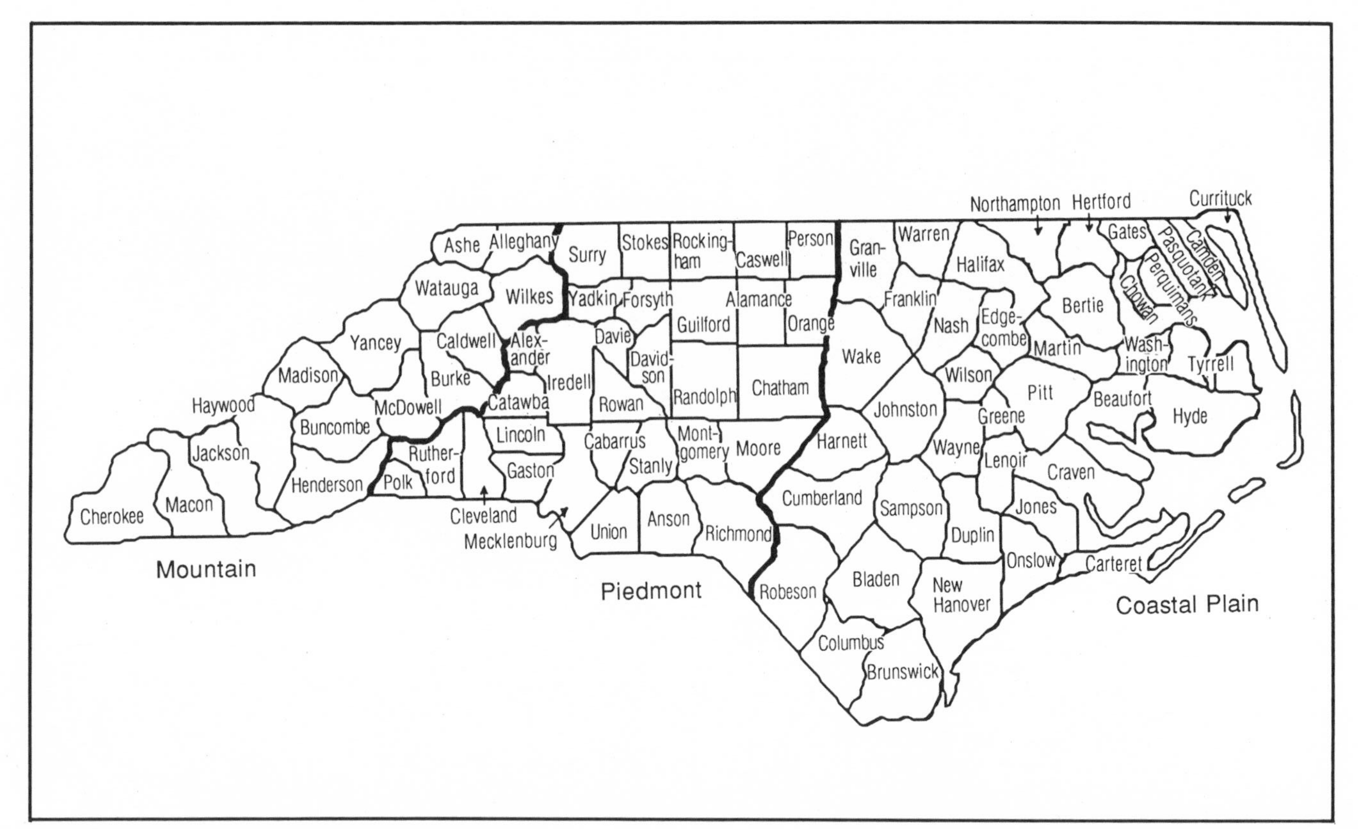

MAP 2-3. *North Carolina Counties and Regions in 1860*

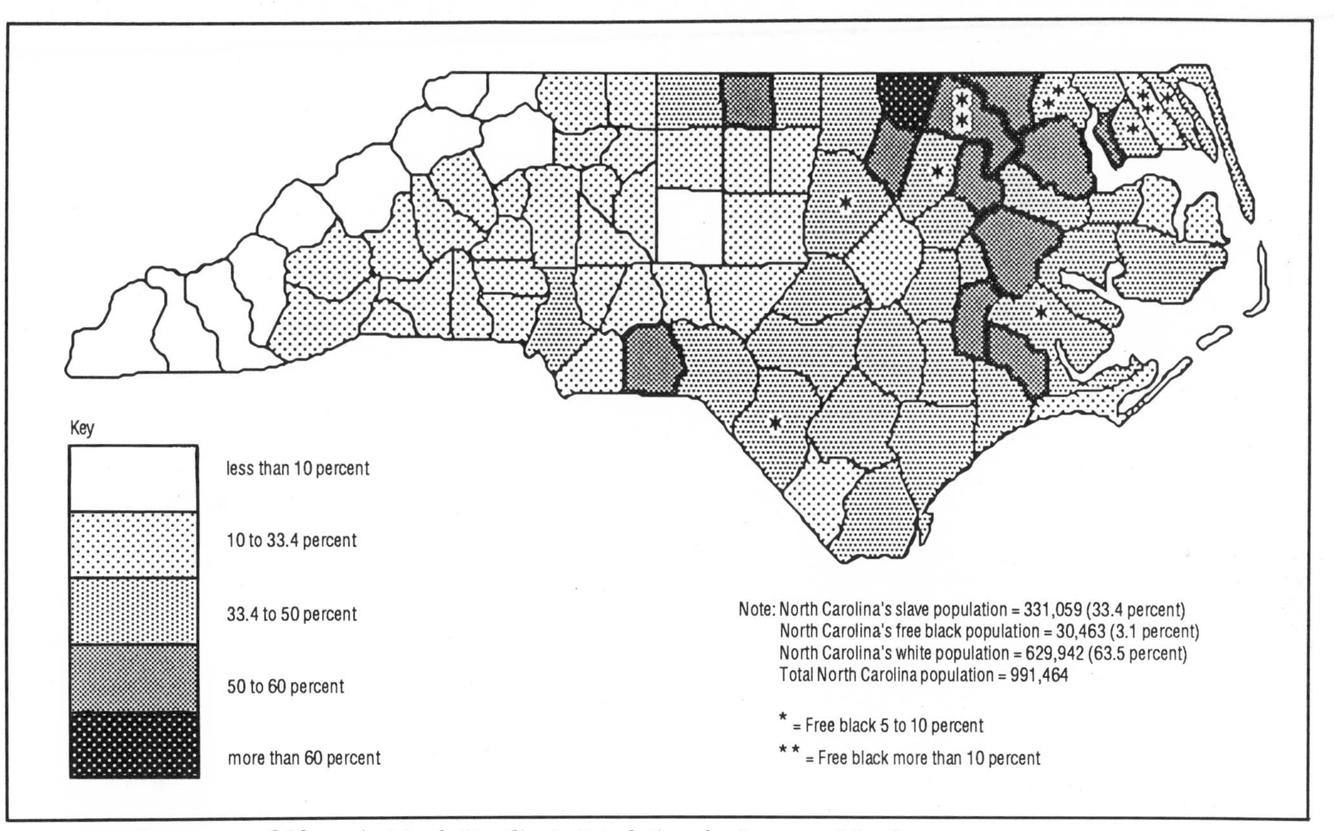

MAP 2-4. *Percentage of Slaves in North Carolina's Population, by County, 1860 Census*

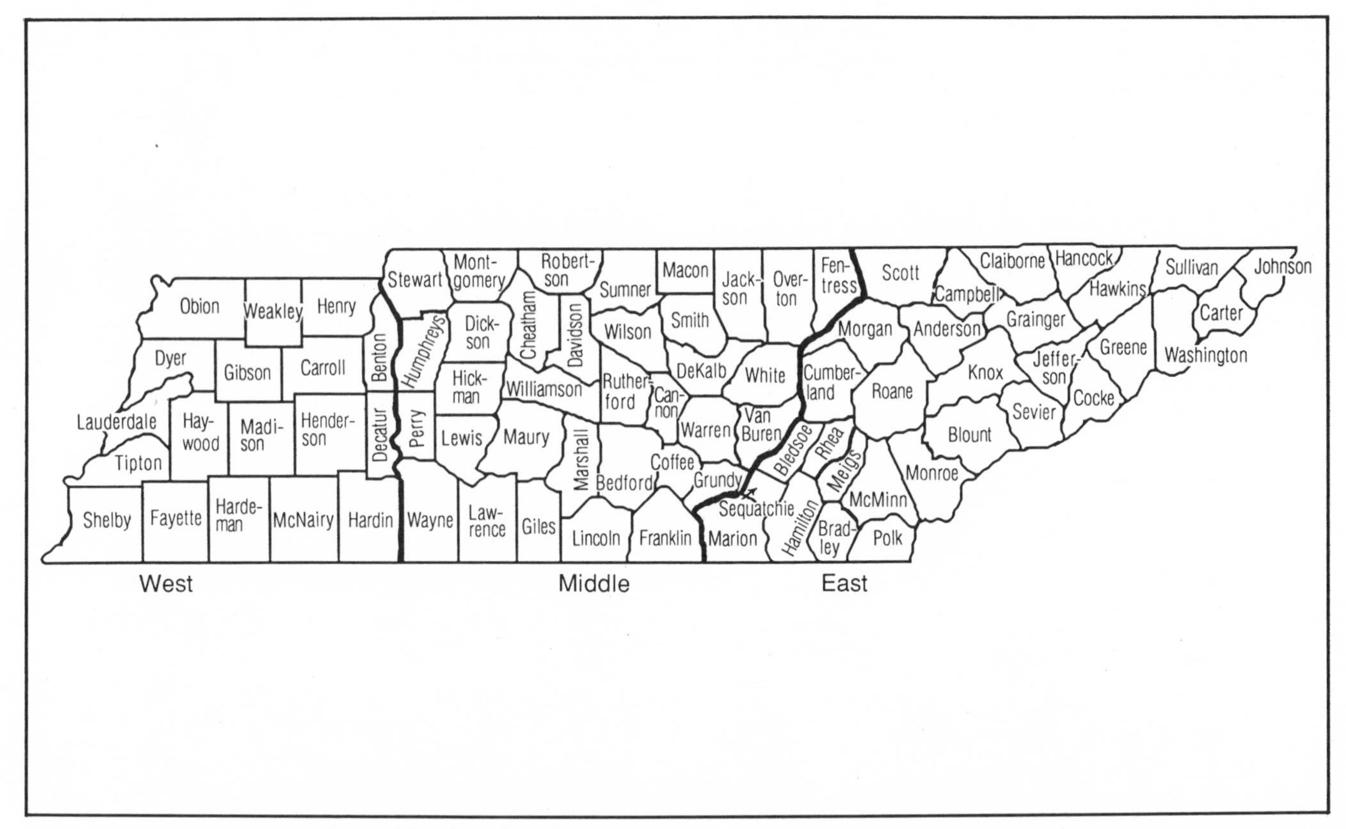

MAP 2-5. *Tennessee Counties and Regions in 1860*

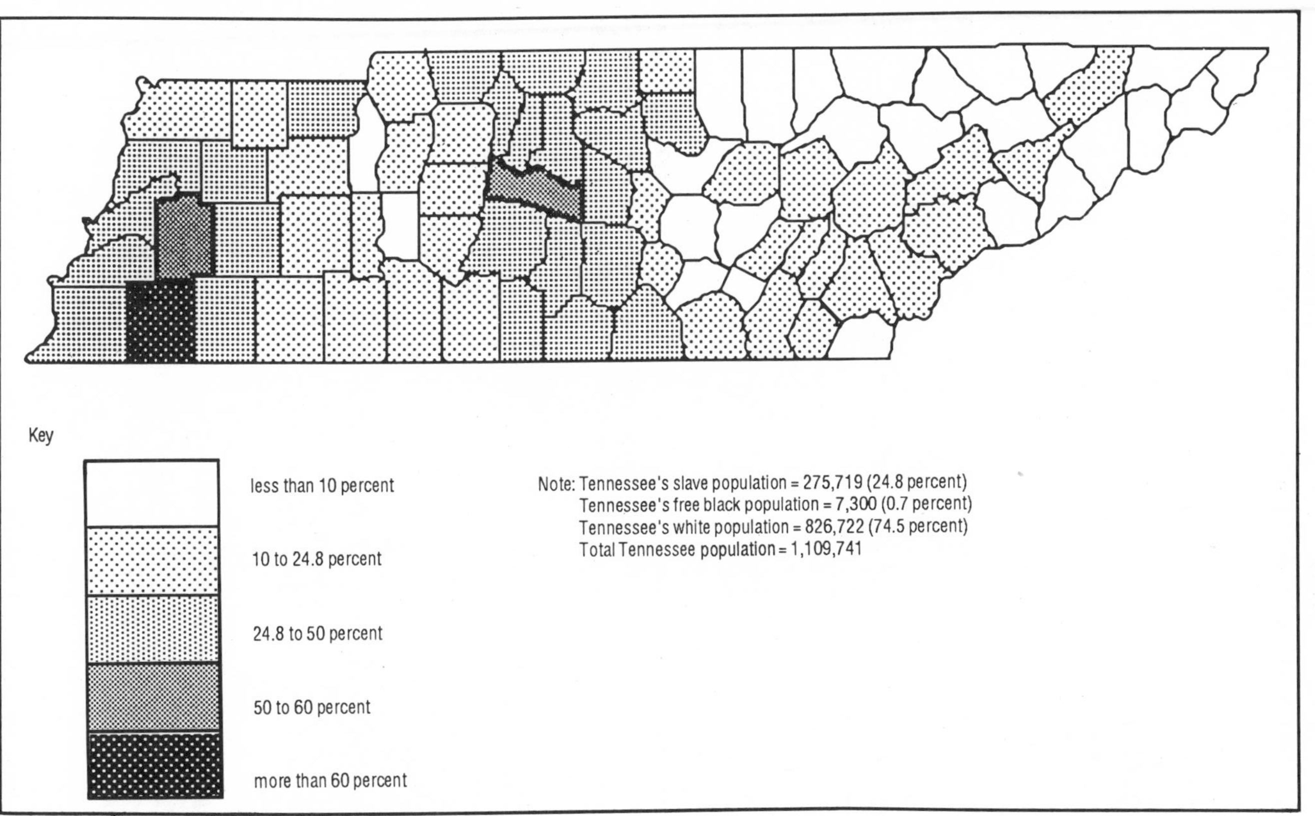

MAP 2-6. *Percentage of Slaves in Tennessee's Population, by County, 1860 Census*

The Blue Ridge bisected Virginia. Slave-based agriculture dominated the east, but only a few counties in the west contained more than incidental numbers of slaves. The lines of division in North Carolina and Tennessee were less abrupt but equally real. Far western North Carolina and eastern Tennessee had very few slaves, the Cumberland valley counties of Middle Tennessee and two strips of central North Carolina counties along the Virginia and South Carolina borders provided plantation environments in regions that included other overwhelmingly white counties, and plantation counties with a strong deep South ambiance clustered in eastern North Carolina and western Tennessee.[1]

Antagonisms between the plantation low country and the yeoman upcountry had a long history in all three states. The two older states of Virginia and North Carolina faced chronic tensions over issues such as legislative apportionment, taxation, internal improvements, popular election of public officials, and property qualifications for voting and officeholding. Protracted east-west constitutional struggles simmered in both states during the antebellum era. Tennessee decided in 1834 to follow the western pattern of democratized procedures on apportionment, taxation, and qualifications. But geography and patterns of economic development tended to divide the long, narrow state into three sections, with prosperous and politically dominant Middle Tennessee pitted against landlocked and isolated East Tennessee and later-settled West Tennessee, which was not cleared of Indians until the 1830s.[2]

In all three states, as in every other state in the Union except South Carolina, competitive political parties developed during the 1830s. These parties were better defined and organized than any that had existed before. Voters' loyalties that were to remain durable for twenty years achieved stable form by 1840. North Carolina and especially Tennessee provided striking examples of vigorous two-party politics between 1840 and 1860. Political mobilization in Virginia lagged somewhat because of property restrictions on eligibility to vote and a dearth of local and state offices subject to popular election before adoption of the 1851 constitution.[3]

The pattern of partisan allegiances that developed bore no uniform relationship to slaveholding or to the conspicuous regional divisions in all three states. Maps 3-1 through 3-3 in the following chapter, which indicate the results by county in the presidential election of 1860, suggest the difficulties in establishing a relationship between party preference and the broad socioeconomic divisions apparent in Maps 2-1 through 2-6. The traditional assumption that Whigs were a planter party should not be applied to the upper South. Only in

North Carolina did high-slaveowning areas display a different pattern of party allegiance than low-slaveholding areas, and there the high-slaveholding areas tended to be Democratic, not Whig. In Virginia and Tennessee, slaveowning bore scant relationship to party affiliation. Considering the three states together, nonslaveholding correlated more clearly with nonvoting than with either party.

A few simple statistics will illustrate the relationship between party and slaveowning. Table 2-1 divides the counties of each state into two categories—those above and those below the statewide average of slave population in 1860. In Tennessee high-slaveowning counties and low-slaveowning counties had almost identical patterns of party preference. Both displayed a slight Democratic edge, although high-slaveowning counties had a slightly greater turnout rate. In Virginia and especially in North Carolina, voter turnout in high-slaveowning counties more sharply exceeded that of low-slaveowning ones. Democrats in Virginia received 4.8 percent more of the 1860 presidential vote than did Whig John Bell in high-slaveowning counties and 7.6 percent more in low-slaveowning ones, which had an 8.3 percent lower voter turnout. Of the three states, North Carolina showed by far the sharpest discrepancies between counties with high and low slaveowning. High-slaveowning counties had a 13.2 percent greater turnout and a decisive Democratic edge of 17.7 percent over Bell. In the low-slaveowning counties, Democrats ran 6 percent behind Bell. In other words, slaveowning bore a demonstrable relationship to party in only one of the three states. And because both North Carolina parties were proslavery "without reservation," effective mobilization of voters, especially at the initial stages of partisan development, must have required an emphasis on issues unrelated to slavery.[4]

Voting patterns in different regions of Virginia, North Carolina, and Tennessee parallel the patterns observed when the counties are arbitrarily divided into high- and low-slaveowning categories. Fewer eligible voters participated in western Virginia than in eastern Virginia, but those who did vote showed slightly greater Democratic proclivities than in the east. Tennessee's three regions, in order of increasing Democratic strength, were East Tennessee, which had a narrow Whig majority; West Tennessee, with a narrow Democratic majority; and Middle Tennessee, which repeatedly produced Democratic margins of more than seven thousand votes between 1856 and 1860 and in which voter turnout stood slightly higher than in the other two regions. In North Carolina, a large cluster of eastern plantation counties voted overwhelmingly Democratic. Despite a smaller cluster of eastern Whig counties adjacent to Albemarle Sound, the east remained a Democratic bastion. Its higher rates of voter turnout

TABLE 2-1.
Voting Patterns in High- and Low-Slaveowning Counties in 1860 (in Percentages)

State	Whig (Bell)	Democrat (Breckinridge and Douglas)	Nonvoting
Virginia: entire state	30.3	36.8	32.2
Virginia: high-slaveowning	34.1	38.9	27.0
Virginia: low-slaveowning	27.9	35.5	35.3
North Carolina: entire state	31.9	36.7	31.3
North Carolina: high-slaveowning	29.1	46.8	24.1
North Carolina: low-slaveowning	34.3	28.3	37.3
Tennessee: entire state	36.8	40.3	22.9
Tennessee: high-slaveowning	37.8	41.6	20.6
Tennessee: low-slaveowning	36.1	39.4	24.5

Note: Data include the entire eligible electorate, both voters and nonvoters. See Chapter 7, n. 2, on sources of data.

than in the west helped to give the state a Democratic majority. Central and western North Carolina had pockets of Democratic strength along the South Carolina and Virginia borders of the piedmont and in some of the mountain counties, but a nucleus of Whig counties in the interior piedmont and adjacent mountains gave the west a slight Whig majority.

Just as slaveowning and intrastate regionalism fail to explain adequately the observed patterns of party allegiance in the upper South, so too ethnic and religious cleavages could not have influenced voters' loyalties in the upper South nearly as much as these factors operated in the North. Although upper South cities attracted significant foreign immigration during the late antebellum period, and pockets of rural German settlement in Virginia's Shenandoah Valley and North Carolina's piedmont dated from the period of original settlement a century before, most white residents of the upper South had British origins and were native born. Consequently, ethnic tensions in the upper South were much less formidable than in the North.

Nor did patterns of religious affiliation in the upper South display as much diversity as in the North. Members of the Methodist and Baptist churches far outnumbered all other religious denominations in these three states and throughout the South.

Mounting evidence suggests that southern partisanship pitted those who welcomed "the social and economic changes associated with the Transportation Revolution" against those who were ambivalent about change or opposed to it—and unhappy about the use of government power to promote it. By appealing to the ideals of economic independence and autonomy, Jacksonians exploited anxieties created by the expansion of the marketplace and the increasing need to buy and sell at a distance. Their rhetoric resonated with eighteenth-century fears about corruption inherent in large-scale economic organization and enterprise. They hoped the nation would return to the "plain and honest path of Republican simplicity." Whigs, by contrast, contended that commercial growth and economic interdependence benefited everybody. Whigs wanted government to promote economic growth by chartering banks, building canals and railroads, and enacting tariffs to raise necessary capital and to spur industrial development. The conflict was not narrowly economic. Alternative visions of the future made some people receptive to change while others found it alarming. Cultural and ideological differences predetermined the responses to many to the changing world of the 1830s. But economic change provided the catalyst for party mobilization.[5]

Differing amounts of wealth in a locality had no more than a tenuous relationship to political allegiances in the upper South. Commercial regions and especially towns often displayed Whiggish tendencies, and more isolated upcountry farming areas often voted Democratic, but such patterns were far from uniform. Prosperous areas might oppose using public money to construct expensive canals or railroads that would primarily benefit less advantageously situated interior regions. Many plantation counties in eastern Virginia and North Carolina thus embraced principles of limited government and exhibited strong Democratic preferences. Likewise, some poorer interior localities favored Whig-supported construction of transportation links to the outside world. Economic aspirations thus help to explain the emphatic Whig loyalties of the central North Carolina piedmont and the Knoxville region of East Tennessee.[6]

Antebellum southerners voted more as members of a community than as individuals. And that community was defined by kinship, "habits of mutuality," and an intricate network of patron-client relationships. Consequently, most southern counties, and especially most voting districts or "beats" within each county, were not politically competitive. Instead, voters "lived in distinct clumps of like minded partisans," and most beats developed "a partisan identity." Local elites or "rural oligarchies" often shaped political preferences, and many ordinary southerners "deferred to the decision of the notables."[7]

Comparisons with the North help to identify the characteristics of antebellum southern voting behavior. In Massachusetts, for example, a distinguishing feature of the emerging second party system in the 1830s was an increase in local party competition. The number of towns that voted overwhelmingly for one party or the other shrunk dramatically. A consensual political order, in which local elites wielded great influence and voting was a "social act," gave way to one in which increasing religious, cultural, and economic diversity provided a basis for greater partisan competition at the local level.[8] But the social and economic order in a typical southern locality remained less diverse than in Massachusetts and therefore less likely to have evolved beyond the consensual elite-dominated phase. The relative absence of ethnoreligious tensions in most southern localities also tended to preserve political unanimity.

No "reductionist model" will prove more than partially successful in explaining party allegiance in the Old South. Party lines "never followed the contours of economic interest with nice exactness." Elite decisions shaped partisan loyalties. Even if the process was generally "not capricious or arbitrary, but consistent with an overall pattern," there was nevertheless plenty of room for slippage.[9]

Although the socioeconomic bases of party loyalty in the Old South remain somewhat inscrutable, there can be no doubt that popular enthusiasm for parties became deeply rooted and genuine. Gross measurements of eligible turnout reached peaks during the second party system never seen before or since. In Tennessee, with no property restrictions on voter eligibility after 1834 and a fiercely competitive political environment, the turnout of eligible voters regularly surpassed 80 percent and sometimes reached over 90 percent. North Carolina developed a pattern of high turnouts in elections for state offices. Voting participation in Virginia, artificially stunted before the reform constitution of 1851, increased sharply thereafter.[10]

The communal and theatrical elements of the second party system did much to stir interest and loyalty of voters. Both candidates for governor typically spent the months before the election traveling together from one county seat to another, giving long speeches and rebuttals in a brutal test of stamina. Candidates for lesser offices followed the same pattern and managed to reach many remote crossroads. Food, drink, music, and other amusements helped to draw swarms of people for political occasions. What reader of antebellum newspapers has not encountered rapturous accounts of the greatest mass meeting in the history of the county, at which an enlightened citizenry listened for hours with perfect attention to the declamations of visiting dignitaries? In a world without radio, television, national magazines, or organized sports, political promoters had an unparalleled opportunity to stir public excitement, and they used it.

But of course there was more to it than that. Politicians commanded attention because they claimed to be able to perform essential services. The mass of voters in antebellum America clung to the eighteenth-century "republican" world view. They feared that freedom, liberty, and equality were constantly endangered by self-seeking conspirators who would put aristocratic privilege ahead of the public good. The great professed goal of political leaders in both parties was to identify and crusade against such "antirepublican monsters." During the 1830s the specter of the "monster bank" seemed to many Americans the greatest threat to liberty, after Andrew Jackson warned about its antirepublican proclivities in one of the most effective state papers in American political history. But others thought the autocratic "King Andrew the First" endangered the republic. In subsequent decades, other antirepublican monsters attracted increasing attention. Even if many "new party professionals" simply pursued power and office as ends in themselves, and did not necessarily share the prevalent republican belief system, they framed their rhetoric in "egalitarian republican language" to stir the passions of ordinary voters. Party leaders deliberately, sometimes cynically, learned to manipulate the "popular dread of manipulation." But the lower rungs on the political ladder were often occupied by men whose party loyalty was rooted in ideological zeal. The "beat leaders" who served as intermediaries between voters and party leaders passionately shared the republican belief system of the mass electorate.[11]

To make sense of the political crisis that culminated in secession, one must analyze the function of political parties in the late antebellum period. A startling conclusion emerges when the function of the national party system is compared with that of parties in Virginia, North Carolina, and Tennessee. At the same time the dynamics of the national party system became pathological, intrastate party competition in the upper South continued to play a healthy integrative role.

The national party system, as it first took shape in the 1830s, functioned to "mediate the rivalries, antagonisms, and conflicts within the society and to resolve them in such a way that conflict would not reach the level of large-scale violence and that the forces of integration would continue to hold the ascendancy over the forces of disintegration or disruption."[12] Increasing societal strain and mob violence wracked the United States during the 1830s. Economic doldrums after 1837 added to public uneasiness. The pace of social and economic change divided those who welcomed change from those who feared it. The developing party system in effect tamed and institutionalized this cleavage. The Democratic party gave "at least the appearance of involvement and participation to those who doubted the benefits of progress," while actually "diverting most challenges to economic development into noisy but harmless rituals." Changes were made "easier to swallow" by forcing the modernizers within the Whig party "to act within the limits set by the will of the people." The second party system thus "knitted up the seams in a straining social fabric."[13]

In other ways, too, the emerging second party system of the 1830s functioned in a unifying manner. An increasingly heterogeneous and geographically scattered nation, which prized local autonomy and freedom from central authority, was bound somewhat more closely together by ties of party loyalty. However much the parties polarized the electorate into two groups, they also functioned symbiotically to create a powerful instrument of national integration. The earnest popular conviction that political parties could thwart the various dangers to American freedom gave them a uniquely important role. So long as they could fulfill such popular expectations, parties clearly performed a stabilizing function.[14]

It may be argued that the party system, though superficially democratic, functioned in a "profoundly conservative" manner. The parties originated at a time when the United States was experiencing "a revolution in market and class relations" marked by "growing inequality" in the distribution of wealth. From this viewpoint, the parties "deflected and coopted new social conflicts as they arose, keeping politics safe for politicians and expanding their followings." The parties thus defused "questions about the fairness of the economic system" and kept disruptive issues "off the political agenda."[15]

The second party system in the South functioned to "prevent any political clash between slaveowners and nonslaveowners which could threaten the security of the slave system." National party leaders also had ample motivation to dampen disagreements regarding slavery. The Whig and Democratic parties each attracted followers both North and South. Sectional controversies potentially threatened both parties. To the dismay of antislavery northerners and southern nationalists of the Calhoun school, both parties remained bisectional coalitions through the 1840s. The party system thereby "deflected the divisive issue of slavery from national politics."[16]

Thus the second party system—at least during the decade after it originated—promoted national integration, defused political conflicts, especially sectional ones, reconciled a substantially skeptical mass public to the rise of industrial capitalism, and provided more orderly channels of political preferment and advancement than had existed before.

But the second party system ceased to function as it once had. Instead, it began to foster sectional polarization. National party leaders who tried to keep the slavery issue out of politics failed to do so. Texas annexation, war with Mexico, and the rise of the territorial issue forced many northern politicians toward at least a qualified antislavery stance, coupled with criticism of the southern wing of the opposite party. Southern politicians played the same game from the opposite point of view. To be sure, party cohesion remained strong on many of the economic issues around which the second party system had formed, but issues relating to slavery cut across party lines. The party system that once dampened "smouldering sectional conflict" began to "fan the fire until it exploded into open warfare." The question, of course, becomes, why did the function of political parties change so drastically during the 1850s?[17]

Some contend that deeply rooted sectional antipathy finally eroded the bisectional bases of support that the parties earlier enjoyed. "Sectional ideology" intruded to shatter the party system "despite the efforts of political leaders of both parties to keep it out."[18] Others argue that social strains caused by rapid economic change and foreign immigration weakened the second party system and that voters' support for parties diminished during the early 1850s because neither party effectively addressed the festering popular discontent. Sectional polarization between 1854 and 1861 could thereby have arisen more as the consequence than as the cause of a malfunctioning party system.[19]

Northern politics experienced kaleidoscopic changes during the early and middle 1850s. Promoters of new partisan issues—antiliquor, antiforeignism, and "reform"—challenged the hegemony of the two parties. Antisouthernism or opposition to "slave power" was at first no more than a subsidiary part of the popular groundswell. Most northern voters who rejected the old party system between 1853 and 1855 supported the "Know-Nothing" insurgency, with its bewitching mixture of antiaristocratic, antiforeign, and reform sentiments. Only when events in Kansas created the impression that northern liberties were directly endangered by a "slave power conspiracy" did the political upheaval in the North begin to coalesce within the Republican party. The latter, benefiting from a more egalitarian and antiaristocratic ethos than northern Whigs ever possessed, and giving at least lip service to the resentments that fueled the Know-Nothing uproar, supplanted both the Whig and Know-Nothing parties and became the majority party in most northern states in 1856. The Republicans' first presidential candidate, John C. Frémont, won a plurality of northern popular votes and a majority of northern electoral votes. The political realignment in the North did not totally eradicate older patterns. Most northern Whigs eventually moved into the new Republican party, joined by an increment of antislavery Democrats and a surge of new voters. But the Republican party, unlike the Whig party, had no need to straddle on sectional issues to conciliate a southern wing. Republicans forthrightly opposed slavery in the territories and promised to curb excessive "slave power." They ridiculed northern Democrats as obedient lackeys of aristocratic slaveowners, conspiring to sell out the interests of free white voters.[20]

The rise of the Republican party deeply stirred the South. Lacking any southern base except in a few scattered localities along the border, the Republican party inevitably presented an ominous and threatening appearance to southerners. Most considered Republican antisouthernism to be insulting and outrageous; many thought it overtly dangerous and potentially subversive of the entire southern social order.

The rise of the Republican party also produced major political reverberations within the South. The southern Whig electorate, most of which had gravitated toward the Know-Nothing or "American" party in 1855 as the national Whig party disappeared, found itself politically isolated by 1856. As the northern wing of the American party shriveled and the Republican party became the only practical political home for northern non-Democrats, southern non-Democrats were left stranded without a national party base. "South Americans" relabeled themselves the "Opposition" or "Southern Opposition" in 1858 and 1859 and "Constitutional Unionists" in 1860. Though not powerless—they held twenty-three seats in the House of Representatives in 1860, almost all from the upper South—the southern Opposition was dwarfed by two larger hostile blocs, the Republican party of the North, organized on the antisouthern platform of opposing slavery in the territories, and the Democratic party, the only remaining national party, which had become increasingly dependent on southern support because of its eroding northern base.[21]

Political arrangements in the deep South changed dramatically during the 1850s. Two-party competition had all but collapsed in the lower South by the end of the decade. The increasingly southernized Democratic party became the vehicle through which the lower South would protect its interests. Factional infighting within the state Democratic parties of the deep South provided leverage for the most extreme Southern Rights proponents. Their insistence on a territorial slave code ultimately split the national Democratic party, and their long-standing belief that the South should secede rather than acquiesce in the election of a Republican president suddenly became fervent majority sentiment in much of the deep South once that dreaded event had occurred.[22]

By any objective standard, southerners exaggerated the danger posed by the Republican party. Northern resentment about excessive southern power—"slave power"—should not have been equated with sympathy toward slaves or a desire to revolutionize the southern social order. The Republicans' principal objective was to break the power of the southern-dominated Democratic party. Thus "for most Republican voters Lincoln's victory and Democratic defeat was the only triumph over the South, the slave power, and slavery they required."[23]

Unfortunately for the peace of the country, many southerners assumed the worst about the Republican party. Partisanship reinforced this dangerous tendency. Southern Democrats insisted that they alone could protect the South from the menace of politicized abolition. Democratic claims presented southern Whigs and their successors with a dilemma. Whigs sometimes asserted that Democratic efforts to protect southern rights were ill conceived and self-defeating. Some Whigs, for example, condemned the Kansas-Nebraska Act on grounds that it greatly increased the external danger facing the South. Other Whigs, however, denounced alleged free-soil tendencies among Democrats and bid opportunistically for the votes of more extreme Southern Rights proponents. The posturing of southern Democrats and Whigs made the Republican party appear monstrous. Ordinary southerners hardly realized that the Republican antislavery program consisted of little more than restricting slavery from the territories, where it had no future anyway, accompanied by the wish or hope that territorial restriction might in the long run create an environment favorable to voluntary emancipation. Instead, the average southerner heard repeatedly that the Republican party constituted a grave menace, that its leaders wanted to annihilate the freedom, liberty, and equality of white southerners, slaveowner and nonslaveowner alike, and that Republicans encouraged reckless fanatics who were hell-bent on unleashing slave rebels.[24]

Similar hyperbole had been a familiar staple of political discourse during the second party system. Politicians North and South had become specialists in identifying menaces to popular liberty that could be averted by electing the right party. When both parties had a national following, such tactics could not readily generate sectional polarization. But the sectionalization of political parties in the 1850s—especially the rise of a northern party that had no base in the South and no means or inclination to defend itself before southern audiences—made traditional political tactics risky and destabilizing. Thus, as suddenly became clear during the weeks after Lincoln's election, the changed party system of the 1850s had produced an unprecedented crisis.

FROM a national perspective, then, the party system and the country itself were headed toward spectacular trouble in 1860. But within the three upper South states that most concern us here, the second party system proved more durable and functioned more effectively than anywhere else in the country. The political balance between the parties did not change greatly, despite a slight Democratic trend in all three states during the 1850s. Narrow Whig majorities in North Carolina and Tennessee in the 1840s became narrow Democratic majorities during the 1850s. Virginia, already a Democratic state, moved more decisively into that party's fold. But by the late 1850s, the Whiggish Opposition recovered some lost ground. It carried twelve of thirty-one seats in the 1859 congressional elections and took advantage of Democratic divisions to deliver the electoral votes of both Virginia and Tennessee to John Bell by plurality votes in 1860. The second party system in the upper South, unlike the deep South, thus survived the upheavals of the 1850s and remained competitive.

Tables 2-2 through 2-6 suggest that patterns of Whig voting in Virginia, North Carolina, and Tennessee remained surprisingly durable at a time when the national party disintegrated. Correlation coefficients higher than .7 and frequently as high as .9 characterized pairs of elections between 1848 and 1860. It appears probable that most Whig voters supported Whig successor parties (American, Opposition, Constitutional Union). Tabulations of Democratic voting, not included here, produce nearly identical results. Party allegiances in these three states of the upper South thus displayed greater continuity than in the North or the deep South.

Tables 2-2 through 2-6 also suggest that greater upheaval occurred

TABLE 2-2.
Virginia: Correlation Coefficients, Whig Voting, 1848–1861

	1851G	1852P	1855G	1856P	1859G	1860P	1860P+R	1861U
1848P	.74	.78	.78	.77	.72	.75	.75	.04
1851G		.81	.77	.71	.69	.65	.66	.20
1852P			.84	.86	.71	.75	.79	.24
1855G				.88	.76	.80	.83	.23
1856P					.71	.77	.81	.34
1859G						.85	.82	−.04
1860P							.96	.03
1860P+R								.12

Note: Whenever pairs of elections exhibit strongly positive correlation coefficients, most voters have probably supported the same party each time (the value of a correlation coefficient may range between +1 and −1). High correlations can mask changes that operate uniformly (for example, a 25 percent decline in Whig voting in each county of a state). But a highly localized political system such as existed in the antebellum South would not often have produced such uniform patterns throughout an entire state. Whenever, on the other hand, pairs of elections exhibit weakly positive correlation values or negative values, significant changes in voting behavior must have occurred.

Tables 2-2 through 2-6 display correlation values from 1848 to 1861 for all three states covered in this study. All eligible voters (adult white males) are included, both those who voted and those who did not. Tables are also provided for Virginia both east and west of the Blue Ridge, a demarcation of great significance during the secession crisis.

The correlations here for Virginia show values of .7 and usually .8 between adjacent pairs of elections between 1848 and 1860. In North Carolina and Tennessee, values as high as .9 may frequently be observed. Correlations taking into account only the votes actually cast, thereby ignoring nonvoters, will produce higher values (often above .95 in North Carolina and Tennessee, with values for Virginia ranging between .8 and .95).

Calculations are based on county-level data and have been weighted in proportion to the number of eligible voters in 1860. The table correlates the Whig vote for president (P), governor (G), and against secession in February 1861 (U). Whig successor parties (American, Opposition, Constitutional Union) are used as the basis for calculations for 1855–60. 1860P+R is the combined Constitutional Union and Republican vote. Antisecession or Union sentiment (1861U) is measured by the vote for "reference," that is, the vote for referring any action of the state convention to popular referendum. See Chapter 7, n. 2, on sources of data.

TABLE 2-3.
Virginia East of the Blue Ridge: Correlation Coefficients, Whig Voting, 1848–1861

	1851G	1852P	1855G	1856P	1859G	1860P	1861U
1848P	.77	.80	.74	.78	.67	.72	.51
1851G		.87	.79	.75	.73	.74	.50
1852P			.84	.85	.78	.78	.52
1855G				.86	.83	.83	.54
1856P					.78	.79	.59
1859G						.85	.44
1860P							.52

Note: Same basis for calculation as Table 2-2.

in voting patterns during the three months between November 1860 and February 1861 than in the previous twelve years. Correlation coefficients far below the 1848–60 norms result when secession crisis voting returns are analyzed. The Union electorates in February 1861 included enough former Democrats and nonvoters to produce distinctly new patterns. Although most Whigs voted pro-Union, a pro-Union surge in low-slaveowning regions obscures the Whig core of Union voting, especially for Virginia and Tennessee. Tables 2-3 and 2-4, with data for the two different halves of Virginia, better show the pro-Union tendencies of Whigs than do the statewide figures in Table 2-2.

A comparative analysis will show that the party system continued to perform a unifying function within each of these three internally diverse states. Until the secession issue arose, party rivalries tended to diminish intrastate sectional antagonisms. Substantial constituencies in various parts of each state impelled partisan organizers to build coalitions. Even as they competed for office and power, politicians thus helped to bind each state together.

Virginia, especially, suffered from severe regional strains. Trans-Allegheny or northwestern Virginia was part of the Ohio Valley. The completion of railroads during the 1850s connecting it to Baltimore, Pittsburgh, and Cleveland weakened its already scant ties to eastern Virginia. Of the three states here considered, Virginia had the greatest intrastate sectional divergences, the least competitive party system, and the least coherently mobilized electorate.[25]

TABLE 2-4.
Virginia West of the Blue Ridge: Correlation Coefficients, Whig Voting, 1848–1861

	1851G	1852P	1855G	1856P	1859G	1860P	1860P+R	1861U
1848P	.78	.75	.79	.78	.69	.69	.71	.27
1851G		.80	.78	.68	.70	.66	.66	.16
1852P			.84	.86	.62	.72	.77	.45
1855G				.91	.70	.78	.83	.43
1856P					.67	.80	.84	.49
1859G						.83	.77	.03
1860P							.92	.29
1860P+R								.40

Note: Same basis for calculation as Table 2-2.

Yet political linkages between the disparate regions of Virginia tended to overcome the tenuousness of its material and cultural bonds. Had it lacked party organization and leadership, Virginia might well have split in 1851. Eastern resistance to legislative reapportionment embittered many westerners. But key leaders and newspaper editors of both parties worked to achieve a compromise that would appease western resentments. A small committee that included former congressman George W. Summers, the leading Whig at the convention, and John Letcher, Democratic congressman and future governor, devised an arrangement to apportion the House of Delegates on the basis of white population but to maintain a "mixed" formula for the state senate that reflected both population and property. The compromise settlement gained endorsements from the two most widely read newspapers in the state, the *Richmond Whig* and its Democratic antagonist, the *Richmond Enquirer*.[26]

The new constitution of 1851 also brought the Old Dominion into line with current procedures elsewhere in the Union. Political competition in Virginia thereby developed a more egalitarian quality. For the first time, all adult white males became eligible to vote, without property qualifications. The state abandoned the archaic county court system, through which courthouse cliques perpetuated themselves in power by appointment rather than by popular election. Also scrapped was the privilege of "plural voting," through which propertyholders in more than one county might increase their political le-

TABLE 2-5.
North Carolina: Correlation Coefficients, Whig Voting, 1848–1861

	1850G	1852P	1854G	1856P	1860G	1860P	1861U	1861C
1848P	.90	.90	.93	.80	.83	.80	.52	.44
1850G		.84	.92	.75	.80	.78	.63	.57
1852P			.89	.85	.86	.87	.56	.52
1854G				.83	.88	.84	.62	.57
1856P					.91	.95	.64	.61
1860G						.93	.70	.66
1860P							.64	.62
1861U								.88

Note: Same basis for calculation as Table 2-2. Antisecession or Union sentiment (1861U) is measured by votes for specific candidates or against a convention. 1861C is the February 1861 vote against holding a convention.

verage. Virginia voters also gained the power, formerly entrusted to the legislature, to elect governors.

The two parties responded to the new democratization by nominating trans-Allegheny leaders to run against each other for governor in 1851. Democrat Joseph Johnson defeated national Whig George W. Summers as both candidates attracted large numbers of first-time voters. Four years later, with the Whig party moribund, Virginia Whigs used the vehicle of the American party to contest for power. Unfortunately for them, the flamboyant eastern champion of western interests, Henry A. Wise, outmuscled more traditional intraparty rivals, secured the Democratic nomination for governor, and solidified his party's already substantial hold on voters of foreign extraction. Wise won handily over the American party candidate, former Southern Rights Whig Thomas S. Flournoy, amid yet another record turnout for a state election. Ready to speak at length on any issue at any time or to write immense missives to fill the columns of the *Richmond Enquirer*, Wise was the most arresting political personality in the state. His skills as a mass leader were unique among antebellum Virginians. But for the political ties between eastern and western Virginia, his meteoric career would have been inconceivable.[27]

By the end of the decade internal strains again gripped Virginia. Intrastate antagonisms, quieted temporarily by the reformed constitution of 1851, intensified. The trans-Allegheny region continued

TABLE 2-6.
Tennessee: Correlation Coefficients, Whig Voting, 1848–1861

	1851G	1852P	1855G	1856P	1859G	1860P	1861U	1861C	1861UU
1848P	.82	.79	.79	.78	.68	.75	.36	.29	.22
1851G		.87	.93	.90	.91	.90	.64	.56	.46
1852P			.87	.90	.87	.90	.53	.37	.22
1855G				.95	.93	.92	.61	.50	.41
1856P					.93	.96	.55	.42	.33
1859G						.96	.70	.55	.43
1860P							.60	.42	.32
1861U								.78	.60
1861C									.77

Note: Same basis for calculation as Table 2-5. 1861UU is the June 1861 vote against separation. County election returns in June 1861 are recalculated to take into account the vote of soldiers in Confederate military encampments. See Chapter 7, n. 2.

to feel neglected by the failure to complete the James River and Kanawha Canal or an equivalent railroad connection to the east. Westerners also resented the constitutional limit of $300 on the value of slaves for purposes of taxation, at a time when the actual value of a prime field hand increased to five times that amount. The 1851 constitution promised further reforms in 1865. Could the state party system ameliorate western grievances before that time? One might have expected the Whiggish Opposition to bid for western votes as it tried to escape its traditional minority position.[28]

Virginia Whigs, however, had traditionally run well in parts of the high-slaveowning east. Even though onetime Whigs such as R. M. T. Hunter, John Tyler, and Henry A. Wise moved into the Democratic party, many counties in eastern Virginia retained Whiggish proclivities through the 1850s (see Map 3-1). Thus Whig or Opposition managers gambled in 1859 that they could win by bidding for eastern votes rather than by taking a pro-western stance. The campaign between Southern Rights Whig William L. Goggin and western Democrat John Letcher, who had recanted earlier emancipationist heresies, degenerated into a proslavery shouting match that Letcher narrowly won, despite modest Opposition gains in the east. A sharp decrease in voting turnout in the west indicated disenchantment with both parties, as did the move of antislavery Whigs in the northwestern panhandle toward the Republican party.[29]

During the 1860 presidential campaign, neither major party in

Virginia could unite all its potential supporters. A substantial fraction of Democrats, centered primarily in eastern cities and parts of the Shenandoah Valley and the northwest, refused to accept the decision to bolt the national Democratic party. The loyal Douglasites, led by Governor Letcher, though heavily outnumbered by Breckinridge supporters, were still numerous enough to throw the state narrowly to John Bell in a plurality vote. Helping to make the outcome unclear for a month were the almost two thousand votes polled for Lincoln, mostly from former Whigs in the northwestern panhandle, who followed the lead of A. W. Campbell's *Wheeling Intelligencer*. Campbell exulted in having established a balance of power between the two major parties and predicted a steady growth of free-soil voting.[30]

INTERNAL strains within North Carolina were not as acute as in Virginia. But issues similar to those that divided Virginia festered in North Carolina: legislative apportionment and taxation that favored the wealthier slaveowning east, property qualifications for voting and officeholding, selection of county officials by appointment rather than by election, and western desires for improved transportation. Although the party system in North Carolina, unlike Virginia's, did have a regional tendency, with Democrats stronger in the east and Whigs in the west, the function of parties was, on the whole, integrative. Despite its western base of strength, the state Whig party hesitated to press western demands. The Whig coalition included a cluster of counties in the far northeast, so that party leaders feared "divisive state issues." Western Whigs therefore failed to get their party to support modification of the provision of the 1835 constitution that gave the east strength in the legislature well beyond what it would have received on the basis of white population. Whigs also hesitated to raise necessary taxes to fulfill their promise to build a railroad linking eastern and western North Carolina.[31]

Whig paralysis offered Democrats an opportunity. By attacking one less significant part of the structure of eastern advantage—the provision in the state constitution that required a fifty-acre freehold to vote for candidates to the state senate—Democrats succeeded in portraying themselves as "the champions of reform and the friends of the common man." Democratic endorsement of "free suffrage" gained sufficient new strength in the west to give the party a statewide majority through the 1850s. At the same time, Democrats pointed out to easterners that they opposed tampering with the system of apportionment that provided the real basis for eastern power.[32]

Additional factors contributed to Democratic success. Even though their party had traditionally opposed spending money on internal improvements, Democratic managers during the 1850s provided crucial support for construction of the North Carolina Railroad. William W. Holden, who edited the most important statewide Democratic newspaper, the Raleigh *North Carolina Standard*, played a key role in devising party strategy on the railroad issue, just as he had on the free suffrage issue. Although Whigs in the legislature voted more consistently for the North Carolina Railroad, the project went ahead during the administrations of Democratic governors, so that their party gained somewhat undeserved credit. By 1856, far western North Carolina, once overwhelmingly Whig, voted for the first time in favor of a Democratic candidate for governor. In yet another way Democrats won political dividends by exploiting the grievances of the west. A powerful western Whig congressman, Thomas L. Clingman, had a burning desire to move up to the U.S. Senate. Embittered by failure to gain the support of his party, Clingman became a political hermaphrodite in the 1850s. He led a faction of Southern Rights Whigs from the west who frequently supported Democratic candidates for state and national office. Clingman finally earned his coveted Senate seat in 1858. By this time he was an avowed Democrat and was elected by Democratic legislators.[33]

The Democratic tide in North Carolina began to ebb in the late 1850s. A sharp increase in state taxes and indebtedness had been required to build the North Carolina Railroad, which remained unfinished in the far west beyond Morganton. Despite western demands that the railroad be completed, the spiraling costs, coupled with the nationwide economic recession in the late 1850s, cooled Democrats' enthusiasm for the cause they had tentatively embraced.

To add to Democratic discomfort, the Whiggish Opposition party overcame its former caution and indecision and in 1860 boldly advocated "ad valorem"—taxing slave property at full value. The state constitution of 1835 exempted slaves under age twelve and over age fifty from taxation and specified that those between the ages of twelve and fifty could be taxed only on a per capita basis. The capitation tax on free white males between the ages of twenty-one and forty-five had to be set at the same rate as the tax on slaves, so that "the nonslaveholding majority could raise the tax on slaves only by raising the tax on itself." Sponsors of ad valorem thus attempted to tap the discontent of nonslaveholding taxpayers, who felt the pinch of state taxes that had more than tripled between 1854 and 1860 and who resented the protected status afforded to slave property. Editor Holden led a minority of Democrats who wanted their party to support ad valorem and thereby prevent it from becoming a partisan issue. But the powerful eastern wing of the Democratic party refused to budge. A strong turnout in the gubernatorial election of 1860 indicated that the ad valorem campaign had stirred public interest. The Opposition ran an impressive race but failed to regain enough western support to win. Many westerners apparently doubted that the Opposition candidate, John Pool, would favor completion of the railroad.[34]

The example of North Carolina illustrates, even more clearly than Virginia, that the second party system remained healthy and functional in the upper South during the 1850s. North Carolina's antiquated constitutional provisions made the formal ground rules of authority less egalitarian than in any other state except neighboring South Carolina. Oligarchy apparently had roots in precedent as well as in law because voters in the Old North State consistently selected officeholders with very high average per capita wealth.[35] But North Carolina traditionalists could not simply stand still. Close two-party competition made North Carolina politicians attentive to popular grievances. To some extent those with complaints were appeased by token concessions such as free suffrage. But issues of undoubted substance—notably, railroad construction and slave taxation—moved to the top of the political agenda during the 1850s.

The electorate of North Carolina apparently found state issues more stirring than national ones. Turnout at gubernatorial elections regularly exceeded the popular vote in presidential contests. The 1860 presidential election, held just three months after the hotly contested ad valorem race for governor, attracted significantly fewer voters to the polls. Such had been the pattern in North Carolina for more than a decade. Even though Stephen A. Douglas had ties to North Carolina through his deceased first wife, a cohesive Democratic party leadership spurred would-be dissidents to line up behind John C. Breckinridge, who carried the state (see map 3-2).[36]

TENNESSEE, unlike Virginia or North Carolina, had an egalitarian constitution and hence no chronic sectional disputes over apportionment, voter eligibility, or slave taxation. Nor was the state afflicted by an obviously discriminatory pattern of internal improvements that favored the lowlands over the uplands. Though it had no railroads as late as 1850, Tennessee by 1860 boasted a substantial rail network that extended over a thousand miles. Heretofore isolated East Tennessee became the site of the key rail line linking Virginia with the Southwest. Chattanooga in lower East Tennessee became a junction for several major rail lines as did Memphis in the Southwest. All regions in the state began to enjoy the good transportation that the Cumberland River had long provided in Middle Tennessee.

But rivalries between its three regions were very much a part of political life in long, narrow Tennessee. During the 1850s, Middle Tennessee, which had long dominated the commercial and political life of the state, found itself challenged by the growing assertiveness of politicians in both East and West Tennessee, who demanded greater recognition in both state parties than they had earlier received, and by the economic and commercial growth of West Tennessee, which by 1860 contained the most wealthy plantation counties in the state and fast-growing Memphis, the largest city.[37]

Tennessee politics during the 1850s were neither as issue-oriented as in North Carolina nor as prone to degenerate into sterile disputes on the slave issue as in Virginia in 1859. Tennessee Democrats tried repeatedly to pin the abolition label on their opponents, hoping especially to gain political advantage from Whig Senator John Bell's votes against both the Kansas-Nebraska Act and the Lecompton constitution. Such accusations appeared to make little impact. Political competition remained close despite the collapse of the national Whig party. The most distinct personality to achieve statewide office in the 1850s was former East Tennessee Congressman Andrew Johnson, the self-styled plebeian. Though never a favorite of conservative party leaders, Johnson had a mass following that made him too formidable to be denied the Democratic nomination for governor in 1853. He was elected and became the first Tennessee Democrat to win reelection to the office in 1855. Although Johnson got less than 51 percent of the vote in both his races, he broke the Whig grip on the state, as became clear in 1856, when James Buchanan became the first Democratic presidential candidate since Andrew Jackson to carry Tennessee. A Democratic legislature soon elevated Johnson to the U.S. Senate. His successor as governor, West Tennessean Isham Harris, won 54 percent of the vote in 1857, but a revived Opposition party ran him a closer race in 1859 and managed to take seven of ten seats in Congress. A healthy increase in voter turnout in 1859 aided the Opposition and indicated that the tradition of two-party competition remained strong. The Opposition may also have benefited by nominating for the first time a candidate from East Tennessee for governor.[38]

Tennessee voting patterns in the presidential election of 1860 duplicated almost exactly those of 1856 and 1859, with a statewide Democratic lead of 5 percent. But Douglas had strong support in Memphis and the adjacent southwestern counties, thereby drawing off more than enough votes from Breckinridge to give native son John Bell a plurality victory (see Map 3-3). Tennessee's strong, stable political parties provided cohesion in a geographically segmented state. Two Tennessee presidents (Jackson and James K. Polk), another future president (Johnson), and two other major presidential candidates (Bell and Hugh Lawson White) were not the only powerful personalities in Tennessee politics during the antebellum era. The state provided as good an example as any North or South of how relentless two-party competition could elevate strong leaders and engage and hold the loyalties of the mass electorate. Of the three states considered here, Tennessee consistently had the highest levels of voter turnout.[39]

A COMPARATIVE glance at the careers of Henry Wise, William Holden, and Andrew Johnson will reveal a great deal about the political environment of their respective states. During the decade before the war, each of these three became a particular symbol and champion of egalitarianism within the Democratic party. Each spearheaded efforts to make the party more attractive to ordinary voters. Each recognized that the party would at its peril neglect the nonslaveowner of the upcountry. Two of the three won gubernatorial elections during the 1850s; the third very much wanted that same chance.

The most conspicuously independent and successful of the three, Andrew Johnson, came from the state with the most democratized political culture. Party leaders distrusted him both because of his political style and because he advocated exotic issues such as expanded public education, free homesteads, popular election of presidents, and limitations on the term of federal judges. But Johnson's rousing stump oratory and tireless personal campaigning gave him a base of loyal support that party leaders could not ignore. Johnson, in turn, remained an orthodox Southern Rights Democrat on most issues before Lincoln's election. He cheerfully supported Breckinridge after the rupture of the party in 1860. But secession brought Johnson to the crossroads of his career.[40]

Like Johnson, Henry Wise was a tireless stump speaker and campaigner with a mass following. Unlike Johnson, Wise operated in a less democratic, more elitist, and more conservative political environment. Consequently, his position in the Virginia Democratic party remained more tenuous. His intraparty rivals derailed Wise's presidential bandwagon in the spring of 1860. The Virginia setting also helps to explain his intermittent espousal of extreme Southern Rights positions when these seemed to offer political advantages.

Thus Wise threatened to lead a secession movement in 1856 if the Republican party's John C. Frémont won the presidential election. Wise later explained that his object had been to awaken northern conservatives and that the tactic had succeeded perfectly. His role in 1860–61 was less ambiguous. Though posturing as a conditional Unionist, Wise masterminded secessionist strategy at the Virginia convention and itched for combat. Virginia's popular leader thus followed a course diametrically opposite to that of Tennessee's Andrew Johnson, who cut loose from the secession-tainted Democratic party in December 1860 and became the most outspoken unconditional southern Unionist in Congress.[41]

Holden had remarkable skills. Only a political genius could have created an egalitarian image for the North Carolina Democratic party, dominated as it was by the planter east. After years behind the scenes and at the press, Holden believed that he deserved the chance to run for governor or U.S. senator. But the gentlemen who controlled the party shunted the editor aside. In 1860 Holden was barely reconciled to his party's stance on the ad valorem issue or to the southern disruption of the Democratic party and the separate candidacy of Breckinridge. The crisis of the Union drove Holden into permanent estrangement from the party he had done so much to build. Outspokenly Unionist before Fort Sumter, when most North Carolina Democrats leaned toward secession, Holden became a very reluctant Confederate supporter. He soon emerged as the most visible and dangerous critic of Confederate rule in North Carolina. When the war ended, Holden finally gained the governorship, first by appointment from Andrew Johnson and then, under the new constitution of 1868, as the elected leader of the Republican party.[42]

PARTIES and partisanship thus shaped the political culture of the late antebellum upper South. More than in any other part of the nation, the second party system there remained a vital force as the sectional crisis intensified. Who in the upper South resisted sectional polarization, and why? It is appropriate now to consider the persistence of sectional moderation there during the 1850s, as the North and the lower South stumbled toward confrontation.

3

THE POLITICAL ORIGINS OF UPPER SOUTH UNIONISM

POLITICAL ties between North and South disintegrated during the 1850s. The Whig party, already weakened by sectional acrimony, lost most of its electorate to the American party between 1853 and 1855. The American party in turn divided when most northern Americans became Republicans during 1856. Finally, in 1860, the Democratic party, the one remaining political organization that commanded loyalty both North and South, ruptured. Northern and southern sectionalism functioned as "two blades of a pair of shears: neither blade, by itself, could cut very effectively; but the two together could sever the bonds of Union."[1]

In hindsight the shearing process appears relentless and the country inexorably headed toward secession and civil war. At the time, however, nobody knew how events would unfold. Moderate political leaders in the upper South, whose prewar perceptions and actions provide the focus for this chapter, recognized that sectional polarization had become a dangerous force. In their gloomier moments they sometimes suspected the worst. But they generally remained hopeful that a crisis could be averted, right up to the weeks after Lincoln's election in November 1860, when events suddenly reeled out of control.

THE Kansas firebrand disrupted an interval of diminished sectional tensions following the Compromise of 1850. Interpreting the repeal of the Missouri Compromise as evidence of a plot to nationalize slavery, North as well as South, many northern politicians resolved to challenge the "slave power conspiracy" and to prevent Kansas from becoming "a dreary region of despotism, inhabited by masters and slaves."[2] The uproar in the North persuaded many southern politicians that slavery was menaced and southern rights endangered. Ammunition provided by their sectional antagonists thus strengthened the hands of more extreme leaders, North and South.

For four years Kansas remained a source of poisonous dissension, beginning with the establishment of the Kansas territory in 1854, continuing through the lawless skirmishing of 1855–56, and culminating in the abortive effort in 1857–58 to admit the territory as a state under the proslavery Lecompton constitution. By late 1858, however, the Kansas issue began to lose its disruptive power. Public affairs in that troubled territory stabilized. A large majority of Kansas residents plainly opposed slavery and soon would seek entry to the Union as a free state.[3]

As southern moderates surveyed the wreckage left by four years of sectional acrimony, they anticipated a brighter future. They assumed that "the slavery agitation must die out, unless new fuel shall be found for the flame." Hoping that the era had ended when "opposition or zeal for the establishment of slavery in a territory" would "be permitted to swallow up all questions of national policy," they looked forward to an "approaching calm in the public mind," when "extremists on either side" would no longer set the political agenda.[4]

Southern moderates, composed primarily of former Whigs from the upper South, had a mixture of motives. They were alarmed by the erosion of national parties and feared the Union would be endangered by continued North-South controversy. "Bitter sectional excitement," warned Congressman John A. Gilmer of North Carolina, would only lead to disunion and civil war. The moderates also hoped that a grateful public would honor those who had stood firm against sectional polarization during the storms of 1854–58. They hoped to play an enlarged role in national politics.[5]

Relatively few southern politicians had withstood the pressures for sectional solidarity in the 1854–58 period. The ethos of their region provided little support for principled dissenters from community opinion. But southern politicians who tried to make the Kansas issue a test of regional loyalty had not entirely succeeded. An undercurrent of southern Whiggish opinion regretted the overturn of the Missouri Compromise and saw no reason for asserting the "abstract" and "barren" right to take slaves into regions where Henry Clay, Daniel Webster, and many other sensible men had long concluded that slavery would never flourish. Southerners who voiced such opinions between 1854 and 1858 found themselves condemned as free-soilers, abolitionists, and worse by the self-appointed political guardians of southern interests. But in Whiggish parts of the upper South, widespread skepticism about Kansas prevented any unanimity.[6]

Thus a small number of southern congressmen "voted against the South" on the most publicized sectional controversies during the 1850s. The group included Senators John Bell of Tennessee and John J. Crittenden of Kentucky and such House members as North Carolina's John A. Gilmer and Tennessee's Emerson Etheridge. Others, who had failed to follow their better judgment, later wished they could retrace their steps. George E. Badger, a Whig senator from North Carolina until 1855, considered his vote in favor of the Kansas-Nebraska Act the greatest mistake of his political career.[7]

When the Buchanan administration tried to get Kansas admitted to the Union in 1858 under the Lecompton constitution, a proslavery subterfuge clearly opposed by a majority of Kansas residents, a small group of southern moderates balked. Southern anti-Lecomptonites argued that the ill-fated campaign to make the territorial issue a test of southern rights had boomeranged and proven counterproductive. It had aroused so much hostility and resentment in the North as to lay the foundation for an antisouthern political party. Further provocations such as Lecompton, southern critics noted, would only strengthen Republicans and weaken the South. Every southern anti-Lecomptonite faced a barrage of criticism for having voted on the same side of a sectional issue with William H. Seward, Joshua Giddings, and the "Black Republicans."[8]

Southern voters, however, shrugged off the highly charged rhetoric. In August 1859, John Gilmer was reelected to his North Carolina seat in Congress by an increased majority after having spent the campaign defending his anti-Lecompton vote. In West Tennessee, Emerson Etheridge, who had voted against the Kansas-Nebraska Act, made a political comeback, narrowly defeating the popular J. D. C. Atkins. In Middle Tennessee, the Opposition dumped Congressman Charles Ready, who had voted for Lecompton. Ready ran for reelection with Democratic support but lost to young Robert Hatton, the rising star in the state Whig-American-Opposition pantheon. Maverick Democrat John Millson of Norfolk, Virginia, an opponent of the Kansas-Nebraska Act, held his seat, and Southern Rights candidates for Congress lost two districts in Virginia's Shenandoah Valley.[9]

Moderates from the upper South, relieved to see the Kansas issue abate, provided scant support for the more bizarre demands put forward by Southern Rights Democrats in the late 1850s. The campaign to revive the African slave trade won few friends in the upper South, which feared the collapse of slave prices. Douglas Democrats from the upper South likewise rejected, as did most of the southern Opposition, the effort to enact a slave code for the federal territories. So, too, the campaign to annex a slave empire in the Caribbean encountered resistance from non-Democrats, especially in the upper South.[10]

EXPECTATIONS that sectional controversy might diminish led some members of the southern Opposition and a scattering of diehard Whigs in the North to try organizing a "United Opposition" across sectional lines. They hoped that a presidential ticket of old Whigs, one northern and one southern, could stand on the common ground of opposition to the alleged corruption and incompetence of the Buchanan administration. Some would-be architects of the United Opposition contemplated complete silence on sectionally divisive issues; others thought it could safely oppose reopening of the African slave trade or seek to attract supporters of Stephen A. Douglas with a popular sovereignty platform.

The political logic underpinning the concept of a United Opposition made sense—up to a point. For the Opposition of the upper South, it offered the prospect of a national party affiliation, which they had badly missed since the demise of the Whig party. Yet most of their presumed northern allies were "Black Republicans," who would have to be repackaged and relabeled so as not to alarm southern voters. It seemed improbable that any such party, starting from a minority position in every southern state except Maryland, could in the near future challenge a united Democratic party. But the bitter quarrel between the Buchanan administration and supporters of Stephen A. Douglas suggested that the Democracy might be vulnerable. The possibility of exploiting Democratic divisions and exercising real power in a successful national coalition party tantalized upper South Opposition leaders. They even hoped that a southern Whig could emerge as the compromise choice should the next presidential election be thrown into the House of Representatives.

Republicans could see both benefits and disadvantages in a United Opposition. The scheme did appear to offer a way to enlarge the party base. Republicans lost the presidency in 1856 because they could not unite all anti-Democratic voters in the North. A coalition of nativists and Whigs who voted for former President Millard Fillmore on the American party ticket held the balance of power in Illinois, Indiana, Pennsylvania, and New Jersey. Some Republicans, notably Horace Greeley, editor of the influential *New York Tribune*, thought a United Opposition party that abandoned the Republican label could attract these voters. Other Republicans knew, however, that a United Opposition would offend party loyalists who wanted unmistakable support for antislavery principles. Republican gains in the 1858 elections in the North also raised hopes that the party might carry the key states of the lower North in 1860 without making further concessions to Fillmore supporters.[11]

Discerning Republicans therefore treated the idea of a United Opposition like a dead cat. Abraham Lincoln calculated that even with "two of the best men living placed upon it as candidates," a ticket pledged only to oppose the slave trade and the "rotten democracy" would prove disastrous. It "would gain nothing in the South," Lincoln thought, except probably Maryland, the only state Fillmore had carried in 1856, "and lose everything in the North." All the northern Democrats who had joined the Republicans "with the object of preventing the spread, and nationalization of slavery" would desert a United Opposition party and render it "utterly powerless everywhere." "If the rotten democracy shall be beaten in 1860," Lincoln concluded, "it has to be done by the North." A southern man could be placed on its ticket but only if he accepted the Republican idea of preventing the expansion of slavery.[12]

Discussion about the possibility of a United Opposition party nevertheless continued during 1859, although the would-be coalitionists had great trouble identifying suitable candidates or devising a satisfactory platform. Horace Greeley, the chief Republican planner, insisted that the candidate must have a record of clear opposition to the Kansas-Nebraska Act, Lecompton, the slave trade, a territorial slave code, and the conquest of new slave territory and that he be unmistakably opposed to enlarging slave territory in the Union. Such antislavery specificity was totally unacceptable to most southerners. The single prominent exception—Greeley's candidate for president—was Edward Bates, a respected former Whig from Missouri. But by placing himself within the ideological consensus of the Republican party, Bates sacrificed most of his potential support in the upper South.[13]

THE already precarious scheme to organize a United Opposition suffered a devastating and unexpected blow on the night of October 16, 1859, when John Brown led eighteen men in a suicidal assault against the federal armory at Harpers Ferry, Virginia. Brown's apparent object was to stir a slave insurrection in the South. At that, he completely failed. But if he also had the political objective of making it more difficult to keep or create party coalitions across sectional lines—though there is no clear evidence that he did—then Brown's raid succeeded brilliantly. It drove a wedge through the already tentative and fragile Opposition-Republican coalition and helped to intensify the sectional polarization that soon tore the Democratic party and the Union apart.

The southern reaction to Brown's raid took time to develop. Although initial news reports from Harpers Ferry suggested that hundreds of abolitionists or slave rebels were involved, it soon became apparent that Brown led only a small group, that it had been overwhelmed, that the survivors were all in custody, and that no slave rebellion had occurred. So southerners at first felt relieved and reassured: an isolated fanatic had led a few deluded followers in an enterprise that proved a complete fizzle. Before long, however, captured documents showed that Brown had a network of northern supporters who had provided him with money and supplies. It then became possible to argue that a far wider conspiracy stood behind Brown. That suspicion was reinforced by his success at gaining the sympathy of many antislavery northerners. Proving to be as effective a publicist as he had been incompetent as a military strategist, Brown portrayed himself as a martyr in a holy cause. Very few northerners actually defended what Brown had done, but growing numbers expressed admiration for his pure motives, his courage, and his willingness to die for his beliefs.[14]

Indignation swept the South during November. The secondary southern response to Brown's raid, fueled by suspicion that many in the North supported or condoned his actions, pushed southern estrangement to unprecedented levels. Brown's raid was "not simply an accident without historical significance, due to the fanatical character of an individual, like Nat Turner's insurrection in Southampton," concluded one worried Virginian. Instead, Brown was an "agent" who had the "sympathy of the masses of the North." Many across the upper South called for military preparation. "You know not how soon the cloud which is rising in the North may overtake us," noted a Southampton County resident. "*We already hear the low mutterings of the distant thunder, and it is now time for us to close the shutter, and prepare for the approaching storm.*" Secessionists celebrated the new mood of southern militance. "We may now see that a great majority of the northern people are so much the enemies of negro slavery, that they sympathise even with treason, murder . . . to overthrow slavery," Edmund Ruffin observed. He hoped the bad sectional feelings triggered by the Brown raid would "have important consequences, in widening the breach, & forwarding the separation of the slaveholding states."[15]

The furor stirred by John Brown had unavoidably political dimensions. For southern politicians who wanted to depict the Republican party as a grave menace, the episode offered an irresistible opportunity. Republicans had always contended that they had no intention of interfering with slavery where it existed. Brown offered a glimpse of the alleged wolf that lurked beneath the sheep's clothing. Southern Democrats asserted that New York Senator William H. Seward, the expected Republican presidential nominee, had inspired or even masterminded the fanatical Brown. Had not Seward's Rochester speech of 1858 proclaimed an "irrepressible conflict" between slave and free society? The Harpers Ferry raid became, in southern eyes, "one of the first fruits of the teachings of Black Republican leaders." The *Richmond Enquirer*, warning against false Republican reassurances, demanded southern vigilance "to resist the consummation of sectional outrage and injustice by the election of a Black Republican President."[16]

The sectional polarization growing out of the Brown raid effectively ended efforts to create a United Opposition. By the winter of 1859, the southern Opposition dared not make any arrangements or alliance with the Republican party, so that "henceforth all talk of an intersectional coalition was just so much hot air." Kentucky Senator John J. Crittenden, one of the several border state Whig moderates whose name had figured prominently in speculation about a United Opposition presidential ticket, observed in January 1860 that he could not carry a single southern state on a Republican ticket and that any ticket including him would fail in the North: "The party would sink me in the Slave States, and I should sink the party in the Free States." Under these polarized circumstances, the southern Opposition decided to act independently. A group that chose to call itself the Constitutional Union party eventually nominated former Tennessee Senator John Bell to run for president.[17]

A PROTRACTED struggle to organize the U.S. House of Representatives further exacerbated the sectional acrimony resulting from the Brown affair. The elections of 1858–59 had produced a House with no party in the majority. Republicans held 109 seats, 21 more than regular Democrats and not far short of half the 237 seats. But thirteen northern anti-Lecompton Democrats, twenty-three southern Opposition men, and four northern Whig-Americans held the balance of power. Furthermore, several nominal Republicans from Pennsylvania stood ready to support a compromise candidate for Speaker.[18]

Three days after Brown was hanged, the new House met for the first time. The Republican nominee for Speaker, John Sherman of Ohio, was not identified with the outspoken antislavery wing of the party. His long future career in Congress would amply demonstrate Sherman's basically conservative temperament and principles. But Sherman had incautiously joined sixty-seven other congressional Republicans in endorsing *The Impending Crisis*, a book written by Hinton Helper of North Carolina, which called for nonslaveowners of the South to challenge the power of slaveowners and rid the South of slavery. Helper contended that the South could achieve economic growth only by abandoning slavery and relying on free white labor. For slaves and free blacks he voiced only contempt. Helper, however, thought southern white yeomen were entitled to wage class warfare.

This idea touched a raw nerve. Democrats insisted that no endorser of Helper's "incendiary" book could serve as Speaker of the House. Their challenge produced an explosive two-month stalemate.[19]

The southern Opposition played a significant role in the Speakership fight. Their twenty-three votes were the largest single bloc not controlled by either of the two major parties. Despite the fiercely sectionalized atmosphere, the southern Opposition spurned calls to support a southern Democrat to prevent the election of a "Black Republican" Speaker. But the southern reaction to the Brown raid and the Helper book placed a formidable barrier between Republicans and the southern Opposition. Some of the latter had apparently been inclined to vote for Sherman but were "frightened" away by his association with Helper.[20]

Instead, the southern Opposition put forward its own candidate, John A. Gilmer. One of the few southerners who voted against Lecompton, the North Carolinian represented a strongly Unionist constituency, which had just reelected him to Congress by an increased majority, shrugging off accusations that Gilmer was a "Black Republican" ally. His stance on Lecompton and his earlier prominence in the Whig and American parties—he had been the American candidate for governor in 1856—gave Gilmer the potential to attract support from some of the more conservative American-Whig-Republicans of the lower North. On December 16, his vote total rose to thirty-six, as thirteen members from Pennsylvania, New Jersey, and New York voted with the southern Opposition. At that point, the eighty-six regular Democrats on the floor could have elected Gilmer Speaker. But they did not. The result, in the judgment of a reporter for the *Raleigh Register*, "stripped . . . the veil of hypocrisy from the Democratic party." It showed the "hollowness and insincerity" of Democratic pleas to put aside all other considerations to defeat the Republican party and thereby "preserve the rights of the South and save the Union." In language that anticipated the rhetoric of the upcoming presidential campaign, the correspondent charged that "their object is to save—not the Union—but the Democratic party—to continue their hold on the Federal offices. If they cannot do this, they spurn all other parties, and would willingly convulse the Union by placing in power those that they claim are the worst enemies of the Republic!" He concluded that some Democrats preferred Sherman's election so as to promote disunion.[21]

The Democratic rebuff of Gilmer "stiffened the backs" of the southern Opposition. Three Tennessee congressmen—Emerson Etheridge, William B. Stokes, and Robert Hatton—won national attention by rejecting appeals for southern unity, castigating Democrats for endangering the Union, and forcefully defending the course of their party. Etheridge's words "appear to carry weight both with his own men and the Republicans," reported the *New York Times*, and Hatton "at once commanded attention" as one of the leading orators in the House. But the southern Opposition remained unwilling to collaborate with the Republican party. The one southern Opposition congressman receptive to an Opposition-Republican agreement, Henry Winter Davis of Baltimore, privately lamented that his party friends "feared to strike a blow" at the Democrats, "the only party which is really dangerous to the country." For Davis the only "practical" course was to unite with rather than oppose the Republicans.[22]

In late January the southern Opposition nearly arranged to gain the Speakership. Spokesmen for the Democrats secretly agreed to support a conservative Opposition-Whig from North Carolina, W. N. H. Smith, who would in turn give Democrats substantial power. But the regular Democrats and the southern Opposition together did not constitute a majority. Southern Opposition managers used some subterfuge to get several northern Whig-Republicans to pledge for Smith, without revealing that the Democrats would join to elect him Speaker. At the last minute, however, the Whig-Republicans backed out when they found themselves voting with the Democrats, so that Smith's candidacy fell a few votes short.

At this point a nucleus of intransigent Republicans, who had promised to vote for Sherman "until the crack of doom," decided to relent. Republican managers thereupon dropped Sherman and brought forward William Pennington of New Jersey, a quasi-Republican Whig-American who had not signed the Helper endorsement. Pennington appeared likely to attract a few crucial extra votes. Henry Winter Davis, who had secretly promised to support a Republican if his vote could tip the balance, found himself put to the test. His lone vote, the only one for Pennington cast by a southerner, proved decisive. Outraged southern Democrats condemned Davis for delivering control of the House to a "Black Republican."[23]

Davis acted deliberately. His vote not only resolved the Speakership controversy, but it also won substantial leverage for his hesitant southern friends. The victorious Republicans agreed to share power with a coalition of anti-Lecompton Democrats, "People's" and "Opposition" Whig-Americans from Pennsylvania and New Jersey, plus the southern Opposition. Sherman had promised, and Pennington honored the promise, to "assign the committees on the basis of recognizing all the opposition whether they voted for him or not—and constitute them as to stifle the negro agitation—and to turn the whole activity of the session on exposure of the administration." Several southern Opposition leaders, who had felt constrained from voting for any Republican, accepted committee chairmanships. Key assignments went to John A. Gilmer, who took control of the Committee on Elections, and Robert Hatton of Tennessee, selected to head the Committee on Naval Expenditures, which would soon investigate some of the misdeeds of the scandal-plagued Buchanan administration. Davis himself rejected a chairmanship and urged Pennington to "put men further south in high places—where they could be seen." It could thus be said that a very attenuated United Opposition had emerged, in spite of all the forbidding circumstances weighing against it.[24]

THE possibility that the 1860 presidential election might be resolved in the House added to the intensity of the Speakership fight. If no candidate received a majority from the electoral college, each state delegation in the House would cast a single vote, with a majority of states needed to decide. Only the three leading vote-getters in the electoral college would be eligible for consideration.

No party controlled a majority of the thirty-three states in 1860. Republicans dominated fifteen House delegations, Democrats commanded fourteen (though Douglas's Illinois was a special case, considering his estrangement from the southern wing of the party), and the southern Opposition claimed only Tennessee. But three other states of the upper South (Maryland, Kentucky, and North Carolina) had delegations evenly divided between the southern Opposition and the Democrats, with Gilmer's committee well positioned to fend off Democratic challenges to Opposition seats in Maryland and Kentucky.

If the House could not select, then the Senate would choose among the top two candidates for vice-president, with the victor in a position to serve as president. Because senators would vote as individuals and choose only between the top two electoral vote candidates for vice-president, some decision would almost certainly result.

Expectations that no candidate could get a majority in the electoral college shaped the contest for the presidency in 1860. It appeared increasingly unlikely by 1859 that any Democratic nominee could, as Buchanan had in 1856, sweep the South and carry enough Northern states to win in the electoral college. Stephen A. Douglas, the obvious choice to maximize Democratic strength in the North, faced bitter opposition in the South. But those candidates better positioned to unite southern Democrats appeared unlikely to win enough crucial northern states. The electoral college dilemma confronting the Democrats appeared insoluble: "No southern candidate could be elected without 42 northern votes. No northern candidate could win without at least 66 southern votes."[25]

Under the circumstances, the southern wing of the old Whig party did not think of itself as merely exercising in a hopeless cause by nominating a presidential candidate. The old Whigs scented opportunity. Party competition in the upper South remained close enough for the Opposition to foresee a respectable bloc of electoral votes and to place third if not second in the electoral college. The Constitutional Union party candidate might then emerge as the logical compromise choice for president. Henry Winter Davis noted that his friends in the southern Opposition plus the few remaining northern Whigs were "playing the old game of trying to elect one of themselves by a minority of the people." Although Davis thought it improbable that a party "in a minority in both ends of the country" could in fact elect a president, the scheme appeared plausible for a time.[26]

Most southern Whigs rallied instinctively behind John Bell, the candidate chosen by the Constitutional Union party convention to run for president. His vice-presidential nominee, Edward Everett of Massachusetts, a respected northern Whig, strengthened Bell's claims to "nationality." Constitutional Union party managers hoped to exploit the division of the Democratic party. When Bell and Everett were selected, in May, the Democratic convention at Charleston had already ruptured. After the Baltimore convention in June failed to reunite the Democratic party, and instead led to the nomination of two Democratic candidates for president, Bell considered himself likely to carry all but two or three slave states.[27]

Throughout the summer, Bell supporters freely discussed their hope that the presidential election would be decided by Congress. The *Louisville Journal* expressed optimism that Bell and Everett could win if Lincoln failed to gain an outright victory. In a widely reprinted speech, the historian George Ticknor Curtis predicted that the House would not be able to choose a president, but that the Senate would unhesitatingly select Everett over Hannibal Hamlin, the Republican nominee for vice-president, so long as Bell ran second in the electoral college behind Lincoln. By the end of the summer, however, the prospects for the Bell-Everett ticket appeared less cheering. Most southern Democrats lined up behind the presidential candidacy of John C. Breckinridge, the nominee of the party's southern wing. Meanwhile, Lincoln's nomination maximized Republican strength in the pivotal states of the lower North that could give him an outright victory in the electoral college. The Constitutional Union party ticket thus faced a double dilemma. Northern non-Republicans had to stop

Lincoln, but even if that happened, Bell had to carry enough states to finish third or second in the electoral college.[28]

Although Breckinridge gained the support of most upper South Democrats, his nomination appeared to some the work of deep South extremists. In certain localities such as the Memphis area of southwest Tennessee and the famed Tenth Legion of the Virginia Democracy in the Shenandoah Valley, party organizers supported Douglas rather than Breckinridge. The Little Giant also displayed strength in scattered other cities and counties where he had the backing, typically, of a newspaper, at least some of the local party apparatus, and voters of immigrant stock. Douglas had a better chance of influencing the result in the upper South than of winning electoral votes. The persistently competitive nature of the region's two-party politics assured that he could play a decisive spoiler's role by siphoning only a fraction of the normal Democratic vote.

Several factors interacted to ensure that a separate Douglas ticket remained on the ballot in the South. First, the Douglas wing of the Democratic party provided a political home for many Irish- and German-American voters, who felt they had no place else to go. Repelled both by the suspected disunionism of the Breckinridge Democracy and the nativist taint of the Bell party, the German counties of the Shenandoah and the Irish wards of Memphis provided a firm popular base for Douglas's candidacy. Second, the bitterness of the party split made reconciliation difficult. The poisonous division of the Democratic party in 1860 left Douglas loyalists vengeful toward what they perceived as the secession-minded bolters. Douglas supporters in the South complained that they had been subjected to "every species of ridicule and contempt, branding us as submissionists and traitors, and thus rendering us, if they could, *socially*, as well as politically, odious among our neighbors and countrymen." They were therefore disinclined to "get upon their knees" and crawl back to "take the political hand of men who have denounced us as no better than abolitionists and free soilers." The Douglasites shrugged off constant taunts from the Breckinridge faction about the ignominy of splitting the Democratic vote and thereby aiding the Whigs.[29]

In fact, many southern Douglas leaders wanted Breckinridge defeated and found Bell a suitable alternative. They knew that the Douglas ticket in the South would improve Bell's chances. But they judged that Bell's success would undermine the disunion movement. Douglas himself instructed his friends to "cultivate good relations" with Bell supporters "for they are Union men." Throughout the campaign, relations between the Bell and Douglas campaigns remained "cordial." Virginia Douglasites hinted that they planned to continue working with the Whigs, so as to produce "a shaking up of the dry bones . . . at the next Spring elections," when congressmen and state legislators would be chosen.[30]

Some awkwardness and mutual discomfort inevitably colored the Bell-Douglas rapprochement. Whigs and Democrats in the upper South had for years hurled political invective at each other. Each regularly purported to find the other tainted with abolitionism and unwilling to defend the interests of the South. Many upper South Whigs gave the familiar litany a new twist by condemning Democrats for repealing the Missouri Compromise, thereby triggering the growth of antisouthern feelings in the North and the sectionalization of national politics. Douglas of course had been the chief, albeit reluctant, architect of that repeal. But just as Douglas's subsequent rejection of the Lecompton constitution divided him from the southern wing of his own party, it facilitated a Whig-Douglas rapprochement in the upper South in 1860. Supporters there of both Bell and Douglas tended to condemn Breckinridge and Lincoln as sectional candidates who would tear the Union apart. A shared perspective on the sectional crisis thus forged an alliance between the upper South Opposition and Douglasites.[31]

Spokesmen for Bell and Douglas in the upper South repeatedly characterized the Breckinridge candidacy as a disunionist conspiracy. The editor of the *Lynchburg Virginian* charged that the "plotters" supporting Breckinridge had seized on a "miserable abstraction" (the issue of protecting slavery in the territories), with deliberate intent to break up the Democratic party and bring about "a speedy dissolution of the Union." George D. Prentice, editor of the *Louisville Journal*, likewise insisted that "they broke up the Democratic party at Charleston and Baltimore for no other purpose under heaven than that Lincoln might be elected and an opportunity thus afforded them for inaugurating their projected rebellion and revolution." Breckinridge supporters in the North furthered the conspiracy by running separate electoral slates, designed to divide the Democratic vote and "give those states to Lincoln."[32]

Were Bell-Douglas complaints about a disunionist conspiracy simply campaign rhetoric? Hardly. The principals themselves became convinced that the danger was real. Bell sent an alarmed letter to his campaign manager in late July, complaining that "a more widespread and determined purpose exists in the South, to attempt a separation of the states in the event of the election of Lincoln, than I had before thought existed." Bell concluded that "artful and able instigators" had laid the groundwork to drive three or four states in the deep South out of the Union. They wanted Lincoln elected to create a pretext for disunion and had split the Democratic party to further their purposes. Douglas saw the situation similarly. He went south in late August and again in October to warn that disunionist Breckinridge supporters hoped "to break up the Union." Recognizing that a perilously large number of southerners regarded the election of Lincoln, by itself, as sufficient cause for disunion, Douglas tried manfully to persuade them to reconsider.[33]

Most Breckinridge supporters in the upper South rejected as "unfounded and absurd" the secession label that Bell and Douglas partisans tried to pin on them. Many of these Unionist professions ring true. But some of the denials had an ominous tone. The *Richmond Enquirer* said it was "supremely ridiculous" to charge Breckinridge supporters with disunionism, but then went on to argue that the election of Lincoln, in and of itself, would be so destructive of southern interests, honor, and equality in the Union as to leave no other feasible response. Thus some Breckinridge supporters rejected disunion per se while at the same time commending it as an appropriate response to an increasingly likely contingency.[34]

The October elections for governor in Indiana and Pennsylvania showed that Republicans had gained strength in the pivotal states of the lower North. Buchanan had carried both with absolute majorities in 1856, but Republican ("People's" in Pennsylvania) candidates won them outright in 1860. If the pattern held for a month, Lincoln would be president. One Bell partisan in Virginia noted in his diary on October 12 that "the Black Republicans had carried Pennsylvania by a large margin. The election of Lincoln to the Presidency seems to be almost certain. I fear that the days of peace and Union in our nation are coming to a close."[35]

The likelihood of Lincoln's election made Bell and Douglas leaders in the upper South very apprehensive. Though obliged to appear hopeful that the election could still turn out favorably, they began to offer reassurances that Lincoln, as president, posed no imminent danger to the South. They noted that the Republican party would not likely control either house of Congress, that Lincoln's appointees required confirmation by the Senate, and that a non-Republican Supreme Court would scrutinize all legislation passed by Congress. They noted too that Lincoln, even if victorious, would not win anything close to a majority of popular votes and that his supporters included many who had no quarrel with the South. George W. Summers pointed out, for example, that support for a protective tariff rather than hostility to slavery made Republicans attractive to many Pennsylvanians. He and others predicted that the responsibilities of governing would fracture the Republican coalition, producing "a reconstruction of the parties" in which southern Unionists might yet "rally the conservatives" from both North and South and win the next presidential election.[36]

But Bell and Douglas leaders knew that many southerners, especially in the Gulf states, saw the matter differently. Reese B. Brabson, Opposition congressman from Chattanooga, observed on October 15 that "the result of the elections in Indiana, Ohio, and Pennsylvania, is very discouraging, and leaves but little hope of Lincoln's defeat." He feared that the deep South would react in an uncontrollable and revolutionary manner. "I am here on the borders of Alabama and Georgia," he wrote, "and feel all the premonitory symptoms of the approaching storm." Congressman John Millson, a Union Democrat from Norfolk, likewise thought the danger of secession real. He predicted that a dissolution of the Union would lead to civil war, in which "Virginia would be the battle ground." Only a decisive defeat of Breckinridge might persuade deep South disunionists to reassess.[37]

Upper South Bell and Douglas partisans addressed the secession issue specifically during the last weeks of the campaign. Bartholomew F. Moore of North Carolina, one of the "most respected and eminent" legal scholars in the South, presented an especially systematic analysis of "the probable consequences of disunion." He cautioned that "excitement, panic, and hatred," fueled by rhetoric about armies marching "over our borders to foment the butcheries of servile insurrection," had run all out of proportion to any "just cause for alarm." Moore soberly examined the three main points of concern about Republican policy—territories, fugitives, and "the agitation of the question of slavery." He warned that disunion would make matters worse in each instance. It would annihilate all claims to western territory, and the absence of "maritime strength" in the South would preclude any hopes of acquiring more territory in the Caribbean or Central America. Likewise, an independent South would face a far greater drain of fugitive slaves. "Great Britain receives with open arms all who can reach Canada," Moore noted. Secession would move the Canada line to the very borders of the slave South because the North would no longer have any obligation to uphold southern rights under the Constitution. Finally, Moore suggested that secession would intensify rather than diminish agitation about slavery. Any attempt "to sunder the Union on account of slavery," he predicted, would in fact trigger "a deep agitation among ourselves." Many southerners would sooner question "the value of slavery" than acquiesce in disunion. Other Unionists shared Moore's cautionary instinct about an internal southern debate over slavery. The editor of the *Lynchburg Virginian* predicted that secession "would create antagonism between slaveholding and non-slaveholding Virginians, that all could see would be fatal to the former."[38]

UNCERTAINTY and anxiety were widespread in the upper South by election day. One worried Virginian believed he was casting his last vote ever for a president of the United States and feared that the country would soon be plunged into civil war. The beautiful sunny late autumn weather appeared incongruous: "One is almost disappointed at thus finding in nature, no sympathy with great political convulsions,—that it has not caught even a shadow from the dark clouds which, long obscuring the political horizon, on this day, gather to a head."[39]

The election returns revealed that voters in the upper South had clung to traditional party allegiances. Maps 3-1 through 3-3 indicate the results by county in the 1860 presidential election. In Virginia (Map 3-1), John Bell carried traditional Whig strongholds such as Loudoun, Augusta, and Kanawha counties. Lincoln's vote was confined to a few counties in the far northwest. Several clusters of Douglas strength—around Petersburg and in parts of the Shenandoah Valley and the northwest—prevented Breckinridge from carrying normally Democratic Virginia. Map 3-2 shows that Bell ran strongest in the North Carolina Whig citadels adjacent to Albemarle Sound and in the Quaker Belt of the central piedmont, while Breckinridge amassed large margins in the Democratic bastions of the coastal plain and in piedmont regions bordering Virginia and South Carolina. A smaller Douglas vote in North Carolina, confined primarily to the Raleigh area, enabled Breckinridge to carry the state. Tennessee's 1860 voting patterns, plotted in Map 3-3, likewise demonstrated persistent Whig and Jacksonian tendencies. John Bell ran well where Whigs maintained an advantage: in the Knoxville region of East Tennessee, in several counties of West Tennessee near the Tennessee River, and in his home base of Nashville and the Cumberland Valley of Middle Tennessee. A united Democratic party could have defeated the native son, but strong support for Douglas in the city of Memphis and adjacent southwestern counties siphoned votes from Breckinridge, enabling Bell to carry the state.

If the combined Breckinridge and Douglas votes are considered Democratic and the Bell vote Whiggish, statistical tests reveal a very high relationship with previous patterns of party voting. The correlation matrices given above in Chapter 2 (see Tables 2-2 through 2-6) clearly suggest that voting behavior in the upper South remained relatively unchanged through 1860. A procedure for estimating how

TABLE 3-1.
Vote Totals and Percentages, 1860 Presidential Election

1860	Virginia	North Carolina	Tennessee
Eligible electorate	246,062	142,385	189,429
Democratic total	90,523	52,187	76,378
Percent of vote cast	54.2	53.4	52.3
Percent of eligibles	36.8	36.7	40.3
Breckinridge	74,325	49,447	65,097
Percent of vote cast	44.5	50.6	44.6
Percent of eligibles	30.2	34.8	34.4
Douglas	16,198	2,740	11,281
Percent of vote cast	9.7	2.8	7.7
Percent of eligibles	6.6	1.9	5.9
Constitutional Union (Bell)	74,481	45,492	69,728
Percent of vote cast	44.6	46.6	47.7
Percent of eligibles	30.3	31.9	36.8
Republican (Lincoln)	1,887	Lincoln not on ballot	
Percent of vote cast	1.2		
Percent of eligibles	0.7		
Voters	166,891	97,679	146,106
Percent of eligibles	67.8	68.6	77.1
Nonvoters	79,171	44,706	43,323
Percent of eligibles	32.2	31.4	22.9

Note: See Chapter 7, n. 2, on sources of data.

voters in one election distributed their votes in a subsequent election, described more fully in Appendix II, also indicates that very few voters switched parties. Tables 3-2 through 3-4 suggest that differences between the 1856 and 1860 elections were primarily the result of voters moving in and out of the active electorate plus the division of the normal Democratic vote in 1860 between the two candidates.

Do the ossified voting patterns mean that people in the upper South regarded the election as routine? Certainly not. Many southerners feared that a Republican president would destroy southern rights or tarnish southern honor. Others feared that a reckless southern response to his election would prove self-fulfilling. But a conviction persisted among southerners of various persuasions that danger

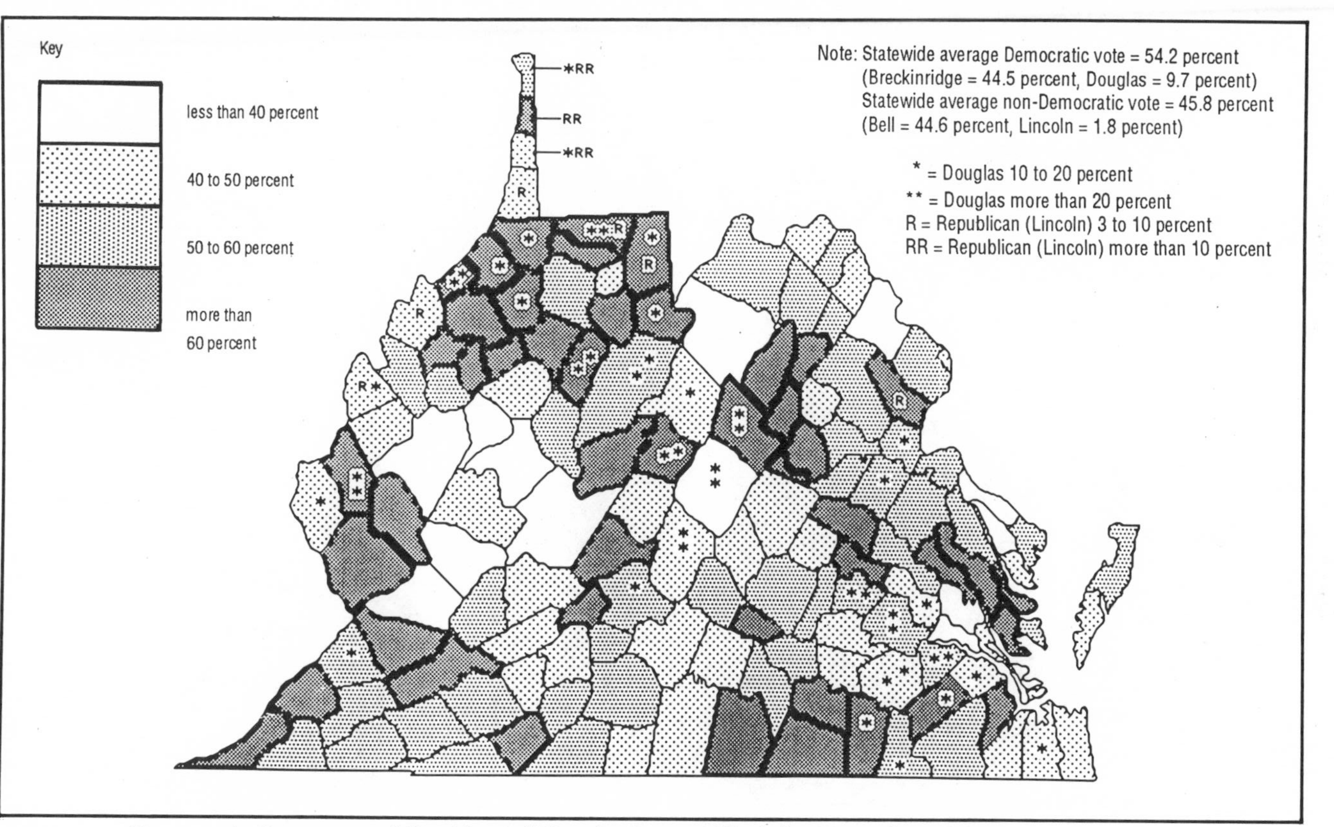

MAP 3-1. *Democratic Percentage of Presidential Vote, by County, Virginia, November 1860*

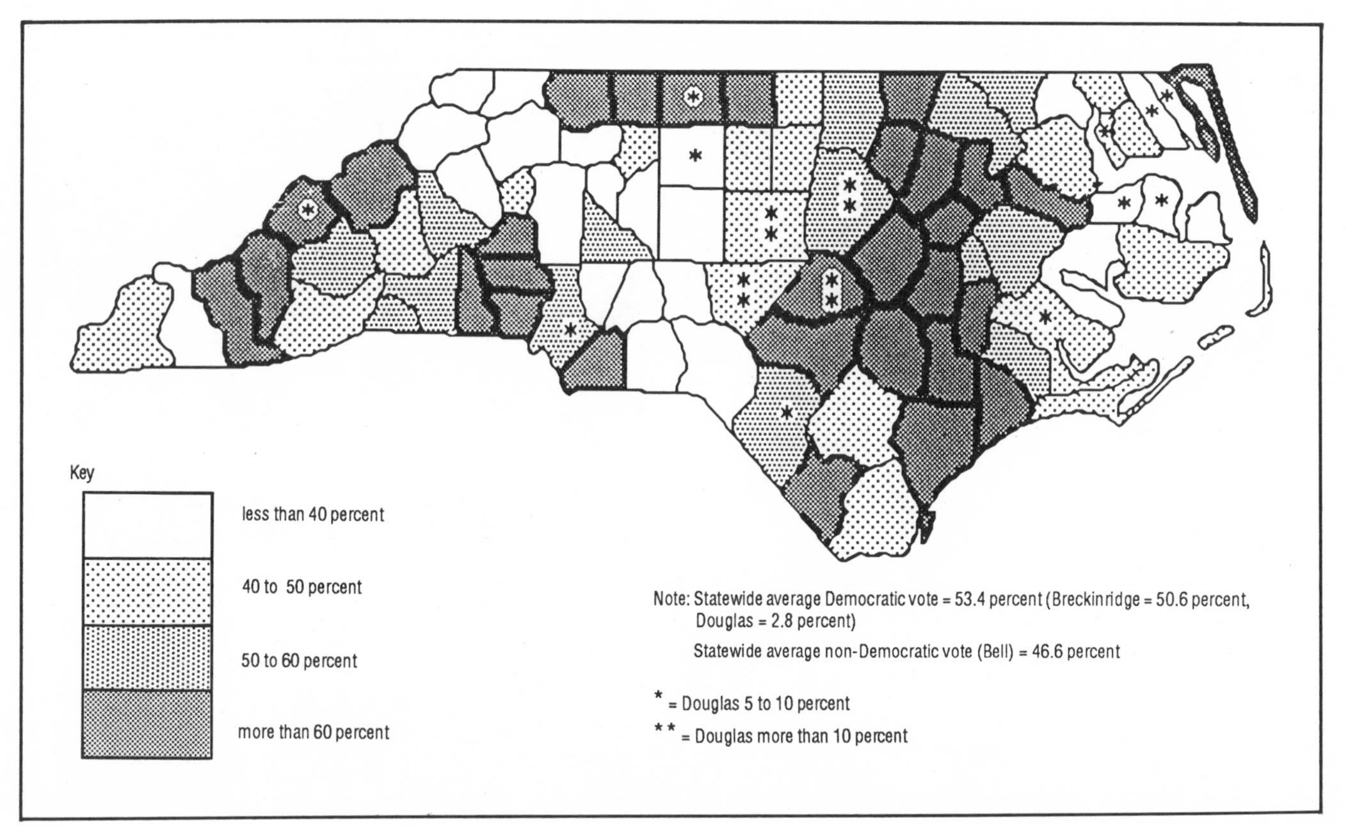

MAP 3-2. *Democratic Percentage of Presidential Vote, by County, North Carolina, November 1860*

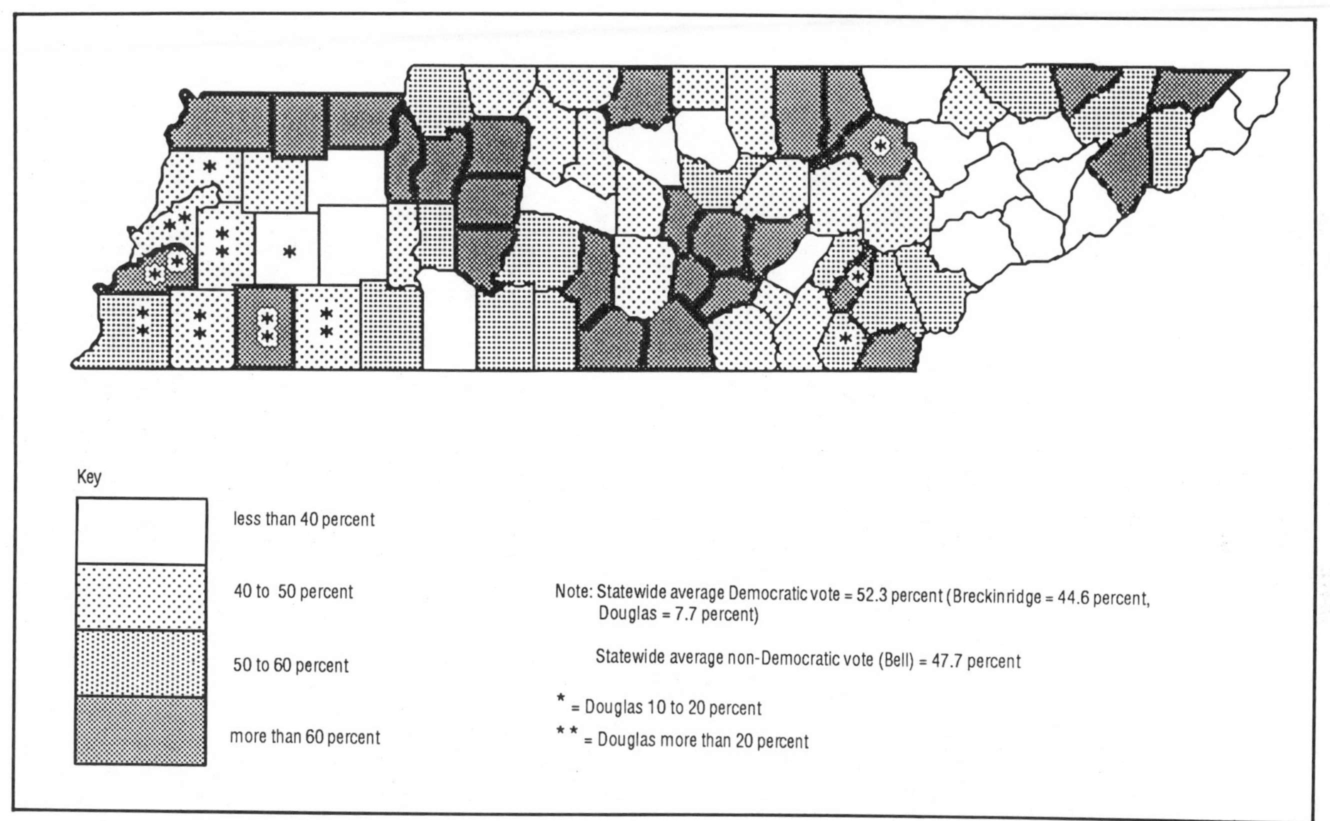

MAP 3-3. *Democratic Percentage of Presidential Vote, by County, Tennessee, November 1860*

TABLE 3-2.
Virginia: Estimated Distribution of Voters, 1856–1860 (in Percentages)

	1856						
1860	Democrat		American		Non-voting		Total
Democrat		34		0		3	37
Breckinridge	29	(28)	−1	(0)	3	(2)	30
Douglas	5	(6)	1	(0)	0	(1)	7
Constitutional Union		0		23		7	30
Republican		0	0	(1)	1	(0)	1
Constitutional Union and Republican	1	(0)	23	(24)		7	31
Nonvoting	4	(5)	3	(2)		25	32
Total		39		26		35	100

Note: To interpret Tables 3-2 through 3-4, read horizontally to see how the 1860 supporters of various candidates had voted in 1856, and read down to see how 1856 voters distributed their votes in 1860. In each instance, the figures on the bottom line and the right-hand margins (the "totals") are known percentages of the entire eligible electorate. The other figures are estimated percentages of the entire electorate. A more complete explanation is available in Appendix II. The system used here, called "ecological regression," often produces illogical estimates, indicating that over 100 percent of Democrats, for example, voted Democratic in a subsequent election, or that fewer than 0 percent voted for the other party. As explained in Appendix II, such results are adjusted here to fall within logical boundaries. The adjustments are indicated in parentheses. The tabulated estimates should be viewed as approximations, designed to show the general contours of voter distribution. All figures in Tables 3-2 through 3-4 are based on county-level data and are weighted proportionate to the eligible electorate in 1860.

could be overcome by voting for familiar and trusted party nominees. That conviction drew them to the polls on November 6.

Although the informed echelon of southern Unionists fully expected Lincoln's election a month in advance, most ordinary white southerners at the beat level probably found the outcome shocking. Supporters of Bell, Breckinridge, and Douglas had spent the summer and fall campaigning across the South to explain how a vote for their candidate would avert a Republican victory. Even after the state elections in October showed Republican majorities in the pivotal states of the North, many southern opinion shapers continued, at

TABLE 3-3.
North Carolina: Estimated Distribution of Voters, 1856–1860 (in Percentages)

1860	1856 Democrat		1856 American		1856 Nonvoting		Total
Democrat	37	(34)	−3	(0)		3	37
Breckinridge	37	(33)	−4	(0)		2	35
Douglas	0	(1)	1	(0)		1	2
Constitutional Union		0	30	(28)	3	(4)	32
Nonvoting	−1	(2)	1	(0)	31	(29)	31
Total		36		28		36	100

least in public, to keep up a brave front. They assured the faithful that a vote for Bell (or Breckinridge, or Douglas) would enable the free men of the South to prevent the result no southerner wanted.

Southern self-deception thus prefigured the calamity that followed the November election. Southerners deluded themselves into thinking that large numbers of northerners, who had stubbornly refused to see the dangers of a Republican victory, would finally come to their senses. For the sake of the campaign, southern politicians had to assume that northerners would deprive Lincoln of an electoral majority. Only such a reassuring belief made it possible to contend that the southern vote would make a difference. And politicians of all stripes wanted their supporters to believe that it would. Few southerners would admit that northerners alone might decide the result. The sudden public discovery that southern votes mattered not at all, and that every southern voter might just as well have stayed home, contributed mightily to the postelection furor in the South.

NOBODY really knew what might happen in the South if Lincoln won the election. The question had lurked just offstage for a long time, with circumstances such that it could not easily be answered. Campaigners for Breckinridge, especially in the upper South, indignantly denied that their candidate was a secessionist puppet. They insisted that he alone favored preservation of the Union with southern rights unimpaired. But the Unionism professed by Breckinridge

TABLE 3-4.
Tennessee: Estimated Distribution of Voters, 1856–1860 (in Percentages)

	1856			
1860	Democrat	American	Nonvoting	Total
Democrat	39 (38)	−2 (0)	3 (2)	40
Breckinridge	38 (33)	−1 (0)	−3 (1)	34
Douglas	1 (5)	−1 (0)	5 (1)	6
Constitutional Union	2	34	1	37
Nonvoting	0 (2)	5 (3)	17 (18)	23
Total	42	37	21	100

supporters in the upper South had a delphic quality. At least some said a Lincoln victory would justify secession, even while predicting that sufficient advance indication of southern resolve would undermine Lincoln in the North.

Controversy about future contingencies intensified as the election approached. The *Richmond Enquirer* stated in October that the southern states had every right to secede if Lincoln won the election and that the federal government had no power to prevent them from doing so. The *Enquirer* furthermore announced that Virginia was "hitched" to the states of the deep South by a shared interest in the slave system and would be "dragged into a common destiny with them, no matter what may be the desire of her people." "Dragging" and "hitching" quickly became staple phrases for the duration of the campaign, as Bell-Douglas partisans across the upper South warned against Breckinridge disunionism. Was the *Enquirer* bluffing? Officially it was, because its editor continued to argue that a united South behind Breckinridge would awaken conservatives in New York and thereby prevent Lincoln from getting an electoral majority. The organizing of militia companies raised similar questions. Was the threat of southern resistance to Lincoln's election a bluff? What would happen if the North called the bluff? None of these questions could be answered conclusively until after November 6. The southern Democratic leaders "were for the Union as long as they could rule it; they preferred to rule it. But if they could not? As yet they were not ready to face that reality."[40]

Should federal authority be defied, everyone knew where it would begin. In 1832–33 and 1850–51, and once again during the previous winter after John Brown's raid, South Carolina had attempted to spur her lethargic southern sister states into action. Virginia's humiliating refusal even to endorse a southern conference in early 1860 led many South Carolinians to conclude that they would never again wait for cooperative action by the other southern states. In October voters selected a militant new legislature, and South Carolina stood on the verge of revolution. But even such an ardent secessionist as Virginia's Edmund Ruffin remained uncertain whether South Carolina would act alone, much as he hoped it might. And it was even less clear whether any other states would follow if South Carolina did take the lead. South Carolina Senator James H. Hammond predicted that hasty action by his state in response to Lincoln's election would be "most impolitic and assuredly abortive." Hammond misread the situation, but he had historical precedent on his side.[41]

4

UNIONISTS ON THE DEFENSIVE

THE furious southern reaction to Lincoln's election made tangible the nagging Unionist nightmare. It quickly became apparent that South Carolina would not act alone. Everywhere in the lower South, radicals seized the initiative. A perilous challenge suddenly confronted Unionists during November and December.

Secessionists stressed the vital need to cut all ties to the Union before Lincoln's inauguration. They insisted that governors call legislatures into session, that legislatures immediately schedule dates for voters to select convention delegates, and that conventions meet promptly. Across the lower South the secessionist strategy worked. The process unfolded in an atmosphere of crisis and haste. Everywhere in the lower South except Texas, state legislatures freed the conventions to do as they pleased without referring their action to popular referendum. What Unionists often called an "epidemic" or "fit of madness" thus seized the lower South. The "infection" or "contagion" spread to the supposedly "conservative" states of Georgia and Louisiana, albeit by narrow margins. Many who had long opposed secession either fell in with the popular current or did nothing to stop it. Others put up feeble "cooperationist" resistance that conceded so much to the radicals as to blur the differences between cooperation and secession.[1]

By December, secession sentiment gripped large parts of eastern Virginia and North Carolina, plus scattered areas in Middle and West Tennessee. As their own states headed toward the "vortex of Revolution," upper South Unionists gasped in amazement. By December, many were losing confidence in their ability to arrest the passionate "excitement." The editor of the *Richmond Whig* noted that the secession tide in Virginia was "exceedingly strong," perhaps even "irresistible." He pleaded with opponents of secession to speak out and try to "change the current." North Carolina Unionists observed that secessionists' "racy and inflammatory appeals" had left Union men with "scarcely any foot hold left to stand upon." Bold secessionist actions contrasted with the "comparatively paralyzed and depressed" behavior of "Conservative men." A prominent Tennessee Unionist warned that "revolutionary feeling" was "gaining ground daily and rapidly" in his state. "You have no conception of the intense pent up feeling here," he informed Stephen A. Douglas. "It needs but a spark to explode it." Some Unionists despaired. One, living near Charlotte, North Carolina, a secessionist hotbed described by an observer as a "young Charleston," could not see "the shadow of a hope" for the Union cause.[2]

THE events that so distressed Unionists produced exactly the opposite response among a small but ardent group of original secessionists, who had long hoped the South would seek independence. Centered in South Carolina and represented most notably by Robert Barnwell Rhett's *Charleston Mercury*, original secessionists valued their cause more than the success of any party. For them secession was no tactic or bluff but an object intrinsically desirable. For thirty years Rhett had urged dissolution of a Union that had become subversive of southern rights and the establishment of "a Confederacy of the Southern States."[3]

Virginia's Edmund Ruffin, the humorless, ascetic, introverted prophet whose flowing white hair fell to shoulder length, was indisputably the most prominent original secessionist in the upper South. Famous for his efforts in behalf of agricultural reform, Ruffin retired from plantation management in 1856 to devote himself to achieving southern independence. He recognized that secession could never attract appropriate leadership as long as prominent southern politicians harbored ambitions to hold high federal office. In his native Virginia, for example, the two leading Democrats, Henry A. Wise and Robert M. T. Hunter, both saw themselves as potential presidential nominees. Ruffin hoped southern leaders would "come to their senses" in 1860, when, he predicted, no southern candidate would get the Democratic nomination. "Still better," he thought, would be the effects of having the Democratic party "defeated and ruptured, and an abolitionist elected." This man who deliberately rejected conventional party politics thus had keen perceptions about the coming national political impasse.[4]

Ruffin's plan for initiating secession was equally astute. From 1856 through 1860, he argued that neither Virginia nor any other upper South slave state would ever take the lead. Instead, the impetus would have to come from states in the deep South, five or six of which should "declare their independence of, and secession from, the present Federal government." Ruffin expected the nonseceding slave states to provide a defensive barrier, preventing any immediate federal attack on the seceding ones. The nonseceding slave states would soon discover themselves a powerless minority in the old Union and choose to join the "new Southern Confederacy." Feelings of friendship and common interests would also draw the southern states together. Because Ruffin expected all remaining slave states except Delaware to join the new government within "a few months," and thereby to confront the North with a united South, he considered his plan unlikely to risk "war or bloodshed." Any attempt by the North "to coerce or conquer the seceding States" would fail. With the fatal exception of the last points, Ruffin earned high marks for prophetic insight into the dynamics of the secession crisis.[5]

FOR every Ruffin in the upper South who had a long-standing preference for southern independence and who therefore welcomed Lincoln's election, dozens of politicians and ordinary citizens deplored that outcome and preferred to stay in the Union. A combination of fear and anger drove them to conclude that the South must leave the Union before Lincoln took power.[6]

Though secessionists generally agreed that a Republican president endangered the South, some saw the threat as more immediate than others. The most alarmist variety of secessionism depicted an imminent Republican effort to unleash John Browns and slave rebels. Hysteria about slave insurrections and abolitionist conspiracies, prevalent in many parts of the South in 1860, continued during the secession winter. The starkest prognostications about the Republican threat were more widely broadcast and accepted in the lower South than anywhere else, especially in the crucial face-to-face nexus between local politicians and ordinary citizens.[7]

At the more official level, in published speeches and newspaper editorials, secessionists tended to emphasize the dangers of slow subversion and strangulation. Breckinridge Democrats had frequently voiced such concerns before the November election. They sneered that their opponents were "submissionists" who would become "the pioneers of Black Republicanism in the South." Breckinridge partisans predicted that Lincoln would shower patronage on southern Bell and Douglas supporters, who would help organize a "Union party." It would gradually become an antislavery party, appealing to those southerners who thought the territorial issue unimportant, or to nonslaveowners who felt they had no stake in the well-being of the slave system. "The contest for slavery" would then "no longer be one between the North and the South" but rather "in the South, between the people of the South." Before long, warned one pro-Breckinridge newspaper, "the struggle shall be transferred to our own soil," and "the armies of our enemies will be recruited from our own forces."[8]

Once Lincoln was elected, secessionists persistently accused him of planning to build an antislavery party in the upper South. "Federal patronage within our limits, will become the nest to hatch black republican eggs, and a nucleus, around which will gather a black republican squad," one North Carolinian predicted. The spread of Republican ideas would stir "jealousy between the slaveholder and the non-slaveholder," and the "minds of the uneducated" would be "systematically demoralized upon the subject." A Virginia secessionist agreed. Southern aspirants for patronage jobs would soon profess political opinions congenial "to the powers that be." Each such appointee would "form a nucleus of sympathizing friends." Soon there would be "Black Republicans upon every stump and organizing in every county." The *Richmond Enquirer* warned that this "gradual and insidious approach under the fostering hand of federal power" would introduce the "irrepressible conflict" to the South, even though "no direct act of violence against negro property" might ever be committed, "no servile war waged," and the Constitution not openly violated.[9]

Secessionists thus saw a fundamental incompatibility between the slave system and the democratic political arrangements in the antebellum South. They judged that the nonslaveowning majority potentially threatened the interests of the slaveowning minority, and they feared that unconstrained political debate would awaken dangerous antagonisms. Rather than self-confident leaders of a region united against an external threat, secessionists appear from this perspective a frightened elite (or spokesmen for a frightened elite), who dreaded an insidious alliance between external critics and the Old South's free white nonslaveowners.

One Tennessee secessionist spelled out in detail his fears about political subversion. The Lincoln administration would first award "postmasterships, mail agencies and government contracts" to those native southerners who were "most moderate on the slavery question." Federal appointees would become "suppliant tools of power" because "gratitude exercises a controlling influence over human actions. Men who get bread and meat put into their own mouths and the mouths of their wives and children, will, naturally be inclined to sympathize in the fortunes of those who bestow these gifts upon them." William H. Seward, soon to become Lincoln's secretary of state, had the tact and skill "to build up a large abolition party" in Tennessee and the border slave states. "Soft language will be used—kind words—proper time given at intervals in the drama. . . . Government officials will softly hint. Money, without measure, will be used to poison the fountains of public sentiment." A "Black Republican ticket" would be "openly run in Tennessee" at the next presidential election. Once that happened, asked the worried secessionist, "what will negro property be worth? Does not every man know that all the negroes among us will, as a matter of self-preservation, have to be carried South?" Seward and Lincoln, having sought their objective in a "slow and conciliatory" manner, would keep resistance from ever becoming a serious obstacle. If the deep South seceded, leaving the slave states of the upper South "a powerless minority" in the Union, the "abolition programme" would take effect even more rapidly.[10]

The dramatic fact of Lincoln's election without any southern support sharpened fears about slow strangulation of the slave system. The *Wilmington Journal* concluded that the North had determined to rule "regardless of the rights or interests or feelings of the South." Having seized the presidency, Republicans soon would control Congress and the federal judiciary. "The South would then be powerless. Her Senators and Representatives might just as well stay at home.— The South would cease to be an element in the Government. It would be a mere tributary appendage." The election showed that "hereafter one section is to rule and the other to submit." The choice facing the South had narrowed to "unconditional submission"—or "resistance to aggression."[11]

Secessionists sometimes offered a broad historical and world view to show that slavery was endangered. They emphasized the vulnerability of the South at a time when abolitionists had triumphed in "the whole civilized world." Outsiders regarded southern slavery with "scorn and contempt" and thought it "a sin and a crime." One secessionist warned that "the anti-slavery feeling of the North" could never be reversed or changed—"You may just as well attempt to dam up the tumbling waters of Niagara, with your little finger, as to attempt any such thing." In this view, Lincoln's election provided conclusive evidence that the only safety for the South lay in withdrawal from a Union pervaded by antislavery sentiment.[12]

Alarms about a threat to white racial hegemony served as a subsidiary theme to buttress arguments that slavery was endangered. "Do you desire the millions of negro population of the South, to be set free among us, to stalk abroad in the land, following the dictates of their own natural instincts, committing depredations, rapine, and murder upon the whites?" asked one newspaper editor. A North Carolinian likewise warned that slaves, now "happy, contented, and faithful," would, under a Republican president, "be aroused to a sense of fancied wrongs" and would begin to act "on the smouldering brutal instincts of their nature." Secessionists thus tried to stir white racial fears. They asserted that Lincoln and his advisers intended to overthrow slavery and give the newly freed blacks "all the privileges of white men—voting with you; sitting on juries with you; going to school with your children, and intermarrying with the white race."[13]

SECESSIONISTS, however, often downplayed the theme of "slavery endangered." They agreed that northern attitudes toward the South were malignant and hostile and would eventually endanger the slave system. But the secession mentality often had its roots in a sense of immediate provocation and a desire to avenge an insult. Some secessionists therefore emphasized their resentment about the attitudes themselves, rather than the long-run erosion of the slave system those attitudes might produce.

A few examples will illustrate. The "Northern people . . . look upon slavery as a scab, as a running sore, and throw contempt upon us in every way," complained one delegate to the Virginia convention. Although northern "hatred of our southern institutions and our system of slavery" threatened eventual abolition, what demanded immediate redress was the affront to southern honor. Defense of honor was "far more precious" than protection of property rights. Other secessionists took a similar view. "Shall we continue to allow the stamp of inferiority for ever to be put upon us?" one asked. "For myself, I can hardly realize the possibility of . . . submitting to such a degradation." A horror of dishonor prompted yet another secessionist to spurn the idea of remaining in the Union. Were he to agree to that, he insisted, "I should feel that I was base enough to bend my knee to my oppressor, to take the yoke upon my neck, and to present my own hand for the shackles of slavery." Hot-blooded young southerners admired "the glorious little game-cock of South Carolina" for maintaining an "unparalleled, and in many quarters incomprehensible, devotion to her lofty sense of honor." They eagerly awaited the "pending affair of honor" between the Confederacy and the "corrupt" North, anticipating that the upper South would fight once hostilities commenced.[14]

An issue more of honor than of substance thus lay at the heart of the sectional crisis and thwarted all efforts to effect a Union-saving compromise. Slavery in the territories, many Unionists complained, was an "abstract" or "barren" issue that did not involve real interests. One noted, for example, that "the territorial question is of no practical value and only involves a point of etiquette and honor." But secessionists insisted that the territorial issue had become a symbol of southern equality in the Union. The Supreme Court had certified a right to take slaves to the territories, and the South would be humiliated and disgraced if it could not exercise that right. A leading secession delegate to the Virginia convention announced that he could not tolerate the refusal of the North to treat southerners "as equals." The South, he maintained, ought not to "permit the brand of inferiority to be marked upon her forehead." Doctrinaire southerners believed they had an absolute right to take slaves to the territories. Only if slave property received the same protection as other forms of property could southerners consider themselves in "the position of an equal." Without that right, secessionists concluded, "we are a dishonored people."[15]

The same mentality also fastened upon alleged northern interference with the recapture of fugitive slaves. The actual trickle of fugitives who made good their escape bothered secessionists far less than the obstruction of a constitutional right. Thus the debate over personal liberty laws had more to do with honor than with pecuniary interest. It seems to me a very extraordinary thing," observed a Virginia secessionist, "when a great principle is at stake, to measure it by the mere matter of dollars and cents. When our ancestors resisted the stamp act, was there any calculation as to the number of cents each man would have to pay? No sir. It was the principle—the violation of their rights—that they resisted." Secessionists thus rejected Unionist efforts to downplay the controversy over runaway slaves. Nor could northern proposals to compensate for lost fugitives satisfy those southerners who saw the issue as one of principle.[16]

Historians who contend that the South had a material interest in taking slaves to new territories surely have overstated their case.[17] Many southerners shared eagerly in the enthusiasm for territorial expansion widespread in mid-nineteenth-century America. Democrats, especially, believed that economic opportunity and social harmony depended upon access to new land. And some racial theorists held that new territory would become an essential escape valve to keep the South from becoming "Africanized." But during the 1850s slaveowners displayed no inclination to take their property to the recently acquired domain in the Southwest, even though the huge New Mexico territory had as thorough a territorial slave code as any southerner could wish. As Unionists often noted, very little unsettled land in the United States had rainfall or soil suitable for plantation agriculture. Nor should one interpret in narrowly material terms southern ambitions to annex parts of the Caribbean or Central America to build an enlarged slave empire. Southern expansionist schemes during the 1850s originated primarily out of a desire to demonstrate sectional resolve. Southern imperialists, fearful of growing northern power, thought the South must assert itself.[18]

It is therefore sensible to question whether "the thirst for territorial expansion was really the force behind secession." What southerners most resented about territorial restriction from the time the issue first became prominent in the 1840s was the "denial of Southern equality in the nation." An urge to vindicate southern rights, rather than "positive desires for expansion," fueled the territorial controversy during the 1850s. Southerners "always understood the problem of slavery in the territories in a way that would have been familiar to any duelist." Secessionists thus acted, as they saw it, to save face. The most persistent theme in secessionist rhetoric "was not the danger of the abolition or restriction of black slavery, but the infamy and degradation of submitting to the rule of a Republican majority." Only on this basis could "the mere election of Lincoln . . . provoke secession."[19]

The response of antebellum Alabamians to the territorial issue reveals much about the entire South. They resented "discriminatory action by the common government." The "contempt for the South" implied by restricting slavery from the territories "became the embodiment of humiliation." Southern self-respect mattered far more than any economic or material justification for the expansion of slave society. "The essence of the case was not what would happen to Southerners when they were excluded from the territories but was the fact that they were to be excluded." Secession was thus not "a remedy for the consequences of free-soil" but rather "revenge for the condemnation implied by the policy and the inequality inherent in it." White southerners "wanted to be treated like Americans." They refused to accept what they considered the "second-class citizenship" that northern voters tried to impose on them in 1860.[20]

"What is our claim?" asked one Southern Rights Democrat. "It is this, in short. . . . We have no wish to propagate slavery, but every man at the South does wish to insist upon his right to enter the territories upon terms of perfect equality with the North, if he chooses to do so. He may not exercise the right but he will not give it up." A Virginia secessionist likewise insisted upon "perfect equality," whether or not western territory was suited for slavery. He would not "surrender the principle" even in the case of "an iceberg or a barren rock," because "by surrendering it, I should be acknowledging an *inequality*."[21]

When Kentucky Senator John J. Crittenden attempted to devise an arrangement that would preserve the Union, he interpreted southern motives similarly. The eminent Unionist thought the territory in the Southwest "a trifle in point of any material value that can be assigned to it" and entirely unsuited for slavery. "That, however, is not so much the question as our right to go there at all," he noted. Southerners insisted upon recognition of their "equal rights" and the "principle of equality." To preserve the Union "on the proper terms of equal respect and equal regard," northerners needed to provide southerners with symbolic recognition of the right to own slaves in the federal territory. Virginia Unionist George W. Summers agreed. The "territorial question" involved a "question of right" much more than "a practical question of value." Resolution of the secession crisis required northern recognition of the presumed southern right.[22]

Concerns about southern honor thus inflated the territorial issue, so that it was "the threat of honor lost, no less than slavery, that led to secession and war." Southerners frequently used words such as degraded, shamed, demoralized, and humiliated when they complained about Republican tampering with their rights. Nearly every white southerner regarded Republican opposition to the expansion of slavery as an insult. "Plain anger" and a determination to maintain "regional self-regard" marked the southern response to the 1860 election. Secessionists believed Lincoln's victory an "overt act" requiring disunion; more moderate southerners wanted to see whether Lincoln would actually try to govern according to his professed principles or whether he would "back down."[23]

Anxiety about the emotional themes of equality, dignity, reputation, duty, and honor reverberated in secessionist pronouncements. The South had to choose between the "humiliation" of losing "her manhood" and the stern path of duty. "Honest men and patriots" must defy Lincoln to "save themselves from dishonor." Henry A. Wise, leader of the Virginia secessionists, thought "*shame and dishonor*" were the worst calamity that could befall the South. Only by refusing to tolerate northern encroachment on their rights could southerners avert the "peril of dishonor." Other grim things could still happen to them: "We may be shattered to pieces—we may be torn and rent asunder—we may be conquered—we may die," but by resisting, southerners could preserve their honor.[24]

Southern militants insisted that the Founding Fathers and the "patriots of '76" would never have submitted to Black Republican injustice. Would "the heroes who illumine our early history" have remained part of a Union that had become subversive of liberty? Would they have endured "the humiliation and ruin of a sectional ascendancy, worse than a colonial vassalage"? Would they have allowed themselves to be denied a "fair proportion of the public domain" on pretexts "as insulting as they are injurious"? Would they have remained in political fellowship with those who denied the

South her equality, "trampled upon her rights, maligned her institutions, slandered her reputation, rejected her demands for justice, insulted her representatives, scorned her remonstrances, and now insolently threatens to subjugate her with the sword if she dare attempt resistance to their domination?" Secessionists warned that "ruin overtakes every people who surrender their rights to their fears, and prefer their ease to their duty." The way to show "true veneration" for the Founding Fathers was not by "living under a Union which is already the instrument of inflicting upon us such degradation—a Union which threatens our future destruction," but rather "by acting in our day and generation, as we believe they would have acted, had they been standing in our places."[25]

Secessionists thus defined an inherently uncompromisable impasse. By simply electing a Republican president, northerners had insulted and dishonored the South. What, Lincoln sourly asked, did southerners want? Ought he to repent "for the crime of having been elected" and "apologize and beg forgiveness"? Nor did it matter that Republicans from Lincoln on down insisted that they harbored no plan to interfere with slavery in the states where it already existed. Many in the South demanded, in addition, "a fundamental change in northern sentiment." But Republicans would not agree to drop their criticisms of slavery or to countenance expansion of a system they thought wrong. Conciliatory Republicans who tried to soothe southern fears drew a line. "You must not ask us to love slavery," one warned. "We cannot do that."[26]

The lower South's leadership of the secession movement strongly suggests that issues of principle and honor mattered more to secessionists than material ones. By almost any standard, a federal government in unfriendly hands posed a greater threat to slavery in the upper than in the lower South. Only in the upper South had the escape of fugitive slaves become a significant problem, and only border regions of the upper South faced the possibility of raids similar to John Brown's. So also, upper South slaveowners had more reason than their lower South counterparts to fear that Republicans might use federal patronage to build an antiplanter or antislavery party. Even the territorial issue, if seen as substance rather than as symbol, mattered more to the upper South. Leading Virginia Unionist George W. Summers pointed out that "the slave migration to the territories, so far as there is any, will be from the border States, and not from the cotton States." Should the states of the deep South refuse to return to the Union even if the states of the upper South received "guarantees satisfactory to themselves," he observed, "such refusal would furnish strong evidence that they left us, not on the ground of the slavery issues and difficulties, but for other causes, and upon a foregone conclusion."[27]

THE two primary reasons why southerners embraced secession after Lincoln's election were "slavery endangered" and "honor violated." But several subsidiary points to justify that choice figured prominently in upper South secession rhetoric. Secessionists often asserted that the upper South could achieve greater prosperity out of the Union. They also argued that the upper South had to choose sides and that it could avert war by uniting promptly with the deep South.

Secessionists predicted that the upper South "would rise at once to the front rank in the race of material greatness and power" if part of an independent South. One Virginian painted a dazzling rhetorical picture: "Capital and enterprise would spring up as if by magic, in our midst; our noble water-falls would whistle with machinery, and the spindles of the North would be transferred to the Potomac, the Rappahannock, and the James; and Norfolk, with her magnificent harbor, would become the grandest commercial emporium of the world." Another Virginia secessionist likewise argued that southern industrial development would always be stunted in the Union. Manufacturers in the northern states, who wanted the southern market for themselves, would always try to destroy southern rivals. But if Virginia seized the opportunity to cut loose from the North, her "material interests" would flourish. Southern and foreign demand for her agricultural and industrial production would quickly compensate for any short-range loss of northern markets. And by separating from the North, Virginia could avoid the potentially disastrous disruption of her successful hybrid system of "mixed" labor, that is, "partly slave and partly free."[28]

North Carolina and Tennessee secessionists, concerned to protect and extend trade links with adjacent states in the deep South, made similarly cheerful prognoses about the economic consequences of disunion. The *Memphis Appeal*, for example, noted that markets for Tennessee "grain, horses, mules, [and] hogs" were "found almost exclusively in the cotton states." United with the deep South, Tennessee would soon see "the smoke of the foundry" and hear "the sound of the loom" as it became "the chief manufacturer for the South." But if commercial ties between Memphis and the deep South were cut, economic disaster would result. The "industrious and energetic laboring men" would be thrown out of work, "the palatial dry goods stores, whose counters now groan with costly fabrics, would be abandoned," new manufacturing, "just springing into a healthy and vigorous life would perish for want of sustenance," and "ere long it would be literally true that the grass would grow in the streets of our flourishing city."[29]

Deep South secessionists did their best to convince the upper South that secession would provide an economic bonanza. Georgia's spokesman at the Virginia convention argued that the lower South already provided the chief market for the upper South's flour, wheat, bacon, pork, mules, and slaves. He dangled the hope that an independent South would adopt sufficiently protective duties on imports to allow "Virginia and the border states" to supplant "New England and New York" as the chief suppliers of manufactured goods in the deep South. By joining the southern Confederacy, the upper South could become "a great manufacturing empire." But if it remained in the Union, it would always be thwarted by northern competition, which had a head start and would prevent the upper South from ever catching up.[30]

Secessionists assumed that the Union was permanently and irrevocably disrupted, so that the upper South must choose sides. To ask, "Shall the Union be preserved?" was to raise a "false issue," warned one secessionist newspaper. The "only question before us" was "*Shall we go North or South?*" Secessionists predicted that if it remained in the Union, the upper South would face a grim future as a helpless minority "without power or influence." The choice lay between joining an independent South or becoming "a despised fag end of a Free Soil Confederacy," unable to fend off insidious abolitionist influences. Though Unionists argued that no choice between North or South was necessary because the deep South would soon reconsider its hasty action, secessionists insisted that the seceding states would never return to the Union. "From the nature of things," one editor reasoned, "the secession of any important part of the Southern States means, virtually, the secession of all who really are Southern, and the Northernization of all who are *not*."[31]

Secessionists further reasoned that the upper South could prevent war by seceding quickly. Although the deep South alone might tempt a federal attack, the North would not dare to fight a united South. Secession of the Upper South would thereby ensure peace. But if the upper South remained in the Union, secessionists warned, just the opposite could result. A "policy of procrastination" would put "the peace of the country in jeopardy" and make possible "the horrors of civil war."[32]

DURING late November and December, many who had not immediately embraced the cause upon Lincoln's election climbed aboard the secession bandwagon. They realized that the lower South would secede before Lincoln's inauguration and set up an independent government. Nor did Congress or the Republican party appear likely to offer sufficient concessions to draw back the seceded states. Efforts to effect a compromise that might save the Union made scant progress before the end of the year, and deep South secessionists insisted that they would never return to the Union in any case. "We ask no compromise and we want none," insisted Mississippi's spokesman to the Virginia convention. "We know that we should not get it if we were base enough to desire it, and we have made the irrevocable resolve to take our interests into our own keeping."[33]

Under the circumstances, some former Unionists concluded that the upper South must secede. The rapid about-face of the widely read *Memphis Appeal* illustrates the process. Immediately after the election, its editor judged that southern rights could best be protected in the Union. "However much we may deprecate the election of a sectional candidate," he cautioned, "we ought at least to give his administration a trial." Nothing Lincoln had yet done justified rash action, and once in office he might prove "conciliatory and conservative." The editor also warned that "insurmountable" difficulties, such as access to and control of the Mississippi Valley, rendered "peaceable secession" what Daniel Webster had labeled it in his famed 1850 speech—"an utter impossibility." But even before the end of November, the editor of the *Appeal* began to reassess. "Two weeks ago we thought that the excitement in the cotton States, in consequence of the late freesoil triumph, would be ephemeral in its duration, and expressed ourselves accordingly. We falsely imagined that a conflict would arise between the conservatives and the extremists, thus consuming much time with the elaborate discussion of the momentous issue. But not so." In mid-December the newspaper concluded that the Union was permanently sundered. It proclaimed that the upper South should join an independent South rather than remain "the southern-tail of a Black Republican Confederacy." The *Appeal* thus completed its hasty journey from Unionism to secession, attacking any who disagreed as collaborators with the Republican enemy.[34]

By late December, secession had become majority sentiment in substantial parts of the upper South. Support for the Union eroded most rapidly in high-slaveowning counties, especially those with Democratic leanings. Many newspapers became strong supporters of secession, the most influential including the *Richmond Enquirer*, the *Richmond Examiner*, the *Norfolk Argus*, the *Wilmington Journal*, the *Raleigh State Journal*, the *Nashville Union and American*, the *Memphis Avalanche*, and, as just illustrated, the *Memphis Appeal*.

Southern Unionists repeatedly used metaphors about clouds, storms, and the cutting off of light to describe the spread of secession. One observed with alarm in early December "the lowering clouds of secession and disunion, which now cover and overspread the political heavens of the South." A few weeks later another depressed Unionist surveyed "the political storm now raging." Much as he wished it would disappear, he could not see "any light ahead." Yet another detected "no single ray of hope." Instead, "darkness and madness sway the hour, and revolution is set on foot in the land." Throughout the upper South as the secession crisis deepened, Unionists employed similar language. Writing to his wife from Washington on a "bright, cheerful" New Year's Day, Tennessee Congressman Robert Hatton drew the obvious contrast: "The sky is dark, politically—dark as midnight."[35]

5

THE UNIONIST ARGUMENT

UNIONISM in the upper South first appeared as an organized force in late December and early January, just as the secession wave crested. Upper South secessionists, imitating the formula used successfully by their counterparts in the deep South, tried to have state conventions held at the earliest possible moment. But the convention campaigns boomeranged. A coalition of antisecessionists formed to block the onslaught. This chapter will analyze the ideas of those who opposed secession in early 1861. Subsequent chapters will move from thought to action and will show how Unionists tried to put their ideas into effect.

The Union coalition in the upper South was not all of one mind. The spectrum of antisecessionist ideas ranged from unconditional Unionism to a qualified willingness to remain in the Union for a short time in the hope of major Republican concessions. Three varieties of Unionism had emerged by midwinter: absolute or unconditional, anticoercionist or extended ultimatumist, and fast ultimatumist. Not until April, when southerners had to choose sides in a war, did Unionists have to declare their ultimate allegiance. But there was never much doubt that a majority of Unionists, if forced to choose, would fight on the side of the South. To the frustration of northerners, opponents of secession in the South typically attached conditions to their Unionism.

A minority of Unionists, however, boldly announced that their position was unconditional. Former Tennessee Governor William B. Campbell declared that "our only safety is in the Union and we must stand by it to the end." He could see "no future but ruin to a broken confederacy." Andrew Johnson warned that there were "many in Tennessee whose dead bodies will have to be trampled over" before the state would secede from the Union. In areas with large concentrations of unconditional Unionists, aspirants for the state convention were told that "the people are going to make every man walk the chalk mark on this question of the Union, and they are not going to be satisfied . . . with any qualified Unionism."[1]

Among those who did qualify their Unionism, the great majority could be called anticoercionists or extended ultimatumists. Anticoercionists would stay in the Union unless the North tried to wage war on the South. They warned that the upper South would certainly secede should the North "attempt, under any pretext, however plausible," to "subjugate . . . by force of arms" the "sister States of the South." Before mid-April, however, anticoercionists often denounced secession with a vehemence equal to that of unconditional Unionists. Robert Hatton, the congressman from Middle Tennessee who sided with his state when the war came, earlier flayed disunionists. Their "reckless selfishness" had made them "practically our enemies, as truly as the most unprincipled fanatics of the North." The "chivalry of the cotton States" had generously "assumed . . . the guardianship of both our interests and our honor; and, for the protection of the one, and the vindication of the other, they counsel that we put in jeopardy our every material interest, and then—commit suicide!" How, he asked sarcastically, "shall we of the border States ever be able to repay our southern brethren for this unselfish and considerate advice?" Hatton's complaints were widely echoed among both conditional and unconditional Unionists in the upper South.[2]

Extended ultimatumists would stay in the Union until all reasonable hope for compromise was exhausted. Unionists at the Virginia convention hoped the states of the upper South could agree on an ultimatum, requiring the North to grant concessions to keep the upper South in the Union. The plan annoyed both secessionists, who saw it as a device for protracted and indefinite delay, and unconditional Unionists, who suspected a plot to remove the state gradually from the Union. Most extended ultimatumists were anticoercionists, and vice versa. The two largely overlapping categories together embraced most conditional Unionists in the upper South.

Relatively few Unionists of the January–February period converted to secession before Lincoln's April 15 proclamation for seventy-five thousand troops. Those who did may be called fast ultimatumists. An important example was James Barbour, a Virginia legislator and convention delegate from Culpeper County in the northern piedmont. Barbour announced in January that his Unionism depended upon prompt Republican concessions to bring back into the Union the seceding states of the deep South whose government was then "in its chrysalis state." When Republicans did not fulfill Barbour's hopes, he concluded that the southern Confederacy was a fait accompli, the Union permanently disrupted, and Virginia's position in it no longer tenable. Barbour was thus the quintessential fast ultimatumist, of whom there were a scattered number in Virginia but few in North Carolina or Tennessee.[3]

By far the larger number of conditional Unionists preferred that the states of the upper South remain in the Union and try to rebuild it. During March and early April fast ultimatumists assailed the more numerous extended ultimatumists and anticoercionists for stubbornly refusing to act. The latter reluctantly joined the secession movement only after April 15 because Lincoln had, in their view, spurned reasonable compromise proposals and forced them to choose sides in a war. What extended ultimatumists would have done without that provocation remains unclear. Although they claimed to favor secession if the North rejected the ultimatum of the upper South, they could hardly have built the mass base or emotional impetus necessary to carry the upper South out of the Union had Lincoln not challenged their anticoercionist principles by calling for troops.

Despite their differences, most Unionists shared a common set of ideas about the secession crisis. With the exception of a few fast ultimatumists, almost all antisecessionists agreed with each of the five following points: first, that the economic interests of the upper South lay in resolving the crisis and restoring the Union, not in joining an independent slave South; second, that men who wanted disunion per se rather than redress for southern grievances had conspired to frighten fellow southerners; third, that secession was a mass delusion; fourth, that southern misunderstanding of northern intentions had created a grave threat of civil war; and fifth, that only the Republican party could correct the misunderstanding and reverse the drift toward war. The remaining part of this chapter will examine, in turn, each of the characteristic Unionist ideas.

FIRST, upper South Unionists saw no economic advantage in joining an independent slave South. They rejected secessionist arguments that an identity of economic interests linked all slaveholding states. Many Unionists hoped that the economy of the upper South would increasingly develop along the pattern of adjoining northern states, with a diversified base of agriculture, industry, and trade. They insisted that the economic interests of the "grain growing states" of the upper South would be sacrificed in a "Cotton Confederacy" led by South Carolina. "Slavery is the great ruling interest of the extreme Gulf States," one Unionist observed, but the states of the upper South had "*great interests besides slavery, which cannot be lightly abandoned*."[4]

Virginia Unionists insisted that the economic consequences of secession would be bleak. The two leading Unionists in the Virginia convention, John B. Baldwin and George W. Summers, warned repeatedly that Virginia's commercial and industrial interests were "bound up with the free states of the border." Baldwin noted that wheat, tobacco, livestock, and garden crops from eastern Virginia were sold in Baltimore and the cities of the Northeast. Summers explained that customers on both sides of the Ohio and upper Mississippi rivers bought the salt and coal produced in his home region, the Kanawha Valley. In the northwestern Virginia panhandle, wedged snugly along the Ohio River between the two free states of Ohio and Pennsylvania, secession appeared economically suicidal. The editor of the *Wheeling Intelligencer* predicted that "it would kill us off as a city more completely than a big fire. . . . We should sink day by day until we got to be a poor, miserable, penniless, decayed country town."[5]

Virginia manufacturing interests had no wish to join a southern nation dominated by free traders, who opposed any protective tariff for industry. One Unionist from Alexandria predicted that an independent South would seek close commercial ties with England and France, which would tend to keep the South an agricultural exporter, dependent on a supply of imported manufactured goods. "What will become," he asked, "of the promised manufacturing industry and enterprise of Virginia and the other border States of which we hear so much?" Virginia Unionists also suspected that deep South secessionists intended to reopen the African slave trade, thereby depressing slave prices and benefiting the slave-importing states in the lower South at the expense of the slave-exporting states in the upper South. Virginia Unionists thus dismissed secessionist assertions about the bright economic future their state would enjoy in a cotton confederacy. They concluded instead that the economic interests of the upper and lower South were "irreconcilably antagonistic" and "in direct collision."[6]

Parts of North Carolina and Tennessee had more significant economic ties with the deep South than did Virginia. In Memphis, Charlotte, and Wilmington, secessionists contended that any political separation between the upper and lower South would prove an economic nightmare. But Unionists in North Carolina and Tennessee echoed many of the same economic themes used by their counterparts in Virginia. They complained that a southern nation based on South Carolina's "Free Trade, and African Slave Trade Doctrines, would be ruinous to us." Many feared that secession would foreclose future industrial development and economic diversification. In Nashville and the adjacent Cumberland Valley region, the largest manufacturing center in Tennessee, secession had few friends. The owner of a Nashville foundry and machine shop complained to Andrew Johnson that "this mad rush after dissolution" was undermining "all commerce and manufacturs and enterprize." Having already laid off many of his hundred-man work force, Thomas M. Brennan implored Johnson "for God sake try to save this Union" and prevent secessionists from completing "the ruin that had been commenced."[7]

Unionists also pointed out that secession directly threatened two major upper South internal improvement projects, the James River and Kanawha Canal and the Southern Pacific Railroad. Virginia's incomplete canal remained an unhappy symbol of how the state government had shortchanged western interests. Extended gradually west to two towns in the Valley by the early 1840s, the canal had never been completed across the thirty-mile gap between the headwaters of the James and the Kanawha, nor had the segment down the latter to the Ohio been built. In 1860, a French and Belgian consortium, Bellot des Meniers and Company, proposed to assume both the assets of the canal company and its obligation to extend the canal to the Ohio. Strongly endorsed by the governor in January 1861, the sale of the canal awaited legislative approval. Unionists complained that the uproar over secession threatened to sabotage the arrangement and "render the entire work utterly useless and valueless."[8]

Secession also rudely interrupted a grandiose effort to build a southern transcontinental railroad from east Texas to southern California. Most of the chief promoters of the scheme were from Tennessee, which had just experienced a fast-paced decade of railroad construction that gave it rail links extending to the seaboard and up and down the Mississippi Valley. By 1860, managers of the Southern Pacific Rail Road Company were negotiating with the same European consortium that had bid to finish the Virginia canal. Only a twenty-seven-mile segment of the railroad had been completed, enabling cotton planters in fertile Harrison County, Texas, to move their crops to the Red River west of Shreveport, Louisiana. But the state of Texas had pledged substantial assistance, and even more liberal aid from Congress was judged a realistic possibility. Compared to the canal project, which included two hundred miles of finished waterway that had been functioning for decades, the railroad would appear to have been more visionary and speculative. It was, however, more in tune with the economic trends of the era. The James River and Kanawha Canal would never be completed, whereas a southern transcontinental railroad eventually would. But the Southern Pacific's 1861 promoters found to their dismay that the spread of secession blighted hopes for congressional aid and European investment. Congress lost interest in subsidizing the project when Texas seceded from the Union, which in turn discouraged the Europeans. Directors of the Southern Pacific, hoping to salvage something, threw themselves into the campaign to save the Union. They hoped that if the upper South remained in the Union, the deep South might be persuaded to return.[9]

Anxiety about the probable economic consequences of joining a cotton confederacy led some upper South Unionists to contemplate a "central" or "middle" confederacy, composed of the "grain growing slave states" and the border free states. Its advocates thought a border confederacy could prevent "armed collision or civil war" and serve as a nucleus for restoration of the Union once the border slave states and adjacent free states agreed on terms of settlement. Prominent Virginia Unionist William Cabell Rives spelled out the idea in a widely reprinted public letter dated December 8. Rives's scheme attracted considerable support and received a further boost in January when the Unionist governor of Virginia, John Letcher, commended it in his message to the state legislature. Although its advocates sometimes mused about the possible advantages of building a new Union without the troublesome states of New England and the deep South, which were considered mutually responsible for the national crisis, the plan to create a border confederacy is best understood as a means to secure peaceful reunion.[10]

Unionists' doubts about the economic effects of secession related closely to their fears about the impact secession might have on the slave system. A few Unionists in northwestern Virginia were free-soilers or close to it, but the great majority of upper South Unionists defended slavery and denied that secession would enhance its safety. Instead they saw the Union as an essential bulwark for slavery, a barrier that prevented Northern antislavery opinion from becoming a more overt danger. Former Governor William B. Campbell of Tennessee thought the seceding states had contrived a "most unfortunate and injurious" means of protecting slavery. A self-designated "pro-slavery man," he condemned secession as "unwise and impolitic, and tending to the ruin and overthrow of negro slavery. The rights of the slaveholder cannot be maintained out of the Union so well as in it, and I fear cannot be maintained at all outside of it."[11]

Unionists thought secession totally unsuited to remedy the problems facing slaveowners in the upper South. Runaway slaves, Unionists noted, were an irritant in the border states, not in the seceding states of the deep South that sat "hundreds of miles" from the free states. Should the entire South secede and the North become a separate country, more slaves would run away and none could ever be recaptured. Bringing "the Canada line down to the banks of the Ohio" would, warned Tennessee Congressman Emerson Etheridge, make the runaway slave problem far worse in the border states, but the cotton states would continue to "feel secure because of their remoteness from danger." Slaveowners would gravitate to the deep South to prevent their slaves from running away, and slavery in the upper South would decline rapidly. "Five years will show a more destructive warfare on slavery in our own midst, brought about by secession," one North Carolina Unionist thought, "than Lincoln could inflict in 25 years of his irrepressible conflict." Several Virginia Unionists predicted that Virginia would not long remain a slave state if detached from the Union.[12]

Unionists likewise observed that raids such as John Brown's posed no conceivable menace to any seceding state, whereas the border slave states would receive no more cooperation from an independent North in protecting their borders than in recovering fugitives. Would it not be better, asked Unionists, to have the federal army on their side, as at Harpers Ferry? Unionists therefore ridiculed claims that secession could protect southerners from northern invasions to "free their slaves."[13]

Nor did Unionists see secession as a rational means of gaining access to more territory. "What do you gain on the territorial question?" asked Virginia's George W. Summers. By seceding, the South would abandon "all connection with and control over" existing territories. Unionists thus charged that secession would "*shamefully surrender all the territories to the North*" and leave the South with the dubious prospect of seizing parts of Mexico, Central America, and the Caribbean. Tennessee Congressman Robert Hatton said such expectations were "a childish fatuity." Great Britain, whose recognition and aid the seceding states were "so earnestly seeking," would "never permit us to touch one foot of it."[14]

Upper South Unionists frequently quoted former Congressman William W. Boyce of South Carolina, who had once called it "stupendous madness" to try to protect slavery by disrupting the Union. "If secession should take place," he warned in 1850, "I shall consider the institution of slavery as doomed." Andrew Johnson agreed with Boyce "that the dissolution of the Union is the beginning of the destruction of slavery." George D. Prentice, editor of the *Louisville Daily Journal*, thought Boyce's reasoning "unanswerable then" and "unquestionable now." If the slave states all left the Union, the North for the first time would become "a united anti-slavery power," no longer bound by "Constitutional obligations" to the "maintenance of slavery." The South would then be "greatly and fatally weakened, and the doom of slavery irrevocably fixed." Prentice concluded that secessionists were "blinded" and guilty of "mad fanaticism" and "amazing stupidity."[15]

Many Unionists thought secession would undermine slavery because they expected war would result from disunion. War, they knew, posed a far more tangible threat to the slave system than did a Republican president in Washington. They recognized prophetically that an invading army would utterly disrupt the authority of slaveowners. William W. Holden, editor of the *North Carolina Standard*, charged that "Civil War will be Abolition!" He foresaw that slavery would be "rendered insecure and comparatively valueless" amid the chaos and disruption of warfare. A Virginia Unionist likewise predicted that slavery would "vanish from our midst" should civil war "sound its horrid tocsin."[16]

THE second characteristic Unionist idea was to blame secession on a deliberate conspiracy. More forthright southern Unionists pointed a finger of blame directly at "Disunion Democrats." The conspirators had spread the absurd idea that Republicans planned to abolish slavery. Anybody in the South who did not agree was labeled a "submissionist" or "abolitionist." Maryland Congressman Henry Winter Davis assailed the southern Democratic party for having harbored a "revolutionary faction" that had poisoned the minds of southerners. A North Carolina Unionist likewise concluded that the "miserable wretched situation" had been brought about by Democratic distortions and "villainy."[17]

Speeches and pronouncements by southern Unionists reverberated with wholesale denunciations of the southern Democratic party. Especially to the large majority of Unionists with Whig antecedents, there seemed compelling evidence of conspiratorial disunionism nurtured by their political opponents. Had not Democrats, "in an evil hour of folly and madness," initiated the fatal train of events in 1854 by repealing the Missouri Compromise—thereby creating such a storm of protest in the North as to allow the Republican party to arise? Had not Democrats also provided the issues—Lecompton, Caribbean adventurism, proposed Cuban annexation, and renewal of the African slave trade—that allowed the Republican party to sustain its growth? Had not its rule-or-ruin southern wing split the Democratic party, thereby paving the way for election of a Republican president? Had not most southern Democrats professed Unionism during the presidential campaign, only to renege after they lost the election? And most sinister, had not certain southern Democrats openly welcomed Lincoln's election because it would provide the needed catalyst for secession?[18]

Upper South Unionists thought South Carolina's prominence and leadership in the secession movement very revealing. Unique and isolated, South Carolina shunned the egalitarian political tendencies that had taken root in the rest of the country. It was the only state with no political parties and no popular vote for governor or for presidential electors. Unionists suspected that South Carolina's action concealed a hidden agenda—perhaps the establishment of an "aristocratic" southern government with a "property qualification," dominated by "cotton lords." A Tennessee Unionist fumed with outrage at the prospect of having to "bow down" to the "*Disunion Despotism* of Calhoun and his successors, the aristocrats of the least oppressed, least democratic and most anti-republican State on this continent!" Unionists asked whether the states of the upper South should "yield their necks to the yoke of 'King Cotton'" and join hands with those who had displayed a "*wicked* disregard" for their interests and views. William H. Polk, brother of the late president, posed several questions to his fellow Tennesseans: "Will you obey the edict of South Carolina? Are we to be dragged out of the Union without even the courtesy of a consultation? Will we submit the neck of our proud state to a yoke shaped in an hour of madness and folly by *political desperadoes*?"[19]

Some Unionists contended that a hidden agenda lay behind the secession movement—that the conspiratorial core of deep South leaders consciously decided to play on popular fears to secure their own selfish objectives. One Virginia Unionist characterized the clamor in the deep South about the election of Lincoln as a subterfuge. The "real ground of dissatisfaction" in the deep South, he surmised, was that secessionists wanted to reopen the African slave trade. Another Virginia Unionist, likewise discounting talk about slavery being "endangered," believed that South Carolina secessionists were motivated by resentment at the tariff and hopes for a free trade alliance with Great Britain. Unionists thus refused to take secessionist complaints at face value. Instead, they suspected that the alleged grievances were "mainly pretexts," a smoke screen for those "*whose aim is disunion*."[20]

Nor did Unionists find persuasive secessionist contentions that southern honor was at stake. Unionists could be just as vehement as secessionists about the need to defend southern honor; they insisted, however, that it had not yet been irreparably violated. William Holden, for example, said the people of the South would "*never submit*" to the loss of "honor and Constitutional right," but he reasoned that southern honor was yet "untarnished" and southern rights "untouched" by any action of the federal government. The *Charlottesville Review* likewise thought the "question of honor" was "paramount to all others." Virginia should go to war rather than "submit to any degradation." But southern rights and honor could still be maintained within the Union, the *Review* concluded.[21]

Many Unionists tried to turn concerns about honor to their advantage by contending that secession involved a dishonorable loss of face and surrender of rights. One North Carolina Unionist condemned secessionists as "deserters who basely run away from their rights in the face of an advancing foe," thereby giving up the national Capitol, the army, the navy, and the fugitive slave law. Another sneered at South Carolina for acting "a dastardly and cowardly part in making like a *rat* out of a falling house, instead of attempting to reform the government." How, asked a leading Virginia Unionist, could his state's honor "be vindicated by a secession from the Union?" His conception of honor required, instead, "that we should stand fast" in the Union and "vindicate our rights." Andrew Johnson agreed: the "duty" of the South was to stay in the Union, "fighting the battle like men."[22]

Unionists also rejected secessionist claims that the Union created by the Founding Fathers had failed and that "two distinct peoples" could no longer live under the same government. The editor of the *Lynchburg Virginian*, quoting Alexis de Tocqueville, stated that fewer real differences divided North and South than England and Scotland or different regions within Canada, France, or Switzerland. He denied that the Founding Fathers were "guilty of the folly of attempting to cement into one confederated nation, such incongruous elements, as would, in the very nature of things, soon go apart." Their work remained "the greatest and highest example of free government," the editor insisted. It might require adjustment "to the somewhat altered circumstances in which we now find ourself," but it was no "failure." Was secession in 1861 a legitimate sequel to the revolution of 1776? He and many other Unionists profoundly disagreed. They charged, instead, that disunion would, "under the mad excitement of the hour," destroy "the work of our fathers" and ruin everything that patriots of the revolutionary era had fought and bled to create.[23]

To clinch the case that the secession movement was a disunion conspiracy, Unionists pointed out that its promoters persistently refused to spell out terms for preserving the Union. One Virginia editor complained that "nothing will satisfy these gentlemen." Because secessionists had rejected all proposed plans of adjustment, he concluded that "*no settlement is wanted*." Maryland Congressman Henry Winter Davis observed that the argument for secession "flits like a neuralgia from point to point—it is never where it was a moment before. . . . The claim is *everything* or revolution!!" One Virginia secessionist boasted: "You may give me a sheet of white paper and let me write it out myself, and I will not agree to it." Secessionists throughout the South were similarly dogmatic. "The truth is our ultra men do not desire any redress of these grievances," Georgia's Alexander H. Stephens observed. Rather than "settlement or adjustment," they were "for breaking up." Andrew Johnson tartly concluded: "It is not guarantees in reference to slavery they want: it is a government South so they can have the absolute control in their own hands."[24]

As secession sentiment suddenly erupted, in apparent defiance of any reasonable calculation of southern interests, Unionists struggled to find language describing the astonishing turn of events. They frequently likened secession to an approaching storm, with clouds that blackened the sky and cut off all light.[25] Unionists also described secession as pathological—a disease, plague, contagion, infection, epidemic, or distemper. They suspected that secessionists lacked key perceptual faculties, that their deafness and especially their blindness prevented them from comprehending reality. Repeatedly, too, Unionists likened secession to a mental aberration. They characterized secessionists (or at least all those outside the small circle of malevolent, conspiratorial plotters) as mad, insane, or crazy. To explain why a distorted grasp of political reality, earlier confined to a few isolated ideologues and fanatics, had suddenly spread throughout the South, Unionists reasoned that mental incapacity (madness or insanity) had acquired the explosively contagious qualities of the worst plague or epidemic. Unionists thus forged their third key idea—that secession was a mass delusion.

Unionists repeatedly pointed to the demented character of secession. Robert Hatton thought that "madmen—drunken madmen" had gained "control of the popular mind" and were "carrying it like a whirlwind to ruin." One of Andrew Johnson's correspondents called secession "a most savagely raging lunacy," and Johnson himself observed that "the public mind seems to have been inflamed to madness, and in its delerium it overbears all restraint." One North Carolinian in early 1861 sent a bitter note to a South Carolina acquaintance: "Christmas was no doubt a very merry one with you in Charleston where every body is drunk or crazy. I hope the new year may be a happy one and that all of you may come to your senses before the end of it." William M. Tredway, a Union delegate to the Virginia convention, told a story to illustrate his "crude notions" about the secessionist psyche: "I told a friend of mine, who is as sober a man as there is in this body, that he was drunk and that I had not seen him sober since he was in Richmond. 'Do you mean to tell me I am drunk,' he said. 'I do not mean to say you are drunk with liquor,' I replied; 'but you are drunk with excitement, with this idea of secession.' Men can get drunk on something else besides whiskey. I have seen men drunk and deranged, who had not taken a drop of liquor; and I tell you there is more derangement now in the country than you are aware of."[26]

Unionists thus considered many southern political leaders as deluded as the rank and file. Secession could not have become such a mass movement, Unionists reasoned, had not men of influence and prominence joined the mob. Even if the small conspiratorial nucleus of original secessionists had acted deliberately, by far the larger segment of prosecession leadership had surrendered its judgment to the same "mad fanaticism" and "wild ultraism" affecting those less sophisticated and more gullible. In trying to explain such behavior, Unionists suggested that deep South leaders had suffered a double shock. Just after losing power in the federal government, they faced a threat of losing it at home too. As one unsympathetic Unionist noted, politicians who had been "clothed in purple and fine linen" and who had feasted on "official patronage" suddenly found their power in Washington eclipsed and their constituencies panicked. In a display of "amazing stupidity," Unionists charged, men of standing who should have known better had embraced a "wild, revolutionary scheme." Temporarily "blinded," they could not see "the abyss into which they are trying to plunge their country."[27]

Unionists observed that some southerners were more susceptible to secession excitement than others. "The young, the ardent, the impulsive," noted the *Louisville Daily Journal*, most frequently contracted the "distemper" or "contagious madness." The "weak" were then "drawn in" while "the timid, conservative majority" was "overawed by violence and clamor into passive acquiescence." Many Unionists commented on the attraction of secession for "young men" who were "full of fight." Southern colleges and universities became centers of secession enthusiasm. A professor at the University of Virginia reported that "secession *feeling* is so predominant amongst our youths, as practically to have extinguished all Union *principle*. They hasten to 'follow a multitude' to folly, and scarce but one vies with his fellows, in frantic ultraism." Ultimately many of "the oldest and wisest men" were also "carried away" and even many ladies were "captivated." Tennessee Congressman Emerson Etheridge observed that "martial music and warlike demonstrations" reinforced the compulsion for unanimity in the seceded states, and "everything that might have invoked calmness or deliberation had disappeared."[28]

Unionists described secessionists as "crazy enthusiasts" who had "a morbid appetite for excitement" and were "ripe for revolution." Parallels with the French Revolution frequently occurred to Unionists as they watched public sentiment "becoming more and more depraved every day." Thus a secession crowd in Richmond was depicted as a "turn out of the faubourgs of Paris—a regular '93' demonstration in the incipiency of the French Revolution, having no guiding star except desire for civil revolution and military excitement." The doctrinaire intensity of secessionists left Unionists feeling "almost under a reign of terror." "If they had the power," one judged, "they would be quite equal to the bloody Jacobins of France."[29]

In contrast to secessionists, Unionists had a cautionary sense, coupled with a deep pessimism about the likely consequences of disunion. "We have terrible times upon us," former Tennessee Governor William B. Campbell wrote, "and if the wild notions of the South shall prevail, we will be a ruined people." Episcopal Bishop James T. Otey of Memphis, Tennessee, expressed similar alarm. "One would think that men engaged in breaking up a great government . . . would feel themselves burdened by the weight of responsibility," he reasoned. Instead, secessionists displayed a very different state of mind: "*They can whip all creation*—Cotton will make them 'princes and rulers in all lands'!" The bishop feared that the "day of judgment" was "near at hand"—that God would make "our own passions—our Covetousness, pride and ambition the executioners of his wrath." Georgia's Alexander Stephens, though soon to cast his lot with the southern Confederacy, had grave trepidations about the disunion movement. "Revolutions are much easier started than controlled, and the men who begin them, even for the best purposes and objects, seldom end them," Stephens noted. "The American Revolution of 1776 was one of the few exceptions to this remark that the history of the world furnishes. Human passions are like the winds; when aroused they sweep everything before them in their fury . . . until those who sowed the wind will find that they have reaped the whirlwind." Leading Virginia Unionist George W. Summers agreed. "It is much easier to destroy than to reconstruct," he observed. "If disunion once begins, none can foresee where it will end."[30]

Unionists thought it essential to treat the deluded people of the South with great care. Tennessee historian A. Waldo Putnam considered secession a "violent fever" that he hoped would "not long endure." He thought "the spread of the contagion might have been stayed" had firm presidential action quickly isolated the "plague-spot" (South Carolina). But by February he concluded that the disease could be controlled only through a nonprovocative "hands-off" policy. Any invasion of the seceded states, Putnam feared, would "cause a commotion" and "awaken a sympathy" in the upper South, where many people suffered from the same "sensitive, nervous, emotional condition." Changing the metaphor to emphasize the same thought, Putnam warned that the "use of force at any point" along the "inflamed borders" of the seceded states would cause flames to "spread and kindle in the Middle Slave States" and "rage furiously" into general warfare. Such a catastrophe "would involve us in a war of desolation, the extent and duration of which no human Ken can limit."[31]

THE fourth principal Unionist idea was, therefore, that southern misunderstanding of northern intentions had created a grave threat of civil war. However much they blamed secessionists for distorting northern intentions, Unionists recognized that popular fear and anger pervading the South would, if not alleviated, soon produce a disastrous tragedy. Unionists themselves, believing southern anxieties either groundless or exaggerated, tried to introduce a less alarmist perspective.

Those wishing to show that Republicans had no plans to interfere with the southern states had plenty of evidence to marshal. Party officials, both prominent and obscure, had made countless reassurances about their conservatism, especially after the Brown raid when Republicans worked to put as much distance as possible between their party and the abortive Harpers Ferry conspiracy. Abraham Lincoln characterized as "malicious slander" all efforts to connect John Brown to the Republican party. "John Brown was no Republican," Lincoln observed in his Cooper Union speech, nor had any investigation implicated "a single Republican in his Harper's Ferry enterprise." The Republican party platform of 1860 directly addressed southern concerns, advocating "the maintenance inviolate of the rights of States, and especially the right of each state to order and control its own domestic institutions," while condemning any "lawless invasion" of a state or territory "as among the gravest of crimes." Republican newspaper editors insisted that the people of the North would not "countenance any infraction of Southern rights." Henry J. Raymond, editor of the *New York Times*, charged that "the most perilous misrepresentations concerning the Republican party" had created the "delusion" that the South was endangered. Those depicting the Republican party as an abolition party, ready to undertake a "violent crusade against the rights of the Southern States and the peace of Southern society," had perpetrated a "fearful falsehood," Raymond insisted. Amasa Walker, a prominent Massachusetts Republican and former lieutenant governor, insisted that Republicans had "never proposed, nor do they wish, to deprive you of your slaves."

Slavery would be "just as safe under Lincoln as under Buchanan." As the secession crisis deepened, Lincoln himself reiterated to southerners his intention "to leave you alone, and in no way to interfere with your institution." He pointedly opened his Inaugural Address by emphasizing the same point: southerners had no "reasonable cause" for "apprehension."[32]

Perhaps the most candid and authentic avowals of northern conservatism took place in private. An occasional surviving manuscript adds credence to the public pronouncements made by prominent Republicans. One North Carolinian received a letter from an old Massachusetts friend, who regretted that "a general delusion prevails in the Southern mind as to the feelings and purposes of the Northern States at the present crisis." The New Englander judged that more than 99 percent of the people in his region were ready "to maintain the just rights of the South." Although many northerners considered it important to prevent slavery from spreading, almost all opposed interference with the rights of slaveowners in states where it already existed. An Ohio Republican likewise wrote to a friend in Tennessee to explain that the "radical Abolition party," which favored the use of federal power to abolish slavery, was a small faction, "much more violent and bitter towards the Republicans than towards the Democratic party." A Pennsylvanian explained to William Holden that the "great issue" in his state during the presidential campaign had been the tariff, not slavery. "There is *no doubt*," he concluded, "about the sentiment of our *people* almost *en masse* being in favor of doing ample justice to the South." Another Pennsylvanian sent Andrew Johnson a similar message. Republicans had used the tariff issue to attract a "large number of Whigs, who cared very little about the Slavery issue, but were in earnest about protection."[33]

Unionists thus insisted that southerners ought not to interpret the results of the 1860 election as indicating that northern majorities hated the South or planned to assault the slave system. Unionists instead depicted the Republican party as a diverse coalition, including many who had been attracted primarily by economic issues such as the tariff, the Homestead Bill, and the Pacific railroad. Presidential candidate John Bell reasoned in a December public letter that perhaps a third of Republicans had no interest in the sectional dispute and "would be sincerely glad to see the slavery controversy between the two great sections of the country speedily terminated." He judged that no more than one-third of Republicans held "extreme" antislavery or antisouthern sentiments, whereas the middle third considered the election of Lincoln, by itself, to have vindicated opponents of the Kansas-Nebraska Act and Lecompton. The moderate majority of Republicans, Bell surmised, would now be "content to cease the war upon Southern interests and feelings."[34]

Immediately after Lincoln's election, many Unionists stated that the South had no basis for either complaint or alarm. Because his victory had been achieved in a manner fully consistent with the Constitution, although with only 40 percent of the popular vote, Unionists judged that he deserved a "fair trial." His election did not endanger the South, ventured the editor of the *Lynchburg Virginian*, because "thousands upon thousands of those who voted for Lincoln did so without caring a straw for the Negro question." Another Unionist wrote a reassuring letter to his son at the University of Virginia: "The Presidential election is over and Lincoln is lawfully elected. I think he is conservative, and that the South has really nothing to fear from his administration. I don't think he has any desire to act against Southern rights. He is anti-slavery it is true; but that is a mere political feeling, which will find its gratification, in embarrassing the spread of slavery; it will not seek to destroy slavery where it already exists." Even if Lincoln "desired to injure Southern institutions," he would not have "the power to do it" because both Congress and the Supreme Court stood in his way.[35]

As the crisis intensified, the most outspoken southern Unionists continued to scoff at southern alarms about Republican intentions. No other political party, Tennessee Congressman Emerson Etheridge insisted, had ever "given stronger guarantees against any desire or any power to interfere with slavery in the States of this Union." He condemned "disunionists and their allies" for deliberately distorting "the most solemn assurance which a political party can make to the world."[36]

However accurate Etheridge's portrayal of Republican purposes, his speech worried most other southern Unionists in Congress. By denying the existence of a threat, they opened themselves to the argument that Republicans need not make concessions. Robert Hatton explained the dilemma: "To say to the Republicans, what we say to our own people at home, relieves them of apprehension, and makes them indisposed to do anything." Unionists thus faced a paradoxical challenge. They needed to calm fellow southerners and downplay fears of imminent danger. But at the same time, Unionists needed to persuade Republicans to take generous remedial action. "It is a difficult road to travel," Hatton observed.[37]

Hatton had good reason to worry. "Stiff-backed" Republicans directed a torrent of abuse at party colleagues "who were inclined to give in and do something." The radicals insisted that southern Unionists themselves should take responsibility for reversing any false impressions. "Should you not tell your people what we have assured you on every proper occasion, that the Republican Party has always repudiated all intention of interfering with slavery or any other Southern institution within the States?" asked New York's David Dudley Field, a leading uncompromising Republican. Many other Republicans shared Field's view. Horace Greeley's *New York Tribune* argued that southern "usurpers" had created a furor about "frivolous" and nonexistent grievances. Republicans, Greeley insisted, should not offer concessions "to the pretexts set up." Influential Republicans such as incoming Secretary of the Treasury Salmon P. Chase suggested that sensible southerners "unite with us" in a simple declaration "that all fears of aggression entertained by your people are groundless."[38]

Even though agreeing with Republicans that there was "no sufficient reason" for secession and that "demagogues" had "deceived and misled" the people of the South, southern Unionists believed that too many northerners, especially Republicans, dangerously underestimated popular disaffection in the South. The most unconditional Unionists, such as Tennessee Congressman Emerson Etheridge and Virginia Congressman Sherrard Clemens, pointed out that many southerners had been "struck blind" by "a sudden frenzy" and had lost all perspective. "Thousands believe honestly that Lincoln and his cohorts are coming down to apply the torch and the knife to the dwellings and people of the South," Etheridge warned. These "apprehensions of danger" were so pervasive, noted Virginia Congressman John Millson, that his constituents would not believe his own explanations to the contrary.[39]

Some conciliatory Republicans and many northern Democrats recognized the validity of Unionist warnings. Republican Congressman Charles Francis Adams of Massachusetts believed that "imaginary dangers" had grown up "into a gigantic reality" and needed to be "dealt with as such." Adams thus advised Republicans to provide reassurances to stem the "panic." Democratic Congressman John Cochrane of New York contended that "civil communities or States" could not be treated as "refractory individuals" and that any use of armed force would be senseless and counterproductive. He favored "reasonable concessions" to the "border slave States" as the only way ultimately to win back the allegiance of the seceded states and restore the Union. Citing the opinion of Alexander Hamilton in *Federalist* No. 16, Cochrane concluded that the secession crisis was one of those occasional outbreaks of popular discontent so widespread as to require extraordinary measures.[40]

Although they welcomed the views of men such as Adams and

Cochrane, astute Unionists worried that many Republicans failed to recognize the "fearful *earnestness*" displayed by both the leaders and the "mass of people" in the seceded states. Frightened by Lincoln's comments in February that the crisis was "only *artificial*" and "would soon pass away" and "nobody be harmed," A. Waldo Putnam warned that "it will not do to allow the impression to remain on the minds of the Northern people that the Southern people or their leaders are engaged in the producing of this terrible disturbance . . . for mere political effect—that is without any provocation or ground of reasonable apprehension of infringement of rights." Instead, thousands of conservative propertyholders in the deep South had, however foolishly, "yielded to the prevalent Southern spirit of action" and thrown their support to the new order.[41]

Unless steps were taken to calm the excitement in the South, Unionists warned, "a terrible war" was inevitable. They feared with good reason that the upper South would "bear the brunt" and be turned into a battleground. Scenes of "blood and carnage" beyond all comprehension would result. "Civil war, with all its train of attendant furies," would desolate the South, Robert Hatton warned. One Virginia newspaper editor urged his readers to consider the "sombre picture" of "wives and children in distress, naked and starving, homesteads in ashes; father, brothers and sons weltering in blood shed in unholy war, and the corpses of neighbors and friends encumbering nameless battle-fields." Unionists rejected secessionist predictions that the North was too cowardly and irresolute to threaten an independent South. "The idea that there will be no war because the Northern people will not fight is absurd," commented prominent Whig Unionist William A. Graham of North Carolina. "The North Western men are bone of our bone and flesh of our flesh, their ancestors in many cases having gone from the old Southern States."[42]

Upper South Unionists certainly were not the only Americans who thought war likely and feared a ghastly bloodletting, but their sense of alarm was as unanimous and unqualified as it was prescient. Many northerners, by contrast, saw secession as a theatrical gesture, designed simply to bluff and intimidate, and believed that secession leaders could call off the upheaval whenever they felt disposed to do so. At the same time, growing numbers of southerners had become intoxicated with the idea of southern independence, persuading themselves that effete Yankees would never dare to fight. Southern Unionists did their best to show that both were deluded and that their mutual delusions threatened unprecedented disaster. They deplored the widespread "apathy and indifference" about the sectional crisis. Both in their private communications and their public pronouncements, Unionists repeatedly insisted that "imminent peril" faced the country. "What spirit broods over us," asked Tennessee Congressman T. A. R. Nelson, "that we cannot arouse to a sense of the danger?" Alarmed Unionists thought they saw what more sectional-minded people both North and South either could not see or refused to recognize.[43]

BUT what could be done to prevent the disaster of civil war? Even though Unionists blamed secessionists for grossly exaggerating the supposed dangers of a Republican president and for acting "rashly" and in "manifest disregard" of the true interests of the South, Unionists agreed that matters had gotten out of hand—that the leaders of the secession movement could no longer control the mass panic they had triggered. Only the Republican party, Unionists insisted, had the power to overcome southern anxiety and reverse the drift toward war. "You hold . . . the Union in your hands," Virginia Congressman John T. Harris told the Republicans: "You can save it; and you alone can." Robert Hatton likened the American government to a burning house. "Flames, fierce as hell, are consuming it. Men of the North, would you prevent its destruction? You have it in your power. Without risk, without sacrifice, without dishonor you can do it. . . . I demand to know if you will longer stand indifferently by, and see it tumble into ruins before you." The belief that a peaceful resolution to the national impasse depended upon conciliatory action by the Republican party was thus the fifth basic Unionist idea.[44]

In asking for Republican assistance, southern Unionists confronted a paradox. Candid Unionists acknowledged that Republicans had never proposed interfering with slavery in the states. But because so many southerners did "whether justly or not, honestly believe" that the Republican party intended to subvert slavery, Unionists argued that secession could not be stopped without Republican aid in the form of tangible concessions and reassurances, not mere words.[45]

But who would define the appropriate concession or reassurance? Some Republicans, led by Charles Francis Adams, offered to support a constitutional amendment protecting slavery in the states. Would this measure give the Unionists the evidence they needed to overcome secession? They thought not. The Unionists regarded Adams's proposal as no more than a preliminary step in the right direction because it involved no real change in Republican policy. Ironically, Unionists insisted, Republicans could show that they did not threaten slavery in the states only by retreating from the one point on which their opposition to slavery was clear and specific—the territories.

Even if logically inconsistent, most discussion of a Union-saving compromise therefore hinged around the territorial issue.

In Unionist eyes, the territorial issue should have been negotiable because it was a "mere abstraction." They believed Republicans wanted to prohibit something that was not going to happen in any event and that southerners contended for a right that had no practical applicability. "This territorial issue is a humbug and a nuisance, which no sensible man should disturb himself about for a single moment," insisted the editor of the *Richmond Whig*. Unionist complaints about the territorial issue could be multiplied ad infinitum. Territorial rights were "of no practical value" because there was not "a foot of territory belonging to the United States adapted to slave labor." It defied "common sense" to quarrel about "a thing that can never be of any use to us." Only a "fool" or a "fit subject for a lunatic asylum" would take valuable slaves to the arid territories. Virginia Unionist John B. Baldwin asserted that it was "infatuation, madness, and fanaticism" to destroy the Union "upon an issue like this."[46]

So why worry about the territories in the first place? A full answer would require a detailed history of North-South sectionalism from 1846 to 1861, but a few familiar facts should be kept in mind. Roger Taney's Supreme Court had defined the territorial issue in such a way that many southerners regarded it as encompassing a matter of "right" and "honor." By specifying, in the *Dred Scott* decision, that no federal law could prevent the taking of slaves to territories, the Supreme Court established a curious and controversial right. Interference with or enforcement of that right was necessarily hypothetical because plantation owners had no incentive to migrate with their slaves to the Rocky Mountains or the deserts of the Southwest. But Southern Rights absolutists insisted that the Democratic party go on record supporting passage by Congress of a territorial slave code, that is, a law to protect slavery in the territories. When northern Democrats refused to commit political suicide by doing so, intransigent southerners bolted the party. And once Lincoln was elected, the same people continued to exploit the same issue. Unionists frequently charged that southern "precipitators" had fastened upon the territorial issue to split both the Democratic party and the Union.

Unfortunately for the Unionists, the territorial issue had assumed a symbolic importance to the Republican party at least equal to that it occupied for southern intransigents. Territorial restriction had become the least common denominator in the Republican antislavery program. Because the territorial issue provided a basis for uniting various elements of the party around a common position, Republicans could not easily heed Unionist pleas for compromise. Zealous Republicans, who wanted to demonstrate their firmness and reliability to antislavery constituents, had to be content with territorial restriction. Because Southern Rights spokesmen said the issue was momentous, Republicans could point to the southern furor and say they were indeed doing something to hurt the slave system. A significant number of Republicans thus contended that the exclusion of slavery from the territories constituted a genuine first step in the direction of abolition—and rather than have to defend the argument on its merits, which would have been difficult, they could simply quote Southern Rights ideologues. The process worked just as well in reverse. One must appreciate the dynamics of this exercise in mutual deception to understand the collapse of the American political system in 1860–61.

Unionists tried to persuade Republicans that their party would lose nothing tangible by modifying its position on the territories. "This territorial question has been settled," Virginia Congressman John Millson observed:

> The battle has been fought, and it has been won by both parties; it has been lost by both parties. You have lost the principle on which your party is founded. You cannot, under existing laws and the existing Constitution, as interpreted by the Supreme Court, prohibit slavery in a Territory. You have lost the battle; we have gained it. But you know that, if your purpose has been to exclude slavery from the Territories, there is not the least probability that slavery will ever be carried into any one of them. Thus, in all that respects practical results, you have gained the battle, and we have lost it. You have lost the principle; we the substance. You have gained the substance; we the principle. We are, then, on equal terms. We are both victors; we are both vanquished. There is nothing, then, to prevent us from making an end of the whole quarrel now, and preclude all controversy on the subject hereafter.[47]

North Carolina's John A. Gilmer advanced the line of argument one audacious step further. He advised Republicans to take the territorial issue away from the extremists:

> Why, sirs, do you think these ultra men insist on what they call protection, because it is of any value to them? Whenever you say to them, take it as you want it, then you hand over to them what will be to them their political winding-sheet. It is not because it is a thing which is really valuable to the South that they desire

> protection, nor is it because it would be any injury to the North if you grant it. They demand it because they think you will refuse it, and by your refusal, they hope the South will be inflamed to the extent of breaking up this government—*the very thing* the leaders desire.

Convinced that the most stringent protection for slavery in the territories "would come as near making slave states, as the drying up of the Mississippi, could be secured by a law of Congress," Gilmer hoped Republicans could sacrifice their symbol and thereby throttle the secession movement. Nor would such a bold move constitute a humiliating surrender to "threats." Instead, Robert Hatton argued, it would enable Unionists to reassure southerners "of your purpose to deal fairly and justly with them." By placing "in our hands the weapons of conciliation and concession," Republicans would enable Unionists to "cleave the armor of our adversaries."[48]

Leading southern Unionists thus earnestly sought Republican assistance. John A. Gilmer privately bewailed the unreasonable behavior of "my maddened brethren of the South" and urged Republicans to treat southern symptoms with an appropriate palliative. "The South is deranged," he wrote to Thurlow Weed, "and only needs a few bread pills to cure their madness." Conceding "this useless and foolish abstraction of Congressional protection to slavery in the Territories" seemed to Gilmer the most potent placebo Republicans could offer. He pleaded with Republicans to recognize that the choice had narrowed to territorial compromise or civil war. He foresaw more accurately than most of his fellow countrymen that any clash of arms would so arouse the states of the upper South as to make reunion impossible, except at the price of massive bloodshed. The peroration of Gilmer's powerful speech in Congress on January 26, 1861, forcefully depicted the horrors of civil war and challenged Republicans to look ahead and consider the likely consequences of inaction: "I can never envy the feelings of the man, North or South, who, when that day of butchery and destruction shall come, will feel in his heart that he stood out on a mere point of etiquette; that if he had yielded a matter of no practical importance to him, or his constituents, all trouble could have been avoided."[49]

Confident that a territorial compromise would stifle secession and set in motion the process of reunion, Unionists denied that the upper South had to choose sides. Even though spokesmen for the seceding states of the deep South talked as if disunion were permanent, Unionists such as John Millson of Virginia predicted that the adoption of "a judicious, wise, moderate course" by the Republican party would hold the remaining slave states in the Union and "induce the return of those who have already withdrawn from it." Congressman J. Morrison Harris of Maryland likewise believed it possible to "bring back those which have gone out."[50]

The Unionists had one final piece of advice for the Republicans. For the policy of compromise and conciliation to work, the federal government must scrupulously avoid any clash of arms with the seceding states. Unionists in the Virginia convention, for example, repeatedly warned against any "coercion" policy. "This Government can never be kept together by force," one insisted. "The very moment you attempt coercion you produce war," another predicted, "and war will end this Union now and forever." Yet another announced that if the federal government attempted to coerce the seceding states, Virginia would "make common cause with them" and that federal armies would have "to march over the dead bodies of countless numbers of Virginia's true sons."[51]

Almost all southern Unionists rejected coercion. Three samples from congressional debate reflect the nearly unanimous anticoercion mentality. James M. Leach, Opposition party Unionist from the western North Carolina piedmont, contended that "if a coercive policy is adopted, all is lost." Whether or not the federal government had the right "to coerce a State," it would be "the height of folly and madness and wickedness, to attempt its exercise" because "the first gun fired for such a purpose would rally every slave State of the Union together." Any military action against the seceded states, warned unconditional Unionist Horace Maynard of East Tennessee, would be "unwise," "ineffective," and "attended with evil, and only evil." "Believe me," he insisted, "the moment you wage war, you array the entire South, as one man, in behalf of the portion that is attacked." Maynard warned about the dangers of treating the people of the seceded states as lawless rebels: "Whole peoples are never consciously wrong, and must not be proceeded against as criminals." Maryland Congressman Edwin H. Webster, echoing his Opposition colleagues Leach and Maynard, recalled the debates between Lord North and the Earl of Chatham (William Pitt), when North insisted that British laws must first be enforced and rebels punished before trying to conciliate the American colonies. "The world knows the result," Webster observed; "the rebellion was successful and the English empire was dismembered."[52]

Considerations about honor figured prominently in the Unionist rejection of coercion. "We have argued and protested against secession, we have denounced our friends for being disunionists, we have done our utmost, in a feeble way, to prevent the present deplorable state of affairs," commented the editor of the *Wilmington Daily Herald*, "but we . . . should dishonor the blood that flows in our veins, and which was freely shed to establish American Independence, if we hesitated to beat back the armed aggressor, come from what quarter he may." The editor of the *Charlottesville Review* felt "the most bitter resentment" toward South Carolina for placing the upper South in a terrible dilemma, but he warned that "the subjection of South Carolina or any other seceding State, in consequence of their determination not to submit to the policy of the Republicans, is a blow at the entire South—subjection to all. We are, thenceforth, humiliated. We are conquered. We could not hold up our heads in the Union any more. We would meet a Northern man as the Saxon met the Norman." Coercion would deny southern equality in the Union. Though their slaves would be lost, their fields devastated, and their young men slaughtered, Virginians would fight to maintain "their feeling of *self-respect*." Coercion would create a situation, warned Maynard, "as when a brother is assailed," and "all his brethren rush to his rescue, not stopping to inquire whether, in the context, he be right or wrong." War waged "on brethren of the same blood and a common lineage," Leach likewise insisted, would turn North Carolina against the Union: "She will do everything that can be done to save the Constitution and the Union, except to tarnish her name, or sully her honor. This she will never do—never!" North Carolinians would not tolerate an armed effort to subjugate their state or "any of her southern sisters."[53]

EVEN amid "the gloom that has settled upon the nation, and the thick darkness that has pervaded our political horizon," some Unionists detected "the first faint glimmerings that precede the dawn of a brighter day." One Virginian hoped "ere long to see a silver lining on the cloud that overhangs us." An anonymous Virginia poet beseeched God

to save our own beloved land,
from *Dissolution's* murderous hand. . . .
Sweep from her sky the gathering gloom,
and fill her days with light and bloom.

A North Carolina poet likewise hoped God could "control the raging storm" and save the country from the "dark and awful" consequences of disunion. But a Unionist newspaper reporter in Washington soberly acknowledged in late January that "the *darkness* is still very great."[54]

Unionists had good reason to fear that they might be whistling in the dark. The dynamics of the secession crisis placed them and their northern allies in the position of trying to reconcile a bitterly polarized situation. A majority of Republicans opposed any compromise or concession. The single most influential Republican newspaper, the *New York Tribune*, had emblazoned on its masthead: "NO COMPROMISE! NO CONCESSIONS TO TRAITORS!" The unwillingness of Republicans to compromise vexed the Unionists. "All the clouds that have, from time to time, come over our hopes of a settlement, grow out of their obstinate action," one fumed. It appeared to Unionists that hard-line Republicans and secessionists interacted so as to strengthen each other. "We spit upon every plan to compromise," roared a prosecession newspaper editor from North Carolina: "A Southern man who would now offer to compromise with the Northern States is a traitor to the South."[55]

In private correspondence Unionists often voiced frustration, rage, and despair. A prominent Memphis Unionist complained that the "majestic work" of the Founding Fathers was being "subverted and overturned" by a few "disappointed, ambitious traitors," who had placed the country on the verge of civil war. He could not see "a gleam of light through the impenetrable gloom that overhangs us." Congressman Robert Hatton of Tennessee likewise confessed to his wife in late December that "my hopes of saving the Government are nearly, if not quite, gone." Advising her to "prepare your mind for the worst," Hatton explained that civil war was "inevitable." Who was responsible? Hatton blamed both "the fool, hot-headed fire-eater" of the South and the "Northern intermeddler" who played into the hands of southern extremists. What most angered him, however, was the "stubborn, stupid, blind" refusal of most Republicans to face reality by granting "liberal concessions" that would "appease the inflamed Southern mind." Hatton had little hope that Republicans would see the danger in time to avert it. Most northerners continued to believe there was "no danger of disunion" even though they were "standing in the very midst" of it. "They will wake up," Hatton sadly predicted, "when it is too late."[56]

Republicans who refused to comprehend the danger were, in the estimate of the southern Unionists, adding to it all the time. "A deep gloom hangs over us all in the South" because Republicans "fold their arms and look coldly on," one North Carolinian noted. The "cold, icy, stoical indifference" of Republicans similarly distressed North Carolina Congressman John A. Gilmer, who vividly described the resulting impasse: "Northern extreme men are working night and day to defeat all Compromises. Southern extreme men do the same thing, and send telegraph dispatches out South to excite and inflame our people to the utmost tension. The fury and madness of the South hourly becomes more and more aggravated. The Southern disunionists visit Northern Representatives at their rooms, talk with them, and tell them to concede nothing—that nothing will be acceptable to the South, and they by concession will only humiliate themselves for no good." The frustrations of trying to mediate between such mutually supportive poles of irreconcilability left Gilmer jangling with nervous apprehension. "We are in real trouble," he scrawled to a friend in early January: "There is real danger at hand. I can't say that I have lost all hope, but . . . the prospects are gloomy in the extreme. I often shed tears in silence."[57]

6

THE UNIONIST OFFENSIVE

UPPER South Unionism coalesced during the first two months of 1861. Though confronted by grave obstacles, Unionists possessed one key advantage: popular support for secession had grown since November but had not yet gained a majority in any upper South state. Unionists faced the task of arresting and reversing the growth of secession sentiment in their home states, while also urging Congress to enact Union-saving measures. The two objectives were, of course, interconnected, but each may best be treated separately. This chapter will focus on the first.

The great Unionist achievement, during a winter otherwise marked by frustration and failure, was the mobilizing of popular majorities across the upper South to thwart secession. Why did the upper South refuse to follow the lead of the lower South? That crucial question requires a two-pronged answer, involving both slavery and party. Relatively smaller concentrations of slaves and slaveowners, plus statewide political arenas in which the two major parties competed on close terms, made the upper South less receptive to secessionist appeals. The combination of fewer slaveowners and more formidable political opposition to the secession-leaning Democratic party kept Virginia, North Carolina, and Tennessee in the Union during early 1861.

Plantation regions dominated the seven seceding states in the deep South. It was no coincidence that the first states to leave the Union had the greatest commitment to slavery. Support for secession, both in the upper and lower South, tended to be strongest in high-slaveowning areas and weakest in the low-slaveowning regions of the upcountry. However formidable the slaveowning interest in Virginia, North Carolina, and Tennessee, a larger share of each state's electorate resided in the upcountry than anywhere in the lower South.

Somewhat less well known, but of comparable importance in understanding the relative weakness of secession in the upper South, was a set of partisan arrangements that differed markedly from those in the lower South. Competitive two-party politics in the upper South gave antisecessionists an indispensable base. The Whig party organization and electorate provided the foundation for what would soon be called the Union party in Virginia, North Carolina, and Tennessee.

Whig and Opposition parties throughout the lower South were much weaker and generally weakest in the upcountry. The tendency for lower South Whigs to reside in the "black belts" enervated whatever latent Unionism they possessed. But in the Upper South, Whigs had greater residual strength, which was by no means confined to plantation regions. In North Carolina, notably, a cluster of low-slaveowning counties in the piedmont regularly provided the largest Whig margins in the state (see Map 3-2). Voters in this Whiggish "Quaker Belt" spearheaded statewide opposition to secession. They gained reinforcements from party loyalists in the mountains and the northeast. Each Tennessee party received comparable support from high- and low-slaveowning regions. But a bloc of strong Whig counties around Knoxville provided a militantly antisecession nucleus for the broader East Tennessee region, and Whiggish counties in the fertile Cumberland Valley of Middle Tennessee proved especially hospitable to a qualified wait-and-see conditional Unionism. Western Virginia was slightly more Democratic than eastern Virginia, but the unique geographical position of the trans-Allegheny, coupled with its long history of estrangement from the east, made the west almost unanimously pro-Union. Whig strongholds in the Virginia valley and western piedmont also rejected secession, including, for example, Jefferson County, the site of John Brown's assault in October 1859. Even in Southampton County, the Virginia tidewater locale where the slave rebel Nat Turner had rampaged thirty years before, Whigs voted overwhelmingly pro-Union. The inability of secessionists to carry even a bare majority in Southampton well illustrated the linkage between Unionism and Whig party loyalties.[1]

Upper South Unionism thus had both a regional and a party base. A popular outpouring of antisecession sentiment among upcountry nonslaveowners provided the most conspicuous element of Union strength. But Unionism had the potential to become a dominant political force because it extended beyond the upcountry to draw support from the Whig rank and file. The latter included a broad spectrum of southerners, among them more than a few slaveowners from the fertile lowlands. Thomas P. Devereux, one of the wealthiest plantation owners in North Carolina, berated South Carolina for her "folly" and confidently awaited a Union-saving compromise. A conservative orientation was especially pronounced among Union Whigs in eastern Virginia, many of whom deplored the democratic revisions in the 1851 Virginia constitution. They blamed secession on the new breed of "worthless, disgusting politicians" who pandered to popular fears.[2]

Although some embraced Unionism to preserve or rebuild existing social hierarchies, the antisecession insurgency in the upper South had unmistakable egalitarian overtones. Far more than in the lower South, class resentments surfaced in late 1860 and early 1861. One of Edmund Ruffin's correspondents told him in late November that secession sentiment in the Southside Virginia counties of Lunenburg and Nottoway had increased greatly since the election but that "disaffection" among "the poorer class of non slaveholders" had also appeared. Some antisecessionists stated flatly that "in the event of civil war or even servile insurrection, they would not lift a finger in defense of the rights of slaveholders." An observer in Hertford County, North Carolina, a tidewater area just below the Virginia border, was similarly "mortified" to find many nonslaveowning "plain country people" unwilling to fight "to protect rich men's negroes." Nor were nonslaveowning Virginians in the Shenandoah Valley willing "to break up the government for the mere loss of an election." Similar reports emanated from West Tennessee, where "the nonslave holders (or a large majority of them) when approached on the subject declare that they will not fight if war fol[l]ows a dissolution of the union." And in towns and cities across the upper South, "workingmen" organized and demonstrated against secession.[3]

Sensitive to the egalitarian stirrings, some secession sympathizers cautioned against trying to rush the states of the upper South out of the Union prematurely. "You cannot unite the *masses* of any southern State much less those of North Carolina against the Union and in favor [of] slavery *alone*," surmised an astute secessionist. Nonslaveowners would resist any movement that appeared controlled by "the *avarice* and the *selfishness* of *Negro Slavocracy*." But by prudently waiting until the federal government attacked the seceding states, secessionists could "change the issue" to "a question of popular liberty." Once the second consideration was introduced, nothing could hold North Carolina in the Union. A Southern Rights supporter from Virginia reasoned along the same lines. "You can't make the great mass of the people, especially the non slaveholders understand . . . the nice principles on which the secessionists are now attempting to act," he observed. Indeed, he feared that secessionist clamor ran the potential danger "of creating a party with sympathies for the incoming administration, here in our midst." He therefore thought it best "to *prepare* for resistance" without seeming to follow the lead of "disunionists *per se*." He foresaw, too, that "the non slaveholder will fight for his section as soon as the slaveholder if you can convince him that *his* political rights are really threatened."[4]

Such caution was appropriate. Large regions of Virginia, North Carolina, and Tennessee opposed secession with at least as much fervor and with even greater unanimity than it was supported in other areas of those states. Spontaneous Union meetings gathered in upcountry locations at the same time secessionists seized the organizational initiative in many plantation districts. For example, a well-attended public meeting on November 29 in Hawkins County, East Tennessee, resolved that "the doctrine of secession" was "subversive of all just principles of government." The meeting reaffirmed Andrew Jackson's view that secession was "treason." An estimated eight hundred to a thousand people likewise gathered on December 28 in intensely Unionist Randolph County, in the North Carolina piedmont, to condemn secession as "unwise and suicidal" and to deplore the "folly and madness" of extremists North and South.[5]

For the Breckinridge wing of the Democratic party, which provided the political backbone for the secession movement, the antisecession groundswell in parts of Virginia, North Carolina, and Tennessee posed a deadly threat. Breckinridge had readily carried most Democratic areas of the upcountry. Any significant slippage of Democratic loyalties there, when coupled with the already manifest disaffection from the party of those who voted for Douglas in 1860, seriously endangered the prospects for statewide secession. It likewise threatened the narrow statewide Democratic majorities in all three states.

Several important Democrats led the Unionist exodus from the Breckinridge Democracy. Congressman Sherrard Clemens from Wheeling, the major town in northwestern Virginia's panhandle, condemned South Carolina's "hot and indecent haste." Her action, Clemens charged, "affords no remedy for alleged grievances but would intensify every one of them." Publicly urged to resign by the local Democratic newspaper editor, Clemens refused to back down. He bitterly announced to a Union meeting that if one had to be a disunionist to be an accepted member of his party, he was "no longer a Democrat." Two other Virginia Democratic congressmen, John T. Harris from the Shenandoah Valley and John Millson of the Norfolk region, likewise broke with the party to oppose secession. In North Carolina, editor William W. Holden insisted that voters who had supported Breckinridge had not endorsed secession. He made a blistering attack on Governor John Ellis, a fellow Democrat, who had called for a state convention and a conference of southern states. Holden charged that secession would bring disastrous consequences—bitter internal strife, chronic warfare, an increase in foreign influence, economic stagnation, high taxes, large standing armies, and a "military despotism." The most prominent Breckinridge Democrat to oppose secession was, of course, Senator Andrew Johnson of Tennessee. Insisting that southern rights could best be protected in the Union, he fiercely criticized South Carolina and her allies for trying to coerce Tennessee and the states of the upper South.[6]

A rank-and-file rebellion against disunionist Democratic leadership doomed immediate secession in Virginia, North Carolina, and Tennessee. Only by embracing secession with near unanimity could Breckinridge supporters have carried the three states out of the Union because most Bell and Douglas partisans opposed secession and Douglas had siphoned enough normal Democratic votes to allow Bell to carry Virginia and Tennessee. But by early 1861 the Democratic party was more gravely divided than it had been in November 1860.

Nowhere in the upper South, therefore, did secession become statewide majority sentiment during the first months after the presidential election. Nor, however, did unconditional Unionism. Many Unionists agreed that the South had grievances against the free states and that redress was in order. Unionists also abhorred the idea of using armed force to challenge secession, and many warned that they would fight on the side of the South if war came. Thus, probably the largest segment of thinking in the upper South during the secession winter favored new constitutional guarantees of supposedly endangered southern rights, coupled with a hands-off policy by the federal government toward the seceding states. Conditional Unionists thus reflected, to use the terminology introduced in the last chapter, a mixture of ultimatumist and anticoercionist ideas.

In Tennessee, for example, only 23.6 percent of voters favored secession in February 1861; 76.4 percent favored either conditional or unconditional Unionism. By using the subsequent June vote to estimate that 35.1 percent of February voters were unconditional Unionists, it may be calculated that 41.3 percent of the February electorate were conditional Unionists. Proportionately fewer unconditional Unionists lived in Virginia and North Carolina, and there was more substantial prosecession sentiment in the two eastern states than in Tennessee. But in all three states, the conditional Unionists stood out as the largest of the three groups.[7]

For Unionists to consolidate their position, they first needed to establish clear demarcations between Unionism and secession. That task was complicated by the conditional nature of much Union sentiment. More Unionists than not could imagine circumstances that would compel them, however reluctantly, to support secession. Some conditional Unionists also flirted with a deliberately ambiguous policy called "reconstruction," which in effect accepted secession as a tactic to achieve reunion.

Virginia Senator R. M. T. Hunter, the chief theoretician of reconstruction, publicized his ideas early in December. He wished to keep the South united, to keep the peace, and to "reconstruct" the Union "upon safe terms." His support for a southern conference made Hunter's proposal attractive to those who had doubts about separate state secession, but his insistence that the South should unite "either within or without the Union" had quasi-secessionist overtones. Because his proposition was put forward at a time when the states of the deep South appeared certain to secede, Hunter in effect advised the upper South to do likewise, at least for tactical reasons. But his alleged motives were to reconstruct the Union—even if the secession of the entire South proved necessary to set that process in motion.[8]

Hunter's formulation temporarily offered his allies in the Democratic party a way to bid for the support of both secessionists and conditional Unionists. A centerpiece of the "reconstruction" scheme, obviously inspired by John C. Calhoun, would have given the slave and free states each a veto power over national policy decisions, along with the right to control the appointment of government officials within each region. Reasoning that the South would be safe in the Union only if the Constitution were amended to encompass the minority veto, Hunter and his followers rejected as inadequate proposed compromises and guarantees regarding the disputed issue of slavery in the territories. "Unless we can have securities of political power," one insisted, "I say this Union ought to be . . . dissolved." Another proposed amending the Constitution to specify that no candidate could be elected president without "a majority of the Southern members of the Electoral College." That requirement would "place the government of the country in the hands of its moderate men" and would offer a strong motive "to ambitious men in all sections, to calm, and not to inflame sectional irritation and prejudice." Concessions of "political power" would be of far more value to the South than any "theoretical acknowledgement of our right of property and our right of equality." These demands for constitutional revision appeared so drastic as to ensure that they could never be enacted. And as it became clear that the lower South considered disunion irrevocable, reconstruction appeared more and more a secessionist subterfuge.[9]

By January Unionists had become contemptuous of the reconstruction ploy. "Let us not deceive ourselves with any such delusion as a reconstruction of the Government, in the event of a separation of the North and the South," warned Congressman William B. Stokes of Tennessee. "Dismemberment will not be followed by a reunion of these States. Disunion means war—civil war." Louisville editor George D. Prentice also erupted angrily at talk of reconstruction. This word "now flowing so glibly from the lips and pens of precipitators here, is that hideous thing DISUNION," Prentice exclaimed. "Let patriots shun it as they would shun the abyss to which it points." John A. Gilmer likewise condemned the idea of reconstruction as "fallacious" and "dangerous," designed by disunionists as a "syren song" to "decoy" and "deceive" the people of the South. "Reconstruction!" he snorted. "You might as well tell me, after you had taken a delicate watch, and put it under the ponderous blows of a forge hammer, that you only did it that you might reconstruct, with perfection, its complex machinery." Virginia Congressman John T. Harris spoke out with similar vehemence: "Reconstruct! Reconstruct! As well try to reconstruct the shattered vase or to tie up Niagara in a handkerchief, and put it in your pocket." As soon as the upper South left the Union, he predicted, secessionists there would adopt the chant used by their counterparts in the cotton states: "We are out forever; we want no guarantees; we will never come back."[10]

By rejecting reconstruction, Unionists in the upper South acquired a more unmistakable identity than their "cooperationist" counterparts in the lower South. Voters in the upper South had no difficulty in differentiating between Unionists and their opponents. Upper South Unionists firmly opposed secession, either as a tactic or in cooperation with other states.

IN considering how Unionists challenged secession in their home states, the place to start is Virginia. For reasons that stretched back over two and one-half centuries, Virginia occupied a unique place in both American and southern consciousness. Home of the first permanent English settlement in North America and incubator of the social system that would come to be called southern, Virginia had been the dominant state in the nation during the revolutionary and early national periods. Rapid western expansion had drained population from Virginia and the older states of the Southeast, but she remained the most populous state in the South, with more whites and slaves in 1860 than any other southern state.

Of all the states in the upper South, Virginia had the strongest inclinations toward secession. A web of social, political, and cultural ties linked her to the deep South. Though few Virginians favored disunion per se, many were electrified by the action of the deep South. Unionists watched with dismay as secession momentum intensified in large parts of the piedmont and tidewater. Their alarm increased by late December and early January, when state conventions in the deep South quickly adopted secession ordinances, without submitting their decision to popular referendum. Fearing that "demagogues and extremists" would capitalize on "popular excitement" to call a convention in Virginia and win control of it, Unionists looked for some alternative or at least delay. "We cannot see what any one, who wishes to preserve the Union can accomplish by a convention," one noted. But public sentiment in favor of a convention increased through December, making Unionists doubtful that they could block it altogether.[11]

The secession issue overshadowed everything else by the time the legislature met in special session in early January. "We shall have two distinctly marked and very zealous parties here," observed former U.S. senator and former ambassador to France William Cabell Rives, "one for secession before the 4th of March," the other hoping the Union could be saved. "The secession party is already strong, and has been rapidly gaining ground up to the present time," he noted, "but I cannot but hope, as soon as a definite plan for pursuing redress in a constitutional method shall be brought forward in opposition to secession, the progress of the latter will be checked."[12]

The unprecedented public excitement in Richmond that greeted the assembling legislature made it appear, at first, that Rives had underestimated secessionist strength. "Times are wild and revolutionary here beyond description," one Virginia legislator reported. Governor John Letcher's message combined a vigorous condemnation of northern encroachment on southern rights with a cautionary warning against calling a convention or acting hastily, but many legislators were swept up in the secession enthusiasm. The Richmond correspondent of the *Wheeling Intellegencer*, the most important unconditional Union newspaper in the state, reported that "nothing is heard but resistance to the General Government, and sympathy with the cause of South Carolina." His editor feared that "nine tenths" of the members of the legislature had "gone crazy." Alexander H. H. Stuart, a state senator and former secretary of the navy, wrote on January 8 that "madness rules the hour. You can hardly imagine the extent of the insanity. I have scarcely a ray of hope left." He reported that several prominent Virginia congressmen had come to Richmond from Washington "to poison the minds of the legislature." Stuart, doubtful that anything could be done "to stay the storm," feared that war might soon erupt.[13]

The strength of Virginia secessionists proved illusory. They wanted the legislature to empower a state convention to secede from the Union, following the example set in the deep South. But a coalition of moderates balked. The legislature did agree to call a convention, but under ground rules that hedged against immediate secession. Only the timing of the convention suited secessionists: an election would be held on February 4, with the delegates then selected to meet on February 13. By apportioning delegates on the "white basis," as in its lower house, the legislature assured that regions west of the Blue Ridge, where secession was weak, would hold a majority. A proposal to give voters the chance to approve or disapprove the holding of a convention failed by a narrow vote. But the legislature did allow voters to decide on February 4 whether any change in the relationship between Virginia and the federal government proposed by the convention should be subject to popular referendum. Thus, at the same time voters chose delegates, they would also vote for or against reference.[14]

At the same time the legislature acted on the convention bill, it invited all other states to appoint delegates to a special meeting in Washington, D.C. The Virginia-sponsored gathering, scheduled for February 4 and soon dubbed the "Peace Conference," raised hopes for a Union-saving compromise. The legislature also dispatched representatives to meet with President Buchanan and the authorities of the seceding states to urge against any hostilities and to invite the latter to attend the Peace Conference. The plan for the Peace Conference, credited to Union Democrat James Barbour, Union Whig George W. Summers, and perhaps others, provided antisecessionists with an excellent basis to argue that peaceful restoration of the Union remained possible. The Unionists who devised the idea of a Peace Conference thus laid a clever and effective trap for secessionists, who found themselves in the awkward position of asserting that the state's peacemaking efforts were futile. The Peace Conference stratagem would pay Virginia Unionists rich dividends on election day in early February.[15]

The action of the legislature pleased Unionists and alarmed secessionists. The editor of the *Wheeling Intelligencer* applauded the legislature's "returning sense of moderation." Giving voters the right to decide whether they wanted a popular referendum on any convention action removed "the deadly feature that was most to be feared." By contrast, the editor of the *Richmond Enquirer* condemned the "stupid" reference amendment, bitterly regretting that the legislature had "emasculated" the convention bill.[16]

The legislature scheduled the election of convention delegates for the same day the Peace Conference would meet in Washington. The contest received national attention as the first clear indication of how the upper South would respond to the secession crisis. Though undertaken in haste and handicapped by midwinter weather and bad roads, the Virginia campaign was intense and spirited. Union ranks included almost all supporters of Douglas in 1860, almost all Whigs who lived west of the Blue Ridge, a large majority of Whigs from the piedmont and tidewater, plus a substantial increment of "moderate Breckinridge men," especially those from the West, who were retrospectively dismayed to find "so many Disunionists" among their former political allies. Unionists worked hard to put old party animosities on the shelf. In counties entitled to more than one representative, Union nominations often went to a Whig and a Douglas Democrat. Opponents of secession began to refer to their coalition as a "party." As the February election approached, they felt encouraged about the prospects of "the Conservative and anti-precipitation Union party."[17]

Union efforts in Virginia were enhanced by authoritative reassurances from Washington about the prospects for a satisfactory settlement of the sectional crisis. Stephen A. Douglas wrote a public letter stating that "there is hope of preserving peace and the Union. All depends on the action of Virginia and the Border states. If they remain in the Union and aid in a fair and just settlement, the Union may be preserved.—But if they secede under the fatal delusion of a reconstruction, I fear that all is lost. Save Virginia, and we will save the Union." Kentucky Senator John J. Crittenden and the four Union congressmen from Virginia—Alexander Boteler, John T. Harris, John S. Millson, and Sherrard Clemens—assessed the situation similarly. Conditional Unionist leader James Barbour urged voters to be guided by the opinions of Douglas and Crittenden, who were "above all men in America . . . devoting their energies to secure a pacific adjustment to the pending controversy."[18]

Unionist success in seizing the middle ground threw Virginia secessionists on the defensive. The case for secession hinged on the assumption that the North would never accept an adequate plan for sectional reconciliation, so that Virginia had to side with the South. But the calling of the Peace Conference and the reassurances from Douglas and Crittenden made many Virginians hopeful. The Southern Rights Democrats who dominated Virginia's congressional delegation—Senators R. M. T. Hunter and James M. Mason, plus eight of the state's twelve representatives—tried desperately to regain the advantage. They issued a statement endorsing Southern Rights convention candidates, declaring that Congress would not enact a suitable compromise, and strongly implying that the Union could be reconstructed only if Virginia seceded quickly.

But the argument that the state's secession could effect a reconstruction of the Union had become untenable by late January. Virginia's spokesman to the seceded states, Judge John Robertson, was told repeatedly that they did not intend to come back. Nor would they attend the Peace Conference. The *Richmond Whig* pronounced the idea of seceding so as to reconstruct an "utter absurdity" and a "ridiculous idea." The reference issue also hindered the secession cause. Unionists supported reference on the obvious democratic grounds of wanting citizens to approve any change in the relationship between Virginia and the federal government. Secessionists argued lamely that the convention might need to act quickly, making it inexpedient to wait for a popular referendum. Only in eastern Virginia did the antireference argument receive much of a hearing. In many counties in northwestern Virginia, all candidates for the convention favored reference.[19]

By the end of January, perceptive secessionists recognized the likelihood of "a defeat in Virginia and all the rest of the border States." An observer from Georgia reported that several economic issues had aided Unionists. The "manufacturing interest of Virginia" suspected that a southern Confederacy would destroy tariff barriers and "establish free trade." Worries that "navigation of the Mississippi will be obstructed and that the slave trade will be reopened" had also weakened the secession cause in the upper South. Unless organizers of the southern Confederacy proceeded "with the greatest caution," they ran the danger of having "the border slave States strongly bound with our foes against us and making common cause with them to conquer."[20]

The election surpassed Unionist hopes. Fewer than one-third of the 152 delegates elected favored secession. The provision to refer the action of the convention to a popular referendum also carried by an emphatic majority, 103,236 to 46,386. Voters east of the Blue Ridge divided almost evenly on reference, 32,294 to 32,009. But western voters overwhelmingly favored it, 70,942 to 14,377. Map 6-1 illustrates that voters in most counties west of the Blue Ridge favored reference by a notably larger margin than the combined Bell, Douglas, and Lincoln vote in 1860. Starred counties are ones in which significant numbers of Breckinridge supporters must have voted pro-Union. Nowhere in the northwestern trans-Allegheny could secessionists achieve even the feeble 31 percent antireference vote they averaged statewide. Except for a handful of ardently Democratic counties in the Valley and the southwest, secession attracted solid

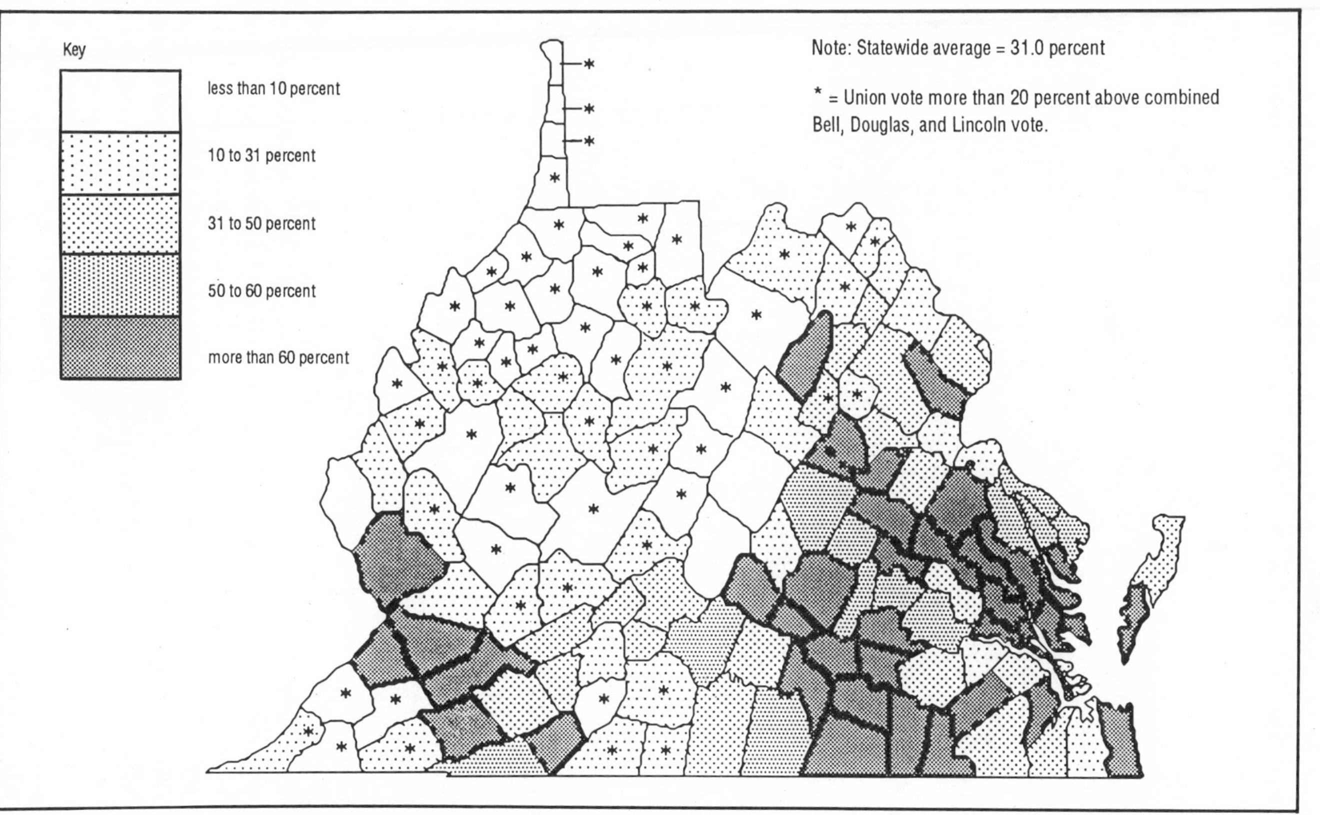

MAP 6-1. *Percentage against Reference (for Secession), by County, Virginia, February 1861*

support only in traditionalist bastions in the piedmont and tidewater, characterized by large slaveholdings or Democratic loyalties (and usually both). Virginia, unlike the states of the deep South, decided against hasty action and chose instead to use its influence to mediate the sectional crisis. "Lord, how dumfounded are the secessionists here!" crowed one Virginia Unionist. "But a few days ago they were high up stairs and clamoring from the house tops. But 'such a getting down stairs, I never did see.' "[21]

Several observers recognized that the Virginia election had "annihilated all existing party organizations" and set in motion a fundamental rearrangement of political forces in the state. The Southern Rights Democrats who dominated the state congressional delegation suffered an obvious popular rebuke after committing their prestige to the secession cause. The *Richmond Whig* applauded the independence of the "masses," who had "ignored old party divisions" and "emancipated themselves from the thraldom of party leaders." As a consequence, the *Whig* predicted the rise of "new organizations" based on "the great question of the day." Conservatives of all earlier political persuasions would unite to form "a new Union party," and the "destructives" would coalesce in a competing minority party: " 'UNION' or 'DISUNION' is the issue; and 'UNIONISTS' or 'DISUNIONISTS' must be the party organizations and designations."[22]

A massive mailing of speeches and documents contributed to the Union victory in Virginia. The effort was coordinated by Joseph C. G. Kennedy, head of the U.S. Census Bureau. Kennedy asked census takers to send him information about secession sentiment in their localities and then arranged to have Union documents sent to areas where they would be useful. He kept a reported twenty clerks at work to address the mailings and lined up southern Unionist congressmen to frank the documents for free delivery. Virginia received first priority, but Tennessee and North Carolina became the principal destinations in February. Robert Hatton reported to his wife that he was "worn out" from "franking and directing documents, speeches, etc., to Tennessee, hoping to influence our election for members of the convention." He dispatched "about fifteen hundred speeches a day" for several weeks. John A. Gilmer, probably the wealthiest of the congressmen involved, later reported that he paid to have speeches reprinted and to hire clerks. Others also paid substantial amounts out of pocket for reprints. "Night after night," from the close of office hours until midnight, the mailing operation continued.[23]

Fragments of his surviving correspondence show that Kennedy, a Pennsylvanian with Whiggish antecedents, worked closely both with upper South Unionists and with conciliatory Republican leaders such as William H. Seward and Charles Francis Adams. Kennedy reassured southern census takers that Lincoln would "satisfy all reasonable men, North and South," and "inaugurate an era of peace and good will." By rejecting secession, the border slave states would be "certain to secure all Southern rights and guarantees." To preserve the interest of southern census takers in the Union cause, Kennedy informed them that they would be paid "at the earliest moment funds are provided by the Treasury. If things settle peaceably, there will be no delay; if revolution comes, God only knows what will follow." The responses Kennedy received from his Virginia census takers filled him with "apprehension." But two days after the Virginia election, a relieved Kennedy jubilantly encouraged southern Unionist congressmen to continue franking documents. More volunteers would "make the work lighter as our hearts are by the result in Virginia."[24]

Howls of protest about the mailing operation soon came from secessionists and Southern Rights supporters, who arraigned "this creature Kennedy" for developing "a system of espionage to pry into the feelings of the people" and for "turning out every man in the Census Bureau who entertains the right of secession." Southern Rights devotees in Virginia complained about the promulgation of "incendiary documents"; those in North Carolina wailed that "Gilmer and company," working with "the Census Bureau and the Black Republicans," were "flooding the state with submission and coercion speeches." Allegations that recipients of a mass mailing of Union documents to eastern Virginia included some free blacks provoked an uproar in the Virginia convention. Secession newspapers made similar accusations during the North Carolina campaign. The complaints were doubtless true. Free blacks and whites were listed together on the same census sheets. Tired clerks could easily, if inadvertently, have dispatched Union documents to free blacks.[25] Secessionists did more than complain. Southern Rights postmasters regularly tampered with the mails, and a secession delegate to the Virginia convention boasted that Union documents in one town had been "collected and publicly burned."[26]

Secessionist obstruction testified to the impact of the mailings, prompting Unionists to follow up on their Virginia victory by blanketing North Carolina and Tennessee. A local political leader told North Carolina Congressman Zebulon B. Vance that "the people seem to want information and want to hear from you." Vance promised to send "thousands of Union documents" into his district, so that "*every man* shall have one." He also urged his friends to help circulate the material. Congressman Gilmer likewise did all he could to place documents "in the hands of each voter" in North Carolina.[27]

TENNESSEE and North Carolina soon followed Virginia's lead in rejecting immediate secession and adding insult to secessionist injury by refusing to countenance state conventions. But as in Virginia, Unionists originally thought the situation dire.

Many Tennessee Unionists had been near despair in early January. Thinking that any hope for "a satisfactory settlement of our national troubles seems to be at an end," one diarist concluded that "*all is lost*." Jordan Stokes, state senator from Wilson County, friend of Robert Hatton, and one of the leaders among Tennessee Unionists, wrote on January 15 that "we are in great danger of drifting into secession. Things get more gloomy daily." The quasi-secessionist governor of Tennessee, Isham G. Harris, thought the only "practical question" was whether to ally with the North or the South.[28]

But by late January a pro-Union groundswell had undermined secession strength in Tennessee. Senator Andrew Johnson's forthright speeches and the slashing editorials in William G. Brownlow's *Knoxville Whig* raised growing doubts about the behavior of the deep South. In the Tennessee legislature, sufficient Union Democrats joined with almost all Whigs to derail the secession express. Legislators did approve a bill to allow a Tennessee convention, but antisecessionists imposed even tighter restrictions than in Virginia. They stipulated that any action by a convention would automatically require a popular referendum, without the voters first indicating they wanted such power. Furthermore, a majority of those who voted in the last election for governor had to approve any act of the convention. The Tennessee legislature also empowered voters, when they cast ballots for convention candidates on February 9, to indicate whether they even wanted a convention to meet. If a convention was approved, it would meet on February 18, but if not, the delegates elected would receive an empty honor. Unionist legislators believed they had "whipt the Seceders out of their boots, and completely unhorsed his Excellency."[29]

In North Carolina too, by late December and early January secessionists appeared to have the advantage. "The outside pressure to drag us out of the Union is terrible," one Union legislator complained to his wife. "All sorts of lies are circulated by telegraph and every bad report . . . constantly paraded in *extras* from the disunion press to excite, intimidate and overawe us." Another influential Union legislator feared that the politicians who had initiated the panic could no longer control it. "Conservative Democrats" were allowing radicals to lead. "If those who would preserve the Union say nothing," he warned, "we go with South Carolina." A Gaston County secessionist noted that sentiment in his area was "unanimous almost for a Southern Confederacy. . . . Every one not for us is against us and is counted an enemy, a 'submissionist,' equal to a Tory." Furthermore, North Carolina Governor John W. Ellis stood firmly with the Southern Rights wing of the Democratic party. His public statements expressed great pessimism about the Union, and his private correspondence shows him to have been an ardent secessionist.[30]

But North Carolina ended up following the pattern established in Tennessee. Despite strong secession sentiment in the heavily Democratic counties of eastern North Carolina that stretched from Wilmington north to the Virginia border, and also in the Charlotte area of the southwest along the South Carolina border, pro-Union feelings predominated in most Whig areas, especially in the dozen plus counties of the central piedmont Quaker Belt. Thus Governor Ellis explained to friends in the deep South that "submissionists" and "tories" had exploited "old party divisions" in North Carolina to stall the drive toward secession. Nor did Ellis have solid support from the Democratic electorate. Just as Andrew Johnson had emboldened Union Democrats in Tennessee to make common cause with Union Whigs, efforts to build Unionist cooperation across party lines in North Carolina received similar stimulus from Democratic editor William W. Holden. He transformed the *North Carolina Standard*, the widely read official journal of the state Democracy, into the most aggressively pro-Union newspaper in North Carolina. By daily characterizing Governor Ellis and other Southern Rights Democrats as pawns in the hands of lower South disunionists, Holden depressed support for secession among the Democratic rank and file. His stance also helped to stir a surge of antisecession feeling among Union Whigs and many previous nonvoters.[31]

Despite Holden's efforts, most North Carolina Democratic legislators inclined toward secession. They could not act unilaterally, however, because the state constitution required a two-thirds majority of both houses of the legislature to call a convention. To get a convention bill approved, Southern Rights advocates in North Carolina had to agree to the same restrictions as in Tennessee. Voters would not only elect delegates to a convention but would also indicate whether they even wanted a convention. And if a convention did meet, any action it approved would require a popular referendum before taking effect. The legislature furthermore specified that the election not take place until February 28 and that a convention not meet before

March 11, thereby defeating in advance the secessionist idea of leaving the Union before Lincoln took office.[32]

In Virginia all Unionists voted to make the action of the convention subject to popular referendum, but in Tennessee and North Carolina the question of whether to hold a convention divided Unionists. Some thought it illogical to be "voting for a man for office and voting against the office [at] the same time." Prominent Unionists such as North Carolina Congressmen Zebulon Vance and James Leach and former Tennessee Congressman Meredith Gentry publicly supported holding a convention, expecting Unionists to control it and thinking it would give them better leverage to win northern concessions. Others, however, noticed apprehensively that "*all* the secessionists" favored a convention. Perceptive observers soon detected a groundswell of opposition to the convention among Union voters. One of Andrew Johnson's hometown cronies explained that "straight out Union men of all partys" had dominated a public meeting, badly outnumbering a clique of secession-leaning Democrats who favored a convention. He reported that "the Whigs are to a man nearly [all] against a Convention," but he feared traditional electioneering efforts by insidious convention supporters to revive "old party prejudices" and "to mix it up with Whiskey & Democracy." Another of Johnson's informants correctly discerned that "a pretty large majority will vote against the call of a Convention." Similar indications appeared in Union areas of North Carolina. "The people generally with whom we have conversed, during the last few weeks, seemed to be opposed to a Convention," noted the editor of the *Salem People's Press*. An observer from nearby Wilkes County in the northwestern piedmont informed Congressman Leach that "the people will vote against a Convention here if things look at all hopeful." He correctly predicted that four-fifths of the voters in his and adjacent counties would reject the convention and that it would lose by a small majority statewide.[33]

Unionists who opposed calling a convention suspected a secessionist "trick." They did not see how a convention, "designed by its active friends as a door through which to carry the state out of the Union," could serve any constructive purpose. Many Unionists considered conventions "the work of our enemies . . . like the Grecian Horse which destroyed Troy and robbed her of her liberties." One Unionist accused secessionists of planning "to keep people aroused against the North—to aggravate and misrepresent the danger to be apprehended from that quarter—to keep our gaze fixed on the Republican party, till between rage and terror, like a herd of maddened buffalo, we rush blind and headlong into the pit they have digged for us.

That pit is a *State Convention*." In a public letter to his constituents, North Carolina state senator Jonathan Worth of Randolph County stated: "Believe not those who may tell you this convention is called to *save* the Union. It is called to *destroy* it. If you desire to preserve the Union vote 'No Convention,' and at the same time, be careful for whom you vote as delegates." Several state legislators from an adjoining area of the intensely Unionist Quaker Belt in North Carolina echoed Worth. "We are satisfied that every artifice will be employed to make you believe that a Convention is to be called to save the Union, and the most ultra secessionists will try to make you believe that they are for the Union," they warned. "Be not deceived. . . . If you would stay in the Union, the safest way is to vote 'No Convention.'"[34]

Unionists in Tennessee and North Carolina successfully turned the election of convention delegates into referenda for or against immediate secession. They charged that Southern Rights candidates had no desire to see the Union restored but were instead making plans to join the Confederacy. The only choice, Unionists bluntly announced, lay between "UNION OR DISUNION!" Some Southern Rights supporters countered that the issue was not "*Union* and *disunion*" but rather "equal rights, on the one hand, and *submission* on the other." But enough southern militants had openly embraced secession to make the disunion label stick. Because only a minority supported immediate secession in North Carolina and especially in Tennessee, the Southern Rights effort faltered in both states.[35]

Existing party organizations in Tennessee and North Carolina played significant roles in the convention election campaigns. A "Union party" originated almost overnight in each state, amid declarations that the old party system was no more. In fact, Union parties were enlarged Whig parties. The great majority of Tennessee and North Carolina Whigs, both leadership and rank and file, opposed immediate secession in January and February 1861. Most prominent Democrats, by contrast, followed the quasi-secessionist Southern Rights leadership of Governors Harris and Ellis. A few conspicuous Democrats, however, did ally with the Union Whigs. In addition to Andrew Johnson, Union party supporters in Tennessee included such well-known Democrats as Andrew Ewing, William H. Polk, Cave Johnson, Harvey Watterson, and William H. Carroll. Breckinridge Democrats in North Carolina remained solidly pro–Southern Rights, with such few exceptions as William Holden and Bedford Brown. Douglas Democrats such as Robert P. Dick, Thomas Settle, and Henry W. Miller also aided the Union party.

The creation of a new political entity, composed primarily of one old party but with a significant increment from the opposing party, required a new name, a renunciation of past party prejudices, and a liberal willingness to nominate candidates from the smaller fragment. The recent building of Republican parties in many northern states had followed a parallel course. Republicans in the 1850s and Union party organizers in early 1861 gave converted Democrats a warm welcome and proclaimed the new organization bipartisan, even though in both instances the majority of its leadership and constituency had Whiggish antecedents.

The mood of bipartisanship especially aided Andrew Johnson, who positioned himself to play a major role in the emerging Union party. During the secession winter he received dozens of congratulatory letters from former Whigs who announced their conversion from political enemies to fervent allies. Johnson's professed new friends included former Whig Governor Neill Brown, incumbent Whig or Opposition Congressman Emerson Etheridge and Thomas A. R. Nelson, and Knoxville newspaperman William G. Brownlow, a particular Johnson nemesis. John W. Richardson, a prominent Whig legislator from Middle Tennessee, acknowledged that he had long opposed Johnson on questions of "party character," but that "all these things have passed away, or at any rate are overshadowed by the tremendous and vital issue" of "Union or Disunion." On that question, Richardson affirmed, "I stand with you." An embattled "Clay Whig" from north Georgia wrote that "all the Whiggery and Dimocracy that devided us in former days is as entirely sunk in to obblovion as if they never had existed on earth." A Chattanooga resident who had for twenty years "spent time and money—and used every honorable means in my power to crush you politically" hailed Johnson and reported that "the old political *partys* are routed crushed —or obliterated—." Johnson's stance had an immense impact in his home region of East Tennessee. "The leaders of the Democratic party are generally for secession though the masses are against it," a leading Whig wrote privately. "But for Johnson's speech we would have had trouble in East Tennessee. The leaders of the party curse him from one end of the state to the other."[36]

Opposing the new Union party in Tennessee and North Carolina was a shrunken Democratic party that claimed to favor Southern Rights but carried the stigma of urging immediate secession. Though giving lip service to bipartisanship, Southern Rights organizers generally had few Whig recruits to display. Their main objective was to consolidate the Democratic electorate. Under normal circumstances, a united Democratic party could expect to receive a narrow but adequate majority vote in both states.

A pervasive prosecession spirit did dominate the Democratic strongholds of eastern North Carolina and along the South Carolina border in the Charlotte area. In several counties secession candidates for the convention ran unopposed. In Duplin County, for example, no Unionist "dared to come out." The few Unionists who voted against the convention there did so at their peril: the "fury of the fire eaters" made it unsafe "for a man to open his mouth." But North Carolina's Democratic party depended upon gains it had made in the western part of the state in the 1850s. And there, popular sentiment strongly opposed secession. Congressman Zebulon Vance received word from Asheville in late January that "the *people*, mind you the *people* are in favor of the Union for a while yet," and they would vote "almost unanimously" against immediate secession. Another of Vance's correspondents concluded that "all the Countys west of the Blue Ridge" were "Union by a large majority." A few western Democrats defied the state party leadership by openly supporting Unionists or even accepting Union nominations for the convention. The secession issue had an even more dismal effect on the Democratic party in Tennessee. Union candidates competed vigorously in every county in the state. Their support often extended across party lines, especially in East Tennessee. Even before the election it was apparent to perceptive observers that the disunion cause in Tennessee would suffer a "disastrous rout" and that "an overwhelming majority" of voters would reject secession.[37]

The dimensions of the Union victories in Tennessee and North Carolina were nevertheless startling. Unionist candidates for the convention in Tennessee gathered almost 100,000 votes, while supporters of Southern Rights drew barely 30,000. Hardly any Southern Rights delegates won convention seats in the February 9 election. Nor would the convention ever assemble: Tennessee voters decided against it by a smaller but decisive margin, 69,772 to 57,708. The intensely Unionist counties in East Tennessee had the highest turnout rate in the state and voted against a convention by a margin of over 80 percent, thereby determining the issue. Despite the durable party proclivities of most Tennessee voters, Union Whigs proved ready to vote for Union Democrats, and vice versa. In county after county, Union candidates from differing party backgrounds ran within a few votes of each other. What Andrew Johnson's son noticed in the legislature in January—that "party lines seem to be entirely obliterated and the only question is Union or disunion"—described well the behavior of the mass electorate a month later.[38]

Three weeks later, on February 28, North Carolina followed the Tennessee pattern by electing a large majority of Union delegates

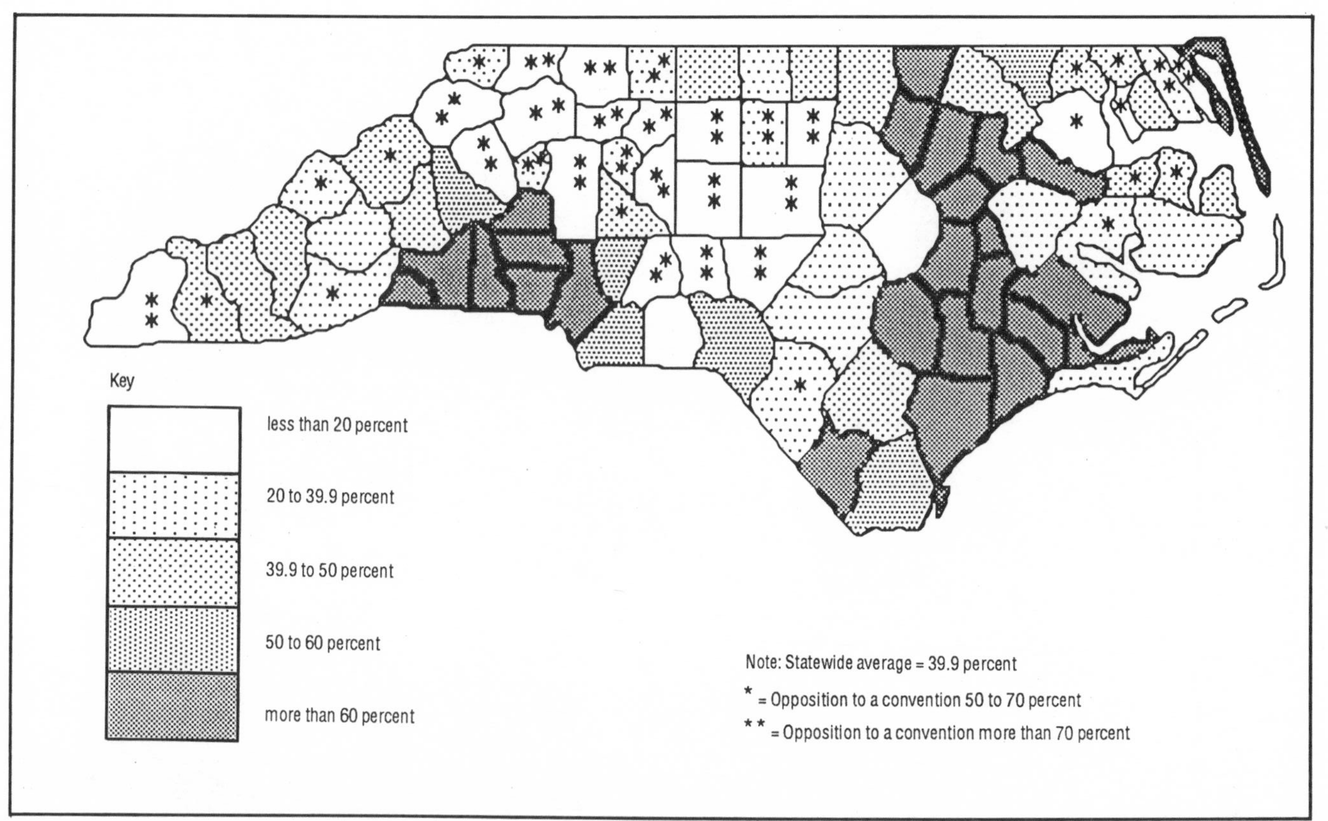

MAP 6-2. *Percentage for Secession, by County, North Carolina, February 1861*

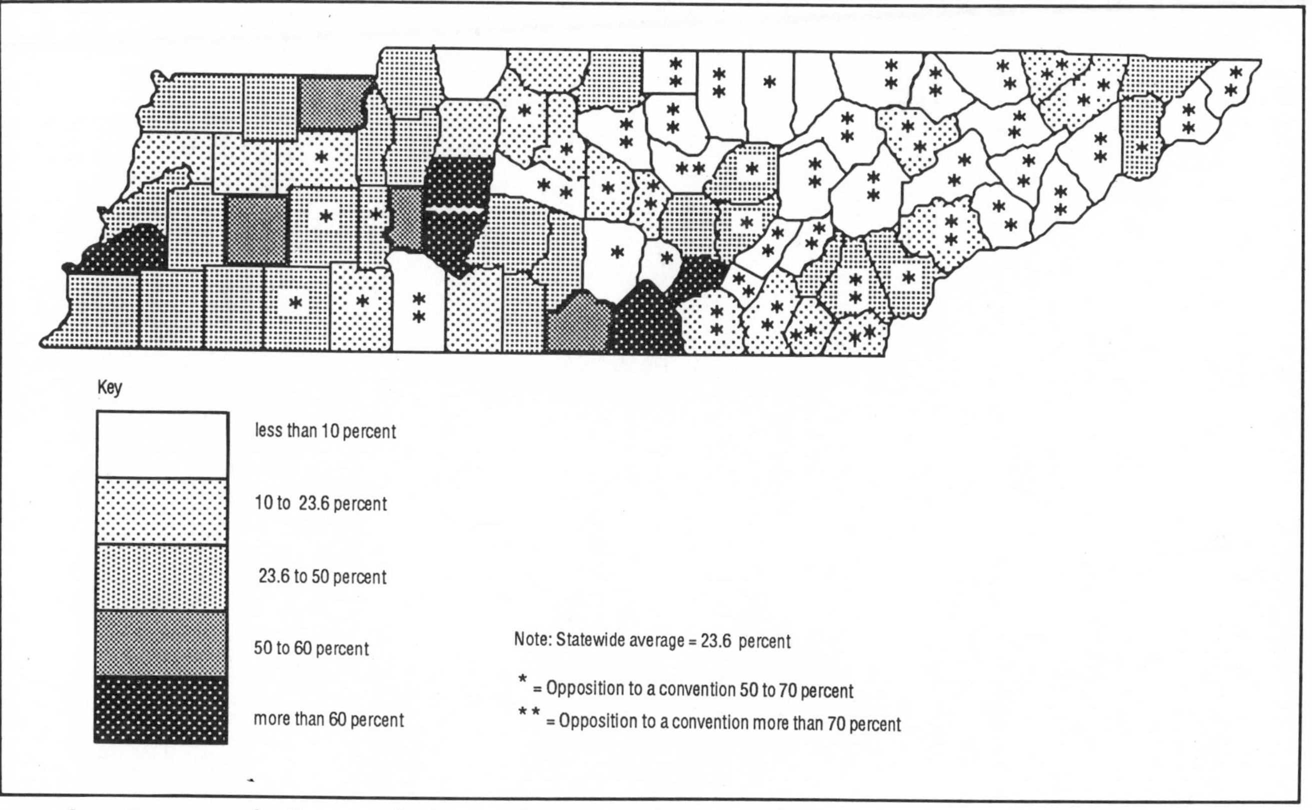

MAP 6-3. *Percentage for Secession, by County, Tennessee, February 1861*

and narrowly refusing, 47,705 to 46,711, to call a convention. Higher turnout rates in areas opposed to a convention also proved decisive in North Carolina. Indicative of the popular mood were the defeats suffered by a number of prominent Democrats who sought election as convention delegates on a Southern Rights platform. Former Governor David Reid, one of the most respected political figures in North Carolina, who lived in dependably Democratic Rockingham County on the Virginia border of the central piedmont, was beaten handily by thirty-year-old Unionist Thomas Settle, a Douglas supporter and future postwar Republican congressman.[39]

Maps 6-2 and 6-3 depict the February elections in North Carolina and Tennessee. It may easily be seen that opposition to a Tennessee convention centered in East Tennessee and in several strongly Whiggish counties of Middle Tennessee, plus the several low-slaveowning Whig counties of West Tennessee adjacent to the Tennessee River. Tennessee secessionists carried only nine scattered counties in Middle and West Tennessee, all but one of which had pronounced Democratic tendencies. In North Carolina, secessionists had a formidable base in the traditionally Democratic parts of the coastal plain and the southwestern piedmont. But Unionists rolled up huge antisecession and anticonvention majorities in the Whiggish piedmont Quaker Belt and in contiguous mountain counties. The traditionally Whig counties around Albemarle Sound rejected secession, as did several normally Democratic counties in the western coastal plain and northern piedmont, regions likely influenced by Holden's *North Carolina Standard*.

The February elections in the upper South provided Unionists with needed uplift. "Is it not most glorious?" former Tennessee Governor Neill Brown asked Andrew Johnson. "The happiest day of my whole life was the 9th inst. when I witnessed the stern verdict of the people of my native state in behalf of the Union. The mad waves of secession found an iron embankment around this proud commonwealth which defied all their fury." Tennessee Congressman Robert Hatton initially thought the secession movement wrecked. "The consternation and dismay of the conspirators here, on the reception of the news of our election was the subject of universal observation and remark," the soon-to-be Confederate general jubilantly observed. "The swords of the wicked and reckless revolutionists," he concluded, had been "turned upon their own breasts." Elated Unionists hoped the example set by the upper South would prove contagious. One East Tennessean predicted that "in less than twenty days you will hear a stir in more than half the Cotton States." The "common people" there would awaken, repudiate the "treasonable" idea of secession, and "with indignation and contempt curse their corrupt leaders."[40]

As they celebrated, however, Unionists cautioned northerners and Republicans not to interpret the upper South elections as affirmations of unconditional Unionism. Virginia legislator James Barbour pointed out to William H. Seward that Unionists generally had insisted "that there was hope of obtaining . . . constitutional guaranties of our slave property rights" and that the published statement by Douglas and Crittenden to that effect had been "the most potent campaign document in this part of the state." If Republicans left Unionists "unsupported," secession was "as inevitable as fate." Barbour, one of the few fast ultimatumists, was more exacting than most southern Unionists, but many shared his concern. An East Tennessee Unionist feared that Republicans would "deceive themselves" by thinking his state would align with the North if forced to choose sides. "When it comes to reducing the question to North and South," he warned prophetically, "you will find it will run like a mighty tide or hurricane sweeping everything before it."[41]

Unionists had good reason to suspect that the North would misunderstand the February vote in the upper South. Many northerners eagerly concluded that the entire South was turning against secession and that the troubles facing the country would soon be over. Charles Francis Adams, Jr., reported from Boston that the news of the Virginia election "sent a regular thrill through the city. The result was announced on Jamaica Pond when we were skating and the huge mass of people flocked together and cheered with one mind." Pennsylvania Congressman Thaddeus Stevens, never an admirer of the South, observed sardonically: "Well, well, well, old Virginia has tucked her tail between her legs and run, and thus ends the secession farce." The Richmond correspondent of the *New York Tribune* interpreted the Union victory as "the first manifestation of Republican sentiment in Virginia," which northern Republicans could best support by rejecting "the timid policy of compromise."[42]

NORTHERNERS were not the only ones who misunderstood the upper South. The February elections there indicated that many experienced politicians, who should have been able to judge popular sentiment in their home states, had badly miscalculated. Southern Rights Democrats looked especially inept. As long as popular majorities in Virginia, North Carolina, and Tennessee had some basis to hope for peaceable reunion, the Southern Rights campaign could only boomerang. He and his convention running mate were "awfully beaten," reported future Confederate General John D. Imboden of

Staunton, Virginia. "The idea got into the minds of the County that we were *immediate* secessionists, and it beat us to death." Those who favored secession "at the proper time" realized retrospectively that "the States Rights party—the immediate secession element—have pursued a suicidal policy." One such eventual secessionist, U.S. Senator Thomas Bragg of North Carolina, concluded that "great blunders have been committed by the extremists—I warned them against it at the outset, but my advice was not heeded." For secessionists, the future looked dubious: "I think it will be hard work to get out now," one commented.[43]

Many Unionist leaders also had misjudged the popular mood. The majority of Unionist politicians and newspapers supported calling state conventions in North Carolina and Tennessee, for fear of alienating conditional Unionists who were willing to support antisecession delegates but who still wanted a convention held. The election results suggested, however, that "the people determined for once to think and act for themselves" and that in so doing they discovered "*their power* over politicians, and party organizations." The high turnouts in Union strongholds in Tennessee and North Carolina revealed an unusual intensity of popular feeling. Randolph County, North Carolina, in the heart of the Quaker Belt, normally cast fewer than 2,000 votes but voted against a convention by a majority of 2,466 to 45. The county sheriff, J. W. Steed, reported: "The people of Randolph believed that all the warm advocates of a Convention wanted to withdraw this State from the Union, and voted accordingly. Not quite all of the 45 who voted 'Convention' are disunionists. Every one of the 2,466 are Union men. We regarded the question as of infinitely greater moment than any on which we had ever before been called upon to vote, and large numbers went to the polls who often neglect the privilege of voting."[44]

Many slaveowners in the upper South reacted nervously to the triumph of "the people." The recent furor about Hinton Helper's book *The Impending Crisis* had revealed a large reservoir of anxiety about the loyalty of nonslaveowning southern whites. The secession crisis rekindled such doubts. Observers noted with dismay "a disposition on the part of the *non* slave holders to back out." Pessimistic secessionists predicted that the convention elections would give "bright visions of coming glory" to Unionist leaders, whose political ambitions would inevitably lead them to sacrifice "the rights of the slaveholder" by creating "a party with supporters for the incoming administration here in our midst." Former Secretary of War John B. Floyd bitterly condemned the willingness of Virginia voters to submit "to the long continued aggressions of the North" and to value "peace and quiet" over an assertion of southern rights. "Far seeing and sagacious men begin already to see symptoms of a coming contest in Virginia for the emancipation of the slaves," he noted. Virginia had dealt "the Southern cause" a "fearful defeat." Historian Roy Franklin Nichols shrewdly assessed the motives of powerful southern Democrats: their "very real and often overlooked fear was loss of power at home" and a "shift of power to poorer farmers and artisans," who would reject the extreme proslavery politics of the 1850s.[45]

A specific case nicely illustrates why upper South slaveowners could become alarmed about the nonslaveowning majority during the secession crisis. William S. Pettigrew, of Washington County, North Carolina, on Albemarle Sound—an eminent large slaveowner, conservative Whig, and heir to one of the great family names in his state—decided to run for the convention as a conditional Unionist, expecting that "he would unite the vote of all parties and not have the shadow of an opposition." Instead, local Unionists challenged Pettigrew by nominating incumbent state legislator Charles Latham. The latter "avowed himself as the poor man's candidate" and circulated rumors that Pettigrew, "the property-holders candidate," would not permit the poor to enter his house, "but would send a servant to meet them at the gate to ask their business." Latham and his friends also spread word that Pettigrew was a secret secessionist who had been urged to run for office by his brother in the South Carolina army. The whispering campaign, conducted behind Pettigrew's back on election day and the day before, gave him no chance to respond. Having aroused what Pettigrew considered "a furious agrarian spirit" in the upper part of the county, Latham handily carried the election, 396 to 276. The convention lost even more decisively, 418 to 238.[46]

Hysterical Southern Rights fulminations about the rise of a Black Republican–abolitionist-submissionist and pro-Lincoln party in the upper South were based upon a kernel of truth. In Tennessee, for example, secessionists tried to woo nonslaveowners by insisting that a Republican president threatened their interests too. Secessionists contended that slavery prevented class antagonisms among whites, thereby making the social and economic status of nonslaveowning southerners enviably better than that of northern workers. Southern white artisans were better paid, secessionists asserted; they were treated with dignity and respect. Secessionists furthermore predicted that Tennessee's material prosperity would be enhanced by joining the Confederacy. The already well-established pattern of selling grain and livestock to the cotton states would expand, and Tennessee would become "the chief manufacturer for the South."[47]

The voting results baffled and frustrated Southern Rights supporters. As they saw it, Unionist nonslaveowners had been misled and had failed to perceive their own best interests. Memphis secessionists, especially, complained bitterly that their city faced a miserable future if isolated economically from the planters of Alabama and Mississippi. The two secessionist newspapers in Memphis warned that economic calamity would "fall most heavily" on the "laboring men" and "artisans," who had "voted in a solid phalanx for the Union ticket." Memphis secessionists attempted to reassure Alabama and Mississippi customers that "the great mass of our property-holders" and "the solid, substantial and reliable business men" had voted secessionist and therefore deserved continued patronage. But the initial response from the deep South was not encouraging. One Alabama newspaper proposed an economic boycott of Tennessee products. Mississippi secessionists sneered that people in Tennessee were "too cowardly" to stand up for their rights and were "willing to be treated as inferiors—*as serfs*." The "dastard Tennesseeans," having submitted their necks "to a yoke worse than death to an honorable people," were "trotting like a cur to the beck and call of Lincoln." The *Memphis Avalanche* despondently agreed that Tennessee had been "plunged" into "disgrace" and "shame." Warning that Unionists had resurrected the heresy of Hinton Helper, the *Avalanche* predicted editorially that "the germ of Abolitionism is budding in our midst and will soon blossom."[48]

Secessionists may well have exaggerated the dangers of internal disunity, but the upper South in 1861 was no monolith and never had been. The survival of a competitive two-party system there institutionalized the means to challenge existing power relationships. Of course, no serious challenge occurred before 1861. But during the preceding decade, popular discontents had spilled decisively into the arena of party politics in the North. There, Know-Nothings and subsequently Republicans had incorporated most of the old Whig party and given the new grouping a politically appealing antiaristocratic ethos; Unionists in the upper South in early 1861 were moving in a parallel direction. The Union party thus threatened to disrupt the ground rules for political competition. For the first time nonslaveholders in the upper South would have found a political framework within which to develop a consciousness of separate interests.[49]

Popular opposition to secession intensified already existing egalitarian tendencies in the upper South. In North Carolina, the election for governor in 1860 stirred much discussion about a proposal to tax slaves as heavily as other property. The issue itself was scarcely radical because it would simply have made North Carolina taxation practices confirm to those of most other slaveowning states, but opponents of ad valorem considered it a blatant attempt to capitalize on the discontent of nonslaveowners. They argued that removal of the traditional tax shelter would drive slaveowners and their slaves out of the state to more profitable agricultural regions in the lower South. The timing of the ad valorem movement also touched a raw nerve, coming as it did amid excitement generated by John Brown's raid on Harpers Ferry, the uproar over Hinton Helper's appeal to southern nonslaveowners, and the ominous polarization of national politics in 1860. Once the secession crisis developed, North Carolina conservatives blamed ad valorem for disunity within the state. Kenneth Rayner, a prominent eastern Whig, deplored "the mischief done last summer by the advocates of 'ad valorem.'" They had "infused among the ignorant poor, the idea that there is an antagonism between poor people and slaveowners—in other words Seward's 'irrepressible conflict,' was insidiously preached; and we shall, I fear have to reap a harvest of trouble from the seeds of mischief then sown." "Wherever '*ad-valorem*' was urged most strenuously," Rayner concluded, "there the feeling of absolute submission . . . prevails most strongly."[50]

The chief culprit in Rayner's eyes must have been William Holden, editor of the *North Carolina Standard*. In 1860 Holden had tempered his enthusiasm for ad valorem when the Whigs made it a party issue, but during the secession crisis he became an outspokenly antiaristocratic champion of Unionism, irrespective of previous party lines. Increasingly in early 1861, Holden defined the struggle in North Carolina as a contest between "the people" and "the oligarchs." He castigated secession as a conspiracy hatched by "enemies of the people," who had "never earned a dime for their own support." "We are not in South Carolina but in *North*-Carolina, where an honest working man is just as much entitled to his opinions, and just as good as the owner of Bank stock or hundreds of negroes," Holden thundered. The editor's antiaristocratic animus led him to identify a bond between himself and other targets of the slaveholders' and secessionists' wrath: "The oligarchs . . . hate Lincoln, not only because he is a black Republican, but because *he* split rails for his daily bread when a young man; they hate Douglas because he worked at the cabinetmaker's trade for his daily bread when a young man; and they hate Holden because, being a printer, he dared to aspire to be Governor of North Carolina."[51]

The secession movement had a similar effect on the thinking of Tennessee's leading antiaristocrat, Andrew Johnson. Most of Johnson's private correspondence for the secession winter has not survived, but two substantial letters he wrote in January provide revealing glimpses. Johnson thought the "ostensible object" of secession—

"to obtain protection in regard to slave property"—was "a pretext and not the real design." The true intention of secessionists was, instead, to form an independent government in the South "as far removed from the people as they can get it." In short, "there is not merely a conspiracy on foot against the existing government; but the liberty of the great mass of the people." Johnson took a cynical view of the clamor about a danger to slave property. "It is not the free men of the north they are fearing most," he explained to a friend, "but the free men South." The "traitors" and "vile miscreants" wanted to have a southern government "so organized as to put the institution of Slavery beyond the reach or vote of the nonslaveholder at the ballot box."[52]

Antisecession egalitarianism in Tennessee cut across party lines and extended well beyond Johnson's home region in upper East Tennessee. A "vary poor man" from Middle Tennessee informed Johnson that "we have differed in our political opinions before hear to fore, but stand as a unit on the present crisis of the Country." He judged that the "Union loving men of all parties are with you," but "the Rich nabob of the South is against you." A Chattanooga admirer told Johnson that "the mountain boys—The wood choppers The rail splitters—In fact the bone and sinew of the country back you—entirely irrespective of party—this day I do believe that 7-tenths of the people of Tennessee are with you—." William S. Speer from Shelbyville, a pro-Union stronghold in Bedford County, Middle Tennessee, likewise told Johnson that "men hitherto your best friends curse you—but two thirds of the old 'yeomanry' are still with you, and nearly all the Whigs." Repelled by proslavery fanaticism, Speer advised Johnson that there were "other interests to look after" besides slavery. William E. Penn, elected as a convention delegate from Henderson County, West Tennessee, sent Johnson a similar testimonial: "Heretofore I was your enemy in *politics* but now we are *together* and I hope will remain so to do battle against *traitors* and scoundrels. The *leaders* of your old party curse you *manfully* and some swear it would not be *well* for you to visit these regions, but the *people* the *real people* are with you and will stand by you to the last." Penn assured Johnson that "the masses of the people in West Tennessee do not believe in ghosts. . . . In other words, we are not yet deranged."[53]

One Tennessean especially exemplified the transcendence of pro-Union egalitarianism over traditional party allegiances in early 1861. Johnson's bitter, long-standing critic, Knoxville newspaper publisher William G. Brownlow, put twenty years of personal and political rivalry behind him to join hands with Johnson on the Union issue. "*Johnson is right*," Brownlow told a mutual friend, "*and I will defend him to the last.*" There were no parties left, Brownlow announced, "but Union men and Disunionists." On the side of the Union stood "the real people, irrespective of parties." Against them was "the Slavery Aristocracy," a group of "overbearing tyrants" who wanted "poor white men" to be their "hewers of wood and drawers of water." Beware, Brownlow warned. The "cotton planters" of the deep South wanted to "drag Tennessee into their scheme" to get the manpower "to fight their battles." While the sons of planters stayed home, the yeomanry of the upper South were to be "shot down like dogs."[54]

Nonslaveowners' resentment about secession reinforced chronic intrastate sectional strains in all three states. Egalitarian resistance to the Southern Rights program flourished in the piedmont counties of North Carolina's Quaker Belt and in the Cumberland Plateau and eastern region of Tennessee. But the most explosive regional antisecession movement occurred in Virginia, where sectional strains had been particularly intense. Far northwestern Virginia, often called the trans-Allegheny, was part of the Ohio Valley. Its residents had long considered themselves neglected and exploited by the rest of the state. Almost all state-sponsored canals and railroads either lay in the east or the Valley. The James River and Kanawha Canal had never been extended beyond the Valley, and the principal western railroad, the Baltimore and Ohio, had been financed out of state and did not connect to eastern Virginia. People living in the four counties of the northwestern panhandle, wedged between Ohio and Pennsylvania, felt that eastern Virginians "know as little about us, and we about them, as Asiatic Russia knows about European Russia, and there is not near as much sympathy between us."[55]

Angered by the failure of the state government to provide tangible benefits for their section, northwestern Virginians were further distressed by what they regarded as a discriminatory state tax system rigged in favor of slaveholders. The 1851 Virginia constitution had exempted from taxation all slaves under the age of twelve and had specified a maximum valuation of $300, for purposes of taxation, on slaves over that age. As slave prices soared during the 1850s, the maximum valuation clause provided an ever-increasing tax windfall for slaveowners. They as a class and the eastern region where most of them lived thus paid lower taxes proportionate to wealth, and nonslaveowners made up the difference. Northwesterners complained that they had become "the complete vassals of Eastern Virginia," taxed "unmercifully and increasingly, at her instance and for her benefit."[56]

Ad valorem slave taxation thus had the potential to become an even more divisive issue in Virginia than in North Carolina because of the uniquely keen sense of regional isolation and resentment in Virginia's northwest. But in contrast to North Carolina, neither Virginia political party before 1861 had dared to champion the west on the ad valorem issue. Exactly the reverse had occurred in the 1859 state elections, when both parties engaged in a proslavery shouting match that totally ignored western grievances. Unhappy northwestern Virginians blamed their political powerlessness on eastern Virginia's success in finding "ready sympathizers in the West here, to second many of her movements." In other words, ties to eastern-dominated political parties meant that western Whigs and Democrats failed to represent the true interests of their section. Instead, they worked to "reconcile us to the yoke of the task-masters."[57]

Secession intensified western resentments. Already believing that the east had long taken unfair advantage of their region, westerners suddenly faced the prospect of having to fight and pay even higher taxes to protect slave interests. Westerners furthermore took an understandably dim view of the military situation they would confront in any war against the North. Virginia's northwest had 450 miles of border with Ohio and Pennsylvania, and because easterners had never been willing to spend state money to provide transportation access across the mountains, the northwest was effectively cut off from the east. A leading Union spokesman predicted that northwestern Virginia would be "the weakest point of a Southern Confederacy, and, therefore, the point of attack. . . . We would be swept by the enemy from the face of the earth before the news of an attack could reach our Eastern friends." Nor did the people of the northwest see any reason to fight their "neighbors" in Pennsylvania and Ohio. "We buy our marketing from them and they receive in exchange our goods, wares, merchandise and manufactures," one observer noted. Northwesterners thus concluded that secession from the North meant economic suicide for their region. "Would you," asked one, "have us . . . act like madmen and cut our own throats merely to sustain you in a most unwarrantable rebellion?"[58]

Efforts by Breckinridge Democratic leaders to align the northwest with the Southern Rights movement therefore triggered an extraordinary political upheaval. When Congressman Albert Gallatin Jenkins, who represented part of the northwest, proclaimed that all true Virginians would follow their state in or out of the Union, even if it meant becoming "rebels," he aroused a storm of controversy. Fellow Democrat Daniel Haymond, of Ritchie County, stated that "Mr. Jenkins will find himself very much mistaken if he thinks all those who voted for Breckinridge are disunionists, or any considerable portion of them." People in western Virginia, Haymond insisted, were "true to the Union" and looked to its perpetuation "as the only security for their liberty and their rights. To destroy the Union, they think, will be the destruction of republican liberty, which they prize above all else."[59]

Democrats such as Jenkins who remained subservient to the eastern wing of the party fared very badly in the convention election in early February. Victorious Unionists laid plans to retire him and other vulnerable Southern Rights Democrats from office. The *Wheeling Intelligencer* called on "Union men of all parties" to form a new "Union party" and make certain that only candidates of genuine loyalty held office. The danger, warned the *Intelligencer*, came from Breckinridge Democrats, who would not dare, after the February election, "to come before the people and advocate secession," but who would instead "plead for votes in strains of melting patriotism" while hiding behind "hermaphrodite resolutions that may mean secession or may not." Such men would "secede at the drop of a hat" once they "had a sure rope" around the necks of their constituents.[60]

Though its instigators obviously had wanted the Virginia convention to concern itself only with national issues, the northwesterners had a different agenda. Their challenge took shape when Waitman T. Willey of Morgantown proposed that the convention address the two western issues—taxation and representation. In addition to demanding that "all property should be taxed in proportion to its value," many westerners hoped to reopen the question of legislative apportionment. The 1851 Virginia convention had finally yielded to western demands that the House of Delegates be apportioned on the "white basis," but state senate districts remained tied to a formula that combined population and property. Discussion about reapportionment bogged down in an inconclusive controversy. Easterners insisted that delegates at the earlier convention had agreed to maintain the 1851 compromise on representation until at least 1865. Although westerners remembered differently, they directed most of their energies to the ad valorem taxation issue.[61]

As secessionist orators lectured about the "irrepressible conflict" between Black Republicans and Southern Rights, northwesterners at the Virginia convention countered by predicting that "if something is not done to make taxation more equal," there would soon be a "dire and awful conflict" within the state. It would not only divide the east and the west but also "the laboring man and the slave owner." The laborer was "burdened with taxes," charged one disgruntled northwesterner, "while opulent slaveowners, resting upon pampered wealth and fortune," were substantially exempt. The leading northwestern delegate, Waitman T. Willey, likewise linked sectional and class considerations in explaining his reasons for raising the taxation issue. He explained to a friend that "the non-slaveholder of East Virginia is as deeply interested in this question as we are." Because the tax exemption for slaveowners penalized nonslaveholders both east and west, Willey predicted that the "taxation question" would cease to be a "sectional question" and would "assume the attitude of a question between classes."[62]

The complaints voiced by western Virginians against the powerful and propertied interests of the east paralleled southerners' complaints about the North. The sectional crisis centered around southern perceptions that they were looked down upon by the North and that their equal rights in the Union were being destroyed. Westerners such as Daniel Haymond likewise complained that the east had "riveted upon their necks the yoke of inequality and oppression," denying their "just rights." Northwestern representatives to the Virginia convention called time and again "for speedy justice to be done" on the issues of taxation and representation. "If you want harmony in Virginia in this crisis," one insisted, "you must acknowledge the people of the West your equals in every respect. Do not discriminate against North Western Virginia."[63]

The more shrill manifestations of western indignation about eastern dominance and mistreatment contained both an antislavery tone and a threat to divide the state. Rephrasing the slogan used by Southern Rights advocates, who called for equality in the Union or independence out of it, western Virginians insisted on "equality, in our state, or in lieu of it, a division of the state." Westerners had become "exceedingly restless and impatient," one warned. "If you refuse much longer to grant their just demands, both in taxation and representation, they may come to the conclusion that this slave interest in Virginia, instead of being a blessing to them, is turned into an engine of oppression." The editor of the *Morgantown Star* was likewise "unwilling that slavery in Virginia shall be used to oppress the people of our section of the State. . . . We people in Western Virginia have borne the burden just about as long as we can stand it. We have been 'hewers of wood and drawers of water' for Eastern Virginia long enough." Unless given "equal laws and equal taxation," he warned, western Virginians would "demand a separation from Eastern Virginia." From the northwestern panhandle came word that the people there were "not willing to be taxed for the support of an army fighting against their country. They love the good old Commonwealth, but they love the Union more." People in the east should understand "that if it is determined to leave the Union, we of the West will cut the feeble cords . . . that bind us together, and remain in the Union."[64]

No document better captures the mood of unconditional northwestern Virginia Unionists than an emotional letter sent to Waitman Willey. Henry Dering of Morgantown, Willey's correspondent, was exasperated by reports that western delegates had been "abused and vilified" by secessionists in Richmond, and he penned a stinging complaint. "We see with pain, the game that is being played, by the Eastern nabobs, to precipitate the old Dominion out of this glorious Union, into the treasonable bosom of King Cotton," he began.

> Talk about Northern oppression, talk about our rights being stolen from us by the North—it's all stuff, and dwindles into nothing when compared, to our situation in Western Virginia. The truth is the slavery oligarchy, are impudent boastfull and tyrannical, it is the nature of the institution to make men so—and tho I am far, from being an abolitionist, yet if they persist, in their course, the day may come, when all Western Virginia will rise up, in her might and throw off the Shackles, which thro this very *Divine institution*, as they call it, has been pressing us down.

Dering contemptuously reviewed the sorry history of state support for internal improvements: "Have we received anything from the treasury to open up our resources—to develop our vast riches, in Western Virginia. No the remorseless craw of old Virginia has been stuffed, to its full, while we have received a tub to the whale, in the shape of a few dollars to build a new turnpike." Embittered by the refusal of easterners to recognize the equality or just rights of the west, Dering concluded with an impassioned plea that Willey move to divide Virginia "and set up a state of our own, and let it belong to the glorious Union founded by Washington, Madison, and Jefferson." The West was "ready for it," he insisted; "it is the sentiment of our people."[65]

7

MEASURING THE UNIONIST INSURGENCY

AN analysis of voting behavior reinforces the evidence already presented about upper South Unionism. The convention elections held in Virginia, North Carolina, and Tennessee in February 1861 afforded a genuine test of popular opinion regarding secession before the issue was overwhelmed by the need to choose sides in a war. The returns from these elections constitute a uniquely valuable source for understanding the response to secession in the upper South.[1] By systematically comparing voting behavior in February 1861 with previous patterns of party voting, and by incorporating data from the censuses of 1850 and 1860, it is possible to identify elements of continuity and to verify the appearance of new alignments.[2] This chapter has been prepared with the general reader in mind. All discussion of statistical procedure is relegated to Appendixes I and II. Readers nevertheless terrified by straightforward graphs and tables will still be able to benefit from reading the concluding segment of this chapter.

Calculations presented above in Chapter 2 suggest that voting patterns in February 1861 differed substantially from earlier ones (see Tables 2-2 through 2-6).[3] The changes appear to have been most abrupt in Virginia. In Tennessee, previous patterns of party voting became a significantly less salient predictor of voting behavior in February 1861. And even in North Carolina, where party lines more closely paralleled the division between Union and secession strength, correlation values fell below previous levels.

What was happening? The following graphs are instructive. In Figures 7-1, 7-2, and 7-3, the counties in each state are divided into two categories: those with Democratic majorities in 1860 (the combined presidential vote for Breckinridge and Douglas) and those with anti-Democratic majorities (the vote for John Bell, or, in the case of Virginia, the vote for Bell plus the small vote for Lincoln). Figure 7-1 shows that the fifty Democratic-minority (or Whig) counties in Virginia displayed somewhat greater Union support, as measured both by the division of participating voters and by the turnout among all eligible voters, than did the eighty Democratic-majority counties. In

FIGURE 7-1.
Virginia Voting Patterns, February 1861: Whig and Democratic Counties Contrasted

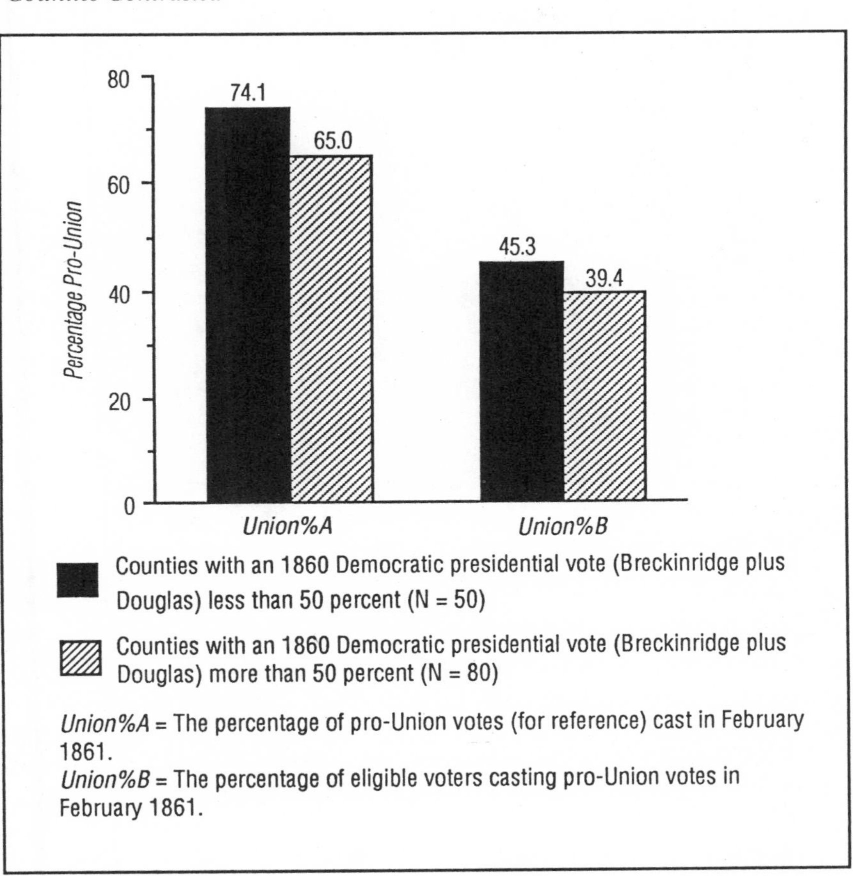

North Carolina, counties with Whig majorities displayed far higher levels of Union support and were also far less likely to favor calling a convention (see Figure 7-2). Tennessee's Whiggish counties likewise reflected very strong pro-Union tendencies. A comparison of the bars farthest to the left on Figures 7-1, 7-2, and 7-3 shows that the Whig-majority counties in Virginia had 9.1 percent higher levels of Union support than the Democratic-majority counties. In North Carolina the difference was 30.5 percent, and in Tennessee it was 18.5 percent. Whig-majority counties in Tennessee opposed the calling of a state convention at a rate of 22.2 percent higher than the Democratic-majority counties; North Carolina had a 36 percent dif-

FIGURE 7-2.
North Carolina Voting Patterns, February 1861: Whig and Democratic Counties Contrasted

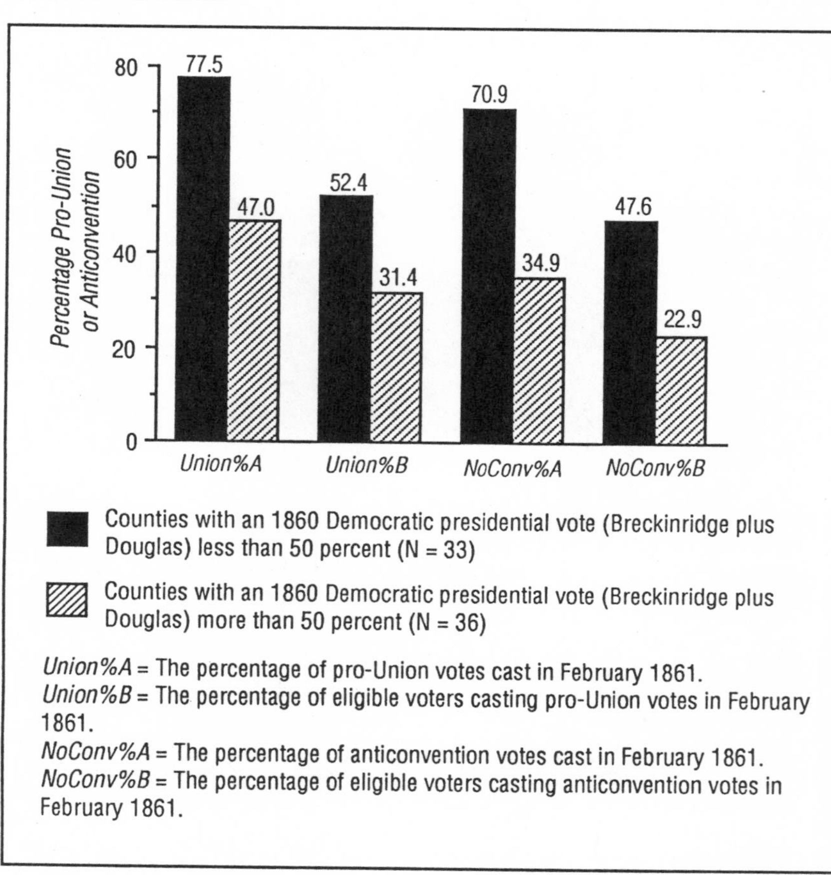

ferential. Even after the war started, Unionism was more persistent among Tennessee Whigs. Whig-majority counties opposed separation in a June 1861 referendum at a rate of 15.7 percent higher than in Democratic-majority counties.

A second series of graphs, organized in a similar manner, will enable the reader to visualize voting patterns in high-slaveowning and low-slaveowning counties in each state (see Figures 7-4, 7-5, 7-6). Counties are divided between those above and below the percentage of the slave population of the entire state (Virginia's slave population in 1860 was 30.8 percent, North Carolina's 33.3 percent, and Tennessee's 24.8 percent). It may be observed that the seventy counties in

FIGURE 7-3.
Tennessee Voting Patterns, February and June 1861: Whig and Democratic Counties Contrasted

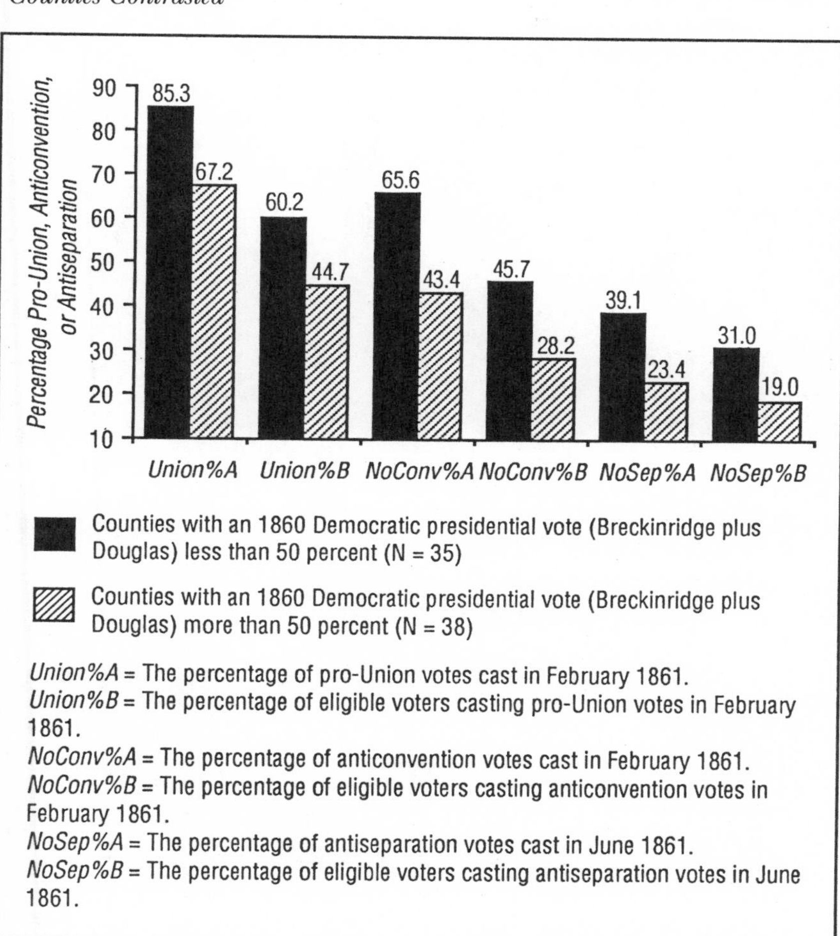

Virginia with slave populations below 30.8 percent voted 81.9 percent pro-Union, whereas the sixty Virginia counties with slave populations above 30.8 percent voted only 45.8 percent pro-Union (see Figure 7-4). North Carolina and Tennesee voters in low-slaveowning counties likewise rolled up heavy pro-Union majorities (71.6 and 80.8 percent, respectively). North Carolina voters in high-slaveowning counties voted only 45.9 percent pro-Union, but those in Tennessee produced a pro-Union figure of 70.2 percent, an anomaly that will be analyzed subsequently. Comparing the vote in each state, we

FIGURE 7-4.
Virginia Voting Patterns, 1860–1861: Low- and High-Slaveowning Counties Contrasted

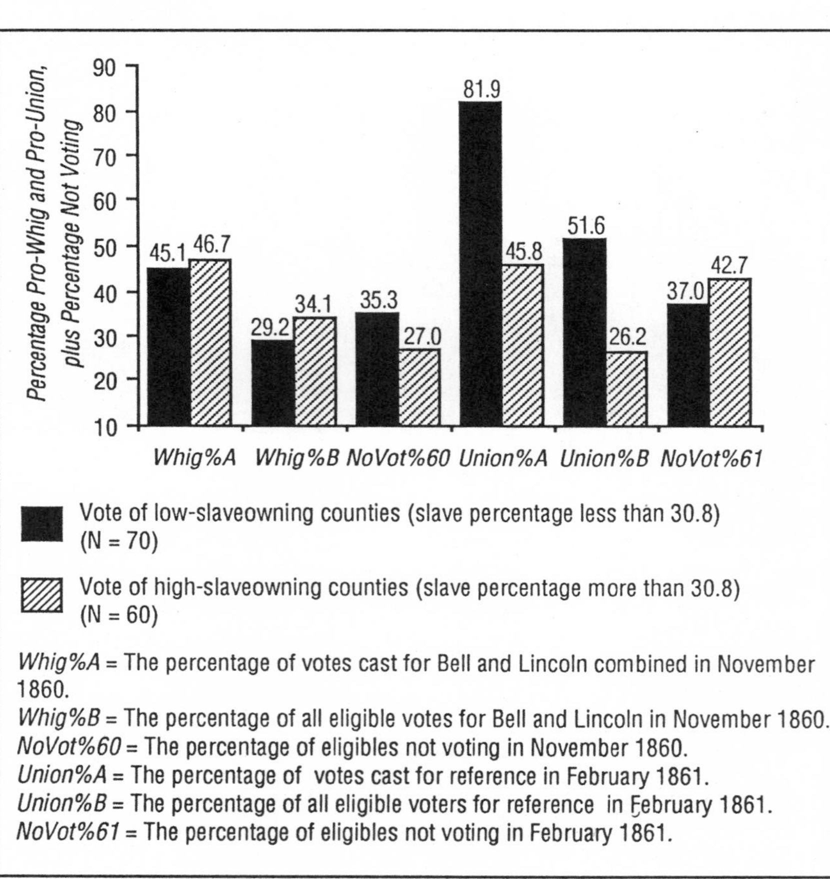

find that low-slaveowning counties in Virginia voted 36.1 percent more pro-Union. In North Carolina the difference was 25.7 percent, and in Tennessee it was 10.6 percent.

The question of calling a state convention polarized voters in the high-slaveowning and low-slaveowning counties of North Carolina and Tennessee even more sharply than did the question of Union versus secession (see Figures 7-5 and 7-6). The great majority of pro-Union supporters in low-slaveowning counties also opposed a convention. Low-slaveowning counties of North Carolina voted 65.6 percent against a convention (close to the pro-Union figure of 71.6

FIGURE 7-5.
North Carolina Voting Patterns, 1860–1861: Low- and High-Slaveowning Counties Contrasted

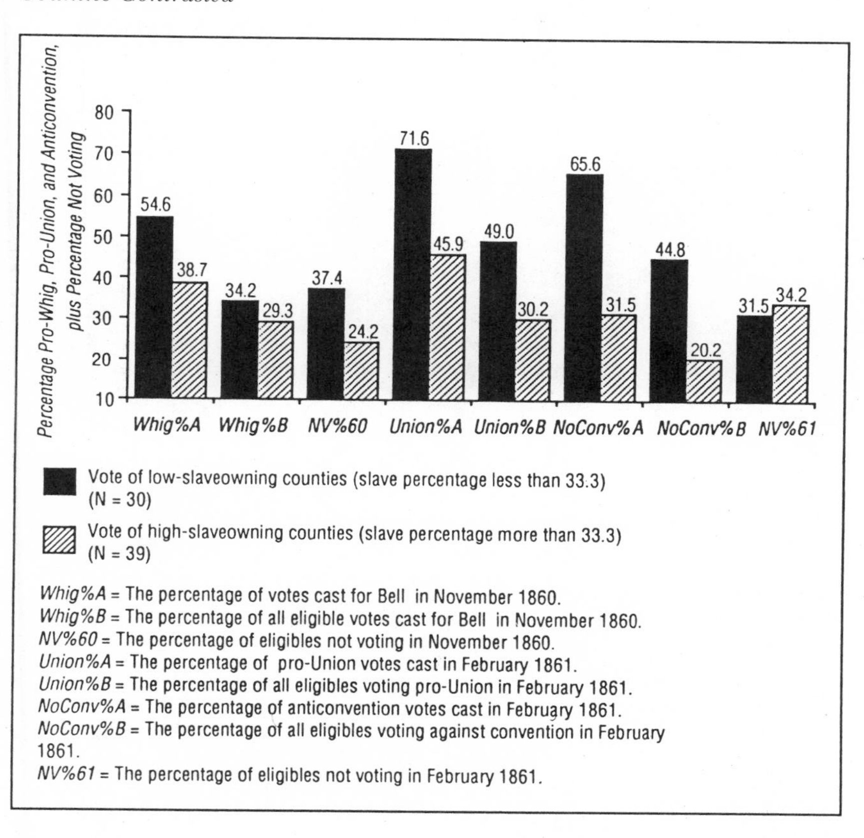

percent). In Tennessee the figures were, respectively, 69.9 and 80.8 percent. But many pro-Union voters in high-slaveowning counties of both states voted in favor of a convention. In North Carolina only 31.5 percent of all voters in high-slaveowning counties opposed a convention (versus 45.9 percent who voted pro-Union). In Tennessee, 32.9 percent of voters in high-slaveowning counties voted against a convention, even though 70.2 percent had voted pro-Union. In other words, fewer than one-third of participating voters in the high-slaveowning counties of each state opposed a convention, whereas two-thirds of the voters in low-slaveowning counties did so. In June, with the war already started, almost half the voters (49.3 percent) in low-slaveowning counties of Tenneseee still opposed secession. By

FIGURE 7-6.
Tennessee Voting Patterns, 1860–1861: Low- and High-Slaveowning Counties Contrasted

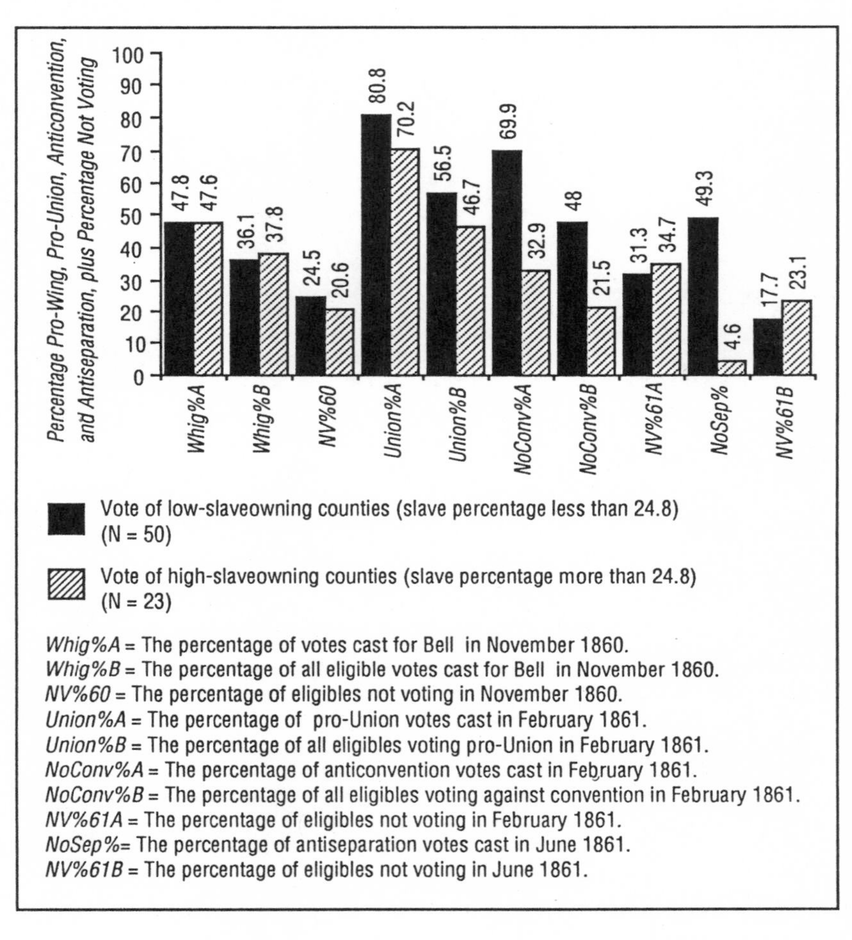

then fewer than one voter in twenty (4.6 percent) in Tennessee's high-slaveowning counties remained a Unionist.

Two other significant matters may be detected in Figures 7-4, 7-5 and 7-6. Before 1861 in only one of the three states did low-slaveowning counties vote differently than high-slaveowning ones. Only in North Carolina did existing party loyalties correlate significantly with slaveownership, allowing John Bell to run 15.9 percent better in low-slaveowning counties than in high-slaveowning ones (see the bars farthest to the left in Figure 7-5). In both Virginia and Tennessee the

Whig (or non-Democratic) percentage vote in the 1860 presidential election was almost identical in the high-slaveowning and low-slaveowning counties (see the bars farthest to the left in Figures 7-4 and 7-6).

In all three states, too, the pattern of turnout in the February 1861 elections reversed the traditional tendency for a higher turnout in high-slaveowning counties than in low-slaveowning counties. Discrepancies in voting rates between high-slaveowning and low-slaveowning counties had been especially marked in Virginia and North Carolina. Figures 7-4, 7-5, and 7-6 reveal that voter turnout in February 1861 in low-slaveowning counties of all three states actually exceeded that of high-slaveowning counties. The margins were 5.7 percent in Virginia, 2.7 percent in North Carolina, and 3.4 percent in Tennessee. Just three months earlier, in the presidential election of 1860, turnout in high-slaveowning counties in Virginia ran 8.3 percent ahead of turnout in low-slaveowning counties. High-slaveowning counties in North Carolina then displayed a turnout advantage of 13.2 percent. The differential in Tennessee stood at 3.9 percent. Figures 7-4, 7-5, and 7-6 indicate that nonvoting in high-slaveowning counties of Virginia soared from 27.0 percent to 42.7 percent. In North Carolina the rate increased from 24.2 to 34.2 percent, and in Tennessee from 20.6 to 34.7 percent.

A third series of graphs makes it possible to consider how both party and slaveowning affected Union sentiment (see Figures 7-7, 7-8, and 7-9). In effect these three graphs combine the relationships depicted separately in the first six graphs. For each state, counties are divided into four different categories. Figure 7-7 on Virginia thus shows that low-slaveowning Whig counties voted 88.2 percent pro-Union, and low-slaveowning Democratic counties produced an only slightly less overwhelming Union vote (77.2 percent). High-slaveowning Whig counties produced a narrow pro-Union margin (53.0 percent), but high-slaveowning Democratic counties solidly favored secession, with only 38.7 percent of voters in favor of remaining in the Union. In North Carolina, low-slaveowning Whig counties strongly opposed secession and a state convention, and high-slaveowning Democratic counties strongly favored both (see Figure 7-8). As might be expected in light of North Carolina's higher level of correlation between voting during the secession crisis and previous patterns of party preference, the high-slaveowning Whig counties voted marginally more pro-Union than low-slaveowning Democratic counties (62.2 to 56.4 percent), and both narrowly favored holding a state convention. Whig counties in Tennessee, high- as well as low-slaveowning, voted very strongly pro-Union, but low-slaveowning Democratic coun-

FIGURE 7-7.
Pro-Union Percentage of Votes Cast in Virginia, February 1861

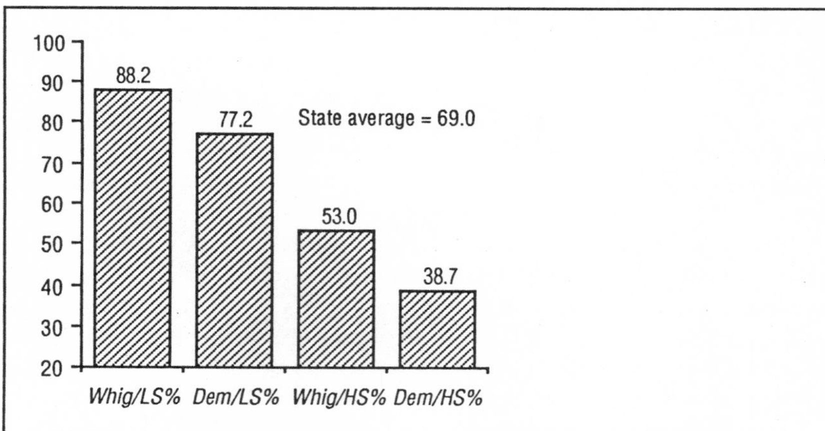

Whig/LS% = The percentage pro-Union in counties with 1860 Democratic presidential vote (Breckinridge plus Douglas) less than 50 percent and slave percentage less than 30.5 (N = 26).
Dem/LS% = The percentage pro-Union in counties with Democratic percentage more than 50 and slave percentage less than 30.5 (N = 44).
Whig/HS% = The percentage pro-Union in counties with Democratic percentage less than 50 and slave percentage more than 30.5 (N = 24).
Dem/HS% = The percentage pro-Union in counties with Democratic percentage more than 50 and slave percentage more than 30.5 (N = 36).

ties also produced solid Union margins. Even high-slaveowning Democratic counties recorded a narrow (54.5 percent) pro-Union advantage. In Tennessee, however, the question of holding a state convention divided the four categories very symmetrically. In low-slaveowning Whig counties 82.7 percent of voters opposed a convention, as did 57.9 percent in low-slaveowning Democratic counties. High-slaveowning counties, by contrast, favored a convention. In high-slaveowning Whig counties 43.9 percent of voters opposed a convention, as did fewer than one voter out of five (19.6 percent) in high-slaveowning Democratic counties. By June the Tennessee electorate overwhelmingly favored separation. The vote was almost unanimous in high-slaveowning counties, both Whig and Democratic. Yet fully 63.9 percent of voters in low-slaveowning Whig counties still opposed that fateful step, as did 36.5 percent of voters in low-slaveowning Democratic counties (see Figure 7-9).

Figures 7-1 through 7-9 thus reveal significant relationships be-

FIGURE 7-8.
Pro-Union and Anticonvention Percentages of Votes Cast in North Carolina, February 1861

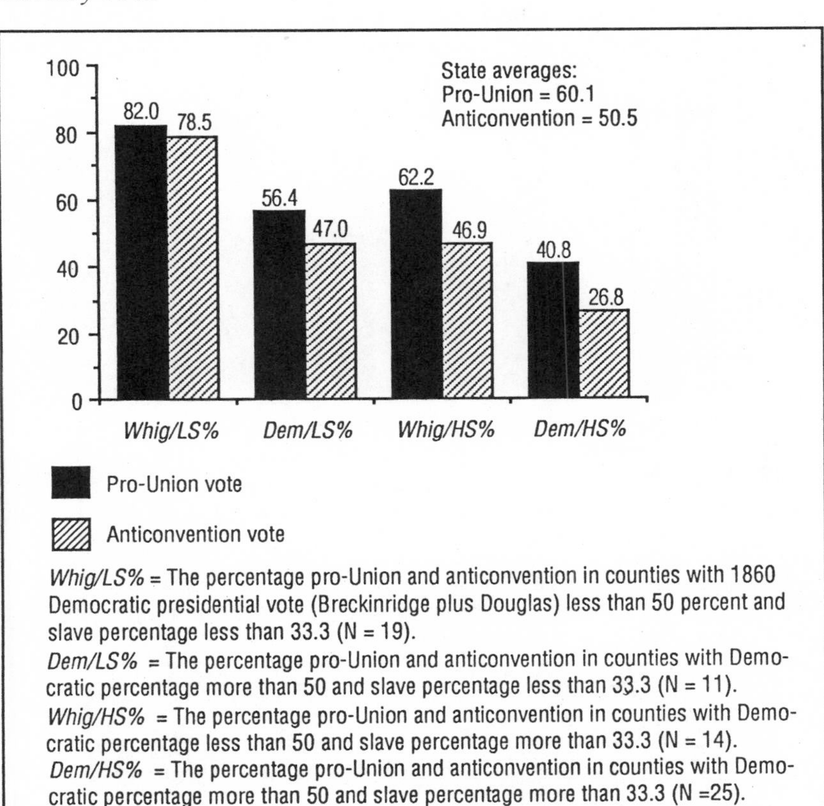
100
80
60
40
20
0
State averages:
Pro-Union = 60.1
Anticonvention = 50.5
82.0
78.5
56.4
47.0
62.2
46.9
40.8
26.8
Whig/LS%
Dem/LS%
Whig/HS%
Dem/HS%
Pro-Union vote
Anticonvention vote
Whig/LS% = The percentage pro-Union and anticonvention in counties with 1860 Democratic presidential vote (Breckinridge plus Douglas) less than 50 percent and slave percentage less than 33.3 (N = 19).
Dem/LS% = The percentage pro-Union and anticonvention in counties with Democratic percentage more than 50 and slave percentage less than 33.3 (N = 11).
Whig/HS% = The percentage pro-Union and anticonvention in counties with Democratic percentage less than 50 and slave percentage more than 33.3 (N = 14).
Dem/HS% = The percentage pro-Union and anticonvention in counties with Democratic percentage more than 50 and slave percentage more than 33.3 (N =25).

tween slaveowning, party, and support for the Union. In all three states, low-slaveowning counties displayed greater levels of opposition to secession and to the calling of a state convention than high-slaveowning counties. Whig counties typically voted more solidly pro-Union than comparable Democratic counties. Party thus remained a major influence during the secession crisis, especially in North Carolina. But the extent of slaveowning in a county had emerged as a powerful determinant of relative support for remaining in the Union.

Graphs most readily illustrate basic patterns, but other, more sophisticated statistical procedures may be employed to analyze voting

FIGURE 7-9.
Pro-Union and Anticonvention Percentages of Votes Cast in Tennessee, February 1861, plus Antiseparation Percentage of Votes Cast, June 1861

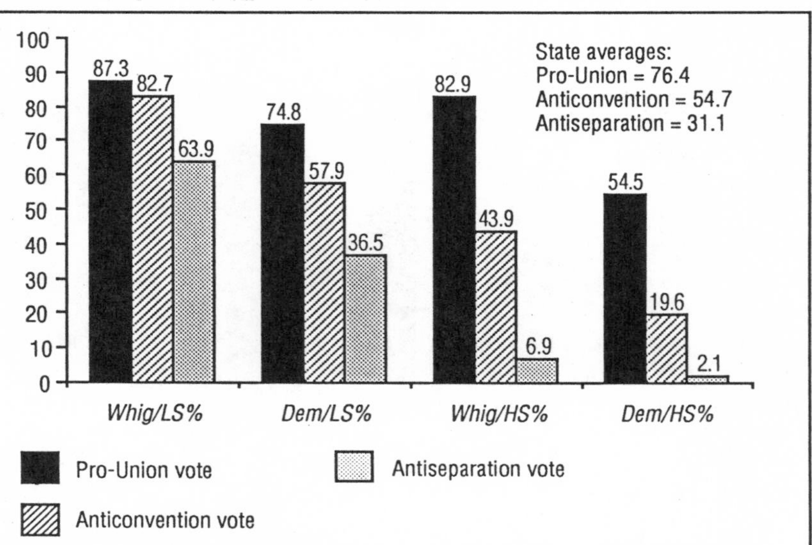

Whig/LS% = The percentage pro-Union, anticonvention, and antiseparation in counties with 1860 Democratic presidential vote (Breckinridge plus Douglas) less than 50 percent and slave percentage less than 24.8 (N = 22).
Dem/LS% = The percentage pro-Union, anticonvention, and antiseparation in counties with Democratic percentage more than 50 and slave percentage less than 24.8 (N = 28).
Whig/HS% = The percentage pro-Union, anticonvention, and antiseparation in counties with Democratic percentage less than 50 and slave percentage more than 24.8 (N = 13).
Dem/HS% = The percentage pro-Union, anticonvention, and antiseparation in counties with Democratic percentage more than 50 and slave percentage more than 24.8 (N = 10).

during the secession crisis. Appendix I provides an explanation of additional techniques used to measure relationships between slaveowning, party, and support for the Union.

Further insights about voting behavior in the upper South in 1860–61 may be obtained by estimating how slaveowners and nonslaveowners divided their votes (see Tables 7-1 through 7-6). Appendix II explains the statistical techniques involved.

We know that 42 percent of Virginia's eligible electorate and 69 percent of those who voted cast Union ballots in February 1861. Among these were an estimated 23 percent of all eligible slaveowners and 36 percent of those slaveowners who voted (see Table 7-1). These slaveowning Unionists provided an estimated 12 percent of all pro-Union votes (see Table 7-2). Similarly, Table 7-1 reports that an estimated 47 percent of all eligible nonslaveowners and 79 percent of those nonslaveowners who voted cast Union ballots. Table 7-2 indicates that the nonslaveowning Unionists contributed an estimated 88 percent of all pro-Union votes.

In Virginia 18.9 percent of the eligible electorate and 31 percent of those voting cast secession ballots in February 1861. Among these were an estimated 42 percent of all eligible slaveowners and 64 percent of those slaveowners who voted (see Table 7-1). These slaveowning secessionists provided an estimated 47 percent of all votes for secession (see Table 7-2). Similarly, Table 7-1 reports that an estimated 13 percent of all eligible nonslaveowners and 21 percent of those nonslaveowners who voted cast secession ballots. Table 7-2 indicates that nonslaveowners constituted 53 percent of all prosecession voters.

Tables 7-1 and 7-2 amplify the findings of Figures 7-1, 7-4, and 7-7. A striking change in Virginia's voting patterns occurred between November 1860 and February 1861. In the presidential election slaveowners and nonslaveowners divided their votes between the parties quite similarly. That is, an estimated 42 percent of slaveowners who voted cast a Whig ballot, as did 47 percent of nonslaveowners. Three months later, 36 percent of the slaveowners who voted cast a Union ballot, compared with 79 percent of the nonslaveowners. To a very significant degree, the February 1861 election aligned slaveowning secessionists against nonslaveowning Unionists.

In North Carolina, as already noted, slaveowners tended to vote Democratic. The estimate here is that only 33 percent of participating slaveowners voted for John Bell in 1860. An estimated 33 percent likewise voted pro-Union in 1861 (see Table 7-3). Only an estimated 26 percent of all eligible slaveowners in North Carolina voted Whig in November 1860. A decline in turnout among slaveowners cut the percentage of eligible slaveowners voting Union to an estimated 22 percent, almost the idential percentage estimated for Virginia (23 percent). A small majority (53 percent) of participating North Carolina nonslaveowners are estimated to have supported John Bell in November 1860, whereas more than two-thirds (69 percent) are estimated to have voted pro-Union in February 1861. Bell received an estimated 35 percent of the vote from all eligible nonslaveowners;

TABLE 7-1.
How Virginia Slaveowners and Nonslaveowners Divided Their Votes: Estimated Percentages for November 1860 and February 1861

	November 1860				
				(Of Those Voting)	
Category	Whig	Democrat	Nonvoting	Whig	Democrat
Slaveowners (N = 52,129)	36	47	20	42	58
Nonslaveowners (N = 193,933)	30	34	36	47	53
All eligibles (N = 246,062)	31.0 (N = 76,368)	36.8 (N = 90,523)	32.2 (N = 79,171)	45.8	54.2
	30.3 (Bell) (N = 74,481)	30.2 (Breckinridge) (N = 74,325)		44.6 (Bell)	44.5 (Breckinridge)
	0.7 (Lincoln)	6.6 (Douglas)		1.2	9.7

February 1861

Category	Union	Secession	Nonvoting	(Of Those Voting) Union	Secession
Slaveowners (N = 52,129)	23	42	35	36	64
Nonslaveowners (N = 193,933)	47	13	40	79	21
All eligibles (N = 246,062)	42.0 (N = 103,236)	18.9 (N = 46,386)	39.2 (N = 96,440)	69.0	31.0

Note: The number of slaveowners and nonslaveowners in the eligible electorate is known, as are the vote totals for November 1860 and February 1861. The percentages provide estimates for the way Virginia slaveowners and nonslaveowners divided their votes in each election. The figures in the two columns to the right are percentages of the vote actually cast, ignoring the nonvoters.

The tables should be read in the following way: the estimates presented here suggest that 47 percent of all eligible nonslaveowners voted pro-Union, 13 percent supported secession, and 40 percent did not vote. An estimated 79 percent of participating nonslaveowners therefore voted pro-Union; only 21 percent supported secession. Tables 7-3 and 7-5 are constructed similarly. See Chapter 7, n. 2, on sources of data.

TABLE 7-2.
Virginia: Estimated Percentages of Slaveowners and Nonslaveowners in Voting Blocs, November 1860 and February 1861

Category	Slaveowners (N = 52,129)	Nonslaveowners (N = 193,933)
Eligible electorate, 1860 (N = 246,062)	21.2	78.8
Whig, 1860 (Bell + Lincoln) (N = 74,481 + 1,887) (Total N = 76,368)	24	76
Democrat, 1860 (Breckinridge + Douglas) (N = 74,325 + 16,198) (Total N = 90,523)	27	73
Nonvoting, 1860 (N = 79,171)	13	87
Union, February 1861 (N = 103,236)	12	88
Secession, February 1861 (N = 46,386)	47	53
Nonvoting, February 1861 (N = 96,440)	19	81

Note: The number of slaveowners and nonslaveowners in the eligible electorate is known, as are the vote totals for November 1860 and February 1861. The percentages provide estimates for the relative concentration of slaveowners and nonslaveowners within each voting group.

An illustration will suggest how to read the table. It is estimated that 12 percent of Union supporters were slaveowners and 88 percent were nonslaveowners. Likewise, an estimated 47 percent of secession supporters were slaveowners and 53 percent were nonslaveowners.

Tables 7-4 and 7-6 are constructed similarly.

the Union cause attracted 46 percent. The latter estimate too is almost identical to the results in Virginia, where an estimated 47 percent of eligible nonslaveowners voted pro-Union.

An unmistakable pattern emerges. In 1860, slaveholders were well positioned to continue wielding power and influence in Virginia's and North Carolina's Democratic and Whig parties. Though only 21 percent of the eligible Virginia electorate, slaveowners constituted an estimated 27 percent of Democratic voters and 24 percent of Whig voters (see Table 7-2). In North Carolina, slaveowners constituted an estimated 36 percent of Democratic voters and 20 percent of Whig voters (see Table 7-4). Even among the North Carolina Whig voters, slaveowners were only slightly less numerous than in the eligible electorate, which was 24.3 percent slaveowning. And the North Carolina Whig party had a long history of balancing off the interests of the low-slaveowning west, where the party base was strongest, to maintain Whig loyalties among voters in a cluster of higher-slaveowning counties adjacent to Albemarle Sound, whose support was essential for statewide Whig victories. Studies of party elites also show, not surprisingly, that slaveowners in Virginia and North Carolina held elective office at rates far exceeding their share of the party electorate.[4]

Three months later slaveowners found themselves politically isolated. The successful Union coalition in Virginia depended on slaveowners for only an estimated 12 percent of its support, whereas slaveowners made up an estimated 47 percent of the defeated secessionists. In North Carolina, slaveowners contributed only an estimated 13 and 9 percent, respectively, to the victorious pro-Union and anticonvention coalitions, while prosecession and proconvention forces gained an estimated 41 and 40 percent of their support from slaveowners. About two-thirds of Virginia and North Carolina slaveowners who voted in February 1861 favored secession (an estimated 64 percent in Virginia and 67 percent in North Carolina); an estimated 81 percent of North Carolina slaveowners favored a convention. As noted already, approximately equal percentages of eligible nonslaveholders voted pro-Union in both states (an estimated 47 and 46 percent, respectively). North Carolina secessionists, however, drew a somewhat more respectable turnout of eligible nonslaveholders (an estimated 13 percent in Virginia, 21 percent in North Carolina). Therefore, though nonslaveowners who voted in North Carolina opposed secession by an estimated 69 to 31 percent margin, the statewide figure in Virginia was almost five to one (an estimated 79 to 21 percent) and it reached seven to one in western Virginia.[5]

Why were North Carolina nonslaveholders somewhat more willing to accept the idea that party loyalty obligated a vote for secession? A basic matter of geography must first be taken into account. Compared to Virginia, a far smaller proportion of North Carolina territory and population lay beyond the mountains in the Ohio-Mississippi watershed. Western North Carolina did have grievances against the eastern-dominated state government, but western regional estrangement in North Carolina diminished during the 1850s, just as

TABLE 7-3.
How North Carolina Slaveowners and Nonslaveowners Divided Their Votes: Estimated Percentages for November 1860 and February 1861

	November 1860				
				(Of Those Voting)	
Category	Whig	Democrat	Nonvoting	Whig	Democrat
Slaveowners (N = 34,658)	26	54	20	33	67
Nonslaveowners (N = 107,727)	35	31	34	53	47
All eligibles (N = 142,385)	31.9 (Bell) (N = 45,492)	36.7 (N = 52,187) 34.8 (Breckinridge) (N = 49,447) 1.9 (Douglas) (N = 2,740)	31.4 (N = 44,606)	46.6 (Bell)	53.4 50.6 (Breckinridge) 2.8 [illegible]

February 1861 (Union versus Secession)

Category	Union	Secession	Nonvoting	(Of Those Voting) Union	(Of Those Voting) Secession
Slaveowners (N = 34,658)	22	45	33	33	67
Nonslaveowners (N = 107,727)	46	21	33	69	31
All eligibles (N = 142,385)	40.4 (N = 57,538)	26.9 (N = 38,277)	32.7 (N = 46,570)	60.1	39.9

February 1861 (No Convention versus Convention)

Category	No Convention	Convention	Nonvoting	(Of Those Voting) No Convention	(Of Those Voting) Convention
Slaveowners (N = 34,658)	13	54	33	19	81
Nonslaveowners (N = 107,727)	40	26	34	61	39
All eligibles (N = 142,385)	33.5 (N = 47,705)	32.8 (N = 46,711)	33.7 (N = 47,969)	50.5	49.5

Note: See Table 7-1 for explanation.

TABLE 7-4.
North Carolina: Estimated Percentages of Slaveowners and Nonslaveowners in Voting Blocs, November 1860 and February 1861

Category	Slaveowners (N = 34,658)	Nonslaveowners (N = 107,727)
Eligible electorate, 1860 (N = 142,385)	24.3	75.7
Whig, 1860 (Bell) (N = 45,492)	20	80
Democrat, 1860 (Breckinridge + Douglas) (N = 49,447 + 2,740) (Total N = 52,187)	36	64
Nonvoting, 1860 (N = 44,606)	16	84
Union, February 1861 (N = 57,538)	13	87
Secession, February 1861 (N = 38,277)	41	59
Nonvoting (Union versus secession) (N = 46,570)	25	75
No convention, February 1861 (N = 47,705)	9	91
Convention, February 1861 (N = 46,711)	40	60
Nonvoting (convention question) (N = 47,969)	24	76

Note: See Table 7-2 for explanation.

northwestern Virginia was becoming increasingly disaffected.[6] North Carolina, in short, was more cohesive. Furthermore, its Democratic party, adroitly managed to appease western discontent, was internally stronger than the Virginia Democratic party. In 1860 Douglas attracted a sufficiently large mass following in Virginia to split the Democratic vote and give John Bell a narrow victory. North Carolina Democratic leaders had better success at keeping the rank and file in line, both in the presidential election and during the secession crisis.[7]

A political earthquake nevertheless struck North Carolina as well as Virginia in February 1861, even though the changes in Virginia's voting patterns appear at first glance more massive. Appendix I does suggest that proconvention, prosecession, and Democratic voting in North Carolina followed somewhat similar patterns. Yet it is essential to realize that prosecession voting in North Carolina was depressed at levels sharply lower than the normal Democratic turnout. Although 37 percent of the North Carolina electorate voted Democratic in November 1860, only 27 percent voted for secession three months later. The overall turnout in the two elections was nearly identical, so a narrow Democratic victory in November was followed by a resounding defeat for secession in February. The sudden erosion of support for secession, relative to previous Democratic strength in North Carolina, was, without doubt, the more important fact than the tendency for secession voting patterns to parallel Democratic voting patterns.

On the whole, voting behavior during the secession crisis in Virginia and North Carolina had much in common. A pro-Union surge in low-slaveowning regions determined the result in both states. In Virginia 37 percent of the eligible electorate voted for Democratic presidential candidates in November 1860, with Breckinridge alone winning over 30 percent. Yet only 19 percent of eligible Virginia voters favored secession. North Carolina secessionists, although supported by a somewhat more respectable 27 percent of those eligible, had no cause for celebration. They too had been badly defeated. In both nominally Democratic states, secession was buried by a pro-Union landslide in which the votes of nonslaveowners proved decisive.

THE case of Tennessee requires separate consideration. There, as suggested in Figures 7-3, 7-6, and 7-9, the level of support shown for secession in higher-slaveowning areas did not match that in Virginia or North Carolina. Why not? One reason is that Tennessee had marginally fewer slaveowners than Virginia or North Carolina (19.5 percent of the adult male population in Tennessee, versus 21.2 percent in Virginia and 24.3 percent in North Carolina). Dividing Tennessee into high- and low-slaveowning counties places in the high category some counties that would have been low in Virginia or North Carolina.

A second and more important reason has to do with the Whiggish loyalties of many Tennessee slaveowners. In November 1860, an estimated 48 percent of all Tennessee slaveowners (and an estimated 57 percent of those participating) supported native son John Bell, one of the largest slaveowners in the state. Yet only an estimated 34 per-

TABLE 7-5.
How Tennessee Slaveowners and Nonslaveowners Divided Their Votes: Estimated Percentages for November 1860, February 1861, and June 1861

November 1860					
				(Of Those Voting)	
Category	Whig	Democrat	Nonvoting	Whig	Democrat
Slaveowners (N = 36,844)	48	37	15	57	43
Nonslaveowners (N = 152,585)	34	41	25	45	55
All eligibles (N = 189,429)	36.8 (Bell) (N = 69,728)	40.3 (N = 76,378) 34.4 (Breckinridge) (N = 65,097) 5.9 (Douglas) (N = 11,281)	22.9 (N = 43,323)	47.7 (Bell)	52.3 44.6 (Breckinridge) 7.7 (Douglas)

February 1861 (Union versus Secession)					
				(Of Those Voting)	
Category	Union	Secession	Nonvoting	Union	Secession
Slaveowners (N = 36,844)	54	20	25	73	27
Nonslaveowners (N = 152,585)	52	15	33	78	22
All eligibles	52.3	16.1	31.5	76.4	23.6

Category	No Convention	Convention	Nonvoting	(Of Those Voting) No Convention	(Of Those Voting) Convention
Slaveowners (N = 36,844)	18	57	25	24	76
Nonslaveowners (N = 152,585)	41	24	35	63	37
All eligibles (N = 189,429)	36.8 (N = 69,772)	30.5 (N = 57,708)	32.8 (N = 61,949)	54.7	45.3

June 1861 (Union versus Separation)

Category	Union	Separation	Nonvoting	(Of Those Voting) Union	(Of Those Voting) Separation
Slaveowners (N = 36,844)	0	85	15	0	100
Nonslaveowners (N = 152,585)	31	48	21	39	61
All eligibles (N = 189,429)	24.9 (N = 47,183)	55.2 (N = 104,471)	19.9 (N = 37,775)	31.1	68.9

Note: See Table 7-1 for explanation.

TABLE 7-6.
Tennessee: Estimated Percentages of Slaveowners and Nonslaveowners in Voting Blocs, November 1860, February 1861, and June 1861

Category	Slaveowners (N = 36,844)	Nonslaveowners (N = 152,585)
Eligible electorate, 1860 (N = 189,429)	19.5	80.5
Whig, 1860 (Bell) (N = 69,728)	26	74
Democrat, 1860 (Breckinridge + Douglas) (N = 65,097 + 11,281) (Total N = 76,378)	18	82
Nonvoting, 1860 (N = 43,323)	13	87
Union, February 1861 (N = 99,150)	20	80
Secession, February 1861 (N = 30,586)	25	75
Nonvoting (Union versus secession) (N = 59,693)	15	85
No convention, February 1861 (N = 69,772)	9	91
Convention, February 1861 (N = 57,708)	36	64
Nonvoting (convention question) (N = 61,949)	15	85
Union, June 1861 (N = 47,183)	0	100
Separation, June 1861 (N = 104,471)	30	70
Nonvoting (Union versus separation) (N = 37,775)	15	85

Note: See Table 7-2 for explanation.

cent of all eligible nonslaveowners (or an estimated 45 percent of those participating) voted similarly (see Table 7-5). It may thus be estimated that 26 percent of the Whig electorate held slaves, compared with 18 percent of the Democratic electorate (see Table 7-6). Still, with slaveowners constituting only 19.5 percent of the entire eligible electorate, they were well situated in both parties. Plenty of Tennessee Democrats were vigorous champions of Southern Rights and chronically purported to find their opponents tainted with abolitionism.

In February 1861, an estimated 73 percent of participating Tennessee slaveowners and 78 percent of participating nonslaveowners opposed secession. An estimated 54 percent of all eligible slaveowners voted pro-Union, as did 52 percent of all eligible nonslaveowners. The Union coalition was an estimated 20 percent dependent on slaveowners' votes; the secession coalition, 25 percent. Candidates opposed to secession understandably ran well in low-slaveowning counties. Yet in a number of populous high-slaveowning counties in Middle Tennessee, a bipartisan conditional Unionist coalition ran candidates for the state convention with little or no opposition.[8] Those candidates were legitimate Unionists by the standard used here, that is, they opposed secession for existing causes at the time of their candidacy. The Middle Tennessee consensus for conditional Unionism assured a crushing statewide defeat for secession.

But the convention issue cut decisively between Tennessee slaveowners and nonslaveowners. An estimated 76 percent of the slaveholders who went to the polls wanted a convention held, compared to only an estimated 34 percent of participating nonslaveowners. Slaveowners constituted only an estimated 9 percent of the victorious anticonvention coalition but a hefty 36 percent of the defeated proconvention coalition. Evidence presented in Appendix I likewise suggests that slaveowning was more important than party in explaining whether voters favored or opposed the calling of a convention. A fault line between conditional and unconditional Unionists, with most slaveowners on the conditional side, thus lay embedded in the Tennessee voting returns. Tennessee slaveowners had tried, with somewhat greater success than their Virginia and North Carolina counterparts, to control the Union juggernaut. But a twelve-thousand-vote margin against a convention severely diminished their achievement.

THE procedure used to estimate how slaveowners and nonslaveowners divided their votes in February 1861 may also be used to estimate how the supporters of various 1860 presidential candidates voted in

February 1861 (see Tables 7-7, 7-8, and 7-9). The reader may again refer to Appendix II for an explanation of the statistical techniques involved.

Table 7-7, for example, indicates that an estimated 80 percent of Virginians who supported John Bell subsequently voted pro-Union. Only an estimated 7 percent of Bell voters favored secession, thus leaving 13 percent as nonvoters. By contrast, an estimated 57 percent of Virginians who supported John C. Breckinridge subsequently voted for secession, an estimated 20 percent voted pro-Union, and 23 percent did not vote.

An inspection of Tables 7-7, 7-8, and 7-9 will reveal that support for secession was confined almost exclusively to Breckinridge Democrats, supplemented by a cluster of Douglas Democrats from southwest Tennessee. But the Democratic electorate was far from unified. An estimated one-sixth (16 percent) of North Carolinians who had voted for a Democratic presidential candidate voted thereafter against secession. In the other two states the proportion of defecting Democrats was twice as large. Estimates suggest that almost one-third (32 percent) of Virginia Democrats spurned disunion and that 35 percent of Tennessee Democrats followed Andrew Johnson's Unionist course. Significant numbers of those who voted Democratic in November 1860 did not vote in February 1861 (an estimated 22, 19 and 27 percent in Virginia, North Carolina, and Tennessee, respectively). Nonvoting Democrats were cross-pressured. They harbored doubts both about secession and about the Whiggish tone and leadership of the antisecession movement.

All evidence suggests that Whigs voted overwhelmingly pro-Union. Estimates presented in Tables 7-7, 7-8, and 7-9 indicate that very few supporters of John Bell subsequently voted for secession in February 1861. In Tennessee, Unionists received an estimated 92 percent of the Whig vote. Virginia and North Carolina Whigs voted almost as monolithically pro-Union (estimates suggest 80 and 81 percent, respectively). Whigs, moreover, were more likely to vote in February 1861 than were Democrats. An estimated 95 percent of Tennessee Whigs voted in February 1861, and their Virginia and North Carolina counterparts displayed turnout rates estimated at 87 percent. Differential rates of party turnout thus contributed significantly to the defeat of secession.

The behavior of former nonvoters also strengthened Union forces. Estimates suggest that very few favored secession and that substantial numbers voted pro-Union. The antisecession coalition of February 1861 included more than one-quarter (26 percent) of nonvoters in November 1860 in North Carolina and around a sixth of such voters

TABLE 7-7.
February 1861 Patterns of November 1860 Virginia Voters (in Percentages)

Party	Percent of Total	Union	Secession	Not Voting
Whig (Bell)	30.3	80	7	13
Republican (Lincoln)	0.7	100	0	0
Democratic	36.8	32	46	22
Breckinridge	30.2	20	57	23
Douglas	6.6	86	0	14
Not voting, 1860	32.2	16	0	84

Note: All aggregate vote totals are known. The percentages listed provide estimates for the way 1860 voters and nonvoters distributed their votes in February 1861. For example, an estimated 80 percent of Bell voters in Virginia subsequently voted pro-Union, 7 percent favored secession, and 13 percent did not vote.

in Virginia (16 percent) and Tennessee (17 percent). Former nonvoters thus played a major role in the Union victories, especially in North Carolina.

The data gathered above also make it possible to estimate the approximate composition of the Union constituency for each state. Table 7-10 tabulates the loyalties in 1860 of those who voted pro-Union in February 1861. Table 7-10 shows that substantial majorities of Unionists in all three states were Whigs. Democrats provided an estimated 30 percent of the Union vote in Virginia, 27 percent in Tennessee, but only 15 percent in North Carolina. Nonvoters in 1860 provided an estimated 20 percent of the North Carolina Union vote, about twice the proportion in Virginia and Tennessee. Although the Whig component was distinctly the largest in each state, it may be said with confidence that the embryonic Union party was a new political grouping. Had it endured, its rise in February 1861 would easily have qualified—to use modern terminology—as a major political realignment.[9]

An exodus of voters from the active electorate in high-slaveowning areas took place just as previously inactive voters from low-slaveowning areas were joining it. The process was especially apparent in North Carolina. The citizens of that state regarded state elections as more important than presidential ones. In the hotly contested gubernatorial election of August 1860, the statewide turnout of eligible

TABLE 7-8.
February 1861 Patterns of November 1860 North Carolina Voters (in Percentages)

Party	Percent of Total	Union	Secession	Not Voting	No Convention	Convention	Not Voting
Whig	31.9	81	6	13	69	18	13
Democratic	36.7	16	65	19	11	70	19
Breckinridge	34.7	11	69	20	6	74	20
Douglas	1.9	90	0	10	80	10	10
Nonvoting, 1860	31.4	26	3	71	26	3	71

Note: See Table 7-7 for explanation.

voters was almost 79 percent, versus 69 pecent in the November presidential election. But only 67 percent of those eligible voted in the February 1861 convention election. The low turnout in 1861 may be traced to counties with slave populations above 40 percent (a category that coincided substantially with the Democratic strongholds in the eastern coastal plain centered around Edgecombe County). In the highest-slaveowning counties, 83 percent of eligibles voted in August, 77 percent in November, but only 66 percent in February. The lowest-slaveowning counties of North Carolina usually experienced smaller turnouts. In counties where no more than one-quarter of the population was enslaved, 74 percent of eligibles voted in August and only 60 percent in November. But turnout in the lowest-slaveowning counties rebounded in February 1861 to 68 percent—a figure 2 percent above that for the highest-slaveowning counties. Never before during the antebellum era had such a reversal of normal turnout patterns occurred.

Estimates of voting behavior in the lowest-slaveowning counties of North Carolina suggest that nonslaveowners opposed secession and a convention by a far larger margin than they normally supported Whig and Opposition candidates (see Table A-11 in Appendix II). In August 1860, Democrats successfully blunted Whig or Opposition appeals for nonslaveowner support by attracting a proportionate share of new voters. But in February 1861, the new voters did not divide: they voted pro-Union with near unanimity. So we must try to visualize a revolving door, through which significant numbers of disillusioned Democrats departed from the active electorate in February 1861. Instead of a state election drawing latent Democrats to the

TABLE 7-9.
February 1861 Patterns of November 1860 Tennessee Voters (in Percentages)

Party	Percent of Total	Union	Secession	Not Voting	No Convention	Convention	Not Voting
Whig	36.8	92	3	5	76	19	5
Democratic	40.3	35	38	27	13	60	27
Nonvoting, 1860	22.9	17	0	83	17	0	83

Note: See Table 7-7 for explanation.

polls, just the reverse occurred. Many reliable Democrats who had stirred themselves to vote in the typically lower-turnout presidential election refused to vote in February. Meanwhile, an influx of up-country nonslaveholders who had not voted in November, and many of whom had not even voted in August, moved into the active electorate. They voted in February against both secession and a state convention.

What did the new voting patterns signify? The results may, to a limited degree, reflect weak turnout for secessionist candidates in eastern Virginia and North Carolina, who either ran unopposed or were considered sure to win and therefore did not poll a full vote. But other, more fundamental forces were clearly at work. There were comparable Union strongholds in both states that experienced strong voter turnout. Moreover, in all three states, voters had to decide secession-related ballot questions—"reference" or "convention"—in addition to selecting candidates. Secessionists should have had at least as much motivation to vote as Unionists. Yet the intensity of opposition to secession in areas where it was weak more than matched the intensity of support for it in areas where it was strong. Southern Rights promoters failed to mobilize their core constituency in high-slaveowning Democratic areas. Nonslaveowners there, and even apparently some slaveowners, abstained rather than enlist under the secession banner.

TAKING into account all the available evidence, we may construct a broad overview of how the secession issue upended the political status quo in the upper South. No Southern Rights Democrat could help but view the situation with alarm. In the three states considered here, between 19 and 27 percent of Democratic voters in 1860 appar-

TABLE 7-10.
Breakdown of Union Voters (in Percentages)

State	Eligible Voters Pro-Union	November 1860 Affiliation of Union Electorate: Whig	Democratic	Nonvoting in 1860
Virginia	42	59 Bell = 57 Lincoln = 2	30 Breckinridge = 15 Douglas = 15	11
North Carolina	40	65	15 Breckinridge = 11 Douglas = 4	20
Tennessee	52	65	27	8

ently did not reappear at the polls in February 1861. An estimated 32 and 35 percent of Democratic voters in 1860 in Virginia and Tennessee, respectively, voted pro-Union, as did 16 percent of North Carolina Democratic voters. But North Carolina Unionists recruited former nonvoters at a rate higher than in Virginia or Tennessee. An estimated 26 percent of nonvoters in North Carolina in November 1860 turned out to vote Union, as did 16 and 17 percent of nonvoters in 1860 in Virginia and Tennessee. And almost all previous nonvoters who opposed secession in 1861 were nonslaveowners.

In all three states secession eroded traditional Democratic support, leaving Southern Rights Democrats hopelessly outnumbered. In Virginia and Tennessee, more than half of 1860 Democrats apparently refused to support secession. An estimated 54 percent of 1860 Virginia Democrats and 62 percent of 1860 Tennessee Democrats either voted pro-Union or did not vote. Never before had the Democratic party in either state experienced such desertion. The new Union party drove a wedge between nonslaveowners and the Democratic party that was unprecedented in the political history of either state. A groundswell of nonslaveowning Democrats, especially in western Virginia and East Tennessee, broke party ranks to oppose secession.

Although North Carolina secessionists held the loyalties of an estimated 65 percent of November 1860 Democratic voters, their prospects were hardly more encouraging. The loss of over one-third of the Democratic electorate crushed hopes for secession. Three out of five Tar Heel voters rejected secession. Unionists mobilized sufficient dissident Democrats and former nonvoters to win almost 70 percent support from the nonslaveholders who voted in February 1861. North Carolina's Democratic party, long the political home for a majority of the state's slaveowners, found itself crippled by the nonslaveowner revolt.

The pro-Union mobilization of nonslaveowners in the upper South certainly did not, by itself, signal an overt challenge to planter hegemony, let alone opposition to slavery. Most upper South Unionists were not trying to subvert the social order in the style of Hinton Helper. They were, however, rejecting the program of Southern Rights Democrats who claimed to champion the slave interest. They were also broadly hinting that they intended to extinguish the political power of the secession-tainted Democratic party at the first possible opportunity. And by refusing even to countenance a state convention, nonslaveowners in North Carolina and Tennessee defied the upper-class slaveowning leadership in the Union coalition itself, thereby alerting aspiring new political entrepreneurs to potential opportunity.[10]

Most fundamentally, the February 1861 elections in Virginia, North Carolina, and Tennessee created a situation within each state very much like what had happened nationally in November 1860. A gnawing sense of political irrelevance was one of the principal sources of southern distress following Lincoln's election. By sweeping the North, Lincoln had accomplished the unprecedented feat of winning the presidency without needing southern support. That stunning demonstration of apparent southern political powerlessness in the Union probably fueled the secession movement as much as any other single factor. For the proud, assertive leaders of the Southern Rights wing of the Democratic party, Lincoln's election was too great a humiliation to bear. Even those who had private doubts about secession soon found that their core constituencies—the substantial slaveowning areas that voted for Breckinridge—demanded radical action.

But then, to the surprise and horror of the Southern Rights leaders in the upper South, the Unionist groundswell in January and February 1861 jeopardized their power at home just as Lincoln had jeopardized their power in the nation. The secession stigma suddenly crippled the Democratic parties of the upper South, the instruments through which Southern Rights leaders had long wielded power. To make matters worse, the challenge to the Democrats came from new political entities, the emerging Union parties, whose most distinguishing characteristic was a base of support in which slaveowners were incidental and irrelevant. Union victories could easily have been achieved in all three states without the vote of a single slaveowner.

Stung by Lincoln's victory, the self-designated custodians of southern interests found themselves facing a situation in the upper South which, to say the least, added insult to injury. And because nobody had demonstrated very conclusively how Lincoln might injure the South—his victory was more of an insult than an injury—the rise of Union party power and the eclipse of Democratic party power was perhaps the true injury.

All things considered, the Union party of 1861 contained in embryo something as close to the outer limits of change in the social basis of political power as could ever be expected from electoral politics. That was its strength and also its weakness. It threatened not only to thwart secession but also to overthrow the structure of power Southern Rights Democrats had amassed in the upper South, while isolating most slaveowners in a minority party. Though led for the most part by a comfortable elite of Whig politicians whose property-holding and social position better fit the secessionist profile, the Union party constituency came closer to being nonplanter, if not yet antiplanter, than any political coalition ever to hold power in a slave-owning state. To flourish, the Union party desperately needed to bring about a peaceful resolution to the crisis that had spawned it. Failing that, it was peculiarly vulnerable to disruption. Leading Unionists well knew that war could destroy their new party even more quickly than it had been formed.

8

THE UNIONISTS AND COMPROMISE

Unionists told voters in the upper South that Congress would soon enact legislation or constitutional amendments safeguarding their rights and thereby making secession unnecessary. Circumstances required that Unionists profess optimism about the chances for compromise. When in public, they articulated their hopes rather than their fears. The actual situation, however, was ominous. Hardly any Republicans would accept the Union-saving compromise preferred by southern Unionists. This chapter will examine what southern Unionists wanted, why they eagerly sought concessions and reassurances about grievances they considered irrational, why Republicans balked at Unionist proposals, and how the near impasse was narrowed if not finally broken.

When Congress convened in early December, efforts to arrange a compromise dominated its agenda. Each house set up a special committee to consider the vexing problem of sectional reconciliation. The Senate Committee of Thirteen quickly deadlocked, unable to find a formula that could attract support from both North and South. The House Committee of Thirty-Three struggled into January to find some basis for agreement.[1]

From the end of December through the first two weeks of January, the chances for a peaceful adjustment dimmed. South Carolina and the federal government appeared close to armed conflict in Charleston harbor. A small federal force, led by Major Robert Anderson, had taken refuge at Fort Sumter on December 26, when South Carolina troops menaced their position at nearby Fort Moultrie on Sullivan Island. Sumter, a still uncompleted coastal fortification, sat on an artificial island near the entrance to the harbor. South Carolina authorities, insisting that no federal forces could remain in the state, demanded Anderson's withdrawal. But President James Buchanan refused to comply, prompting southern members of his cabinet to depart in protest. Anderson, an instant hero in northern eyes, symbolized an unwillingness to acquiesce in secession. On January 9, South Carolina forces fired on a federal ship, the *Star of the West*, as it attempted to resupply Anderson's beleaguered contingent. War spirit swept the North, and hostilities appeared imminent. Only when Buchanan worked out a temporary truce with South Carolina did the war fever subside.[2]

Sectional polarization accompanying the war scare left Unionists frustrated and disconsolate. Caught between the secessionism of the deep South and what they regarded as the intransigence of the North, Unionists found scant grounds for hope that compromise legislation could be enacted. The despairing letters mentioned earlier, written by Robert Hatton and John A. Gilmer, date from the grim period in late December and early January. At this juncture, too, the Virginia legislature assembled in Richmond amid a frenzy of prosecession enthusiasm.

Yet Unionists had no choice but to promote a sectional compromise. By late January, as war fever ebbed and an antisecession undercurrent began to strengthen in the upper South, they finally succeeded in placing the compromise issue at the center of public discussion. Feverishly, they struggled to gain Republican support for mreasures designed to reassure worried southerners.

ONE compromise plan attracted more attention than any other. Senator John J. Crittenden of Kentucky, heir to the "great Pacificator," Henry Clay, sponsored a proposal known ever since as the Crittenden Compromise. The author's prestige and eminence, surveyed in Chapter 1, assured his ideas a wide audience.

Concerned primarily to alleviate southern fears, Crittenden drafted a series of irrevocable amendments to the Constitution, protecting the slave system from any conceivable challenge. Crittenden's compromise forbade any federal interference with slavery in the states where it existed, in federal forts, dockyards, and arsenals, and in the District of Columbia unless approved by both Maryland and Virginia. He included a gratuitous slap at the rights of black citizens that echoed the *Dred Scott* decision. Crittenden also proposed legislation to compensate owners who lost fugitive slaves and to punish persons who obstructed their return.

The key part of Crittenden's compromise addressed the territorial issue. He proposed amending the Constitution to prohibit slavery in territories north of 36° 30′, the old Missouri Compromise line, but to require that Congress not interfere with slavery south of 36° 30′ and to enjoin territorial governments there to protect it. The language covered both existing territory and any "hereafter acquired." Crittenden himself neither favored nor expected new territorial acquisitions, but he included the "hereafter acquired" clause to placate expansion-minded Democrats.

The Crittenden Compromise attempted to encompass both poles of the divisive territorial controversy. Crittenden deftly combined Republican exclusion of slavery from territories north of 36° 30′ with a Southern Rights territorial slave code south of 36° 30′. Southerners would give up their theoretical right promised in the *Dred Scott* decision to take slaves to territory north of 36° 30′, while Republicans would concede that territory south of 36° 30′ remain open to slavery and that southerners enjoy a federally protected right to own slaves there. Crittenden thus tried to revive a solution to sectional polarization "that had been officially dead and buried for a number of years." Republicans had coalesced to bar slavery from *all* territories, whereas southerners had grown accustomed since the *Dred Scott* decision to denouncing *any* territorial restriction "as a gross injustice to their section."[3]

The Crittenden Compromise secured remarkably wide approval outside Republican ranks. Buchanan, the lame-duck president, gave it his blessings, as did his bitter intraparty rival, Stephen A. Douglas. Less than a year before, the latter had so adamantly opposed a territorial slave code that southerners bolted from the Democratic party. Nor had Crittenden or most of his allies in the southern Opposition ever before endorsed "protection." Unionists such as John A. Gilmer thought the demand "a useless and foolish abstraction," put forward by a coalition of conspiratorial disunionists and men who had lost their senses. Nobody, indeed, could endorse the Crittenden Compromise without in some way sacrificing earlier views and strict consistency.[4]

Crittenden's formulation quickly became the upper South's preferred basis for settlement. Democrats, including many with secessionist inclinations, vowed that its prompt passage would preserve the Union. Almost all southern Unionists agreed that Crittenden's would have a more salutary effect than any other compromise proposal. It would, thought T. A. R. Nelson of East Tennessee, "be satisfactory to a large majority of the Southern States, perhaps all of them but one." William B. Stokes, the announced unconditional Unionist from Middle Tennessee, preferred the "Crittenden resolutions" because "the general impression seems to be that they will satisfy reasonable men everywhere." East Tennessee's Horace Maynard explained that the Crittenden Compromise was "the offer of the Union men of the South . . . who were opposed originally to the repeal of the Missouri Compromise line." Recalling how a handful of southern Unionists had, at great political risk to themselves, refused to support the Kansas-Nebraska Act and Lecompton, Maynard urged Republicans to "reciprocate" in the interests of peaceful reconciliation.[5]

Upper South Unionists repeatedly emphasized that the Crittenden Compromise provided the means to arrest secession not only in their states but in the deep South as well. Congressman James M. Leach from the North Carolina piedmont argued that it would induce the border states "not only to remain in the Union but to exert their good offices as mediators and peacemakers." Only the Union men of the South, argued Horace Maynard, could persuade the seceded states to return to the Union "without the firing of a gun" or "the shedding of a drop of blood." If this was what Republicans wanted, they had to give upper South Unionists the means to succeed: "We can do all of this; you cannot; you never can. . . . I beg that you will trust us." Convinced that the safety and well-being of their states could be secured by allowing their "maddened brethren" of the deep South the "empty right" of territorial protection, Unionists such as John A. Gilmer happily embraced the Crittenden Compromise. Its rapid passage would, they hoped, stop the secession movement dead in its tracks and prevent civil war.[6]

By endorsing the Southern Rights position for territory south of 36° 30′ and by applying it not just to existing but to future territory, Crittenden defined what many in the upper South would thereafter consider the minimum acceptable terms for settling the sectional crisis. The tendency was especially marked among Breckinridge Democrats, who had run a presidential candidate in 1860 on a platform demanding protection for slavery in all territories. But many supporters of Douglas and Bell—plus the two former candidates themselves, who had both earlier spurned "protection"—now concluded that a symbolic recognition of the idea would appease wounded southern pride and undermine the secession movement. Thus the Virginia, North Carolina, and Tennessee legislatures all pronounced the Crittenden Compromise the basis for any adjustment. Many upper South newspapers, even those with strong Union proclivities, announced that they would accept "nothing less."[7] Only the tiny minority of southern Unionists who were already Republicans or moving in that direction actually opposed the Crittenden Compromise.[8]

Southern Unionists maintained that Republicans could accept the Crittenden Compromise with no real loss either of substance or of face. "You have got the flesh and the marrow of the Territories, will you not divide the bone?" asked Congressman John T. Harris of Virginia. "I think the judgment of the people, north as well as south, will say you ought to do it." Former Governor Neill S. Brown of Tennessee used a similar metaphor. The Crittenden Compromise was "a mere peace offering and not of fat lambs either, but of mere hide and hoofs." If Republicans were "wise," he thought, they would embrace "Crittenden's proposition or something equivalent." They already controlled "all the territories that are valuable" and would sacrifice "no practical advantage." T. A. R. Nelson thought Republicans could vote for the Crittenden Compromise "without any sacrifice of honor and principle." Slavery already existed in New Mexico; the South only wanted northerners "to acknowledge the fact that slavery is there, and to say that you will not interfere with it. What do we give you as compensation for that? We offer you that slavery shall be forever prohibited north of that line; and if there is any concession in this matter, I maintain that it is a concession from the South to the North." In other words, the South would abandon the *Dred Scott* decision north of 36° 30′ if Republicans would simply recognize that slavery already existed south of that line "without their agency, and for which they are in no conceivable form responsible." Southern Unionists often asserted that the Crittenden Compromise would simply restore the pre-1854 status quo before the Kansas unpleasantness. Because Republicans had coalesced to protest repeal of the Missouri Compromise, they should agree to its restoration.[9]

Despite Unionist blandishments, hardly any Republican of stature would accept the Crittenden Compromise. Even though a minority of Republicans had begun to edge toward some territorial compromise, Crittenden asked more than they were prepared to give. They balked at protecting slavery in any territory. Moreover, they regarded the "hereafter acquired" clause as an invitation to conquer slave territory in Central America and the Caribbean. Republicans dreaded the prospect of further southern filibustering in the Caribbean region or a future southern ultimatum to annex Cuba.

Beyond tangible fears of Caribbean imperialism lay deep-rooted Republican concerns about honor and principle. Territorial policy indicated to many southerners whether they enjoyed the same rights as other American citizens. Republicans proved equally unwilling to renounce the core idea around which their political organization was built—opposition to slavery expansion. They would not, argued Salmon P. Chase, "consent to surrender a principle" so recently endorsed by voters in the North. Abraham Lincoln considered demands that he break his pledges and betray his friends "dishonorable and treacherous." Such an ignominious reversal would, he contended, establish a precedent subversive of "all popular government."[10]

Republicans reacted indignantly when told the Crittenden Compromise would merely restore the old Missouri line of 1820. Unlike the Crittenden Compromise, the Missouri Compromise applied only to territory owned by the United States. And though the 1820 measure prohibited slavery north of 36° 30′, it did not overtly protect or countenance slavery south of that line. To Republicans, these differences were fundamental. Even those Republicans who wished to make some gesture of reassurance toward the South dismissed the Crittenden plan out of hand.[11]

A revealing interchange between Representatives T. A. R. Nelson of Tennessee and John L. N. Stratton of New Jersey illustrated the gap that separated southern Unionists and conciliatory Republicans. Nelson, an East Tennessee Unionist, attempted to make the case that the Crittenden plan would reestablish the Missouri Compromise line, "adapted to the changed condition of the country." He contended that Republicans could accept it with no sacrifice "of honor or principle." Because slavery already existed in New Mexico by territorial law, passage of the Crittenden Compromise would not expand or enlarge the slave system. Stratton, one of the dozen or so Whig-Americans from New Jersey or Pennsylvania who were more open to compromise than any other Republicans, interrupted Nelson's speech to ask whether "he and his friends would be satisfied with the restoration of the Missouri compromise line in its original form." Stratton said he would be "willing to give the Missouri compromise line as an amendment to the Constitution, in its original language." In other words, Stratton would not protect slavery south of 36° 30′, nor would he make any reference to future territorial acquisition. In reply, Nelson stated that "so far as I am personally concerned, I would be glad to receive the Missouri compromise line as it originally was. I doubt, however, whether that would be satisfactory to the entire South." Disaffected southerners required, he insisted, "a recognition, on principles such as we have in the Crittenden resolution, of the existence of slavery there, and its protection." Nelson hoped that Republicans would not "consider that I am asking too much when I ask this. Intelligent as they are, they know but little of the true state of feeling in the South."[12]

Crittenden's failure to provide a plan Republicans could support thus boomeranged. When Republicans rejected the Crittenden Compromise, secessionists insisted that all hope for saving the Union had ended. Unionists scrambled desperately to prove secessionists wrong. The resulting search for alternatives to the Crittenden Compromise led to the formulation of two new schemes of adjustment, both drafted by committees of northern and southern representatives, with an eye to finding some way to attract conciliatory Republicans. Table 8-1 summarizes the key features of the Crittenden Compromise and the major alternative proposals. It should serve as a guidepost to assist readers of this chapter.

THE Border State plan was devised by an ad hoc committee of fourteen congressmen from the upper South and lower North, who met first on December 28 and then again on January 3 and 4. Chaired by Crittenden, the members of the border state committee included several other leading southern Unionists—John A. Gilmer of North Carolina, Robert Hatton of Tennessee, J. Morrison Harris of Maryland, and John T. Harris of Virginia. The border state committee decided to change the Crittenden Compromise in several ways. It specified that neither Congress nor a territorial legislature could restrict slavery in any existing territory south of 36° 30′. Rather than require use of federal power to protect slavery, the Border State plan forbade federal interference with it. And it said nothing about territory "hereafter acquired." The Border State plan thus modified Crittenden's handiwork so as to make compromise more palatable to Republicans. The revised plan also contemplated amending the Constitution only to prohibit interference with slavery in states where it already existed. Its other parts were to be enacted as legislation, not constitutional amendment. Subsidiary features of the Border State plan included revision of the Fugitive Slave Law to make personal liberty laws unnecessary and reassurances about the safety of slavery in the District of Columbia. The Border State plan did attract limited Republican support, as will be explained more fully in the next chapter. But most Republicans voted against a modified version sponsored by Tennessee Congressman Emerson Etheridge that reached the House floor on January 7. That vote took place just as the situation in Charleston harbor appeared ready to explode into war, chilling any northern interest in compromise.[13]

Although southern supporters of the Border State plan preferred the Crittenden Compromise, and although few Republicans at first agreed to the Border State plan, it nevertheless represented an important development. Through it the most respected southern Unionists in Congress offered Republicans an alternative to Crittenden's original proposal. By January deep South secessionists insisted that they would refuse any compromise. Since the logic behind Crittenden's overture had been to make the seceding states reconsider, indications that those states would accept no terms led upper South Unionists to think about interim strategies. Bringing the states of the deep South back into the Union remained an essential objective for upper South Unionists. But their immediate need was passage of a compromise sufficient to "arrest the secession stampede" in the upper South. Southerners on the border state committee agreed that the new package would suffice. Were Republicans to "give us the border state report," Robert Hatton wrote privately, Tennessee would

TABLE 8-1.
Proposed Secession Crisis Compromises in Historical Perspective

	Status of Slavery in Territory North of 36° 30′	Status of Slavery in Territory South of 36° 30′	Status of Slavery in Territory "Hereafter Acquired" South of 36° 30′	Status of Slavery in States Where It Already Existed
Missouri Compromise (1820)	Prohibited by law	Not addressed (by implication allowed)	Not addressed	Not addressed
Dred Scott decision (1857)	Slavery legal in all federal territories		Not addressed	Not addressed
Crittenden Compromise (as amended)	Prohibited by constitutional amendment	Congress prohibited by constitutional amendment from interfering with slavery; territorial government required to protect slavery		Protected by constitutional amendment

Border State plan	Prohibited by law (Etheridge version: by constitutional amendment)	Congress and territorial legislature prohibited by law from interfering (Etheridge version: by constitutional amendment)	Not addressed (no restrictions on annexing new territory) (Etheridge version: no new territory without ⅔ of both Houses, or ⅔ of Senate if by treaty)	Protected by constitutional amendment
Committee of Thirty-three	Not addressed	All such territory to be admitted forthwith as a state (New Mexico)	Not addressed	Protected by constitutional amendment
Peace conference proposal	Prohibited by constitutional amendment	Congress and territorial legislature prohibited by constitutional amendment from interfering	Not addressed, but at least half the senators from both slave and free states must approve any new territory	Protected by constitutional amendment

have no trouble deciding between "safety and honor, in the Union, or ruin and shame in a cotton Republic—in which *cotton* is to be king, a few nabobs the ruling power, and our rights and honor treated with sovereign contempt." Hatton thus confidently expected to use the Border State plan to "whip out disunion in Tennessee." Crittenden reportedly stood ready to abandon his earlier proposal for protection of slavery in present and future territory south of 36° 30′ if Republicans would accept the Border State plan.[14]

The House's Committee of Thirty-Three developed a third major compromise proposal. This group, headed by the conservative Ohio Republican and former Whig Thomas Corwin, experienced great difficulty in reaching a consensus and came perilously close to failure. A coalition of moderates from both North and South, including several Republicans, finally agreed on January 14 to allow Chairman Corwin to report to the House that a majority of its members favored two provisions: a constitutional amendment assuring the safety of slavery in states where it already existed, plus legislation to admit New Mexico into the Union as a state, thereby terminating the territorial status of all area claimed by the South in the Crittenden and Border State plans. The Corwin committee thus cleverly attempted to sidestep an overt territorial compromise. In addition, the Committee of Thirty-Three proposed legislation to repeal all state laws obstructing the Fugitive Slave Law, to allow a jury trial for alleged fugitives in the state from which they allegedly had fled, and to give federal judges power to extradite persons from one state to another. Of the three major compromise proposals, Corwin's attracted the most substantial Republican support. The constitutional amendment won the backing of eleven of the sixteen Republicans on the committee; New Mexico statehood attracted seven of the sixteen.[15]

Unionists of course supported the constitutional amendment protecting slavery in the states, a feature shared by all the major compromise plans. Such an amendment, Robert Hatton observed, would "put forever at rest" southern apprehensions that "the ultimate purpose of the Republican party" was "to destroy the institution of slavery in the States." To Virginia Congressman Sherrard Clemens, Republican support for the amendment provided a "little gleam of hope in the midst of all the darkness of this hour." Tennessee Congressman T. A. R. Nelson likewise welcomed the amendment, saying that additional compromise measures were needed only because of "the excitement that prevails in the country."[16]

The other principal Committee of Thirty-Three proposal, New Mexico statehood, had less intrinsic appeal to Unionists. Southern anxieties about the territories grew out of the need to assert southern equality in the Union. The issue was abstract and symbolic rather than tangible. Few southerners expected that slavery could expand to the West and new slave states be created there. The admission of New Mexico to the Union, even if technically as a slave state, would not have provided the symbolic reassurances southerners craved. The perceived need to vindicate southern honor and equality by giving slaveowners official access to some federal territory would still have festered.

The most forthcoming southern Unionists, such as John A. Gilmer and Robert Hatton, therefore tried to rekindle support for the intermediate of the three compromise proposals, the Border State plan. Gilmer, for example, urged Republicans to consider the Crittenden Compromise, if modified to remove language about "territory hereafter to be acquired." But, he continued, "if you will not give us the Crittenden proposition, give us the border-States proposition." Unlike many other southern Unionists, Gilmer thus openly encouraged Republicans to negotiate. He even said he could accept the report of Corwin's committee, if modified either to allow or protect slavery in territory south of 36° 30′. Gilmer thereby stressed the need for territorial compromise, rather than simply admitting New Mexico into the Union as a state. His bottom line became, in effect, the Border State plan, which encompassed the least dogmatic territorial compromise. Although the Crittenden Compromise best suited upper South Unionists, and although many insisted that Republicans swallow their objections to it, an accommodation based on the Border State plan began to emerge.[17]

For several weeks in late January and early February, the architects of compromise appeared close to success. "Leading Republicans and Southern conservative men" were in "close consultation," the *New York Times* reported on January 16. Two days later, Republican Senators William H. Seward of New York and James Dixon of Connecticut met privately with the two leading promoters of sectional adjustment, Senators Douglas and Crittenden. A large dinner party, hosted by Douglas, brought the four together again on January 24. There Seward delivered an enigmatic toast—"Away with all parties, all platforms of previous committals, and whatever else will stand in the way of restoration of the American Union!"—to which Crittenden responded "with such emphasis" that his glass "shivered to fragments." During the last week of January and first week of February, Crittenden and Douglas sent a series of timely messages to Virginia and Tennessee, holding out hope that Congress would pass a satisfactory compromise.[18]

The focus for negotiation was no longer the Crittenden Compromise itself, but rather a modified version along the lines of the Border State plan. John A. Gilmer wrote privately on January 22 that "we will pass in substance Mr. Crittenden's plan." The qualifying phrase almost certainly pointed to the Border State plan. The Washington reporter for the *Louisville Journal* reported that the "strongest Southern Union men" were working to amend the Corwin report along the lines of the Border State plan so as to cover the territorial question. "*An adjustment will be agreed upon in a very few days*," he insisted on January 28. Horace Greeley's *New York Tribune*, a leading opponent of compromise, warned on January 29 that "a compromise on the basis of Mr. Crittenden's is sure to be carried through Congress either this week or the next, provided a *very few more Republicans* can be got to enlist in the enterprise." Republicans were not, of course, enlisting in behalf of the original Crittenden proposal, but by the end of January some were receptive to the Border State plan, and even more were ready to accept the Corwin package. Conspicuous among the supporters of compromise by the end of January were some of the most prominent members of the New York commercial community. Moses H. Grinnell, John Jacob Astor, Jr., Hamilton Fish, William H. Aspinwall, James DeP. Ogden, Richard M. Blatchford, and numerous others stated that the time had come to offer the "truly conservative citizens" of the upper South "a stand point to which they can rally." Though conceding that the Crittenden Compromise had become the best known and most popular of the proposed formulas, the New Yorkers judged the Border State plan "far preferable."[19]

Between January 21 and early February, a parade of southern Unionists in Congress delivered speeches about the need for compromise, making a decided impact on moderate Republicans. The *New York Times* considered the speech by Tennessee's Emerson Etheridge "one of the noblest and boldest proclamations of devotion to the Union ever pronounced." It reasoned that "if the North is ever induced to yield anything further on the subject of Slavery, it will be at the instance of such men as these—rather than upon the demand of men in arms against the Government. Such men indeed deserve to be sustained in their unequal contest, by whatever of aid and support the North can give them." The *Boston Advertiser* likewise commended "the noble stand taken by the true men of the Border States" and emphasized the need "to give them our aid in their gallant struggle." One reporter had never seen "such an effect as was produced" by John A. Gilmer's "appeal to the Republican side to come forward and save the Union men of the border states." This "honest appeal of a great heart" was judged the "most effective" speech of the session.

When Gilmer finished, "dozens of Republicans and Southern Union men rushed forward to congratulate him." Conciliatory Republicans told newspaper reporters that "some compromise must be made to keep John A. Gilmer from being carried down by the secession tide." The person just quoted may well have been William H. Seward. The day after Gilmer spoke, Seward used identical words in a letter to Lincoln, writing that "the appeals of the Union men in the border States are very painful, since they say that without it their States must all go with the tide."[20]

Indications that Lincoln might support Union-saving measures especially cheered southern Unionists. Congressman William Kellogg of Illinois came back from a visit to Lincoln in late January "full of compromise" and telling southern Unionists that "something must and will be done soon" on which they could "stand." He thereupon introduced into the House a series of constitutional amendments, encompassing the basic ideas of the Border State plan, which supporters of compromise hailed as "an auspicious omen." Kellogg's supposed closeness to Lincoln naturally created the impression that he acted at Lincoln's instigation. After talking with Kellogg, Robert Hatton concluded that "we will get I think, at least, the Border State propositions."[21]

By the second week of February, Unionists grew increasingly optimistic. The action of Virginia and Tennessee put the compromise issue in a new light. Republicans, though disinclined to appease the seceding states, had to pay greater respect to appeals from states in the upper South that had repudiated disunion. Senator Henry Wilson of Massachusetts told one Unionist that "Virginia must now have all she requires." Virginia Governor John Letcher, visiting Washington just after the convention election, decided "the signs all look well —much more favorable than I supposed when I went to the City." Encouraged by interviews with Douglas and Crittenden, Letcher concluded that "we shall have a settlement upon perfectly fair terms, and in a short time." North Carolina Congressman Zebulon B. Vance likewise wrote on February 11 that an agreement "upon the basis of the Crittenden or Border state propositions . . . sufficient to satisfy all the border states" soon would be adopted by Congress.[22]

DESPITE indications that Congress would soon pass a compromise agreement, the prompt action Unionists expected did not materialize. Republicans remained badly divided, and indications that Lincoln favored a compromise were, as will be explained in the next chapter, very misleading. Fortunately for the Unionists, the Peace Conference assembled in Washington on February 4.[23] Conciliators both North and South hoped it might adopt a settlement plan that would win broad support in Congress. Thomas Corwin therefore held off a House vote on his proposals. He promised southern Unionists that if the Peace Conference agreed on an adjustment he could accept, he would substitute it for the recommendation he had brought from the Committee of Thirty-Three.[24]

By arranging for the Peace Conference, Unionists secured a reprieve. The tactic temporarily helped to undermine support for secession in the upper South. But heightened expectations that a satisfactory Union-saving formula could be agreed upon and enacted made Unionists hostage to the success of the Peace Conference. Should it deadlock or should Congress prove unreceptive to its suggestions, Unionists would find themselves in a difficult position.

Just as the Peace Conference met in Washington, the men organizing the Confederate States of America gathered in Montgomery, Alabama. Their audacious behavior increased pressures on the Peace Conference delegates to "speedily submit some plan satisfactory to the border states." If the Peace Conference failed to agree, one prominent Virginia Unionist warned, "despair will seize upon the public mind of this state," control of the Virginia convention would fall into the hands of "rash men," and "no one can say what will be the result." Rather than break up without any result, he concluded, "it would be far better to take something short of our utmost demands."[25]

On February 6, the Peace Conference established a committee including one member from each state represented to draft a proposal for consideration of the entire body. Headed by James Guthrie of Kentucky, head of the Louisville and Nashville Railroad and a prominent Democratic moderate with presidential ambitions, the committee met through February 14 and reported the next day. The Guthrie committee encountered predictable southern pleas for the Crittenden Compromise and Republican refusals to accept it. As the committee deliberated, evidence accumulated that it would recommend a compromise similar to the Border State plan. The Washington correspondent for the most influential newspaper in Guthrie's home state reported on February 13 that the Border State plan seemed "to find most favor" in the Peace Conference: "Southern men say of it that 'it is not quite what they would like to have, but still it would do,' and Northern men say 'it is a little farther than we desired to go, but we are willing to accept it.'" The reporter predicted that because the Border State plan was "less liable to objection from either section" than either the Corwin or Crittenden resolutions, it would "probably be the basis of any arrangement that shall be agreed upon by the Peace Conference, and will find ample support in Congress."[26]

The report of Guthrie's committee, as anticipated, differed significantly from Crittenden's original plan to protect slavery in territory "now held or hereafter acquired" south of 36° 30′. The committee instead proposed a constitutional amendment to forbid interference with the right to hold slaves in territory south of 36° 30′. As may be appreciated by reviewing Table 8-1, the new proposal closely resembled the Border State plan. Crittenden originally specified that territorial governments south of 36° 30′ must protect slavery, whereas the Peace Conference committee suggested that neither Congress nor a territorial government interfere with slaveowning south of that line. Although the distinction may appear trivial, abandoning protection of slavery was essential to enlist any Republican support. The full Peace Conference subsequently amended the committee report to apply specifically to present territory only and to require that half the senators from both the free states and the slave states approve any acquisition of new territory. Subsidiary features of the Peace Conference plan, all to be included in a single multisectioned constitutional amendment, prohibited Congress from interfering with slavery in the states, or in the District of Columbia without the consent of Maryland, and promised full compensation to slaveowners unable to recover fugitives because of "violence and intimidation." The proposed amendment could not be altered without the consent of all the states.[27]

By avoiding "protection" and "hereafter acquired," the Peace Conference plan eliminated the two features of the Crittenden Compromise that Republicans found most objectionable. But relatively few Republicans had accepted the similarly crafted Border State plan. Most Republicans still opposed any territorial compromise, and they were even less inclined to heed the Peace Conference idea that territorial compromise be engrafted into the Constitution, rather than legislated as in the Border State plan. But to sweeten the bitter pill of territorial compromise for Republicans, the Peace Conference did propose more specific safeguards against territorial expansion than the Border State plan.

Southern Unionists, though badly outnumbered, played a leading role in drafting the scheme just described and in getting it before the Peace Conference for consideration. Fourteen free states and only seven slave states were represented at the conference. The seceding slave states did not send delegates, nor did Arkansas. Moreover, only four of the seven slave states represented (Kentucky, Maryland, Delaware, and Tennessee) had delegations with dependable Unionist majorities. The other three (Virginia, North Carolina, and Missouri) sent delegations in which Southern Rights supporters outnumbered Unionists. But the Virginia election, held on the day the Peace Conference assembled and followed five days later by the even more decisive Union victory in Tennessee, validated Unionist claims to serve as honest brokers or mediators. "Now that our people have by their votes crushed the secessionists and their treasonable plots," one Virginia Unionist reasoned, Republicans would respond favorably to compromise overtures.[28]

Southern Unionist delegates at the Peace Conference consulted with political allies in their home states before accepting the compromise language. A group of Virginia Unionists in Richmond scrutinized the Peace Conference plan and found it generally acceptable. Robert Eden Scott of Fauquier County, who represented a substantial slaveowning area where secession sentiment had almost overwhelmed conditional Unionism, would have preferred "a more explicit *protection* of slavery." Others too regretted modification of the Crittenden Compromise. But leading Unionists judged that a majority at the Virginia convention would endorse the Peace Conference plan if it was "tendered quickly."[29]

Convinced that the agreement could satisfy their states, southern Unionists at the Peace Conference appealed for northern support. They urged northerners to recognize that the people of the South were "excited and anxious" and "apprehensive that their rights were in danger." Anyone who said there was "no danger" and no need to offer reassurances was "sadly mistaken." Secession could be stopped only if southerners were "calmed down and quieted." Virginia's George W. Summers thought it useless "to tell them that they have no cause for fear" or to "discuss now whether they are right or wrong." Disavowing any desire to use "threats and intimidation," the Unionists asked northerners to "consider our circumstances" and "deal with things as they are." "Will you not do something," pleaded Summers, "which will enable us to go back to our excited people and say to them, 'the North is treating us fairly.'"[30]

During debate about the key provision of the Peace Conference plan, Southern Rights delegates tried to incorporate Crittenden's original language about protection of slavery in the territories. It alone provided "terms of perfect equality with the North," and it alone would have any effect upon the lower South. "Unless you use language . . . which will satisfy the seceded States" and "induce them to return to the Union," warned Daniel M. Barringer of North Carolina, "your labors will have been in vain."[31]

In rebuttal, southern Unionists demonstrated their determination to close the gap separating them from moderate Republicans. They insisted that prohibiting federal interference with slavery in territory south of 36° 30′ would satisfy the upper South. To ask for more would risk breaking up the conference, securing no agreement, and plunging the country into a war for which "our soil is to be the battle ground." Former Governor Charles S. Morehead of Kentucky explained that he "voted for the Crittenden amendment in the committee" and thought "the North ought, in justice to us, to adopt that amendment." Recognizing, however, that it could not serve as a basis for agreement, Morehead decided to accept what he could get. Likewise, Robert L. Caruthers, the Tennessee state supreme court justice who came from Robert Hatton's hometown of Lebanon, acknowledged that "the report is not such as we wish it might be," but insisted that "if you will give us these propositions Tennessee will adopt them" and thereby "sink secession" beyond any hope of recovery. Virginia's William C. Rives and George W. Summers agreed that the committee report, "though not satisfactory to Virginia in all respects," would nevertheless win approval there and throughout the upper South. Summers protested against the "impracticable" idea of refusing to accept less than the Crittenden Compromise.[32]

Replying to Southern Rights delegates who insisted upon appeasing the seceded states, Unionists contended that an agreement satisfactory to the upper South would eventually force the lower South to return to the Union. Against mounting evidence to the contrary, Unionists hoped the new government taking shape in Montgomery would not endure. Thomas Ruffin of North Carolina thus predicted that enactment of the Peace Conference plan would "not only satisfy and quiet the loyal states of the South" but also "bring back the seven States which have gone out." Southern moderates and a united North thereupon defeated the Crittenden language, seventeen states to three, with only the three Southern Rights delegations in the minority.[33]

Peace Conference Republicans, however, had reservations about the emerging compromise. Samuel Ryan Curtis, a congressman from Iowa who played an important role on the Committee of Thirty-Three, thought slavery south of 36° 30′ could be "tolerated" but given no more encouragement than that. As noted in Table 8-1, the Missouri Compromise of 1820 simply prohibited slavery in territory north of 30° 30′. Nobody ever doubted that the Missouri Compromise tacitly sanctioned slavery in territory south of 36° 30′, or that the Northwest Ordinance of 1787 likewise allowed slavery in territory south of the Ohio River. Kentucky, Tennessee, Alabama, Mississippi, and Arkansas, carved from the regions in question, had all entered the Union as slave states. But the Missouri Compromise and the Northwest Ordinance, written so as not to offend northern and antislavery sensibilities, accepted slavery in southern territories by implication only. Curtis, unhappy with language that explicitly forbade federal interference with slavery south of 36° 30′, asked southerners to accept the precedents of 1787 and 1820.[34]

Southern Unionists rejected Curtis's overture, just as they had the Southern Rights effort to insert Crittenden's phraseology. Committee chairman James Guthrie of Kentucky explained that the change proposed by Curtis "would not be satisfactory either to the South or to myself." Unionists asked the northern delegates to "give us the report as it came from the Committee, without substantial alteration." Some Republicans heeded Unionist pleas to kill the Curtis substitute. Judge Stephen T. Logan, a moderate Republican from Springfield, Illinois, and former law partner of Lincoln's, argued that more explicit reassurances would enable southern Unionists to say they had been treated as equals, not inferiors. Five northern delegations joined the seven southern ones to preserve the formula agreed to by the committee.[35]

The majorities that apparently upheld the Peace Conference plan were, however, deceptive. Unfortunately for the plan's moderate supporters, only nine states had voted against both major amendments, and only eight stood ready to sustain the territorial compromise on a straight yes-or-no vote. The three Southern Rights delegations (Virginia, North Carolina, and Missouri) combined with eight nonconciliatory northern ones to defeat the Peace Conference territorial formula, eleven to eight. Only the four southern Unionist delegations (Delaware, Maryland, Kentucky, and Tennessee) and four moderate-dominated northern ones (Pennsylvania, New Jersey, Ohio, and Rhode Island) favored the compromise. The vote, "taken in the midst of much partially suppressed excitement" during which "the announcement of the vote of different states occasioned many sharp remarks of dissent or approval," occurred on Tuesday, February 26, less than a week before Lincoln's scheduled inauguration. It appeared that the Peace Conference had failed. Some southern Unionists reportedly wept after the decisive vote.

But when the delegates reassembled the next morning after a night of bargaining, moderates resurrected the defeated compromise. Illinois switched from opposing to favoring the territorial arrangement, Missouri abstained, and the previously anticompromise New York delegation deadlocked when one of its Republican members failed to attend. A precarious nine-to-eight majority thus approved the territorial compromise, with two states, Indiana and Kansas, abstaining on both the original vote and the reconsideration. All the subsidiary sections of the Peace Conference plan thereupon passed by more comfortable margins. The conference then adjourned without risking a vote on its entire handiwork.[36]

The Peace Conference resolutions passed on Wednesday, February 27. Its supporters hoped Congress would quickly vote, by the requisite two-thirds majority of each house, to send the proposed constitutional amendment to the states, three-fourths of which would need to ratify it before it could take effect. That objective was far more difficult and improbable than winning agreement from a bare majority of Peace Conference delegates, few of whom held elective office. The brute fact of the calendar further diminished any hope for rapid action. The session of Congress had to end, by law, no later than the coming Monday at noon. Nor could a special session of the next Congress be held soon because new House members in several states would not be elected before summer. So prospects for ratification of the proposed Peace Conference amendment were remote. But announcement of the agreement came in time to aid North Carolina Unionists, whose state voted on the convention issue the next day. It also enabled southern Unionists to go home and say that many moderate northerners favored tangible reassurances.[37]

Secessionists, on the other hand, characterized the Peace Conference plan as "a cowardly and ruinous submission" that planted "the brand of inferiority" on the slave states remaining in the Union. It was, declared the *Richmond Enquirer*, "a plan entirely similar in principle and practical application with, and only inferior in candor to, the Chicago platform." Aided by southern accomplices, Republicans had contrived a "cunning device" for "seducing Virginia to aid in coercion." The *Enquirer*, like other major secession newspapers, argued its case with rhetorical flourish: "We have asked for bread and they have given us a stone; for fish and they have given us a serpent; and yet there are men in Virginia, and unfortunately in the Convention, who will gladly accept the stone and serpent and return thanks to Black Republican bounty for providing so dainty a repast." Secession delegates at the Virginia convention, echoing the *Enquirer*, insisted that the Peace Conference plan was based on the principle of southern "inequality." One denounced it as "an attempt to cheat, swindle, and defraud the South," and another pronounced it "mean and despicable," suited only "to be scorned and spit upon."[38]

WITH submission of the Peace Conference plan to Congress on February 27 and North Carolina's election the next day, southern Unionists breathlessly concluded an intense two-month effort. They had good reason to feel a sense of accomplishment. They had set in motion forces that appeared likely to thwart secession and to alter dramatically the balance of political power in the upper South, so long as war could be prevented.

Unionists hoped, above all, that their efforts had impressed upon Republicans and the incoming Lincoln administration the need to adopt a southern policy based on conciliation and compromise. Confident that Republicans had the power to keep the upper South "firm" and to undermine secession in the deep South, Unionists challenged them to act in the same nationalistic spirit as had voters in the nonseceding slave states. By providing "honorable terms," Republicans could "quiet all apprehension."[39]

But thoughtful Unionists realized that the upper South remained in a precarious position. By February, it must be reemphasized, representatives from the seceding states had started to fashion an independent Confederate government. Many Unionists, such as North Carolina Congressman Zebulon B. Vance, realized that Republicans would not make concessions "sufficient to bring back the Gulf States" and that the latter were in no moood to return in any case. The question would then become, Vance surmised, whether "we could finally force the Gulf States back," or whether they would succeed in "dragooning" the states of the upper South out of the Union. He suspected that the Confederate government would, "if other means fail," seek "to get up a collision," knowing that war "would sweep away all vestige of reason among our people" and knowing too that the upper South could not "stand on the side of the North in that war." To prevent such a disaster, Vance would "give them the forts, repeal the Revenue and other laws and let them go in peace." But he did not envision permanent separation. He and other Unionists hoped that leaving the seceding states alone "to bear the burdens of a separate existence" would set in motion a counterrevolution in the deep South. Many people there "now disposed to *accept the revolution*" would, Unionists believed, eventually change their minds and seek to rejoin the Union. For peaceable reunion thus to come about, however, Republicans would have to continue the same passive policy they had criticized Buchanan for adopting. Persuading Republicans to do that would confront Unionists with their sternest test.

9

THE UNIONISTS, THE REPUBLICAN PARTY, AND PRESIDENT-ELECT LINCOLN

SOUTHERN Unionists clearly required Republican cooperation. They could not alone calm widespread southern fear and resentment. The Union could be peacefully restored, Unionists insisted, only if leading Republicans acted promptly to defuse the powder keg.

A conciliatory vanguard, led by New York Senator William H. Seward and his alter ego, Thurlow Weed, recognized the seriousness of the secession crisis during the month after Lincoln's election. But most Republicans initially opposed offering any concessions, thinking it outrageous to subvert the American political system into a "Mexicanized" one, in which those who failed at the polls might attempt forcible resistance.

As the secession epidemic spread, however, Republicans found it harder to ignore the danger. The deep South made the situation vastly more dangerous by precipitately abandoning the Union. The likelihood of war intensified efforts to find some peaceful accommodation. Conciliatory Republicans proved responsive to appeals from southern Unionists, who made it plain that they abhorred the secession furor and considered it based on a dangerous distortion of what the Republican party stood for. Here were southerners who approached Republicans not in a menacing spirit, but rather with urgent recommendations about steps needed to keep secession from spreading. Even though Republicans felt bruised by having to provide any reassurances, the alternatives appeared increasingly grim.

The balance of forces within the Republican party put the president-elect in a position to tip it in either direction. Though he took pains to conceal his role from public view, Abraham Lincoln worked hard to block any significant Republican concessions. His opposition prevented conciliatory Republicans from reaching an agreement with southern Unionists. Repeatedly, Lincoln cautioned his friends to oppose compromise "as with a chain of steel." Considering it "out of the question" to "shift the ground" upon which he had been elected, Lincoln vowed to remain "inflexible" on the territorial issue. As his March 4 inauguration approached, the Republican party remained bitterly divided between no-compromise Republicans, who wanted Lincoln to maintain his hard-line stance, and the conciliatory element, which pinned its hopes on changing his mind.[1]

THROUGHOUT the presidential campaign Republicans scoffed at the idea that southerners might disrupt the Union. Republicans persuaded themselves that threats of secession in the event of Lincoln's election were empty, designed to bluff and intimidate northern voters. Even after the election, most Republicans continued to underestimate the extent of southern disaffection. They belittled the secession movement as "bluff," "brag," or "bluster," likely to subside only if ignored. The few Republicans who thought otherwise needed somehow to convince other party members that secession gravely endangered the Union, that it posed an imminent danger of war, and that Republicans could not responsibly afford to remain aloof.[2]

Foremost among the minority of worried Republicans was William Henry Seward.[3] For more than two decades, since his election as governor of New York in 1838, Seward had occupied a prominent position in national politics. As U.S. senator from New York since 1849, Seward first led the antislavery Whigs and then became a power in the new Republican party. His greatest disappointment occurred in May 1860, when the Republican National Convention passed him over to nominate for president a more "available" candidate. Party activists concluded that Abraham Lincoln had greater appeal to conservative former Whigs and nativists in such pivotal states as Illinois, Indiana, and Pennsylvania, which were universally regarded as essential for a Republican victory. This political strategy succeeded brilliantly, although the secession crisis soon demonstrated, ironically, that Lincoln was a more doctrinaire Republican than Seward.

The New Yorker, grieved but still ambitious, campaigned loyally for Lincoln in 1860. He thereby made a strong bid for appointment as secretary of state, an honor often conferred on the most formidable figure in the president's party. Lincoln, recognizing Seward's stature, offered him the top cabinet post. Seward soon accepted, even though recognizing that he and Lincoln perceived the secession crisis differently. Public announcement in early January of his forthcoming role made Seward appear a spokesman for the new administration. His position obliged him to develop a Union-saving formula agreeable both to Lincoln and to southern Unionists.[4]

A slender man with a stooped appearance, Seward had a prominent nose, red hair turning gray, shaggy eyebrows, and alert eyes. Listeners considered his "hoarse voice" poorly suited for formal declamation, but his speeches read well and were widely reprinted. Seward's most valuable personal characteristics were his equanimity, "calmness of disposition," and "self-control." He shrugged off personal attacks and instead cultivated the broadest possible range of friendly social relations. Seward was a master conversationalist and raconteur, who sparkled especially with small groups over dinner. Never did he make harsher demands on himself than during the secession winter. A visitor in late February 1861 noted that Seward was "thin and worn and much aged since last Summer."[5]

For Seward as for almost all Republicans, the extent and seriousness of the secession crisis came as a rude shock. During the presidential election campaign, he had barnstormed across the North commending Lincoln as "a soldier on the side of freedom in the irrepressible conflict between freedom and slavery." Seward, who brushed aside complaints that such rhetoric would inflame the South, expected no southern resistance to Lincoln's election.[6] Sooner than other Republicans, however, Seward realized his miscalculation. Within two weeks after the election, while most of his party still imagined that the troubles would blow over, Seward traveled to Albany to consult about the crisis with his political manager and close friend, Thurlow Weed, editor of the *Albany Evening Journal*.

Thirty years earlier, during the Anti-Masonic excitement in upstate New York, young Weed and Seward discovered that they enjoyed each other's company and found their political talents complementary. The tall, soft-spoken Weed, with "deep eyes set under shaggy brows," was a gifted manager, content to work behind the scenes. Seward especially valued Weed's "cool, realistic judgment." The editor had an instinctive sense for public opinion and a unique ability to tailor winning political strategies. Weed, in turn, prized Seward's attributes for political leadership—"his magnetism, his grasp of fundamental issues, his ability to express his thoughts in clear and compelling fashion." Weed's biographer has written evocatively about the rapport that bond the two together. The "voluble, beak-nosed little fellow with the thin, beardless face" was always "brimful of energy and ideas. . . . Weed loved him with a deep and manly affection, and for over forty years his devotion to Seward's interests was a guiding factor in his life."[7]

Through Weed, Seward hinted that Republicans might have to

Thurlow Weed (Thurlow Weed Papers, Department of Rare Books and Special Collections, University of Rochester Library)

modify their key tenet of party orthodoxy—the restriction of slavery from all federal territories. The New Yorkers hoped to undercut a favorite secessionist argument. The refusal by Republicans to respect southern rights or equality in the territories meant, secessionists insisted, that Republicans would endanger slavery in the states where it already existed. Weed therefore asserted that Lincoln's election ended the territorial controversy. Never again as in Kansas would a territorial government seek to impose slavery on unwilling free-soil settlers. Thus the need for specific legislation prohibiting slavery from the territories no longer existed. Weed went even further. He thought Republicans should, in some way, acknowledge a southern right to take slaves to territories south of 36° 30′, though he regarded this right as meaningless because the climate and rainfall in the Southwest were entirely unsuited for plantation slavery. Weed first seriously floated this trial balloon in an editorial in his *Albany Evening Journal* on November 30.[8]

An outburst of disagreement greeted Weed's alleged "compromise" of party "principle." "Stiff-backed" Republicans pounced on the "weak-kneed" Weed, indignant about his "backing down." The hornet's nest of criticism prompted both Weed and Seward to deny that Weed's editorializing met with Seward's approval. The denials, however necessary to maintain Seward's power within the party, were specious. Weed and Seward were "never in closer communication" than during the secession winter; the two "were working together like the two hands of one man." Even though Weed made more explicit procompromise overtures, Seward ambiguously echoed Weed's view that Republicans no longer need worry about the spread of slavery to the territories. Seward's new assessment was "similar to that of the Northern Whig compromisers of 1850" and "entirely inconsistent with what he had been saying for the past twelve years."[9]

Seward deliberately adopted a deceptive facade. Assuming an air of jaunty optimism, he initially affected unconcern about secession. Thanks to Henry Adams, we have memorable glimpses of Seward, "chipper as a lark," telling hilarious stories, cheerfully swearing that "everything was going on admirably," and lightheartedly satirizing events in the South. His demeanor was thus in sharp contrast to that of most other public figures during the secession winter. Bewilderment, disbelief, fear, and despair became the order of the day in Washington as the crisis worsened. Because he believed most Republicans blind to impending disaster, Seward dared not reveal his forebodings. Forthright advocacy of a conciliatory strategy to arrest the secession movement and hold the upper South in the Union thus fell to Weed. Only gradually did astute young Henry Adams discern that

"Weed's motions, compromises and all, had been feelers on Seward's part."[10]

At first Seward and Weed had few important Republican allies. But Weed did gain welcome support from James E. Harvey, the influential columnist for the *Philadelphia North American*. The South was infested, Harvey complained, with "lying demagogues," who had "grossly misled" people and created false alarm about Republican intentions. Sooner than most Republicans, however, Harvey decided that his party had primary responsibility to alleviate the crisis. Even if Republicans were the victims of misrepresentation, he reasoned, they alone could set the record straight. The "brave and patriotic Union men of the South" needed assistance in trying to "arrest the secession stampede."[11]

Like Weed, Harvey thought Republicans should endorse a "seeming concession" on the territorial issue. Reestablishing the Missouri Compromise line would allow southerners the theoretical right to hold slaves in federal territory south of that line. The concession would be symbolic, designed simply to give southern Unionists "enough to stand upon to show their people that the charge[s] made against the Republicans by demagogues who desire disunion are unfounded, and that the rights of the South are not to be violated." Harvey felt that Republicans would not sacrifice "any real principle" because slaveowners did not actually desire to settle in the western territories anyway. "I am as much and more truly opposed to the extension of slavery," he explained to a friend, "than these infernal philanthropists, who are constantly shouting their faith at the corners."[12]

Conciliatory Republicans hoped to divide the South. They thought the secession movement could be sidetracked and eventually reversed if the upper South remained in the Union. They therefore urged northerners to recognize that "bold, true-hearted Union men" in the upper South were "standing firmly and nobly against the madness which seeks to involve the whole South in the treason of South Carolina." By distinguishing between the "true Patriots" trying to save the Union and the "traitors" trying to destroy it, Weed sought to challenge the idea that any Republican concession countenanced secession. Quite the reverse, Weed insisted: Republican inflexibility played into the hands of disunionists, who opposed any Union-saving compromise. But "in the border Slave States," Weed emphasized, "there are tens of thousands of anxious, devoted Union men who ask only that we should throw them a plank which promises a chance of safety."[13]

IN searching for a suitable "plank," Seward privately recommended that Lincoln appoint to his cabinet two or more Unionists from the upper South who had no previous ties to the Republican party. Without specifically compromising on any issue, Lincoln could thereby indicate his readiness to treat the South fairly. Seward made the suggestion after Lincoln had already offered him appointment as secretary of state, thus challenging him to indicate what authority Seward might wield in the new administration. If Lincoln agreed to appoint southern Unionists to the cabinet, Seward could expect to play an influential role in formulating a conciliatory policy toward the South.[14]

Unwilling to fuel public curiosity by conferring personally with Lincoln, Seward arranged for his friend Weed to visit Springfield as an intermediary. The New Yorkers deliberately tried to provoke a discussion of southern policy. Just before he headed west, Weed printed the most procompromise editorial he had yet written, arguing that the Republican party should make concessions to secure an honorable settlement of the crisis. Confident that Republican victory in the presidential election assured against further efforts to spread slavery to the territories, Weed reasoned that stubborn opposition to all compromise served neither his party's nor the national interest. If war nevertheless occurred, Republicans should be able to say that "we have done our duty in endeavoring to preserve peace."[15]

According to Weed's subsequent recollection, Lincoln spoke guardedly about Weed's "heavy broadside," stating that "he hoped to find my apprehensions unfounded." Reluctant to discuss southern policy, Lincoln instead turned the conversation to "cabinet-making." But Weed insisted the two questions were related. Picking up on the idea posed in Seward's letter, Weed urged Lincoln to appoint at least two non-Republican Unionists from the upper South. He mentioned four names: two former congressmen, John Minor Botts of Virginia and Balie Peyton of Tennessee, and two current congressmen, Henry Winter Davis of Maryland and John A. Gilmer of North Carolina. All four were strong Unionists with Whig antecedents.[16]

The idea of conciliating the South by appointing southerners to the cabinet had already become the subject of widespread newspaper speculation. Several of Lincoln's correspondents also raised the idea, but Lincoln himself had misgivings. He did not think it prudent to appoint cabinet members from states that might yet secede, nor did he consider it likely that any prominent non-Republican southerner would accept such an offer. But Weed persisted. He urged especially the appointment of at least one person from a slave state beyond the five that bordered on the free states. Finally, according to Weed, "Mr. Lincoln yielded so far as to say that he would write a letter to the Hon. John A. Gilmer, then a member of Congress from North Carolina, briefly stating his views of the duty of the government in reference to important questions then pending, and inviting him, if those views met his approval, to accept a seat in the cabinet." Weed himself was "authorized to see Mr. Gilmer" to discuss the possible appointment.[17]

Gilmer represented a somewhat atypical southern district. Guilford and adjacent counties of the North Carolina piedmont had long proven more hospitable to modest landownings and yeoman farmers than to plantation slavery. A substantial number of Quakers in the region opposed slavery on principle. During the 1840s and 1850s, successful coal-mining operations began in the area. The improvement of water transportation on the Deep River and the construction of the North Carolina Railroad also stimulated hopes for economic diversification and industrial development. North Carolina had long experienced internal tensions because the western part of the state felt slighted by and underrepresented in the eastern-dominated government. First the Federalists and later the Whigs had taken advantage of this cleavage to build a base of support in the west. Economic aspirations, ethnoreligious factors, and geographic circumstances thus all intersected to make the Guilford County area emphatically Whiggish. Efforts to unite voters behind the Democratic party on a strict Southern Rights platform made no headway here. Memories of local valor and sacrifice in the battle of Guilford Courthouse during the Revolution still nourished an intense nationalism and love of the Union.[18]

Gilmer himself, a "bluff, frank and cordial" man of medium height and powerful physique, had deep roots in the Greensboro region. His Scotch-Irish family had lived in the area since before the Revolution. Both his grandfathers had fought at Guilford Courthouse. Born during Jefferson's presidency, in 1805, Gilmer was named for the Virginian's deposed predecessor and rival, John Adams. His parents thereby gave their son an unmistakable identification with the Federalist loyalties of the region. The oldest of twelve children, Gilmer "lived the life of a country boy" until his late teens. He soon emerged as a prototype of the self-made man. After studying with the eminent Greensboro judge and legal scholar Archibald D. Murphey, Gilmer opened his own practice and became by all accounts a hardworking and successful lawyer. An advantageous marriage to the daughter of a prominent local Presbyterian minister further secured Gilmer's rising status. By 1850 he had become wealthy, partly through land and slaves inherited by his wife, partly through successful investments in railroad building and coal mining, and partly through his extensive caseload on the legal circuit, where his talents and modest fees had produced a booming and "very lucrative" business.[19]

Gilmer's successful legal career led him into politics. Considered "a man of influence in all the counties where he practised," Gilmer cultivated a common touch and gained "a powerful hold on the popular affection." Elected as a Whig to the state assembly in 1846 and soon to the state senate, he vigorously championed internal improvements, tried to secure more equitable representation for western North Carolina, and vehemently opposed the disunionism of extreme Southern Rights advocates in the 1850 crisis. Gilmer ran an unsuccessful race for governor in 1856 as the candidate of the American party.

His political career assumed a new dimension a year later, when Gilmer won a seat in Congress. He there joined the handful of southern Whigs who had survived the collapse of their national party in the 1850s. When the Whiggish Opposition in the upper South made substantial gains in the 1859 congressional elections, notably in Kentucky, Tennessee, and North Carolina, Gilmer became a leader among the two dozen southern Whigs or "South Americans" in the House of Representatives. He gained a degree of national visibility when promoted unsuccessfully by his party for Speaker.

If any possibility ever existed for a peaceful transition from the Old South to the New, Gilmer had plausible credentials to play a conspicuous role. Though a large slaveowner, he was no narrow-minded champion of plantation society. When Gilmer and his Whiggish friends thought about the future, they envisioned railroads, coal mines, manufacturing, and economic diversification. Their ideas about political economy derived from Henry Carey's liberal economic nationalism rather than the crabbed sectionalism of John C. Calhoun. They aspired to develop North Carolina along the lines of Pennsylvania rather than neighboring South Carolina.[20] Chafing impatiently at extremism in defense of the old order, they looked forward to the day when sensible men North and South would rescue political affairs from the agitators and fanatics who plagued both sections. They indiscriminately abhorred abolitionists and secessionists, believed that a majority of Americans did likewise, and hoped that moderates from all parts of the country could make common cause. They knew of no irrepressible conflict.

Lincoln, although still worried about the effects of appointing someone "who opposed us in the election," evidently decided he could safely afford to include one southern Unionist who had "a *living* position in the South." Of the four candidates proposed by Weed, only Gilmer came from farther South than a border state and currently held elective office. His main liability was widely shared among Whig Unionists in the upper South: he had affiliated with the American party since the mid-1850s. Lincoln realized that Gilmer's appointment would thus offend "our German friends" but assumed that "we could appease them." But Gilmer's record had several features to commend him to Lincoln's attention. He was among the few southerners who had voted with the bloc of Republicans and Douglas Democrats to thwart the Buchanan administration's plan to admit Kansas as a slave state in 1858 under the Lecompton constitution. Gilmer also had been appointed chairman of the Committee on Elections by the quasi-Republican House leadership in 1860. And just a week before Weed arrived in Springfield, Lincoln received an earnest letter from Gilmer, written on behalf of the beleaguered southern Unionists in Congress.[21]

Gilmer suggested that Lincoln issue a public reassurance about his conservative intentions. He contended that "a clear and definite exposition" of the president-elect's views would alleviate a great deal of "misunderstanding." Warning that "apprehensions of real danger and harm to them and their peculiar institution" had "seized the people of my section," Gilmer urged Lincoln to disavow any intention of interfering with slavery where it already existed. He also suggested delicately that "a generous and patriotic yielding on the part of your section" would "settle and quiet the disturbing question of slavery in the Territories."[22]

The idea that Lincoln should make a statement to reassure the South found wide favor in November and December. A number of his correspondents had broached the idea to Lincoln even before the election, and many southern Unionists and northern moderates grasped at it once serious troubles developed in the South. For example, one group appealed to Lincoln to recognize that southern demagogues "had poisoned the minds of the masses in regard to yourself and the designs of the Republican Party." Even if it was too late to calm the cotton states, a statement from Lincoln could "have a powerful effect in the Northern slave states, and might arrest the epidemic now so fearfully and rapidly spreading."[23]

But Lincoln had a fatalistic sense that any reassurances from him "would do no good" and might do "positive harm." Secessionists, thinking a new statement evidence of his "timidity," would "clamor all the louder." In a series of "private and confidential" letters to prominent individuals who raised the idea, Lincoln pointed out that his conservative sentiments already were "in print, and open to all who will read." Even moderate southerners had paid no attention, he complained, and instead continued to depict him as "the worst man living." Why, Lincoln asked, should he expect "that any additional production of mine would meet a better fate?"[24]

A private letter sent to his old Whig friend Alexander Stephens of Georgia poignantly illustrated the distance between Lincoln and southern Unionists. "Do the people of the South," Lincoln inquired, "really entertain fears that a Republican administration would, *directly*, or *indirectly*, interfere with their slaves, or with them, about their slaves? If they do, I wish to assure you, as once a friend, and still, I hope, not an enemy, that there is no cause for such fears. The South would be in no more danger in this respect, than it was in the days of Washington. I suppose, however, this does not meet the case. You think slavery is *right* and ought to be extended; while we think it is *wrong* and ought to be restricted. That I suppose is the rub. It certainly is the only substantial difference between us."[25]

By the time Gilmer heard from Lincoln, he had returned home to North Carolina for the Christmas recess. Then, rather than what he hoped would be a conciliatory public letter to quiet the sectional crisis, Gilmer received a cryptic and unexpected invitation to visit Springfield. Gilmer had no reason, as yet, to believe that Lincoln had other purposes than to discuss southern policy. But why a face-to-face meeting? Unless managed secretly, a trip to Springfield would create problems for any southern politician. Gilmer instead promptly dispatched a torrent of fresh advice, pleading with the president-elect to recognize that excitement was spreading "with fearful rapidity through all the slave states." He thought Georgia, Florida, Alabama, and Mississippi were sure to join South Carolina in the "stampede" to get out of the Union. But Lincoln might still confine the secession contagion to the five most extreme states of the deep South by taking a flexible position on the territorial issue and by endorsing a constitutional amendment reaffirming the safety of slavery in the states.[26]

Gilmer penned his earnest appeal to Lincoln before discovering why he had been invited to Springfield.[27] Only upon his return to Washington, probably on January 1 or 2, did Gilmer receive from Seward the unexpected news of his prospective appointment to the cabinet. A few days later Thurlow Weed arrived in Washington to twist the North Carolinian's arm. Gilmer must have found the offer highly perplexing. Lincoln had sent a definite signal that he wanted to aid southern Unionists. But Gilmer had just returned from the superheated South and believed that the appointment by itself would accomplish little. The new administration needed first to provide more specific indications of its conservative character. Until a more substantial segment of southern opinion became persuaded that a Republican president did not endanger the South, any individual southerner who accepted a cabinet position would squander his political influence and destroy his political base. Gilmer explained to Weed that he could not risk a visit to Springfield to see Lincoln.[28]

Despite his great personal trepidation, Gilmer recognized the need to proceed carefully. Without actually rejecting the appointment, he suggested to Seward two other possible nominees, Meredith Gentry of Tennessee and Randall Hunt of Louisiana, neither of whom then held elective office. Lincoln presently informed Seward that Gilmer remained the preferred candidate. Seward, hopeful that Gilmer "would not decline," doubtless renewed his solicitation of the reluctant North Carolinian. Gilmer meanwhile wrote confidentially to friends in North Carolina and consulted with other southern Unionists in Congress. At least some thought Gilmer should consider Lincoln's overture. His predecessor in Congress, Edwin G. Reade, an intense Unionist, "strongly urged Mr. Gilmer to accept."[29]

Within days after insiders would have heard about the prospective Gilmer appointment, Maryland Congressman Henry Winter Davis endorsed the idea in a letter to his cousin David Davis, one of Lincoln's closer Illinois advisers. North Carolina and "her old territory Tennessee" were "the limits of loyalty for the present," Davis warned. Lincoln could avert civil war "*only* by getting the confidence and support" of those two crucially situated states. To do that, he needed to act with "all possible forbearance" and to appoint to the cabinet a man from North Carolina "who has the ear and confidence of her people." Davis, whose congressional responsibilities made him well informed about the characters and capabilities of his colleagues among the southern Opposition, thought the choice lay between Gilmer and former Whig Senator George E. Badger. Though Badger was better known nationally and more experienced, Davis noted that Gilmer was "a man of great personal popularity and ability" and a "mainstay" among Union supporters in North Carolina. Gilmer's greatest advantage over Badger, Davis judged, was his currently active political involvement, making him "freshest from the people." Realizing that the upper South was currently "very much excited" but looking boldly ahead to the time when it might be reconciled to supporting at least the threat of armed force against the deep South, Davis pointedly defended the appointment of Badger or Gilmer as essential "to give the administration any hope of using North Carolina as a base of operations and a source of supplies and men." He concluded his important letter with an unusually clearheaded piece of advice: "You may think it very impertinent of me to write in this way—but it is a matter of life or death. Mr. Lincoln's administration is to be summed up in history in the suppression of the Southern rebellion. He may dismiss *every* political question he has been discussing for years and open the history of revolts and their suppression for his daily reading."[30] Gilmer and most other southern Unionists would, of course, have blanched at Davis's readiness to threaten the seceding states with armed force. But they surely would have agreed that Lincoln had conferred a heavy responsibility on Gilmer, involving issues of great magnitude.

The cabinet offer to Gilmer was, from its inception, thoroughly enmeshed in a titanic struggle for domination of the Republican party. Although substantially hidden from public view, the contest involved the highest stakes and was therefore waged with appropriate ferocity. To a certain extent, the controversy involved naked power considerations. Seward and Weed wanted a compatible, perhaps compliant, cabinet composed primarily of former Whigs. A coalition of former Democrats, however, led by former Ohio Governor Salmon P. Chase and the Francis P. Blair family, plus a vocal faction of New York "Barnburners" (former Democrats who originally broke with their party in 1848 to support the Free Soil party), demanded strict limits on Seward's influence. The alignment of two key participants in the struggle, Horace Greeley and Simon Cameron, resulted from factors other than previous party ties. Greeley, editor of the *New York Tribune* and apostle of Republicanism to hundreds of thousands of readers, had once collaborated with Weed and Seward to build the New York Whig party. But a bitter quarrel with his former allies, which culminated in Greeley's efforts to sabotage Seward's presidential candidacy and in Weed's reciprocal success in preventing Greeley from filling the Senate seat Seward vacated to join Lincoln's cabinet, placed the New York editor prominently in the Chase-Blair camp. Senator Cameron, political boss of Pennsylvania and reputed spoilsman, had nominal Democratic antecedents, but his campaign to secure the treasury portfolio horrified the moralistic Chase-Blair-Greeley faction, not least because Chase himself coveted the same honor (Montgomery Blair, the ambitious son of Francis P. Blair, Sr., also had hopes for a cabinet appointment). Seward, Weed, and Cameron, finding themselves under attack from a common enemy, labored together to promote Cameron's cabinet aspirations and to diminish the prospects for Chase and Montgomery Blair. The latter and their allies directed intense fire at the more vulnerable Pennsylvanian but hoped that a successful assault on Cameron might, in addition, create such a rift between Lincoln and Seward as to force the New Yorker out of the cabinet too.[31]

By mid-January, the battle lines had formed. The competing claims of Chase and Cameron to the Treasury Department gave the contest a focus, rather like a position in chess when all the powerful pieces take aim at one square. But much more than the treasury post was at stake. The contestants acted as if Lincoln's nomination and election had only delayed the real struggle for ascendancy within the party. Rejecting Lincoln's efforts to mediate, the warring factions acted as if one or the other must dominate.[32]

Southern policy, the inexorable challenge confronting the Lincoln administration, figured prominently in the intraparty conflict. Despite his clever dissimulation and refusal to take any public stance inconsistent with Republican orthodoxy, Seward was emerging as the most eminent proponent of a conciliatory approach within the party. This circumstance added to the intensity of the struggle between the Seward forces and the Blair-Chase-Greeley faction. Republicans identified with Seward and Weed thought the secession crisis could be resolved only with the support of upper South Unionists. Conciliatory Republicans searched for the elusive formula acceptable both to southern Unionists and the Republican rank and file. Greeley, by contrast, emblazoned the masthead of the *Tribune* with the slogan: "NO COMPROMISE! NO CONCESSIONS TO TRAITORS!" and launched an editorial vendetta against his former crony, Weed. The Blair family, meanwhile, insisted that the federal government should respond to the crisis of 1860–61 just as it had done in 1832–33, when South Carolina tried to nullify the tariff. A stern Jacksonian threat to use armed force would, the Blairs argued, overawe the traitors and bring the South to its senses. Francis P. Blair, Sr., urged the free states to "crush out in embryo" the "military tyranny" launched by secessionist conspirators.[33]

John A. Gilmer's willingness to take a cabinet seat became doubly important for Seward's conciliatory faction because Lincoln displayed little interest in appointing any other southern non-Republican. Seward therefore engaged in gentle persuasion and allowed the North Carolinian time to await developments. "I still think well and have hopes of Gilmer," he wrote to Lincoln in mid-January. Lincoln reaffirmed Seward's authorization to pursue the matter and expressed the hope that "Mr. Gilmer will, on a fair understanding with us, consent to take a place in the Cabinet." In early February, Lincoln mentioned to a visitor his inclination "to select a cabinet officer from North Carolina" and specified that Gilmer had been "recommended." Again, later in February, when urged by a different visitor to appoint a southern Republican to the cabinet, Lincoln demurred and expressed his preference for a moderate non-Republican such as Gilmer. For two months, the job could have been Gilmer's for the asking.[34]

If the reluctant Gilmer would not serve, Lincoln had a substitute in mind. Thurlow Weed discovered during his Springfield visit that Gilmer stood in the way of Montgomery Blair, the Maryland Republican and son of Andrew Jackson's close friend, who was eager for a cabinet appointment. After Lincoln hinted that he intended to appoint Blair, Weed remonstrated sarcastically, "Has he been suggested by any one except his father, Francis P. Blair, Sr.?" Lincoln subsequently proposed, according to Weed's recollection, that "if Mr. Gilmer should come in," Blair "would be excluded." A cabinet seat was thus reserved, paradoxically, either for Gilmer or for one of the most outspoken opponents of a conciliatory southern policy. Seward and Weed doubtless made much of this curious circumstance in trying to overcome Gilmer's hesitancy.[35]

As the secession movement intensified, Republicans debated what to do. A howl of protest against any compromise echoed through Free Soil strongholds in the North where the Republican party was strongest. For example, Julian M. Sturtevant, president of Illinois College, told Illinois Senator Lyman Trumbull that "to concede *anything at all* is to concede principle." Sturtevant predicted that "the solid phalanx of thoughtful, conscientious, earnest, religious men who form the backbone of the Republican party, will never follow Mr. Seward nor any other man in the direction in which he seems to be leading. We want the Constitution as it is, the Union as the Fathers framed it, and the Chicago Platform. And we will support no man and no party that surrenders these or any portion of them." Constituents from Bloomington, Illinois, also entreated Trumbull to stand firm: "Compromise and our party is ruined. Sustain our constitution and enforce the laws, and a glorious future awaits us. . . . Never, never entangle us with the yoke of bondage that would be brought upon us by compromises and amendments. Give us a monarchy, make us subjects to the British crown, give us anything sooner than make us the servile dupes of a deluded slave oligarchy."[36]

Nor did hard-line Republicans shrink from the prospect of war. The people "are ready for coercion," Carl Schurz informed Lincoln after touring upstate New York and New England. The "rank and file," in Schurz's view, were "far ahead of their leaders." Lincoln's law partner, William Herndon, also itched for a fight. "Cowardly compromises" were wrong, he insisted. The time had come for a showdown between liberty and slavery: "Let the one or the other now die." Herndon's motto was "no flinching, no dodging, no backing down." He promised to "help tear down" the Republican party and "erect another in its stead" if the "cowards and timid men" managed to "patch up some kind of momentary truce." A Massachusetts Republican agreed, believing that "a time must *sometime* come when the *strength* of Freedom and slavery must be tried, and the almost universal consent and, with many, the ardent desire, is that that trial may come *now*. . . . A short campaign, bloody though it may be, will settle the whole matter." A Chicagoan likewise observed that "the Secessionists are for fight, and I believe I do not err when I say that 99/100 of all the Republicans in this section and a large portion of the Democrats are for giving them what they want and plenty of it." Ardent young Republicans in Massachusetts warned: "Let them try to prevent the inauguration of Lincoln and we will see how long slavery will exist *anywhere*."[37]

Other hard-line Republicans still expressed confidence that the furor would blow over if no effort was made to appease it. James Shepherd Pike, influential correspondent for the *New York Tribune*, argued that any conciliatory initiative would be humiliating and counterproductive. The "wild delerium of the secession epidemic" could not be "propitiated by ordinary methods," he insisted. With people acting "so contrary to every dictate of self-interest and sound judgment," no reasonable approach would work. Secessionists themselves would have to recognize "the dangers and disasters of revolution" and awaken "to save themselves from utter ruin." Thus, Pike concluded, "the Republicans and the Free States are entire masters of the situation if they but stand firm. A fire that kindles quick goes out quick." Many Republican politicians shared Pike's perspective. Salmon P. Chase considered "*all propositions* for compromise" to be "ill timed and ill advised. They weaken instead of strengthening the Union men in the South." Charles Sumner opposed "any offer now, even of a peppercorn. . . . We must stand firm."[38]

Conciliatory Republicans agreed that secession was pathological but argued that their party should help find an antidote. "Insanity is sweeping over the whole South like a dreadful epidemic, and is still on the increase," observed John D. Defrees, chairman of the Indiana State Republican Committee. Writing to Lincoln while on an early January visit to Washington, Defrees noted that Republicans in Congress were divided between those who would "stand firm" and "yield not an inch" and those who favored "the semblance of a compromise." Indicating his own agreement with the latter, Defrees explained to Lincoln that "those in favor of some kind of compromise say that they would not do it to satisfy the extremists of the South—but the real Union men of that part of the country." Another prominent Indiana Republican, Richard W. Thompson, presented Lincoln with a similar analysis. Republicans were "mistaken," he concluded, in thinking "that all the threats of the South are mere *bluster*." Reckless politicians, who had created widespread popular fear in the South, could no longer control the situation. It did Republicans no good, Thompson reasoned, to stand aloof and point the finger of blame at southern politicians, much as they deserved it. Instead, Republicans had a paramount interest in alleviating the popular frenzy. By supporting a compromise, Republicans would sacrifice no "principle" but would instead stem the "tide of secession" before it engulfed the upper South. Only in that way could civil war be averted and a Union preserved for Lincoln to govern.[39]

An anonymous Illinois Republican, writing in the *National Intelligencer*, asked Republican members of Congress not to follow blindly the many letters from their constituents "urging you to make no concessions." He too would have written "another letter of this character" had he not visited Washington and become more broadly informed about the crisis. Because of what he learned there, he cautioned against "attempting to enforce our principles at this time." He reasoned that "leading politicians of the South, who knew better, but who had an end to gain by it, represented the Republican party to be a band of 'Abolitionists,' whose object was to abolish slavery in the South." This "false and inflammatory" characterization had produced unexpected consequences: "The people have become maddened and cannot be reasoned with." Even the leaders who had instigated the "phrenzy" or "tornado" could no longer control it. Only if Republicans themselves made "concessions" to show that they had been misrepresented and intended the South no wrong would southern Unionists be able to counteract the mass delusion and keep secession from growing to uncontrollable proportions. The conciliatory Illinois Republican, thus believing the choice lay between modification of his party's "dogma" regarding slavery in the territories and "disruption of the Union," urged Republicans to overcome "the pride of consistency." For him, the choice was clear: "I love my party but I love my country more."[40]

The Illinois writer used the familiar analogy of an ungraded school to demonstrate his point. South Carolina had "caused a great deal of trouble in the school and richly deserved to be reprimanded." The average Republican understandably favored the traditional remedy for such insubordination. The contributor to the *National Intelligencer* warned, however, that any use of force would make a bad situation far worse. Although "stout lads" such as Virginia, Kentucky, and Tennessee "admit South Carolina is in the wrong," a "feeling of gallantry" led them "to protect her from merited chastisement." The teacher, poor "Uncle Sam," thus confronted a class that was "all in a hubbub." Although he "might be able to whip them all at once, it would probably be a larger job than he would like to engage in, as long as it can be avoided." The Illinois Republican thus asked whether it would not be wise "to get these big lads out of the way first, if by any conciliatory means it can be done?"

Conciliatory Republicans struggled during January and February to formulate more acceptable compromise proposals than Crittenden's. They played key roles on both the Committee of Thirty-Three and the ad hoc border state committee. The territorial section of the Border State plan—prohibiting slavery in western territory north of 36° 30′ and prohibiting interference with it south of that line—was officially introduced by Republican James R. Hale of Pennsylvania. Allied with Hale on the committee was John T. Nixon of New Jersey, another of the conservative Whig-Republicans who had tried to play a balancing role in the Speakership fight the year before.

Also assisting behind the scenes was Thurlow Weed, who proceeded to Washington in early January to supervise several delicate matters. In addition to consulting with Seward and Gilmer, Weed encouraged Leonard Swett, a political ally of Lincoln's from Illinois, to exert a conciliatory influence on the president-elect. In a letter to Lincoln that Weed reportedly prepared for Swett, affairs in Washington were described as "steadily progressing from bad to worse" because Republicans opposed all suggested compromises. Such an approach, Weed suggested through Swett, played into the hands of secessionists and baffled the "conservative men" from the upper South who were trying desperately to prevent secession from spreading to their states. The true southern Unionists believed that "something must be done or they will be overwhelmed." Weed tried to assume a low profile, but other newspapers reported his procompromise efforts. Soon Weed's own *Albany Evening Journal* commended the Border State plan for including several "entirely acceptable" features and providing a reasonable basis from which to negotiate an "ultimate agreement."[41]

Conciliatory Republicans who favored the Border State plan had difficulty winning support for the measure within their party. Influential John Sherman of Ohio, a member of the border state committee, rejected the package because the committee would not require a two-thirds majority of both House and Senate to annex new territory. Despite support from some southern Unionists, Sherman's idea encountered Democratic opposition. A secret House Republican caucus on Saturday, January 5, afforded doctrinaire Republicans such as Thaddeus Stevens of Pennsylvania and Owen Lovejoy of Illinois an opportunity to subject the Border State plan to withering fire. The caucus rejected all compromise.[42]

The next Monday, January 7, a version of the Border State plan unexpectedly came up for a procedural vote in the House. Tennessee Unionist Emerson Etheridge, acting on his own initiative, drafted a series of constitutional amendments that combined Hale's territorial measure with Sherman's strictures against new territory (see Table 8-1). Etheridge's request to suspend the rules so that his amendments could be introduced required a two-thirds vote and thus failed when it received only a bare majority, eighty-three to seventy-eight. Almost all those opposing it were Republicans. Only the handful of Middle Atlantic Whig-Republicans supported the Etheridge-Hale proposal. Three of the five Republicans on the border state committee, including Sherman, voted against it. Immediately the telegraph wires south crackled with the news: "Republicans in House to-day refused to consider Etheridge's compromise, which is Crittenden's considerably weakened." The "last hope" of compromise was thus "extinguished," secessionists asserted.[43]

Conciliatory Republicans also received a sharp rebuff from Lincoln. Congressman Hale had written to the president-elect to urge aid for the "true and loyal men" of the South in their struggle "against demagogues and traitors who have inflamed the apprehensions of the people almost to madness." But uncompromising Republicans appealed to Lincoln to stand firm and prevent any concessions. Congressman Elihu B. Washburne of Illinois, a political ally of Lincoln's, informed him on January 7 that "great commotion and excitement exist to-day in our ranks in regard to a *compromise* that is supposed to be hatching by the Weed-Seward dynasty. Weed is here and one great object now is to obtain your acquiescence in the scheme to sell out and degrade the republicans." Washburne warned Lincoln that Illinoisan Leonard Swett was "acting under the direction of Weed," seeking Lincoln's support for a compromise. "No word of caution from me to you can be necessary," Washburne concluded. "If you waver, *our party has gone*." Lincoln did exactly as Washburne wished. He sent a stern "confidential" letter to Hale, protesting against any "surrender to those we have beaten." It would be "the end of us"—that is, the Republican party—"and of the government," Lincoln vowed, if southern troublemakers managed to "extort" a compromise.[44]

LINCOLN could not so easily reject the compromise proposal framed by the House Committee of Thirty-Three, which attracted substantial Republican support because it deftly sidestepped the territorial question. Admitting territory south of 36° 30′ into the Union as a state would have extinguished the territorial status of all regions claimed by the South in the Crittenden or Border State plans.

Ohio Republican Thomas Corwin guided the fractious House Committee of Thirty-Three. Corwin, a prominent former Whig, had served in both houses of Congress, as governor of Ohio, and as secretary of the treasury in the Fillmore administration. He had only reluctantly abandoned his Whig affiliation and was regarded as one of the more conservative Republicans. Tall, heavy-set, and forceful, the sixty-seven-year-old Corwin was well suited by background and temperament to head the House Committee of Thirty-Three. His experience, maturity, and national outlook gave him a perceptive grasp of the deepening crisis.

Corwin noted to Lincoln on December 24 that the situation had become extremely dangerous. "There is an epidemic [of] insanity raging all over this country," Corwin grumbled, "and I am not sure we can prevent the lunatics from destroying each other." He promised that his committee would not "make slavery the normal condition of all territory *to be conquered*." But he suggested a willingness to consider lesser compromise measures such as bringing all western territories into the Union as states, thereby ending the controversy.[45]

Corwin and Massachusetts Congressman Charles Francis Adams devised a proposal with two major points: first, a constitutional amendment affirming the safety of slavery in the states, as already proposed by Seward to the Senate Committee of Thirteen, and second, admission of the New Mexico territory into the Union as a state, a plan championed by Maryland's Henry Winter Davis. Republicans on the Committee of Thirty-Three urged Adams to present the package to the entire committee. He agreed but confessed in his diary that he did so at "great hazard" to himself.[46]

Thus did the procompromise faction of the Republican party ensnare (or so it seemed to the hard-liners) the heir to the most prestigious pedigree in American politics. Son of John Quincy Adams, who spent the last years of his life making antislavery a political force, Charles Francis Adams represented the most intensely Republican state in the Union. A moralistic opponent of slavery, he had been

Martin Van Buren's vice-presidential running mate on the Free Soil ticket in 1848. His implausible role during the secession crisis resulted from several influences, the most important of which was a cordial personal relationship between William H. Seward and the entire Adams family. Many evenings, even amid the growing chaos of the secession winter, Seward could be found visiting the Adams household to enjoy a relaxing hand of whist. Henry Adams left indelible vignettes of Seward, comfortably situated with boots off and cigar lit, fortified with good wine, patting Abigail Adams on the head "like a little girl." Similar behavior by any other visitor "would make our dear mother furious," Henry Adams wrote to his brother, but Seward was "so hopelessly lawless that she submits and feels rather flattered, I think." Seward hypnotized the Adamses with "his grand, broad ideas that would inspire a cow with statesmanship if she understood our language."[47]

Adams and the Republicans on the Committee of Thirty-Three announced that their willingness to accept the compromise package depended on its winning southern support. Without that, they would vote to report to the House that the Committee of Thirty-Three could not agree. Some southern Unionists did give the Adams-Corwin proposal serious consideration. John A. Gilmer described its provisions to William A. Graham, prominent North Carolina Whig and 1852 vice-presidential nominee, and asked "whether we should accept of these now, and advise the South to remain in the Union?" But as explained in the previous chapter, most southern Unionists thought Republicans should make an explicit compromise on the territorial issue. The Unionists thereupon tried with little success to interest Repubicans in the Border State plan. Adams and most other House Republicans, hoping to avoid a territorial compromise and suspicious that the border state committee had been created to upstage the Committee of Thirty-Three, feared that any restoration of the Missouri line would become a means for protecting slavery in present and future territory south of 36° 30′.[48]

An impasse thus developed between conciliatory House Republicans, most of whom believed the Adams-Corwin package the most they could support, and southern Unionists, whose minimal terms were encompassed in the Border State plan, and many of whom still insisted they were doomed without prompt Republican acceptance of the Crittenden Compromise. Few Republicans, however, would support the Border State plan, and many still opposed even so mild a compromise as the Adams-Corwin proposal. They contended that its passage would exhibit irresolution toward secession without in any way stopping it.

These foreboding developments, coinciding with the war scare of early and middle January and the continued spread of secession across the South, placed Seward in a miserable position. To counteract the not erroneous impression that an impasse had developed, he announced that he would speak in the Senate on January 12. For several days Washington buzzed with anticipation. Seward, regarded as the spokesman for the new administration, was expected to suggest a way out of the maze.

In his speech, Seward urged a moratorium on discussion of polarizing issues—slavery in the territories, the right of secession, and coercion. He offered instead a broad statement about the benefits of the Union and the necessity of its preservation. He reminded southerners that their rights within the Union were secure, even though outright abolition was the tendency of the age elsewhere in the world. Disunion, he warned, would surely lead to war and to calamities that would make any presently perceived difficulties trivial by comparison. Seward offered several specific suggestions for promoting restoration of the Union. The centerpiece of his plan was the constitutional amendment specifically protecting slavery in the states, followed by a constitutional convention "one, two, or three years hence," if, on sober second thought, additional constitutional changes appeared necessary. He also proposed admitting the existing western territories as two big states, with provisions for future subdivision, thereby sidestepping the divisive territorial question. Seward thus embraced the essential features of the Adams-Corwin plan. He also supported a repeal of northern personal liberty laws, accompanied by an amendment to the Fugitive Slave Law, so that bystanders would no longer have to aid in the search for fugitives. Finally, he advocated a federal law to prohibit invasions of one state by citizens of another, and he urged construction of two railroad routes to the Pacific, one northern and one southern.[49]

Reactions to Seward's speech differed widely. Secessionists and Southern Rights advocates, relieved that Seward had steered clear of a territorial compromise, dismissed his proposals as "fraudulent and tricky." Senator James M. Mason of Virginia, telegraphing a prominent secessionist, detected "no offer of concession worth consideration." Southern Unionists, believing an outright territorial compromise necessary to arrest the spread of secession, gave the speech no more than qualified approval. The *Alexandria Gazette*, for example, thought the value of Seward's speech would be in "inducing conservative men to *go farther*"—and much faster than "one, two, or three years hence." Andrew Johnson, more generous than many, thought the speech "rather conciliatory in its character," conceding enough to be taken "as a favorable indication." Northern moderates of all political persuasions praised the speech. James E. Harvey, the influential columnist for the *Philadelphia North American*, commended Seward for speaking "bravely and well" and for "rising above narrow prejudice and bigoted constructions of party platforms to meet a national exigency such as never presented itself before." But northern antislavery ideologues accused Seward of compromising on matters of principle. "I deplore Seward's speech," Charles Sumner wrote to Salmon P. Chase. "He sent it to me four days before he made it, and I supplicated him to change its tone and especially to abandon every proposition of concession. . . . He did not hearken to me." Leading abolitionist Wendell Phillips declared that Daniel Webster's support for the Compromise of 1850 had been "outdone, and Massachusetts yields to New York the post of infamy which her great Senator has hitherto filled."[50]

Comparisons with Webster were soon silenced by John Greenleaf Whittier, who had most tellingly pronounced in verse the collapse of Webster's reputation in northern antislavery circles.[51] Whittier took a very different view of Seward's speech. Especially sensitive to the threat of war, the Quaker poet penned the following lines:

> TO WILLIAM H. SEWARD.
> Statesman, I thank thee!—and if yet dissent
> Mingles, reluctant, with my large content,
> I cannot censure what was nobly meant.
> But, while constrained to hold even Union less
> than Liberty and Truth and Righteousness,
> I thank thee in the sweet and holy name
> Of Peace, for wise calm words that put to shame
> Passion and party. Courage may be shown
> Not in defiance of the wrong alone;
> He may be bravest who, unweaponed, bears
> The olive branch, and strong in justice, spares
> The rash wrong-doer, giving widest scope
> To Christian charity and generous hope.
> If, without damage to the sacred cause
> Of Freedom and the safeguard of its laws—
> If, without yielding that for which alone
> We prize the Union, thou canst save it now
> From a baptism of blood, upon thy brow
> A wreath whose flowers no earthly soil has known,
> Woven of the beatitudes, shall rest;
> And the peacemaker be forever blest![52]

Henry Adams, who closely observed him during the secession winter, witnessed only one moment when the normally "immovable" Seward "felt what was said of him"—and that was when "he opened the envelope and read the sonnet which the poet Whittier sent to him from Amesbury."[53]

Two days after Seward's speech, the Committee of Thirty-Three met for what was agreed would be its final session. Southern moderates still found the Adams-Corwin proposals inadequate, but they also opposed breaking up "without any report at all." Finally, the committee decided on a close vote that Chairman Corwin could simply present his own summation to the House. Charles Francis Adams, disgusted by what he considered southern intransigence, withdrew his support for New Mexico statehood and the constitutional amendment regarding slavery in the states. Instead, he filed a minority report, complaining that the seceding states would accept no terms other than an "unacceptable" constitutional amendment "to protect and extend slavery."[54]

The experience left Corwin deeply pessimistic. He wrote to Lincoln: "If the states are no more harmonious in their feelings and opinions than these 33 representative men then, appalling as the idea is, we must dissolve and a long bloody civil war *must* follow. I cannot comprehend the madness of the time. Southern men are theoretically crazy. Extreme Northern men are practical fools. The latter are really quite as mad as the former. . . . I have looked on this horrid picture, till I have been able to gaze on it with perfect calmness." To an old friend from Virginia, Alexander H. H. Stuart, a colleague in the Fillmore cabinet, Corwin tried to identify the source of the trouble. "Behold Nine Millions of the South acting on a stupendous mistake as to facts and yet to them they are facts, and yet I *know* they are all mistaken. They believe Northern people *hate* slavery, that they *hate them*, want to deprive them of their property. All and each of these have no foundation in truth."[55]

It appeared that the best terms Republicans would offer (the Adams-Corwin proposals) were less than moderate southerners would accept and that the least terms moderate southerners could accept (the Border State plan) were more than most Republicans would offer. And it remained unclear whether Lincoln, who had torpedoed every previous compromise proposal, could tolerate even the Adams-Corwin package. Was there no way, Adams wondered, "to combine the preservation of our principles with a policy sufficiently conciliatory to bridge over the chasm?" Reconsidering his own role, Adams decided to reaffirm his support for the Committee of Thirty-Three's proposals and to take the floor of the House to explain his views.[56]

In his speech on January 31, Adams contended that southerners suffered from "apprehensions of things that [would] never come to pass." The idea that "any considerable number of men in the free states" wanted "to interfere in any manner whatever with slavery in the States" struck Adams as "madness" that was rooted in "panic, pure panic." But he disagreed with his Republican colleagues who thought the "uneasiness" of the South should be "neglected or ridiculed." When fears pervade "the bosoms of multitudes of men," an "imaginary evil grows up at once into a gigantic reality, and must be dealt with as such." Conciliatory action to allay apprehension seemed to Adams the appropriate course for Republicans, just as Chatham and Burke had urged the British government to do in 1775. At the risk of displeasing many friends "whose good opinion has ever been part of the sunlight of my existence," Adams called for rapid admission of New Mexico as a state and for passage of a constitutional amendment protecting slavery in the states. But Adams condemned southern demands to protect slavery in territory "hereafter acquired." This condition, he reasoned, was deliberately contrived so Republicans must reject it or dishonor themselves. To accept it would "disgrace," "degrade," and "humiliate us in the dust forever"—"rather than this, let the heavens fall."[57]

Adams's speech predictably got bad reviews from both hard-line Republicans and secessionists. Massachusetts Senator Charles Sumner, until recently a regular visitor in the Adams household, thought his colleague had "ruined himself." Southern Rights devotees, realizing that Adams hoped to undercut the Crittenden Compromise, considered his proposal an insidious subterfuge. But conciliators North and South strongly commended Adams. Seward "received the speech with the most generous praise," Adams recorded in his diary, "calling it what he had tried to say and not said so well." George D. Prentice, editor of the *Louisville Journal*, wrote that Adams had made "the most finished and masterly as well as the most significant expression of the spirit of conciliation that has yet been made on the Republican side." Tennessee Congressman T. A. R. Nelson thought Adams "deserved the very highest degree of credit" for making a peace offering "which may peril his popularity at home." And Robert Hatton, writing to his wife as Adams spoke, thought the "admirable speech" would "do great good." The "prospect of an adjustment," Hatton declared, was "brightening." Other southern Unionists hailed Adams's "spirit of conciliation" and suggested that the combination of his proposed constitutional amendment with an "adjustment of the territorial question" would "restore peace to the country."[58]

Adams soon had reason to feel encouraged. The Virginia and Tennessee elections showed that strong pro-Union sentiment persisted in the upper South. Although southern Unionists still sought more than he had offered, Adams hoped they might yet see the merits of his approach. Several Unionists indeed offered private assurances that their states would accept the Adams-Corwin package.[59]

The Virginia and Tennessee elections also made Republicans more disposed to aid southern Unionists. Conciliatory Republican newspapers lauded them for inaugurating "the remarkable change that has come over the face of political affairs within the last few days." Republicans had an "imperative duty," argued the *Boston Daily Advertiser*, to strengthen loyal southerners. With their aid, secession could be stopped, the South divided, and the cotton states eventually reconciled to the Union. The *New York Times* likewise editorialized: "We have evidence now of a Union Party in the Southern states. The government has friends, the Constitution has supporters there with whom to treat. Conciliation and compromise become now acts of friendly arrangement, instead of surrender to open and defiant enemies."[60]

Hopes grew among conciliatory Republicans that the worst of the crisis had passed. "Everything is going to simmer down," Henry Adams reported to his brother. "The ancient Seward is in high spirits and chuckles himself hoarse with his stories. He says it's all right. We shall keep the border states, and in three months or thereabouts, if we hold off, the Unionists and Disunionists will have their hands on each other's throats in the cotton states. The storm is weathered."[61]

Seward still was acting out his self-assigned role by displaying more good cheer than the situation warranted, but he did have reason for celebration. The voters of Virginia and Tennessee, vindicating his decision to pursue a conciliatory strategy, had provided a welcome reprieve. He faced severe problems, however, in taking advantage of the opportunity offered by these states. He could not support the concessions Unionists there wanted and expected unless he could persuade the president-elect to modify his hard-line views.

On January 27, Seward sent Lincoln an analysis of developments in the South. He reported that "Union men in the Border states" talked as if their states "must all go with the tide" unless they were offered "concession or compromise." Seward explained that he had tried "almost in vain" to calm them. He judged, however, that they overestimated the immediate danger because an antisecession reaction was occurring in the upper South. But Seward thought the situation in the lower South bleak: Lincoln would confront "a hostile armed Confederacy" when he took office and would have to "reduce it by force or conciliation." Considering force an inadmissible option,

Seward advised Lincoln to be "forbearing and patient" and to write a "wise and winning" inaugural address. He also warned Lincoln that most Republicans still remained "reckless now of the crisis before us." They thought compromise or concession "intolerable" but offered no credible alternative. The "fate of our country" depended, Seward concluded, upon Lincoln's ability to approach the South in a "generous and hopeful" manner.[62]

At the same time Lincoln was receiving very different advice from Salmon P. Chase, leader of the rival Republican faction. He identified the greatest danger facing Lincoln as "the disruption of the Republican party through Congressional attempts at compromise." Chase, who eagerly aspired to become Lincoln's secretary of the treasury, insisted that the "watchword" for the party should be "Inauguration first—adjustment afterwards." He warned that passage of the least objectionable compromise proposals, the Adams-Corwin plan, would produce ugly political repercussions. "I know the temper of the people," Chase emphasized, "and I know that the Republican Party will be defeated in Ohio next fall if the pledge given at Chicago is violated by the passing of an enabling act for the admission of New Mexico as a Slave State or by the proposal by Congress of the Amendment to the Constitution recommended by the Committee of 33."[63]

Chase articulated fears widely shared by "stiff-backed" Republicans. Pennsylvania Congressman Thaddeus Stevens, "mortified and discouraged" by evidence of Seward's influence, gloomily predicted that "our platform and principles are to be sacrificed to peace," so that the party would "soon cease to exist." There were "too many weak knees" among Republicans, Stevens confided to Chase. George C. Fogg, one of Lincoln's Illinois promoters, sent the president-elect a bitter letter while visiting Washington. Treachery of the worst sort was afoot, Fogg warned. Seward regarded both the Republican party and "its *principles*" with "utter contempt" and was ready "to yield everything." In private conversation, Fogg reported, Seward talked of the Republican party as having "*fulfilled its mission, and not being worth preserving*." Lincoln received repeated complaints about Seward's readiness "to meet by compromise the demands of the slave powers," thereby endangering the party.[64]

Seward and Weed enlisted leading Republicans from the New York commercial community to show Lincoln that a conciliatory policy would help rather than hurt the party. In a long formal letter, they warned against risking both Union and party by refusing to compromise on the territorial question. Many voters who had supported Lincoln, they insisted, believed that a strict no-compromise policy would bring disastrous consequences. "In a mere party view and looking solely to our party organization," the New Yorkers judged, "sound policy requires that some action shall be taken." Recognizing that "any concessions or compromises, no matter how unimportant they may be," could not be adopted "without incurring the opposition and hostility of the extreme wing of our party," they contended that the political dividends would far outweigh the losses. By supporting the Border State plan, which they considered "far preferable" to other proposed bases of settlement, Lincoln could hold the upper South in the Union. To lose the upper South without making "a broad liberal and substantial offer of settlement" would, the New Yorkers warned, wreck the party.[65]

Lincoln's sympathies clearly lay with Seward's critics. One January visitor, for example, found the president-elect "*firm as a rock*," convinced that any countenance he gave to compromise measures would simply increase southern demands for more concessions. Lincoln told another visitor "who wanted him to make some back-down declaration" that he "would sooner go out into his back yard and hang himself." He was determined to keep the Republican party from becoming "a mere sucked egg—all shell and no principle in it." Lincoln therefore sent a fierce reminder to Seward that he remained "inflexible" on the territorial question and wanted "no compromise which *assists* or *permits*" the extension of slavery. He thereby poured cold water on rumors initiated by Republican Congressman William Kellogg of Illinois, who had returned to Washington from a trip to Springfield predicting that Lincoln would endorse the Border State plan. Lincoln did not, however, follow Chase's suggestion to disown categorically the work of the House Committee of Thirty-Three. He indicated to Seward a grudging willingness to accept New Mexico statehood "if further extension were hedged against." And he said nothing about the constitutional amendment regarding slavery in the states.[66]

Seward concluded, after hearing from Lincoln, that the only feasible course of action was to gain a Republican consensus in favor of a national convention. So far as immediate strategy was concerned, Seward in effect capitulated to Chase's policy of "inauguration first—adjustment afterwards." Why did Seward not instead try to enlist Republicans in behalf of New Mexico statehood, after finding that Lincoln would accept it? Apparently, Seward saw no advantage in risking an open party rupture to pass legislation that most southern Unionists considered inadequate in any case. For weeks, Seward had reassured hard-line Republicans behind closed doors that he supported measures such as New Mexico statehood only for effect and "*had no idea of bringing them forward*" because "there were not *three* men on our side of the Senate who would support them." Union victories in Virginia and Tennessee may also have convinced Seward that he could safely procrastinate.[67]

CONCILIATORY Republicans, however, needed to sustain expectations that Lincoln would offer reasonable concessions and make every effort to preserve the peace. Those expectations received a rude jolt when the president-elect spoke out in public for the first time since the election. He left Springfield on February 11 to travel by train to Washington. That same evening, in Indianapolis, Lincoln asserted the right to retake forts, enforce laws, and collect duties in the seceded states. He denied that such action would constitute "coercion." Four days later, in Pittsburgh, he declared the crisis an "*artificial one*," gotten up without justification by "designing politicians," and sure to subside if people would "keep cool."[68]

Lincoln's speeches caused distress both for what they said and what they did not say. A case could indeed be made that the crisis was rooted in unreasonable fears and resentments, but Lincoln seemed almost naive in suggesting that it might painlessly dissipate. And though Lincoln disavowed any intention of sending armies south to subdue rebels, his readiness to maintain federal authority in the seceded states appeared likely to trigger armed conflict. Equally distressing to conciliators was Lincoln's silence regarding Union-saving initiatives. The impression grew that Lincoln would make no concessions to southern Unionists. All at once, Seward's Union-saving schemes began to crumble. His supposed influence in the new administration appeared barren.

The Adams family watched the unfolding drama with morbid fascination. Complaining in his diary that Lincoln's speeches had diminished his estimate of the man, Charles Francis Adams feared that "in this lottery, we may have drawn a blank." His son, Charles Francis Adams, Jr., wrote two long letters recounting in detail how grim the situation looked to conciliatory Republicans. The younger Adams, upon arriving in Washington on February 20, ate dinner with his father and brother, "the European Henry," whose "brow was black" and who was evidently "a burdened man." "At dinner my father was pleasant, but—but—as the meal went on I felt my face growing longer and longer till it took up nearly the whole of my body." Young Adams found that "my father, certainly, and he tells me, Seward are more depressed than at any previous time." Lincoln's speeches had left Virginia Unionists "in despair." The Virginians said they could "do nothing" to prevent secession if Lincoln followed the policy he declared at Indianapolis.[69]

The bitter struggle between Seward and his antagonists in the party was thus coming to a head: "Lincoln gets to Washington and meets Seward on Saturday. A tremendous influence headed by Chase is now at work to force Seward out and Lincoln has not declared himself." The sympathies of the Adams clan were emphatically pro-Seward. "If Lincoln throws his whole weight in support of Seward," reported young Charles Francis Adams, "the party will unite and follow out a conciliatory policy which will, in view of the late elections, keep Virginia steady and save us the country without the loss of anything save many fair words." Should Lincoln, however, "throw himself into the hands of the extreme Republicans" and adopt "the coercion policy," Seward would refuse to serve in the cabinet and war would break out within a month. Summarizing what he had learned from his father and his brother Henry, young Adams wrote: "Within ten days they tell me the question will be decided and they look blue as they say so. The new shallow will be tided over and the future before us, or Union, Administration and party go to one eternal smash."

A few glimpses reveal what lay behind Seward's "cool and calm" facade. "I have had to feel my own way in the dark and amid the tempest," he wrote irritably to one friend. Charles Francis Adams confided to his diary on February 19 that Seward "seemed to be more discouraged than I had yet seen him. . . . My wonder is that he keeps up his spirits as he does." Thurlow Weed, who conversed with Lincoln as the president-elect traveled to Washington, sent a cryptic letter to Seward explaining that his "solicitude in reference to the country" remained unabated. Fearing the coming "ordeal," Weed pointedly advised Seward: "You have a delicate duty before you."[70]

As he restlessly awaited Lincoln's appearance in Washington, Seward braced himself for a maximum effort to win the confidence "of the person on whom all depends." His rivals had made plans to install the president-elect in a private home until Inauguration Day; Seward thwarted that scheme and arranged for Lincoln to stay at Willard's Hotel. When General Winfield Scott warned Seward about possible dangers facing Lincoln in Baltimore, Seward dispatched his son Frederick to arrange for Lincoln's secret trip to Washington. After Lincoln's early morning arrival in the capital, on Saturday, February 23, Seward undertook to play the role of host. He escorted Lincoln to introductory meetings with President Buchanan, the members of his cabinet, and General Scott. Seward also prevailed upon

Lincoln to make himself available for a long evening meeting with delegates from the Peace Conference. The next day Seward accompanied Lincoln to church and then entertained him at home until late afternoon. On Monday Seward conducted the president-elect to the Capitol for courtesy introductions to members of both houses of Congress and the Supreme Court. Seward also took time during the hectic weekend to scrutinize and comment on Lincoln's projected Inaugural Address.[71]

The president-elect, badly fatigued from an endless round of receptions and speeches that marked his circuitous trip east, faced a vexing situation in Washington. Hard-line Republicans led by Horace Greeley and Francis P. Blair, Sr., demanded that he stand firm, while Seward's allies, including many southern Unionists and Lincoln's old rival, Stephen A. Douglas, tried to move him in a conciliatory direction. Hordes of office-seekers plus the merely curious besieged Willard's Hotel. "It was bad enough in Springfield," Lincoln told a reporter, "but it was child's play compared to this tussle here. I hardly have a chance to eat or sleep." Photographs taken in late February show Lincoln with an expressionless face, near exhaustion.[72]

Three paramount issues dominated Lincoln's agenda during his first frantic week in Washington—the choice of a cabinet, the text of his Inaugural Address, and the possible adoption of conciliatory legislation by Congress during its final few days in session. All three matters interconnected, but each may best be analyzed separately.

Lincoln had a roster in mind for the cabinet, but certain details remained to be ironed out. He had already revealed his intention to appoint Seward and Edward Bates of Missouri, his two most formidable challengers for the Republican presidential nomination. He had also decided to offer seats to Gideon Welles of Connecticut and Caleb Smith of Indiana. Of the three remaining positions, Cameron and Chase contended for the treasury post. Fearing the political consequences of excluding either from the cabinet, Lincoln had determined to try to include both. In all likelihood, therefore, only one other position remained unfilled. It would go either to John A. Gilmer or to Montgomery Blair, or possibly to a different non-Republican southerner if Gilmer remained unwilling. Consideration of several southerners, Gilmer foremost among them, must have figured prominently in discussions between Lincoln and Seward.[73]

A series of newspaper reports during the week before the inauguration indicated that Gilmer was expected to hold a seat in the cabinet. Several dispatches indicated that he had been offered the position of secretary of the navy, a post traditionally filled by a North Carolinian, and that Gilmer's promoters, chief among them Seward, had also approached other southern Unionists, either to find an alternative candidate in case of Gilmer's refusal or as part of an effort to rekindle Lincoln's interest in appointing more than one non-Republican southerner to the cabinet. Maryland Congressman Henry Winter Davis, former presidential candidate John Bell, and leading Virginia Unionist George W. Summers all were rumored to be under consideration for a position. Lincoln, however, apparently planned to choose either Gilmer or Blair. Gilmer remained, as he had since December, uncomfortably implicated in the struggle to shape Lincoln's cabinet.[74]

Senator Thomas Bragg of North Carolina remarked in his diary on February 26 that "the moderate and extreme Republicans" were still quarreling about the cabinet and that a position had probably been "tendered to Gilmer." Bragg expected that Gilmer would accept "unless he fears the indignation of the people of North Carolina." Bragg defined the problem that became ever harder to surmount. Several circumstances intersected during the last week before the inauguration to drive a wedge between southern Unionists and the new administration and to persuade Gilmer to refuse the cabinet offer.[75]

It became apparent that Republicans would not supply the "bread pills" that Gilmer considered essential to undermine secession and preserve the peace. A cryptic note from Gilmer to Lincoln establishes that the North Carolinian made his acceptance of a cabinet post contingent on Lincoln's acceptance of compromise on the territorial question. Gilmer implored the president-elect "to do what I have so anxiously urged on you . . . nothing below." The appeal, which probably referred to the modified territorial compromise of the Border State plan, was, of course, doomed to disappointment.[76]

Gilmer's willingness to serve in the cabinet must also have been chilled when Chase won the protracted and bitter struggle for the treasury portfolio. Lincoln, having been buffeted by the contest for two months, finally decided to poll Republican members of the Senate. As he apparently expected and preferred, they overwhelmingly supported Chase. For southern Unionists, the Chase appointment was ominous. It signified, most of all, that Seward would not dominate the new administration. Anyone who knew about the "irrepressible conflict within the Republican party" during January and February could recognize the triumph of the Chase-Blair-Greeley combination over the Seward-Weed-Cameron group on the crucial issue of the treasury office, even though Cameron finally consented to take the supposedly less prestigious position of secretary of war. Available evidence strongly suggests that the appointment of Chase had a decisive effect upon Gilmer.[77]

Gilmer's decision to refuse the cabinet offer provided inflexible Republicans with a double victory because the militaristic Montgomery Blair eagerly accepted the final cabinet position. Rather than Gilmer, Lincoln designated an unabashed coercionist to represent the upper South. The appointment, which seemed a calculated insult to the conciliatory lobby, was interpreted by Henry Adams as "the death-blow to the policy of Mr. Seward." The latter's inability to recruit a representative southern Unionist, or to keep Chase and Blair out of the cabinet, led many southerners to fear the worst about the new administration.[78]

Gilmer's doubts about the future surely were intensified when he read the text of the Inaugural Address that Lincoln brought to Washington. Gilmer hoped that Lincoln might heed "the wishes and views of the loyal conservative men of the South." But the draft Gilmer saw had a very different character. In it, Lincoln flatly refused to support any compromise measures or to "shift his position." Worse, the draft promised to reclaim federal property in Confederate hands and closed with an ominous threat to defend the Union by force if necessary.[79]

Lincoln also gave Seward a copy of his proposed Inaugural Address. The New Yorker promptly told Lincoln to rewrite the document in a more conciliatory manner and proposed numerous changes. A tone of desperate earnestness marked the letter Seward sent to the president-elect. He warned bluntly that the original draft would, if delivered, drive Maryland and Virginia out the Union. Insisting that he had developed a better understanding of the situation in the South than any other Republican, Seward urged Lincoln to reconsider:

> I, my dear sir, have devoted myself singly to the study of the case here—with advantages of access and free communication with all parties of all sections. . . . You must, therefore, allow me to speak frankly and candidly. . . . I know the tenacity of party friends, and I honor and respect it. But I know also that they know nothing of the real peril of the crisis. It has not been their duty to study it, as it has been mine. Only the soothing words which I have spoken have saved us and carried us along thus far. Every loyal man, and, indeed, every disloyal man in the South, will tell you this.

Lincoln, however, gave no indication that he intended to modify the Inaugural Address. The original hard-line text remained the official statement of Lincoln's views as Inauguration Day approached.[80]

The week before the inauguration also marked the final days of the long struggle to get Congress to enact conciliatory legislation. But divisions within the Republican party made passage of any measure very difficult. A scattered number of Republicans favored a territorial compromise. Although repelled by the "protection" and "hereafter acquired" features of the Crittenden Compromise, they could accept the Border State plan, which forbade federal interference with slavery in New Mexico, the territory where it already existed. This outer limit of Republican procompromise sentiment also reappeared in the Peace Conference plan, which likewise attracted limited Republican support. Somewhat larger numbers of Republicans supported the Adams-Corwin plan to admit New Mexico as a state and to amend the Constitution to safeguard slavery in the states. But because few southerners thought the Adams-Corwin proposal adequate, it remained in limbo as the Peace Conference debated. A majority of Republicans believed compromise unnecessary and humiliating. To avoid presenting the appearance of rigid inflexibility, most "stiff-backed" Republicans by late February claimed to favor a national convention to amend the Constitution, as provided in Article Five. Anticompromise Republicans in effect told conciliators to persuade the requisite twenty-three state legislatures to call such a convention.

When Lincoln arrived in Washington, on Saturday, February 23, the Peace Conference remained in session. Though many of its Republican delegates considered southern fears groundless and concessions inappropriate, some proved receptive to appeals from southern Unionists and helped to engineer an agreement. On the morning of Wednesday, February 27, the Peace Conference finally passed its plan. It has been alleged that Lincoln influenced the crucial switch of the Illinois delegation, which enabled the Peace Conference to avert failure and created a bare majority in favor of territorial compromise, but that seems unlikely. Reports about Lincoln's interviews with Peace Conference members indicate that his position on the territories remained unyielding. One delegate remembered Lincoln saying that he believed he would betray his party if he ever agreed "to allow slavery to be extended into the territories." Judge Stephen T. Logan of Illinois, the supposed conduit for Lincoln's alleged procompromise manipulations, also denied that he acted with Lincoln's approval.[81]

Hasty congressional consideration of the Peace Conference plan followed during the hectic last few days of the session. Southern Rights Virginian Robert M. T. Hunter tried to substitute the Crittenden Compromise for the Peace Conference plan, but Crittenden himself interposed. Describing the Peace Confernce plan as the "best hope" for peace and compromise, the Kentuckian vowed to vote for it rather than the proposal he had authored. Nor did Crittenden complain because the Peace Conference had deleted the "hereafter acquired" clause: the country would be better off without further territorial "aggrandizement." But only one Senate Republican, Edward D. Baker of Oregon, endorsed submission of the Peace Conference amendments to the states. Baker wanted to sustain the loyal men of the upper South, "who implore me for the love of a common Union to do something to satisfy the doubts and fears of their people." He contended that slavery already existed "nominally" in New Mexico, so that the Peace Conference plan would open no new territory to slavery. Other Republicans disagreed. Caught between the upper and nether millstones of Republicans who thought it conceded too much and southern Democrats who insisted on the Crittenden Compromise, and hopelessly ensnarled in end-of-session deadlines, the Peace Conference plan finally came to a vote in the Senate long after midnight in the last hours of the congressional session, when it lost ignominiously, seven to twenty-eight.[82]

The House demonstrated greater support for the Peace Conference plan, though not the two-thirds needed to pass a constitutional amendment. In what many regarded as a test vote, the House on March 1 divided ninety-three to sixty-seven in favor of suspending the rules and opening debate on the measure. Thomas Corwin and Charles Francis Adams joined the conciliatory Republicans from New Jersey and Pennsylvania in favoring consideration, though by far the larger bloc of Republicans voted against it. Southern Rights Democrats in the House, some complaining bitterly about the "insidious propositions" and "miserable abortion," but no doubt also looking ahead to the summer's congressional elections, voted substantially in favor. Southern Unionists of both parties of course voted eagerly and unanimously for the Peace Conference plan.

Long-delayed consideration of the Adams-Corwin package also took place during the last week of the congressional session. On Tuesday, February 26, and the following day, Corwin tried to get the House to pass the constitutional amendment protecting slavery in the states where it already existed. But Republican support for the measure had eroded, and it failed to receive a two-thirds majority when the House first voted on the twenty-seventh. The House favored it by a majority of 123 to 71, but Republicans opposed it, 37 to 68. Conciliatory Republicans were outraged. "I can scarcely imagine a more remarkable exhibition of folly," Charles Francis Adams complained in his diary. "A united vote would have carried with it the proof of a conciliatory spirit. . . . On the other hand a negative vote carried on with so much vehemence and passion leaves an implication at least of a desire to keep open a chance of direct interference at some favorable moment hereafter." But the next morning, Thursday, February 28, the House voted to reconsider its action. And by a bare two-thirds majority, 132 to 65, the House reversed its action of the day before and passed the amendment. Republican opposition diminished just enough to make the difference, as the second vote found 7 more Republicans in favor and 6 fewer opposed. A majority of Republicans still voted against the amendment, 44 to 62, but the provocation Adams feared had been substantially averted.[83]

Lincoln may well have used his influence in favor of the amendment, as some surmised at the time. He reportedly told delegates from the Peace Conference that "he was willing to give a constitutional guarantee that slavery should not be molested in any way directly or indirectly in the States." His position on the amendment thus contrasted with his continuing opposition to the territorial compromise contemplated in the Peace Conference plan.[84]

But the second major Adams-Corwin proposal, the New Mexico statehood bill, suffered a different fate. On March 1, the House tabled it by a vote of 115 to 71, despite efforts by conciliatory Republicans to depict it as a complement to the constitutional amendment. The New Mexico bill, which needed only a simple majority to pass, failed because southerners were reluctant to accept it. Crittenden privately passed word that he opposed New Mexico statehood. With southern House members divided almost evenly, Republican support for the measure collapsed: 26 Republicans voted for New Mexico statehood and 76 opposed it. Had southerners wanted the New Mexico bill, enough Republicans would have come forward to pass it.[85]

By late February Republicans had coalesced behind the dubious expedient of merely favoring a national convention. Both in the Peace Conference and in the House of Representatives, majorities of Republicans specified a national convention as the appropriate means to alleviate southern grievances. Republicans who actually opposed compromise could claim to support a convention without offering specific terms or concessions. This approach, too, was agreeable to Lincoln. Thus Seward, leader of the conciliatory Republicans, apparently concluded that Republican endorsement for a convention looked better than nothing at all. Seward may also have feared the effects of an unsuccessful effort to get Republicans to accept more, such as nearly happened when the House voted on the constitutional amendment protecting slavery in the states.[86]

The circumstances under which Seward took a public stance in favor of a national convention jeopardized his standing among upper South Unionists. A special Senate committee of five members, including Seward and Republican Lyman Trumbull of Illinois, was assigned to prepare a report on the Peace Conference plan for the entire Senate. Seward and Trumbull submitted a minority report on February 28, favoring a national convention to amend the Constitution rather than Senate passage of the constitutional amendments proposed by the Peace Conference. Seward's action astonished his covert allies in the upper South, who thought he understood the necessity for a territorial compromise. His position on the Peace Conference plan thus caused an uproar. "Many of our conservative friends are greatly disturbed by it," reported a Union delegate to the Virginia convention. One of Seward's principal Virginia allies, James Barbour, decided that he had been treated treacherously and warned the Virginia convention not to allow itself to be deceived further by "one of the shrewdest and smartest men in this Union." Former President John Tyler, the quasi-secessionist leader of the Virginia delegation to the Peace Conference, sarcastically said of Seward: "After midnight conferences with our friends, pretendedly inclining to compromise and settle it, why he proposes a *National Convention*." To Tyler, Seward was a designing "spider" who had deceitfully spun a web to trap unwary Virginians. Southern moderates, hard-pressed to answer Southern Rights criticism that the Peace Conference was a sellout, found their position made even more precarious by Seward's action. While secessionists raged about the impropriety of collaborating with "the great arch-enemy of the South," Unionists bitterly recognized that neither the Lincoln administration nor the Republican party would accept any territorial compromise.[87]

By the weekend before Lincoln's scheduled Monday inauguration, it appeared that he had embraced and strengthened the powerful no-compromise wing of the Republican party. With the single exception of his probable role in reversing the House vote on the constitutional amendment regarding slavery in the states, Lincoln had disappointed conciliatory Republicans and southern Unionists. The identities of the cabinet appointees, which began to become known, showed that no-compromise Republicans had gained two key seats. Though the text of the Inaugural Address remained secret, hard-line Republicans who had seen it or heard reports about it were jubilant. And territorial compromise appeared dead, with only the uncertain palliative of a national convention to take its place.[88]

WITH conciliatory Republicans apparently defeated, southern Unionists had good reason to fear the worst. Three surviving documents are especially revealing. Robert Hatton, the sincere young Unionist from Middle Tennessee, wrote a very pessimistic letter to his wife on Friday, March 1, as the congressional session approached its end. "We are getting along badly with our work of compromise—badly!" he reported. "We will break up, I apprehend, without any thing being done. God will hold some men to a fearful responsibility. My heart is sick."[89]

Probably that same day, Lincoln met with a delegation of Virginians, including Sherrard Clemens, the Union Democrat who represented the panhandle of northwestern Virginia in Congress and at the Virginia convention. Clemens sent a bitter letter to a friend, describing the interview with Lincoln. The president-elect impressed Clemens as poorly informed—he "*did not know* what the Adams amendment was until I told him." Lincoln certainly did know about the amendment, and he may well have been responsible for House passage of it, but he may not have recognized the "Adams" designation. Lincoln's apparent ignorance upset the Virginians, thereby poisoning the interview. Clemens also doubted that Lincoln would offer concessions sufficient to hold the upper South in the Union. Beneath the facade of an informal western storyteller, who "as he talks to you *punches* you under your ribs" and "swears equal to uncle Toby," Clemens thought he detected "an abolitionist of the Lovejoy and Sumner type." He grimly predicted that Lincoln would drive Virginia and the Union slave states to secede.[90]

A third glimpse at the nightmarish prospect facing southern Unionists by the weekend before the inauguration came from the pen of former Governor John M. Morehead, one of the North Carolina delegates to the Peace Conference. During his stay in Washington, Morehead became well informed about the complex drama then unfolding. He must have consulted directly with Gilmer because the two were longtime political allies and lived in the same town of Greensboro. Morehead returned to North Carolina soon after February 27, when the Peace Conference concluded its labors. There he anxiously awaited news from Washington. Few persons in the South had a better basis to evaluate what they learned. A letter from him to North Carolina's other Union delegate at the Peace Conference, Thomas Ruffin, shows that Morehead expected nothing but bad news regarding the cabinet, the Inaugural Address, and the new administration's southern policy. "I am exceedingly anxious to see the inaugural," Morehead told Ruffin. "I fear its effect very much. Chase is in the Cabinet, it is said, if so there is danger. . . . The South refused seats in it I expect; and it was said the inaugural would demand the return of all property seized, the collection of duties, etc., etc. If so, I fear all hope is gone."[91]

10

THE UNIONISTS AND PRESIDENT LINCOLN—THE MARCH 1861 RAPPROCHEMENT

A BEHIND-THE-SCENES drama of great importance to southern Unionists was enacted without their knowledge the weekend before the inauguration. On Saturday, March 2, just two days before Lincoln was to take office, Seward sent him a letter declining to serve as secretary of state. He did not specify reasons, but events during the preceding week needed no amplification. Seward wanted assurances that the administration would pursue a conciliatory southern policy, notwithstanding the inclusion of Blair and Chase in the cabinet. He calculated that Lincoln would hesitate to start his presidency amid such an open and visible rupture of the party. Of course, Seward was bluffing: any hope for the policies he favored depended more than ever on the effectiveness of his own counsel within the administration.[1]

The bluff worked. Lincoln decided to make substantial last-minute revisions in the Inaugural Address. By one account, he "rose before dawn" on Inauguration Day to alter the document. In that all-important statement of his intended policies, Lincoln accepted Seward's advice to delete both a reaffirmation of Republican orthodoxy on the territorial issue and a threat to recapture federal property in the seceded states. Instead, Lincoln incorporated a variety of suggestions Seward had made to give the speech a more conciliatory tone. The vow to seek "a peaceful solution of the national troubles, and the restoration of fraternal sympathies and affections" used Seward's exact phraseology. Seward also inspired Lincoln's eloquent peroration, telling southerners, "We are not enemies, but friends. We must not be enemies."[2]

Following the inauguration ceremony, Lincoln and Seward met at the White House and had "a long and confidential conversation." Seward probably conferred with Thurlow Weed later that same evening. The next morning Seward countermanded his resignation. The agreement between Lincoln and Seward obviously involved southern policy. Lincoln must have provided assurances that he would heed Seward's concerns.[3]

The conciliatory cause also received last-minute aid from Congress. Though Republicans rejected territorial compromise, they offered an oblique alternative by organizing three western territories—Dakota, Colorado, and Nevada—without reference to slavery. In effect, Republicans quietly accepted an idea long championed by Stephen A. Douglas. They conceded that "popular sovereignty" would prevent slavery from spreading just as effectively as overt prohibition. Republicans thus offered the South a significant symbolic concession. They also, in the same context, chose not to repeal the New Mexico territorial code, which allowed slavery. They had tried to do so in 1860, before the presidential election. Even though secession gave them a majority in both houses, "they left the matter untouched."[4]

In addition, Congress finally approved the Adams-Corwin constitutional amendment regarding slavery in the states. Long deferred by the fruitless struggle to enact a territorial compromise, the amendment did not reach the floor of either house until the last week of Congress. Finally, however, moderates North and South rallied behind it, hoping to salvage the most significant conciliatory initiative that still had a chance to gain congressional approval. Obstructed both by inflexible Republicans who wanted no concessions and by secessionists who spurned the amendment as an inconsequential insult, the conciliatory coalition guided it to heart-stoppingly narrow and last-minute victories in both the House and Senate. House passage of the amendment may have resulted from Lincoln's intervention. Douglas, a leading promoter of conciliation, then kept the Senate in session all night before the inauguration to secure action on the Adams-Corwin measure. It finally carried twenty-four to twelve, exactly the two-thirds majority required, with eight of the twenty Republicans present voting in favor. Lincoln stated in his Inaugural Address that he had "no objection" to the amendment because protection for slavery in the states was already implied in the Constitution.[5]

Although southern Unionists would have preferred an explicit territorial compromise, they welcomed the actions of Congress. Congressman Thomas A. R. Nelson of Tennessee commended the establishment of new territories without restrictions on slavery and declared that the constitutional amendment would "remove the only real ground of apprehension in the slave States." Believing the North had demonstrated its good intentions, Nelson argued that "the people in the border states ought to be satisfied, or at least to acquiesce, in what has been done." So, likewise, Andrew Johnson announced that passage of the three territorial bills and the constitutional amendment enabled him to "go before the people of the South and defy disunion." John A. Gilmer thought Congress had helped to restore a "plain common sense view of things" for deluded southerners. He expressed hearty satisfaction with the "perpetual guaranty against Congressional interference with Slavery in the States" and the "territorial organization without the Wilmot Proviso." With such tangible evidence of northern conservatism, he asked, "what more does any reasonable Southern man expect or desire?"[6]

As the session ended, southern Unionists also expressed relief that Congress had not enacted legislation authorizing the president to use military force against secession. Discussion of a "force bill" in the House between February 19 and 21 had severely agitated Virginia Unionists, several of whom sent vehement complaints to Seward. The offending measure indicated that the new administration would pursue a coercive policy, Unionists claimed; it had done them "more injury than an invading army" and made secessionists "clap their hands with joy." Several days later, twenty House Republicans voted with a solid bloc of Democrats and southern Unionists to set the measure aside. When its sponsors succeeded in reviving the force bill, Virginia Unionist Congressman Alexander R. Boteler went directly to Lincoln to protest. According to Boteler's subsequent recollection, the president-elect indicated that he would try to stop the bill. That same night, the House once again blocked it. Unionists thus were confident that Lincoln could not legally use force against the seceding states and that he had not wanted any such authority in the first place. Their confidence would, in the short term, help to keep secession stifled in the upper South. After April 15, however, Unionists would feel bitterly disillusioned and betrayed.[7]

As long as Congress remained in session, efforts to promote sectional reconciliation focused on the territorial issue. After Lincoln's inauguration, however, the territorial issue attracted less attention. Because it involved complex and inscrutable questions about future power relationships between North and South, deeply polarizing challenges to party identities and organizations, as well as touchy considerations of honor and rights, the territorial issue was not resolved, nor could it have been.

The Confederate government's establishment cut short debate about the distant future and raised instead several more urgent questions. Although the deep South had proclaimed its independence, popular majorities held the upper South in the Union. As of March, eight states in the upper South, with twice the white population of the lower South, stood aloof from the secession experiment. The campaign for united southern action before Lincoln's inauguration boomeranged, leaving the South more divided than ever before. To that extent, the secession movement had failed.[8] The situation required reassessment in all quarters. Would the lower South persist in its quest for independence? Would the eight states of the upper South remain in the Union, even if the seven states of the lower South refused to return? Most immediately, would the federal government allow southerners to determine their allegiance, or would it challenge secession with armed force?

Upper South Unionists, who had struggled during January and February to enact a territorial compromise, recognized by March that peace was their greatest priority. They knew that any collision of arms between the federal and Confederate governments would destroy all their accomplishments. They had worked to diminish sectional excitement in the upper South, to promote a transfer of power there to antisecessionists, and, above all, to leave the door open for the deep South to reconsider its hasty action. The southern Unionist plan for peaceful reunion obviously required time, patience, and a sustained relaxation of sectional tensions.

Unionists therefore implored the Lincoln administration to avoid an armed clash with the southern Confederacy. They urged abandoning Fort Sumter, in the harbor of Charleston, South Carolina, and Fort Pickens, in the harbor of Pensacola, Florida, the two outposts in the seceded states remaining in federal hands. So, too, they advised against trying to collect customs duties in deep South ports. Unionists would thereby deprive the Confederacy of any chance to begin hostilities. Although appearing to favor de facto recognition of Confederate independence, Unionists expected, instead, that a passive policy would eventually produce a counterrevolution in the deep South, followed by peaceable restoration of the Union. "Our Gulf State brethren may not come back, this year or the next," reasoned the editor of the *Richmond Whig*, but he felt "fully assured" that they would "ultimately come—that is, within the course of a very few years." A serious movement "in favor of Reconstruction" could be expected in all the seceded states before the end of the year.[9]

A particularly important exposition of the southern Unionist formula for peaceful reunion may be found in a series of letters written by John A. Gilmer. Called home to North Carolina at the end of the congressional session by "the extreme and dangerous illness of a member of my family," Gilmer wrote four long letters to Seward within a week after his return, as well as two others to Stephen A. Douglas, who was, like Gilmer, deeply implicated in Seward's schemes to save the Union. "I am here in the very midst of the South," Gilmer warned, "and I beg you to weigh well the suggestions which I make to you."[10]

Gilmer implored Seward against trying to hold Sumter and Pickens. Federal control over the two forts gave Confederate leaders both a pretext for fighting and, in Sumter, a locale in which federal forces faced overwhelming disadvantages. Gilmer described the nervous impetuousness among secessionists, who were more and more inclined toward violent action to maintain their flagging revolution. Their "only hope," he noted, "is that some sort of collision will be brought about between federal and state forces." In each of his four crucial letters to Seward, Gilmer repeatedly stressed the same point: "The seceders in the border states and throughout the South ardently desire some collision of arms." They would "give a kingdom for a fight."

Gilmer believed that any fighting in the near future would reunite the South. Anxieties about federal interference with slavery had become closely tied to the supposed threat of "coercion," loosely defined to include any use of federal force against the seceding states. Persistent alarms about an armed federal invasion of the South, even if unsubstantiated, tended to keep southern Unionists on the defensive. As Gilmer explained to Seward: "The only thing now that gives the secessionists the advantage of the conservatives is the cry of coercion—that the whipping of a slave state, is the whipping of slavery."

But Gilmer expected that hysteria about "coercion" would gradually diminish, especially in the upper South, as the administration demonstrated its pacific intentions. "The great point is to avoid a collision," he emphasized. "There must be no fighting, or the conservative Union men in the border slave states of North Carolina, Tennessee, Missouri, Kentucky, Virginia, Maryland, and Delaware who are at this time largely in the majority, will be swept away in a torrent of madness." Only by surrendering the forts, Gilmer insisted, could Lincoln hope to secure reunion.

As Gilmer well realized, the southern forts confronted the new administration with a cruel quandary. Sumter, although rendered militarily useless by the superiority of Confederate forces elsewhere in Charleston harbor, had become a highly publicized symbol. Its abandonment, appearing to acquiesce in secession, would have enraged many in Lincoln's own party. How, then, did Gilmer reconcile his undoubted hope for reunion with a policy that appeared to accept the permanency of secession? The question was not one he could responsibly evade.

Gilmer saw no contradiction. He believed the lower South could not successfully maintain its independence. He shared the view, widespread among those who looked for a conciliatory resolution to the secession crisis as well as among many secessionists themselves, that the cotton Confederacy would wither unless buttressed by the manpower and resources of the upper South. Gilmer envisioned a process requiring perhaps two years to achieve results. As Unionists consolidated their grip on the upper South, an internal reaction would begin within the seceded states. He confidently expected that the fling at independence would prove disappointing. Secessionists had promised boundless prosperity and a smoother functioning of the slave system. Gilmer, like other southern Unionists, thought the actual experience of going "out into the cold for a while" would provide such a contrastingly harsh taste of reality in the deep South as to destroy the novelty of secession.

Allowing the cotton states de facto independence would, Gilmer assured Seward, promote the ascendance of Unionists in the upper South. "Let the Union seem quietly to settle down with the free states and the border slave states," he urged. The "Union Conservative men" in the upper South could solidify control over their states "before the lapse of sufficient time to be construed into acquiescence in secession." Eventually, Gilmer predicted, the upper South would prove willing "to unite cordially with the free states" in providing external pressure against the deep South, to stimulate the anticipated counterrevolution there. The essential prerequisite was an interval of time to allow new leadership to emerge in the upper South and to diminish enthusiasm for secession in the deep South.

Gilmer thus advocated what others called a "hands-off" policy. The phrase was coined by the influential newspaper writer James E. Harvey, who contended, in an important and widely reprinted column on March 24:

> The cotton States are determined to try a separate government. Resistance to it here will unite and consolidate the south, and enable it to do what could not be done in a condition of peace—extort money by forced loans to carry on their government. If left severely alone to work out this problem in their own way, no human power can prevent the destruction and disintegration of the cotton confederacy. . . . If the Administration keeps its hands off and ignores the very existence of the cotton States, the peo-

> ple who have been deceived and betrayed will soon rise up in their might to crush out the treason and seek a return to the Union, in which their prosperity and protection were so well secured.

Harvey's passive hands-off approach was exactly what southern Unionists wanted. One influential Virginian, Alexander H. H. Stuart, stated that the policy outlined in Harvey's article "would put every thing to rest."[11]

A similar explanation of the hands-off policy appeared in the *New York Times* on March 21. Rejecting both peaceable separation and "a resort to force," editor Henry J. Raymond concluded that "the true policy of the Government is unquestionably that of *masterly inactivity*." To restore the Union, the government must appeal "to the minds of the people, to their judgment, their political sagacity, their common sense." The people of the South could not be forced to return to the Union; they should instead be made to realize that "their interests require it." By adopting a policy that would "prevent war" and "satisfy the South of his determination to respect their rights," Lincoln could "eventually bring back every Southern State." Raymond confessed that "this may seem a long process," but he thought it "the only one which contains the slightest promise of success." When written, analyses such as Harvey's and Raymond's were thought to reflect administration policy.[12]

EVEN though Lincoln had rewritten his Inaugural Address in a conciliatory manner, secessionists tried to interpret it as a "declaration of war." Lincoln announced his intention "to hold, occupy and possess the property and places belonging to the Government, and to collect the duties on imposts." Secessionists, confident that these objectives could be secured only by force, trumpeted that coercion and civil war were imminent. They insisted that the upper South must choose whether to fight with the "sister states of the South" or on the side of the "Black Republican invader." No other choice remained: "There is left no middle course."[13]

Unionists responded cautiously to the secessionist onslaught. They carefully disavowed support for Lincoln, his party, or the platform on which he ran for office. But they concluded that the inaugural was "*not a war message*" and that it was "not unfriendly to the South." They noted that Lincoln had endorsed the constitutional amendment protecting slavery in the states and had pleaded for the preservation of peace. Sharp-eyed Unionists recognized that Lincoln had omitted any mention of excluding slavery from the territories. Nor had he threatened to recapture federal property held by secessionists. They also noticed that Lincoln's promise to enforce laws and collect revenue in the seceded states contained a key qualification: he would do so only "as far as practicable," and he reserved the right to modify his approach to secure "a peaceful solution of the national troubles." Hence, Unionists concluded, alarms about coercion were false.[14]

Unionists in the Virginia convention confronted a secessionist clamor for several days after Lincoln's inauguration. One Union delegate reported that the address had been "grossly distorted" and that "our ranks are being sadly thinned by desertions." He advised the administration to withdraw its men from the forts in the seceding states and to abstain from trying to collect the revenue. A peace policy would "reassure the weak and give additional strength to the strong." By giving an "unambiguous indication" of his conciliatory intentions, Lincoln could enable Virginia Unionists to "sweep the state in the spring elections" and lay the foundation for "a restoration of the Union." But if the administration provoked an armed clash in the South, Virginia Unionists would be "swept away like chaff before the wind" and would not be able to carry a single district east of the Blue Ridge.[15]

Authoritative reports from Washington soon encouraged the Unionists. On March 6 and 7, Stephen A. Douglas took the floor of the Senate to defend Lincoln's Inaugural Address as a "peace offering." Douglas, who almost certainly knew about the earlier hard-line version, commended the speech as more conciliatory than he had dared to hope. He insisted that Lincoln favored peaceful reunion. The administration would, Douglas suggested, even abandon Fort Sumter rather than risk provoking an incident there. Circumstantial evidence suggests that Douglas, in making predictions about Sumter, echoed information he had received from Seward.[16]

Douglas's speech electrified upper South Unionists. It was "opportune" and had been "of much service to us," they reported. Although the inaugural had "caused a decided swing of the pendulum" toward disunion in Virginia, the Douglas speech "brought about a reaction." Within a week his friends in the Virginia convention reported that "everything here is right" and "Virginia is safe." A prominent North Carolina Unionist likewise observed that Lincoln's inaugural had stirred "a powerful reaction in favor of the Secessionists," but that Douglas's "patriotic speech" had produced "a counter reaction in our favor." Southern Douglasites applauded the prospective withdrawal from Sumter. The "great and only effective weapon" secessionists had was the popular dread of "coercion." If Lincoln abandoned the southern forts, it would deprive the seceding states of the opportunity to start a war and would "more completely *put to rout* the disunion party, than all the guns and soldiers in the world"—Unionists would "overwhelm them everywhere." But nagging worries remained. "Ultra Republicans" were sure to oppose evacuation of Sumter. Would Lincoln have sufficient nerve to breast the expected "blast of opposition" from them? Or would he change his policy under pressure and decide for coercion?[17]

Douglas's interpretation of the Inaugural Address received partial confirmation from the best possible source, Lincoln himself. The president could not have appreciated hearing that he might abandon Sumter, but he did provide more generalized reassurances about his peaceful intent. On Wednesday, March 6, two southern Unionist congressmen from East Tennessee, Horace Maynard and T. A. R. Nelson, sought an audience with the president. Lincoln invited them to meet privately with him at the White House the following evening. All accounts of the meeting agree that the Tennesseans asked Lincoln "how his inaugural was to be understood," whereupon Lincoln assured them "*that it meant peace*" and promised to do "all in his power to avoid a collision." Lincoln specified that he would not attempt to recapture federal property then held by Confederates. And even though the federal government badly needed money, he thought it best "to forego the collection of the revenue for a season, so as to allow the people of the Seceding States time for reflection." Lincoln hoped they would soon "recede from the position they have taken." One of the congressmen, probably Nelson, professed to be "quite satisfied with the assurances of the President."[18]

Soon afterward, Lincoln had an interview with a Virginia legislator, Joseph Segar, "a Commissioner for the Union members of the Virginia Convention." Segar, who also consulted with members of the cabinet, returned to Richmond with "every assurance that the policy of the Administration is peace and conciliation." What may have been another version of the same interview quoted Lincoln as promising a member of the Virginia convention that he would "prevent the shedding of blood." The visitor judged Lincoln "a peace man," who would "not allow himself to be drawn into adopting a war policy to please a few radical republicans."[19]

For several weeks in March after the brief postinaugural uproar, Unionists became cautiously optimistic that the administration would preserve the peace. If so, they thought the crisis could be surmounted, the Union restored, and their political dominance in the upper South solidly secured. Thus the new Union party began to display vigorous signs of strength and potential permanency. A firm determination to ignore "old party divisions" characterized the new mood. Union Whigs supported Union Democrats for federal patronage jobs, and vice versa. Habitual political rivals exchanged compliments. Governor Letcher of Virginia, a Union Democrat, thought an oration by prominent Union Whig John B. Baldwin would "place him among the first men of his generation." The *Richmond Whig* in turn strongly commended "Honest John Letcher," the man whose election it had tenaciously opposed two years before. Dozens of former Whigs likewise wrote to Andrew Johnson to applaud his "noble and patriotic course," to note the disappearance of old party lines, and to announce their conversion from political enemies to friends.[20]

Virginia Unionists expected that the legislative and congressional elections in late May would create a watershed in their state's political history. "At as early a date as the Constitution and the laws allow," the *Richmond Whig* confidently predicted, "retribution, swift and sure, will overtake the faithless dynasty which now abuses the confidence of Virginia." Unionists believed that "if the peaceful and conciliatory policy of the President is not deviated from a clear majority of sixty thousand votes in the State will be shown at the Congressional election in May against the Secessionists." The Virginia election thus loomed as an event of first importance. It gave conciliators an early opportunity to demonstrate their strength. Henry Adams, who made himself well informed on the subject, reported that "the Virginia Congressional elections which were to come in May, would have been the decisive point."[21]

The new Union party resurrected the political fortunes of Virginia's leading Whigs, whose careers had been blighted by the traditional Democratic proclivities of their state's voters and by the unhappy history of the national Whig party. Only during the presidency of Millard Fillmore had someone who pleased them occupied the White House, and since then, of course, the Whig party had itself disintegrated. Virginians such as Alexander H. H. Stuart and John Minor Botts, who had achieved national prominence during the 1840s and early 1850s, thus languished in relative political obscurity by 1860. Virginia Whig publicists complained that a brilliant constellation of political talent was being wasted. "What a commentary upon the galling party tyranny that has been exercised by our masters in Virginia,—soon, thank Heaven, to be our masters no longer,—that such men as these are kept out of the public service," commented the editor of the *Lynchburg Virginian*.[22]

Foremost among the Union Whigs was George W. Summers, of Charleston in western Virginia. Although his aristocratic bearing gave Summers an eastern appearance, nobody had more persistently challenged the power of "Old Virginia." From his advocacy of gradual emancipation thirty years earlier through his efforts to secure a more democratic state constitution in 1850–51, Summers had fought an uphill and generally losing battle. He ably led the Whigs in 1851, when the governorship first became an elective office, but his candidacy fell short. His party and its several successors during the 1850s could never assemble a statewide majority, failing especially to attract Jacksonian nonslaveowners in the fast-growing west. Summers, well into his middle years, appeared to have no political future.[23]

The secession crisis suddenly vaulted Summers to prominence, confronting him with multiple responsibilities. The legislature selected him as one of two Whig Unionists on the five-member Virginia delegation to the Peace Conference in Washington, where he helped formulate an agreement. He also won an overwhelming mandate to represent his home county at the Virginia convention and quickly became the Unionist floor leader there upon returning from Washington. For the first time in his career, Summers commanded an effective majority. The breakaway faction of Union Democrats, headed by Governor Letcher, plainly stood ready to join him and the more numerous Union Whigs in building Virginia's Union party. Secessionists remarked bitterly about the power wielded by a man whom they correctly identified as "the most intimate and confidential of Mr. Seward's Richmond allies." The heir apparent to quasi-secessionist James M. Mason in the U.S. Senate, Summers had attained national stature by March 1861. He personified the Union cause in the largest and most important state of the upper South.[24]

As the May election approached, the Unionist alliance in Virginia coalesced formidably. Congressman Alexander R. Boteler, the incumbent Whig Unionist from the lower Shenandoah Valley, received assurances that he could expect votes from "every Union man" whether Whig or Democrat. "Not even the most rabid secessionists doubt your reelection by a large majority," one supporter noted. The *Richmond Whig*, the leading Union newspaper in the state, exhorted its readers "not to be bamboozled" by former party distinctions. The only issue in the coming contest, insisted the *Whig*, was "between those who are yet struggling to save the Union if it can be honorably done, and those who are seeking to destroy it." The *Whig* gave ringing endorsements to John T. Harris and John S. Millson, two Union Democrats seeking reelection to Congress. They had "stood up manfully for the Union, and it is our duty to stand up manfully for them. Let Union men of all shades of opinion give them a cordial, hearty, and effective support." The *Whig* insisted that only "your strongest

Union men," regardless of party, should run for office in the spring elections: "It matters not whether they have heretofore been Whigs or Democrats. Let there be established a thorough *entente cordiale* between Union men of all shades of opinion. Let there be a generous magnanimity displayed and where necessary a fair division of candidates, with a view to remove all suspicion of any bias by reason of old party ties."[25]

Thoughtful Unionists recognized the need to subordinate traditional party allegiances. "I think I am about as deeply imbued, with real old fashioned Henry Clay principles, as any man, in this whole district," wrote one northwestern Virginian. But he professed readiness, in selecting a candidate for Congress, to "unite upon that man, no matter who he may be, or of what party he belongs to," so long as he was "a genuine Union man." Whig Unionists and Douglas Democrats needed to agree on a single candidate because division of the Union vote might elect "a Breckinridge secessionist." It would be "sheer folly," this Unionist reasoned, "to nominate a Douglas and a Bell man too." Though hoping the Union nominee would be a Whig, he stood ready, if necessary, to vote for "the veriest Democrat, in all the land."[26]

A similar rearrangement of political forces started to occur in Tennessee and North Carolina, both of which faced elections in August. Like Virginia, Tennessee would choose a new legislature and congressional delegation. In addition, Tennessee Unionists had the opportunity to oust incumbent Governor Isham G. Harris, a Southern Rights Democrat who had aided secessionists.

Tennessee Unionists moved rapidly to build a new party after winning their handsome victory in the convention election of February 9. They displayed unprecedented bipartisanship. "Past party affiliations should be *forgotten*, absolutely and unqualifiedly," insisted the *Nashville Republican Banner*. "Let us unite on good and well known and well tried Union men, irrespective of all other considerations. The parties of last year and the past are literally dead." A Union Whig activist calculated that nominating a candidate for governor "from the late Democratic party" would help "to hold the parties in their present position, as 'Union' and 'Disunion' parties," and would solidify the support of the "many Union Democrats now in our ranks." Elkenah D. Rader, a Union Democrat from strongly Democratic Sullivan County, in East Tennessee, had "never Seen Sutch a revolution." The local "Union Party" was "gaining strength." Leading Union Whigs promised to support "any Union Democrat for any office." Whig Congressman T. A. R. Nelson had just made a speech, Rader reported to Andrew Johnson, in which "he sustains you like a brother." Although local secessionists boasted that they would "egg" Johnson if he tried to speak there, Rader and the Unionists promised that "blood will be spilt" should any such indignity occur. "The battle in Tennessee this Summer will be fierce," Rader predicted, "but the victory will be great."[27]

Conclusive evidence indicates that leading Union Democrats and Whigs in Tennessee were "co-operating" together "for future good." John Bell "made advances" to Andrew Johnson and was reported gratified that Johnson had "received his approach properly." Johnson and Union Whig Congressman Emerson Etheridge established themselves as brokers for federal patronage in Tennessee. Jeptha Fowlkes, railroad promoter and behind-the-scenes political wirepuller, regarded it as "vastly important" that the two "act unitedly" and place in office men who would best advance the Union cause.[28]

North Carolina's scheduled congressional elections in August stimulated a parallel party realignment. Whig Unionists regretted that so many leading Democrats were "the most *ultra disunionists*" but strongly applauded the few such as editor William W. Holden who put Union ahead of party. Their success in the convention election of February 28 persuaded Union Whigs to maintain a warm welcome for Union Democrats in the emerging Union party. Former U.S. Senator George E. Badger, a Union Whig, marveled that he and two Union Democratic running mates won a landslide victory as convention delegates in normally Democratic Wake County, with Badger himself leading the ticket. Traditional party loyalties in the Raleigh area had been superseded by something more fundamental, Badger concluded: "It was the strength of the Union feeling that did it." In Orange County, directly west of Raleigh, long an arena for close two-party competition, a bipartisan Union ticket swept to victory by a four-to-one margin, the "most lopsided" election there since political parties originated in the 1830s. A "life-long Whig" from Orange reported that "party spirit is completely dead with the people, and they will vote for the Union candidate, no matter what he has been heretofore." Professing readiness to support a Union Democrat for Congress, if necessary, he admonished other Whigs: "Let us bury party and support any man that is sound on the Union question." Holden's *North Carolina Standard*, traditionally the newspaper of record for North Carolina Democrats, likewise urged citizens "to disregard all former party associations" and to nominate a strong Union man for Congress, "without regard to his former political connections or opinions."[29]

For the political realignment in the upper South to fulfill its potential, southern Unionists believed that a parallel movement must also occur in the North. They hoped a new Union party, with strength in both North and South, would emerge to bridge the sectional abyss. When some southern Unionists talked about a national Union party, they had in mind an anti-Republican coalition that would bring together all those in the North who had opposed Lincoln, plus enough disaffected Republican moderates and conservatives to tip the balance of power. One common Unionist argument against secession was the expectation that such a coalition could defeat the Republicans in 1864. Others thought the Republican party would collapse long before that. The ferocious struggle within the Republican party persuaded a Virginia newspaper editor that its disruption was "imminent."[30]

But significant numbers of southern Unionists thought that by pursuing a conservative course once in power, the Lincoln administration could become part of the contemplated national Union party. John A. Gilmer was an important example. As early as December, he frankly urged Lincoln to "come as far South as you can. You may divide from your many party friends, but by the preservation of the peace of the country you will nationalize yourself and your party." Soon afterward, Gilmer likewise encouraged Thurlow Weed to help build "a great national party." Although he refused a seat in Lincoln's cabinet, Gilmer still hoped upper South Unionists could collaborate with the conciliatory wing of the Republican party. The letters he wrote to Seward in March and April 1861 offered candid advice about how the administration, through "wise management," could strengthen the Union cause in the upper South before deciding how to deal with the seceded states. Considered together, Gilmer's letters strongly suggest that he and Seward shared some agreement about the future. Gilmer, believing that Seward understood the necessity of a hands-off approach, hoped the secretary of state could exercise a controlling influence toward that end within the new administration. If, as informed observers expected, disagreements about southern policy led Blair and perhaps Chase to resign from the cabinet, Gilmer could scarcely then have refused active participation.[31]

One other prominent upper South Unionist wrote even more explicitly about the formation of a "national conservative party." State legislator James Barbour of Culpeper, Virginia, visited Washington in January and had extensive consultations with both Seward and Douglas. Soon after the Virginia elections in early February, he advised Seward: "Come forward promptly with liberal concessions. . . . You may lose a portion of your own party North. But you place yourself and the new administration at the head of a national conservative party which will domineer over all other party organizations North and South for many years to come. You above all men have it in your power to bring the really conservative elements North and South into an organization the most useful and the most powerful yet seen in this country. But to be done at all this must be done promptly." Barbour outlined the same idea to Douglas: "On the basis of events now transpiring a new party *can* and ought to be entrenched which will command this country for 25 years. The course of the shrewd partisan and the wise patriot is now upon the same line. You and Mr. Seward have the capacity to see and know this."[32]

The February elections in the upper South stirred considerable speculation about including Republicans in a national Union party. The Washington reporter for the *Louisville Daily Journal* predicted that Lincoln would want to "nationalize his administration." If rebuffed by the no-compromise wing of the party, he would let them "go to the wall" and seek allies instead from the "Conservatives" of the "Border Slave States." The "radicals" would thus be "reduced to the proportions of the old abolition party of 1848, when it was led by Van Buren." One North Carolina Unionist thought that Lincoln would "be hailed as the savior of his country" and would become part of "the most powerful political party that has ever existed" if he followed the policy of letting the secessionists alone. The *Richmond Whig* announced, in a widely reprinted editorial, that "the conservative Whigs and Democrats of the South and the conservative Republicans of the North must unite to form a new Union party." The *Whig*'s editor considered partisan realignment imminent: "We predict that before the 4th of July this will be the arrangement of parties. The Republican organization cannot exist on its present basis. Lincoln and Seward will have the sagacity to see this, and they will promptly give the cold shoulder to the extreme men of their party and try to establish a national party, which will repudiate the wild absurdities of the Abolition school. A political necessity will constrain them to abandon not only the extreme dogmas of their party, but also to adopt a new name significant of the policy of the new party, and this name must be the UNION PARTY."[33]

Although most Republicans, including Lincoln, regarded such discussion as a prescription for party suicide, the idea of a Union party generated comment throughout the secession crisis. Its persistence resulted in large part from expectations that the responsibilities of power would impel a conservative course upon Lincoln. If then abandoned by radical Republicans, who opposed all conciliation, he would need new political allies. Proponents of a Union party sought to demonstrate to Lincoln that alienating the inflexible wing of his party would win more political support than it would lose, so that the pursuit of what conservatives considered sound public policy would prove politically advantageous to the new president.[34]

Indeed, many observers believed that a Union party would develop either with or without Lincoln. An article in the *New York Times* noted that "the question pending is one as to whether Mr. Lincoln shall become the head of the great 'Union Party' of the country, or whether a party upon that issue shall be permitted to grow up in hostility to his Administration." To this writer, the correct decision seemed apparent. If Lincoln initiated "a policy satisfactory to the Union men of the Border States" he would gain "a strong body of supporters in the South," and his party would become "a national and not a sectional one." The new administration had to choose, in other words, between "the party issues of the *past*" and "the necessities of the future." In this view, the Union party of the upper South would either collaborate with the new administration to effect a conservative southern policy, or the Union party would become the nucleus for an antiadministration coalition made up of southern Unionists and northern conservatives. People were "waiting in almost breathless anxiety," the writer in the *Times* concluded, "to see whether the Administration is to become powerful and successful by allying itself with the union sentiment of the country, or is to be broken down and ruined at the very outset, and rendered utterly powerless for any good."[35]

A number of prominent Democrats indicated a willingness to work with Republicans in an intersectional Union party. Andrew Johnson and Representative John Cochrane of New York helped draft "a conciliatory manifesto, to be signed by as many leaders of all parties as will sign it, setting forth the basis of the formation of a Union party." Their design was "to include in the proposed party all who approve the policy of compromise." John B. Haskin, anti-Lecompton Democratic congressman from New York City, urged Republicans to satisfy the needs of the border slave states that had proved their devotion to the Union. By so doing, Republicans could "build up a great Union party, which will have the power South and North to sustain Mr. Lincoln's administration."[36]

Expectations that a Union party would supersede the Republican party became most intense in late February. Believing that "the two or three hundred thousand voices in the North, in favor of coercion and involving the nation in the horrors of civil war, shall henceforth be disregarded," the *New York Herald* predicted that "over a million Union loving citizens in the States of Virginia, Kentucky, Tennessee, Missouri, Maryland, and Delaware, will rally in their places, to the support of the government which will assume the reins of power next week, and a new party will arise out of the ruins of those that will have ceased to exist." The architect of this "great Union party," according to the *Herald*, was the incoming secretary of state, William H. Seward.[37]

However inaccurate the *Herald*'s predictions about administration policy, it correctly identified Seward as the key promoter of the evanescent Union party. The man who only a year before had been the odds-on favorite to receive the Republican presidential nomination decided early in the secession winter that his party would need a broader and more national political base. Without announcing his objective in so many words, the wily New Yorker strove to implement an alliance between the upper South Unionists and conciliatory Republicans.

Did Seward contemplate a formal effort to unite under the aegis of a "Union party" or a looser collaboration toward common ends? The evidence is not conclusive. For obvious reasons he could not advocate openly what most of his party colleagues and the rank and file of Republicans considered abhorrent. But he did on several occasions make cryptic warnings that narrow party interests should not be allowed to stand in the way of sectional reconciliation.[38] Seward's pattern of activity during the secession crisis certainly suggests that, at the very least, he wanted the Lincoln administration to seek allies outside the Republican party. His efforts to get non-Republican southern Unionists appointed to the cabinet have already received close scrutiny in Chapter 9, as have Seward's close contacts with Crittenden and Douglas, the elder statesman among southern Unionists and the acknowledged leader of the national Democrats. Seward also used secret collaborators from outside the Republican party to remain informed about developments within President Buchanan's cabinet, to communicate with the new Confederate government, and to exert influence among upper South Unionists.[39]

Seward's relationships with Virginia Unionists illustrate how adept he had become at building bridges beyond the Republican party and creating expectations that he would throw his support behind a new national Union party. Seward met secretly with Democrat James Barbour and several Whigs, including George W. Summers and Robert Eden Scott. By persuading the Virginians that the new administration would support a satisfactory plan of settlement, Seward paved the way for the Union triumph in the February convention election. Later, using agents and intermediaries such as James C. Welling and William W. Seaton, editors of the Whiggish *National Intelligencer*, and John Cochrane, a prominent Democratic congressman from New

York, Seward kept Unionist leaders in the Virginia convention reassured about administration policy.[40]

Seward was "starting out afresh for a *Union Party*!" the well-informed Washington correspondent James E. Harvey noted privately. Seward's enemies within the Republican party reached similar conclusions. One bitterly condemned him for abandoning the party and working for "new combinations, under the name of a 'Union party,' or something of that kind." Henry Adams, who became fully aware of Seward's "Union party" idea by floating trial balloons for it in a newspaper column he anonymously penned, recorded the outburst of one unidentified Republican senator: "God damn you, Seward, you've betrayed your principles and your party; we've followed your lead long enough."[41]

One particular episode reveals much about Seward's likely aims. On March 3, 1861, the day before Lincoln's inauguration, the commanding general of the United States Army, Winfield Scott, addressed a letter to Seward. Judged either by its timing or its contents, Scott's was an extraordinary document. The recipient had just submitted his tactical refusal to serve in the cabinet as a desperate gambit to change Lincoln's southern policy. Scott's letter, obviously written in response to Seward's direct solicitation, outlined several different courses of action available to the administration. In mentioning one possibility, Scott used five words that subsequently made the letter famous: "Erring sisters, depart in Peace!" The general, however, did not advocate acquiescing in secession. Nor did he see merit in the forceful options of blockading southern ports or trying "to conquer the seceded States by invading armies." War would bring ruinous costs, "frightful" destruction of life and property, and the impossible task of trying to rule a conquered South. Instead, Scott argued that secession could be peacefully overcome only if Lincoln's administration were to "assume a *new* designation—the Union Party" and to adopt the conciliatory measures desired by southern Unionists. It could thereby gain the "early return of many, if not all the states which have already broken off from the Union." By immediately placing the letter before Lincoln, Seward indicated his own agreement with Scott's assessment.[42]

Informed observers understood Seward's thinking. The Confederate commissioners in Washington reported its basic features to their superiors in Montgomery. Seward, they judged, stood ready to "merge" the Republican party into a "Union party," so as to hold the upper South and to stir a Unionist backfire in the seceded states. They quoted Seward as saying that he had defeated Virginia Senators Mason and Hunter in their home state and looked forward to doing the same to Jefferson Davis and other deep South secessionists. Though contemptuous of Seward's hope that "the people of the cotton states" would "rebel against their leaders," the Confederate commissioners had a good grasp of his plan for peaceful reconstruction. Likewise, the British minister to America, Lord Lyons, a friend of Seward's, reported to his government:

> Mr. Seward's real view of the state of the country appears to be that if bloodshed can be avoided until the new government is installed, the seceding States will in no long time return to the Confederation. He seems to think that in a few months the evils and hardships produced by secession will become intolerably grievous to the Southern States, that they will be completely reassured as to the intentions of the Administration, and that the Conservative element which is now kept under the surface by violent pressure of the Secessionists will emerge with irresistible force. From all these causes he confidently expects that when elections are held in the Southern states in November next, the Union party will have a clear majority and will bring the seceding States back into the Confederation. He then hopes to place himself at the head of a strong Union party, having extensive ramifications both in the North and in the South, to make "Union" or "Disunion" not "Freedom" or "Slavery" the watchword of political parties.[43]

The question of federal appointments in the nonseceded southern states required that the new administration make some rapid decisions about cooperating with Unionists. In Maryland, Kentucky, Missouri, and far northwestern Virginia, a relative handful of avowed Republicans demanded recognition and control over federal patronage. Lincoln, however, had ample reason to disappoint the border state Republicans. Southern apprehensions about a Republican president resulted in part from a belief that federal appointees would establish a hostile fifth column of nonslaveholding Republicans in the South. Non-Republican Unionists warned that their cause would suffer as a consequence of any such policy. Seward, eager to repair the damaging impression made by the cabinet appointment of the militaristic border state Republican Montgomery Blair, urged Lincoln to fill a pending Supreme Court vacancy with an eminent non-Republican southern Unionist—either John J. Crittenden, the retiring Kentucky senator, or George W. Summers, the Union leader at the Virginia convention. Unionists responded enthusiastically to rumors about the Crittenden appointment, but inflexible Republicans thwarted the plan.[44]

Unionists did, however, exercise a major influence over federal appointments in the upper South in March 1861. Although an occasional prominent border state Republican such as Cassius M. Clay of Kentucky won a federal office, the administration, for the most part, consulted with and appointed non-Republican Unionists. Indeed, members of Lincoln's cabinet asked leading Unionists such as Congressmen John A. Gilmer and John Millson, and former U.S. Senator George E. Badger, to recommend suitable postmasters, federal marshals, and district attorneys. Attorney General Edward Bates agreed to give Andrew Johnson and Congressman Emerson Etheridge control over Tennessee appointments. Even the hard-line cabinet members, Montgomery Blair and Salmon P. Chase, who doubtless hoped to build a southern Republican party, solicited advice from non-Republican Unionists. Despite mutual distrust, circumstances forced the administration to collaborate with southern Unionists. Secessionists insisted that consultation regarding patronage marked the first step in the direction of slow strangulation, but their complaints rang hollow. Just the month before, the men being consulted had received the most emphatic endorsement from voters in the upper South.[45]

THE great issue in March 1861, however, was not patronage but peace. Southern Unionists most needed to prevent any fighting. Their concern focused especially on the two remaining outposts in the seceded states that remained in federal hands—Fort Pickens, on Santa Rosa Island outside the harbor of Pensacola, Florida, and Fort Sumter, on an artificial island within the harbor of Charleston, South Carolina. Sumter, located in sight of the city that could well consider itself the cradle of the Confederacy, was easily the most important. It had been in the public eye ever since late December, when a contingent of federal troops, led by Major Robert Anderson, fled there from the mainland, bringing South Carolina and the U.S. government close to war. Sumter thus had become a symbol of northern determination not to tolerate permanent secession. Popular sentiment in the North strongly favored its continued federal occupation. But southern Unionists saw the matter differently. They wanted the forts abandoned to minimize the chances of a violent clash between the federal government and the infant Confederacy. They feared that any bloodshed would unite the still divided South and make peaceful reunion impossible.

Lincoln discovered as soon as he took office that he would soon have to make decisions about Sumter. The fort's commander, Major Robert Anderson, reported on February 28 that he had only six weeks of food supplies remaining. The Confederates meanwhile threatened to resist any federal resupply mission, insisting that Sumter properly belonged to South Carolina. Their reinforcements in the Charleston area put Sumter in grave military jeopardy. Confederate batteries at the mouth of the harbor had the fort within easy range, thereby blocking any relief or support from federal ships in the Atlantic. General Winfield Scott calculated that defense of the fort against Confederate attack would require twenty-five thousand troops and a naval fleet. Scott's advice pointed inexorably toward abandoning Sumter. For one thing, the requisite troops and ships could not be gathered and coordinated for months, long after Anderson's food would be gone. So also, Scott's assessment indicated plainly that a decision to try to retain Sumter was, under the circumstances, a decision for civil war.[46]

Scott's military advice dovetailed with Seward's political calculations. Nor was the convergence mere coincidence. The two were "working like hand in glove" at this juncture, in the words of Seward's biographer. When Lincoln polled his cabinet in mid-March for advice about Fort Sumter, Seward replied with "the fullest explanation he ever made" of his secession crisis policy.[47] Seward argued that holding the fort meant war and that war would, at least at present, drive the upper South into the arms of the Confederacy and make reunion impossible. Instead, he would "deny to disunionists any new provocation or apparent offense," allowing Unionists to show that "alarms and apprehensions" were "groundless and false." By continuing to conciliate the slave states of the upper South, Lincoln could bind them more securely to the Union and enlist "their good and patriotic offices" to revive Unionism in the deep South. Latent "patriotic sentiment" there would, given time, "rally the people of the seceding states" to reverse their course. To those who thought such advice passive or unpatriotic, Seward recalled the parallel situation facing Great Britain in 1775. A plea for conciliation was exactly what "Chatham gave to his country under circumstances not widely different."[48]

Seward's defense of a hands-off policy also addressed the partisan considerations known to trouble Lincoln. Seward acknowledged that some party members thought "conciliation toward the slave states" tended to "demoralize the Republican party." He suggested, however, that civil war posed a greater danger for the party, risking "a popular disavowal both of the war and the administration which unnecessarily commenced it." Seward's approach, reinforced by Scott's military prognoses, drew support from three other cabinet members, with only Montgomery Blair unequivocally favoring an effort to hold Sumter.[49]

Lincoln, who had promised in his Inaugural Address "to hold, occupy, and possess the property and places belonging to the government," resisted the idea that Sumter be abandoned. He indicated as much soon after his inauguration, when visited by a delegation of Unionists from the Virginia convention.[50] The cabinet discussion of mid-March may, however, have moved him away from his commitment to Sumter. A memorandum in the Gideon Welles Papers would appear to be "a resume of conflicting views" about Sumter, presented by Lincoln to the cabinet on or about March 18. The arguments in the memorandum favoring withdrawal outweigh the objections. Lincoln recapitulated the conciliatory case for withdrawal—that it would "gratify and encourage" Unionists while at the same time working to undermine secessionist claims that Republicans planned to coerce the seceded states. Trying to hold the fort would, by contrast, trigger a "bloody conflict" over a position of scant military value. Would abandoning Sumter cause Republicans to lose confidence in the administration? Perhaps not. Any such "first impression" would change, for Republicans would "discover the wisdom of the course."[51]

While Lincoln and the cabinet wrestled with the Sumter dilemma, Seward empowered at least two individuals to inform George W. Summers that the fort soon would be evacuated. Seward knew, of course, that Unionists would react very favorably. They shared his hope that a hands-off policy would lead eventually to peaceful restoration of the Union. Summers soon reported that the news had "acted like a charm" and given the Virginia Unionists "great strength." He noted that "a reaction is now going on in the State. . . . We are masters of our position here, and can maintain it if left alone." Summers thereupon expressed confidence, in a speech to the Virginia convention, "that a pacific policy has been wisely determined on at Washington, and that the troops in Fort Sumter are now or will soon be withdrawn."[52]

Seward did not confine his secret diplomacy to Virginia and the upper South. Using Supreme Court justice and Alabama native John A. Campbell as a secret go-between, he conveyed to the Confederate government of the lower South the same message: Sumter soon would be evacuated. Seward hoped thereby to forestall any rash Confederate action. In effect, he offered Sumter as a gift rather than requiring Confederates to fight for it.[53]

Did Seward send word south about Fort Sumter on his own authority? Or did he act with Lincoln's knowledge and approval? An analysis of Seward's efforts to reassure the Virginia Unionists suggests the difficulties in reaching a conclusive answer. One of Seward's Virginia go-betweens, James C. Welling, an editor of the *National Intelligencer*, sent a letter informing George W. Summers about the prospective evacuation of Sumter and specifically attributing the information to Seward. Welling believed that Seward had acted "not only in perfect good faith but by authority of the President." Seward "honestly believed in the truth of his statements when he made them," Welling asserted, "for they were made with the full knowledge and consent of Mr. Lincoln." Did Welling himself speak to Lincoln? He did not so indicate. Available evidence about Seward's other go-between, New York Congressman John Cochrane, suggests that Seward initially may have worked behind Lincoln's back in telling Virginia Unionists that Sumter would be abandoned. But the record concerning Cochrane suggests also that Seward believed he was conveying correct information, even if he did act without authorization. Cochrane, who visited Richmond in mid-March, confirmed that the prospective Sumter evacuation delighted Summers. Seward thereupon enlisted Cochrane to show the president why he should honor Seward's promises. Such, at least, is a reasonable interpretation of Seward's note of March 19, introducing Cochrane to Lincoln as someone with whom he could "converse freely," and reporting that Cochrane had just received "a noble letter from Summers, which was written upon explanations made to him by Mr. Cochrane from me." The "noble letter" is not in the Lincoln Papers, but copies of a letter written that same day by Summers to Welling, the other go-between, have survived. In the letter to Welling, Summers said that assurances about Sumter's evacuation had strengthened the Unionists. He admonished Welling to "do your utmost . . . to preserve a pacific policy; everything depends upon it." By March 19, if not before, Lincoln thus received full information about Seward's contacts with the Virginians and about his pledges regarding Sumter.[54]

REPORTS about the administration's peaceful purposes and the imminent evacuation of Fort Sumter went far toward repairing the damage the conciliatory cause had suffered when territorial compromise bogged down, Chase and Blair won cabinet seats, and secessionists interpreted the inaugural as a war message. Unionists regained confidence that "the peace of the country will not be further disturbed, and that the times will change greatly for the better in the course of a few months."[55] From mid-March to early April, it appeared that the secession cause in Virginia, Tennessee, and North Carolina had suffered a mortal blow.

Virginia, the upper South state with the strongest indigenous secession movement, remained unmistakably within the Union. Initial reports about Lincoln's Inaugural Address, "indicating, as was thought, a rigorous and cruel policy of coercion toward the Seceded States," left some Virginians "terribly excited." But a week later, "the sober second thought" had "assumed sway." Indications that the administration would pursue "a peaceful and conciliatory policy" had "disarmed our people of much of their resentment." News about the "probable evacuation of Fort Sumter" reassured those with "feeble knees" that the sectional crisis would be resolved amicably. As the new agricultural season began, people in Virginia were "calming down and beginning to attend to their ordinary avocations." They "commenced their year's work" hoping for "peace and quiet."[56]

Leading Virginia Unionists insisted that they retained support from overwhelming popular majorities. They discounted a referendum held in Petersburg between March 13 and 15, indicating apparent gains for secession. Slave traders there and in Richmond had spent large sums of money to influence the result, Unionists charged. As late as April 13, Jubal Early, Union delegate to the Virginia convention and future Confederate general, labeled as a "fallacy" the idea that there had been "a change in popular sentiment." Secessionist mobs led by "bands of music in the streets" of Richmond did not represent "the masses of the people of Virginia." Only those areas that had voted against reference two months before favored secession, Early insisted.[57]

Out-of-state observers also judged that Virginia would not secede. After taking "a brief trip into the interior of Virginia" in late March, a reporter for the *Washington Evening Star* rejected claims by the "Richmond disunion newspapers" that a "considerable change" of opinion had taken place since the election in early February. If anything, the reverse was true. Many who had been "uncertain" about the policy of the Lincoln administration no longer feared that it would be "aggressive." Another observer reported that "without some decidedly and unequivocally hostile demonstration by the Administration, *immediate secession* in Virginia is as dead as a door nail." Confident that Virginia's Unionism offered a "powerful motive to the Republican party to preserve the peace," he hoped Lincoln would soon withdraw troops from the southern forts. A Tennessee doctor diagnosed Virginia's progress in clinical terms: "The fever is gradually subsiding—and soon our sick patient will be convalescent."[58]

Continued Union strength was especially evident in western Virginia. "The people here are very much calmed down in the last two weeks," reported a resident of Hampshire County in the upper Potomac Valley. So long as Lincoln made no "attempt to coerce," people would soon "almost forget that there is a black republican president." "If there is a secessionist here now that was not one before the election I have not heard of him," the westerner noted. Instead, local secessionists, "aware that they could not force the people to break up this Union," had begun to talk as if they were good Unionists too. An observer from Morgantown in the far northwest found "the masses" in his region were "solid as the Rock of Gibraltar." They had "settled down calmly and determined that no power shall take them out of the Union." People were "outraged," he added, "that they had no *opportunity* to vote down the calling of a convention as other states have had." Asked by convention delegate Waitman T. Willey to provide an updated assessment of the "Union spirit" in the northwest, another Morgantown resident replied: "I tell you in sober earnestness that it is as intense, as it can be, and that a large majority of our people are warm Union men. There has been no decline in that respect since you left, but on the contrary an increase in Union feeling."[59]

Virginia Unionists commended the administration for initiating a southern policy based on "diplomacy rather than bayonets and bullets," but secessionists and their allies such as Senators Mason and Hunter were allegedly thrown into "a perfect agony of apprehension" by reports about withdrawal from Sumter. "They say there is no shadow of a chance to push secession any further, and every Southern man who favored it will be tomahawked," reported the *New York Times*. John Letcher, the Unionist governor of Virginia, also found secessionists "disheartened" and grumbling against Lincoln for refusing "to aid them in carrying out their plans."[60]

Secessionists were "praying for" an armed clash involving federal forces. "They are absolutely agog for it," one prominent Virginia Unionist observed. "No matter what the form, so collision can take place and force be used or blood spilt, is all they require." Occasional open avowals hinted at less restrained private views. The *Richmond Enquirer*, for example, predicted that an "actual conflict of arms" would drive many "qualified submissionists" to "take sides at once with their Southern brethren." And Virginia Congressman Roger A. Pryor encouraged Confederates to "STRIKE A BLOW!" As soon as "blood is shed," he promised, "old Virginia will make common cause with her sisters of the South." But from mid-March to early April,

Unionists believed the Lincoln administration, by carefully avoiding armed conflict, would disappoint secessionists.[61]

As in Virginia, so also in the two other pivotal states of the upper South. Former Tennessee Governor William B. Campbell wrote to an Alabama relative, describing Lincoln's inaugural as "decidedly conservative and peaceful" and predicting that the administration would "do nothing coercive or aggressive in the rebellious states." Campbell observed that the "feeling of sympathy" toward the seceded states was "daily weakening in Tennessee." The "coarse and vulgar abuse of Tennessee" by the press in the deep South was creating "an estrangement which will be universal and deep-seated." News of the administration's apparent intentions regarding Fort Sumter added to Unionist confidence. Andrew Johnson predicted that there would be "nothing left of Secessionists" in Tennessee once Sumter was abandoned. Robert Hatton tersely summarized the situation in Middle Tennessee on March 27: "All is quiet here. Secession is making no headway. Can't for the present. Trust it never may." A newspaper editor in Hatton's district likewise detected "the dawn of a brighter day." The country was "gradually yet surely, emerging into the light of peace. . . . The curtains of war are being drawn from the heavens, and the sunlight begins to break down upon us." Confident that Lincoln would make no attempt "to coerce," the editor concluded that secession would spread no further, so that the seceded states would, "after a few years of Independent existence, return to the glorious union of our Fathers."[62]

Even in West Tennessee, a region more inclined to identify with the lower South than any other part of the state, secession sentiment was reported "coming down" by mid-March. "Our people will not consent to go into a Southern Confederacy," concluded a Trenton resident. Jeptha Fowlkes, a hardheaded crony of Andrew Johnson's, reported from Memphis: "If no act of violence and no new cause of irritation be furnished, the secession feeling will rapidly lessen. The evacuation of Fort Sumpter and promises of Peace by the Administration is doing a vast deal to bring men to reason and to a common sense view of the issues before the Country!" Confident likewise that "the policy of the Administration is peace," West Tennessee Congressman Emerson Etheridge predicted that "next August Tennessee will give secession another blow more terrible than ever before."[63]

North Carolina Unionists also felt encouraged. State senator and future governor Jonathan Worth concluded that "Lincoln's Inaugural breathes peace to any candid mind." Considering "the Revolution arrested," he anticipated that people in the seceding states would "recover from their mania." Other North Carolina Unionists reported that secessionists had exhausted "every known and imaginary artifice to carry their point" and were by March sustained only by the possibility that Lincoln intended war. "Their only hope is a collision," a Raleigh resident advised Stephen A. Douglas. Even from the Charlotte area, a center of disunion strength, came a report in early April that pursuit of "a wise and cautious let-alone policy" by the administration would undermine support for secessionists. The leading historian of North Carolina antebellum politics has concluded that "between February 28, when they voted overwhelmingly for the Union, and April 15, the Unionism of most North Carolinians endured. In March and early April, North Carolina did not drift toward secession. . . . Throughout March and early April, Unionists believed that the 'let alone' policy had been adopted by the Lincoln administration and that North Carolina would remain in the Union for the indefinite future."[64]

A few fateful weeks later, William A. Graham, the elder statesman among North Carolina Unionists, recalled the misleading interval during March and early April, when "the public mind in all the eight slave holding States that had not yet seceded, was settling down in the conviction that the forts were to be evacuated and repose was to be allowed, so favorable to conciliation and harmony." Jonathan Worth likewise believed that "Union men had gained strength" in North Carolina until the very moment of Lincoln's proclamation for seventy-five thousand troops. "If he had withdrawn the garrison of Fort Sumter," Worth believed, "this State and Tennessee and the other slave States which had not passed an ordinance of Secession, would have stood up for the Union."[65]

Although secessionists tried frantically to demonstrate that a reversal of popular opinion had occurred in the upper South since the February elections, Unionists became increasingly contemptuous of their opponents' "trailing and howling after South Carolina." The *Salisbury Carolina Watchman* tartly observed that "the secessionists are increasing their noise and agitation as their numbers decrease." Jonathan Worth believed the secession taint had fatally handicapped his political opponents: "Democracy has fought for months with the rope around its neck. Its votaries should now have their coffins made and say their prayers." Virginia Unionists agreed. "The out-and-out secessionists are perfectly rampant," reported one local correspondent to the *Richmond Whig*; "the poor defeated, demoralized, despairing crew who have ruled us to ruin us, have seen the hand writing on the wall, and knowing that their days are numbered, still in their death agony cry out[:] we are the men, and ours are the doctrines that will save you." Governor Letcher dismissed as "the last effort of expiring treason" a flurry of secessionist "instructions" to the Virginia convention. "How sadly they have been mistaken in their calculations," he commented with evident satisfaction. "They are doomed to certain and overwhelming defeat." The *Whig* castigated attempts by "rowdy demonstrations in the galleries and lobbies, and by mobs in the streets of the Capitol" to "overawe and bully the union delegates." It explained the resort to "intimidation and terror" as evidence of "desperation."[66]

Failure at the polls forced secessionists to consider extreme measures. The diary of David Schenck provides a glimpse of secessionist anguish and turmoil upon discovering that Unionists firmly controlled the upper South. Schenck lived in Lincolnton, North Carolina, not far from Charlotte, an overwhelmingly Democratic and prosecession region. Secessionists carried the vote on February 28 in Lincolnton by a margin of 334 to 1. Then came the astonishing revelation that a coalition of Whigs, "abolition sympathizers," and "old Federalists" had teamed up to place North Carolina on the side of "submission." This result, Schenck noted, "has changed the feeling from one of excitement to a deep feeling of desperation, quiet but determined." The prospect of seeing his home state and Virginia "succumb ignobly to the yoke" made Schenck favor "resistance to the death by means legal if possible but illegal if necessary."[67]

Virginia secessionists likewise found apparent Unionist dominance hard to bear. Future Confederate general John D. Imboden of Staunton suspected that Unionists would "submit to the dishonor of standing by and seeing war made on the seceded states." Believing former Governor Henry A. Wise the only convention member who had "the true spirit which should animate Virginia at this time," Imboden contemplated "fearful times here in Virginia," possibly even "a war amongst ourselves." Ardent Southern Rights enthusiast G. D. Gray of Culpeper Courthouse had thought at the end of December that his county was "almost a unit for secession." Then came the reversal of January and February. Culpeper voted for "reference," 532 to 365, and sent prominent Unionist James Barbour to the convention. "Exasperated" and "sadly depressed about old Virginia," Gray concluded that the only chance for secession lay "in Revolution or else in conflict of the Government with the Seceded states." Willing "to peril all in the struggle," Gray, like Imboden, clung to the hope "that Gov. Wise will raise the standard of Revolution if all else fail."[68]

Rumors about irregular military action or even a secessionist coup surfaced in Virginia from time to time. Alfred M. Barbour, superintendent of the federal armory at Harpers Ferry and soon to be elected as a Union delegate to the Virginia convention, confidentially informed his superiors in Washington on January 21 that he feared an attack. Though reticent about his source of information and uncertain whether his concern was "well founded," Barbour requested protection from "a company or more of regular U.S. soldiers." At about the same time Alexander H. H. Stuart, a state senator and soon an important Union delegate in the convention, urged Governor Letcher to investigate whether "certain rash and ill-advised citizens" were plotting to seize federal installations in the state. In private conversation, Stuart also reported rumors that a movement was afoot to remove Letcher and reinstate former Governor Wise. When Wise found out about Stuart's suspicions, he and a friend threatened to turn it into a test of honor. Rumors persisted that "there would be rebellion in Virginia" if the convention did not "act speedily." O. Jennings Wise, editor of the *Richmond Enquirer* and son of the former governor, allegedly told a member of the convention that if it did not pass a secession ordinance, "it ought to be driven from its hall at the point of a bayonet." Another prominent secessionist editor delighted a crowd by advocating the same bayonet policy against the convention.[69]

Suspecting that some secessionists plotted a coup d'etat to overthrow the convention or even the state government, Unionists had reason to remain vigilant. But their opponents' desperation also seemed to acknowledge that Unionists commanded a popular majority statewide. The *Charlottesville Review* humorously advised "thoughtful fire-eaters" about "the utter injudiciousness of making a rumpus." Having had things "their own way so long," they did not understand "the functions of a minority." Their "harnessing" was therefore a "tedious" process: "It is like taking pigs to a new pen. They squeal the whole distance." The spirit among secessionists was well depicted by Governor Letcher's hometown friend and frequent correspondent James D. Davidson of Lexington: "The Secession party here are straining every nerve to its utmost tension, to disorganize the conservative party. That party knows that what it does must be done quickly, and it is pressed to the utmost point of endurance. It can't stand such extreme tension long, and unless it is relieved from it, by an early success in their machinations, a terrible reaction will befall them: and well they know it." Therefore, concluded Davidson, "let Conservatism stand fast, and hold designing men and their sensation measures, at bay, and time will do its work, of peace to the country, and vengeance to her foes."[70]

Union delegates in the Virginia convention remained unperturbed.

They continued drafting a proposal to set before the planned border state conference in June. Convinced that no emergency threatened and confident that their efforts would help maintain the peace, Unionists expected to adjourn the convention after completing their proposal and not to reconvene until late summer or fall. They believed themselves destined to play a large role in restoring the Union. More immediately, they looked forward to sweeping the state elections in May.[71]

UNFORTUNATELY for the Unionists, the administration's commitment to a conciliatory southern policy was no more than tentative. Lincoln remained undecided about Fort Sumter and kept his own counsel. Though upper South Unionists thought the administration had adopted a policy of "letting the secessionists alone," a groundswell of opposition arose from within the Republican party to any such "humiliation." If Lincoln fulfilled the hopes of southern Unionists, he would split his party. He doubtless feared a repetition of John Tyler's dismal term in office two decades before, which featured the anomaly of a president repudiated by his own party. But keeping the Republican party together might plunge the country into war. Lincoln had reason to hesitate before choosing between two such unhappy alternatives.[72]

While Lincoln pondered, new complexities began to develop. Commercial uncertainty and reduced international commerce rapidly undermined national finances during the secession crisis because the federal government in that arcadian age still supported itself primarily by taxing imports. Treasury officials scrambled to arrange loans as a stopgap measure. Coincidentally, the departure of low-tariff congressmen from the deep South enabled Republicans to fulfill a campaign pledge by enacting a protective tariff. Supporters of the bill also depicted it as a timely revenue measure. Increased federal tariff rates were, therefore, due to take effect on April 1.[73]

But doubts about the new tariff soon arose. A violent clash between federal and Confederate authorities appeared likely should the federal government try to collect tariff revenues in the deep South. Unionists therefore urged a passive approach, fearing the impact of any armed confrontation. The new tariff thus provided an additional exhibition of apparent federal helplessness in the face of secession.

To make matters worse, the federal government continued to run out of money. American trade remained depressed by political uncertainties, and revenue collections therefore lagged. In late March as in January, the Treasury Department again had to float substantial loans. Its principal creditors, the powerful and influential large merchants of New York City, had strenuously opposed passage of the new tariff and now urged its repeal. Although initially hopeful that political turmoil in the deep South would bring more interior commerce and hence international trade to New York, they concluded during March that considerable New York trade would be siphoned off to secession ports, where the old lower tariff rates would remain in effect. Nor were they reassured by supporters of the new tariff, who insisted that few imports would be diverted south because southern ports had inadequate facilities and poorer access to interior customers. The Confederate Congress added to merchants' anxieties by indicating that it would soon move to lower the southern tariff, thereby giving importers added incentive to ship to the South rather than New York.[74]

By late March, the *New York Times*, until then a bastion of support for a hands-off policy, suddenly began to editorialize belligerently about the Confederate threat to New York trade. Economic analyst Henry Varnum Poor, who wrote a series of incisive editorials for the *Times* during the secession winter, had been confident in January and February that southern troubles posed no danger to northern commerce or prosperity. Instead, secession would create economic havoc in the seceding states. On March 22 and 23, however, the *Times* abruptly reassessed the situation, concluding that secession posed an economic menace to the North and to its international trade. It urged the federal government "at once to shut up every Southern port, destroy its commerce, and bring utter ruin on the Confederate states." Depressed foreign trade and fears of even greater disruption so exasperated the New York commercial community that the *Times* could remark: "A state of war would almost be preferable."[75]

The interconnecting issues of tariff and revenue collection thus illustrated the difficulty of maintaining a hands-off policy. Keeping the peace entailed increasingly unpleasant side effects. Hoping to improvise and muddle through, Lincoln on March 18 asked three of his cabinet members whether federal ships might try to collect revenue outside the ports of the seceding states. Whatever the merits of Lincoln's plan, upper South Unionists strongly opposed it. They contended that attempts to collect revenue at sea were unlawful, "impracticable," and likely to cause fighting. The spectacle of a disintegrating Union and a paralyzed federal government fueled northern demands for a more decisive policy to thwart secession. As pressures to "do something" intensified, it became ever harder to defend what looked like a "do nothing" policy of abandoning forts and failing to collect revenue.[76]

Formulation of federal policy toward the seceded states required, furthermore, that the Lincoln administration judge the international ramifications of any steps it took. Would a hands-off policy toward the South achieve desired results before France and Great Britain considered recognizing or aiding the Confederate states? The question became increasingly hard to avoid during March as the newly established government at Montgomery began to function. If the federal government relinquished Fort Sumter, the most important symbol of its sovereignty over the deep South, how could it deny that the seceding states had established a de facto government? Many in the North began to have worries of the sort expressed by a Cincinnati newspaper, which feared that "England and France, and the other great commercial nations" would "recognize the Government of the Confederate States." When Lincoln defended his policies to Congress the following summer, he noted that abandoning Sumter would have tended to "insure" foreign recognition of the Confederacy and thereby bring about "our national destruction." This outcome, Lincoln contended, "could not be allowed."[77]

Lincoln also remained unpersuaded that the deep South would voluntarily return. Even if a conciliatory policy would hold the upper South in the Union, would it also draw back the seceded states? To get a better idea of the situation in the deep South, Lincoln sent Stephen A. Hurlbut, an Illinois friend who had been born and raised in Charleston, South Carolina, down for a brief visit to his home city. Hurlbut left on March 21 and returned on the twenty-seventh with the conclusion that the seceding states were "irrevocably gone" and were "'de facto' a Nation." In South Carolina itself, Hurlbut found "an unanimity of sentiment which is to my mind astonishing." There was "no attachment to the Union" and "positively nothing to appeal to." Hurlbut, to be sure, went to a city where any significant Union sentiment would have been hard to find, but if he had toured more extensively in the deep South during late March, he would not likely have changed his assessment. The new Confederacy looked more permanent all the time. Upper South Unionists who realized the strength of pro-Confederate opinion in the deep South were greatly troubled. Jeptha Fowlkes, the Tennessee railroad promoter, reported alarming evidence to Andrew Johnson. Travelers from the lower South, in conversation with Fowlkes, displayed "much *less* disaffection" than he had expected. He feared that people there were "settling down to remain out of the Union."[78]

By late March the spirit and determination of the deep South forced some observers to begin thinking about permanent division of the country. Even though Seward and most southern Unionists continued to hold out hope for peaceful reunion, others discerned momentum toward peaceful separation. The respected *National Intelligencer* published a long editorial on March 21 entitled "The Past, the Present, and the Future," raising the question of what the federal government should do if the seceding states did not return voluntarily to the Union. If "developments of the ensuing year" showed that people in the deep South still wished to remain out of the Union, the editors advised that "it would seem to be the part of wisdom and sound policy for the people of the United States to acquiesce in that desire." To arrange terms for peaceful separation, they recommended holding a national convention. The editorial immediately became "the principal topic of conversation" in Washington and was reported to be "causing a sensation in political circles." Rumors surfaced that the editorial reflected administration thinking (Seward's closeness to James C. Welling and William W. Seaton, editors of the *National Intelligencer*, was no secret).[79]

Seward, of course, shared the administration's goal of restoring the Union. But the *New York Times* reported "growing sentiment throughout the North *in favor of letting the Gulf States go*." James E. Harvey, Washington correspondent for the *Philadelphia North American*, noted that "the opinion is fast gaining ground among public men that, if the cotton States cannot live with us *amicably*, and their people really desire to go, to try the experiment of a separate government, it is better and wiser that a convention of the States should be called, so as to let them depart in peace, and forever." One such public man was Hurlbut, whom Lincoln had just sent out on southern reconnaissance. Hurlbut's March 27 report specifically advocated surrendering national jurisdiction over the deep South by a national convention, rather than going to war.[80]

Discussion about peaceful separation or the recognition of Confederate independence placed upper South Unionists in an awkward position. They had urged the administration to follow a conciliatory policy to achieve peaceful reunion, not separation. Unionists hoped a noncoercive approach would bring back the seceded states—and they very much wanted the seceded states brought back. They believed a Republican president could do little to hurt the South, so long as all southern states remained in the Union. But a Union with nineteen free states and only eight slave states looked unappealing. The decline of slavery in several border slave states made proslavery Unionists all the more anxious about the future.

Most Unionists, therefore, either never discussed recognizing Confederate independence or struggled to reconcile it with their formula for peaceful reunion. For example, one Unionist newspaper editor in Tennessee concluded that recognition of southern independence would be "exceedingly politic under the circumstances" because it was "the surest way to prevent bloodshed." The "restoration of the whole Union" could still be achieved, once people in the deep South came to their senses. "We are perfectly willing that the uncertain Cotton State Experiment shall be fairly tested," reasoned editor C. D. Steele of the *Gallatin Courier*. "We think it will prove a failure—a terrible failure—in which event the necessity of a reconstruction of the old Union will become apparent to the Confederate states." Charles W. Button, the editor of the *Lynchburg Virginian*, likewise thought it best to recognize that the seceded states had established "a separate and independent government." His reasons were forthright: "We want peace, and desire, above all things, to avoid everything that is likely to induce a collision." But he too held out hope that the mediating leverage of the upcoming border state conference would "pave the way for the return of the seceding States upon terms that will not be wounding to their honor." John Minor Botts suggested calling a national convention to amend the Constitution so as to allow states to withdraw and thereby prevent civil war. He also expressed the hope that the seceded states would, within a year, seek readmittance to the Union.[81]

But what if the seceded states decided to stay out? That, surely, was the question that most bedeviled Lincoln. Yet it was not a question southern Unionists even liked to consider. Two of the few to do so were John Bell, who later claimed that he privately advised Lincoln to let the seceded states "go in peace" rather than try to force them back into the Union, and William A. Graham, who likewise thought "peaceable separation" far preferable to war. Their premises were universally shared by other southern Unionists. Bell believed, for example, that "the policy of *coercion* by the use of the bayonet, could not succeed" and that the deep South "could never be subjugated or reduced to submission" even if "overrun and desolated by fire and sword." So the conclusion he and Graham reached—to acquiesce in Confederate independence "if upon a candid comparison of opinions our differences should be found to be irreconcilable"—was one most southern Unionists would have been driven toward, albeit reluctantly. It was not, however, a conclusion they could reasonably expect Lincoln to accept.[82]

If peaceful reunion was beyond reach, then the choice lay starkly between peaceful separation and war. Ominously, as far as Republicans were concerned, secessionists and quasi-secessionists were already making exactly that point. The *Richmond Enquirer* stated that Lincoln must either "recognize the independence of the seceded States" or attempt to conquer them by armed force. Senator James

M. Mason of Virginia insisted that the only way to preserve peace was to admit, as Lincoln had refused to do in his Inaugural Address, that the Union was "broken" and "at an end" and that the seceding states had successfully established "their separate and independent existence" under a new government. That, Mason announced, "is the peace policy; and none other."[83]

Former U.S. Senator Henry S. Foote, of Nashville, Tennessee, a prominent Mississippi Unionist only a decade before and warm supporter of Stephen A. Douglas in 1860, converted to secession in early 1861 after deciding the Union had irrevocably ruptured. He judged that the Lincoln administration was trying to pursue a hopelessly contradictory policy. It wanted to preserve peace so as to keep the border states in the Union and place no obstacles in the way of the cotton states, should they experience a change of heart. Yet at the same time, it persisted in viewing the Union as unbroken and the seceded states as still subject to federal law. Unless the administration quickly abandoned its claims to the deep South and recognized Confederate independence, Foote warned, an armed confrontation would follow and "in all probability result in the most sanguinary and destructive conflict that the world has yet known." In a public letter to John J. Crittenden, leader of the upper South moderates, who had been trying to find a formula to achieve peaceful reunion, Foote made an urgent plea that Crittenden work instead for peaceful separation. "*The Federal Union is gone*," Foote insisted. Neither he nor Crittenden had any hand in destroying it, but they could do nothing now to resurrect it. Would it not be better, Foote asked, "to have *two Governments* and *two Unions*," than to experience the horrors of civil war?[84]

11

REVERSAL OF THE HANDS-OFF POLICY

"P. S. What delays the removal of Major Anderson? Is there any truth in the suggestion that the thing is not to be done after all? This would ruin us." George W. Summers thus appended a cautionary postscript to his important letter of March 19, assuring Secretary of State William H. Seward that the promised evacuation of Fort Sumter had "acted like a charm" to strengthen Unionists at the Virginia convention. This speck on the horizon grew larger. Soon it would produce the biggest and most ominous cloud darkening the skies for southern Unionists during the secession winter.[1]

By the end of March the speck had become an irritating presence. "It is settled on all sides that the Administration have decided to remove the troops from Sumter. Why then delay?" asked the *Lynchburg Virginian*. "Why defer the execution of their purpose, until *necessity* shall seem to divest the movement of all merit as being in the interest of peace? Such blundering, and dilly-dallying is inexcusable. It embarrasses the Union men of the Border States, and is playing directly into the hands of the Secessionists." Henry W. Miller, about to accept a Union party nomination to run for Congress in North Carolina, sent a worried letter to Stephen A. Douglas to inquire about the same problem. Miller was troubled by "the tardiness of the Administration in carrying out its promised policy with reference to Fort Sumter." The continued "suspense and uncertainty" were beginning to hurt: "Union men who have been firm and true heretofore, are beginning to *despair and doubt the faith of the Administration*." Virginia Unionist Alexander H. H. Stuart likewise complained that "the undecided course of the administration has weakened and is weakening us daily," and Jeptha Fowlkes, the Tennessee railroad promoter, privately condemned the administration's "hesitation and uncertainty." "You can't *lead* without boldness and decision," Fowlkes told Andrew Johnson.[2]

As some Unionists suspected, a struggle was taking place within the administration. The prospect of abandoning Sumter displeased Lincoln. Many earnest Republicans opposed any such "concession to traitors." The financial and international ramifications of a conciliatory policy also began to look increasingly bleak. And Lincoln had growing doubts—reinforced by Stephen A. Hurlbut's letter of March 27—that the deep South would ever voluntarily rejoin the Union.

By late March two very different definitions of the available choices had emerged. On one hand, Seward and most southern Unionists said the choice lay between (1) holding the forts and trying to collect the revenue, which ran the strong risk of a collision that would unite the South and prevent reunion; and (2) conciliation, hands-off, masterly inactivity, which offered the only hope for reversing deep South secession and stimulating voluntary reunion. But a growing body of Republican opinion said Lincoln must choose between (1) voluntary separation, which was the inevitable result of a hands-off policy; and (2) enforcement of federal laws in the seceded states, hoping that secessionists might yet acquiesce, but recognizing that reestablishment of federal authority in the deep South might require the use of force.[3]

Each of the contending groups—those who favored a hands-off policy and those who did not—agreed on the paramount object of reunion but disagreed about the relative risks of using armed force. Seward and the southern Unionists insisted that a coercive policy would make disunion permanent and so argued that only voluntary means could ever restore the Union. The hard-line Republican critics of a hands-off policy contended, by contrast, that a coercive policy offered the only chance of holding the Union together because a hands-off policy would never bring back the seceded states. Thinking the risks of full-scale war less foreboding than what they perceived as the fatal drift toward peaceable separation, stiff-backed Republicans wanted an energetic display of federal authority. In short, Seward and southern Unionists saw war as the greatest danger to reunion, while hard-line Republicans saw fear of war as the greatest danger to reunion.

Southern Unionists and their northern critics each interpreted the national predicament from the perspective of trying to protect their party base. Southern Unionists chose to run the risks of voluntary separation because they knew that war would explode their fragile political coalition and destroy their power. Most persuaded themselves that peaceful reunion remained feasible and that no choice between forcible reunion and voluntary separation need be made. The anticompromise Republicans chose to run the risk of war because they knew that adoption of a hands-off policy by the Lincoln administration would produce upheaval among the Republican rank and file, potentially disrupting the party.

One may learn a great deal about the climate of opinion within which Lincoln had to make his decision by examining leading northern newspapers. The place to start is the *New York Tribune*, edited by Horace Greeley. No other newspaper came close to the *Tribune* in reaching a wide audience among people the administration depended upon for support. Its famous weekly edition had a circulation of 287,750 by April 1861, and Greeley estimated that a million people read each issue. The *Tribune* both reflected and helped to shape the thinking of a large segment of the Republican electorate throughout the North.[4]

The *Tribune* had steadfastly opposed compromise since the crisis began. Even peaceful separation would be preferable to compromise, Greeley suggested. He remained confident, however, that the Union would endure without compromise and without war. If northerners stood firm and refused to appease secessionists, the furor would cease. But if northerners temporized, secessionists would increase their demands and reunion would become more difficult.[5]

Greeley's assessment of the situation gave him a callous view of southern Unionists. Until late in the secession crisis, he too looked forward to peaceful reunion. But he condemned as dangerously wrongheaded the approach they favored. He bitterly accused Unionists of trying to "dictate terms" that amounted to little more than northern "surrender," insisting that the North allow the secessionists to do "exactly as they please, and never draw a trigger on them," while also demanding "degrading and revolting amendments to the Constitution" that would make slavery "a truly national institution." Southern Unionists were, in Greeley's eyes, dishonest accomplices to the secession movement. Under the pretense of trying to save the Union, they were in fact "shielding the seceders" and playing "directly into their hands."[6]

The behavior of the "Union party, so called," the *Tribune* charged, simply gave countenance to "the current Southern assumption that Republicanism menaces the rights and safety of the South" and that a powerful faction of the Republican party consisted of "blind fanatics." Confident that few people in the upper South honestly held any such distorted ideas, the *Tribune* insisted that the strength of secession sentiment there had been "unduly magnified" and that "the loyal men of the South" held an impregnable majority. "*Virginia will not leave the Union* . . . no matter on what pretext," the *Tribune* confidently asserted. The North therefore need not offer any "sugar-plum" or "fig-leaf" of compromise, nor adopt "the nostrums of the Union-saving quacks." Real Union sentiment would flourish in the upper South as soon as purported Union leaders there admitted that slavery was an economic albatross and took steps to encourage free labor. Greeley thus indignantly chastised the leader of the Virginia Unionists, George W. Summers, for having renounced the antislavery principles he had articulated thirty years before as a young state legislator.[7]

James Gordon Bennett's *New York Herald* had a daily circulation of over eighty thousand in 1861, making it by far the largest daily in the world. Major participants in national politics considered it essential reading. Soon after Lincoln's inauguration, former President James Buchanan reminded Bennett to redirect the *Herald* to his Pennsylvania home: Buchanan professed himself "quite lost without it." Though officially nonpartisan, the *Herald* tended to take a Democratic slant. Its influence was especially great in the South, where it was judged "a great authority" not just by the politicians "but with the people as well." The *Herald*'s coverage of southern news was therefore doubly important. It not only informed the North about the South but also provided southerners with what they considered reliable news about their home region.[8]

During the secession crisis, the *Herald* took an outspokenly pro-compromise position, consistently berating the Republican party and the Lincoln administration for refusing to offer essential concessions. The *Herald* warned incessantly that the upper South would soon follow the cotton states out of the Union unless the Crittenden Compromise were rapidly adopted. Such exaggerated fears about the danger of upper South secession, though widespread in January, were much less excusable in February and March. Yet the *Herald* continued to trumpet a distorted view of the upper South. By late March and early April, it concluded that a great change in public sentiment had occurred in Virginia since the convention election in February. It reported an "irresistible ground swell" in favor of secession because the Lincoln administration had failed to offer any conciliatory terms. Why did the *Herald* so exaggerate secession strength? In concluding that Virginia secessionists were "fighting most zealously on the offensive" whereas Unionists were "nearly silenced," the *Herald* referred to the "very active and earnest daily newspapers" in Richmond for corroboration. In other words, it interpreted the hysterical prosecession stance of O. Jennings Wise's *Richmond Enquirer* and John M. Daniel's *Richmond Examiner* as a reasonable sample of public opinion in the upper South. By any standard of good journalistic practice, the *Herald*'s Virginia coverage was lazy and inaccurate. But it was influential. One Unionist in the Virginia convention condemned the *Herald* as "the leading disunion and sensation journal in this country."[9]

To see how the *Herald*'s coverage of events in the upper South helped to shape the perceptions of informed northerners, one must refer back to the *Tribune*. However different the principles and perspectives of the two newspapers, the *Tribune* by early April found itself having to explain why Unionists had lost ground in Virginia. To do so required a flagrant sleight of hand because Greeley had insisted for months that ordinary Virginians displayed far more unconditional Unionism than their timid leaders. But he proved equal to the demands of the occasion. Greeley blamed his favorite targets, "the shilly-shally Unionists in the Virginia Convention." By wasting weeks "in hair-splitting talk" and taking an "equivocal position" that failed to satisfy real Unionists in Virginia, Summers and his allies had allowed secessionists—who "had a definite purpose and marched straight toward their object"—to seize the initiative. Greeley thus concluded, in effect, that treacherous and incompetent leaders had sabotaged Virginia Unionism, forcing the administration to try to save the Union by its own means and without their aid.[10]

Greeley therefore condemned as "foolishness" Seward's efforts "to shape public policy to suit the border slave states." That approach would "ruin the Republican party" and "rend it asunder." Instead, Greeley urged the administration "to prepare to meet force with force." Only such a "proud and manly" refusal "to submit to degrading terms" could preserve "the honor and independence of the United States." Should the Republican party "prove unequal to the occasion," he predicted, "another party will supersede it, even as it superseded the effete and emasculate Whig Party."[11]

The *Tribune*'s growing readiness to confront the Confederacy militarily was echoed in other Republican newspapers by late March and early April. The conciliatory *Boston Advertiser* and *New York Times*, unhappily confessing doubts about the prospects for peaceful reunion, suggested that Lincoln might have to risk civil war. More militant Republican journals openly advised Lincoln to "let the sword do its work!" Though war would be "a terrible evil," disunion would be an even greater evil. If war had become the only way to preserve the Union, "then, horrible as it may be, let us have it quickly and decidedly. The sooner it is begun, the sooner it will be over."[12]

With the independent Confederacy displaying every sign of vitality and permanence, Republican opinion turned decisively against a hands-off policy. The undoubted disappearance of Unionism in the lower South also tended to obscure its persistence in the upper South. Northern newspapers with sharply differing editorial policies mistakenly agreed that Unionism was collapsing in the upper South. Yet even if northerners had understood the situation in the upper South, they would not likely have thought that Unionists there had a credible plan for restoring the Union.

A letter preserved in the papers of Salmon P. Chase provides a fascinating glimpse of how one Republican, who knew more about the strength of upper South Unionism than most of his party colleagues, could still by early April favor "immediate action." William P. Mellen of Cincinnati, a political ally of Chase's, had once lived in Kentucky. On April 6, he sent the new secretary of the treasury a substantial account of impressions he had received the previous week while on a business trip to Memphis, Nashville, and Louisville. "Thinking you might be glad to know the political feeling as manifested to me on such a trip," Mellen explained, "I took pains to ascertain it as fully as possible."

> I don't think I heard five men on the whole trip *express* themselves in favor of secession. In the cars, at the Hotels, at Counting Houses and on the streets there was almost perfect unanimity of sentiment against the precipitate action of the Cotton States and of the whole secession movement. Many of the Southern men were as bitter in their denunciation as are the best Republicans here. . . .
>
> There was a secession convention near Memphis while I was there (on Monday) [April 1] which was attended by the Mayor and some other prominent and respectable citizens, but they really attended it for effect in the business relations between Memphis and Northern Alabama and Mississippi. There is probably much more honest secession feeling in Memphis than in any other large town in Tennessee, through which I passed, and yet it amounts to nothing beyond a rabble. . . .
>
> But there was much diversity of sentiment as to the ultimate course to be pursued by the non-seceding slave states. Generally they say that unless the North conceed what they claim as their "equal rights," they will favor dissolution. But they give no assurance whatever that, even if all is granted which they demand, they will then sustain the government in any coercive measures against the confederate states. They all to a man would regard any coercive action on the part of the Government against Cottondom prior to the Border state Convention as entirely destructive to the Union cause in all the loyal slave states, and a secession victory in all of them made certain. And yet not one whom I questioned would say that in case this action were avoided until after their Convention, and then the ultimatum adopted by that Convention granted by the Northern States, they would join in, or even permit the North to execute the laws in conflict with the

Confederacy in case *force* should be necessary to such execution. The *real* fact is that there is *no* good feeling in the South toward the present administration as such and *very little* toward even the Democracy of the North. They profess to approve of the pacific and conciliatory action of the present Administration as eminently wise, and yet denounce it as "imbecile" and "contemptable"—they want the present Union preserved and yet would resist the only possible means of preserving it. . . .

I have given you these *facts*, that you may make your own deductions. To my mind the conclusion is *irresistable,—The Administration has nothing to gain by delay*. Whatever policy is to be adopted will be strengthened rather than otherwise by immediate action. The North itself is somewhat divided and the old Democratic party is hoping to recuperate through throwing itself body and soul into the arms of the border slave States, and these states will only take them to use them. All their sympathies, and prejudices, and notions are with their sister Slave states and with them they will go, right or wrong, whenever *action* becomes imperative. They condemn the action of the Cotton States, charge them with "rule or ruin" notions, and all that, not because it is *wrong*, but because it *divides* the Slave power, and lessens its ability to command such concession as by united and well matured action, they *hoped* for in the Union.[13]

Mellen deftly pinpointed the hazards and contradictions inherent in the hands-off policy. He recognized the strength of southern Unionism but realized that it would evaporate if the federal government and the Confederate states went to war. Because he believed peaceful reunion impossible and thought force alone would bring back the seceded states, Mellen saw no reason to continue tailoring federal policy to suit upper South Unionists. They wanted the Union preserved "yet would resist the only possible means of preserving it." Like most others who saw "nothing to gain by delay," he did not emphasize and probably did not comprehend the high price required to implement an active policy, though he did recognize that war would tend to unite the slave states. The significance of Mellen's letter, rather, is to demonstrate how an unusually well-informed Republican could, by early April, find "immediate action" preferable to continued hands off.

LINCOLN had already reached similar conclusions. Events on March 28, the day after he received the account of Hurlbut's Charleston visit, led the president to rethink the entire southern dilemma. By March 29, he decided that voluntary peaceful means could never secure reunion.

The catalyst that changed Lincoln's mind involved the other deep South trouble spot—Fort Pickens, on Santa Rosa Island offshore from Pensacola, Florida. Of couse, Fort Sumter in Charleston harbor had attracted far more attention.[14] But the Confederate government, preparing to challenge federal control of both forts, had begun to send reinforcements to Pensacola too. Pickens, situated so that it could be defended by federal ships, was less vulnerable than Sumter to Confederate attack. Indeed, it remained in federal hands throughout the war.[15]

If the reason for abandoning Sumter was to avoid inevitable military defeat, no comparable case could be made for Pickens. But if the reason for abandoning Sumter was to adopt a hands-off policy toward the seceded states, as southern Unionists desired, then the case for abandoning Pickens was equally valid. Unionists, indeed, had begun to make just this point once they received Seward's assurances about Sumter. Leading Virginia Unionists George W. Summers and John B. Baldwin, insisting that evacuation of Pickens as well as Sumter was necessary "for purposes of pacification," secured overwhelming endorsement for such a policy from the Virginia convention. The "Poetical Editor" of the *Nashville Daily Patriot* likewise urged Lincoln to give up both forts. If he did so:

> You will have clipped this new Republic's wing,
> And dimmed her day star in its earliest dawn.
> She wants a row as sure as you are born,
> And means to have it, if you do not bring
> Your troops away. . . .
> From Sumter and from Pickens too.[16]

General Scott's advice about the military difficulty of holding Sumter had impressed Lincoln. To compensate for the loss, the president ordered additional federal troops landed at Pickens. He could thereby preserve one clear symbol of federal control within the seceded states to show that his administration did not acquiesce in secession or recognize the Confederate government, regardless of what happened at Sumter.[17]

But then, probably on March 28, Scott proposed abandoning Pickens as well as Sumter—and for reasons that were frankly political rather than military. Claiming that "recent information from the South" made it uncertain "whether the voluntary evacuation of Fort Sumter alone would have a decisive effect" in holding the upper

South in the Union, Scott recommended that Lincoln please "our Southern friends" by surrendering "both the forts." To do so would "instantly soothe and give confidence to the eight remaining slave-holding states, and render their cordial adherence to the Union perpetual." Scott also held out hope that "the liberality of the act" would weaken support for secession in the deep South, thereby improving the chances for peaceful reunion. Nor was Scott alone implicated. As Seward's biographer has noted, "Owing to the intimacy between Scott and Seward, it was assumed that Scott's recommendation was really Seward's, adroitly and tentatively made in this way in order to avoid hazarding the Secretary of State's influence within the administration."[18]

Scott's proposal boomeranged. A distressed Lincoln called his cabinet into session late on Thursday evening, the twenty-eighth, to explain the new development. Nobody supported Scott, and Montgomery Blair criticized the general for "playing politician." The cabinet agreed to meet again the next day. Thursday night "Lincoln's eyes did not close in sleep." On Friday, the twenty-ninth, Lincoln told a friend he was "in the dumps," and on Saturday he "keeled over with a sick head ache" for the first time in years. Scott had inadvertently called into question the still unresolved Sumter issue and confronted the president with a "horrible dilemma." Lincoln had probably leaned toward the view that Sumter must be abandoned. But if Scott's advice about Pickens resulted from political rather than military calculations, what about his ostensibly military advice regarding Sumter? Might there be a way to hold Sumter? And if so, should it be tried?[19]

An alternative military analysis of the Sumter situation did exist. It came from naval officer Gustavus V. Fox, brother-in-law to Montgomery Blair, the cabinet member who steadfastly opposed abandoning Sumter. Fox believed that small, fast New York tugboats could run past Confederate guns and provision or reinforce Fort Sumter under cover of night. Sent by Lincoln to survey the situation first-hand, Fox returned on March 25 claiming that his plan was entirely feasible—so long as a strong naval force backstopped the resupply ships and drove off any hostile Confederate craft.[20]

When the cabinet reassembled at noon on Friday, March 29, a decisive juncture had been reached. Lincoln had concluded that "he must try to relieve Sumter," even though "relief meant war."[21] Dominant cabinet sentiment, which two weeks before had favored evacuation of Sumter, now shifted. Chase and Gideon Welles joined Blair in advocating a resupply mission. "Irrespective of this fresh advice," his secretaries recalled, Lincoln's mind "was already made up." The president ordered preparation of the naval expedition recommended by Fox, "ready to sail as early as the 6th of April next," only eight days away.[22]

Seward, who readily grasped that his peace policy was in grave danger, suddenly had to improvise. The hostile reception afforded Scott's recommendation to abandon Pickens showed that "it would be suicidal to come out positively in favor of it now." Seward knew that he must try to salvage withdrawal from Sumter to keep the promises he had made both to Unionists and to the Confederate government. Relinquishing both forts would have made a more consistent peace policy, but if one must be held, Seward strongly favored Pickens. He therefore put forward a two-pronged proposal in the cabinet meeting on the twenty-ninth: abandon Sumter but send a naval expedition to the Gulf to maintain "the possessions and authority of the United States." Though proclaiming a readiness to fight, Seward doubtless hoped that this "new and vigorous move" would preserve "his policy of peace and procrastination."[23]

Seward not only proposed sending ships to Florida; he took personal responsibility for organizing an expedition under the command of Captain Montgomery Meigs and Lieutenant David D. Porter, with orders to proceed as rapidly as possible to Pensacola harbor and prevent any attack on Pickens or Santa Rosa Island, on which the fort stood. Seward and Scott secretly arranged the Pensacola venture, with the acquiescence of Lincoln. Simon Cameron and Gideon Welles, the secretaries of war and the navy, knew nothing about it. So far as they were aware, the only naval expedition being organized was Fox's.[24]

At the same time Seward energetically prepared to reinforce Pickens, he continued trying to change Lincoln's thinking about Sumter. Seward had every reason to expect that the Confederates would use force to repel any federal resupply mission in Charleston harbor, thereby destroying his precarious peace policy. Fort Pickens's lesser vulnerability to Confederate attack made the chances of any "collision" there correspondingly lower. But how could Lincoln be dissuaded from persisting with Fox's Sumter expedition? Facing a deadline only days away, Seward had to act quickly.

On Monday morning, April 1, Seward presented to Lincoln a now-famous memorandum, entitled "Some Thoughts for the President's Consideration." The principal idea encompassed in the "Thoughts" was to "CHANGE THE QUESTION BEFORE THE PUBLIC FROM ONE UPON SLAVERY, OR ABOUT SLAVERY" to a question of "UNION OR DISUNION." Seward reasoned that Fort Sumter, "although not in fact a slavery or party question," was "so regarded" both North and South. In other words, most opposition to abandoning Sumter came from Republicans, some of whom so resented such an apparently humiliating capitulation to the proslavery Confederacy that they had threatened to split the party. Southern Unionists therefore suspected that narrow partisan considerations and antislavery intransigence prevented the anticipated evacuation of Sumter. Seward reasoned that the administration should demonstrate its readiness to reach across partisan and sectional barriers. By yielding Sumter, it would show southern Unionists that federal policy was designed neither to put Republican party interests ahead of national interests nor to interfere with slavery. By thus distinctly raising "the question of Union or disunion," the administration could win broad support for a program to "defend and reinforce all the Forts in the Gulf."[25]

Seward then made the proposal for which his "Thoughts" have achieved greatest notoriety. He advised Lincoln to threaten war against the European powers, particularly Spain and France, if they did not provide "satisfactory explanations" of their activities in the Western Hemisphere. A revolution in the island republic of Santo Domingo had occurred only a few days before, under circumstances that suggested a Spanish effort to reacquire control of her former colony. France and other European powers were also known to be considering intervention in Mexico. All were watching with undoubted interest the bid by the states of the deep South to achieve independence.

Seward reasoned that his Pickens expedition could serve several purposes at once. It would alert European governments not to misinterpret abandonment of Sumter. Holding Pickens and making a strong naval demonstration in the Gulf would indicate that the federal government had not acquiesced in Confederate independence. It would also remind European governments that the United States intended to uphold the Monroe Doctrine and maintain its ascendancy in the Caribbean area. Seward wished "to rouse a vigorous continental spirit of independence . . . against European intervention." He proposed supplementing his Pickens expedition by recalling additional troops "from foreign stations," assigning them to the Gulf, and being "prepared for a blockade."

Was this a plan for war? No! Seward's proposal can be understood only by recognizing that his paramount concern was "the American domestic crisis" and that "his foreign policy proposals followed logically from his domestic proposals." His great hope was to maintain peace "both at home and abroad." Faced with the necessity of demonstrating a continued federal presence in the seceded states, Seward gladly preferred Pickens to Sumter. Here a clash might be delayed or even averted. And in the interim, Seward calculated that a surge of "patriotism" would tend to strengthen the Union cause. By showing that the administration put national interests ahead of party interests, and by loudly cautioning European countries against meddling in the Western Hemisphere, Seward hoped to weaken the secession cause and keep open the possibility of peaceful reunion. He may also have hoped, depending on how the Confederate government reacted, either to drive a wedge between it and its would-be European allies or to depict it as a Trojan horse through which European power would be reestablished in the Western Hemisphere. But Seward's purposes could not have been served by war.[26]

Seward's "Thoughts" have traditionally gotten low marks from historians. Even those who treat Seward sympathetically have described the April 1 proposals as "fantastic" and "wild"—a "slap-dash improvisation" that showed "Seward was at the end of his tether." It was not "a serious outline for national and international action" but instead "a gorgeous and dangerous scheme," the "reckless invention of a mind driven to desperate extremes, as the sole means of escape from ruin."[27] Had Seward in fact contemplated a foreign war, such criticisms might ring true. The evidence, however, is quite conclusive that he wanted a foreign *crisis* rather than a foreign *war*. Seward's objective remained consistent. He still hoped to secure peaceful reunion by relying on southern Unionism.[28] Insofar as circumstances already reviewed tended to make that hope a forlorn one, Seward may fairly be criticized. But his failing, if such it was, lay in clinging too long to a hands-off policy, not in proposing startling new departures.

The "Thoughts" were a fizzle. Lincoln, replying to Seward the same day, rejected the idea that "the reinforcement of Fort Sumter would be done on a slavery or party issue, while that of Fort Pickens would be on a more national or patriotic one." Nor did he approve a show of belligerence toward the European powers. Though Lincoln's reply effectively closed the issue, the last echoes of Seward's overture appeared in print a few days later in the columns of two newspapers owned by his intimate friends, Henry J. Raymond of the *New York Times* and Thurlow Weed of the *Albany Evening Journal*. Both had huddled with Seward the night before he presented the "Thoughts" to Lincoln. Apparently they considered coordinating a front-page article in the April 1 *New York Times* to reinforce Seward's private appeal but decided against it. Two days later, however, Raymond listed the pros and cons of the Sumter issue. Although half-persuaded that national disintegration could be prevented only by using armed force, Raymond still advised Lincoln to consider openly embracing the hands-off policy, thereby disarming "the fears of War which now unite, by outward pressure, the Southern people," and making it possible "to organize a Union Party in every Southern State." The next day Weed warned that a get-tough policy would have disastrous effects in the South. Many Unionists would consider their rights "infringed" if the federal government used force to challenge secession. He pleaded instead for "reconciliation."[29]

THE same day Seward presented his "Thoughts," he also sought assistance. Who might help persuade Lincoln to reconsider? To George W. Summers in Richmond, Seward sent a telegram, stating: "The President desires your attendance at Washington as soon as convenient." Summers, suspicious that the telegram was a secessionist trick, replied guardedly. He thought his presence necessary at the convention and hoped that nothing was so urgent "as to preclude the more satisfactory communication by letter." Summers did not yet realize that Lincoln intended to try to hold and resupply Fort Sumter, or that Seward was trying desperately to change the decision. The telegram was indeed real. It was the first premonitory warning that the abyss lay just ahead.[30]

Two days later, on April 3, Allan B. Magruder, a Virginia-born lawyer who practiced in Washington, appeared at the state capitol in Richmond, where the Virginia convention was meeting, to see Summers. The visitor reported that he had been enlisted by Seward to bring Summers to Washington. Seward had taken Magruder to meet Lincoln, who explained that he wanted to consult with Summers on a matter "of the highest importance." Lincoln charged Magruder: "Tell Mr. Summers, I want to see him *at once*, for there is no time to be lost; what is to be done must be done quickly. . . . If Mr. Summers cannot come himself, let him send some friend of his, some Union man in whom he has confidence." The summons came at an inopportune moment. Unionists were pushing for a showdown vote against immediate secession. Summers met hastily and secretly with the circle of influential Union Whigs—John Janney, Robert E. Scott, Samuel Price, Alexander H. H. Stuart, and John B. Baldwin—and it was decided that Baldwin would represent them in Washington while Summers stayed in Richmond. Baldwin and Magruder left forthwith on the night train. They were in Seward's office early the next morning.[31]

The subsequent secret interview between Baldwin and Lincoln, held in a private room at the White House late in the morning on Thursday, April 4, has long been a controversial enigma. Of the two participants, only Baldwin left an account. But soon afterward Lincoln briefly described the interview to another visiting Virginia

Unionist, John Minor Botts. In 1866, Baldwin and Botts gave contradictory versions of the interview, under circumstances less than ideally suited for seeking historical truth. Both testified at length before the Joint Committee on Reconstruction, then investigating conditions in the postwar South. Baldwin, although a firm Unionist before the war started, had become a loyal Confederate and served in the Confederate Congress. By 1866 he was Speaker of the House of Delegates, the acknowledged leader in what was dubbed the "Baldwin legislature" of the restored state government. Botts had remained an unconditional Unionist throughout the war, which subjected him to many unpleasant experiences, including a term in jail. He believed the postwar Virginia legislature was improperly dominated by "a few leading and designing politicians" and "lawyers of reputation" who had supported the Confederacy. Botts, in short, had ample motive to impeach the veracity of Baldwin, and he testified to an audience inclined to find fault with southern state governments. Botts alleged that Baldwin spurned Lincoln's offer to evacuate Fort Sumter if the Unionists would permanently adjourn the Virginia convention and, furthermore, that Baldwin and his close friends conspired to prevent Lincoln's offer from becoming known to the convention. Baldwin, on the other hand, insisted that Lincoln never made such an offer. He enlisted corroborative testimony from surviving Unionist leaders of the Virginia convention.[32]

In trying to tiptoe through this minefield of contradiction and possible misinformation, one must keep the 1861 context firmly in mind. It was Seward's idea to bring Summers or another Union leader from the Virginia convention to meet Lincoln. Seward's chief object at the time was to change Lincoln's mind about Fort Sumter. Lincoln must have been no more than a reluctant collaborator in the exercise, despite the apparent eagerness to see Summers that he conveyed to Magruder.[33]

Baldwin's version of the interview, presented in 1866, deserves careful scrutiny. He recalled that Lincoln immediately said: "Mr. Baldwin, I am afraid you have come too late," and expressed the wish that Baldwin "could have been here three or four days ago." Baldwin, who had ridden all night on a train and had gotten from Richmond to Washington as fast as was physically possible, found Lincoln's comment perplexing and could not get him to explain it. Instead, Lincoln changed the subject and asked Baldwin: "Why do you not adjourn the Virginia Convention?" This unexpected and discomfiting inquiry prompted Baldwin to explain that Unionists controlled the convention and could keep control "if you help us," that is, by adopting "a conservative policy." If the convention were in fact adjourned, Baldwin predicted, another would soon be called. The stigma of having adjourned the convention without having secured "any kind of settlement" would so hurt the Unionists that any subsequent convention would have a secessionist majority.[34]

Baldwin insisted that Lincoln neither offered to withdraw federal troops from Fort Sumter if the Virginia convention would adjourn nor made any "overture" or comment "from which I could infer it." Baldwin "would not have thought it a practical scheme" if it had been offered, but he would have welcomed it as the "foundation" for additional "negotiation" or at least "temporizing." Baldwin went to Washington "full of hope and confidence" about finding some basis for reaching "an understanding with Mr. Lincoln" to preserve the peace; he was "much depressed and disappointed" when the interview provided no clear indication why he had been invited.[35]

His friends strongly corroborated Baldwin, both in general and on the specific point about Lincoln offering no terms or arrangement. As soon as Baldwin returned to Richmond, they had "cross-examined" him "as to all the details and incidents of the conversation . . . with a view to refresh your memory, and draw from you all the information as to the President's probable intentions and policy, which you had been enabled to gain." Price recalled that "your narrative of the conversation between Mr. Lincoln and yourself was circumstantial and minute. You seemed to give the language of each, and sometimes you described Mr. Lincoln's manner and gestures." So far as they could judge, Lincoln had made no offer linking abandonment of Sumter to adjournment of the convention, or anything equivalent. "That would have made too deep an impression to have been forgotten by any of us," Summers recalled. Stuart likewise observed that "such an important fact could not have escaped my notice or faded from my memory."[36]

A strong case can be made for the integrity of Baldwin's testimony and that of his corroborative witnesses. Baldwin himself pointed out that he had no motive "without authority to reject, or . . . to suppress any proposition or suggestion coming from the President, and having for its object the preservation of peace and the restoration of the Union." Nor did he have any motive to conceal information from the other Unionists who had selected him to represent them in Washington and to whom he reported on his return. They were "my intimate, personal and political friends and associates," Baldwin recalled. "It was my habit, and, on the occasion referred to, it was my duty . . . to observe and remember every word that passed in order to make a fair report on my return." Five years later Baldwin described his trip to Washington and meeting with Lincoln as "a subject of more interest to me than anything that ever happened to me" and insisted that upon returning he had repeated "over and over to the gentlemen who had concurred in sending me" his recollection of the interview. Consequently, "it impressed itself deeply on my mind."[37]

At first glance it would appear that Botts's recollection leaves much to be desired. Botts misdated the Baldwin interview with Lincoln, placing it on April 5 rather than April 4. Botts also put into Lincoln's mouth certain words that could not have been spoken to Baldwin—a remark about an antisecession vote in the Virginia convention that did not take place until the afternoon of April 4, hours after the interview occurred. If attributable at all to Lincoln, the comment must have been made to Botts himself rather than to Baldwin.[38]

But there are definite reasons to conclude that Botts's account has substantial validity. In March, at a time when Lincoln saw no way to hold Sumter, he may have told other unspecified Virginia Unionists that he would evacuate the fort if the convention passed a resolution promising not to secede. Botts believed Lincoln had made a similar offer to Baldwin to trade a fort for a state. Baldwin, who insisted Lincoln had made no such offer, acknowledged that Botts honestly believed otherwise, having "derived that impression from conversation with Mr. Lincoln."[39]

It would appear wise to assume that both Baldwin and Botts gave fair reports, five years after the fact, of what they believed Lincoln had told them in April 1861. Did Lincoln mislead Botts? No conclusive answer is possible, but a good deal of evidence points toward such a conclusion. Stuart, Baldwin's brother-in-law, believed that Lincoln had given Botts "a different version of the interview," so Baldwin too probably saw the matter in that light. Lincoln certainly had every motive to want an unconditional Unionist leader such as Botts to think that he had bent over backward to reach an accommodation with the conditional Unionists in the convention.[40]

If Lincoln gave Botts a misleading version of what had occurred, most of the heretofore incongruous aspects of the Baldwin interview become explicable. The whole idea for the interview, one must remember, was Seward's. He persuaded Lincoln to meet with a Virginia Unionist. It seems unlikely that Lincoln promised to do more than listen and consult. Circumstances obviously weighed heavily against any agreement between Lincoln and the Virginia Unionists. Seward could only hope that something helpful might develop. Before the interview, Seward told Baldwin that "he would not anticipate at all what the President desired to say." When the two had a "long talk" afterward, Seward impressed Baldwin as "extremely earnest" to preserve the peace but not offering any more specific terms than Lincoln did. Lincoln, who had made up his mind to resupply Fort Sumter and knew that the fleet would soon sail, had reason to hope the Virginia convention would adjourn but to remain reticent about why he wanted it adjourned. He also had reason to dismiss as "too late" Baldwin's vigorous defense of a hands-off policy.[41]

At no point during the critical six weeks between March 4 and April 15 did a Unionist in a position of authority have a better opportunity to discuss southern policy with Lincoln. Baldwin clearly tried to make the case for a noncoercive policy as effectively as he could. Never, the articulate attorney recalled, "did I make a speech on behalf of a client in jeopardy of his life, with such earnest solemnity and endeavor." He beseeched Lincoln to withdraw federal troops from both Sumter and Pickens. The president could then make a statement to the country, explaining that the United States had a perfect right to keep troops there, but that in the interests of achieving peaceful reunion, he would waive the right and call for a national convention to "settle this thing . . . by consultation and votes instead of by appeal to arms." Baldwin also tried to suggest why Virginia Unionists favored amending the Constitution. The secession of the deep South states had left the Union slave states "helpless in the hands of the North." By staying in the Union "despite all the obligations of association and sympathy" with fellow southerners, Unionists in the upper South had gained "a claim on the States of the North which is of a high and very peculiar character." The North should therefore agree to constitutional changes consistent with its promises "not to injure us in our peculiar rights" or, in other words, a territorial compromise. Lincoln could thereby assure that the upper South would stay in the Union, while giving Unionists "a stand-point from which we can bring back the seceded States."[42]

Lincoln listened attentively to arguments he had decided a week before to reject. At points he made comments or asked questions indicating his reservations. He worried about where to find the funds to run the government if $50 million per year in import revenues were lost. He led Baldwin to understand that "his friends would not be pleased" by the withdrawal of troops from Sumter and Pickens, nor by the idea of doing so voluntarily rather than "on the ground of military necessity." And, perhaps most significant, Lincoln hinted that his Sumter plans were different than what the Unionists hoped and expected. "He said something about feeding the troops at Sumter," Baldwin recalled. "I told him that would not do," that "if there is a gun fired at Sumter—I do not care on which side it is fired—the thing is gone," and that "Virginia herself, strong as the Union majority in the Convention is now, will be out in forty-eight hours."

"Oh, sir," Lincoln replied, "that is impossible."

Baldwin retorted: "Mr. President, I did not come here to argue with you; I am here as a witness. I know the sentiments of the people of Virginia and you do not." Baldwin was, however, "too late" to impress Lincoln, who had decided that the risks of the Sumter resupply mission were preferable to the risks of following the hands-off policy.[43]

One of Baldwin's corroborative witnesses, Samuel Price, believed Lincoln did not comment about Baldwin's being late at the beginning of the interview but only at "another point in the conversation" after Baldwin had explained the policy he thought should be followed. Price recalled that Lincoln initially greeted Baldwin with the question: "Why do you not adjourn that Convention?" Price's recollection of what Baldwin told his friends immediately afterward suggests that Lincoln may never have made the offer he later reported to Botts. In telling Botts that Baldwin "wouldn't listen to it at all; scarcely treated me with civility," Lincoln provided a version of the interview that may well reflect Baldwin's peremptory response to the naked suggestion that the convention be adjourned. If Baldwin emphatically rejected the idea—and if Lincoln concealed his reasons for wanting the convention adjourned without ever renewing the fort-for-a-state offer that he perhaps made to other Virginians weeks earlier—that could have produced the discrepancy in the two accounts, as well as the ominously unsatisfactory tone of the occasion.[44]

Price also thought Lincoln had remarked, after listening to Baldwin's defense of a hands-off policy: "I wish you had come sooner." Price vividly recalled his horror upon hearing Lincoln's comment: "When this remark of his was repeated to me, I remember that it chilled the very blood in my veins. I was, as you know, an intense Union man, and thought I saw that unless the Union party was upheld by the National Administration, that Virginia would inevitably take position with her Southern sisters; and, I inferred from this remark of Mr. Lincoln, that he had taken a step, which he could not retrace, inconsistent with the view you were urging upon him, and which would result in war and bloodshed." Price's recollection, even if intensified by the traumatic events of the ensuing years, rings true. The abortive Baldwin interview was indeed "too late." So failed the last card Seward had to play in trying to change Lincoln's mind about Sumter.[45]

Later the same day that Baldwin visited—Thursday, April 4—Lincoln met with Captain Gustavus Fox to make final plans for the Sumter expedition. He also notified Major Robert Anderson, the Union commander at Fort Sumter, to expect an effort to reprovision the outpost by the eleventh or twelfth. Thus on the afternoon of April 4, Lincoln moved decisively to implement the decision he had first reached on March 29. Several northern governors, including Andrew Curtin of Pennsylvania, were also at the White House on April 4. If troubles developed in the South, as he had good reason to expect, Lincoln wanted to have additional troops available to defend Washington.[46]

On Saturday, April 6, Seward's secret fleet left New York for Fort Pickens. It included a powerful warship, the *Powhatan*, that Fox believed he had obtained for the Sumter expedition.[47] That same day, Lincoln dispatched a messenger to Governor Francis W. Pickens of South Carolina, informing him that an attempt would be made to reprovision Fort Sumter. Lincoln stipulated that if no resistance were encountered, there would be "no effort to throw in men, arms or ammunition . . . without further notice." The ships headed for Fort Sumter left New York between April 8 and 10. Fox still expected the *Powhatan* would rendezvous with his modest fleet outside Charleston harbor and be ready for action by Friday night, April 12. Lincoln would risk war, but in such a way that the first shot must come from the other side.[48]

So far as Lincoln was able, he concealed these portentous developments from public view. Reporters found that they were "looked upon as spies and excluded from the departments." State Department clerks were said to "hold their tongues for fear of dismissal." The cabinet was "impenetrable," and most observers could "glean nothing" from the principals. But sharp-eyed reporters in New York and Washington could discern that some major move was afoot. Increasingly the press bristled with a mix of fact, rumor, and speculation during the first two weeks of April. Naval preparations were taking place, but for what purpose? Sumter, Pickens, the Gulf forts, Texas, Santo Domingo—all were listed by one source or another as possible destinations.[49]

The fate of southern Unionism was sealed by decisions made in late March and early April. Lincoln concluded that he must try to achieve reunion in a manner the Unionists considered catastrophic. All that remained was for the consequences of his decision to unfold.

12

THE UNIONISTS, FORT SUMTER, AND THE PROCLAMATION FOR SEVENTY-FIVE THOUSAND TROOPS

Two weeks after the interview between President Lincoln and John B. Baldwin, upper South Unionism lay in ruins and Virginia, North Carolina, and Tennessee had effectively seceded from the Union. A political coalition strong enough to dominate each state in early April was thoroughly routed. The extraordinary final phase of the secession crisis in the upper South will be examined here by tracing developments in the three state capitals—Richmond, Nashville, and Raleigh.

Because the Virginia convention remained in session in Richmond, one must start by trying to find out what happened there during the fateful month of April. Any historian reading the convention debates and private letters written by Unionists between mid-March and early April will receive a shock: Virginia Unionists thought the situation under control and had little sense of working against a deadline. Believing that peacekeeping and reunion would be a protracted process, they acted deliberately. Their principal task, as they saw it, was to lay the groundwork for a border state conference, at which delegates from all upper South states would formulate a Union-saving compromise based on the Peace Conference plan. They planned to adjourn the convention by mid-April, as soon as it finished drafting the proposed compromise, and to reconvene in the fall. Hoping to benefit in the interim from public anticipation of a successful settlement, just as they had in February, Virginia Unionists purposefully scheduled the border state conference to meet shortly after the state elections in May. At those elections, they expected to capture the state legislature, to oust many incumbent congressmen, and, in the words of George W. Summers, to "bury Secession and Secessionists in Virginia."[1]

Confident that the administration was committed to a peace policy and would soon withdraw its troops from Sumter, Virginia Unionists shrugged off secessionist alarms and warlike news reports during the first week of April. Stephen A. Douglas received word from a friend in Richmond that "everything is going straight here notwithstanding newspaper telegrams. We have a decided majority and a firm and unflinching one." The same day Baldwin secretly conferred with Lincoln, the convention decisively rejected immediate secession, ninety to forty-five. "That vote decided that Virginia would not commit the suicidal act of secession," exulted one Union delegate: "The harpoon went into the vital spot of the whale, and . . . it will be but a little while before his white belly appears on the surface."[2]

By Friday afternoon, April 5, Baldwin had returned to Richmond and was present at the convention. The circle of Unionist leaders quickly learned about his disquieting interview with Lincoln, though they kept it a closely guarded secret. But his return coincided with a growing volume of newspaper stories reporting military preparations and a change in administration policy. That same night a delegation of Virginians including John Minor Botts and Joseph Segar met with Lincoln and the cabinet to urge a peacekeeping arrangement by which the federal government would promise not to use military force in the South and the Confederate government would promise to seek no treaties with foreign powers. A national convention would then attempt to devise terms for reunion, or, if that proved impossible, peaceful separation. Lincoln would not, however, promise to preserve the military status quo in the South, leading Segar to predict that the country was "on the brink of civil war." Segar's distress was all the more significant in light of his having interviewed Lincoln in mid-March and found him soundly committed to a policy of "peace and conciliation." Newspaper reports about the Botts-Segar interview stirred discussion at the convention on Monday, April 8, and telegraphic accounts probably reached some people in Richmond much sooner.[3]

By Saturday afternoon, April 6, a bloc of moderate Unionists led by William Ballard Preston, a former secretary of the navy, had become alarmed enough to propose sending a three-member delegation to meet officially with Lincoln. Fearing that the administration was tempted to pursue a "coercive policy" against the seceded states, Preston hoped Virginia might yet influence Lincoln to maintain the peace. The proposal provoked bitter controversy. Unconditional Unionists, primarily from the northwest, professed to see "a cat in the meal tub here"—that is, a pretext for renewed secessionist clamor. Unionists such as John Jackson feared that an "unsatisfactory answer" from Lincoln would be used to create a secession stampede. He bluntly warned that northwesterners would sooner divide the state than join a southern Confederacy. Action on Preston's proposal was delayed until Monday, April 8, after what one Unionist called "the most unfortunate debate that has occurred within this Hall since the Convention met."[4]

Monday brought newspaper reports about "unusual movements of men and munitions of war." Evidence accumulated that "a large military expedition" was "fitting out in the Northern ports." Preston's Unionist allies insisted that an official interview with Lincoln concealed no "cat in the meal tub" or secessionist plot. It would, instead, offer the president an opportunity to dispel rumors and to offer reassurances that "the peace of the country" would not be disturbed after the convention's pending adjournment. Baldwin, Summers, and their immediate circle joined the unconditional Unionists in voting against the proposal, but Preston won over enough other conditional Unionists to carry his plan with the solid bloc of secessionist votes. The convention selected Preston, Richmond secessionist George W. Randolph, and Baldwin's brother-in-law Alexander H. H. Stuart, also from Staunton, to confer with Lincoln in Washington. News reports about the convention's action gave the president ample warning that he could expect visitors from Virginia. "There is great impatience at the mysterious and hesitating policy of the administration," one Unionist reported to his wife, "and if our commissioners do not bring us assurances of a pacific policy we shall have trouble yet."[5]

Throughout the upper South during the first and second weeks of April, Unionists began to doubt that the Lincoln administration remained committed to a hands-off approach. A Kentucky correspondent of Seward's reported on April 4 that John J. Crittenden had expressed among "intimate friends . . . his apprehension that he has been deceived by false assurances of a peaceful policy," though in speaking publicly to the Kentucky legislature, Crittenden "suppressed the utterance of any forebodings." Doubts increased the second week. Convention delegate James B. Dorman, a Douglas Democrat and close friend of Governor Letcher, realized sooner than many of his colleagues that disaster lay just ahead. "I have seen this thing coming on for several days," he wrote privately on April 9. "In *strict confidence* I have little *heart* for any thing with my apprehensions of what is soon to be upon us." A North Carolina newspaper editor complained to John A. Gilmer that Unionists had been "cheated, imposed upon, and deceived" by Lincoln and that "secessionists were right in their conjectures concerning him." The editor feared that "the friends of the Union" would be "*driven off*," and the upper South "*driven out*." Why, he asked, "has not Sumpter been evacuated and thus strengthened us? Why has not Pickens been evacuated and thus rendered us impregnable?" The accumulating evidence that the administration had rejected a conciliatory policy threw Gilmer himself into a profound depression. "I am so deeply distressed that my heart seems to melt within me," he wrote to Seward on April 12. "I cannot but still believe that the course I suggested would have been wise, and the results, had it been pursued, most beneficial. . . . If what I hear is true that we are to have fighting at Sumter or Pickens, it is what the disunionists have most courted, and I seriously apprehend that it will instantly drive the whole South into secession."[6]

Many Unionists refused at first to believe that Lincoln had reneged on the promises of peace and a withdrawal from Sumter that he had apparently made in March. Jubal Early, irritated by "false rumors," announced that he would ignore "telegraphic dispatches." But the latter became increasingly foreboding. Heavy rains and severe flooding starting on April 9 isolated Richmond for the rest of the week. The mail was cut off, travel obstructed, outside newspapers unavailable, but, as one Unionist lamented, "the telegraph lines are yet in operation."[7]

Unionists did their best to carry on as if no serious difficulties impended. Despite severe objections from former Governor Henry A. Wise, the de facto leader of secession forces at the Virginia convention, Unionists voted to exempt Forts Jefferson and Taylor (on Key West and Dry Tortugas) from a resolution protesting against federal reinforcement of forts in the seceded states. Clearly hoping that the federal fleet was headed to offshore forts, rather than to Charleston or Pensacola, Union leaders Summers and Baldwin argued that Jefferson and Taylor protected national commerce in the Gulf, thereby posing no threat to the Confederacy.[8]

Summers told William C. Rives that Unionists remained "hopeful calm and firm," though "machinations are going on against us all the time." They had "stood the telegrams pretty well—got up I presume for effect, as they were." Other Union leaders likewise refused to credit sensational reports. Robert Young Conrad, chairman of the Committee on Federal Relations, reported to his wife on April 10 that "telegrams are read in the house, and rumors are circulated—none of which I listen to but with a smile of incredulity." Conrad recognized, however, that many delegates thought otherwise. Telegraphic dispatches "disturb many and it was some of these that led to Preston's mission." The next day Conrad remained confident that all telegraphic rumors of war were "utterly untrue" and that "our troubles may yet end without a fatal termination." Only on Saturday, the thirteenth, did he acknowledge that "the telegraph is beginning to tell some—though not the whole—truth."[9]

Telegraphic reports on the thirteenth told, of course, about the fall of Fort Sumter, which had been shelled by Confederate guns since before dawn on Friday, the twelfth. Early in the afternoon on the thirteenth, Anderson surrendered his forces. Fox's fleet never had a role to play, except to carry Anderson's small contingent north after the surrender. But predictions that Virginia would secede as soon as the first shot was fired proved premature. Virginia Unionists suspected that South Carolina had provoked the fighting at Sumter and sought more information before deciding how to react. Triumphant pro-Confederate mobs in the streets of Richmond made Unionists all the more determined to stay calm and act deliberately. Conrad wrote his wife a contemptuous description of the "great parade of mobocracy" that fired one hundred guns in honor of South Carolina and forced their way into the state capitol building, where the convention met, to raise a Confederate flag. Jubal Early, the future Confederate general, insisted that Virginia's "masses" still opposed secession, Richmond mobs notwithstanding.[10]

Although recognizing that the fight at Sumter weakened their position, Union leaders still expected the convention to call a border state conference. William C. Rives reasoned that it was "more incumbent than ever" for "Virginia and the other border slave states to maintain their mediatorial position." By assembling promptly in conference, "they could yet command the peace between the two warring sections" and "lay the foundation for . . . the final re-construction of the Union on principles of justice and equality to all." Some Unionists, however, favored a popular referendum, allowing voters to choose between a border state conference and direct state secession. Unionists fully expected to win majority support for the border state conference in such a referendum but judged the tactic necessary to hold the state together. James B. Dorman explained that "Eastern Virginia will not submit to remain in the Union nor can be kept quiet without a chance to vote on secession" and that "Trans Allegheny Virginia will not go with the State unless they have a chance at least for consultation and concert with Kentucky etc."[11]

Meanwhile, what of the three commissioners the convention had dispatched to visit Lincoln? Heavy rains that washed out rail connections between Richmond and Washington blocked their departure for several days. Not until Thursday, April 11, were they able to take a boat from Norfolk to Baltimore. The commissioners did not, therefore, reach Washington until Friday the twelfth, nor did they meet with Lincoln until the thirteenth. Lincoln told them that "if, as now appears to be true," an "unprovoked assault has been made upon Fort Sumter," he would try to hold all federal outposts in the seceded states and to "repossess, if I can," those already captured. In so doing, he would "repel force by force." Lincoln's comments, news of which spread quickly among convention delegates after the commissioners returned to Richmond on Sunday, the fourteenth, weakened the Unionists. Stuart, the Union member of the delegation, judged Lincoln's response "in the highest degree unsatisfactory," though he hoped the president intended no "general war."[12]

The same train that brought the commissioners back from Washington on Sunday evening also brought unverified reports of an even more ominous development—that Lincoln planned to raise an army to fight the Confederacy. Next morning the Richmond newspapers printed copies of Lincoln's proclamation, dated April 15, calling upon each state to provide from its militia a proportionate share of seventy-five thousand troops. It justified the use of armed force on grounds that "combinations too powerful to be suppressed" by ordinary means prevented enforcement of federal law in the deep South. Lincoln also called Congress into special session on July 4.[13]

Many Unionists at first thought the proclamation a "forgery" or a "mischievous hoax." The flagrant prosecession bias displayed by the *Richmond Enquirer* and the *Richmond Examiner* made Unionists distrust anything these newspapers reported. Stuart, who had received from Seward what he considered satisfactory reassurances about the administration's peaceful purposes, first read the proclamation at breakfast on Monday, the fifteenth. He "did not for a moment believe that it was authentic," nor could he believe Lincoln "guilty of such duplicity." Stuart therefore telegraphed Seward to ask whether it was a "fabrication."[14]

The convention met at 10 A.M. on Monday, the fifteenth, under circumstances of extreme tension. Only the question of "the authenticity of the proclamation" prevented the convention from immediately going into secret session. Unionists such as Jubal Early, clinging desperately to the hope that the document was forged, contended that it could not be authenticated until printed in a newspaper Unionists trusted, such as the *National Intelligencer*, edited by Seaton and Welling, copies of which had not yet arrived in Richmond. Early reasoned that "it may be true; but if it is true, it is certainly an evidence that the administration and its officers have lost all prudence, discretion, and good sense." He hoped that a "statesman" as able as Seward could not have been "guilty of the blunders which appear in that proclamation." Baldwin supported Early, arguing that he had "no hesitation, when it comes to war or subjugation against the South, as to what position I shall occupy," but wanting to be absolutely sure about "the genuineness of the information, upon which we are called to act." The convention therefore adjourned for the day at 12:45 P.M.[15]

Before the convention reassembled on Tuesday, the sixteenth, all doubt about the proclamation's authenticity was resolved. The incredulous Stuart, who initially thought it "a sensation document, gotten up by some mischievous persons," reported to the convention that Seward had replied "late last night" to confirm that it was indeed genuine. Copies of the *National Intelligencer* and other nonsecessionist papers, containing the same astonishing proclamation, also reached Richmond.[16]

As its first order of business on the sixteenth, the convention went into secret session. That same day Governor Letcher received—and indignantly refused—a request from the War Department to supply troops for the federal army. Virginia Unionists made one last effort to delay the inevitable. On the morning the secret session began, Robert E. Scott, a leader among the heretofore dominant Union Whigs, proposed allowing the people of Virginia to choose by referendum between immediate secession and cooperation with the other states of the upper South through the mechanism of the already planned border state conference. What Scott proposed was, in form, similar to what Dorman had favored during the interval after Sumter had fallen and before the proclamation became known. But though Dorman on the fourteenth saw the referendum as a Unionist gambit to appease ardent secessionists in the east and prevent them from splitting the state, Scott defended the identical measure on the sixteenth from exactly the opposite perspective. He no longer believed the Union could be preserved, regarding "dissolution as inevitable." He insisted, however, that immediate secession would divide the state, which it certainly did do. Scott contended that cooperative action with the other border states would keep the state together and would also allow valuable time for military preparation. He assumed that other border states would also favor secession and that all could better protect their interests by acting in concert. No longer was a border state conference a means for preserving the Union: "I think it a straight road to secession," said Scott, "and I am frank to avow it."[17]

Scott's "cooperation" position was designed to maximize dwindling Unionist strength, but desertions from Union ranks proved so great that even Scott's quasi-secessionism could not attract majority support. Dorman, for example, abandoned the Unionists entirely. He had feared on the fourteenth that Unionists would oppose his referendum idea; on the sixteenth he noted that "the extreme Union men would be *glad enough to get off with that now*" and vowed not to help them. The mood of the convention was epitomized by William T. Sutherlin of Pittsylvania County, who contended: "I have a Union constituency which elected me by a majority of one thousand, and I believe now that there are not ten Union men in that county to-day." Baldwin was left to mourn the "rabid" fever that had "seized" many Unionists. Though debate continued into a second day, Scott's referendum proposal failed, sixty-eight to seventy-nine. As soon as the vote took place, Scott announced his own support for immediate secession, as did several other of his supporters. Unionists had reached a dead end. By an eighty-eight to fifty-five majority later that same day, Wednesday, April 17, the convention voted in favor of the secession ordinance.[18]

THE action of the convention, though taken in secret, soon became known. Most people in Richmond expressed delight. Thousands participated in a huge torchlight procession a few nights later.[19] Although it had substantial Union sentiment before April 15, Richmond was a center of secessionist activity. Two of the most vehemently prosecession newspapers in the upper South were published there, and secessionist mobs periodically appeared in the streets. In late February, for example, an "immense crowd" of a thousand to fifteen hundred surrounded the American Hotel, the lodging of Samuel McD. Moore of Rockbridge County, who had just made a strong Union speech in the convention. Secession leaders dissuaded the group from burning an effigy of the "traitor," but Unionists continued to suffer indignities. They and their wives became targets for "hissing and howling" directed at antisecessionists by the "dregs of the populace." Some Unionists considered moving the convention to a different city when it next met.[20]

Though secessionists did not go out of their way to advertise the fact, they received enthusiastic and tangible support from the slave traders of eastern Virginia. Sending slaves south was one of the most lucrative businesses in Richmond. One trader in 1860 reportedly made profits exceeding $100,000; the group overall had "millions of money under their control, including one bank." Samuel McD. Moore regarded it as "the most potent money power that has ever existed in Virginia." Promoters of the slave trade had obvious reasons for wanting Virginia to ally with the seceded states. Unionists could point out that few Virginia products were sold in the deep South, but slaves were the major exception to that generalization. The prospect of a seven-state nation in the deep South, in relationship to which Virginia would be part of a foreign country, did not please slave traders. Their support for a united South was intensified when the new Confederacy established a policy of refusing slave imports—either from Africa or from the upper South. The threat to bar upper South slaves, which Unionists denounced as more overt "coercion" than anything the government in Washington had attempted, had its desired effect. Virginia traders predicted that the ban on slave imports would "break us up." Moore observed bitterly that "the interest of these people is entirely with the seceded states, and to promote it, they would sacrifice every other interest in the state, without the least scruple."[21]

Unionists made several specific complaints about prosecession activities by slave traders. Samuel McD. Moore and others charged they had "gotten up" the mobs that paraded in the streets and insulted Union delegates to the convention. In this and other ways, the traders were "spending money freely, in order to influence the public mind in favor of immediate secession." John Minor Botts, narrowly defeated as an unconditional Unionist candidate to the convention, contended that "the gamblers and nigger traders of Richmond spent ten thousand dollars" on election day to defeat him. Unionists further charged that slave traders were pressuring Union newspapers to change their editorial stance or deliberately buying them out to achieve the same goal. The latter approach proved very effective. Secessionists embarrassed Governor Letcher by purchasing the *Lexington Valley Star*, his hometown newspaper. The only Union newspaper in Richmond, the *Whig*, suffered the same fate in late March. Secessionists "purchased the stock of the concern" and fired editor Robert Ridgway. Having suddenly lost control of the *Whig*, which circulated throughout the state, Unionists found themselves needing to establish a new Richmond newspaper.[22]

A most audacious and risky effort to drive Virginia out of the Union was overtaken by the dramatic events of mid-April. On Tuesday morning, April 16, a "Southern Rights" assembly convened at Metropolitan Hall in Richmond. Around two hundred fervent secessionists, primarily from eastern Virginia, met that day behind closed doors. Weeks before, when promoters of the gathering made their plans, nobody could have predicted that so much else would be occurring on that same date.

The idea of holding a Southern Rights meeting, as explained later to Edmund Ruffin by two of the principal organizers, Willoughby Newton and David Chalmers, developed in March, when "some of the ardent and active secessionists then in Richmond consulted together, and began a private movement." Newton, a former congressman and outspoken Southern Rights ideologue from Westmoreland County in the Northern Neck, had for years championed the cause of southern independence. Only one other Virginian had stronger secessionist credentials than Newton, and he was no longer available to help. Edmund Ruffin had fled to South Carolina rather than remain in a country ruled by a "Black Republican" president. Newton and like-minded fire-eaters such as Chalmers, from Halifax County, stayed behind in hopes of rousing Virginia from its torpor. By March they believed "popular sentiment . . . in favor of immediate secession" was growing rapidly. But they had little hope that a convention so dominated by "submissionists" and "traitors" would ever take "patriotic action." They shared an equally low regard for the governor, John Letcher, who had become a firm Unionist even though elected to office as a Southern Rights Democrat.[23]

The promoters of the meeting had a circular letter "secretly printed" and sent copies to hundreds of "reliable men" through the state who were "known to be true to the South." It urged recipients to convene in Richmond on the sixteenth "to consult with the friends of Southern rights as to the course Virginia should pursue in the present emergency." Of the nine who signed the document, four were members of the convention. Easily the most prominent name on the list was that of former Governor Henry A. Wise.[24]

Southern Rights orgnizers hoped originally to keep their movement hidden from public view. But copies of the mailed circular reached unfriendly hands and were thereupon printed in Union newspapers. Unionists condemned what looked like a plan "to overawe and intimidate" the convention. "What do these secessionists mean to do," inquired Alice Janney, wife of the Unionist president of the convention. Were they "gathering their forces . . . to drive you all from the city," so they could "seize the government there and set up for themselves?" The response to the circular in northwestern Virginia was especially hostile. The *Wheeling Intelligencer* warned that supporters of the project included "some of the most active and desperate disunion agitators in Virginia," who had "staked everything on secession." Though uncertain whether to expect a secessionist "*coup d'etat* like that by which Louis Napoleon took possession of the throne of France," the editor of the *Intelligencer* predicted that the Union majority in the state would not "submit quietly to disunion usurpation, should it come to that."[25]

The Southern Rights undertaking warranted Unionist suspicions. Although its revolutionary nature was "carefully concealed," the organizers fully expected to use "physical force" to accomplish their purposes. Several companies of Richmond volunteers were "relied upon for support." The plan called for Governor Letcher to be "arrested or kidnapped, carried off, and confined in secret, for the time necessary." George W. Summers and other Union leaders in the convention also were to be "seized and imprisoned." Lieutenant Governor Robert L. Montague, an avowed secessionist, may have been party to the plot. He, at least, was judged by the conspirators as someone who "could be relied upon." Arrests of "submissionists" in the convention were to continue, if necessary, until the "revolutionary party" could declare "the secession of the state." Rarely in American history, it seems fair to say, has a state government faced so serious a threat.[26]

There is excellent reason to accept Henry A. Wise's claim that the scheme was his idea. Though weakened by ill health and frustrated by political setbacks, Wise craved attention. And he remained able to command it thanks to his unmatched oratorical skills. Ironically, the tall, gaunt former governor, whose long hair and clean-shaven face emphasized his angular features, regarded the secession cause with deep ambivalence. Long hopeful that progressive leadership could enable Virginia and the South to modernize and remain comfortably within the Union, he feared that disunion "made no sense." In the end, the conflicted Wise masterminded a revolution that his sober self considered doomed and verging on treason. His reckless zeal both masked and resulted from insoluble contradictions.[27]

Surviving manuscripts show clearly that Wise had, since January, been writing to friends about the possibility of staging a coup to install a genuine prosouthern government in Virginia. He had gotten it into his head that Republican leaders had deliberately provoked the secession crisis to drive off the lower South and then "unite with Canada and force their boundary down to North Carolina and Tennessee!—you may rely on this." Republicans were determined to hold the upper South, Wise suspected, "to retain our iron and coal for their furnaces." He had no doubt that "this whole treason is instigated by the fanatics of Old England and the game is to get the paw of the British lion upon us," so that Republicans were witting or unwitting British agents. Wise's correspondence and speeches in early 1861 also reflect an obsession with the federal armory at Harpers Ferry and the naval installations at Norfolk and Fortress Monroe, which he feared would be reinforced and used as jumping-off points to coerce Virginia. Chafing impatiently at the failure of many secessionists to measure up to his standard of "active and immediate resistance," he called for "bold and decisive action." He proposed the assembling in Richmond, "seemingly spontaneously," of men who were "true to the South" and who would not shrink from "revolution." However vague on particulars, Wise's fascination with extralegal armed force was startlingly clear. As the weeks dragged on and Virginia remained within the Union, he began to plan in earnest.[28]

In urging friends to attend the Southern Rights meeting, Wise claimed that its purpose was to effect a "thorough organization of a Resistance party for the spring elections." But Wise clearly feared that voters would remain obstinate. He reasoned that it was "folly to tender naked secession to Virginia and risk final defeat forever," until the "popular head and heart" had been trained to appreciate that Virginia could not safely remain in "this house of bondage with the North, whose freedom is tyranny." Such an educational campaign would necessarily take time. Wise's temperament was impelling him by early April toward a shortcut or a quick fix, rather than the long haul. He wanted to be prepared "for any emergency, mild, middle, or extreme," and hoped this secessionist meeting would "put a cold sweat" on Unionists in the convention. But until the startling events of mid-April, few Unionists sweated. They thought Wise a charismatic genius—a "Red Republican" who "misleads the rash, and blinds the reckless"—and they credited him with doing "more mischief than any one in the State." They judged, however, that nobody in the convention, outside of Wise's circle of twenty "devoted followers," was "influenced by anything he says." Unionists hoped that Wise's mass following remained similarly limited.[29]

As news of the Southern Rights circular leaked out, John M. Daniel's *Richmond Examiner* came close to advocating openly the use of force "to overthrow and disperse the vile tyranny" imposed on the state by the convention and Governor Letcher. Armed revolution, Daniel explained, would soon be "the only resort left to a betrayed people." He predicted that glory would await "any hundred honest men—men of character and faith," who would "take weapons in their hands and their lives in their teeth" and act boldly to liberate Virginia from Unionist oppression. Unionists were unsure whether to be alarmed or amused. The *Lynchburg Virginian* responded by asking who would volunteer to lead the hundred brave patriots. With a "dictator" such as Cromwell or Napoleon, secessionists could have "a regular French revolution done up on the most approved style." The obvious candidate, suffocating in the Unionist-dominated convention, declared on April 11 his readiness to "leave my seat upon this floor" to fight. Itching "to defend Southern rights and Southern slavery," Henry A. Wise prepared to free his native state from the submissionist toils that bound it.[30]

Such was the situation the week before the Southern Rights enthusiasts were to gather in Richmond. As it happened, of course, the prospective coup coincided with the decisive moment of the secession crisis. External events undermined Virginia Unionism, producing the results that Southern Rights conspirators wanted, without requiring the extraordinary tactics that at least some of them contemplated. Edmund Ruffin's informants told him that "some of the most zealous secessionists" in the convention successfully urged the conspirators "to postpone action" because of strong indications that a majority would soon vote for secession. That did happen. It "rendered all private or revolutionary action superfluous and improper," so that the Southern Rights meeting "strictly speaking . . . did nothing." But Ruffin also learned that the leading conspirators intended to use force quickly if the convention did not act.[31]

Substantial evidence suggests that persons involved with the Southern Rights movement had infiltrated and gained leadership over secessionist mobs and militia companies in Richmond. When news of the fall of Fort Sumter reached Richmond on Saturday afternoon, the thirteenth, a huge armed crowd surged into the streets. They commandeered artillery for a hundred-gun salute on the public square in front of the capitol, serenaded past the governor's house, and then forced their way into the capitol building—where the convention was then meeting—to raise a Confederate flag on the roof. "The rejoicings, with processions, torches, fire works, bonfires, and music were kept up until midnight." A Union caucus with Governor Letcher, scheduled to meet in the capitol at 8 P.M., was "not very largely attended" because some members "did not care to venture" through the mob, which controlled the building both inside and out and kept up a constant "clamor." "The worst of this matter," complained Robert Young Conrad, "is that men of standing and influence, including some members of the Convention openly countenance all these proceedings and avow the purpose to establish a provisional revolutionary government, and supersede the Convention, and other regular authorities. I understand that several highly respectable men harangued them to this effect."[32]

By Monday morning, the fifteenth, the public square and all parts of the capitol remained "crowded with people, looking earnest and excited." One leading secession delegate to the convention, Marshall Ambler of Louisa County, told Robert Young Conrad that "he had been engaged for more than twenty four hours in suppressing a plan to break up the Convention, by violence, which had been formed by 250 men, and was to be carried out to day." Ambler warned the plotters that "they would have to pass over him and his friends in the Convention." Secessionists such as Ambler argued that the events of the weekend assured the prompt secession of Virginia, making it counterproductive to risk the desired result by acting against the convention or the governor. Appeals such as his were apparently persuasive. The crowd even agreed not to hoist another Confederate flag over the capitol.[33]

The next morning, Tuesday, April 16, the Southern Rights meeting convened behind closed doors, amid much flamboyant secession rhetoric. The delegates were impatient, to say the least. Suspicions increased that Southern Rights leaders planned more than speeches. That same day, convention delegate James B. Dorman sent a "strictly private" letter to a friend, explaining that secessionists would no longer accept anything short of immediate disunion. "One thing is certain," Dorman wrote, "unless a secession ordinance is submitted and that by another day, *there will be an open revolution in Eastern Virginia*. This *I know*." Had Unionists refused to budge, secessionists would have "retired from the Convention, appealed to the people, and called Jeff Davis to their aid." But the conspirators decided on the sixteenth that the convention itself would soon vote for secession. Test votes that afternoon showed that secessionists had at least a thirteen-vote majority, which they used to enforce a ten-minute rule to limit debate.[34]

Instead of directly seizing power, Wise and his friends insisted that Governor Letcher act as if secession were accomplished and Virginia at war. They pressed him to seize the federal armory at Harpers Ferry and the Gosport Navy Yard in Norfolk. When Letcher contended that the convention must first ratify secession and authorize military action, Southern Rights leaders ordered volunteer troops to attack the two federal facilities. The readiness of substantial military forces to heed extralegal authority offers the most tangible indication that the Southern Rights movement was no mere bluff or exercise in political theatrics. Only the next morning did Letcher decide to approve the already initiated military action. Aided by federal incompetence, Southern Rights irregulars took control of the most important federal military installations in Virginia by the end of the week.[35]

On April 17, the day of secession, the conspiratorial Wise added to the charged atmosphere by announcing to the secret session of the convention that "blood will be flowing at Harpers Ferry before night" and that Virginia troops were also attempting "to capture the Navy yard." He brushed aside complaints by Baldwin and others about the dangers of exercising power without constitutional warrant. Wise insisted that the doctrine of *salus populi suprema lex* justified "overriding" legal and constitutional restraints to defend the people against threatened invasion. Baldwin, unimpressed, rejected Wise's "higher law" views. Warning that revolutions endangered popular liberty even while professing to enlarge it, Baldwin predicted that "we are in danger of emerging from this revolution anything but a free people."[36]

The Southern Rights conspiracy raises fascinating hypothetical questions. If the administration had decided against trying to hold Sumter—or if it had even held back or delayed the proclamation for seventy-five thousand troops—Wise and his friends would have been put to a far more severe test. They would then have confronted a Unionist majority in the convention, supported by a Unionist governor and a majority of Virginia voters. What the conspirators would have done under such different circumstances is impossible to judge, but they might well have overplayed their hand. An irregular movement against one of the federal installations would have been front-page news across the country. (A similar situation in North Carolina in January became only a brief sensation when secessionists relinquished control over Fort Caswell after holding it overnight.[37]) Had Southern Rights conspirators in Virginia actually tried to maintain control over a federal installation, or to move forcibly against the governor or the convention while calling for Confederate aid, that would have produced a grave crisis. Could it have happened?

Most of those involved in the conspiracy underestimated the persistent strength of Unionism in Virginia before April 15. They were utterly convinced that popular sentiment would regard a secessionist coup as an act of liberation and deliverance. They presumed that the entire state stood ready to follow the lead of Southern Rights enclaves in "Old Virginia." Henry A. Wise, by far the most accomplished politician among the Southern Rights conspirators, should have known better. But even he appeared eager to see whether secessionists could exploit the advantages of greater boldness and audacity.

John Minor Botts believed that Lincoln's proclamation "came just in the very nick of time to save the disorganizers the task of a revolutionary movement." Had Lincoln not issued the proclamation, he "might have received a call from the executive of this state for the aid of the general government to sustain the lawful authorities of Virginia." Federal troops might then have entered Virginia to challenge a secessionist coup and to protect or restore the state government and the convention. Under such circumstances, Botts speculated, nothing could have "driven Virginia or the other Border States into a participation with the Cotton States."[38]

There is no evidence that Lincoln or his cabinet ever considered waiting for Virginia secessionists to do something rash enough to hurt their cause. But articles about the Southern Rights meeting and its possibly subversive intent did appear in a number of newspapers, both in and out of Virginia, and Seward, at least, had received warning about "the secret circular of Governor Wise and his clique."[39] Might Seward or Botts have raised the subject during early April conversations with Lincoln? We do not know.

FURTHER perspective on the brief history of southern Unionism may be gained by looking at developments in the capital cities of the two other states with which this study is particularly concerned. In Nashville and Raleigh, an apparently overwhelming Unionist advantage collapsed as soon as the proclamation became known. Both therefore illustrate the striking reversal of public opinion that occurred in large parts of the upper South in mid-April.

Nashville and Raleigh, unlike Richmond, had solid pro-Union majorities before April 15. In each the Union side benefited from a strong popular base. Each also supported three emphatically Union newspapers, which set the tone for like-minded editors in outlying parts of the state. The intangible elements of energy, vitality, and initiative—qualities secessionists displayed in Richmond—were Union attributes in Nashville and Raleigh. But because neither Tennessee nor North Carolina called a convention, events in their capital cities during the secession crisis attracted far less out-of-state attention than Richmond received.

The initial surge of "revolutionary feeling" in Nashville greatly alarmed Unionists. An "outburst of ultra Southern sentiment" at a meeting in late December convinced one Unionist that Tennessee soon would be "ready to join South Carolina." Southern Rights supporters in Nashville and throughout Tennessee took strong exception to Andrew Johnson's unconditional Unionist speech of December 18–19. Many of his former allies and leading Democratic newspapers such as the *Nashville Union and American* turned against Johnson for his "fatal blunder."[40]

But the balance of forces in Nashville and across the state tipped decisively against secession in January and February. The great majority of Whigs became Unionists, as did enough Democrats to constitute a definite majority of the active electorate. Southern Rights newspapers in January began to charge "maneuvering politicians" with "denouncing the citizens of our more Southern sister States as traitors," thereby giving "aid and comfort to the Black Republicans." Would-be secessionists, recognizing the risks of overtly endorsing disunion, contended instead that southerners must stand together to win Republican concessions. Any "Union demonstrations," they warned, simply encouraged Lincoln and Seward to deny the South her just rights.[41]

Outspoken Nashville Unionists spurned such gratuitous Southern Rights advice. They believed the deep South states had seceded because of Unionist timidity. "Our friends in Georgia and Alabama," observed Union Whig John Lellyett, had "tried to compromise with treason. They tried to soothe a raging wolf by patting him gently and allowing him to taste a little of their blood by way of compromise." The lesson for Tennessee Unionists was plain: "We must meet the domineering career of this raging fanaticism in Tennessee by presenting a bolder, more threatening and determined front, or we may be speedily overwhelmed, and bound hand and foot." Lellyett had no use for a qualified Unionism that demanded "impossible conditions." How, he asked, "can we expect to obtain any concessions amid such an uproar of treasonable confusion?" Similarly unequivocal Unionism appeared in the *Nashville Democrat*, a Douglas newspaper whose editor, William R. Hurley, claimed to have the largest circulation in the city by January. The *Democrat* said very unkind things about "wicked precipitators" and "cotton traitors." Having lost power in the Union, they wanted a new southern government they could dominate. Because few "cotton lords" intended to risk "their noble and elegant bodies before the mouth of a cannon," an essential feature of the plan for southern independence was to have "the poor, honest working man . . . do the fighting." Hurley challenged the "leaders of the so-called Union party" to repudiate the "Secession party" and to "stand by the flag of the Union—punish the traitors—and save the country."[42]

Unconditional Unionists such as Lellyett and Hurley were in a minority in Nashville, but before April 15 they had powerful allies. The Whig elite in Nashville took a firm Union stance. Recent presidential candidate John Bell and former Governor Neill S. Brown both wrote long public letters, urging southerners to await "a sober second thought" and warning against hasty action. The election of a president by a political party that opposed slavery and did not even pretend to have a national base had, they acknowledged, created understandable southern apprehensions. But they considered secession a drastic remedy, suitable only for the unlikely contingency that the South faced "intolerable evils" and the "certainty of tyranny and oppression." Bell warned that the secession movement was led by persons who had "long cherished" the "delusive vision" of an independent South and who now had "a pretext more plausible than any heretofore presented to attempt the accomplishment of it." Influential Democratic leader Andrew Ewing, recognizing that many Democratic voters approved Andrew Johnson's course and opposed secession, made common cause with Whig Unionists.[43]

Henry S. Foote, one of the colorful figures of antebellum American politics, led Nashville secessionists. A former U.S. senator and governor of Mississippi, the diminutive, fiery Foote had few peers in the rough and tumble of public debate. Legends had grown up around his achievements during the 1850–51 crisis, when Foote broke the back of secession in Mississippi, thereby intensifying a poisonous personal feud with the leader of the rival Southern Rights faction, Jefferson Davis. Foote moved to Nashville in 1859. He soon played a conspicuous role in Stephen A. Douglas's presidential campaign, believing the Illinois senator the one genuinely national candidate available. Until 1861, Foote thus remained a symbol of southern Unionism.[44]

But Foote decided during the secession winter that the Union had been shattered irretrievably. Unlike most Tennesseeans, he saw no hope for its peaceful restoration through reassurances or compromise. The only choice, he concluded, lay in recognizing the existence of two nations—one northern and one southern. Foote therefore became a Southern Rights candidate for the Tennessee convention, forcefully articulating the theory of what might be called contingent secessionism in a series of speeches and public letters.

Even though Foote originally regarded secession as reckless and likely to result in civil war, his firsthand knowledge of political dynamics and public opinion in the deep South convinced him that the seceding states had acted in earnest. Capitulation to the new order by leading deep South Unionists such as Jeremiah Clemens of Alabama and Alexander Stephens of Georgia deeply impressed him. For a short time Foote wondered whether the Union might possibly be "reconstructed" on southern terms. Confederate adoption of the U.S. Constitution with only a few modifications provided the basis for such hope. Northern states, by requesting admission into an enlarged Confederacy, could thus rebuild a new Union. By late March, Foote knew better. It would be "a great mistake," he then observed, "to indulge the faintest hope that the Union of our fathers, as it formerly existed, will ever again be restored."[45]

Foote's initial efforts to explain that Tennessee must choose between North and South failed miserably. The voters of Nashville on February 9 trounced Foote and the rest of the Southern Rights ticket for the state convention by a margin that averaged six to one. By a narrower margin, voters also opposed even calling a state convention. Nashville's Whigs, over 60 percent of the electorate, voted solidly Unionist. Many Democrats, including large numbers of workingmen of immigrant ancestry, also spurned secession. Seeing the disaster coming, Foote tried to arrange a face-saving withdrawal of the Southern Rights ticket a week before the election. But Unionists, confident of victory, refused to make any concessions.[46]

The February 9 election results in Nashville and throughout Tennessee crippled the secession movement for the next two months. Southern Rights advocates, powerless and without leverage, were reduced to complaining that "Union-shriekers" had deceived the voters. Instead of demanding that Republicans support the Crittenden Compromise or the Peace Conference plan, Unionists had shamefully backed down. Such "reckless treachery" was leading Tennessee "into the meshes of unconditional submission."[47]

Nashville Unionists bristled in response. An anonymous contributor to the *Patriot* declared that the only danger facing the "great masses" of the state came from a despotic "Southern oligarchy," who wanted "to brow-beat Tennesseeans into submission to their behests," to "rule us with a rod of iron," and to "grant us no rights but that of fighting its battles." Nashville residents expected the Lincoln administration to act "with prudence and discretion." After consulting with Lincoln in Washington, John Bell returned to tell his Nashville friends that "there was fair and reasonable ground to expect that peace would be preserved." News reports in mid-March about the prospective abandonment of Fort Sumter appeared to substantiate Unionist hopes about Lincoln's policy.[48]

A reviving interest in appointment to federal office demonstrated the ebbing of secession sentiment in Nashville. Southern Rights advocates had once insisted that no southerner could hold office under Lincoln "without bringing personal odium upon himself" and showing that he was "disloyal to his section." But the apparent failure of secession in Tennessee prompted a reconsideration. Jesse B. Clements, an avowed member of the Nashville "Post Office Clique," sought reappointment as federal marshal for Middle Tennessee. He acknowledged to Andrew Johnson that his "more *fire eating* friends" thought it would be "disgracefull for any Democrat to hold office under Mr. Lincoln's Black Republican administration," but he had "a different opinion." "Somebody has to and will hold public offices," Clements rationalized, and "I never have seen the good sense in my giving up the office to a political opponent if I could hold it myself."[49]

Clements's appeal was not successful. Johnson, who had to divide federal patronage appointments with Congressman Emerson Etheridge, a Whig Unionist, agreed to replace Clements with Herman Cox, a Union Whig from Nashville. But Johnson appeased the Nashville "Post Office Clique" by allowing them to maintain control of the patronage-rich post office itself. He arranged to elevate William McNish from chief clerk to postmaster. The appointment came as a bitter surprise to two unconditional Nashville Unionists, John Lellyett and William R. Hurley, both of whom had sought the job. The latter complained that secessionists in the post office had "done all in their power" to impede circulation of his strongly pro-Union newspaper, the *Nashville Democrat*, forcing him to use a private express company. The Post Office Clique, Hurley bluntly told Johnson, were "the worst enemies you and I have had in this city." And Johnson had independent verification that Postmaster Samuel R. Anderson and his clique "were very harsh and bitter towards you" and "doing all they can against you." They maintained ostensibly correct relations with Johnson only because "they assert the road to office from the President is through you."[50]

Johnson, a habitual lone wolf, apparently chose to hedge his bets. Though his political fortunes were by March linked to the emerging Union party, he hesitated to cut loose entirely from his previous base in the Democratic party. Secessionists suffered such a lopsided rout in February that he may have feared the Union coalition would fly apart, allowing old party lines to reappear. By supporting the entrenched network of Democratic wirepullers in the state capital, and throwing at least one other major appointment to a secession-tainted Democrat—John L. Hopkins as district attorney for East Tennessee—Johnson apparently hoped, as one Unionist critic saw it, to use "patronage as a kind of cement to unite the two divisions of his party—the patriots and the traitors." In demanding the McNish and Hopkins appointments, Johnson certainly alienated many Unionists. And he may not have gained much leverage for himself. As soon as McNish took office, he refused to appoint someone Johnson wanted and launched a campaign to take away the public printing contract that helped to support the financially struggling *Democrat*. McNish subsequently became Nashville's Confederate postmaster.[51]

Quarrels about federal patronage show that the question of Tennessee's remaining in the Union was considered settled—more settled, indeed, than in North Carolina and Virginia, where Unionists still faced formidable secessionist opposition and where markedly less competition for federal office occurred in March 1861. In Tennessee, however, Unionists enjoyed such an overwhelming advantage that they began to jostle for leadership of the Union party.

At the state level, the struggle pitted Andrew Johnson against Knoxville editor William G. Brownlow. Bitter personal enemies for twenty years, they had found themselves allied in the fight against secession. But their entente could not long survive the huge Union victory of February 9. Jealous of Johnson's growing power and influence, Brownlow lashed his long-standing rival for appointing Democratic cronies while allegedly ignoring Union Whigs. More candidly, Brownlow complained about Johnson's choice of Union Whig allies. It became apparent by mid-March that Johnson was collaborating closely with West Tennessee Congressman Emerson Etheridge. The presumption was that Johnson would support Etheridge for governor if the latter would support Johnson's reelection to the Senate. Brownlow, ambitious himself for the governorship, declared his own candidacy, denounced the scheme "to monopolize the power and the patronage of the Union party in Tennessee," and proceeded to smear both Johnson and Etheridge.[52]

Before mid-April Nashville secessionists had only a Jeremiah role to play—predicting that Lincoln would soon disappoint the Unionists. Henry Foote correctly perceived by the end of March that a decisive impasse was imminent. But Nashville Unionists remained unperturbed. In a manner that was enacted concurrently at county seats across the state, they held a convention on April 1, county court day, to select delegates for the state Union party convention in May. Despite complaints from some Unionists of Whig antecedents, the county Union meeting supported Nashville Democrat Andrew Ewing as its preferred candidate for governor. John Bell agreed to take the nomination for his old seat in Congress. The Unionists' strategy for the upcoming campaign was simple—to keep the secession label firmly attached to their opponents. The *Nashville Republican Banner* warned that the "secession organization," consisting primarily of former leaders of the "now defunct" Democratic party, might attempt a campaign "so equivocal and vague in its features as to offer them the hope of securing for their nominees the support of many Union men, especially Union Democrats." To counter such a threat, Unionists would "have to remove the veil" secessionists had "thus thrown over their real designs and purposes, and expose them to the public gaze."[53]

Nashville Unionists worried about reports in early April that the administration had adopted a coercive policy but concluded that Lincoln and his cabinet could not have made such a "suicidal" choice. "The effect in the South of the inauguration of a war would be disastrous to the friends of the Union," reasoned the *Nashville Republican*

Banner. War would "paralyze their strength, and amount to a virtual reinforcement of the enemies of the Union. The Administration is certainly wise enough to see a thing so patent as this. . . . Their policy is to preserve the Union—war would destroy it."[54]

As happened throughout the upper South, Nashville was thrown into "a blaze of excitement" by the proclamation calling for troops. Local Unionists, at first astonished and bewildered, soon began to sputter with rage. They denounced the request as "inexcusable, mad . . . detestable . . . insane, aggressive, and malignant." Expressing a bitter sense of betrayal, they condemned the Lincoln administration for having "well nigh, if not entirely blasted all the hopes of preventing war and ultimately preserving the Union." Even if still inclined to blame the "miserable secessionists" for having initiated the trouble, most Unionists considered Lincoln's policy outrageous. Unconditional Unionists watched in hopeless dismay as public sentiment suddenly switched from Union to secession. Former Governor William B. Campbell received a letter from a friend in Nashville, reporting that "the events of the last few days" had totally transformed popular allegiances. The "most influential and strongest Union men of yesterday" were "to day carried by the vortex of circumstances into that powerful stream of public opinion on which they float too weak and powerless to stem the current." Before long, Campbell's friend mourned, the rampaging stream would "inundate the whole country in a most horrid civil war."[55]

Neill Brown, Andrew Ewing, and John Bell were thus "brought over by the injudicious and suicidal acts of the present imbecile Administration to the defense of a united South." Soon secession flags were "floating in the breeze all over the city." At a huge outdoor meeting on Saturday, April 20, leaders of the Southern Rights and Union parties met together to make common cause. They unanimously adopted resolutions condemning "the armed invasion of Southern soil," commending "the manly spirit of patriotic resistance" that had "everywhere displayed itself," and calling upon Tennessee to join with a "united South" to "repel the usurpations of the Federal Government." Henry Foote elicited "long loud and repeated cheers" when he spoke to the assembled throng.[56]

In most parts of Middle and West Tennessee, including the Nashville area, the formal ratification vote on secession in June was a mere formality. The issue was decided during the days after Lincoln's proclamation.[57] The few remaining unconditional Unionists in Nashville were "silenced by the mob" and "afraid to say anything on the street." By early May a correspondent wrote to William B. Campbell that "we are all one way in the river counties and that for secession and war. Such excitement and such unanimity I never witnessed before."[58]

THE secession winter in North Carolina's capital city became a nightmare for advocates of southern independence. When South Carolina Congressmen William W. Boyce and John D. Ashmore tried to speak at a meeting, a group of Raleigh "workingmen" disrupted the visiting dignitaries by burning tar barrels, ringing bells, and shouting. Another crowd shot down a Confederate flag raised by local disunionists, chopping the flagpole into small pieces. A group of secessionists traveling by railroad through the city imprudently labeled Raleigh "a d——d Abolition hole"; only the speedy departure of the train prevented a riot. Meanwhile, local Unionists sponsored a series of large and well-attended meetings, featuring hours of fervent Union rhetoric and group singing of patriotic songs such as "The Star Spangled Banner" and "The Flag of the Union." The latter supplied the suddenly popular tune, "Dixie," with appropriate alternative lyrics:

> to live and die for Union. . . .
> look away, look away, look away, see the flag![59]

When called upon to vote in February for delegates to a state convention, Raleigh's citizenry delivered a crushing majority for candidates of the "Constitutional Union Ticket," a coalition of Democratic and Whig Unionists. Douglas Democrat Quentin Busbee and the outspoken Union Democratic newspaper editor William W. Holden ran a joint campaign with former U.S. Senator George E. Badger, a leading Whig. The Union candidates polled between 694 and 712 votes, while their three secessionist opponents gathered between 74 and 81. Voters also decisively opposed the calling of a convention, 544 to 222. Badger noted that he and his Union colleagues had rolled up their margins even though running against "very popular men." On election night, an "immense procession" wound through the city, "giving out with loud voice the song of 'The Flag of Union.'"[60]

Raleigh secessionists complained bitterly about the "submissionist" victory. It had been gained, they charged, by pitting "class against class," by holding up "to public gaze the *rich* man and the poor as natural enemies," and by appealing "to the worst passions of the *mob*." The "abusive" and "unmanly vituperation" in William Holden's *North Carolina Standard* had "borne full fruit." Secessionists described the election night procession of exultant Unionists as "a horde of fanatical howlers," who had "paraded the streets of the city . . . carrying transparencies, singing election songs," and giving "three groans for John W. Ellis" as they passed the governor's house. "Mob law and violence," secessionists warned, would soon result.[61]

Unionists moved promptly to consolidate their new power. Raleigh's incumbent congressman, Lawrence O'B. Branch, came from a politically prominent family. His uncle had been a member of Andrew Jackson's cabinet, and Branch himself was a powerful and influential insider, more moderate than many southern Democrats. His Unionist credentials were still sufficiently untarnished that he was offered the treasury portfolio in December 1860 when President James Buchanan replaced several quasi-secessionist members of his cabinet. Yet during the spring of 1861 Branch was in deep political trouble in his home district. His endorsement of "States Rights" candidates to represent Raleigh in the abortive North Carolina convention alienated him from the successful Unionist coalition and led to demands that Branch publish the private letter in which he had expressed his views. When finally extracted, the document showed Branch to have worried that "what is called the Union party is drifting into unconditional and uncomplaining submission" and to have thought that North Carolina would be "ruined" if it did not call a convention. By the time the letter appeared in print, in late March, Branch was a marked man. The future Confederate brigadier general, later killed at Antietam, faced political extinction. Unionists in his district, determined to elect a congressman of their own persuasion, had begun to rally around the candidacy of Henry W. Miller, a Douglas Democrat and former Whig, who had played a leading role in the Unionist resurgence in the area. States Rights supporters thereupon endorsed Branch for reelection, which, in the eyes of Unionists, fixed "the black spot of disunion" upon him.[62]

Henry W. Miller, reviled by his secessionist relatives as someone who "lacked the true *Southern* feeling" and had "an especial spite against Slave holders," was a fitting choice to represent the burgeoning antiaristocratic Union party in the Raleigh area. He offended his plantation-owning kin by doubting whether nonslaveowning North Carolinians should be expected "to fight for our negroes." Miller wrote to Stephen A. Douglas on March 31 to explain the situation and to ask for advice:

> There is being expressed a strong desire, on the part of the Union men of this District, that I should take the field in opposition to the Secession Candidate for Congress. I think it very probable I shall be forced to do so. Before taking this step, I am

> anxious to learn the opinions of some one, in whom I have confidence, as to the future policy of the Administration toward the Seceded States. If it is the determination of the Administration to withdraw the forces from Sumter and Pickens, and to make no attempt to collect the revenue in the Seceded States, by means of armed vessels &c, in other words, if its policy is peace and the policy is promptly carried out, we can overwhelm the Secessionists in this State.

But Miller was troubled by "the tardiness of the Administration in carrying out its promised policy in reference to Fort Sumter." He also reported growing public "anxiety" about "the threatening state of things" at Fort Pickens. Continued "suspense and uncertainty" had begun to hurt the Unionists.[63]

Whether or not Miller received the reassurances he sought, he accepted the Unionist nomination for Congress and began his campaign during the first two weeks of April. The initial indications were superficially auspicious. The Whig newspaper in Raleigh grumbled about the Union nomination going to a Democrat but soon was admonished by one of its readers to "bury party" and support Miller: "I am in favor of him and all the Whigs around me are strongly in his favor." They would vote "for the Union ticket and for no other." William Holden's *North Carolina Standard* endorsed Miller's challenge in bold terms. "*No disunionist can represent this District in Congress,*" Holden editorialized:

> Democracy and Whiggism have nothing to do with this contest. The issue is *Union* or *Disunion*. Democratic principles and Whig principles will always exist, but the parties that were once organized on those principles have perished.—The old Whig party perished in 1852, and the work of destroying the Democratic party was commenced at Charleston in 1860. That work went on, and the party in this State was *finished* by Governor Ellis and the disunionists during the last Legislature. Two new parties have since been formed—one at Goldsborough *by the politicians*, and the other all over the State by the *people*; the former being for disunion, and the latter opposed to it.[64]

That editorial was printed on Saturday, April 13, even as news of fighting at Fort Sumter crackled across the telegraph lines. Monday brought word of Lincoln's proclamation for seventy-five thousand troops. On Tuesday, April 16, Henry Miller renounced his candidacy and urged "united resistance" to Lincoln's "declaration of war against the South." William Holden concurred: "The proclamation of Mr. Lincoln, calling for troops to make war on the Southern States, dissolved the Union so far as we are concerned, and summoned every true Southern man to arms." The proclamation "as by a stroke of lightning, made the North wholly North and the South wholly South."[65]

13

FORCED TO CHOOSE SIDES: SOUTHERN UNIONISTS AFTER THE PROCLAMATION

UNIONISTS of all descriptions, both those who became Confederates and those who did not, considered the proclamation calling for seventy-five thousand troops "disastrous." Having consulted personally with Lincoln in March, Congressman Horace Maynard, the unconditional Unionist and future Republican from East Tennessee, felt assured that the administration would pursue a peaceful policy. Soon after April 15, a dismayed Maynard reported that "the President's extraordinary proclamation" had unleashed "a tornado of excitement that seems likely to sweep us all away." Men who had "heretofore been cool, firm and Union loving" had become "perfectly wild" and were "aroused to a phrenzy of passion." For what purpose, they asked, could such an army be wanted "but to invade, overrun and subjugate the Southern states." The growing war spirit in the North further convinced southerners that they would have to "fight for our hearthstones and the security of home." Words of bitter condemnation poured from Maynard's pen. "Never was published a more unfortunate state-paper. It has done more, and I think I speak considerately, to promote disunion, than any and all other causes combined."[1]

Had Lincoln "inadvertently" misjudged the impact his proclamation would have in the upper South? Could he, some Unionists wondered, still define his purposes so as to dampen the "flame of excitement and apprehension"? When John Bell heard about the proclamation, he concluded that armed force was needed "mainly for the protection of the Capitol and other points threatened, and that no invasion of the South was then meditated." So Bell "waited with eager hope and expectation" for word that soldiers would be used only for strictly limited defensive purposes. But no such explanation ever came. Instead, reports arrived daily that northerners were determined "to wage a war for the subjugation of the South." A week after the proclamation as sectional polarization became so intense as to leave "scarcely a ray of hope for the preservation of the Union," Bell sadly endorsed Tennessee's military preparations. William Holden, probably the most outspoken Unionist in North Carolina before April 15, saw matters much as Bell did. "If Mr. Lincoln had only insisted on holding the federal property, and had called in good faith for troops to defend Washington City, the Union men of the border states could have sustained him," Holden thought. "But he 'crossed the Rubicon' when he called for troops to subdue the Confederate States. This was a proclamation of war, and as such will be resisted."[2]

The unconditional Unionist John Minor Botts, though somewhat more inclined than Bell or Holden to give Lincoln benefit of the doubt, nevertheless shared much of their resentment at the proclamation. Botts agreed with Bell and Holden that a prompt statement of limited defensive objectives would have "retained the support of the Union party of the South," which was instead "paralyzed by this single dash of his pen." Because the proclamation devastated support for the Union in the upper South and played into the hands of "demagogues with which the land was filled," Botts considered it "in many respects the most unfortunate state paper that ever issued from any executive since the establishment of the government."[3]

The proclamation and the northern response to it persuaded many Unionists to repudiate their earlier position and join hands with secessionists. "I was as strong a union man as any in the state up to the time [of] Lincoln's proclamation calling for 75000 volunteers," one North Carolinian noted. "I then saw that the South had either to submit to abject vassallage or assert her rights at the point of a sword." A Virginia Unionist likewise thought Lincoln's "villainous" course left the South "no alternative but to fight out our independence." Having earlier wished that South Carolina could be "pushed into the ocean" for initiating the trouble, he admitted that his opinions about that state were "little changed." But to show support for the southern war effort, he enlisted in the "Home guard" and rode "16 weary miles through a hot sun . . . to vote against Lincoln," that is, for the secession ordinance. Jonathan Worth, a state senator and leading North Carolina Unionist, observed that his state became "a unit" as soon as the proclamation was issued. Amid a seemingly universal determination "to resist to the death," Worth sadly realized that he had "no other alternative but to fight for or against my section." So also, Callaway Campbell, a prosperous young Virginian farming in northwestern Georgia, just across the border from East Tennessee, grimly concluded that "we are now upon the eve of a most terrible war." Though he had bitterly opposed secession, Campbell's ultimate loyalties were not in doubt: "Lincoln's base and blind course has destroyed all hope of reconciliation or reconstruction and no matter what differences of opinion we may have had, we shall be found shoulder to shoulder to defend our homes from all invasion. No matter how much we may regret it, it is now a fixed fact that there are to be two nations, a Northern and a Southern one and it does not take me long to decide which I shall uphold."[4]

The bombardment of Fort Sumter, by itself, did not destroy Unionist majorities in the upper South. Because only three days elapsed before Lincoln issued the proclamation, the two events, viewed retrospectively, appear almost simultaneous. Nevertheless, close examination of contemporary evidence, as suggested in the previous chapter, shows that the proclamation had a far more decisive impact. North Carolina Congressman W. N. H. Smith judged that "the Union feeling *was strong* up to the recent proclamation," and a Union delegate to the Virginia convention stated flatly that "*the conflict at Charleston could not have carried us out*." John A. Gilmer likewise remained confident until April 15 that Unionists could "overcome the disunionists in North Carolina" and throughout the upper South. The "fight at Charleston," he reported to Seward, "had done us no harm." Jonathan Worth also thought that "a large majority up to the time of issuing Lincoln's proclamation were firm for the Union." But then "Lincoln prostrated us. He could have devised no scheme more effectual than the one he has pursued, to overthrow the friends of the Union here."[5]

In Lexington, Virginia, home of Governor Letcher, Unionists still held the upper hand as of Saturday, April 13, when news of the fall of Sumter arrived. Secessionists raised a Confederate flag in front of the courthouse, but the "more numerous Unionists"—who included many "working men"—built a higher "Union pole" with an "eagle on it," to fly the American flag. When a few secessionist cadets from the Virginia Military Institute objected, a scuffle ensued and "the Unionists handled them roughly." But on Tuesday, April 16, after news of the proclamation reached Lexington, the same men who had raised the Union pole cut it down. A month later, Rockbridge County voted 1,728 to 1 for secession.[6]

In a letter written on April 15, after hearing about the fighting at Fort Sumter but before news of the proclamation reached him, William C. Rives, the elder statesman among Virginia Unionists, advised his friends to remain calm. They should stick to their plan for calling a border state conference and not be "hurried into any act of desperation and rashness." But the proclamation persuaded this influential Unionist that separation had become "inevitable," so that neither he nor Virginia could maintain "a position of neutrality." Reluctantly accepting a commission as one of five Virginia commissioners to the Confederate government, Rives decided that "we must make good our independence, or submit to a government resting on force and the arbitrary will of a sectional majority."[7]

The April 15 issue of the *Louisville Daily Journal* illustrates dramatically the impact of the proclamation. A long article, clearly written over the weekend by editor George D. Prentice, bitterly condemned the "revolutionists" of the deep South for attacking Fort Sumter. Because the secession movement was "flagging" and "in danger of perishing," its promoters had deliberately and cynically taken up arms in the hope that a new "Lexington" would reunite the South. Prentice, thinking that no "widespread fighting" would result from the troubles at Charleston, held out hope that the administration in Washington would react "with prudence and self-control." If it did, he judged, "the consequences of the collision at Charleston may yet overwhelm the authors of the enormity instead of the loyal men of the South against whom it was levelled." But just before the paper went to press, a "telegraphic report" of the proclamation arrived. Outraged at Lincoln's "hare brained and ruinous" change of policy, Prentice inserted his indignant reaction just below the masthead on the editorial page. "We are struck with mingled amazement and indignation. The policy announced in the Proclamation deserves the unqualified condemnation of every American citizen." Lincoln either had deceived the Unionists or had acted impulsively in response to events at Charleston. In either case, he was unfit to govern.[8]

Former Unionists again and again identified the proclamation as the decisive element that forced them and their states to abandon the Union. "Lincoln's arrogant and infamous usurpation of power" confronted James B. Dorman with a stark choice: "The issue presented is of a *fight* and the question simply is 'which side will you take?'" William S. Pettigrew of Washington County, North Carolina, saw matters similarly: "Lincoln threw off the mask on the 15th and revealed his real intention of subjugating the South." John H. Bills of Hardeman County, Tennessee, noted in his diary on April 16 the arrival of "old Abe Lincoln's proclamation of war against the South. . . . He calls for 75,000 volunteers to subdue *them*. Not one of which will he get from the slave states. *Now* the South will be a unit. However wrong the leaders may have acted, no one will see the south coerced into submission." Two months later, Bills's voting district, which had produced a Unionist majority in February, voted unanimously for secession.[9]

Stunned by the proclamation, Unionists tried to discern Lincoln's objectives. Many concluded, after the events of mid-April, that Lincoln had deliberately chosen "to drive off all the Slave states, in order to make war on them and annihilate slavery." Indignant Unionists wondered whether secessionists had correctly suspected Lincoln of planning to use armed force to carry on "the old John Brown business of *freeing* our slaves and punishing us for the sin of having held them." They speculated that Lincoln knew Union men "were about to gain strength enough in the South to stay Secession" and therefore decided perversely "to drive us all into rebellion," ignite "servile insurrection," and "desolate our section." Although other Unionists made a less sinister assessment of Lincoln's actions, it did little to improve their estimate of the man. Jonathan Worth of North Carolina complained bitterly that Lincoln was a "fool" who had misjudged "the feverish state of the popular mind" in the South and had thereby set in motion forces that crushed "the Union men in the Slave States." How, asked Worth, could Lincoln not have known "that he was letting loose on us a torrent to which we could oppose no resistance. It may be said, theoretically, that this should not have been the effect. Statesmen should have common sense. All sensible men knew it would be the effect."[10]

Upper South Unionists considered themselves betrayed. Throughout March, seemingly authoritative reports indicated that the administration intended to pursue a peace policy toward the seceded states, avoiding any armed "collision." Lincoln "allowed it to go forth to the world that Fort Sumter was to be evacuated." Unionists concluded that the hands-off policy would receive a fair trial, thereby restraining "the war spirit of the Southern people." The attempt to resupply Sumter thus appeared to be "double dealing," and the proclamation was a "declaration of war against the South." Lincoln had "basely falsified" assurances earlier given to southern Unionists and proceeded "to levy a war of the most gigantic proportions." The editors of the *Salisbury Carolina Watchman* protested: "This, to our apprehension, is *rank usurpation*, and as freemen, we cannot submit to it. Toward the Union men of the border states this conduct is infamous. To the South as a whole it is a gross and intolerable wrong—to the Union party, in particular, it is *treachery* and *fraud*." The editor of the *Alexandria Gazette* made a similarly harsh evaluation of Lincoln's behavior. "It is against the friends of the Union at the South, that the Administration has struck its hardest blows." Although a majority of over fifty thousand in Virginia had opposed secession, the consequences of the proclamation were such that "secession, if put to a vote now, would be carried by a tremendous majority." The theme of betrayal also pervaded Jonathan Worth's rueful letters during the weeks after the proclamation: "Union men feel that just as they had got so they could stand on their legs, Lincoln had heartlessly turned them over to the mercy of their enemies."[11]

Unionist reactions to the events of mid-April ran the gamut from outrage and defiant bravado to a deep sadness and intimation that the upper South was doomed. Exemplifying the militant mood, an embittered Virginia supporter of Stephen A. Douglas sounded a howl of indignation. He hoped "the God of battles" would "*crush to the earth and consign to eternal perdition*, Mr. Lincoln, his cabinet, and all 'aiders and abettors,' in this cruel, needless, *corrupt betrayal* of the conservative men in the South." The reporter who wrote a weekly column about affairs in Loudoun County, Virginia, a Union stronghold west of Washington, D.C., on the Potomac River, conveyed a similar message, even if phrased more circumspectly: "It is said 'thou shalt not speak evil of the ruler of thy people,' but since the issuing of the President's proclamation this injunction of Holy Writ has not been much respected in these parts." Having "knocked away the props that have upheld the Union party in this county," Lincoln would find "as sturdy a set of rebels" there as in any other part of the South. A resident of Lynchburg, Virginia, summarized the feelings of many former Unionists: "His proclamation is one of war and the South will be united to a man and will meet his menaces with defiance. We will maintain our rights or we will die in the effort to maintain them."[12]

In contrast, however, many Unionists expressed only sadness and dread after hearing about the proclamation and seeing the sectional polarization that followed it. As the nation—often referred to metaphorically as a "ship"—appeared to disintegrate, pessimistic Unionists looked to the future with foreboding. He had "stood by the ship . . . as long as a plank remains," one Tennessee Unionist noted in his diary, "but now all is lost." An elderly North Carolinian had hoped "that the good sense and virtue of the people would save the ship from the rocks," but he too feared the situation hopeless. "We are," he concluded, "a ruined people." Jonathan Worth, forced by circumstances to embrace the Confederate cause, did so "with sorrow." He unburdened himself in two letters to his son: "I tremble for you and for myself—for everybody who has any property. Peaceable secession would soon annihilate slavery. War, long continued, will ruin every peaceful citizen and end in the total overthrow of civil liberty and the abolition of slavery." Worth thus feared the worst: "I think the South is committing suicide, but my lot is cast with the South and being unable to manage the ship, I intend to face the breakers manfully and go down with my companions." To a friend in the North, Worth explained his hopeless predicament: "I am filled with horror at the condition of our country. . . . I see no hope of any good and stable government except in the *united* government we are pulling down."[13]

No upper South Unionist had been more centrally enmeshed in the struggle against secession than John A. Gilmer. The letter he sent to Seward on April 21 is thus one of special significance and poignancy. Unlike many other last letters sent North the week after the proclamation, its tone was not bellicose but reflective and despairing. His hopes of saving the Union shattered and his only son already serving in a Confederate volunteer company, Gilmer took a bleak view of the future. "All hope is now extinguished," he mourned. Instead of pursuing the policy he had expected, the administration had done "the very thing which the disunionists most desired." "As matters now stand," he sadly concluded, "there is a United North against a United South, and both marching to the field of blood."[14]

VIRGINIA, North Carolina, and Tennessee all effectively seceded from the Union and joined the Confederacy within days after the proclamation became known. Popular sentiment shifted unmistakably from majority Union to majority secession. The governors of all three states immediately refused to send troops to fight in the Union army and instead worked feverishly to organize and enlist forces to oppose Lincoln. Seizing the opportunity to demonstrate its sudden claim to upper South loyalties, the Confederacy quickly moved its capital to Richmond. So the question of statewide allegiance was promptly resolved. The formal process of secession necessarily took longer, and it followed a somewhat different pattern in each state. But the end result was the same.

In Virginia, the convention promptly passed a secession ordinance on April 17, but its action did not receive formal validation until ratified by popular vote on May 24. By that time the entire Confederate government was installed at Richmond, making the result of the referendum a foregone conclusion. In Tennessee, Governor Harris called the legislature into special session, which met on April 25. The legislature quickly arranged to put the question of secession to popular referendum on June 8. Overwhelming prosecession sentiment in Middle and West Tennessee left no doubt about the result of the referendum. Governor Ellis called the North Carolina legislature into special session on May 1. It ordered the election on May 13 of an unrestricted convention, to meet on May 20. That convention immediately proclaimed North Carolina out of the Union and rejected a proposal to submit the decision to popular referendum.[15]

Public opinion in each state reversed itself overwhelmingly. The only significant opposition to secession in the Virginia referendum of

May 23 occurred in the far northwest, adjacent to the Ohio and Pennsylvania borders. Unanimous secession affirmations were the order of the day almost everywhere else, including many counties subsequently included in southern and eastern parts of West Virginia. The completely polarized Virginia pattern—a cluster of overwhelmingly antisecession counties in the trans-Allegheny but hardly any other antisecession votes, let alone majorities, elsewhere in the state—does not invite elaborate statistical comparison with the pro-Union vote of February. The absence of accurate statewide voting returns is also a handicap. Still, on the basis of evidence available, including approximations for some counties, it may be said that secession was ratified by a majority of close to 100,000 votes—132,201 to 37,451. Historian Richard O. Curry estimated that in the trans-Allegheny of northwestern Virginia, the vote was 10,021 for ratification and 30,586 against; in the entire future state of West Virginia, he found a total of about 19,121 for ratification and 34,677 opposed. It may thus be concluded that the approximate vote for secession in the present state of Virginia was 113,080 in favor and only 2,774 opposed. The vote east of the Alleghenies was 122,180 in favor and 6,865 opposed.[16]

It is impossible to develop any statistical analysis of the change from Union to secession sentiment in North Carolina after April 15. Unlike Virginia and Tennessee, no statewide referendum on secession ever took place. The only election occurred on May 13, when North Carolina voters selected delegates for a state convention. Because most former Union leaders either acquiesced in or actively supported the new order, almost all convention candidates endorsed secession and many ran unopposed, thereby depressing voter turnout. The only contested issue in North Carolina was whether to label the departure of the state from the Union as "secession" or "revolution." Former Union Whigs preferred "revolution" but were outvoted at the convention. The delegates then unanimously adopted the ordinance of secession, and a majority opposed even going through the formality of securing popular ratification. Yet despite the unanimity displayed by North Carolina's political leaders, pockets of grass-roots unconditional Unionism remained.[17]

In Tennessee, however, the June 8 popular vote on secession does lend itself to statistical analysis. Unlike Virginia, complete returns are available. Also unlike Virginia, opponents of secession did attempt to campaign statewide. But overall voting patterns in Tennessee and Virginia were sufficiently similar that an analysis of Tennessee data will shed light on developments in Virginia and probably North Carolina as well. In Tennessee the eastern region became, of course, the counterpart to northwestern Virginia, opposing separation 15,782 to 32,323. Middle Tennessee voted for separation, 58,063 to 8,143, as did West Tennessee, 30,626 to 6,717. Thus the state overall voted for separation 104,471 to 47,183, with a margin of 88,689 to 14,860 in Middle Tennessee and West Tennessee combined.

Tennessee counties with high concentrations of slaveowners voted very differently in June 1861 than did counties with low concentrations of slaveowners. Map 13-1, showing voting patterns in June 1861, substantially resembles Map 2-6, showing concentrations of slaves in 1860. Counties with higher than average slaveholdings in Middle and West Tennessee voted for secession in June with near unanimity. Some traditionally Democratic counties with few slaves also embraced secession in June (note, for example, the contiguous Middle Tennessee bloc of Cannon, Coffee, Grundy, Van Buren, and Warren counties). Opposition to secession nevertheless ran deepest in other low-slaveowning regions—especially East Tennessee, but also the cluster of counties, principally in West Tennessee, adjacent to the Tennessee River. Figures 7-6 and 7-9 show that by June, high-slaveowning counties in Tennessee overwhelmingly favored secession, 58,796 to 2,830, whereas low-slaveowning counties only narrowly supported it, 45,675 to 44,353. In voting for convention delegates in February, high- and low-slaveowning counties of Tennessee had not divided as sharply as in Virginia and North Carolina because of the presence of many conditional Union Whigs in the higher-slaveowning counties of Middle and West Tennessee. But the question posed in February of whether to hold a convention had divided more clearly between high-slaveowning and low-slaveowning counties and had thereby prefigured the June vote.

Data in Table 13-1, Table A-4 in Appendix I, and Table A-10 in Appendix II reinforce the maps and graphs. By all measurements, the secession referendum of June 1861 divided slaveowners from nonslaveowners more than it divided Whigs from Democrats. Party remained a significant explanatory factor, as Whigs demonstrated greater qualms about secession, but ownership of slaves had more explanatory value. The June 1861 pattern resembled the anticonvention vote of February 1861 much more than the antisecession vote of February 1861.[18]

It is important, however, not to exaggerate the polarization between Tennessee slaveowners and nonslaveowners on the separation issue in June. Obviously, a state in which 19 percent of the eligible electorate owned slaves and 55 percent voted for separation required that large numbers of nonslaveowners support separation. Estimates of individual voting behavior, explained in Table 7-5, suggest that 85

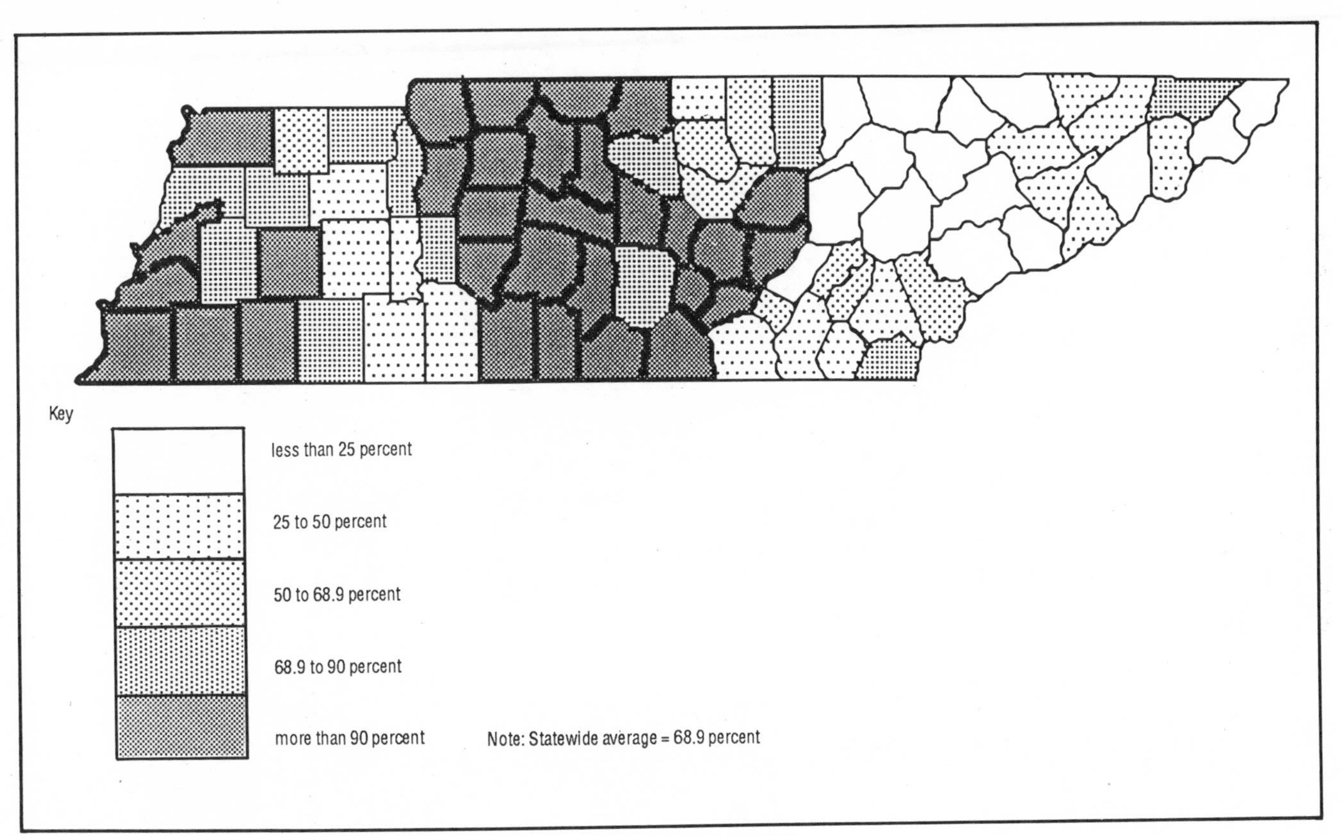

MAP 13-1. *Percentage for Separation, by County, Tennessee, June 1861*

TABLE 13-1.
Tennessee: Secession Crisis Correlation Coefficients

	Slaveowner	Whig	Democratic
Union, February 1861	−.21	.60	−.39
Secession, February 1861	.29	−.45	.62
Anticonvention, February 1861	−.46	.42	−.33
Proconvention, February 1861	.58	−.28	.46
Antiseparation, June 1861	−.66	.32	−.36
Proseparation, June 1861	.64	−.32	.51

Note: Calculations are based on county-level data, weighted according to the eligible voters in 1860. "Slaveowner" = the percentage of adult males owning slaves. "Whig" = the percentage of eligible voters supporting John Bell in 1860. "Democratic" = the percentage of eligible voters supporting John C. Breckinridge and Stephen A. Douglas. Voting returns for June 1861 have been compiled in the manner explained in Chapter 7, n. 2, which also discusses sources of data. See Table 2-2 on interpreting correlation coefficients.

percent of slaveowners voted for secession and 15 percent did not vote, whereas 48 percent of nonslaveowners voted for secession, 31 percent voted against it, and 21 percent did not vote.

Very much at work here was the process of community solidarity and affirmation discussed in Chapter 2. Communities that favored secession often did so en masse—with near or total unanimity. Prosecession localities in Middle and West Tennessee decisively outnumbered those localities, mostly in East Tennessee, where antisecession solidarity was nearly as intense. So the discovery that voters in low-slaveowning counties divided almost equally on the secession issue should not be read to mean that individual nonslaveowners divided equally statewide. Those nonslaveowners who lived in high-slaveowning counties voted with few exceptions for secession or else did not vote. As a result, nonslaveowners were divided, to be sure, but over 60 percent of those voting favored secession. Slaveowners who voted were almost unanimously prosecession, but an increment of slaveowners, doubtless Union Whigs, did not vote. The low-slaveowning counties included all of East Tennessee, where voters opposed secession by a two-to-one margin. But voters in low-slaveowning counties in Middle and West Tennessee voted for secession by an even larger margin. Thus the most profound polarization in Tennessee was geographical. East Tennessee, like trans-Allegheny Virginia, in effect and in spirit seceded from the remainder of the state when the state seceded from the Union. Tennessee did not divide into two states only because no federal army could aid East Tennessee Unionists early in the war. Once federal armies did seize parts of Middle and West Tennessee early in 1862, the federally imposed government under Andrew Johnson needed to keep the state together, in the hope that votes from East Tennessee Unionists would provide a sufficient base for a Union party, once peace came and military rule ended.

POPULAR sentiment favoring resistance to Lincoln had its roots in the home communities of the South. Original Unionists and original secessionists joined hands to prepare for war. The impulse to defend the home community against threatened aggression united people who had earlier disagreed. Themes of community solidarity and patriotic unanimity pervaded the countless mass meetings, public pledges of financial support, martial parades, and ritualistic presentations of battle flags from the ladies to the local volunteer soldiers. Few even tried to swim against such a fierce popular current. As East Tennessee Unionist Oliver P. Temple observed: "Sympathy with friends and kindred became the bond that united the South. Tens of thousands of men who had no heart for secession, did have heart for their neighbors and kindred. This almost universal fellowship and sympathy drew men together in behalf of a cause which one-half of them disapproved."[19]

The few who would not bow to local feeling risked very unpleasant consequences. George W. Eastham, who lived in Smithville, Tennessee, "a Confederate community," was "the only Union man in the vicinity in which he lived." He had six sons of military age. The oldest five fought for the Confederacy and four died. But Eastham persuaded the youngest—"the only one I could controll"—to join the Union army. For his defiance of community norms, and notwithstanding the sacrifice of his older sons, Eastham was threatened, mobbed, and eventually driven into exile. Even if "not molested or injured," avowed Unionists were "socially tabooed and ostracized." A Unionist from Murfreesboro, Tennessee, sadly recalling "the bitterness and hatred which was manifested towards me and other Union men and our families," stated that his "most intimate friends and business associates" would no more recognize him on the street than they would "a dog."[20]

Intense pro-Confederate pressures often prevented Unionists from voting against secession. Henry C. Sinclair, a merchant and farmer from Franklin, Tennessee, was "one of the few that were original unconditional Union men" in Williamson County. At the election in June 1861, however, he "voted a blank ticket." Sinclair explained: "The times were dangerous. There were but few Union men in Franklin and we were watched. I had to vote some way. I was afraid to vote against ratification as I knew it would be found out." Other Unionists simply "staid away from the polls" on election day. One Murfreesboro, Tennessee, voter explained that he and other Union men were "afraid of the excited state of the public mind" and so "did not vote at all." Unionists in one district in Loudoun County, Virginia, decided "it was too dangerous to vote," thereby allowing secessionists to claim a unanimous victory.[21]

Some Unionists cast prosecession ballots. James M. Haynes, a substantial propertyholder in Rutherford County, Tennessee, was "intimidated" into voting for secession. At the polls on election day he "used some expression not favorable to the cause of rebellion and secession and a very intense feeling was expressed against him." Though not directly threatened, Haynes considered himself in danger. "As long as I was there I felt that it would not be safe to refuse to vote," so Haynes voted against his convictions, explaining that "I can vote with you, but my feelings are not with you." No Union votes were cast in Haynes's district. Another isolated Unionist in a different district in Rutherford County likewise voted for secession in response to even more direct threats. John J. Neely, a farmer and schoolteacher, recounted: "At the time of the election the feelings of the community had been worked up to a fever heat. The district was almost unanimously Democratic. I was known as an outspoken Union man. I lived within about a mile of the polls. Threats were made that if I did not go to the polls and vote for ratification I would be killed." Neely reluctantly voted against "his sentiments and wishes" to "save my life as I believed." Several pacifistic Mennonites from Rockingham County, Virginia, in the Shenandoah Valley, cast pro-Union ballots but were then escorted back to the polls by armed secessionists, who compelled them to change their votes.[22]

A few brave souls nevertheless refused to bend to community pressures. Starling Proctor of Orange County, North Carolina, denounced by a Confederate lieutenant for being "a darned old Union son of a bitch" who "ought to be hung," went after his tormentor and "knocked him down with a hoe." Joseph R. Thompson, a farmer and distiller from Rutherford County, Tennessee, defiantly voted against ratification of the secession ordinance. A few days before the June 1861 election he was told that "no Union man would be allowed to vote" in the district where he lived. "That made me angry and excited," he recalled. "I had never been deprived of my right to vote any way I pleased and I never intended to be. I did not know but I might have trouble and therefore took my gun with me to the polls. At the door of the house where the election was being held I met one of my neighbors, a strong secessionist, and he said to me: 'Joe how are you going to vote?' I said 'I am going to vote as I d——m please.' I voted against ratification." Young Amasa Hough also voted against ratification in Loudoun County, Virginia. When secessionists then threatened to hang him, Hough swam across the Potomac River on election night to reach safety in Maryland.[23]

In some southern localities, however, sentiment in the home community was either openly divided or pro-Union, giving wartime Unionists a far more supportive environment. Indeed, large parts of East Tennessee and northwestern Virginia were as inhospitable for "rebels" as Confederate areas were for Unionists. And Confederates never effectively controlled parts of the Quaker Belt in piedmont North Carolina. Wartime Unionism also persisted in a few areas in Middle and West Tennessee, where a scattered number of political leaders remained unconditionally Unionist, in contrast to North Carolina and to Virginia east of the Alleghenies. Parts of Bedford County, south of Nashville, were a "stronghold of loyalty" during the war. At least some votes were cast against secession in most Bedford voting districts in June 1861, and even though prosecession voters had a solid overall majority, 1,595 to 727, Unionists carried six of the nineteen districts. Prominent Bedford County politicians such as Edmund Cooper and William H. Wisener supported the Union side.[24]

The town of Liberty in DeKalb County likewise illustrated the persistence of Unionism in some Middle Tennessee communities. Here leadership must have played a significant role: Liberty was the home of Congressman William B. Stokes, who became colonel of the Fifth Tennessee Cavalry Regiment (USA). Union candidates carried Liberty in February 1861 by a vote of 206 to 4, and voters likewise opposed calling a convention, 205 to 5. By June the Union majority in Liberty diminished only slightly (170 to 30), as voters resisted the secession tidal wave that engulfed most other parts of Middle Tennessee. Stokes's Fifth Tennessee soon drew recruits from local Unionists. John Davis of Liberty, for example, had three sons in the Fifth, one of whom died, as well as three nephews. Adjacent towns in DeKalb and Smith counties also had Union tendencies. Alexandria, in DeKalb County, maintained a Union majority in June 1861, albeit by a reduced margin.[25]

Just as parts of Smith and DeKalb counties remained strongly Unionist and provided the soldiers for a Union cavalry regiment, parallel pockets of Union strength existed in West Tennessee. Carroll and Henderson counties, on the west bank of the Tennessee River, were centers of Whig Unionism, in which solid popular majorities continued to oppose the Confederacy throughout the war. Men from these counties constituted the backbone of the Seventh Tennessee Cavalry Regiment (USA) under Colonel Isaac R. Hawkins. Below Carroll County on the Mississippi border lay McNairy County, where areas of Union strength remained despite a majority vote cast for secession in June 1861. An outspoken Unionist, Fielding Hurst, who was imprisoned for his last-ditch opposition to secession, subsequently organized the Sixth Tennessee Cavalry Regiment (USA), which attracted local men fleeing from Confederate service.[26]

Southern Claims Commission documents in the National Archives reveal that ties of kinship and locality sustained Unionism in these West Tennessee counties. Jane Read, for example, lived two miles outside Lexington in Henderson County. Her two sons served in Company A of Hawkins's Seventh Cavalry and died in Andersonville Prison. Unionism was pervasive where the Read family lived. Captain Thomas A. Smith of Company A testified that "all that neighborhood was that way," and another witness reported that five or six first cousins of the dead Read brothers had served in the Seventh. Similar patterns occurred in McNairy County. In one area just above the state border north of Corinth, Mississippi, two politically active brothers, David and George Mickey, supported Stephen A. Douglas in 1860 and then became unconditional Unionists. One prominent local Unionist recalled: "I think I can remember every man in my vicinity who was in favor of secession. I think there were just ten of them." Confederates used their power in late 1861 to conscript the local McNairy County militia into regular service as the Fifty-second Tennessee Infantry (CSA). But when Union gunboats came upriver in early 1862, members of the Fifty-second deserted en masse. Among the deserters were many future members of Hurst's Sixth Cavalry (USA).[27]

Correspondence between former Tennessee Governor William B. Campbell and Francis H. Gordon, a local Union leader in Smith County, Tennessee, well illustrates how Union sentiment persisted in some areas after April 15 but suffered for lack of effective statewide leadership. Smith County, located east of Nashville in the foothills of the Cumberland Plateau, was a classic Union Whig locality. The original home of Campbell, who still lived in adjacent Wilson County, Smith regularly polled Whig majorities of 70 percent or higher. Though its slaveowning percentage (25.8) slightly exceeded the statewide average, Smith County emphatically opposed secession before the proclamation. In the election of February 1861, Union delegates won by margins of approximately 1,900 to 200, and the voters rejected a convention, 1,829 to 303.[28]

Soon after the proclamation appeared, Campbell sent a cautionary letter to Gordon, a political ally who had reportedly "defended Lincoln's policy" and talked of raising soldiers to sustain the president. Gordon protested that the rumors were inaccurate and probably planted by a secessionist. Explaining that he opposed both "Republicanism and . . . secession," Gordon criticized Lincoln's "war policy" as "imprudent to say the best for him." Whatever Lincoln's "ultimate object," he had overpowered "the conservative men in the Border Slave States" and played "exactly into the hands of Jeff Davis." Gordon reluctantly agreed with Campbell's pessimistic assessment of Union prospects in the state: "I have no doubt you are correct as to the storm raging in our State. It will sweep every thing before it. Tennessee will likely be draged out of the Union into the Southern despotism. I fear all is lost."[29]

Gordon nevertheless hoped to maintain "*armed neutrality* of the *Border States*" rather than "going into the Southern Confederacy." He explained to Campbell, "in confidence," why such a stance made far greater sense for Smith County. Unlike "the people of the towns and cities," who were "turning fast to disunion and for a Southern Confederacy," the nonslaveowning "country people" in his area remained "against disunion and against war." If "forced" against their will to support secession and serve in "a southern army," many would rebel: "They say they will fight for the Union and against any disunionists south or north. One of those men told me yesterday, that there are at least four hundred such men in Smith." Though few were abolitionists, they were "not willing to fight for slavery."[30]

A month later, Gordon prodded Campbell to come out against secession. "We have been still long enough," he reasoned. Smith County Unionists had initially followed Campbell's advice to keep quiet and organize "home guards" for local defense. But during "the last few days," Gordon reported on May 24, several speakers including Congressman William B. Stokes had taken the stump in towns around the county, with the result that "secession is almost dead here." The people were readily convinced that secession had been "inaugurated to *enslave* them." Young men of "no experience or personal influence" had successfully challenged prominent secession speakers. Though condemning the "fraud and usurpation of secession" and urging people to vote against it in June, Smith County Unionists insisted that they too opposed Lincoln and were ready "*to defend our homes and fight the Northern invader.*" They hoped that Kentucky, Missouri, western Virginia, and Maryland would join Tennessee in a stance of armed neutrality.[31]

But even though Gordon had confidence that secession could be decisively defeated in his immediate home area, he recognized that Unionists had "the great disadvantage of no strong newspapers" and suffered also because most prominent Unionists in Middle Tennessee had either come out for secession or, like Campbell, lapsed into silence since the proclamation. He pleaded with Campbell to act. "The secession papers will kick up and some of them pounce on you," Gordon reasoned, but Campbell's "influence with the people" would "control at least twenty thousand votes" and embolden many other "true men" who would "take the stump as soon as you come out."

Gordon's urgent plea to Campbell reflected a belief in the power of political leadership in the second party system. Gordon himself was a person of influence in his immediate neighborhood and believed he could sway votes locally. He thought a cue from leading Tennessee Whig Unionists such as Campbell and Balie Peyton would prompt many other local leaders and their constituents to reject secession. "I doubt whether you are fully aware of the immense influence you have with the people, and therefore of the great responsibility resting on you in this crisis," Gordon wrote. His plea was far from unreasonable. By speaking out boldly and unequivocally, Andrew Johnson had certainly made it easier for rank-and-file Democrats, especially in East Tennessee, to vote Unionist in February. Others echoed Gordon's judgment. Emerson Etheridge reported from West Tennessee that Union sentiment in his congressional district remained strong, even though many Union leaders in Nashville and Memphis, where "all the mischief has been done," had "yielded to mob pressure." Imploring Campbell not to "desert us now," Etheridge calculated that a public avowal of his Unionism would be worth twenty-five thousand votes and that a statewide majority against secession could still be obtained.[32]

But Unionists such as Gordon and Etheridge overestimated the potential strength of their cause and exaggerated the influence that any Union leader still possessed. There is solid evidence that vigorous local Union leadership made it feasible for voters who were so inclined to vote Unionist without fear. But only in a few localities in Middle and West Tennessee did the Union constituency of February remain relatively intact in June. The pressures to switch were immense. Unionists and Union-inclined communities were "trumpeted far and near as being abolitionists and Lincolnites" and subjected to intense pressure "to *force* us into the current." In Smith County, for example, despite pockets of unconditional Unionism, secession carried in June by more than a two-to-one margin, 1,418 to 676. Secessionist recruiters worked hard to enlist soldiers into the Confederate armies. When Confederates lost control of Middle Tennessee in 1862 and some of these local soldiers returned home, secessionists threatened them "with disgrace and even violence" if they did not reenlist. Confederate cavalry raiders aided by "numerous rebel citizens" kept life miserable for Smith County Unionists.[33]

The overall situation in Tennessee and the seceding states of the upper South was well described by A. O. P. Nicholson, the state's other U.S. senator. Unlike his colleague Andrew Johnson, Nicholson had remained a Southern Rights loyalist through the secession winter. In early May he tried to explain to a northern friend that the proclamation had brought about a dramatic "revolution in public sentiment" in Tennessee. "I know that my State was regarded at the North as unalterably fixed in the Union," Nicholson wrote, "but I declare to you that to-day there is only a small portion of our State in which a man can safely avow himself a Union man." Tennessee was now "virtually out of the Union and in a condition of revolution." Its withdrawal from the Union and alliance with the Confederate States would soon be "overwhelmingly ratified by the people." They regarded the proclamation and subsequent decrees from Washington as "clear and palpable acts of usurpation," thought Lincoln a "tyrant," and saw "the northern people as enemies bent on their subjugation or extermination." Nicholson pinpointed the new perspective on the sectional crisis that had swept Tennessee since mid-April: "It is no longer the negro question but a question of resistance to tyranny." People saw the issue as one of "liberty or death." A "military spirit" was sweeping the state, and volunteers by the thousands were "actively drilling and preparing" for armed conflict. Unless the North recognized the unity and determination of the South, there would be "no escape from a bloody civil war."[34]

Just as Nicholson wrote, delegates to the state convention of the Union party assembled in Nashville "under peculiar circumstances." When appointed, one month before, they represented "the dominant Party in the State—a party which a few weeks previous had triumphed in a warmly contested election by an overwhelming and unprecedented majority." But "since their appointment events had transpired in the country which rendered it necessary for that party to abandon the position which it then occupied." Hiram K. Walker, editor of the *Nashville Republican Banner*, blamed the changed circumstances on the "insincerity" of Lincoln and his advisers, who had promised "to pursue a peace policy." Instead, the administration had taken the "perfidious and suicidal" step of issuing the proclamation. As a consequence, "the once Union party of Tennessee" was "a Union party no longer," and the convention "disclaimed being a Union convention." With war "imminent" between the federal government and the seceded states, members of the Tennessee Union party "saw that they had no alternative but to choose sides." In Walker's estimation, "they could not debate as to which side their honor and their duty required them to take." They decided, "in common with the Union men of Virginia and the other Border Slave States," to "defend themselves and the whole South against an arrogant and overbearing Northern majority."[35]

Adjacent to the article in the *Republican Banner* on May 3, explaining the awkward position of the state Union party, was an excerpt from the *Lebanon Herald*. It reported that "war spirit" in Wilson County had reached "a high pitch," that people had united to resist "the coercive policy of Mr. Lincoln," and that Robert Hatton, whose career so aptly illustrates the paradoxical history of southern Unionism, was a Unionist no longer. Instead, the outspoken antisecessionist, first introduced in the Prologue to this study, was "in the Country getting up a company to go to the wars." The *Herald* noted that "Col. Hatton did all he could to stay the tide of war that is now sweeping over the land, but having failed, he is now ready to do all he can to defend Tennessee and the South against any invading foe. He will soon have a full Company ready for service, and should war continue, he and his brave followers will be found in the thickest of the fight."[36]

EPILOGUE: RETHINKING THE SECESSION CRISIS

WRITING in late April 1861, shortly after the war began, Henry Adams tried to decide whether the secession crisis could have had any other result. "What would have been the end of the matter," he wondered, if "the conciliatory policy had become the policy of the Government?" Adams knew that a great deal depended upon the actions of the upper South. Elections in Virginia scheduled for late May were, he recounted, to have been a "decisive point" in the campaign to achieve reunion without war.[1]

The question posed by Adams deserves more careful consideration than it has usually received. Had armed "collision" been averted, the Virginia elections in late May would have strengthened Unionist control of the legislature, given Unionists a majority of the state's twelve seats in the U.S. House of Representatives, and sent George W. Summers to the U.S. Senate in place of the Southern Rights Democrat, James M. Mason. An even more one-sided Union victory could reasonably have been expected in Tennessee in August, where Governor Isham G. Harris faced sure defeat. Unionists in North Carolina would also have gained at least one more congressional seat in the August elections.

By summer, too, the border state conference would have met at Frankfort, Kentucky. There is scant reason to believe that the conference would have eroded Union strength in the upper South. To be sure, conditional Unionists in the Virginia convention tenaciously insisted that their continued adherence to the Union depended upon northern acceptance of Virginia's "ultimatum," consisting of new constitutional amendments "necessary for the security of her rights and institutions." But they also pledged themselves to cooperate with the states of the upper South in preparing the ultimatum. Therein lay a formidable obstacle to any unequivocal action by the conference. Of the eight states that were to have sent delegates to it, only Arkansas and Virginia would likely have supported a threat of secession in default of new guarantees.[2] North Carolina and Tennessee, by voting against holding a state convention, had demonstrated a firmer attachment to the Union. And Unionists thoroughly dominated Delaware, Maryland, Kentucky, and Missouri, the four border slave states that did not secede even after the war started. It appears unlikely that the eight states of the upper South could have agreed to the sort of ultimatum discussed in the Virginia convention.

Secessionists recognized as much. They had little hope that the border state conference would take any decisive action. Twice within the previous ten years, during the 1850 crisis and after the John Brown raid, Southern Rights advocates had failed ignominiously in trying to unite the South by means of a conference. The decision by secessionists to move on a state-by-state basis after Lincoln's election reflected the proven inefficacy of conferences. So too did efforts by Unionists and deep South "cooperationists" to postpone secession until a southern conference could be held. During March and early April, when it appeared that the upper South would remain in the Union, at least for the time being, and that the border state conference would indeed convene in Kentucky in late May, few secessionists expected that the meeting would do anything to aid their cause. One Southern Rights activist in Virginia disgustedly predicted that it would produce no more than a "milk and water ultimatum." Another thought the conference would "succeed in tacking the border States as a tail to the Northern Confederacy, and thus abolitionize them all."[3]

The consolidation of Unionist control over the states of the upper South would have tended to make secession an increasingly illegitimate option. State loyalty would have worked to the advantage of Unionists throughout the upper South had war been averted or postponed in April 1861. When the deep South seceded, those still opposed tended to accept the inevitable and support the new regime. At the time the war broke out, the reverse process had not yet happened in the upper South, where secessionists remained active and ardent, even if outnumbered. But had the peace been preserved, Unionists expected the clamor would soon begin to subside. They counted on the powerful southern impulse to maintain "community consensus," through which dissenters usually yielded to majority opinion.[4]

None of these developments, to be sure, would have brought back the seceded states or enabled the federal government to solve its problems of collecting the revenue or preventing the European powers from recognizing the Confederacy. War could ultimately have resulted, and probably would have, because Lincoln and the Republican party firmly opposed peaceful separation. But one may well imagine circumstances in which the introduction of armed force would have evoked less overwhelming southern opposition.

Imagine, for example, that the spontaneous Southern Rights convention had actually attempted to seize power in Virginia. Its leaders were certainly contemplating just such a rash step. Assume further that a conspiratorial force had indeed captured the governor and broken up the convention. Would Unionists then have turned to the federal government for assistance? They might have had to. And the Lincoln administration would probably have responded vigorously. The U.S. Constitution fairly bristles with authority to provide armed force under such circumstances. It gives the federal government broad power to "suppress Insurrections," to protect states against "Invasion" and "domestic Violence," and to guarantee to each state "a Republican Form of Government."

The hypothetical troubles in Virginia might have led directly to war, especially if those who attempted the coup d'état requested or received armed assistance from the Confederacy. But it might have been a very different war, with popular majorities in the upper South supporting the Union side. Such a conflict would have had less potential to become a protracted revolutionary upheaval. A short, decisive war in which the deep South fought alone might not have lasted long enough to undermine the slave system or to allow emancipation to emerge as a northern war aim.

The course of events in Kentucky illustrates how Unionists elsewhere might have reacted, had the war started without seeming to require that the upper South join in "coercing" the lower South. Kentucky's Union party, in contrast to those of Virginia, North Carolina, or Tennessee, rejected both secession and coercion. It retained power by championing a policy of armed neutrality and by trying to mediate between the federal and Confederate governments. However unsuccessful the attempted mediation, it well served the political needs of Kentucky Unionists. They swept statewide elections in May and June, gaining undisputed control over the state legislature. Quasi-secessionist Governor Beriah Magoffin bowed to the popular will. Supporters of Kentucky's prosecession Southern Rights party either acquiesced to majority sentiment in the state or emigrated south behind Confederate lines. Months later, in September, when Confederate armies moved above the Tennessee border to occupy several positions in southern Kentucky, the state legislature requested federal protection. That request was promptly granted.[5]

To say that the conciliatory policy did not work obscures the fact that it scarcely received a fair trial. Less than a month after William H. Seward persuaded Abraham Lincoln to seek voluntary reunion through conciliatory means, the president changed his mind. Concluding that the choice had narrowed to disunion or forcible reunion, he decided to risk a confrontation with the Confederates at Fort Sumter.

Upper South Unionists and their northern allies remained hopeful about the chances for peaceful reunion. They either believed forcible reunion impossible or believed it could not be considered until public sentiment in the upper South became more unconditionally pro-Union. The elapse of time would, Seward calculated, either bring peaceable reunion or so isolate the deep South Confederacy as to make the use of force feasible.

Most upper South Unionists absolutely opposed the use of force. By the end of March some therefore began to see peaceful separation as the lesser of evils. But other Unionists such as John A. Gilmer indicated privately to Seward that they might eventually support the use of force under more promising circumstances.

Historians have long criticized Seward for having "greatly underestimated the force and stamina of the secession movement" and for relying upon "the kind of qualified Unionism" that prevailed in the upper South. Frederic Bancroft considered Seward's southern allies weak and vacillating: his alliance with such "broken reeds" made him an unintended dupe of secessionists. Kenneth Stampp judged Seward guilty of "incredible blindness" in believing that the Union could be peacefully reunited. Seward's policy of "appeasement" and pursuit of peace "at any price" impressed Allan Nevins as evidence of "a profound moral defect."[6]

This study suggests the need for reassessment. Who "greatly underestimated the force and stamina of the secession movement"? Seward recognized its strength far sooner than most other Republicans. He realized that the states of the lower South were, for the present, estranged. But if secession could be prevented from spreading to the upper South, he believed the Union could be restored. That a seven-state Confederacy would either grow or perish was an idea widely held by knowledgeable observers both in Washington and Montgomery. While Seward took steps to limit secession, inflexible Republicans insisted that it had been "gotten up for effect" and would soon blow over if ignored. They condemned him for regarding seriously an illusory threat.

The accusation that Seward misconceived the character of Unionism in the upper South is likewise untenable. Through personal contacts and an aggressive search for accurate information, he knew more about the upper South than any other official in the Lincoln administration. He well knew that antisecession victories in February depended greatly on support from conditional Unionists. He therefore recognized, as many Republicans failed to do, that upper South Unionism was not yet reliable. Seward's memorandum to Lincoln on March 15 pointed out that "while the people of the border states desire to be loyal, they are at the same time sadly, though temporarily, demoralized by a sympathy for the slave states. . . . This sympathy is unreasonable, unwise, and dangerous, and therefore cannot, if left undisturbed, be permanent. It can be banished, however, only in one way, and that is by giving time for it to wear out, and for reason to resume its sway. Time will do this, if not hindered by new alarms and provocations."[7]

Seward therefore did his best to demonstrate the folly of militaristic Republicans such as Montgomery Blair and his father, Francis P. Blair, Sr., who believed secession a minority coup and expected loyal southerners to sustain the Union cause as soon as federal armies arrived to crush the conspirators.[8] Seward realized that the initiation of hostilities between the federal government and the Confederacy would, under existing conditions, transform nearly the entire South into a hostile armed camp.

Seward also realized, however, that the antisecession groundswell had potentially transformed the political landscape of the upper South. He knew that a new Union party stood on the verge of dominating the whole region. He had established ties with several key leaders of that party. His expectation that time would favor the cause of the Union was based on much more than naive hope.

There were, to be sure, other ways in which the passage of time might weaken the prospects for reunion. The nub of the dilemma facing the Lincoln administration in March was to judge whether the advantages of inaction outweighed the disadvantages. A truly momentous debate thus raged behind closed doors. Yet the terms of that debate have never been well understood. And the argument in favor of delaying a showdown, based upon expectations that the upper South would tend to become more unconditionally pro-Union, has eluded most historians.

Seward favored conciliatory inaction because he was extremely pessimistic about the likelihood of forcible reunion. Keenly aware that war would unite the South, he suspected that war would divide the North. If the administration were to "take up the sword," he predicted, then "an opposite party" would "offer the olive branch." He did not allow himself to see that the passions generated by the firing on Fort Sumter and the proclamation for seventy-five thousand troops would produce an outburst of patriotic unanimity in the North, such as to make forcible reunion possible, though at a ghastly price in blood and treasure. Seward's policy required no use of force unless and until the upper South could be counted on to sustain the Union.[9]

Lincoln, by contrast, appears to have judged that the eclipse of Unionism in the deep South made peaceful reunion impossible. No surviving evidence indicates how he expected the outbreak of war to affect the upper South. He may have underestimated the latent pro-Confederate sympathies of states that had recently rejected secession. Or he may have concluded that the Union could be restored only by fighting against an enlarged Confederacy and that it was better to fight sooner than later.

Lincoln certainly saw political, diplomatic, and economic dangers resulting from a hands-off policy. Restlessness within his own party would have burst into open revolt had he abandoned Fort Sumter. Foreign encouragement or recognition of the Confederacy would have become a greater threat as long as the administration appeared unwilling to challenge secession. And the commercial and financial consequences of secession looked increasingly grim by late March. Lincoln may well have decided to try resupplying Fort Sumter to avoid the likely and, to him, unacceptable consequences of continued inaction, but without fully knowing what would result from sending the resupply fleet.

A war of vast dimensions necessarily appears unavoidable in retrospect. Once the limited war aim of restoring the old Union was supplanted by the revolutionary war aim of creating a new Union in which slavery would have no place, it became difficult to realize that reasonable men could have considered peaceful reunion a legitimate possibility during the months before the war started. Lincoln's wartime leadership and posthumous stature have likewise functioned to make us see the secession crisis through his eyes. No outcome other than a "violent and remorseless revolutionary struggle" appears credible.[10]

Pronorthern historians, both early and modern, have therefore generally heaped ridicule on the efforts of those who opposed a military confrontation with the Confederacy in March and April 1861. Even though more Americans died in the Civil War than in all other American wars combined from the Revolution through Vietnam, we so prize the preservation of the Union and the achievement of emancipation that we cheerfully justify the high price that was paid. We reject as unprogressive or unpatriotic any suggestion that alternatives existed. Yet by so doing, we make it harder to understand what actually happened in 1861.

The historian's advantage of hindsight, David Potter cautioned, "is really a disadvantage in understanding how a situation seemed to the participants." Relying on our own "omniscient twenty-twenty vision," we credit Lincoln and his Republican allies for accepting a war "whose magnitude they could not know" and for choosing results "which they could not foresee." Had the war ended differently and the Confederacy secured its independence, "the Monday morning quarterbacks of the historical profession would have been in the position of saying that the rash choice of a violent and coercive course had destroyed the possibility of a harmonious, voluntary restoration of the Union—a restoration of the kind which William H. Seward was trying to bring about." For Potter, "the supreme task of the historian, and the one of most superlative difficulty, is to see the past through the imperfect eyes of those who lived it."[11]

It bears repeating that the issue under discussion in early 1861 was how best to achieve reunion. Nobody in the Lincoln administration or the Republican party then endorsed the use of federal power to destroy slavery. To say that black freedom could have been achieved only through war and that a war for black freedom was a war worth fighting is to ignore entirely the limited Union war aims of 1861.

We cannot know whether Seward's hands-off policy would have averted or diminished the "baptism of blood" that Whittier so gracefully deprecated. But it is dangerously ahistorical to see the outbreak of the Civil War as simply the first chapter of a morality tale and Lincoln as a secular saint or giant among pygmies. The haunting might-have-been that intrigued Henry Adams deserves more than a patriotic put-down, and his epitaph on Seward's policy remains entirely pertinent in a world infested with weapons of mass destruction: "Like all such attempts at wisdom and moderation in times of heated passions and threatening war, it was swallowed up and crushed under the weight of brute force, that final tribunal to which human nature is subjected or subjects herself without appeal. Yet it is right to make the effort even if overruled."[12]

SOUTHERN Unionism has remained a mysterious enigma precisely because it vanished abruptly. War splintered the antisecession coalition that took shape in Virginia, North Carolina, and Tennessee in early 1861. Any phenomenon so transitory appears dubious and its proponents insincere. Conspicuous Unionists such as Zebulon B. Vance and Jubal Early immediately went to war, as did Robert Hatton. Elder statesmen whose careers symbolized Whig Unionism and nationality—John Bell, William C. Rives, George E. Badger, and William A. Graham—sadly cast their lot with the Confederacy. William W. Holden read Lincoln's proclamation and decided he had no choice but to side with his state. John B. Baldwin and John A. Gilmer eventually held seats in the Confederate Congress. George W. Summers resigned from the Virginia convention, returned home, and refused ever to participate in political affairs again. Only in East Tennessee and northwestern Virginia did more than a handful of pre–April 15 Unionist leaders maintain their allegiance after the war started. Residence in those distinctive regions made possible the wartime and Reconstruction political careers for unconditional Unionists such as Waitman T. Willey, William G. Brownlow, and especially Andrew Johnson.

Yet for almost all these men, whatever their future course, and for the great majority of the quarter million voters in Virginia, North Carolina, and Tennessee who rejected secession in February 1861, a conviction persisted that the events of April could and should have been avoided, or at least handled very differently. That conviction united southern Unionists, even as the proclamation shattered their movement, destroyed their party, and engulfed them in war. Many indeed sided with the Confederate States of America, but they did so with reluctance.

APPENDIX I:

MULTIPLE REGRESSION—PARTY, SLAVERY, AND SECESSION

A STATISTICAL procedure known as multiple regression enables the historian to measure the relative influence of two or more factors on an electoral outcome. In other words, one may determine the amount of change in voting produced by each of two or more different variables, while taking into account the influence of every other variable.[1] Multiple regression thus allows more precise and sophisticated assessment of the relative influence of party and slaveowning on secession voting than do Figures 7-7 through 7-9. There is no need for the reader to feel burdened by the statistical technique to appreciate the common-sense results revealed by multiple regression. One should first look at Tables A-1 through A-4, which display multiple regression figures for all three states and for the two halves of Virginia.

An example will illustrate how multiple regression tables should be interpreted. Anyone studying the crisis of the Union in the upper South will quickly recognize that secession sentiment bore some relationship both to the Democratic proclivities and to the concentration of slaveowners in each county. Multiple regression allows the researcher to find out whether party or slaveowning more heavily influenced the susceptibility to secession. Thus, in the case of Virginia (see Table A-1), multiple regression suggests that even though both factors were statistically significant, the percentage of slaveowners better predicted the secession vote than the percentage of Breckinridge Democrats (standardized regression coefficients or so-called beta weights of .650 and .384 respectively).[2] In other words, every 10 percent increase in slaveholding produced a 6.5 percent increase in secession voting, when taking into account or controlling for the impact of the other explanatory variable in the equation (voting for Breckinridge). And every 10 percent increase in the Breckinridge vote produced a 3.8 percent increase in voting for secession, when taking into account the impact of slaveowning. Multiple regression also shows that the two factors together explained an impressive 68 percent of total variance in voting on secession (coefficient of multiple determination, or Total R^2, equals .681). Multiple regression thus validates the common-sense assumption that slaveowning and Breckinridge support had something to do with secession and allows the researcher to determine both how much and the relative weight of the independent or explanatory variables (slaveowning and party).

Multiple regression also helps to reveal influences that may be hidden if considered in isolation. Look again at Table A-1. The low *r* value (.027), or Pearson's correlation coefficient, appears to suggest that the percentage of Whig voters in a Virginia county, by itself, reveals nothing about the Unionist

TABLE A-1.
Multiple Regressions: Virginia

Dependent Variable	Independent Variable	Simple *r* (Pearson's)	Beta	Total R^2	R^2 Change
Union	Slaveowner, 1860	−.665	−.795	.442	
	Whig, 1860	.027	.335	.537	.095
Union	Slaveowner, 1860	−.665	−.763	.442	
	Whig, 1860	.027	.326	.537	.095
	Douglas, 1860	.347	.274	.611	.074
Secession	Slaveowner, 1860	.735	.650	.541	
	Breckinridge, 1860	.529	.384	.681	.140

Note: "Union" and "Secession," the dependent variables, derive from February 1861 voting data. The independent variables likewise derive from November 1860 voting data (the percentage support for presidential candidates in each county) and from 1860 census data about the percentage of slaveowners in each county. All calculations are based on county-level data and have been weighted in proportion to the number of eligible voters in 1860. All eligible voters (adult white males) are included, both those who voted and those who did not. See Chapter 7, n. 2, on sources of data.

proclivities of the county (coefficient of determination, or R^2, equals *r* times *r*, or .027 times .027, which equals .001). But multiple regression takes into account the strongly inverse relationship between Union strength and the concentration of slaveowners, so that the Whig factor is revealed to carry respectable weight, albeit secondary to slaveowning (beta weights of −.763 and .335, respectively). The common sense of this hidden influence may be stated as follows: Virginia counties with high concentrations of slaveowners strongly tended to vote more heavily for secession, but counties with high concentrations of Whigs tended to vote more pro-Union than counties with equal numbers of slaveowners but fewer Whigs. Viewed separately, one tendency obscures the other. Thanks to multiple regression, both influences may be considered together and accurately weighed.

Multiple regression also forces the analyst to recognize that one of two or more apparently significant explanatory variables may eclipse the others when considered together. Look, for example, at Table A-3 on prosecession and proconvention voting in North Carolina. Viewed in isolation, the distribution of slaveowners appears quite significant. Positive relationships to slaveowning at *r* values of around .5 produce bivariate R^2 values of around .25. But the multiple regression equations show that the pattern of Breckin-

TABLE A-2.
Multiple Regressions: Virginia, East and West of the Blue Ridge

Dependent Variable	Independent Variable	Simple *r* (Pearson's)	Beta	Total R^2	R^2 Change
Union (east)	Slaveowner, 1860	−.521	−.437	.272	
	Whig, 1860	.518	.430	.452	.181
	Douglas, 1860	.208	.199	.492	.040
Secession (east)	Breckinridge, 1860	.693	.531	.480	
	Slaveowner, 1860	.614	.399	.613	.133
Union (west)	Douglas, 1860	.385	.404	.148	
	Slaveowner, 1860	−.251	−.551	.235	.087
	Whig, 1860	.287	.526	.445	.210
Union (west)	Whig + Republican, 1860	.399	.517	.160	
	Slaveowner, 1860	−.251	−.472	.334	.174
	Douglas, 1860	.385	.367	.467	.113
Secession (west)	Breckinridge, 1860	.449	.508	.202	
	Slaveowner, 1860	.393	.458	.408	.206

Note: Same basis for calculation as Table A-1.

ridge voting in 1860 greatly reduces the explanatory value of the slaveowning variable. What is the common sense of this result? About two-thirds of North Carolina slaveowners were Democrats (see estimates in Tables 7-3 and A-6). Counties with larger concentrations of slaveowners did tend to vote for secession and for a convention, but in about the same pattern that they normally voted Democratic.

The example just cited also suggests why multiple regression alone has the potential to mislead. Table A-3 shows that prosecession, proconvention, and pro-Breckinridge voting all display similar patterns. Yet it is also essential to realize that prosecession voting was depressed at levels sharply lower than the normal Democratic turnout—a point emphasized in Chapter 7. Data presented in Table 7-4 show that 35 percent of the North Carolina electorate (49,447 voters) favored Breckinridge in November 1860, yet only 27 percent (38,227 voters) supported secession three months later. Since the overall turnout in the two elections was nearly identical, a narrow Breckinridge victory in November was followed by a resounding secession defeat in February. As suggested in Chapter 7, the inability of North Carolina secessionists to poll a full Democratic vote mattered more than the congruence between secession voting patterns and Breckinridge voting patterns.

TABLE A-3.
Multiple Regressions: North Carolina

Dependent Variable	Independent Variable	Simple *r* (Pearson's)	Beta	Total R^2	R^2 Change
Union	Whig, 1860	.639	.583	.408	
	Slaveowner, 1860	−.464	−.378	.548	.140
Union	Whig, 1860	.639	.563	.408	
	Slaveowner, 1860	−.464	−.429	.548	.140
	Douglas, 1860	.229	.278	.622	.074
Secession	Breckinridge, 1860	.800	.762	.640	
	Slaveowner, 1860	.466	.072	.644	.004
No convention	Whig, 1860	.615	.545	.379	
	Slaveowner, 1860	−.558	−.477	.601	.222
No convention	Whig, 1860	.615	.527	.379	
	Slaveowner, 1860	−.558	−.522	.601	.222
	Douglas, 1860	.182	.248	.660	.059
Yes convention	Breckinridge, 1860	.794	.714	.631	
	Slaveowner, 1860	.524	.156	.649	.018

Note: Same basis for calculation as Table A-1.

SEVERAL conclusions may be drawn from these multiple regression tables. In all three states, an antisecession surge in low-slaveowning regions in February 1861 disrupted patterns of party loyalty that had endured for a generation. The deviation from previous voting patterns was greatest in Virginia, the most sprawling and diverse of the three states and the one in which the partisan loyalties of the electorate were somewhat less rigid than in the other two. Partisan influences nevertheless remained significant. Areas of Whig strength in Virginia did tend to vote more strongly pro-Union, and secessionists clustered in Breckinridge strongholds. Virginia's Douglas Democrats strengthened the pro-Union coalition, as did their less numerous North Carolina counterparts.

What we know about statewide voting patterns in Virginia should, however, be supplemented by separate multiple regression analyses for eastern and western Virginia, as divided at the Blue Ridge (see Table A-2). Although slaveowning overwhelms party as an explanatory factor in statewide secession crisis voting, the partisan loyalties of a county do become more signifi-

TABLE A-4.
Multiple Regressions: Tennessee

Dependent Variable	Independent Variable	Simple *r* (Pearson's)	Beta	Total R^2	R^2 Change
Union	Whig, 1860	.599	.679	.359	
	Slaveowner, 1860	−.206	−.358	.481	.122
Secession	Democrat, 1860	.620	.592	.385	
	Slaveowner, 1860	.291	.213	.429	.045
No convention	Slaveowner, 1860	−.457	−.580	.209	
	Whig, 1860	.423	.552	.499	.290
Yes convention	Slaveowner, 1860	.575	.523	.331	
	Democrat, 1860	.462	.394	.483	.153
Antiseparation	Slaveowner, 1860	−.657	−.766	.432	
	Whig, 1860	.318	.489	.659	.227
Proseparation	Slaveowner, 1860	.642	.585	.412	
	Democrat, 1860	.511	.435	.597	.185

Note: Same basis for calculation as Tables A-1 and A-3. "Antiseparation" signifies opposition to separation and "Proseparation" signifies support for separation in June 1861 voting.

cant explanatory factors when each region is analyzed separately. In other words, the relative concentration of slaveowners best explains statewide voting in Virginia because of a powerful tendency for counties with fewer slaveowners to vote pro-Union. But in explaining differences in voting behavior within each region, it may be seen that partisan loyalty equals and in some instances exceeds the explanatory value of slaveowning (note respective beta weights and R^2 change in Table A-2). A high-slaveowning county in eastern Virginia was far more likely to poll a strong secession vote than a low-slaveowning county in western Virginia. But a Whig county in eastern Virginia was more likely to show some Union strength than a Breckinridge county, just as a Breckinridge county in western Virginia was more likely to show pockets of secession support than a Whig county. Table A-2 also shows that the relationship between Union strength and voting for Douglas, already apparent in the statewide results in Table A-1, was distinctly stronger in western Virginia. Western Douglas supporters, such as Governor Letcher and his allies, were outspoken antisecessionists.

Secession crisis voting in Tennessee and North Carolina somewhat more closely approximated earlier patterns of party voting than in Virginia (see Tables A-3 and A-4). Patterns of Democratic support explained substantial amounts of secession strength in both states, especially in North Carolina; patterns of Whig support likewise substantially explained Union strength. Compared with Virginia, slaveowning was a less powerful predictor of Union and secession voting patterns in Tennessee and North Carolina.

The question of calling a state convention did, however, sharply divide slaveowning and nonslaveowning voters in Tennessee. Partisan affiliation rather than slaveholding was a better predictor of voting patterns for convention candidates in Tennessee, but the question of holding a convention became more like the statewide Virginia pattern on secession. That is, the percentage of slaveowners in a Tennessee county better predicted support for a convention than did the percentage of Democrats (beta weights of .523 and .394, respectively). The pattern of opposition to calling a convention was inversely related to the concentration of slaveowners and positively related to the concentration of Whigs (beta weights of −.580 and .552, respectively).

The percentage of slaveowners in a Tennessee county became by far the best predictor of voting behavior in June 1861. Opposition to separation had a strongly inverse relationship to slaveowning and a positive but weaker relationship to Whig voting (beta weights of −.766 and .489). The two variables together accounted for 65.9 percent of the total variance in the statewide vote against separation (R^2 = .659). Support for separation was positively related both to slaveowning and to Democratic voting (beta weights of .585 and .435). Together the two variables explained 59.7 percent of the variance in the proseparation vote (R^2 = .597).

In North Carolina, the county-by-county percentage of Breckinridge support best predicted by far the pattern of support for secession or for the calling of a convention. Patterns of Whig partisanship likewise carried greater weight in explaining opposition to secession, although the concentration of slaveowners did carry a substantial inverse relationship to North Carolina Union strength. And, similar to Tennessee, the opposition to calling a state convention in North Carolina was accounted for as much by an inverse relationship to slaveowning as by Whig loyalties (note the comparable beta weights of −.522 and .527).

APPENDIX II: ECOLOGICAL REGRESSION—ESTIMATING VOTER BEHAVIOR

A STATISTICAL technique known as ecological regression allows the historian to estimate patterns of voting between two elections or to estimate how identifiable groups within the electorate divided their votes in any particular election. In other words, one may estimate how Virginia voters who supported John C. Breckinridge in November 1860 distributed their votes at the secession crisis election in February 1861. Likewise, one may estimate how Virginia slaveowners and nonslaveowners divided their votes in either election. Such information, even if estimated, allows the historian to make educated guesses about matters of great interest. Data in Tables 3-2 through 3-4 and 7-1 through 7-10 are based on ecological regression analysis.[1]

Ecological regression estimates should take into account all eligible voters. The total number of eligibles in 1860 and 1861 for any state or county may be closely approximated by using the 1860 census to discover the number of white males aged twenty or older. Slaveowners and nonslaveowners also may be tabulated with census data. Most voting returns, as suggested in Chapter 7, are available through the Inter-University Consortium of Political and Social Research (ICPSR), though somewhat greater ingenuity is required to locate and interpret secession crisis vote totals.

The reader should now examine the segment of Table A-5 entitled "Virginia West of the Blue Ridge: Union versus Secession (February 1861)." This table presents estimates for the voting behavior of slaveowners and nonslaveowners. If read horizontally, the bottom line shows that 53 percent of the eligible voters in Virginia west of the Blue Ridge voted Union, 10 percent voted secession, and 37 percent did not vote. So also, the vertical column on the right side of the table shows that 8 percent of the adult males living west of the Blue Ridge owned slaves, whereas 92 percent did not. These figures on the bottom line or the right-hand margin (the "totals" or "marginals") are known, and when added together (either horizontally or vertically) equal 100 percent. But the cell entries, suggesting how slaveowners and nonslaveowners divided their votes, are estimates, and they should be read as general indications of voting behavior, not precise measurements. We know that 53 percent of the eligible electorate in western Virginia voted Union; the regression estimates are that 4 percent of the eligible electorate both owned slaves and voted Union, whereas 49 percent owned no slaves and voted Union. Because of specific assumptions explained in the table, I have slightly modi-

TABLE A-5.
Estimated Voting Behavior of Virginia Slaveowners and Nonslaveowners, 1860–1861 (in Percentages)

Virginia East of the Blue Ridge:
Presidential Election (November 1860)

Category	Whig	Democratic	Not Voting	Total
Slaveowners	12 (11)	27 (20)	−1 (7)	38
Nonslaveowners	23 (24)	11 (18)	28 (20)	62
Total	35	38	27	100

Virginia West of the Blue Ridge:
Presidential Election (November 1860)

Category	Whig	Democratic	Not Voting	Total
Slaveowners	7 (4)	2	−1 (2)	8
Nonslaveowners	21 (24)	34	37 (34)	92
Total	28	36	36	100

Composite Estimate for the Entire State:
Presidential Election (November 1860)

Category	Whig	Democratic	Not Voting	Total
Slaveowners	7	10	4	21
Nonslaveowners	24	27	28	79
Total	31	37	32	100

Virginia East of the Blue Ridge:
Union versus Secession (February 1861)

Category	Union	Secession	Not Voting	Total
Slaveowners	4 (8)	23 (16)	11 (14)	38
Nonslaveowners	25 (21)	6 (13)	31 (28)	62
Total	29	29	42	100

TABLE A-5. *continued*

Virginia West of the Blue Ridge: Union versus Secession (February 1861)

Category	Union		Secession		Not Voting		Total
Slaveowners	4	(3)	3	(2)	1	(3)	8
Nonslaveowners	49	(50)	7	(8)	36	(34)	92
Total		53		10		37	100

Composite Estimates for the Entire State: Union versus Secession (February 1861)

Category	Union	Secession	Not Voting	Total
Slaveowners	5	9	7	21
Nonslaveowners	37	10	32	79
Total	42	19	39	100

Note: Patterns of slaveowning and voting in eastern and western Virginia were so dissimilar that more useful ecological regressions were achieved by dividing the state at the Blue Ridge. Figures in parentheses represent recalculations based on three assumptions: that no more than 80 percent of eligible slaveowners voted in November 1860, that no more than 65 percent of eligible slaveowners voted in February 1861, and that 20 percent fewer slaveowners voted for secession than for a Democratic presidential candidate. Estimates for the entire state are extrapolated from the separate estimates for each region. See Chapter 7, n. 2, on sources of data.

fied the original estimates, as indicated within the parentheses. Likewise, we know that 92 percent of the eligible electorate in western Virginia owned no slaves; the regression estimates are that 49 percent of the eligible electorate were nonslaveowners who voted Union, 7 percent of eligibles were nonslaveowning secessionists, and 36 percent of eligibles were nonslaveowners who did not vote. Again, I have slightly modified the original estimates. It bears repeating that the cell entries are estimates, whereas the marginals are known percentages of the entire eligible electorate.

Table A-8, to take a related example, illustrates how ecological regression may be used to estimate voters' transitions between pairs of elections. We have already noted that in western Virginia, 53 percent of eligible Virginia voters cast Union ballots in February 1861, 10 percent voted for secession, and 37 percent did not vote. These figures may be found in the right-hand vertical margin of the middle segment of Table A-8 entitled "West of the

TABLE A-6.
Estimated Voting Behavior of North Carolina Slaveowners and Nonslaveowners, 1860–1861 (in Percentages)

Presidential Election (November 1860)							
Category	Whig		Democratic		Not Voting		Total
Slaveowners	11	(6)	19	(13)	−5	(5)	24
Nonslaveowners	21	(26)	18	(24)	37	(26)	76
Total		32		37		31	100
Union versus Secession (February 1861)							
Category	Union		Secession		Not Voting		Total
Slaveowners		5		11		8	24
Nonslaveowners		35		16		25	76
Total		40		27		33	100
Convention versus No Convention (February 1861)							
Category	No Convention		Convention		Not Voting		Total
Slaveowners	2	(3)	12	(13)	11	(8)	24
Nonslaveowners	32	(31)	21	(20)	22	(25)	76
Total		34		33		33	100

Note: Figures in parentheses represent recalculations based on two assumptions: that no more than 80 percent of eligible slaveowners voted in November 1860, and that February 1861 nonvoters on the convention question were the same persons as February 1861 nonvoters on the Union versus secession issue.

Blue Ridge." The horizontal margin, or bottom line, displays the distribution of votes in western Virginia in November 1860: 29 percent for Breckinridge, 7 percent for Douglas, 27 percent for Bell, 1 percent for Lincoln, and 36 percent not voting. Regression estimates of cell entries suggest, among other things, that Bell, Douglas, and Lincoln supporters in western Virginia voted overwhelmingly pro-Union. Substantial numbers of Breckinridge supporters also voted pro-Union, the estimates suggest, but other Breckinridge partisans supplied almost all the votes cast for secession in western Virginia. An

TABLE A-7.
Estimated Voting Behavior of Tennessee Slaveowners and Nonslaveowners, 1860–1861 (in Percentages)

Presidential Election (November 1860)

Category	Whig	Democratic	Not Voting	Total
Slaveowners	11 (9)	8 (7)	0 (3)	19
Nonslaveowners	26 (28)	32 (33)	23 (20)	81
Total	37	40	23	100

Union versus Secession (February 1861)

Category	Union	Secession	Not Voting	Total
Slaveowners	13 (10)	5 (4)	1 (5)	19
Nonslaveowners	39 (42)	11 (12)	31 (27)	81
Total	52	16	32	100

Convention versus No Convention (February 1861)

Category	No Convention	Convention	Not Voting	Total
Slaveowners	4 (3)	14 (11)	1 (5)	19
Nonslaveowners	33 (34)	16 (19)	32 (28)	81
Total	37	30	33	100

Union versus Secession (June 1861)

Category	Union	Secession	Not Voting	Total
Slaveowners	0	15	4	19
Nonslaveowners	25	40	16	81
Total	25	55	20	100

Note: Figures in parentheses represent recalculations based on two assumptions: that no more than 85 percent of eligible slaveowners voted in November 1860 and that no more than 75 percent of eligible slaveowners voted in February 1861.

TABLE A-8.
Virginia: Estimated Distribution of Voters, 1860–1861 (in Percentages)

East of the Blue Ridge

1861	1860 Breckinridge	Douglas	Democrat	Whig	Nonvoting	Total
Union	−5 (0)	2	−3 (2)	28 (25)	4 (2)	29
Secession	24 (23)	1	25 (24)	5	−2 (0)	29
Nonvoting	13 (9)	2	15 (11)	2 (5)	26	42
Total	32	5	37	35	28	100

West of the Blue Ridge

1861	1860 Breckinridge	Douglas	Democrat	Whig	Republican	Nonvoting	Total
Union	13	8 (7)	21 (20)	25	2 (1)	6 (7)	53
Secession	11 (10)	0	11 (10)	−1 (0)	−1 (0)	1 (0)	10
Nonvoting	5 (6)	−1 (0)	4 (6)	4 (2)	0	29	37
Total	29	7	36	27	1	36	100

Entire State

1861	1860 Breckinridge	Douglas	Democrat	Whig	Republican	Nonvoting	Total
Union	6	6	12	24	1	5	42
Secession	17	0	17	2	0	0	19
Nonvoting	7	1	8	4	0	27	39
Total	30	7	37	30	1	32	100

Note: The very different patterns of voting in eastern and western Virginia required separate ecological regression calculations for the two halves of the state. Parenthetical figures suggest ways to recalculate logically impossible values. Estimates for the entire state are extrapolated from the separate calculations for each region. "Democrat" = the combined Breckinridge and Douglas vote. "Whig" = the Bell vote. "Republican" = the Lincoln vote.

TABLE A-9.
North Carolina: Estimated Distribution of Voters, 1860–1861 (in Percentages)

	1860										
1861	Breckinridge		Douglas		Democrat		Whig		Nonvoting		Total
Union	−4	(4)	3	(2)	−1	(6)	27	(26)	15	(8)	40
Secession	28	(24)	−2	(0)	26	(24)	−2	(2)	2	(1)	27
No convention	−9	(2)		2	−7	(4)	25	(22)	17	(8)	34
Yes convention	33	(26)	−1	(0)	32	(26)	0	(6)		1	33
Nonvoting	11	(7)	1	(0)	12	(7)	7	(4)	14	(22)	33
Total		35		2		37		32		31	100

Note: Parenthetical figures suggest ways to recalculate logically impossible values. Recalculations are also based on the assumption that 6,000 Breckinridge supporters voted pro-Union and that 3,000 voted anticonvention. "Democrat" = the combined Breckinridge and Douglas vote. "Whig" = the Bell vote.

estimated 25 percent of the electorate voted for John Bell in November and then pro-Union in February; 13 percent voted for Breckinridge and Union; 8 percent for Douglas and Union, and 2 percent for Lincoln and Union. In addition, an estimated 6 percent of the eligible electorate voted pro-Union in February after having sat out the presidential election. Because the original estimates exaggerate the total number of Douglas and Lincoln voters, I have placed slightly modified figures in parentheses to overcome logical impossibilities.

Tables 7-1 through 7-10 in Chapter 7 are designed to make the data in Appendix II easier to interpret. For an analysis of Tables A-5 through A-11, the reader should therefore consult Chapter 7.[2]

TABLE A-10.

Tennessee: Estimated Distribution of Voters, 1860–1861 (in Percentages)

	1860			
1861	Democrat	Whig	Nonvoting	Total
Union, February 1861	11 (14)	37 (34)	5 (4)	52
Secession, February 1861	19 (15)	−2 (1)	−1 (0)	16
No convention	1 (5)	32 (28)	4	37
Yes convention	28 (24)	4 (7)	−1 (0)	31
Nonvoting, February 1861	11	2	19	32
Antiseparation	−7 (4)	24 (17)	8 (4)	25
Proseparation	44 (33)	9 (16)	2 (6)	55
Nonvoting, June 1861	3	4	13	20
Total	40	37	23	100

Note: Figures in parentheses suggest ways to recalculate logically impossible values and also to take into account the greater anticonvention and antiseparation voting among East Tennessee Democrats than suggested in the original regression equations. "Democrat" = the combined Breckinridge and Douglas vote. "Whig" = the Bell vote. "Antiseparation" signifies opposition to separation and "Proseparation" signifies support for separation in June 1861 voting.

TABLE A-11.
Estimates of 1860–1861 Voting Behavior in Twenty-two Lowest-Slaveholding (Less Than 25 Percent) North Carolina Counties

August 1860 Election (Governor)

Category	Whig	Democratic	Not Voting	Total
Slaveowners	6	5	2	13
Nonslaveowners	35	28	24	87
Total	41	33	26	100

November 1860 Election (President)

Category	Whig	Democratic	Not Voting	Total
Slaveowners	6	6	1	13
Nonslaveowners	28	20	39	87
Total	34	26	40	100

February 1861 Election (Union versus Secession)

Category	Union	Secession	Not Voting	Total
Slaveowners	6	4	3	13
Nonslaveowners	43	15	29	87
Total	49	19	32	100

February 1861 Election (Convention versus No Convention)

Category	No Convention	Convention	Not Voting	Total
Slaveowners	5	4	4	13
Nonslaveowners	40	19	28	87
Total	45	23	32	100

APPENDIX III: STATISTICS, SECESSION, AND THE HISTORIANS

IT is revealing to compare the findings of this book with other quantified studies of secession. Because most earlier work has focused on the lower South, this appendix will help to illuminate the unique qualities of secession crisis voting behavior in the upper South.

An ambitious dissertation by Jerry C. Oldshue, completed in 1975, pioneered the use of modern statistical techniques to analyze secession. Though handicapped by the difficulties in gathering reliable data for North Carolina and Tennessee, Oldshue did undertake to study the three upper South states considered here. He also examined five states in the lower South—Georgia, Alabama, Mississippi, Louisiana, and Texas. Oldshue concluded that a "very large proportion" of Breckinridge voters favored secession and that concentrations of slaves also had a significant positive relationship to secession sentiment. He briefly analyzed the results each state, separately assessed the upper and lower South, and then divided the entire South into regions of high, medium, and low slaveowning (over 45 percent; 20–45 percent; less than 20 percent). In general, Oldshue's findings on the upper South anticipate my own. His study was, however, set up in such a way that the only 1860 voters it included were those who supported Breckinridge; 1860 Bell, Douglas, and nonvoters were excluded from the analysis. Oldshue also deleted many counties from his analysis, either because voting returns appeared to conflict (favoring both a convention and Union delegates), or because counties were statistical "outliers"—typically, Democratic counties in the upper South that voted strongly antisecession.[1]

Better conceptualized than Oldshue's, and stronger both in its application of statistical technique and in its explication of the statistical results, is a study of secession in the deep South by Peyton McCrary, Clark Miller, and Dale Baum. The McCrary team's work, focused on Alabama, Mississippi, and Louisiana, with supplementary information about Texas, provided a constructive model and many helpful hints for analyzing upper South data. McCrary and his associates used an elaborate grouping of social and economic variables, including the percentage of slaveowners, to try to pinpoint patterns of support for party and secession voting. The best combination of these variables explained only 28.4 percent of the variance (R^2) in aggregate secession strength in Alabama, Mississippi, and Louisiana. Knowing the pattern of Breckinridge voting increased the R^2 by 17.3 to 45.7 percent. The ostensibly antisecession, or "cooperation," voters of the deep South defied statistical analysis. The best mix of socioeconomic variables explained only

16.4 percent of their variance (R^2), and knowing the pattern of Bell voting increased the explanatory percentage by only 2.8 percent to 19.2 percent.[2]

By comparison, statistical analysis of secession voting in the states of the upper South considered here generally yielded more satisfying results. In Virginia, as noted in Appendix I, the percentage of slaveowners and the pattern of Breckinridge voting together explained 68.1 percent of the variance (R^2) in secession voting; the percentage of slaveowners and the patterns of Bell and Douglas voting explained 61.1 percent of the variance in Union voting. Breckinridge voting explained 64.0 percent of the variance in North Carolina secession voting and 63.1 percent of the variance in support for a state convention. So, too, party (Whig) and slaveowning together explained 54.8 percent of the variance in North Carolina Union voting and 60.1 percent of the variance in North Carolina's opposition to a state convention. These figures rise to 62.2 and 66.0 percent, respectively, when including the patterns of 1860 Douglas support. In Tennessee, slaveowning and party (Democratic) together explained 42.9 percent of the variance in support for secession and 48.3 percent of the variance in support for a convention; slaveowning and party (Whig) together explained 48.1 percent of the antisecession variance and 49.9 percent of the variance in opposition to a state convention.

The research design used here to study the upper South, though similar to McCrary's, is not identical. Each state here is analyzed separately. The statistics for all three states are not aggregated or combined. Although reasonably clear patterns for secession crisis voting are apparent in each of the three states, considering all three together would tend to blur the analysis. Slaveowners in North Carolina were considerably more likely to be Democrats than Whigs; the reverse, to a lesser extent, was true in Tennessee. Several relatively low-slaveholding counties in Virginia's Shenandoah Valley voted strongly for Douglas, as did the highest slaveholding counties in Tennessee adjacent to Memphis. Each state had an idiosyncratic political history and pattern of voter behavior.

A variety of other socioeconomic variables, in addition to the percentage of slaveowners in a county, were subjected to computer analysis during the course of this study. It became apparent, however, that slaveowning regularly muscled aside most other socioeconomic factors in explaining the variance of secession crisis voting. Such potentially interesting considerations as the percentage of small farms in a county, per capita investment in manufacturing, and concentrations of various religious denominations usually produced trivial increases in explained variance when entered into multiple regression equations that included slaveowning. The multiple regression tables printed in Appendix I reflect recalculations using only slaveowning and pertinent political variables to get accurate beta weights.

Efforts to identify the socioeconomic bases of party preference in the upper South likewise yielded meager statewide results, which is not at all surprising, given the heterogeneous origins and constituencies of those antebellum parties. Nor were Douglas supporters in any state an easily identifiable group. The greatest amount of explained socioeconomic variance for any pre-1861 political grouping in any of the three states was a figure of 41 percent for North Carolina Democratic voters, the principal element of which was a strong positive relationship to slaveowning. All other attempts to explain party allegiance on the basis of aggregate socioeconomic variables produced R^2s in the high teens and low twenties, nothing to write home about or to clutter a book with. It might be noted, however, that 1860 nonvoters, especially in Virginia and North Carolina, could be "explained" at quite significant levels—50 percent and more—by an inverse relationship to slaveowning and a positive relationship to small farms. In other words, Virginia and North Carolina nonvoters in 1860 tended to be nonslaveowners who lived on small farms, or to be more precise, since multiple regression deals only with units of analysis rather than individuals, it should be said that nonvoters tended to live in low-slaveowning counties with smaller than average farm size.

We may confidently conclude that the secession elections in Virginia, North Carolina, and Tennessee differed very significantly not only from earlier upper South elections but also from the secession elections in the lower South analyzed by McCrary, Miller, and Baum. To be sure, the secessionist constituencies in the upper and lower South had something in common. McCrary found that two-thirds of secession voters were Breckinridge Democrats and that the prosecession constituency bore a definite positive relationship to slaveowning. Slaveowning and Breckinridge voting each explained about 17 percent of lower South secession support, and the inclusion of McCrary's additional socioeconomic variables increased the R^2 to 45.7 percent.[3] In the three upper South states studied here, almost all secessionists were Breckinridge Democrats, and they too were more likely to be slaveowners than the average upper South voter. Except for scattered Southern Rights Whigs in "lower Virginia" and some of the Douglas Democrats in the Memphis area, upper South secessionists were almost a Breckinridge monolith. As noted in Appendix I, the Breckinridge percentage of each county's 1860 presidential vote best predicted secession strength in North Carolina. It alone explained more variance in North Carolina (R^2 = .640) than McCrary could for the deep South with a sophisticated array of political and socioeconomic variables. In Tennessee, which featured the anomaly of secession strength in the Memphis region, where Douglas had run strongly, the appropriate political yardstick with which to measure the relationship between party and secession is the combined 1860 Douglas and Breckinridge vote. The two variables, 1860 Democratic voting and slaveowning, together explained about as much variance (R^2 = .429) in Tennessee as McCrary did for Alabama, Mississippi, and Louisiana with these two and a variety of additional socioeconomic variables. In Virginia, slaveowning by itself explained an eye-opening 54 percent (R^2 = .541) of the variance in secession voting. Breckinridge strength and slaveowning together explained a far higher amount of variance (R^2 = .681) in Virginia secession voting than anywhere in the deep South.

The sharp differences between the upper and lower South become most visible when comparing the antisecessionists in each region. Many lower South "cooperationists" would have been considered secessionists in the upper South. Indeed, Mills Thornton, one of the most able students of deep South secession, insists that cooperation in Alabama was simply a dispute about means, not ends—about *how* to secede, not *whether*. Furthermore, the cooperationists of the deep South were an extraordinarily miscellaneous group, whose heterogeneity blunted the sharp statistical tools employed by McCrary's team. Whiggish in Mississippi and Louisiana, the cooperationists of Alabama were the Douglas voters combined with a breakaway faction of Breckinridge Democrats from northern Alabama. McCrary's aggregate multiple regressions showed scant relationship between cooperation and lower levels of slaveholding. With the partial exception of Alabama, cooperation did not divide along class lines or enlist a disproportionate number of nonslaveowners.[4]

But in the upper South, the Unionists of February 1861 were both more formidable and more susceptible to measurement. As noted in Appendix I, North Carolina and Tennessee present somewhat comparable patterns, with Whig loyalty being by far the best single predictor of Unionism, as shown by the relative beta weights. An inverse relationship to slaveowning raised the respective R^2 figures to .548 and .481. In Virginia, the inverse relationship to slaveowning loomed largest in explaining the Union vote. By also taking into account patterns of Whig and Douglas voting, over 61 percent ($R^2 = .611$) of the variance in Union strength in Virginia may be explained and 62.2 percent ($R^2 = .622$) in North Carolina.

In all three states, ecological regression estimates using slaveowner and nonslaveowner as dependent variables suggest that nonslaveowners voted heavily Unionist (see Chapter 7 and Appendix II). By contrast, majorities of slaveowners in Virginia and North Carolina who voted in February 1861 favored secession. Although a majority of Tennessee slaveholders voted pro-Union, their plans to control the Unionist movement were thwarted by the refusal of nonslaveowners to vote for the calling of a convention, which slaveowners emphatically favored. Contributing powerfully to Union strength in the upper South was a higher turnout among Whig voters than Democrats, exactly the opposite of the pattern that McCrary, Miller, and Baum found in the deep South.

The statistical analysis here of upper South Unionism and secessionism does bear greater resemblance to one state study of secession in the lower South—Michael P. Johnson's book on Georgia. Secession divided that state "along lines which coincided roughly with an interest in slavery and the established order," Johnson contended. Slaveowners feared the rise of an anti-planter party in Georgia once Lincoln held power in Washington. They therefore favored secession both to protect themselves from external danger and to guard against any challenges to their power within the state. Thus, "the internal crisis of the South necessitated secession."[5]

Surely Johnson was correct to say that privileged Georgians worried that class resentment might become politically threatening. A polity in which all adult white males could vote, and most usually did, was not one that a wealthy and privileged minority could automatically expect to dominate. Important subsequent research by Steven Hahn, Fred Siegel, and J. William Harris has demonstrated conclusively that the potential for dissatisfaction toward planters was embedded in the structure of antebellum Georgia society. Even if ties of family and community, loyalties to political parties, and appeals to white racial solidarity all tended to subordinate such tensions, they lurked and festered.[6]

But did voting behavior in Georgia during the secession crisis manifest the overt politicization of class tensions? Unfortunately, Johnson propounded his interpretation with a boldness that his statistics hardly warranted. The differing levels of support for secession between high- and low-slaveowning areas in Georgia were much less pronounced than in the upper South. High-slaveowning counties voted 55 percent for secession, only 9 percent more than low-slaveowning counties (Johnson's percentages divided the voters, not the entire eligible electorate). Nor did multiple regression adequately sustain Johnson's thesis: the amount of variance in the secession vote explained by the combined pattern of Breckinridge support and the concentration of slaveowners was a disappointingly low 23 percent ($R^2 = .228$), again in contrast to the upper South. Counties with Democratic majorities in Georgia gave a 53 percent vote for secession; counties with Whig majorities followed closely behind at 49 percent. Whig counties, however, were markedly wealthier than Democratic counties and had an average of 18 percent more slaveowners (50 to 32 percent). Plainly, no strong polarization between slaveowners and nonslaveowners on the secession issue could take place in Georgia as long as secession sentiment ran stronger among Democrats than Whigs, even though many more Whigs were slaveowners.[7]

The most important evidence to sustain Johnson's case was the strong prosecession pattern in towns and cities, especially those with a habit of Democratic voting, coupled with the high turnout rates and relatively low secession vote totals (34 percent) in the small number (thirteen) of Georgia counties with fewer than 15 percent slaveowners. Heavier support for secession among wealthier, more cosmopolitan urbanites and low support for it in the atypical "white" counties provided the foundation for Johnson's interpretation.[8] But the over 80 percent of Georgia voters who lived neither in the cities nor in the whitest upcountry counties tend to disappear from his analysis because their votes failed to provide stronger secession margins in high-slaveowning areas.

In short, Johnson's arresting interpretation of Georgia loses much of its force when weighed against the evidence presented in this study about the upper South. Compared with the antisecession wave that swept the upper South in February 1861, Georgia Unionism was a lifeless shadow. Its leaders were irresolute, paralyzed, and inclined to acquiesce in secession. The cooperationist campaign before the January 2 election for convention delegates was almost nonexistent. Everything that Johnson has written about Georgia containing the ingredients for an antiplanter party would apply far better to Virginia, North Carolina, or Tennessee. If Georgia secessionists thought they faced a serious internal challenge, their upper South allies could have shown them the genuine article.[9]

A more judicious and statistically sophisticated comparative effort to identify class conflict during the secession crisis has, unfortunately, never been published.[10] Believing that "the issue of secession created a political arena for the development of class consciousness," Paul D. Escott used research techniques employed in this book to analyze voting behavior in eight states: the three from the upper South studied here, plus Georgia, Alabama, Mississippi, Louisiana, and Texas from the lower South. His multiple regression equations, using as explanatory variables the percentage of support for Breckinridge and the percentage of slaveowners to explain variations in the level of support for secession, of course paralleled this study's findings about the upper South. Like the McCrary team, Escott found that Alabama presented more evidence of class voting ($R^2 = .517$) than did Mississippi ($R^2 = .365$) or Georgia ($R^2 = .339$). Louisiana ($R^2 = .478$) and especially Texas ($R^2 = .604$) also appear to have experienced significant class voting.

But other evidence still suggests that class polarities in upper South voting behavior during the secession crisis were far more pronounced than in the lower South. It should be recalled that the McCrary team found little consistent pattern among antisecessionists in the lower South. Only in northern Alabama, according to McCrary and Escott, did participating lower South nonslaveowners consistently oppose secession. In Mississippi, Escott estimated that a large majority of nonslaveowners did not even vote, so that Mississippi cooperationists actually included more slaveowners than nonslaveowners. And in Georgia, where Escott identified tendencies that partially corroborate Michael Johnson's analysis, over 40 percent of participating nonslaveowners apparently supported secession.[11]

On balance, upper South Unionism differed in kind rather than degree from lower South cooperationism. One had momentum, that precious attribute so prized by modern campaign managers; the other did not. A solid regional and political base anchored the Unionist insurgency in the upper South. Though strongest in the upcountry, it was by no means confined to those regions. Upper South Unionists likewise expanded their Whiggish base to add both estranged Democrats and previous nonvoters. Its leaders had good reason to hope that the antisecession coalition could lay the foundation for a new Union party that would politically dominate the upper South—if peace could be preserved and the Union restored.

NOTES

ABBREVIATIONS

CG, 36:2, A513
Congressional Globe, 36th Cong., 2d sess., Appendix, p. 513.

CWAL
Roy P. Basler, ed., *The Collected Works of Abraham Lincoln*, 8 vols. plus index (New Brunswick: Rutgers University Press, 1953–55).

Campbell, *Attitude of Tennesseans*
Mary Emily Robertson Campbell, *The Attitude of Tennesseans toward the Union, 1847–1861* (New York: Vantage Press, 1961).

Chittenden, *Report*
Lucius E. Chittenden, *A Report of the Debates and Proceedings in the Secret Sessions of the Conference Convention, for Proposing Amendments to the Constitution of the United States, Held at Washington, D.C., in February, A.D., 1861* (1864; rpt. New York: Da Capo Press, 1971).

DAB
Allen Johnson and Dumas Malone, eds., *Dictionary of American Biography*, 20 vols. (New York: Charles Scribner's Sons, 1928–36).

Drake, *Hatton*
James Vaulx Drake, *Life of General Robert Hatton, Including His Most Important Public Speeches; Together, with Much of His Washington and Army Correspondence* (Nashville: Marshall and Bruce, 1867).

Dumond, ed., *Southern Editorials*
Dwight Lowell Dumond, ed., *Southern Editorials on Secession* (New York: Century, 1931).

Johnson Papers
LeRoy P. Graf and Ralph W. Haskins, eds., *The Papers of Andrew Johnson*, 7 vols. to date (Knoxville: University of Tennessee Press, 1967–).

OR, I:51:2, p. 7
The War of the Rebellion: A Compilation of the Official Records of the Union and Confederate Armies, 70 volumes in 128 (Washington, D.C.: U.S. Government Printing Office, 1880–1901), Ser. I, vol. 51, pt. 2, p. 7.

Perkins, ed., *Northern Editorials*
Howard Cecil Perkins, ed., *Northern Editorials on Secession*, 2 vols. (New York: D. Appleton-Century, 1942).

Reese, ed., *Virginia Convention*
George H. Reese, ed., *Proceedings of the Virginia State Convention of 1861*, 4 vols. (Richmond: Virginia State Library, 1965).

Shanks, *Secession Movement in Virginia*
Henry T. Shanks, *The Secession Movement in Virginia, 1847–1861* (1934; rpt. New York: Da Capo Press, 1970).

Sitterson, *Secession Movement in North Carolina*
Joseph Carlyle Sitterson, *The Secession Movement in North Carolina* (Chapel Hill: University of North Carolina Press, 1939).

Duke	William R. Perkins Library, Duke University, Durham, N.C.
HSP	Historical Society of Pennsylvania, Philadelphia
LC	Manuscripts Division, Library of Congress
MHS	Massachusetts Historical Society, Boston
NA	National Archives
NCDAH	North Carolina Division of Archives and History, Raleigh
RG	Record Group
SHC-UNC	Southern Historical Collection, University of North Carolina at Chapel Hill
TSLA	Tennessee State Library and Archives, Nashville
UVA	Alderman Library, University of Virginia, Charlottesville
VHS	Virginia Historical Society, Richmond

PREFACE

1. David M. Potter, *Lincoln and His Party in the Secession Crisis* (New Haven: Yale University Press, 1942, 1962), Preface to the 1962 edition, xxix.

2. Eugene D. Genovese, *The Political Economy of Slavery: Studies in the Economy and Society of the Slave South* (New York: Pantheon, 1965), 5.

3. William M. Clark to Lewis Thompson, Jan. 10, 1861, Lewis Thompson Papers, SHC-UNC. Quotations in the next paragraph draw from the same letter.

4. William B. Campbell to A. C. Beard, Mar. 15, 1861, copy, Campbell Family Papers, Duke.

5. William K. Scarborough, ed., *The Diary of Edmund Ruffin*, 2 vols. to date (Baton Rouge: Louisiana State University Press, 1972–), 1:557–59 (entries of Feb. 27, 28, Mar. 1, 2, 3, 1861).

6. Ibid., 2:8 (entry of Apr. 23, 1861).

7. See the discussion under "Studies of the Secession Crisis and the Late Antebellum South" in the Bibliographical Essay. As explained there, I have a special regard for David Potter's exemplary study, *Lincoln and His Party in the Secession Crisis*. See also my introduction to Chapter 9, below, and the commentary in note 1 of that chapter.

8. Shanks, *Secession Movement in Virginia*; Sitterson, *Secession Movement in North Carolina*; Campbell, *Attitude of Tennesseans*.

9. See William J. Evitts, *A Matter of Allegiances: Maryland, 1850–1861* (Baltimore: Johns Hopkins University Press, 1974); Jean H. Baker, *The Politics of Continuity: Maryland Political Parties from 1858 to 1870* (Baltimore: Johns Hopkins University Press, 1973); Harry A. Volz III, "Party, State, and Nation: Kentucky and the Coming of the American Civil War" (Ph.D. dissertation, University of Virginia, 1982); William E. Parrish, *Turbulent Partnership: Missouri and the Union, 1861–1865* (Columbia: University of Missouri Press, 1963).

10. James M. Woods, *Rebellion and Realignment: Arkansas's Road to Secession* (Fayetteville: University of Arkansas Press, 1987); see also Jack B. Scroggs, "Arkansas in the Secession Crisis," *Arkansas Historical Quarterly* 12 (1953): 179–224.

PROLOGUE

1. Drake, *Hatton*; Charles M. Cummings, "Robert Hopkins Hatton: Reluctant Rebel," *Tennessee Historical Quarterly* 23 (1964): 169–81; Charles Faulkner Bryan, Jr., "Robert Hatton of Tennessee" (M.A. thesis, University of Georgia, 1971); Bernard Barton Threatte, "The Public Life of Robert Hatton (1855–1862)" (M.A. thesis, Vanderbilt University, 1931).

2. Dixon Merritt, *History of Wilson County* (Lebanon: Benson Printing Co., 1961), 316–18. Figures cited on slave population and per capita wealth come from the 1860 census, prepared in machine-readable form by the Inter-University Consortium for Political and Social Research (ICPSR), Ann Arbor. Per capita wealth is the total value of property in the county, divided by the number of adult white males aged twenty and older.

3. Bryan, "Hatton," 61–72; Robert Hatton to his wife, Dec. 3, 28, 1859, Feb. 8, 1860, Jan. 1, Feb. 12, 1861, all in Drake, *Hatton*, 173, 185, 232, 316–17, 340–41; Bertram Wyatt-Brown, *Southern Honor: Ethics and Behavior in the Old South* (New York: Oxford University Press, 1982), passim; Edward L. Ayers, *Vengeance and Justice: Crime and Punishment in the Nineteenth-Century American South* (New York: Oxford University Press, 1984), 9–33, esp. 27–28; Ian R. Tyrrell, "Drink and Temperance in the Antebellum South: An Overview and Interpretation," *Journal of Southern History* 48 (Nov. 1982): 485–510, esp. 497–501.

4. *New York Times*, Jan. 16, 1860.

5. *Johnson Papers*, 4:157, 159; Chittenden, *Report*, 110, 304, 436.

6. Hatton to his wife, Dec. 5, 14, 21, 1860, Jan. 1, 15, 1861, Hatton diary entry of Dec. 8, 1860, all in Drake, *Hatton*, 298, 301, 305–6, 310, 316, 321.

7. Hatton to his wife, Jan. 30, Feb. 8, 1861, in Drake, *Hatton*, 323, 325; *CG*, 36:2, A170–74.

8. H. L. Carrick to William B. Campbell, Feb. 1, 1861 (quoted), Jordan Stokes to William B. Campbell, Jan. 29, 1861, both in Campbell Family Papers, Duke; B. W. Harris to Isham G. Harris, Jan. 31, 1861, Isham G. Harris Papers, TSLA; Merritt, *Wilson County*, 318; *Nashville Weekly Patriot*, Feb. 11, 1861.

9. Hatton to William B. Campbell, Feb. 16, 1861, Campbell Papers.

10. Hatton to T. A. R. Nelson, Mar. 27, 1861, T. A. R. Nelson Papers, McClung Collection, Lawson McGhee Library, Knoxville, Tenn.; Drake, *Hatton*, 345–47; *Lebanon Herald*, quoted in *Nashville Daily Patriot*, Apr. 5, 1861; *Nashville Weekly Patriot*, Apr. 8, 1861; *Gallatin Weekly Courier*, Apr. 3, 1861.

11. *Gallatin Weekly Courier*, Apr. 3, 1861; *Nashville Daily Patriot*, Apr. 13, 1861; *Lebanon Herald* quoted in *Nashville Republican Banner*, Apr. 12, 1861; Bryan, "Hatton," 120–21; Drake, *Hatton*, 345–46.

12. *Gallatin Weekly Courier*, Apr. 17, 1861; Campbell, *Attitude of Tennesseans*, 293. Vote totals in June 1861 are recalculated to include for each county a proportionate share of prosecession votes cast by Confederate soldiers at military camps. See Chapter 7, n. 2.

13. Drake, *Hatton*, 351.

CHAPTER 1

1. "Speech at Cincinnati," Feb. 12, 1861, *CWAL*, 4:199, repeated from a Sept. 17, 1859, speech at Cincinnati, *CWAL*, 3:453.

2. "Farewell Address at Springfield," Feb. 11, 1861, *CWAL*, 4:190.

3. David M. Potter, *Lincoln and His Party in the Secession Crisis* (New Haven: Yale University Press, 1942); Kenneth M. Stampp, *And the War Came: The North and the Secession Crisis, 1860–61* (Baton Rouge: Louisiana State University Press, 1950). For an able summary of the historiographical puzzle, see Richard N. Current, *The Lincoln Nobody Knows* (New York: Hill and Wang, 1958), 76–130, 293–97.

4. Robert W. Johannsen, *Stephen A. Douglas* (New York: Oxford University Press, 1973), 4–5, 588, 659–60; Damon Wells, *Stephen Douglas: The Last Years, 1857–1861* (Austin: University of Texas Press, 1971), 6–8.

5. Frederic Bancroft, *The Life of William H. Seward*, 2 vols. (New York: Harper and Brothers, 1899–1900), 1:184–205, quotation on 184, 2:70–90.

6. Martin Duberman, *Charles Francis Adams, 1807–1886* (Stanford: Stanford University Press, 1960), xv, 47, and passim.

7. Edward Chalfant, *Both Sides of the Ocean: A Biography of Henry Adams, His First Life, 1838–1862* (Hamden, Conn.: Shoe String Press, 1982), 187–250; Henry Adams, "The Great Secession Winter of 1860–61," *Proceedings of the Massachusetts Historical Society* 43 (1910): 656–87.

8. Albert D. Kirwan, *John J. Crittenden: The Struggle for the Union* (Lexington: University of Kentucky Press, 1962), 15, 33, passim, and esp. 366–434 on the secession crisis.

9. Joseph H. Parks, *John Bell of Tennessee* (Baton Rouge: Louisiana State University Press, 1950).

10. Joshua W. Caldwell, "John Bell of Tennessee," *American Historical Review* 4 (July 1899): 655; Parks, *John Bell*, 357–58; Oliver P. Temple, *East Tennessee in the Civil War* (1899; rpt. Freeport, N.Y.: Books for Libraries Press, 1971), 230–32.

11. Bell to William B. Campbell, Aug. 10, 1854, *Tennessee Historical Magazine* 3 (1917): 223–25; Parks, *John Bell*, 283–388.

12. Temple, *East Tennessee in the Civil War*, 233–36; Caldwell, "John Bell," 664; Joseph H. Parks, "John Bell and Secession," *East Tennessee Historical Society Publications* 16 (1944): 30–47.

13. John Bell Brownlow to Oliver P. Temple, Jan. 17, 1894, Oliver P. Temple Papers, University of Tennessee, Knoxville; Johnson to Blackston McDannel, Oct. 15, 1845, quoted in Robert W. Winston, *Andrew Johnson: Plebeian and Patriot* (1928; rpt. New York: Barnes and Noble, 1969), 65–66. Winston's book and the first three volumes of the *Johnson Papers* are the indispensable sources on Johnson's career through 1860.

14. "To the Freemen of the First Congressional District of Tennessee," Oct. 15, 1845, *Johnson Papers*, 1:270–71; John Bell Brownlow to Oliver P. Temple, Sept. 8, 1892, Temple Papers.

15. "From William G. Brownlow," Dec. 13, 1843; "To the Freemen of the First Congressional District of Tennessee," Oct. 15, 1845, *Johnson Papers*, 1:123–24, 246–47, 253.

16. "Introduction," ibid., xxvi–xxvii.

17. E. Merton Coulter, *William G. Brownlow: Fighting Parson of the Southern Highlands* (1937; rpt. with introduction by James W. Patton, Knoxville: University of Tennessee Press, 1971), v–xi, 133.

18. Temple, *East Tennessee in the Civil War*, 147–66, quotations on 151, 152, 154, 162; Joseph C. McDannel to Andrew Johnson, Dec. 29, 1860, *Johnson Papers*, 4:102–3.

19. Horace W. Raper, *William W. Holden: North Carolina's Political Enigma* (Chapel Hill: University of North Carolina Press, 1985), passim.; William C. Harris, *William Woods Holden: Firebrand of North Carolina Politics* (Baton Rouge: Louisiana State University Press, 1987), passim.; Paul D. Escott, *Many Excellent People: Power and Privilege in North Carolina, 1850–1900* (Chapel Hill: University of North Carolina Press, 1985), 90–93.

20. George W. Atkinson and Alvaro F. Gibbens, *Prominent Men of West Virginia*, 2 vols. (Wheeling: W. L. Callin, 1890), 1:214–17.

21. James M. Callahan, "George William Summers," *DAB*, 18: 206–7; William H. Gaines, Jr., *Biographical Register of Members: Virginia State Convention of 1861, First Session* (Richmond: Virginia State Library, 1969), 73–74; A. Clinton Loy, "George W. Summers and His Relation to the Formation of the State of West Virginia" (M.A. thesis, West Virginia University, 1937); Francis P. Gaines, Jr., "The Virginia Constitutional Convention of 1850–51: A Study in Sectionalism" (Ph.D. dissertation, University of Virginia, 1950), 190–94; Clement Eaton, *The Mind of the Old South*, rev. ed. (Baton Rouge: Louisiana State University Press, 1967), 3–23, esp. 19. The Lewis Summers and George W. Summers Papers at the University of West Virginia contain little of interest after 1843.

22. J. Lewis Peyton, *History of Augusta County, Virginia* (Staunton, Va.: S. M. Yost & Son, 1882), 379–85, quotation on 380. See also Gaines, *Biographical Register of Members*, 14–15.

23. H. W. Howard Knott, "John Brown Baldwin," *DAB*, 1:536.

24. Rev. R. L. Dabney, "Memoir of a Narrative Received of Colonel John B. Baldwin, of Staunton, Touching the Origin of the War," *Southern Historical Society Papers*, 44 vols. (Richmond: Southern Historical Society, 1876–1923), 1:443–55, quotation on 448; see also John B. Baldwin, *Interview between President Lincoln and Col. John B. Baldwin, April 4th, 1861: Statements and Evidence* (Staunton, Va.: "Spectator" Job Office, 1866); Allan B. Magruder, "A Piece of Secret History: President Lincoln and the Virginia Convention of 1861," *Atlantic Monthly* 35 (1875): 438–45.

25. Peyton, *Augusta County*, 382–84; Jack P. Maddex, Jr., *The Virginia Conservatives, 1867–1879: A Study in Reconstruction Politics* (Chapel Hill: University of North Carolina Press, 1970), 39–42.

26. Robert Hatton Diary, Dec. 22, 1859; Robert Hatton to Sophie Hatton, Dec. 23, 1859, both in Drake, *Hatton*, 184–85; Gerald S. Henig, "Henry Winter Davis and the Speakership Contest of 1859–1860," *Maryland Historical Magazine* 68 (Spring 1973): 1–19; Henry Winter Davis to Samuel F. Du Pont, two letters from July 1860 (W9-10344 and W9-10345), Aug. 15, 24, 1860 (copies), Samuel F. Du Pont Papers, Eleutherian Mills Historical Library, Greenville, Del.

27. Robert Hatton to Sophie Hatton, Feb. 8, 1860, in Drake, *Hatton*, 232; Charles Faulkner Bryan, Jr., "Robert Hatton of Tennessee" (M.A. thesis, University of Georgia, 1971), 74–75; *New York Times*, Dec. 23, 1859.

28. Alexander H. Stephens to the Voters of the Eighth Congressional District of Georgia, Aug. 14, 1857, in Ulrich B. Phillips, ed., *The Correspondence of Robert Toombs, Alexander H. Stephens, and Howell Cobb, American Historical Association Annual Report, 1911*, 2 vols. (Washington, D.C.: U.S. Government Printing Office, 1913), 2:412; *Paris* (Tenn.) *Weekly Sentinel*, Apr. 3, 1857, Apr. 11, 1860; *Memphis Avalanche*, Aug. 15, 1860, Jan. 30, 1861; *CG*, 36:1:441; (Jackson) *West Tennessee Whig*, Jan. 27, 1860; *Nashville Weekly Patriot*, Apr. 14, 1859; Andrew Johnson, "Exchange with John Bell," Feb. 24, 1858, *Johnson Papers*, 3:83; note on Etheridge, ibid., 88.

29. *CG*, 36:2:A112–13.

30. "Southern Rights," Dresden (Tenn.), Apr. 1, 1861, in *Memphis Avalanche*, Apr. 6, 1861; Robert Johnson to Andrew Johnson, Apr. 29, 1861, *Johnson Papers*, 4:414–16; John B. Brownlow to Oliver P. Temple, Mar. 1, 1891, Temple Papers; R. G. Payne to unknown, Apr. 16, 1861, in Horace Greeley, *The American Conflict: A History of the Great Rebellion*, 2 vols. (Hartford: O. D. Case, 1866), 1:484.

31. Herman Belz, "The Etheridge Conspiracy of 1863: A Projected Conservative Coup," *Journal of Southern History* 36 (Nov. 1970): 549–67, quotation on 556.

32. John Livingston, *Portraits of Eminent Americans Now Living: With Biographical and Historical Memoirs of Their Lives and Actions*, 4 vols. (New York: Cornish, Lamport, 1853–54), 1:342–56, quotations on 347, 355–56; *New York Times*, Dec. 17, 1859. Gilmer's decency toward his slaves is attested to in D. F. Caldwell et al. to Andrew Johnson, June 3, 1865, Case Files of Applicants for Presidential Pardons, RG 94, NA. Gilmer distributed "the larger

part of his estate" in 1865 to provide more than sixty former slaves with "lands, clothing, farming implements, horses, mules, waggons, &c."

33. *Baltimore Clipper*, quoted in *Salisbury* (N.C.) *Carolina Watchman*, Feb. 5, 1861; Gerald W. Johnson, "John Adams Gilmer, 1805–1868," in Bettie D. Caldwell, ed., *Founders and Builders of Greensboro, 1808–1908* (Greensboro: J. J. Stone, 1925), 94–102, quotations on 100–101.

34. Henry Winter Davis to David Davis, Jan. 5, 1861, photocopy, David Davis Papers, Chicago Historical Society.

35. J. G. deRoulhac Hamilton, "John Adams Gilmer," *DAB*, 7:307–8. On the cabinet offer to Gilmer, see Daniel W. Crofts, "A Reluctant Unionist: John A. Gilmer and Lincoln's Cabinet," *Civil War History* 24 (Sept. 1978): 225–49, excerpted in Chapter 9 below.

CHAPTER 2

1. Alison Goodyear Freehling, *Drift toward Dissolution: The Virginia Slavery Debate of 1831–1832* (Baton Rouge: Louisiana State University Press, 1982), 11–35; Shanks, *Secession Movement in Virginia*, 1–17; Marc W. Kruman, *Parties and Politics in North Carolina, 1836–1865* (Baton Rouge: Louisiana State University Press, 1983), 6–14; Sitterson, *Secession Movement in North Carolina*, 1–22; Paul H. Bergeron, *Antebellum Politics in Tennessee* (Lexington: University Press of Kentucky, 1982), x, 38–41; Campbell, *Attitude of Tennesseans*, 11–33.

2. Fletcher M. Green, *Constitutional Development in the South Atlantic States: A Study in the Evolution of Democracy* (Chapel Hill: University of North Carolina Press, 1930), 171–296; Chilton Williamson, *American Suffrage: From Property to Democracy* (Princeton: Princeton University Press, 1960), 223–41; Ralph A. Wooster, *Politicians, Planters, and Plain Folk: Courthouse and Statehouse in the Upper South, 1850–1860* (Knoxville: University of Tennessee Press, 1975), passim.; Bergeron, *Antebellum Politics in Tennessee*, x, 38–41.

3. William G. Shade, "Political Pluralism and Party Development: The Creation of a Modern Party System, 1815–1852," in Paul Kleppner et al., *The Evolution of American Electoral Systems* (Westport, Conn.: Greenwood Press, 1981), 77–112; William G. Shade, "Political Culture and Party Development in Virginia, 1828–1852" (paper delivered at the American Historical Association Convention, December 1982); Lynwood M. Dent, Jr., "The Virginia Democratic Party, 1824–1847" (Ph.D. dissertation, Louisiana State University, 1974), 288–89, 369–79; Francis P. Gaines, Jr., "The Virginia Constitutional Convention of 1850–1851: A Study in Sectionalism" (Ph.D. dissertation, University of Virginia, 1950), chaps. 7 and 8.

4. Harry L. Watson, *Jacksonian Politics and Community Conflict: The Emergence of the Second American Party System in Cumberland County, North Carolina* (Baton Rouge: Louisiana State University Press, 1981), 292–93, 296, 319.

5. Ibid., 206–7, 298–300, 322; Kruman, *Parties and Politics in North Carolina*, 6–10; J. Mills Thornton III, *Politics and Power in a Slave Society: Ala-*

bama, 1800–1860 (Baton Rouge: Louisiana State University Press, 1978), chap. 1; Harry L. Watson, "Conflict and Collaboration: Yeomen, Slaveholders, and Politics in the Antebellum South," *Social History* 10 (Oct. 1985): 290–93. See also Daniel Walker Howe, *The Political Culture of the American Whigs* (Chicago: University of Chicago Press, 1979); Marvin Meyers, *The Jacksonian Persuasion: Politics and Belief* (Stanford: Stanford University Press, 1957).

6. Watson, *Jacksonian Politics*, 309; Charles G. Sellers, "Who Were the Southern Whigs?" *American Historical Review* 59 (Jan. 1954): 344 (n. 45); Kruman, *Parties and Politics in North Carolina*, 7–8, 85, 141–42. For suggestive parallels in New York State during the 1840s, see Lee Benson, *The Concept of Jacksonian Democracy: New York as a Test Case* (Princeton: Princeton University Press, 1961), 294–95, 299–301, 304–6, 313–15.

7. Steven Hahn, *The Roots of Southern Populism: Yeoman Farmers and the Transformation of the Georgia Upcountry, 1850–1890* (New York: Oxford University Press, 1983), 50–85; Thornton, *Politics and Power in a Slave Society*, 158–60; Watson, *Jacksonian Politics*, 310–11; Whitman H. Ridgway, *Community Leadership in Maryland, 1790–1840: A Comparative Analysis of Power in Society* (Chapel Hill: University of North Carolina Press, 1979), 20–43, 127–35; Paul F. Bourke and Donald A. DeBats, "Identifiable Voting in Nineteenth-Century America: Toward a Comparison of Britain and the United States before the Secret Ballot," *Perspectives in American History* 11 (1977–78): 280–86; Bruce Collins, *White Society in the Antebellum South* (New York: Longman, 1985), 21–22; Watson, "Conflict and Collaboration," 283–85.

8. Ronald P. Formisano, *The Transformation of Political Culture: Massachusetts Parties, 1790s–1840s* (New York: Oxford University Press, 1983), 45–54, 128–48, 157, 167–68, quotation on 129.

9. Watson, *Jacksonian Politics*, 213, 311; Watson, "Conflict and Collaboration," 293.

10. Bergeron, *Antebellum Politics in Tennessee*, 44–46, 55–56, 74–75, 78, 119, 135; Harry A. Volz III, "Party, State, and Nation: Kentucky and the Coming of the American Civil War" (Ph.D. dissertation, University of Virginia, 1982), 96, 223, 260; Paul E. McAllister, "Missouri Voters, 1840–1856: An Analysis of Ante-Bellum Voting Behavior and Political Parties" (Ph.D. dissertation, University of Missouri-Columbia, 1976), chap. 3; Donald Arthur DeBats, "Elites and Masses: Political Structure, Communication and Behavior in Ante-Bellum Georgia" (Ph.D. dissertation, University of Wisconsin, 1973), chap. 8.

Incontrovertable evidence also now exists to show persistent patterns of party voting with very high levels of continuity from one election to another, both North and South, from the late 1830s into the early 1850s. In several upper South states, the patterns remained stable throughout the antebellum era. See Shade, "Political Pluralism," 77–112; Kruman, *Parties and Politics in North Carolina*, 44, 183, 239; Volz, "Kentucky and the Coming of the American Civil War," 97, 128–29, 226–29, 261–66, 344–46, 398–99, 446–47, 459–62; and Tables 2-2 to 2-6 below.

11. Michael F. Holt, *The Political Crisis of the 1850s* (New York: Wiley,

1978), ix–x, 5; Kruman, *Parties and Politics in North Carolina*, 3–6; Thornton, *Politics and Power in a Slave Society*, 155–61; Formisano, *Transformation of Political Culture*, 324–26; Sean Wilentz, "On Class and Politics in Jacksonian America," *Reviews in American History* 10 (Dec. 1982): 54–58.

12. David M. Potter, "Roy F. Nichols and Rehabilitation of American Political History," in Don E. Fehrenbacher, ed., *History and American Society: Essays of David M. Potter* (New York: Oxford University Press, 1973), 210.

13. Watson, *Jacksonian Politics*, 324. See also Watson, "Conflict and Collaboration," 293–96; Formisano, *Transformation of Political Culture*, 316–18, 328, 336–40.

14. Formisano, *Transformation of Political Culture*, 266–67; Kruman, *Parties and Politics in North Carolina*, 3–4; Watson, *Jacksonian Politics*, 321–24.

15. Formisano, *Transformation of Political Culture*, 253, 261, 329, and 321–43 passim; Wilentz, "Class and Politics," 52–53, 57. Wilentz considers the process more overtly antidemocratic than does Formisano.

16. William J. Cooper, Jr., *The South and the Politics of Slavery, 1828–1856* (Baton Rouge: Louisiana State University Press, 1978), xiii; Holt, *Political Crisis of the 1850s*, 37–38; Watson, *Jacksonian Politics*, 323.

17. Holt, *Political Crisis of the 1850s*, x, 50–52, 56–58; Cooper, *The South and the Politics of Slavery*, passim; Kruman, *Parties and Politics in North Carolina*, 104–5, 137–39.

18. Eric Foner, *Politics and Ideology in the Age of the Civil War* (New York: Oxford University Press, 1980), 34–45, quotations on 35–36.

19. Holt, *Political Crisis of the 1850s*, 101–38; Formisano, *Transformation of Political Culture*, 321–43.

20. Formisano, *Transformation of Political Culture*, 330–40; Ronald P. Formisano, *The Birth of Mass Political Parties: Michigan, 1827–1861* (Princeton: Princeton University Press, 1971), 217–65; Holt, *Political Crisis of the 1850s*, passim, esp. 191, 209–12; Michael F. Holt, *Forging a Majority: The Formation of the Republican Party in Pittsburgh* (New Haven: Yale University Press, 1969), 123–74; Michael F. Holt, "The Antimasonic and Know Nothing Parties," in Arthur M. Schlesinger, Jr., ed., *History of U.S. Political Parties*, 4 vols. (New York: Chelsea House and R. W. Bowker, 1973), 1:575–76, 593–620, 680–737; Stephen E. Maizlish, "The Meaning of Nativism and the Crisis of the Union: The Know Nothing Movement in the Antebellum North," in Maizlish and John Kushma, eds., *Essays on Antebellum American Politics* (College Station: Texas A&M University Press, 1982), 166–82.

William E. Gienapp, *The Origins of the Republican Party, 1852–1856* (New York: Oxford University Press, 1987), offers the most valuable and thorough new synthesis of the topic. Though emphasizing the ultimate centrality of the "slave power" issue, Gienapp ably demonstrates that nonsectional irritants disrupted the party system before 1856.

21. Holt, *Political Crisis of the 1850s*, 207–9, 241–52.

22. Ibid., 118–19, 230–36. The best account of political developments in a deep South state during the decade before the war is Thornton's study of Alabama, *Politics and Power in a Slave Society*.

23. Holt, *Political Crisis of the 1850s*, 8, 216; see also Formisano, *Birth of*

Mass Political Parties, 8. For a contrasting view—that southern alarm about the Republican party was well founded—see Eric Foner, *Free Soil, Free Labor, Free Men: The Ideology of the Republican Party before the Civil War* (New York: Oxford University Press, 1970), 301–17.

24. Chapter 3 below considers Whig opposition to Southern Rights extremism. For a good case study of the 1859 Virginia gubernatorial campaign, in which the Opposition attempted unsuccessfully to ride the Southern Rights issue to victory, see William S. Hitchcock, "The Limits of Southern Unionism: Virginia Conservatives and the Gubernatorial Election of 1859," *Journal of Southern History* 47 (Feb. 1981): 57–72. See also John V. Mering, "The Slave-State Constitutional Unionists and the Politics of Consensus," *Journal of Southern History* 43 (Aug. 1977): 395–410.

25. Freehling, *Drift toward Dissolution*, 241–42.

26. Gaines, "Virginia Constitutional Convention," chap. 6 and 197–213; F. N. Boney, *John Letcher of Virginia: The Story of Virginia's Civil War Governor* (University, Ala.: University of Alabama Press, 1966), 36–52; Freehling, *Drift toward Dissolution*, 237.

27. Shanks, *Secession Movement in Virginia*, 44–49. A major and much needed new biography of Wise has recently been published: Craig M. Simpson, *A Good Southerner: The Life of Henry A. Wise of Virginia* (Chapel Hill: University of North Carolina Press, 1985).

28. See the concluding section of Chapter 6 below.

29. Shade, "Political Culture and Party Development in Virginia"; Dent, "Virginia Democratic Party," esp. chaps. 6 and 10. On the 1859 campaign see Hitchcock, "Limits of Southern Unionism," 57–72; William G. Bean, "John Letcher and the Slavery Issue in Virginia's Gubernatorial Contest of 1858–59," *Journal of Southern History* 20 (1954): 22–49; William G. Bean, "The Ruffner Pamphlet of 1847: An Antislavery Aspect of Virginia Sectionalism," *Virginia Magazine of History and Biography* 61 (1953): 260–82.

30. Shanks, *Secession Movement in Virginia*, 103–19.

31. Thomas E. Jeffrey, "'Free Suffrage' Revisited: Party Politics and Constitutional Reform in Antebellum North Carolina," *North Carolina Historical Review* 59 (Winter 1982): 32–33; Thomas E. Jeffrey, "Internal Improvements and Political Parties in Antebellum North Carolina, 1836–1860," *North Carolina Historical Review* 55 (Spring 1978): 135–38.

32. Jeffrey, "'Free Suffrage,'" 28, 40; Jeffrey, "Internal Improvements," 112, 135, 146–47; Kruman, *Parties and Politics in North Carolina*, 86–103.

33. Jeffrey, "'Free Suffrage,'" 29; Jeffrey, "Internal Improvements," 135–48; Thomas E. Jeffrey, "'Thunder from the Mountains': Thomas Lanier Clingman and the End of Whig Supremacy in North Carolina," *North Carolina Historical Review* 56 (Autumn 1979): 366–95; Marc W. Kruman, "Thomas L. Clingman and the Whig Party: A Reconsideration," ibid. 64 (Jan. 1987): 1–18; Kruman, *Parties and Politics in North Carolina*, 65–85.

34. Donald C. Butts, "A Challenge to Planter Rule: The Controversy over Ad Valorem Taxation of Slaves in North Carolina, 1858–1862" (Ph.D. dissertation, Duke University, 1978); Donald C. Butts, "The 'Irrepressible Conflict': Slave Taxation and North Carolina's Gubernatorial Election of 1860,"

North Carolina Historical Review 58 (Winter 1981): 44–66, quotation on 45; Jeffrey, "Internal Improvements," 147–49; Kruman, *Parties and Politics in North Carolina*, 184–96.

35. Wooster, *Politicians, Planters, and Plain Folk*, 35–42, 126–27; Kruman, *Parties and Politics in North Carolina*, 46–50.

36. Sitterson, *Secession Movement in North Carolina*, 161–75; Kruman, *Parties and Politics in North Carolina*, 196–200.

37. Bergeron, *Antebellum Politics in Tennessee*, 123, 161.

38. Ibid., 103–47, esp. 131–34.

39. Ibid., 165.

40. The first three volumes of the *Johnson Papers* are the indispensable source on Johnson's career through 1860.

41. Simpson, *Good Southerner*, brilliantly analyzes Wise's career. See the *Richmond Semi-Weekly Enquirer*, Jan. 31, 1860, for Wise's version of his 1856 tactics.

42. William C. Harris, *William Woods Holden: Firebrand of North Carolina Politics* (Baton Rouge: Louisiana State University Press, 1987), esp. 82–106.

CHAPTER 3

1. David M. Potter, *The Impending Crisis, 1848–1861*, completed and edited by Don E. Fehrenbacher (New York: Harper & Row, 1976), 62.

Thomas Hart Benton apparently originated the "shears" idea. Stephen A. Douglas then used it during 1860 campaign speeches in Norfolk and Chicago. See *Norfolk Southern Argus*, Aug. 27, 1860; *Lynchburg Virginian*, Oct. 15, 1860; Robert W. Johannsen, *Stephen A. Douglas* (New York: Oxford University Press, 1973), 796.

2. "Appeal of the Independent Democrats," *National Era*, Jan. 28, 1854.

3. Potter, *Impending Crisis*, 145–69, 199–204, 294–327; Michael F. Holt, *The Political Crisis of the 1850s* (New York: Wiley, 1978), 203–9.

4. William A. Graham to Nathan Sargent, Nov. 17, 1858, Graham to New York Whigs, Feb. 21, 1859, both in J. G. deRoulhac Hamilton and Max R. Williams, eds., *The Papers of William Alexander Graham*, 7 vols. to date (Raleigh: North Carolina State Department of Archives and History, 1957–), 5:56–58, 90–91; *Richmond Whig*, July 6, 1859; Holt, *Political Crisis of the 1850s*, 207–9.

5. *CG*, 35:1, A282.

6. William J. Cooper, Jr., *The South and the Politics of Slavery, 1828–1856* (Baton Rouge: Louisiana State University Press, 1978), 353–58; William E. Ames, *A History of the National Intelligencer* (Chapel Hill: University of North Carolina Press, 1972), 312, 316; Joseph H. Parks, "The Tennessee Whigs and the Kansas-Nebraska Bill," *Journal of Southern History* 10 (1944): 308–30; *Lynchburg Virginian*, Dec. 11, 1860.

7. John Bell to William B. Campbell, Aug. 10, 1854, in *Tennessee Historical Magazine* 3 (1917): 223–25; Joseph H. Parks, *John Bell of Tennessee* (Baton Rouge: Louisiana State University Press, 1950), 283–301, 319–32; Parks,

"The Tennessee Whigs and the Kansas-Nebraska Bill." Crittenden, though out of office when the Kansas-Nebraska Act was passed, "made no secret of his opposition to it." He led the fight against Lecompton (Albert D. Kirwan, *John J. Crittenden: The Struggle for the Union* [Lexington: University of Kentucky Press, 1962], 314, 325–35). On George Badger, see *Fayetteville Observer*, Oct. 22, 1860, quoted in Sitterson, *Secession Movement in North Carolina*, 129; Henry Winter Davis to David Davis, Jan. 5, 1861, David Davis Papers, Chicago Historical Society.

8. *CG*, 35:1, 1698–1702, A456–58.

9. *North Carolina Weekly Standard*, May 11–Aug. 17, 1859; *Greensboro Patriot*, May 6–Aug. 19, 1859; *New York Times*, July 27, Aug. 9, 1859; Charles Faulkner Bryan, "Robert Hatton of Tennessee" (M.A. thesis, University of Georgia, 1971), 61–72; *National Intelligencer*, July 19, Dec. 22, 1859. Millson voted for Lecompton.

10. Robert E. May, *The Southern Dream of a Caribbean Empire, 1854–1861* (Baton Rouge: Louisiana State University Press, 1973), 194, 201–3.

11. Richard H. Sewell, *Ballots for Freedom: Antislavery Politics in the United States, 1837–1860* (New York: Oxford University Press, 1976), 348–54; *National Era*, Jan. 6, 20, 27, Mar. 17, Apr. 21, June 9, Aug. 4, 25, 1859.

12. Abraham Lincoln to Nathan Sargent, June 23, 1859, *CWAL*, 3:387–88.

13. Marvin R. Cain, *Lincoln's Attorney General: Edward Bates of Missouri* (Columbia: University of Missouri Press, 1965), 90–107; Parks, *John Bell*, 341–44; *New York Tribune*, Dec. 9, 1858, Jan. 24, Apr. 26, July 25, 1859; *National Intelligencer*, July 11, 12, 19, Aug. 17, 24, 31, 1859.

The only slave state where the United Opposition scheme found much favor was Maryland, which had experienced political upheaval in the 1850s substantially parallel to that of the urban Northeast. And even in Maryland, few besides Henry Winter Davis clearly recognized that Republicans would necessarily dominate any United Opposition (Gerald S. Henig, "Henry Winter Davis and the Speakership Contest of 1859–1860," *Maryland Historical Magazine* 68 [Spring 1973]: 3–5).

14. Potter, *Impending Crisis*, 378–82. See Stephen Oates, *To Purge This Land with Blood: A Biography of John Brown* (New York: Harper & Row, 1970), for the most compelling biography of Brown; also see Jeffery Rossbach, *Ambivalent Conspirators: John Brown, the Secret Six, and a Theory of Slave Violence* (Philadelphia: University of Pennsylvania Press, 1982), for a thoughtful analysis of Brown's allies.

15. Kent Blaser, "North Carolina and John Brown's Raid," *Civil War History* 24 (Sept. 1978): 197–212; John Coles Rutherfoord Diary, Nov. 1859, Rutherfoord Family Papers, VHS; "S. W. C." (Seth W. Cobb), Nov. 28, 1859, in *Petersburg Press*, Dec. 1, 1859; William K. Scarborough, ed., *The Diary of Edmund Ruffin*, 2 vols. to date (Baton Rouge: Louisiana State University Press, 1972–), 1:357 (diary entries of Nov. 18, 19, 1859).

16. John C. Rutherfoord Diary, Nov. 1859, Rutherfoord Family Papers; *Richmond Semi-Weekly Enquirer*, Jan. 3, 1860; Blaser, "North Carolina and

John Brown's Raid," 203; Roy Franklin Nichols, *The Disruption of American Democracy* (New York: Macmillan, 1948), 266–67.

17. Sewell, *Ballots for Freedom*, 355; George D. Prentice to Orville H. Browning, Jan. 9, 1860, quoted in ibid., 352; John V. Mering, "The Slave-State Constitutional Unionists and the Politics of Consensus," *Journal of Southern History* 43 (Aug. 1977): 395–410.

18. Pennsylvania Republicans were formally members of the People's party, an American-Republican coalition. New Jersey Republicans likewise belonged to the Opposition party and preferred the designation of Whig-American rather than Republican. "Americans" were a stronger, more persistent force in those two states than elsewhere in the North. The "People's" and "Opposition" labels allowed Republicans to benefit from American support, in exchange for certain concessions. See the account of one of the principals: John T. Nixon, "The Circumstances Attending the Election of William Pennington of New Jersey, as Speaker of the Thirty-Sixth Congress," *Proceedings of the New Jersey Historical Society*, 2d ser., 2 (1872): 204–20. See also Michael F. Holt, *Forging a Majority: The Formation of the Republican Party in Pittsburgh, 1848–1860* (New Haven: Yale University Press, 1969), 242–44, 253–55, 265–69, 282–83, 286; Charles Merriam Knapp, *New Jersey Politics during the Period of Civil War and Reconstruction* (Geneva, N.Y.: W. S. Humphrey, 1924), 11–23, 38–39.

19. The best short accounts of the Speakership fight are Nichols, *Disruption of American Democracy*, 271–76, and Potter, *Impending Crisis*, 386–91.

20. *New York Times*, Dec. 12, 1859; Henry Winter Davis to Samuel F. Du Pont, Dec. 27, 1859, Samuel F. Du Pont Papers, Eleutherian Mills Historical Library, Greenville, Del.

21. *Raleigh Register*, Dec. 24, 1859 ("Gaston," reporting from Washington, Dec. 17, 1859); Robert Hatton Diary, Dec. 22, 1859, in Drake, *Hatton*, 184; John A. Gilmer to Edward J. Hale, Feb. 4, 1860, Edward J. Hale Papers, NCDAH.

22. Davis to Samuel F. Du Pont, Dec. 20, 27, 1859, Du Pont Papers; *New York Times*, Dec. 23, 1859, Jan. 12, 16, 1860; *National Intelligencer*, Dec. 22, 1859, Jan. 8, 1860; *New York Herald*, Jan. 8, 1860; *CG*, 36:1, 336–37, 364–70, 440–44.

23. Davis to Du Pont, Feb. 3, 1860, Du Pont Papers; John A. Gilmer to Edward J. Hale, Feb. 4, 1860, Hale Papers; Henig, "Henry Winter Davis and the Speakership Contest," 1–19; Nixon, "Election of William Pennington," 204–20.

24. Davis to Du Pont, Feb. 3, 1860, Du Pont Papers; Henig, "Henry Winter Davis and the Speakership Contest," 10, 16. On the importance of the committees, see Allan Nevins, *The Emergence of Lincoln*, 2 vols. (New York: Charles Scribner's Sons, 1950), 2:118–19.

25. Thomas B. Alexander, "The Civil War as Institutional Fulfillment," *Journal of Southern History* 47 (Feb. 1981): 11; Nichols, *Disruption of American Democracy*, 319.

26. Davis to Du Pont, Dec. 20, 1859, Du Pont Papers.

27. Bell to Alexander R. Boteler, July 30, 1860, Alexander R. Boteler Papers, Duke University; Parks, *John Bell*, 344–88.

28. *Louisville Journal*, Aug. 13, 1860, in Dumond, ed., *Southern Editorials*, 159–62; *Lynchburg Virginian*, Sept. 8, 10, 1860, reprinting Curtis's speech of Aug. 3, 1860.

29. *Weekly Montgomery Confederation*, Aug. 17, 1860, in Dumond, ed., *Southern Editorials*, 162–64.

30. Douglas to Charles H. Lanphier, July 5, 1860, in Robert W. Johannsen, ed., *The Letters of Stephen A. Douglas* (Urbana: University of Illinois Press, 1961), 497–98; Johannsen, *Douglas*, 787–88; *Lynchburg Virginian*, Aug. 23, Oct. 23, 24, 1860. For an opposite interpretation, see John V. Mering, "Allies or Opponents? The Douglas Democrats and the Constitutional Unionists," *Southern Studies* 23 (1984): 376–85.

31. *Lynchburg Virginian*, Aug. 30, Oct. 22, 1860.

32. Ibid., Sept. 5, 1860; *Louisville Journal*, Aug. 13, 1860, in Dumond, ed., *Southern Editorials*, 159–62.

33. John Bell to Alexander Boteler, July 30, 1860, Boteler Papers; Parks, *John Bell*, 377–78; Johannsen, *Douglas*, 786–91, 797–803, esp. 790–91, 797–99.

34. William C. Harris, *William Woods Holden: Firebrand of North Carolina Politics* (Baton Rouge: Louisiana State University Press, 1987), 93–94; Shanks, *Secession Movement in Virginia*, 112–15; Sitterson, *Secession Movement in North Carolina*, 171–73; Campbell, *Attitude of Tennesseans*, 123–25, 134–35; *Richmond Enquirer*, July 10, 1860, in Dumond, ed., *Southern Editorials*, 140–42.

35. Elliott L. Story Diary, Oct. 12, 1860, VHS.

36. *Lynchburg Virginian*, Oct. 18, 22, 24, 27, 30, 1860; *Memphis Appeal*, Oct. 17, 25, 1860.

37. Brabson to Alexander Boteler, Oct. 15, 1860, Boteler Papers; *Lynchburg Virginian*, Oct. 24, 1860.

38. *Raleigh Register*, Oct. 22, 1860; Dan T. Carter, *When the War Was Over: The Failure of Self-Reconstruction in the South* (Baton Rouge: Louisiana State University Press, 1985), 187–90 (on Moore); *Lynchburg Virginian*, Nov. 1, 1860.

39. John C. Rutherfoord Diary, July 16, Nov. 6, 1860, Rutherfoord Family Papers.

40. *Richmond Enquirer*, Oct. 15, 1860; Shanks, *Secession Movement in Virginia*, 113–14; Nichols, *Disruption of American Democracy*, 319.

41. Stephen A. Channing, *Crisis of Fear: Secession in South Carolina* (New York: Simon and Schuster, 1970), 94–130; Scarborough, ed., *Ruffin Diary*, 1:482 (diary entries of Oct. 31, Nov. 3, 1860); James H. Hammond to Isaac Hayne, Sept. 19, 1860, quoted in Channing, *Crisis of Fear*, 242–43.

CHAPTER 4

1. Notable modern studies of secession in the deep South include J. Mills Thornton III, *Politics and Power in a Slave Society: Alabama, 1800–1860* (Baton Rouge: Louisiana State University Press, 1978); Stephen A. Channing, *Crisis of Fear: Secession in South Carolina* (New York: Simon and Schuster, 1970); William L. Barney, *The Secessionist Impulse: Alabama and Mississippi in 1860* (Princeton: Princeton University Press, 1974); Michael P. Johnson, *Toward a Patriarchal Republic: The Secession of Georgia* (Baton Rouge: Louisiana State University Press, 1977); and Walter L. Buenger, *Secession and the Union in Texas* (Austin: University of Texas Press, 1984). Uncertainties about how Georgia and Louisiana voted on secession are explored in Michael P. Johnson, "A New Look at the Popular Vote for Delegates to the Georgia Secession Convention," *Georgia Historical Quarterly* 56 (1972): 259–75; Charles B. Dew, "The Long Lost Returns: The Candidates and Their Totals in Louisiana's Secession Election," *Louisiana History* 10 (1969): 353–69; Charles B. Dew, "Who Won the Secession Election in Louisiana?" *Journal of Southern History* 36 (1970): 18–32.

2. *Washington National Republican*, Jan. 18, 1861, in Perkins, ed., *Northern Editorials*, 2:858; Robert Ridgeway to John J. Crittenden, Dec. 16, 1860, John J. Crittenden Papers, LC; David F. Caldwell to Abraham Lincoln, Dec. 31, 1860, Abraham Lincoln Papers, LC (microfilm edition); Henry W. Miller to William A. Graham, Dec. 29, 1860, William A. Graham Papers, SHC-UNC, in Max R. Williams and J. G. deRoulhac Hamilton, eds., *The Papers of William Alexander Graham*, 7 vols. to date (Raleigh: North Carolina State Department of Archives and History, 1957–), 5:203–5; Felix K. Zollicoffer to Stephen A. Douglas, Dec. 31, 1860, Stephen A. Douglas Papers, University of Chicago; W. C. Kerr to Benjamin Sherwood Hedrick, Dec. 26, 1860, Benjamin S. Hedrick Papers, Duke. For Charlotte as a "young Charleston," see John M. Morehead to Thomas Ruffin, Mar. 5, 1861, Thomas Ruffin Papers, SHC-UNC, in J. G. deRoulhac Hamilton, ed., *The Papers of Thomas Ruffin*, 4 vols. (Raleigh: Edwards and Broughton, 1918–20), 3:137–38.

3. Ulrich B. Phillips, *The Course of the South to Secession*, ed. E. Merton Coulter (1939; rpt. New York: Hill and Wang, 1964), 132–34; Laura A. White, *Robert Barnwell Rhett, Father of Secession* (New York: Century, 1931).

4. Avery O. Craven, *Edmund Ruffin, Southerner: A Study in Secession* (Baton Rouge: Louisiana State University Press, 1932), 5–11; William K. Scarborough, ed., *The Diary of Edmund Ruffin*, 2 vols. to date (Baton Rouge: Louisiana State University Press, 1972–), 1:66, 144, 220–25 (entries of May 13, 1857, Jan. 11, Aug. 11, 14, 16, 1858).

5. *DeBow's Review* 23 (Dec. 1857): 605–7; *Charleston Mercury*, Mar. 10, 1860, in Dumond, ed., *Southern Editorials*, 50–55; Scarborough, ed., *Ruffin Diary*, 1:407, 410, 424 (entries of Feb. 24, Mar. 16, May 30, 1860), 633–35 (Ruffin to W. L. Yancey, Oct. 29, 1860).

6. Scarborough, ed., *Ruffin Diary*, 1:482–83 (entries of Nov. 3, 7, 1860).

7. These alarms usually coincided with times when southern power in national politics appeared precarious. Rehearsals for the more widespread

clamor of 1860–61 occurred in 1850–51 and 1856. See William L. Barney, *The Road to Secession: A New Perspective on the Old South* (New York: Praeger, 1972), 146–50; Barney, *Secessionist Impulse*, 163–80; Charles B. Dew, "Black Ironworkers and the Slave Insurrection Panic of 1856," *Journal of Southern History* 41 (Aug. 1975): 321–38; Thornton, *Politics and Power in a Slave Society*, 155–61; *CG*, 36:2, A113.

8. *Richmond Enquirer*, July 10, 1860, *Charleston Mercury*, Oct. 11, 1860, *New Orleans Delta*, Nov. 1, 1860, all in Dumond, ed., *Southern Editorials*, 140–42, 178–81, 203; Barney, *Secessionist Impulse*, 123.

9. *Wilmington Journal*, Jan. 3, 1861; Reese, ed., *Virginia Convention*, 1:256–57; *Richmond Enquirer*, July 10, 1860, in Dumond, ed., *Southern Editorials*, 141.

10. *Nashville Weekly Patriot*, Jan. 28, 1861 (letter to the editor, dated Jan. 22, 1861).

11. *Wilmington Journal*, Oct. 23, Nov. 13, 16, 1860.

12. Reese, ed., *Virginia Convention*, 1:255, 3:34–35.

13. *Salisbury Banner*, Feb. 19, 1861, *Raleigh State Journal*, Feb. 20, 1861, both quoted in Sitterson, *Secession in North Carolina*, 214, 221; *Wilmington Journal*, Jan. 3, 1861.

14. Reese, ed., *Virginia Convention*, 1:270, 2:10, 237–45, 3:96; Francis R. Rives to William C. Rives, Jr., Mar. 13, 1861, William C. Rives Papers, LC.

15. James Barbour to William C. Rives, Feb. 7, 1861, Rives Papers; Reese, ed., *Virginia Convention*, 1:258; Chittenden, *Report*, 93–94.

16. Reese, ed., *Virginia Convention*, 3:100.

17. Eugene D. Genovese, *The Political Economy of Slavery: Studies in the Economy and Society of the Slave South* (New York: Pantheon, 1965), 3–10, 243–70; Barney, *Secessionist Impulse*, 14–16, 19–24; Barney, *Road to Secession*, 6–21.

18. The standard study of late antebellum southern imperialism is Robert E. May, *The Southern Dream of a Caribbean Empire, 1854–1861* (Baton Rouge: Louisiana State University Press, 1973). May's recent contribution, *John A. Quitman: Old South Crusader* (Baton Rouge: Louisiana State University Press, 1985), suggests that both southern expansionism and secession were desperate tactical responses to growing northern power, rather than objectives of intrinsic value.

19. Michael F. Holt, *The Political Crisis of the 1850s* (New York: Wiley, 1978), 223, 241–42; Kenneth S. Greenberg, *Masters and Statesmen: The Political Culture of American Slavery* (Baltimore: Johns Hopkins University Press, 1985), 140–41.

20. Thornton, *Politics and Power in a Slave Society*, 220, 226–27.

21. Chittenden, *Report*, 294–95; Reese, ed., *Virginia Convention*, 3:667–70.

22. *CG*, 36:2, 266–67; Reese, ed., *Virginia Convention*, 1:616.

23. Bertram Wyatt-Brown, *Southern Honor: Ethics and Behavior in the Old South* (New York: Oxford University Press, 1982), passim, quotation on 5; Bertram Wyatt-Brown, "Honor and Secession" (paper delivered at the Southern Historical Association convention, Memphis, Nov. 1982), esp. 10–

12; Bertram Wyatt-Brown, *Yankee Saints and Southern Sinners* (Baton Rouge: Louisiana State University Press, 1985), 126–27, 183–213.

24. *Nashville Union and American*, Oct. 12, 1860, in Dumond, ed., *Southern Editorials*, 181–84; *Memphis Appeal*, Jan. 22, 1861; Henry A. Wise, public letter dated Dec. 31, 1860, in *Richmond Semi-Weekly Enquirer*, Jan. 8, 1861.

25. Reese, ed., *Virginia Convention*, 1:258, 270, 2:94–95; *Memphis Appeal*, Jan. 22, 1861.

26. Abraham Lincoln to John A. Gilmer, Dec. 15, 1860, *CWAL*, 4:152; Nathan Street to Charles Francis Adams, Feb. 3, 1861, Adams Family Papers, MHS; Amasa Walker to William G. Brownlow, Feb. 11, 1861, in *Brownlow's Weekly Knoxville Whig*, Feb. 16, 1861.

27. Reese, ed., *Virginia Convention*, 1:614–15.

28. Ibid., 200, 740, 750, 752–53.

29. *Memphis Appeal*, Jan. 22, 1861; see also *Memphis Avalanche*, Jan. 21, 1861.

30. Reese, ed., *Virginia Convention*, 1:70–73.

31. *Memphis Appeal*, Jan. 22, 1861; Reese, ed., *Virginia Convention*, 1:104, 197, 755; *Wilmington Journal*, Nov. 19, 1860; see also Reese, ed., *Virginia Convention*, 1:396, 2:103; *Richmond Semi-Weekly Examiner*, Mar. 8, 19, 1861.

32. *Memphis Appeal*, Jan. 11, 17, 1861; Reese, ed., *Virginia Convention*, 1:759, 2:103; Scarborough, ed., *Ruffin Diary*, 1:538–40 (entry of Jan. 31, 1861).

33. Reese, ed., *Virginia Convention*, 1:56.

34. *Memphis Appeal*, Nov. 10, 17, 25, Dec. 11, 14, 15, 18, 1860.

35. *Alexandria Gazette*, Dec. 5, 25, 1860 ("Aliquis" in Loudoun County, Dec. 21, 1860), Jan. 4, 1861 ("Aliquis" in Loudon County, Jan. 1, 1861), Jan. 19, 1861 ("S." in Prince William County, Jan. 14, 1861); Robert Hatton to his wife, Jan. 1, 1861, in Drake, *Hatton*, 316.

CHAPTER 5

1. William B. Campbell to William Shelton, Jan. 11, 1861, Campbell Family Papers, Duke; Andrew Johnson, speech of Feb. 5–6, 1861, *Johnson Papers*, 4:252; *Wheeling Intelligencer*, Jan. 19, 1861.

2. *CG*, 36:2, A142, A583, A172–73.

3. Reese, ed., *Virginia Convention*, 2:675–79.

4. Bartholomew F. Moore to his daughter, Dec. 1860, typescript, Bartholomew F. Moore Papers, NCDAH; *CG*, 36:2, A105.

5. Reese, ed., *Virginia Convention*, 3:554, 568–70, 580–82; *Wheeling Intelligencer*, Feb. 2, 1861, in Perkins, ed., *Northern Editorials*, 2:902.

6. *Alexandria Gazette*, Dec. 24, 1860; *Richmond Whig*, Jan. 4, 1861; Shanks, *Secession Movement in Virginia*, 131, 164; Frederick Fein Siegel, "A New South in the Old: Sotweed and Soil in the Development of Danville, Virginia" (Ph.D. dissertation, University of Pittsburgh, 1978), 235–41.

7. Henry W. Miller to William A. Graham, Dec. 29, 1860, William A. Gra-

ham Papers, SHC-UNC, in Max R. Williams and J. G. deRoulhac Hamilton, eds., *The Papers of William Alexander Graham*, 7 vols. to date (Raleigh: North Carolina State Department of Archives and History, 1957–), 5:203–5; Sitterson, *Secession Movement in North Carolina*, 198; Brennan to Johnson, Jan. 7, 1861, *Johnson Papers*, 4:128–29.

8. *Richmond Semi-Weekly Enquirer*, Jan. 8, 1861; *Alexandria Gazette*, Jan. 12, 1861.

9. The prewar efforts of the Southern Pacific Rail Road Company to build a southern transcontinental line still await modern scholarly scrutiny. See the brief summaries in Robert R. Russel, *Improvement of Communication with the Pacific Coast as an Issue in American Politics, 1783–1864* (Cedar Rapids, Iowa: Torch Press, 1948), 268–70; A. B. Armstrong, "Origins of the Texas and Pacific Railway," *Southwestern Historical Quarterly* 56 (Apr. 1953): 489–97. Various newspapers, especially in Memphis, New Orleans, and Texas, contain a wealth of information: see *Memphis Avalanche*, Sept. 18, 1858, Feb. 23, 1859; *Memphis Appeal*, Mar. 23, Apr. 5, 10, 16, 1861. The Morton-Halsey Papers, UVA, are also illuminating. Jeptha Fowlkes, the most zealous promoter of the Southern Pacific, had close ties to Unionist leader Andrew Johnson during the secession crisis. See Fowlkes to Johnson, Mar. 10, 13, 17, 21, 23, 1861, *Johnson Papers*, 4:378–80, 388–89, 401–2, 422–23, 425–26.

10. John H. B. Latrobe to William C. Rives, Dec. 15, 1860, Rives to Latrobe, Dec. 28, 1860, Alexander Rives to William C. Rives, Dec. 28, 1860, William C. Rives Papers, LC; William C. Rives to Alexander Boteler, Dec. 8, 1860, printed public letter, copy in VHS; *Richmond Whig*, Jan. 22, 1861; *Richmond Semi-Weekly Enquirer*, Jan. 8, 1861; James B. Dorman to John Letcher, Nov. 18, 1860, S. C. Moorman to James D. Davidson, Dec. 20, 1860, Letcher to Davidson, Mar. 9, 1861, James D. Dorman, notes for a speech, late March 1861, James D. Davidson Papers, Wisconsin State Historical Society, copies in U. B. Phillips Papers, Yale University. Several significant letters from the Davidson Papers are printed in Bruce S. Greenawalt, ed., "Unionists in Rockbridge County: The Correspondence of James Dorman Davidson Concerning the Virginia Secession Convention of 1861," *Virginia Magazine of History and Biography* 73 (1965): 78–102. See also Zebulon B. Vance to W. W. Lenoir, Dec. 26, 1860, Zebulon B. Vance Papers, SHC-UNC, in Frontis W. Johnston, *The Papers of Zebulon Baird Vance*, 1 vol. to date (Raleigh: North Carolina State Department of Archives and History, 1963), 1:77–78.

11. William B. Campbell to A. L. Beard, Mar. 15, 1861, Campbell Papers.

12. *CG*, 36:2, A111–13; Bartholomew F. Moore to his daughter, Apr. 15, 1861, typescript, Moore Papers, NCDAH; Reese, ed., *Virginia Convention*, 1:366–67, 469, 505, 616–19.

13. *CG*, 36:2, A111–13.

14. Reese, ed., *Virginia Convention*, 1:616; *CG*, 36:2, A172.

15. Andrew Johnson, speech of Feb. 5–6, 1861, *Johnson Papers*, 4:238–39, 258–59; *Louisville Daily Journal*, Jan. 26, 1861, in Dumond, ed., *Southern Editorials*, 422–25. Boyce had become a secessionist by 1860–61.

16. *North Carolina Standard*, Feb. 5, 1861, in Dumond, ed., *Southern Editorials*, 446–47; Reese, ed., *Virginia Convention*, 1:505.

17. *CG*, 36:2, A137, A182; James C. Johnston to Johnston Pettigrew, Jan. 2, 1861, Pettigrew Family Papers, SHC-UNC.

18. *CG*, 36:2, A197; John Minor Botts, in *Richmond Whig*, Jan. 28, 1861; *Alexandria Gazette*, Dec. 29, 1860 ("C. D.," Fauquier County, Dec. 21, 1860). The analysis in Chapter 3 of national political developments between 1854 and 1860 should suggest that the conspiracy theory about secession was, at best, oversimplified, as were the similar Republican perceptions about a "slave power conspiracy." We now know that conspiratorial fears echoed and reechoed in American political thinking from the Stamp Act Crisis through the Civil War and beyond. Unionists who suspected a secession conspiracy could point to Alabama's William L. Yancey and several others, but they lacked evidence for widespread premeditation. The most penetrating recent analysis of secessionist thought emphasizes that disunionists likewise harbored pervasive conspiratorial fears. See Kenneth S. Greenberg, *Masters and Statesmen: The Political Culture of American Slavery* (Baltimore: Johns Hopkins University Press, 1985), 107–46.

19. Daniel H. Kelly to T. A. R. Nelson, Dec. 30, 1860, Andrew J. Fletcher to Nelson, Jan. 21, 1861, W. C. Kyle to Nelson, Feb. 6, 1861, Nathaniel G. Taylor to Nelson, Jan. 3, 1861, Dr. William R. Sevier to Nelson, Dec. 11, 1861, T. A. R. Nelson Papers, McClung Collection, Lawson McGhee Library, Knoxville, Tenn.; *Brownlow's Knoxville Whig*, Jan. 28, 1861, quoted by Campbell, *Attitude of Tennesseans*, 175; A. Waldo Putnam to Andrew Johnson, Dec. 22, 1860, *Johnson Papers*, 4:73–74; William H. Polk to "My Dear Sir" (draft), Jan. 29, 1861, William H. Polk Papers, NCDAH.

20. Reese, ed., *Virginia Convention*, 1:173–77, 495–99, 2:189–90; *CG*, 36:2, A111–13, A172, A136; Bartholomew F. Moore to his daughter, Apr. 15, 1861, typescript, Moore Papers; public letter from William C. Wickham, *National Intelligencer*, Feb. 12, 1861.

21. *North Carolina Standard*, Dec. 5, 1861; *Charlottesville Review*, Jan. 25, 1861, in Dumond, ed., *Southern Editorials*, 415–19.

22. Letter from James G. Ramsey, Mar. 27, 1861, in *Salisbury Carolina Watchman*, Apr. 2, 1861; James C. Johnston to Johnston Pettigrew, Jan. 2, 1861, Pettigrew Family Papers; Reese, ed., *Virginia Convention*, 1:363–64; Andrew Johnson, speech of Dec. 18–19, 1860, in *Johnson Papers*, 4:41–43.

23. *Lynchburg Virginian*, Apr. 2, 1861.

24. *Charlottesville Review*, Jan. 25, 1861, in Dumond, ed., *Southern Editorials*, 416; Henry Winter Davis to Samuel F. Du Pont, mid-Dec. 1860, transcription, Samuel F. Du Pont Papers, Eleutherian Mills Historical Library, Greenville, Del.; A. Clifton Loy, "George W. Summers and His Relation to the Formation of the State of West Virginia" (M.A. thesis, West Virginia University, 1937), 43; Granville D. Hall, *The Rending of Virginia: A History* (Chicago: Mayer & Miller, 1902), 94; Alexander H. Stephens to J. Henly Smith, Dec. 31, 1860, in Ulrich B. Phillips, ed., *The Correspondence of Robert Toombs, Alexander H. Stephens, and Howell Cobb, American Historical Association*

Annual Report, 1911, 2 vols. (Washington, D.C.: U.S. Government Printing Office, 1913), 2:526–27; Andrew Johnson to Sam Milligan, Jan. 13, 1861, in *Johnson Papers*, 4:160.

25. *CG*, 36:2, 581.

26. Robert Hatton to Sophie Hatton, Dec. 31, 1860, in Drake, *Hatton*, 315; John Lellyett to Andrew Johnson, Jan. 23, 1861, Andrew Johnson's speech of Feb. 5–6, 1861, both in *Johnson Papers*, 4:184, 235; James C. Johnston to Johnston Pettigrew, Jan. 2, 1861, Pettigrew Family Papers; Reese, ed., *Virginia Convention*, 1:722.

27. *Louisville Daily Journal*, Jan. 26, 1861, in Dumond, ed., *Southern Editorials*, 422–25; Reese, ed., *Virginia Convention*, 1:350, 722; *CG*, 36:2, A136; Dr. William A. Sevier to T. A. R. Nelson, Jan. 17, 1861, Nelson Papers.

28. *Louisville Daily Journal*, Jan. 26, 1861, in Dumond, ed., *Southern Editorials*, 424; Reese, ed., *Virginia Convention*, 1:184, 2:714; John B. Minor to Mary Minor Blackford, Apr. 8, 1861, Blackford Family Papers, UVA; *CG*, 36:2, A115.

29. Alexander W. Campbell reporting from Richmond, Feb. 26, 1861, in *Wheeling Intelligencer*, Mar. 2, 1861; *CG*, 36:2, A173; Alexander H. H. Stuart to William C. Rives, Jan. 15, 1861, James D. Davidson to Rives, Feb. 1, 1861, both in Rives Papers; Alice Janney to John Janney, Apr. 4, 1861, John Janney Papers, held by Lucas Phillips, Leesburg, Va.; *Alexandria Gazette*, Jan. 28, 1861.

30. William B. Campbell to William Shelton, Jan. 11, 1861, Campbell Papers; James T. Otey to Edward C. Burks, Mar. 12, 1861, in James E. Walmsley, ed., "The Change of Secession Sentiment in Virginia in 1861," *American Historical Review* 31 (1925): 97–99; Alexander Stephens to unknown, Nov. 25, 1860, in Phillips, ed., *Correspondence of Toombs, Stephens, and Cobb*, 504–5; *Alexandria Gazette*, Jan. 24, 1861.

31. A. Waldo Putnam to Andrew Johnson, Feb. 18, 1861, *Johnson Papers*, 4:310–12.

32. Abraham Lincoln, Cooper Union Speech, Feb. 27, 1860, Speech at Cincinnati, Feb. 12, 1861, Inaugural Address, Mar. 4, 1861, all in *CWAL*, 3:538, 4:199, 262–63; William B. Hesseltine, *Three against Lincoln: Murat Halstead Reports the Caucuses of 1860* (Baton Rouge: Louisiana State University Press, 1960), 156; Lee Benson, *Toward the Scientific Study of History* (Philadelphia: J. B. Lippincott, 1972), 292–303; *New York Times*, Nov. 26, Dec. 25, 1860; Augustus Maverick, *Henry J. Raymond and the New York Press for Thirty Years* (Hartford: A. S. Hale, 1870), 401–2, 422–23; Amasa Walker to William G. Brownlow, Feb. 11, 1861, in *Brownlow's Knoxville Whig*, Feb. 16, 1861.

33. C. Hammond to Josiah T. Smith, Jan. 28, 1861, Josiah Townsend Smith Papers, Duke; Ira P. Sperry to Francis H. Gordon, Mar. 2, 1861, in *Nashville Republican Banner*, Apr. 4, 1861; "W. H. M." to William W. Holden, in *North Carolina Weekly Standard*, Feb. 13, 1861; John Griffen to Andrew Johnson, Jan. 7, 1861, *Johnson Papers*, 4:130–47, quotations on 130, 136–37.

34. John Bell, public letter to A. Burwell, Dec. 6, 1860, in *Lynchburg Virginian*, Dec. 14, 1860, and *Nashville Weekly Patriot*, Dec. 10, 1860.

35. *Raleigh Register*, Nov. 10, 1860; *Lynchburg Virginian*, Nov. 9, 1860; John W. Crisfield to his son Henry Page, Nov. 11, 1860, Henry Page Papers, SHC-UNC.

36. *CG*, 36:2, A112–13, A115.

37. Hatton to William B. Campbell, Jan. 24, 1861, Campbell Papers.

38. Ibid.; Chittenden, *Report*, 467–70, 165, 261, 263, 430; *New York Tribune*, Feb. 13, 1861. The term "stiff-backed" entered the secession crisis vocabulary through publication of a private letter written by prominent Republican Senator Zachariah Chandler, urging a "stiff-backed" stance and cheerfully contemplating the prospect of a little "blood-letting" (Robert Gray Gunderson, *Old Gentlemen's Convention: The Washington Peace Conference of 1861* [Madison: University of Wisconsin Press, 1961], 72–74).

39. *CG*, 36:2, A115, A137, A182, A104, A108, A77.

40. *CG*, 36:2, A126; *New York Herald*, Apr. 1, 1861. "When the sword is drawn," Hamilton warned, "the passions of men observe no bounds of moderation."

41. A. Waldo Putnam to Andrew Johnson, Feb. 18, 1861, *Johnson Papers*, 4:310–12; Abraham Lincoln, speeches in Pittsburgh and Cleveland, Feb. 15, 1861, *CWAL*, 4:211, 215–16; John Minor Botts, public letter to Jonas C. Hewitt et al., Feb. 21, 1861, in *Wheeling Intelligencer*, Feb. 27, 1861.

42. *CG*, 36:2, 583, A152, A174, A199; *Wellsburg Herald*, in *Wheeling Intelligencer*, Feb. 4, 1861; William A. Graham, "Notes for a Speech Given as a Candidate for the Secession Convention," Feb. 1861, Williams and Hamilton, eds., *Graham Papers*, 5:219; Bartholomew F. Moore to his daughter, Jan. 17, 1861, typescript, Moore Papers.

43. *CG*, 36:2, A106, A136; *Louisville Daily Journal*, Jan. 31, 1861, in Dumond, ed., *Southern Editorials*, 434–38.

44. *CG*, 36:2, A153, A137, A171; Robert Hatton to Sophie Hatton, Dec. 21, 1860, in Drake, *Hatton*, 310.

45. *CG*, 36:2, 581.

46. *Richmond Whig*, Mar. 2, 22, 1861; John Monroe to David Pugh, Mar. 24, 1861, John Monroe Papers, Duke; James Barbour to William C. Rives, Feb. 7, 1861, Rives Papers; Reese, ed., *Virginia Convention*, 2:197–201.

47. *CG*, 36:2, A77.

48. *CG*, 36:2, A77, 580–83, A170; John A. Gilmer to Thurlow Weed, Jan. 12, 1861, Thurlow Weed Papers, University of Rochester; John A. Gilmer to Dr. D. H. Albright, Jan. 8, 1861, John A. Gilmer Papers, NCDAH.

49. Gilmer to Weed, Jan. 12, 1861, Weed Papers; *CG*, 36:2, 580–83.

50. *CG*, 36:2, A80, A118.

51. Reese, ed., *Virginia Convention*, 1:284, 402–4, 483, 436–40.

52. *CG*, 36:2, A199, A167, A219.

53. *Wilmington Daily Herald*, Jan. 3, 1861, and *Charlottesville Review*, Jan. 4, 25, 1861, in Dumond, ed., *Southern Editorials*, 386–91, 415–19; *CG*, 36:2, A167, A199.

54. *Lynchburg Virginian*, Dec. 13, 1860; James D. Davidson to William C. Rives, Feb. 1, 1861, Rives Papers; *Alexandria Gazette*, Dec. 21, 1860; *Greens-*

boro Patriot, Jan. 31, 1861; *Wheeling Intelligencer*, Jan. 24, 1861; Horace Maynard to John M. Fleming, Jan. 14, 1861, in *Brownlow's Weekly Knoxville Whig*, Jan. 26, 1861.

55. Kenneth M. Stampp, *And the War Came: The North and the Secession Crisis, 1860–61* (Baton Rouge: Louisiana State University Press, 1950), 141–47 and passim; *Charlotte Bulletin*, quoted in Sitterson, *Secession in North Carolina*, 200–201, from the *North Carolina Whig*, Jan. 29, 1861.

56. Rolfe S. Saunders to Oliver P. Temple, Jan. 4, 1861, Oliver P. Temple Papers, University of Tennessee, Knoxville; Robert Hatton to Sophie Hatton, Dec. 21, 1860, in Drake, *Hatton*, 310–11.

57. Platt K. Dickinson to Mrs. John G. Dabney, Jan. 8, 1861, Platt K. Dickinson Papers, SHC-UNC; John A. Gilmer to Dr. D. H. Albright, Jan. 8, 1861, Gilmer Papers.

CHAPTER 6

1. Daniel W. Crofts, "Secession Crisis Voting Behavior in Southampton County, Virginia" (paper presented at the Fifth Citadel Conference on the South, Charleston, S.C., Apr. 10, 1987; to be published in a forthcoming anthology of papers from that conference).

2. Beth G. Crabtree and James W. Patton, eds., *"Journal of a Secesh Lady": The Diary of Catherine Ann Devereux Edmondston, 1860–1866* (Raleigh: North Carolina Department of Cultural Resources, Division of Archives and History, 1979), 6, 13–14, 38, 54 (entries of July 16, Nov. 6, 1860, Jan. 13, Feb. 18, Apr. 20, 1861); Conway D. Whittle to Lewis N. Whittle, Feb. 2, 1861, Lewis N. Whittle Papers, SHC-UNC.

3. William H. I'Anson to Edmund Ruffin, Nov. 28, 1860, Edmund Ruffin Papers, VHS; Kenneth Rayner to Thomas Ruffin, Dec. 25, 1860, in J. G. deRoulhac Hamilton, ed., *The Papers of Thomas Ruffin*, 4 vols. (Raleigh: Edwards and Broughton, 1918–20), 3:108–9; John D. Imboden to John McCue, Dec. 3, 1860, McCue Family Papers, UVA; W. H. Johnson to T. A. R. Nelson, Jan. 19, 1861, T. A. R. Nelson Papers, McClung Collection, Lawson McGhee Library, Knoxville, Tenn.

4. C. B. Harrison to Lawrence O'B. Branch, Dec. 2, 1860, Lawrence O'B. Branch Papers, Duke, in W. Buck Yearns and John G. Barrett, eds., *North Carolina Civil War Documentary* (Chapel Hill: University of North Carolina Press, 1980), 11–13; John D. Imboden to John McCue, Dec. 3, 1860, McCue Family Papers.

5. *Brownlow's Weekly Knoxville Whig*, Jan. 12, 1861; *Fayetteville Observer*, Jan. 7, 1861.

6. *Wheeling Intelligencer*, Nov. 23, 26, Dec. 15, 1860; *North Carolina Weekly Standard*, Nov. 28, Dec. 5, 12, 1860; Andrew Johnson, speech of Dec. 18–19, 1860, *Johnson Papers*, 4:3–51.

7. Most statistical measurements of Union and secession sentiment are

presented in Chapter 7 below and in Appendixes I and II. See also Chapter 13 for reasons why more reliable post-Sumter statistics are available for Tennessee.

8. R. M. T. Hunter to George Booker, Dec. 14, 1860, George Booker Papers, Duke. Hunter's public statement, dated Dec. 10, 1860, and published in the *Richmond Enquirer*, Dec. 12, 1860, is reprinted in Charles Henry Ambler, ed., *Correspondence of Robert M. T. Hunter, 1826–1876*, Vol. 2 of *Annual Report of the American Historical Association for the Year 1916* (Washington, D.C.: U.S. Government Printing Office, 1918), 337–51, esp. 345, 348, 350. A useful study of Hunter in the secession crisis is William S. Hitchcock, "Southern Moderates and Secession: Senator Robert M. T. Hunter's Call for Union," *Journal of American History* 59 (Mar. 1973): 871–84.

9. Reese, *Virginia Convention*, 1:259, 2:84–85; Hitchcock, "Southern Moderates and Secession," 880–81.

10. *CG*, 36:2, A138, 580–81, A153; *Louisville Daily Journal*, quoted in *National Intelligencer*, Feb. 5, 1861.

11. *Lynchburg Virginian*, Dec. 14, 17, 1860; James D. Davidson to John Letcher, Jan. 3, 1861, James D. Davidson Papers, Wisconsin State Historical Society, copy in U. B. Phillips Papers, Yale University; Alexander Rives to William C. Rives, Dec. 28, 1860, William C. Rives Papers, LC.

12. William C. Rives to William C. Rives, Jr., Jan. 3, 1861, Rives Papers. Governor Letcher had agreed to call the legislature to consider both the national crisis and the proposal by a European consortium to purchase the James River and Kanawha Canal (Shanks, *Secession Movement in Virginia*, 142).

13. Edward C. Burks to Rowland D. Buford, Jan. 7, 1861, in James E. Walmsley, ed., "The Change of Secession Sentiment in Virginia in 1861," *American Historical Review* 31 (1925): 83; *Wheeling Intelligencer*, Jan. 11, 14, 1861 (Richmond correspondent, Jan. 8, 1861, in the latter); Shanks, *Secession Movement in Virginia*, 144; Alexander H. H. Stuart to John B. Baldwin, Jan. 8, 1861, in Baldwin's pardon application file, Virginia, RG 94, microfilm series M1003, NA; Stuart to William C. Rives, Jan. 15, 1861, Rives Papers.

14. Shanks, *Secession Movement in Virginia*, 150–51.

15. Barbour is identified as the author of the Peace Conference plan in the *Washington Evening Star*, reprinted in the *Alexandria Gazette*, Jan. 25, 1861; George W. Summers to John J. Thompson, Jan. 8, 1861, in *Richmond Whig*, Jan. 22, 1861. See David M. Potter, *Lincoln and His Party in the Secession Crisis* (New Haven: Yale University Press, 1942), 307–9, and Chapter 9 below for evidence of collusion between Virginia Unionists and New York Senator William H. Seward, who masterminded the conciliatory Republican strategy.

16. *Wheeling Intelligencer*, Jan. 14, 1861; *Richmond Semi-Weekly Enquirer*, Jan. 15, 1861; *Alexandria Gazette*, Jan. 15, 1861 (Richmond correspondent).

17. James B. Dorman to John Letcher, Nov. 27, 1860, Jan. 13, 1861, James D. Davidson to Letcher, Jan. 28, 31, 1861, all in Davidson Papers,

copies in Phillips Papers; C. B. Anderson to Stephen A. Douglas, Jan. 21, 1861, Stephen A. Douglas Papers, University of Chicago.

18. Public letter from Stephen A. Douglas, Jan. 31, 1861, in *Petersburg Express*, Feb. 2, 1861, copy in *Richmond Whig*, Feb. 4, 1861; *Richmond Whig*, Jan. 29, 1861; *Alexandria Gazette*, Jan. 30, 1861.

19. *Richmond Enquirer*, Jan. 25, 1861; Shanks, *Secession Movement in Virginia*, 150–53; *Richmond Whig*, Jan. 29, 1861.

20. Junius Hillyer to Howell Cobb, Jan. 30, Feb. 9, 11, 1861, in Ulrich B. Phillips, ed., *The Correspondence of Robert Toombs, Alexander H. Stephens, and Howell Cobb, American Historical Association Annual Report, 1911*, 2 vols. (Washington, D.C.: U.S. Government Printing Office, 1913), 2:535–36, 538, 541–42.

21. James D. Davidson to James B. Dorman, Feb. 13, 1861, Davidson Papers, copy in Phillips Papers; Shanks, *Secession Movement in Virginia*, 153–57.

22. *Richmond Whig*, Feb. 13, 1861; Alexander Rives to William C. Rives, Jr., Feb. 11, 1861, Rives Papers; James Barbour to William H. Seward, Feb. 8, 1861, John S. Pendleton to Seward, Feb. 15, 1861, both in William H. Seward Papers, University of Rochester.

23. John A. Gilmer to Thomas Corwin, June 4, 1865, Gilmer to J. B. Stewart, Aug. 14, 1865, both in Gilmer's pardon application file, North Carolina, RG 94, microfilm series M1003, NA; Robert Hatton to his wife, Jan. 30, Feb. 17, 18, 1861, in Drake, *Hatton*, 323, 342–43; John A. Gilmer to Andrew Johnson, Mar. 1861 (erroneously listed as Feb. 28, 1861), *Johnson Papers*, 4:110.

24. William R. Leonard, "Joseph Camp Griffith Kennedy," *DAB*, 10:335–36; Joseph C. G. Kennedy to Charles Francis Adams, Feb. 4, 1861, Charles Francis Adams, diary entry of Feb. 4, 1861, both in Adams Family Papers, MHS; Alexander H. H. Stuart to Joseph C. G. Kennedy, Apr. 1, 1861, Seward Papers; Joseph C. G. Kennedy to T. A. R. Nelson, Jan. 28, Feb. 6, 1861, Nelson Papers; John A. Gilmer to *Raleigh Register*, Feb. 28, 1861, in *North Carolina Semi-Weekly Standard*, Mar. 20, 1861; Joseph C. G. Kennedy to Virginia census takers, Jan. 9, 30, 1861, in *Richmond Semi-Weekly Enquirer*, Feb. 1, 5, 1861.

25. *Richmond Semi-Weekly Enquirer*, Feb. 1, 5, 1861; *CG*, 36:2, 836; *Raleigh Weekly State Journal*, Feb. 20, 1861 (telegraphed report from Washington dated Feb. 8, 1861); Reese, ed., *Virginia Convention*, 1:96–100; "States Rights" to Lawrence O'B. Branch, Feb. 21, 1861, Lawrence O'B. Branch Papers, Duke; T. Allan to Howell Cobb, Feb. 11, 1861, in Phillips, ed., *Correspondence of Toombs, Stephens, and Cobb*, 2:540–41; Roy Franklin Nichols, *The Disruption of American Democracy* (New York: Macmillan, 1948), 400, 474.

26. Reese, ed., *Virginia Convention*, 1:100 (Jeremiah Morton with reference to Harrison County); Harvey M. Watterson to Andrew Johnson, Feb. 5, 1861, *Johnson Papers*, 4:203; J. C. L. Gudger to Zebulon B. Vance, Jan. 27, 1861, in Frontis W. Johnston, ed., *The Papers of Zebulon Baird Vance*, 1 vol. to date (Raleigh: North Carolina State Department of Archives and History, 1963), 90–91; H. W. Folsom to T. A. R. Nelson, Feb. 11, 1861, Nelson Papers.

27. Calvin J. Cowles to Zebulon B. Vance, Feb. 20, 1861, Calvin J. Cowles

letterbook, NCDAH; Zebulon B. Vance to C. C. Jones, Feb. 11, 1861, Zebulon B. Vance Papers, SHC-UNC; John A. Gilmer to *Raleigh Register*, Feb. 28, 1861, in *North Carolina Semi-Weekly Standard*, Mar. 20, 1861.

28. John Houston Bills Diary, Jan. 4, 8, 1861, SHC-UNC; Jordan Stokes to William B. Campbell, Jan. 15, 1861, Campbell Family Papers, Duke; *Nashville Union and American*, Jan. 8, 1861.

29. Robert Johnson to Andrew Johnson, Jan. 13, 1861, Return J. Meigs to Johnson, Feb. 7, 1861, John W. Richardson to Johnson, Feb. 8, 1861, all in *Johnson Papers*, 4:157–60, 264, 266; ibid., 178, n. 3; Campbell, *Attitude of Tennesseans*, 158–60.

30. James G. Ramsay to his wife, Jan. 9, 1861, James G. Ramsay Papers, SHC-UNC; Jonathan Worth to Charles Beatty Mallett, Dec. 19, 1860, in Charles Beatty Mallett Papers, SHC-UNC; David Schenck Diary, Feb. 1, Mar. 18, 1861, SHC-UNC; John W. Ellis, Annual Message, Nov. 1860, Ellis to Robert N. Gourdin, Dec. 17, 25, 1860, Jan. 3, 1861, Ellis to Isham W. Garrott, Jan. 30, 1861, all in Noble J. Tolbert, ed., *The Papers of John Willis Ellis*, 2 vols. (Raleigh: North Carolina State Department of Archives and History, 1964), 2:509–15, 534–35, 546–47, 551–52, 574–75; Sitterson, *Secession Movement in North Carolina*, 190.

31. John W. Ellis to Robert N. Gourdin, Dec. 17, 25, 1860, Jan. 3, 1861, all in Tolbert, ed., *Ellis Papers*, 2:534–35, 546–47, 551–52; *North Carolina Standard*, Dec. 1860 to Apr. 1861, passim.

32. Sitterson, *Secession Movement in North Carolina*, 206–8; Marc W. Kruman, *Parties and Politics in North Carolina, 1836–1865* (Baton Rouge: Louisiana State University Press, 1983), 201–7.

33. James W. Harold to Andrew Johnson, Jan. 27, 1861, William M. Lowry to Johnson, Jan. 31, 1861, John W. Richardson to Johnson, Feb. 8, 1861, Joseph H. Thompson to Johnson, Feb. 10, 1861, all in *Johnson Papers*, 4:188–92, 265–67, 269–71; Zebulon B. Vance to G. N. Folk, Jan. 9, 1861, in *Raleigh Register*, Jan. 16, 1861, reprinted in Johnston, ed., *Vance Papers*, 1:81–83; James R. Leach, public letter of Jan. 9, 1861, in *Salem People's Press*, Jan. 25, 1861; ibid., Feb. 22, 1861; Calvin J. Cowles to James R. Leach, Feb. 16, 1861, Cowles to "Bro. Andrew," Feb. 16, 1861, Cowles to Thomas F. Houston, Feb. 25, 1861, all in Cowles letterbook. Voters in Johnson's Greene County overwhelmingly rejected a convention, 2,648 to 357 (*Johnson Papers*, 4:289, n. 5).

34. *Salisbury Carolina Watchman*, Feb. 5, 26, 1861; John W. Richardson to Andrew Johnson, Feb. 8, 1861, *Johnson Papers*, 4:265–67; Jonathan Worth to his constituents in Randolph and Alamance counties, North Carolina, Feb. 1861, in J. G. deRoulhac Hamilton, ed., *The Correspondence of Jonathan Worth*, 2 vols. (Raleigh: Broughton, 1909), 1:132; W. D. Dowd, Alexander Kelly, and E. G. L. Barringer to their constituents in Moore and Montgomery counties, North Carolina, Feb. 15, 1861, circular, enclosed in pardon application of Alexander Kelly, RG 94, microfilm series M1003, NA, copy of the original in NCDAH.

35. *North Carolina Standard*, Feb. 6, 1861; *Raleigh Weekly State Journal*, Feb. 13, 1861; Sitterson, *Secession Movement in North Carolina*, 211.

36. "Introduction," *Johnson Papers*, 4:xx–xxi, xxx; John W. Richardson to Johnson, Feb. 8, 1861, Clisbe Austin to Johnson, Mar. 29, 1861, William Crutchfield to Johnson, Jan. 14, 1861, all in ibid., 265–67, 448–50, 165–67; W. C. Kyle to T. A. R. Nelson, Feb. 6, 1861, Nelson Papers.

37. Kinsey Jones, witness for Samuel Sullivan, Southern Claims Commission Records, Duplin County, North Carolina, RG 217, NA; J. C. L. Gudger to Zebulon B. Vance, Jan. 27, 1861, J. P. Eller to Vance, Jan. 28, 1861, both in Johnston, ed., *Vance Papers*, 1:90–91, 93; Calvin J. Cowles to James M. Leach, Feb. 16, 1861, Cowles letterbook; *Salem People's Press*, Feb. 22, 1861; Robert Johnson to Andrew Johnson, Jan. 13, 1861, Return J. Meigs to Johnson, Feb. 7, 1861, both in *Johnson Papers*, 4:157–60, 263–64.

38. *Nashville Republican Banner*, Mar. 5, 1861; Campbell, *Attitude of Tennesseans*, 175–79. Original county-by-county returns for the delegate vote are in the Tennessee State Library and Archives, Nashville. Analyses of the February 1861 voting returns in Virginia, Tennessee, and North Carolina appear in Chapter 7 and Appendixes I and II.

39. Sitterson, *Secession Movement in North Carolina*, 211–29; Kruman, *Parties and Politics in North Carolina*, 207–13, 273–78; *Salem People's Press*, Mar. 15, 1861; *North Carolina Semi-Weekly Standard*, Mar. 13, 1861 (letter from "H.," in Wentworth, Rockingham County, Mar. 4, 1861).

40. Neill S. Brown to Andrew Johnson, Feb. 17, 1861, *Johnson Papers*, 4:300–302; Robert Hatton to William B. Campbell, Feb. 16, 1861, Campbell Papers; E. A. Millard to T. A. R. Nelson, Feb. 17, 1861, Nelson Papers.

41. *Richmond Whig*, Feb. 4, 8, 1861; *Richmond Dispatch*, Feb. 11, 1861; *Lynchburg Virginian*, Feb. 6, 1861; James Barbour to Seward, Feb. 8, 1861, Seward Papers, in Frederic Bancroft, *The Life of William H. Seward*, 2 vols. (New York: Harper & Bros., 1899–1900), 2:534–36; E. A. Millard to T. A. R. Nelson, Feb. 17, 1861, Nelson Papers. Barbour, who had conferred secretly with Seward and devised the Peace Conference stratagem, represented a high-slaveowning region of the Virginia piedmont.

42. Charles Francis Adams, Jr., to Charles Francis Adams, Feb. 6, 1861, Adams Papers; Stevens quoted in *Richmond Dispatch*, Feb. 9, 1861; *New York Tribune*, Feb. 23, 1861 (report from Richmond dated Feb. 19, 1861).

43. John D. Imboden to Greenlee Davidson, Feb. 15, 1861, Davidson Papers, copy in Phillips Papers; W. J. Yates to Lawrence O'B. Branch, Feb. 26, 1861, Branch Papers; Thomas Bragg Diary, Mar. 1, 1861, SHC-UNC; *Nashville Republican Banner*, Feb. 15, 1861.

44. "A Democrat," *North Carolina Semi-Weekly Standard*, Apr. 17, 1861; Quentin Busbee to Stephen A. Douglas, Mar. 11, 1861, Hamilton Jones to Douglas, Mar. 10, 1861, John A. Gilmer to Douglas, Mar. 8, 10, 1861, all in Douglas Papers; J. W. Steed to E. J. Hale and Sons, in *Fayetteville Observer*, Apr. 15, 1861.

45. George B. Moffett to John D. Imboden, Jan. 25, 1861, John D. Imboden Papers, UVA; Imboden to John S. McCue, Dec. 3, 1860, McCue Family Papers, UVA; John B. Floyd to "My dear Sir," Feb. 7, 1861, Burwell Family Papers, UVA; Richard I. Cocke to Charles Ellis, Apr. 6, 1861, Munford-Ellis Papers, Duke; Nichols, *Disruption of American Democracy*, 343, 349–50. See

also Kenneth Rayner to Thomas Ruffin, Feb. 24, Mar. 6, Dec. 25, 1860, in Hamilton, ed., *Ruffin Papers*, 3:70–72, 108–9.

46. Caroline Pettigrew to J. Johnston Pettigrew, Feb. 23, 1861, William S. Pettigrew to James C. Johnston, Mar. 12, 1861, memorandum in William S. Pettigrew's handwriting, Mar. 1861, all in Pettigrew Family Papers, SHC-UNC.

47. *Memphis Appeal*, Jan. 22, Apr. 1, 1861; letter from Congressman William T. Avery, in ibid., Mar. 27, 1861; Campbell, *Attitude of Tennesseans*, 172, 174–75.

48. *Memphis Appeal*, Jan. 22, Feb. 10, 13, 15, Mar. 12, 1861; *Memphis Avalanche*, Jan. 25, Feb. 11, 1861; *Tuscumbia* (Ala.) *Constitution* and *Hernando* (Miss.) *Press*, in *Memphis Avalanche*, Feb. 15, 1861.

49. Kruman, *Parties and Politics in North Carolina*, astutely analyzes the effects of a persistently competitive two-party system in antebellum North Carolina. Michael F. Holt, *The Political Crisis of the 1850s* (New York: Wiley, 1978), 219–59, demonstrates the applicability of Kruman's findings elsewhere in the upper South. On the Republican antiaristocratic ethos, see ibid., 183–99; Ronald P. Formisano, *The Birth of Mass Political Parties: Michigan, 1827–1861* (Princeton: Princeton University Press, 1971), 325–31.

50. Kenneth Rayner to Thomas Ruffin, Dec. 25, 1860, Hamilton, ed., *Ruffin Papers*, 3:108–9.

51. *North Carolina Semi-Weekly Standard*, Mar. 9, 13, 16, 1861.

52. Andrew Johnson to Sam Milligan, Jan. 13, 1861, Johnson to John Trimble, Jan. 13, 1861, both in *Johnson Papers*, 4:160–65.

53. R. W. Whittington to Andrew Johnson, Feb. 18, 1861, Andrew Johnson Papers, LC (microfilm edition); William Crutchfield to Johnson, Jan. 14, 1861, *Johnson Papers*, 4:165–67; William S. Speer to Johnson, Feb. 17, 1861, William E. Penn to Johnson, Feb. 18, 1861, both in the Johnson Papers. Penn's prognosis was correct for his home area, if not for all of West Tennessee. A Union Whig stronghold before the war, Henderson County supplied many soldiers for the Union army and became dependably Republican after the war ended.

54. "Introduction," *Johnson Papers*, 4:xxx, xxxiv–xxxv; Joseph C. McDannel to Johnson, Dec. 29, 1860, ibid., 102–3; *Brownlow's Weekly Knoxville Whig*, Jan. 12, 19, 1861, *Nashville Democrat*, in ibid., Feb. 2, 1861; *Daily Knoxville Whig*, Jan. 19, 28, 1861; Campbell, *Attitude of Tennesseans*, 174–75.

55. *Wheeling Daily Intelligencer*, Dec. 28, 1860, in Perkins, ed., *Northern Editorials*, 2:895–98.

56. "Old Dominion," in *Clarksburg Guard*, quoted in *Wheeling Daily Intelligencer*, Jan. 16, 1861; *Wheeling Daily Intelligencer*, Dec. 28, 1860, in Perkins, ed., *Northern Editorials*, 2:895–98; Richard O. Curry, *A House Divided: Statehood Politics and the Copperhead Movement in West Virginia* (Pittsburgh: University of Pittsburgh Press, 1964), 21–34. The quarter of a million residents of the trans-Allegheny included only 6,448 slaves, fewer than 2.5 percent of the region's population and only 1.3 percent of the slave population in Virginia (ibid., 147–48).

57. *Wellsburg Herald*, Apr. 1, May 6, 1859; Shanks, *Secession Movement in*

Virginia, 56–62; William S. Hitchcock, "The Limits of Southern Unionism: Virginia Conservatives and the Gubernatorial Election of 1859," *Journal of Southern History* 47 (Feb. 1981): 57–72; *Wheeling Daily Intelligencer*, Dec. 28, 1860, in Perkins, ed., *Northern Editorials*, 2:895–98.

58. Reese, ed., *Virginia Convention*, 1:370; "Bell-Everett," in *Wheeling Daily Intelligencer*, Jan. 22, 1861.

59. *National Intelligencer*, Dec. 31, 1860; letter from Daniel Haymond, Jan. 5, 1861, in ibid., Jan. 12, 1861.

60. *Wheeling Daily Intelligencer*, Feb. 18, Mar. 23, 1861.

61. Reese, ed., *Virginia Convention*, 1:767. See Francis P. Gaines, Jr., "The Virginia Constitutional Convention of 1850–51: A Study in Sectionalism" (Ph.D. dissertation, University of Virginia, 1950).

62. Reese, ed., *Virginia Convention*, 2:15; Waitman T. Willey to Francis H. Pierpont, Mar. 26, 1861, Waitman T. Willey Papers, University of West Virginia.

63. Henry Dering to Waitman T. Willey, Mar. 26, 1861, Willey Papers; Reese, ed., *Virginia Convention*, 2:127, 3:525–28.

64. Henry Dering to Waitman T. Willey, Mar. 26, 1861, Willey Papers; Reese, ed., *Virginia Convention*, 3:525–28; *Morgantown Star*, Jan. 12, 1861, in *Wheeling Daily Intelligencer*, Jan. 14, 1861, and *National Intelligencer*, Jan. 15, 1861; "Democrat," *Wellsburg Herald*, in *Wheeling Daily Intelligencer*, Jan. 19, 1861.

65. Henry Dering to Waitman T. Willey, Mar. 19, 1861, see also Dering to Willey, Mar. 26, 1861, Willey Papers.

CHAPTER 7

1. I am indebted to Professor Dale Baum of Texas A&M University for giving an earlier version of this chapter a close, critical reading. Baum also offered helpful suggestions about material appearing in the Appendixes.

Professor Paul Escott of the University of North Carolina at Charlotte provided a reassuring evaluation after I rewrote this chapter and the Appendixes.

Professor Lee Benson of the University of Pennsylvania prodded me to think more carefully about making quantitative historical writing accessible to the general reader. Although Benson and I do not agree about some of the statistical techniques employed here, this chapter has benefited from his counsel.

2. A generous subvention from Trenton State College enabled me to purchase the basic core of county-level data used in this study from the Inter-University Consortium for Political and Social Research (ICPSR), Ann Arbor, Michigan. Calculations using the Statistical Package for the Social Sciences (SPSS or SPSS-X) were performed at the Princeton University Computer Center and through the New Jersey Educational Computer Network (NJECN).

Demographic and socioeconomic data from the 1850 and 1860 censuses, plus election returns for all congressional, gubernatorial, and presidential elections between 1848 and 1860, had to be reorganized into symmetrical county units, so as to overcome irregularities created by county subdivisions. The total number of county units in this study falls somewhat short of the actual number of counties in each state by 1860 because the county units necessarily are defined by the boundaries of the 1848–50 period. In almost all instances, happily, the result is simply to keep together segments that divided during the 1850s.

The ICPSR does not, however, hold information about the special secession elections of 1861. For Virginia, the measurement of Union strength used here was the vote for "reference" (see Reese, ed., *Virginia Convention*, 1:792–96). Missing returns from eight counties were calculated or estimated from a variety of sources. Most data on North Carolina used in this study were compiled by Marc W. Kruman, who has a special grasp of North Carolina antebellum politics. His findings are summarized in *Parties and Politics in North Carolina, 1836–1865* (Baton Rouge: Louisiana State University Press, 1983), Appendix B, 273–78. Kruman also made a county-by-county estimate of Union and secession strength by evaluating patterns of voting both for delegates and for and against a convention. Estimates are included here for several counties that Kruman judged too contradictory to analyze.

County-level data about Tennessee voting for or against a convention in February 1861 and for or against separation in June 1861 are printed in Campbell, *Attitude of Tennesseans*, 288–94. Though voting returns for delegates in February 1861 were never officially compiled, reports from most counties are filed at the TSLA. That information is combined here with evidence from many different newspapers and manuscripts to create a county-by-county figure for Union and secession strength, comparable to Kruman's work for North Carolina. The pro-Union majority in February may thus be estimated at 99,150 to 30,586.

Published returns in newspapers and in the Campbell book for the June 1861 election were distorted by the sudden concentration of Confederate soldiers in several Middle and West Tennessee counties near the Kentucky border. Thus Sumner County, which normally cast 2,500 votes, showed 6,500 voters in June 1861 because Camp Trousdale produced a prosecession majority of 3,885 to 2 (see *Clarksville Jeffersonian*, June 12, 1861). To correct this problem, all votes from military camps in June 1861 were distributed in proportion to the civilian prosecession vote. A county that cast 1 percent of the statewide prosecession vote in June 1861 would thus also be credited with 1 percent of the approximately 12,500 prosecession votes from Confederate military camps.

3. The correlation coefficients (*r*) displayed in Tables 2-2 through 2-6 will, if squared, reveal the coefficients of determination (R^2). R^2 is a measurement of the explanatory value of the independent variable.

Correlation coefficients of .9, for example, produce R^2 values of .81, and correlation coefficients of .2 produce R^2 values of .04. Correlations of .9 would make it possible to predict, or account for, 81 percent of the county-by-county variation in Whig voting at a second election on the basis of what was known about the pattern of Whig voting in the first election. Unless Whig voting had uniformly declined or increased in all counties of a state, high coefficients of determination (R^2) would suggest that most Whig voters in the first election continued to vote Whig in the second election and that relatively few other voters had voted Whig in the second election. Correlations of .2 would account for only 4 percent of the variation between two elections. If a pair of elections exhibits low coefficients of determination (R^2), voting patterns must have changed significantly.

4. Kruman, *Parties and Politics in North Carolina*, 46–50; Ralph A. Wooster, *Politicians, Planters, and Plain Folk: Courthouse and Statehouse in the Upper South, 1850–1860* (Knoxville: University of Tennessee Press, 1975), 35–42.

5. Supplementary estimates, separating North Carolina into regions of high, medium, and low slaveowning, suggest that a majority of nonslaveowners who voted in the high-slaveowning (and typically high-Democratic) areas favored secession. But nonslaveholders voted by an estimated three-to-two majority against secession in the medium-slaveholding areas and three to one against it in the low-slaveholding areas.

6. John C. Inscoe, "Slavery, Sectionalism, and Secession in Western North Carolina" (Ph.D. dissertation, University of North Carolina at Chapel Hill, 1985).

7. The differing degrees of nonslaveowners' support for secession in Virginia and North Carolina may also to some extent reflect the discrepancies between the measurements of Union and secession voting employed here. In Virginia, a vote against "reference" was the most meaningful statewide indication of antisecession sentiment. In much of Virginia west of the Blue Ridge, convention candidates divided mainly on the question of unconditional or conditional Union, with all favoring reference. In eastern Virginia, conditional Unionists favoring reference typically opposed secessionists who were against it. Little purpose is served by trying to add the votes won by conditional Unionists in the west to those won by secessionists in the east. Indeed, some conditional Union candidates in the west were less conditional than avowed Unionists in the east. In North Carolina, by contrast, the measurement of Union sentiment is based for the most part on a county-by-county evaluation made by Marc Kruman. His formula used the voting for delegates whenever it appeared to represent more accurately the division between Union and secession sentiment than did the vote for or against a convention. It is probable that some nonslaveowning North Carolina Democrats, who in Virginia might have voted for reference, felt obliged to vote for the local Democratic candidate for the state convention, even though that person took a tough Southern Rights position.

8. In Middle Tennessee, Democrats substantially outnumbered Whigs (44 to 35 percent of the eligible electorate in the 1860 presidential vote), but a large majority of slaveowners were Whigs (estimates suggest approximately 70 percent). Jacksonian hill counties of Middle Tennessee's Highland Rim surrounded Whig-majority citadels in the fertile slaveowning lowlands of the Cumberland Valley.

9. On the phenomenon of party realignment, see V. O. Key, Jr., "A Theory of Critical Elections," *Journal of Politics* 17 (1955): 3–18; Walter Dean Burnham, *Critical Elections and the Mainsprings of American Politics* (New York: Norton, 1970); James L. Sundquist, *Dynamics of the Party System: Alignment and Realignment of Political Parties in the United States*, rev. ed. (Washington, D.C.: Brookings Institution, 1983). On the striking and durable relationship between low levels of slaveowning, opposition to secession, and postwar Republicanism in Tennessee, see V. O. Key, Jr., *Southern Politics in State and Nation* (New York: Knopf, 1949), 75–78.

10. Appendix III compares the findings of this book with other quantified studies of secession and explores further the great differences between voting behavior in the upper South and the lower South during the secession crisis.

CHAPTER 8

1. Roy Franklin Nichols, *The Disruption of American Democracy* (New York: Macmillan, 1948), 414–16; David M. Potter, *Lincoln and His Party in the Secession Crisis* (New Haven: Yale University Press, 1942), 170–76; Don E. Fehrenbacher, *The Dred Scott Case: Its Significance in American Law and Politics* (New York: Oxford University Press, 1978), 544–50.

2. Kenneth M. Stampp, *And the War Came: The North and the Secession Crisis, 1860–61* (Baton Rouge: Louisiana State University Press, 1950), 83–103; Nichols, *Disruption of American Democracy*, 433–52; Philip S. Klein, *President James Buchanan* (University Park, Pa.: Pennsylvania State University Press, 1962), 354–95.

3. *CG*, 36:2, 112–14, 264–67; Albert D. Kirwan, *John J. Crittenden: The Struggle for the Union* (Lexington: University of Kentucky Press, 1962), 374–406; Potter, *Lincoln and His Party*, 101–11; Fehrenbacher, *Dred Scott Case*, 544–50, quotations on 545.

4. Robert W. Johannsen, *Stephen A. Douglas* (New York: Oxford University Press, 1973), 814–39; John A. Gilmer to Thurlow Weed, Jan. 12, 1861, Thurlow Weed Papers, University of Rochester.

5. *CG*, 36:2, A107, A137, A166–67.

6. *CG*, 36:2, A198–99, A167; John A. Gilmer to Thurlow Weed, Jan. 12, 1861, Weed Papers.

7. Shanks, *Secession Movement in Virginia*, 145–46; Sitterson, *Secession Movement in North Carolina*, 209; *Nashville Republican Banner*, Jan. 25, 1861, in Dumond, ed., *Southern Editorials*, 413–14.

8. Henry Winter Davis to Samuel F. Du Pont, undated letter (late Jan. or early Feb. 1861), Feb. 14, 1861, transcriptions, both in Samuel F. Du Pont Papers, Eleutherian Mills Historical Library, Greenville, Del.; *CG*, 36:2, A183; *Wheeling Intelligencer*, Jan. 15, 1861.

9. *CG*, 36:2, A153, A107; Neill S. Brown to Andrew Johnson, Feb. 17, 1861, *Johnson Papers*, 4:300–302.

10. Chittenden, *Report*, 428; *CWAL*, 4:200–201 (fragment of speech intended for Kentuckians, Feb. 1861).

11. Stampp, *And the War Came*, 136–58; Fehrenbacher, *Dred Scott Case*, 544–50; Potter, *Lincoln and His Party*, 219–23.

12. *CG*, 36:2, A107–8.

13. *CG*, 36:2, 279–82.

14. *Philadelphia North American*, Jan. 7, 1861 ("Independent"—James E. Harvey—Jan. 6, 1861); Robert Hatton to William B. Campbell, Jan. 24, 31, 1861, Campbell Family Papers, Duke.

15. Patrick M. Sowle, "The Conciliatory Republicans during the Winter of Secession" (Ph.D. dissertation, Duke University, 1963), 194–253; Norman A. Graebner, "Thomas Corwin and the Sectional Crisis," *Ohio History* 86 (Autumn 1977): 229–47; R. Alton Lee, "The Corwin Amendment in the Secession Crisis," *Ohio Historical Quarterly* 70 (Jan. 1961): 1–26.

16. *CG*, 36:2, A171, A104, A108.

17. *CG*, 36:2, 581; Robert Hatton to William B. Campbell, Jan. 24, 31, 1861, Campbell Papers.

18. *New York Times*, Jan. 16, 1861; Kirwan, *Crittenden*, 404; Johannsen, *Douglas*, 827–29; Frederic Bancroft, *The Life of William H. Seward*, 2 vols. (New York: Harper & Brothers, 1899–1900), 2:22; Potter, *Lincoln and His Party*, 303–6; Thomas Fitnam to James Buchanan, Jan. 25, 1861, James Buchanan Papers, HSP; "A Table Talk with Seward," clipping from the *Philadelphia Times*, scrapbook I, Alexander R. Boteler Papers, Duke.

19. John A. Gilmer to Jesse J. Yeates, Jan. 22, 1861, in *OR*, I:51:2, p. 7; *Louisville Journal*, Jan. 23, 29, 31, 1861 ("L. A. W.," Jan. 19, 26, 28, 1861); *New York Tribune*, Jan. 29, 1861; James Ford Rhodes, *History of the United States from the Compromise of 1850 to the Final Restoration of Home Rule at the South in 1877*, 7 vols. (New York: Macmillan, 1893–1906), 3:288; Elizabeth Blair Lee to Samuel Phillips Lee, Jan. 24, 1861, Blair-Lee Papers, Princeton University, in Virginia Jeans Laas, "'On the Qui Vive for the long letter': Washington Letters from a Navy Wife, 1861," *Civil War History* 29 (Mar. 1983): 42; Moses H. Grinnell to Seward, Jan. 28, 1861, William H. Seward Papers, University of Rochester; James A. Hamilton et al. to Lincoln, Jan. 29, 1861, Abraham Lincoln Papers, LC (microfilm edition); Philip S. Foner, *Business and Slavery: The New York Merchants and the Irrepressible Conflict* (Chapel Hill: University of North Carolina Press, 1941), 248–60.

20. *New York Times*, Jan. 25, 1861; *Boston Advertiser*, Jan. 31, 1861; *Philadelphia North American*, Jan. 24, 26, 29, 1861 ("Independent"—James E. Harvey—Jan. 23, 25, 28, 1861); *National Intelligencer*, Feb. 4, 1861; *Baltimore Clipper*, quoted in *Salisbury* (N.C.) *Carolina Watchman*, Feb. 5, 1861; Seward to Lincoln, Jan. 27, 1861, Lincoln Papers, in John G. Nicolay and John Hay, *Abraham Lincoln: A History*, 10 vols. (New York: Century, 1890), 3:365.

21. *CG*, 36:2, 690–91; Hatton to William B. Campbell, Jan. 24, 31, 1861, Campbell Papers.

22. Alexander Rives to William C. Rives, Jr., Feb. 11, 1861, William C. Rives Papers, LC; John Letcher to James D. Davidson, Feb. 11, 1861, John

Letcher Papers, Lexington, Va. (privately held), quoted in F. N. Boney, *John Letcher of Virginia: The Story of Virginia's Civil War Governor* (University, Ala.: University of Alabama Press, 1966), 104; Zebulon B. Vance to C. C. Jones, Feb. 11, 1861, Zebulon B. Vance Papers, SHC-UNC.

23. Two invaluable sources illuminate the history of the Peace Conference. A Vermont delegate, Lucius E. Chittenden, the self-styled James Madison of the Peace Conference, preserved and later published full notes on its secret proceedings (Chittenden, *Report*, esp. 3–8). A splendidly researched modern monograph on the Peace Conference supplements Chittenden's *Report*: Robert Gray Gunderson, *Old Gentlemen's Convention: The Washington Peace Conference of 1861* (Madison: University of Wisconsin Press, 1961).

24. *Louisville Journal*, Feb. 4, 11, 1861 ("L. A. W.," Jan. 31, Feb. 7, 1861); W. N. H. Smith to Thomas Ruffin, Feb. 20, 1861, in J. G. deRoulhac Hamilton, ed., *The Papers of Thomas Ruffin*, 4 vols. (Raleigh: Edwards and Broughton, 1918–20), 3:131–32. Corwin ended up trying to get approval for his own approach in late February. He specified on February 20 that he could wait no longer than several days, but it took the Peace Conference another week to agree. Corwin may also have decided that the prospective terms of the Peace Conference settlement could not gain enough Republican support to pass (Sowle, "Conciliatory Republicans," 374–75, 429–32).

25. Alexander Rives to William C. Rives, Feb. 17, 20, 1861, Rives papers.

26. Chittenden, *Report*, 21–23; Gunderson, *Old Gentlemen's Convention*, 49–50; *CG*, 36:2, 862–65; Kirwan, *Crittenden*, 406; *Louisville Journal*, Feb. 16, 1861 ("L. A. W.," Feb. 13, 1861).

27. Gunderson, *Old Gentlemen's Convention*, 62, 86; Chittenden, *Report*, 43–45, 291, 336.

28. Alexander Rives to William C. Rives, Jr., Feb. 11, 1861, Rives Papers; Gunderson, *Old Gentlemen's Convention*, 26, 40–41. The central role of southern Unionists at the convention is explored in two essays: Robert Gray Gunderson, "William C. Rives and the 'Old Gentlemen's Convention,'" *Journal of Southern History* 22 (1956): 459–76; Patrick Sowle, "The Trials of a Virginia Unionist: William Cabell Rives and the Secession Crisis, 1860–1861," *Virginia Magazine of History and Biography* 80 (Jan. 1972): 3–20.

29. Alexander Rives to William C. Rives, Feb. 17, 1861, James Barbour to Rives, Feb. 18, 1861, both in Rives Papers.

30. Chittenden, *Report*, 135, 151–54.

31. Ibid., 292–93, 294–95, 320–21.

32. Ibid., 293, 295, 127, 296–97, 436, 304–5, 138, 152–53.

33. Ibid., 126–27, 421, vote on 298. Two subsequent votes on the Crittenden Compromise won the support of Kentucky and, in one instance, Tennessee (ibid., 418–24). Each state had one vote, as at the Constitutional Convention of 1787. A majority of members in each state's delegation determined the vote of the stage. Virginia Unionists William C. Rives and George W. Summers could thus be outvoted by the Southern Rights trio of James A. Seddon, John Tyler, and John W. Brockenbrough (Gunderson, *Old Gentlemen's Convention*, 46–48).

34. Chittenden, *Report*, 298–99.

35. Ibid., 298–99, 304–8, vote on 322. On Logan, see Gunderson, *Old Gentlemen's Convention*, 12, 35, 142 (n. 40).

36. Gunderson, *Old Gentlemen's Convention*, 86–90; Chittenden, *Report*, 437–42.

37. Gunderson, *Old Gentlemen's Convention*, 93–102; telegrams from John A. Gilmer and John M. Morehead, Feb. 27, 1861, in *Raleigh Semi-Weekly Register*, Mar. 2, 1861, reprinted from "extra" edition of Feb. 28, 1861.

38. *Richmond Semi-Weekly Enquirer*, Mar. 2, 5, 1861; Reese, ed., *Virginia Convention*, 1:265, 336, 347.

39. Quotations in this and the next paragraph are drawn from Zebulon B. Vance to C. C. Jones, Feb. 11, 1861, Zebulon B. Vance Papers, SHC-UNC; W. W. Lenoir to Zebulon B. Vance, Feb. 5, 1861, Zebulon B. Vance Papers, NCDAH, in Frontis W. Johnston, ed., *The Papers of Zebulon Baird Vance*, 1 vol. to date (Raleigh: North Carolina State Department of Archives and History, 1963), 97–98; A. Waldo Putnam to Andrew Johnson, Feb. 14, 18, 1861, Andrew Johnson Papers, LC (microfilm edition), the latter printed in *Johnson Papers*, 4:310–12.

CHAPTER 9

1. Lincoln to Lyman Trumbull, Dec. 10, 1860, Lincoln to William Kellogg, Dec. 11, 1860, Lincoln to Elihu B. Washburne, Dec. 13, 1860, Lincoln to John A. Gilmer, Dec. 15, 1860, all in *CWAL*, 4:149–53.

Anyone who writes about the Republican party during the secession winter will find his way illuminated by three fine studies: David M. Potter, *Lincoln and His Party in the Secession Crisis* (New Haven: Yale University Press, 1942); Kenneth M. Stampp, *And the War Came: The North and the Secession Crisis, 1860–61* (Baton Rouge: Louisiana State University Press, 1950); and Patrick M. Sowle, "The Conciliatory Republicans during the Winter of Secession" (Ph.D. dissertation, Duke University, 1963), which has never received the recognition it deserves.

Stampp, who celebrated the role of hard-line, no-compromise Republicans, concluded that conciliators such as William H. Seward displayed "incredible blindness" in believing the Union could be peacefully restored (*And the War Came*, 272). In my judgment, Stampp projected backward from the undoubted outpouring of northern patriotic unanimity, once the war had started in April, to assume that northerners were equally hostile to a Union-saving compromise in late January and February. Sowle ("Conciliatory Republicans," 303–26, 345–66) has convincingly challenged Stampp.

Potter gave fuller and more sympathetic attention than Stampp to the conciliatory Republicans. But in contending that Lincoln and Seward worked together to achieve peaceful reunion, Potter understated the differences in Republican thinking about southern policy. Sowle has shrewdly observed: "Potter interprets the secession winter not as a period of bitter feuding between two Republican factions, but as a time in which Lincoln rallied the party behind his ideas about the crisis. . . . Seward is considered not Lincoln's rival, but his Washington agent" ("Conciliatory Republicans," 511–12).

Sowle's dissertation, which made use of important manuscript collections unavailable to Potter—in particular, the papers of Lincoln, Seward, Thurlow Weed, and Charles Francis Adams—provides the best available analysis of the intraparty struggle over southern policy between conciliatory and uncompromising Republicans. See also Richard N. Current, *Lincoln and the First Shot* (Philadelphia: J. B. Lippincott, 1963), esp. 198–99, which criticizes Potter along the same lines as Sowle. For a more thorough analysis of relevant secession crisis historiography, see Daniel W. Crofts, "Secession Winter: William Henry Seward and the Decision for War," *New York History* 65 (July 1984): 229–56, esp. 230–37.

2. Potter, *Lincoln and His Party*, 1–19, 76–80.

3. For an understanding of Seward's political career, the standard modern biography, Glyndon G. Van Deusen's *William Henry Seward* (New York: Oxford University Press, 1967), does not supplant the earlier study by Frederic Bancroft, *The Life of William H. Seward*, 2 vols. (New York: Harper & Brothers, 1899–1900). See also Frederick W. Seward, *Seward at Washington, as Senator and Secretary of State: A Memoir of His Life, with Selections from His Letters*, 2 vols. (New York: Derby and Miller, 1891); Walter G. Sharrow, "William Henry Seward: A Study in Nineteenth Century Politics and Nationalism, 1855–1861" (Ph.D. dissertation, University of Rochester, 1965); Major L. Wilson, "The Repressible Conflict: Seward's Concept of Progress and the Free Soil Movement," *Journal of Southern History* 37 (Nov. 1971): 534–56, in Wilson, *Space, Time, and Freedom: The Quest for Nationality and the Irrepressible Conflict* (Westport, Conn.: Greenwood Press, 1974), 211–37. My own essay, "Secession Winter," synthesizes and updates the findings of Bancroft, Potter, and Sowle on Seward's role in the secession crisis.

4. On the cabinet offer to Seward, see Lincoln to Lyman Trumbull, Dec. 8, 1860, Lincoln to Seward, Dec. 8, 1860, *CWAL*, 4:148–49; Harry Draper Hunt, *Hannibal Hamlin of Maine: Lincoln's First Vice-President* (Syracuse: Syracuse University Press, 1969), 128–32.

5. Charles Francis Adams, Jr., to Richard H. Dana, Jr., Feb. 28, 1861, Richard H. Dana, Jr., Papers, MHS; Henry Adams, "The Great Secession Winter of 1860–61," *Proceedings of the Massachusetts Historical Society* 43 (1910): 659, 678, 685; Van Deusen, *Seward*, 7, 255–59; Bancroft, *Seward*, 1:184, 189–93, 2:77–85.

6. *Lynchburg Virginian*, Sept. 10, 1860; Bancroft, *Seward*, 1:545–53.

7. Glyndon G. Van Deusen, *Thurlow Weed: Wizard of the Lobby* (Boston: Little, Brown, 1947), 213, 239–41; William E. Gienapp, *The Origins of the Republican Party, 1852–1856* (New York: Oxford University Press, 1987), 151–52.

8. Seward to Weed, Nov. 15, 1860, telegram, Thurlow Weed Papers, University of Rochester; *Albany Evening Journal*, Nov. 19, 30, Dec. 1, 17, 1860; *CG*, 36:2, 658; Sowle, "Conciliatory Republicans," 18–19.

9. Bancroft, *Seward*, 2:26–30; Potter, *Lincoln and His Party*, 65–74, 81–88;

Sowle, "Conciliatory Republicans," 18–21, 34–36, 58–59, 164–68; *CG*, 36:2, 657–58.

10. Seward to his wife, Jan. 18, 1861, in Seward, *Seward*, 2:497; Henry Adams to Charles Francis Adams, Jr., Dec. 9, 1860, Jan. 26, 1861, Adams Family Papers, MHS (microfilm edition), in J. C. Levenson et al., eds., *The Letters of Henry Adams*, 3 vols. (Cambridge, Mass.: Belknap Press of Harvard University Press, 1982), 1:204–5, 225; Bancroft, *Seward*, 2:37.

11. *Philadelphia North American and United States Gazette*, Nov. 13, 29, Dec. 4, 6, 8, 1860, Jan. 7, 1861 (all of Harvey's columns in the *North American* ran under the byline "Independent"); James E. Harvey to Lincoln, Nov. 8, 29, Dec. 5, 1860, Lincoln Papers, LC (microfilm edition); James E. Harvey to Thurlow Weed, Dec. 9, 24, 1860, Weed Papers. Harvey was also a part-time correspondent for the *New York Tribune*, though he obviously did not share Horace Greeley's view of the secession crisis. Fuller discussion of Harvey's role may be found in Daniel W. Crofts, "James E. Harvey and the Secession Crisis," *Pennsylvania Magazine of History and Biography* 103 (Apr. 1979): 177–95.

12. *Philadelphia North American*, Jan. 7, 1861; James E. Harvey to Henry C. Carey, Dec. 14, 1860, Henry C. Carey Papers in the Edward Carey Gardiner Collection, HSP.

13. *Albany Evening Journal*, Jan. 9, 17, 28, Feb. 2, 1861; Potter, *Lincoln and His Party*, 280–85, 295–96.

14. Thurlow Weed Barnes, *Memoir of Thurlow Weed* (Boston: Houghton Mifflin, 1884), 301–2; Seward to Lincoln, Dec. 16, 1860, in Seward, *Seward*, 2:482; Seward to Lincoln, Dec. 25, 1860, Abraham Lincoln Papers, LC; Charles Francis Adams, diary entry of Dec. 27, 1860, Adams Papers; Sowle, "Conciliatory Republicans," 168–70; Potter, *Lincoln and His Party*, 164–65.

15. *Albany Evening Journal*, Dec. 17, 1860; Harriet A. Weed, ed., *Autobiography of Thurlow Weed* (Boston: Houghton Mifflin, 1883), 603–4; Sowle, "Conciliatory Republicans," 170–71; Potter, *Lincoln and His Party*, 165–67.

16. Weed, ed., *Autobiography*, 602–14. Weed's account of the meeting was corroborated by Leonard Swett, who was also present. See Barnes, *Memoir of Weed*, 291–95; Leonard Swett to the editor of the *Chicago Tribune*, July 13, 1878, in *Chicago Tribune*, July 14, 1878, photocopy in Dec. 1860 file of David Davis Papers, Chicago Historical Society.

17. Editorial in *Illinois State Journal* (written by Lincoln), Dec. 12, 1860, Lincoln to John D. Defrees, Dec. 18, 1860, Lincoln to Seward, Dec. 29, 1860, Jan. 12, 1861, all in *CWAL*, 4:150, 155, 164, 173; Weed, ed., *Autobiography*, 611; Weed to the editor of the *New York Tribune*, June 25, 1878, in *Chicago Tribune*, July 8, 1878, photocopy in the Dec. 1860 file of the David Davis Papers. This chapter incorporates many parts of my article "A Reluctant Unionist: John A. Gilmer and Lincoln's Cabinet," *Civil War History* 24 (Sept. 1978): 225–49.

18. The best source on the Greensboro region during the 1840s and 1850s is the local newspaper, the *Greensboro Patriot*. For comments on railroads, see Jan. 2, 1847, Jan. 26, Mar. 9, Aug. 24, 1850, Mar. 8, June 24, July 12, 19, 1851; see also Cecil K. Brown, *A State Movement in Railroad Develop-*

ment: The Story of North Carolina's Efforts to Establish an East and West Trunk Line Railroad (Chapel Hill: University of North Carolina Press, 1928). On mining see Hugh Waddell to William A. Graham, June 10, Dec. 27, 1851, in J. G. deRoulhac Hamilton and Max R. Williams, eds., *The Papers of William Alexander Graham*, 7 vols. to date (Raleigh: North Carolina State Department of Archives and History, 1957–), 4:117, 227–28; *Greensboro Patriot*, Feb. 10, Mar. 10, 1855, May 2, 1856, Jan. 23, 1857, May 13, 1859. For a well-annotated overview of North Carolina Whig politics, see Max R. Williams, "The Foundations of the Whig Party in North Carolina: A Synthesis and a Modest Proposal," *North Carolina Historical Review* 47 (Spring 1970): 115–29. See also a historically sensitive account of race relations in modern Greensboro: William H. Chafe, *Civilities and Civil Rights: Greensboro, North Carolina, and the Black Struggle for Freedom* (New York: Oxford University Press, 1980).

19. Three biographical sketches of Gilmer are of particular value: John Livingston, *Portraits of Eminent Americans Now Living: With Biographical and Historical Memoirs of Their Lives and Actions*, 4 vols. (New York: Cornish, Lamport, 1853–54), 1:342–56; Gerald W. Johnson, "John Adams Gilmer, 1805–1868," in Bettie D. Caldwell, ed., *Founders and Builders of Greensboro, 1808–1908* (Greensboro: J. J. Stone, 1925), 94–102; J. G. deRoulhac Hamilton, "John Adams Gilmer," *DAB*, 7:307–8. Quotations in this and the following paragraph are from Livingston.

20. On ties between North Carolina and Pennsylvania Whigs, see *Greensboro Patriot*, Feb. 3, 1860; Kenneth Rayner to Henry C. Carey, Dec. 14, 1856, Oct. 14, 26, 1858, Rayner to William D. Lewis, Apr. 27, 1859, all in Carey Papers.

21. Lincoln to Seward, Dec. 29, 1860, Jan. 12, 1861, *CWAL*, 4:164, 173. For Gilmer's position on Lecompton, see Gilmer to William A. Graham, Feb. 23, 1858, Graham Papers, NCDAH, in Hamilton and Williams, eds., *Graham Papers*, 5:37–39; *CG*, 35:1, A282–85, 1698–1702, A401–4, A452–58.

22. Gilmer to Lincoln, Dec. 10, 1860, Lincoln Papers, in David Mearns, ed., *The Lincoln Papers: The Story of the Collection with Selections to July 4, 1861*, 2 vols. (Garden City, N.Y.: Country Life Press, 1948), 1:330–32. See also Thomas Corwin to Lincoln, Dec. 11, 1860, Lincoln Papers.

23. Thomas Corwin to Lincoln, Oct. 28, Nov. 4, 1860, Nathan Sargent to Lincoln, Dec. 12, 1860, Lincoln Papers; Potter, *Lincoln and His Party*, 134–38; Norman A. Graebner, "Thomas Corwin and the Sectional Crisis," *Ohio History* 86 (Autumn 1977): 232–33.

24. Lincoln to William S. Speer, Oct. 23, 1860, Lincoln to George T. M. Davis, Oct. 27, 1860, Lincoln to George D. Prentice, Oct. 29, 1860, Lincoln to Truman Smith, Nov. 10, 1860, Lincoln to Nathaniel P. Paschall, Nov. 16, 1860, Lincoln to Henry J. Raymond, Nov. 28, 1860, Lincoln to John A. Gilmer, Dec. 15, 1860, all in *CWAL*, 4:130, 132–33, 134–35, 138–40, 145–46, 151–53.

25. Lincoln to Stephens, Dec. 22, 1860, *CWAL*, 4:160. Lincoln prepared a similar private response to Gilmer, noting the same "only substantial difference" and refusing to make a public statement (Lincoln to Gilmer, Dec. 15, 1860, *CWAL*, 4:151–53).

26. Gilmer to Lincoln, Dec. 29, 1860, Lincoln Papers. Lincoln earlier drafted a reply to Gilmer's December 10 letter, rejecting the idea of modifying Republican opposition to slavery in the territories. He sent the reply to Thomas Corwin of Ohio, the prominent Republican moderate who headed the House Committee of Thirty-Three, with instruction to deliver it or not, as he "might deem prudent." Corwin did not give Gilmer the letter, at least not before the North Carolinian went home for Christmas (Lincoln to Gilmer, Dec. 15, 1860, Lincoln to Montgomery Blair, Dec. 18, 1860, *CWAL*, 4:151–53, 155; Gilmer to Lincoln, Dec. 20, 1860, Corwin to Lincoln, Dec. 24, 1860, Lyman Trumbull to Lincoln, Dec. 24, 1860, all in Lincoln Papers). See also Howard K. Beale, ed., *The Diary of Edward Bates, 1859–1866, American Historical Association, Annual Report, 1930*, 4 vols. (Washington, D.C.: U.S. Government Printing Office, 1933), 4:167 (entry for Dec. 16, 1860); Henry Winter Davis to Samuel F. Du Pont, mid-Dec. 1860, transcription, Samuel F. Du Pont Papers, Eleutherian Mills Historical Library, Greenville, Del.

Before leaving Washington, Gilmer telegraphed Lincoln on December 20 to ask whether he could expect a response to his letter of December 10. Lincoln apparently replied by telegram to Gilmer on December 21 (*CWAL*, 4:153). Lincoln's telegram was forwarded to Gilmer in North Carolina. On December 29, Gilmer received a letter dated December 26 from his clerk in Washington, who reported receiving and reading, as he had been authorized to do, a letter from Lincoln to Gilmer. The clerk reported that Lincoln wanted Gilmer to visit Springfield (Gilmer to Lincoln, Dec. 29, 1860, Lincoln Papers).

27. Lincoln explained to Seward on December 29 that he made no direct mention of the cabinet when inviting Gilmer to Springfield: "I wrote him, requesting him to visit me here; and my object was that if, on full understanding of my position, he would accept a place in the cabinet, to give it to him" (*CWAL*, 4:164).

28. Gilmer to Seward, Jan. 3, 1861, Weed to Seward, Jan. 9, 1861, both in William H. Seward Papers, University of Rochester; Gilmer to Weed, Jan. 12, 1861, Weed Papers; Weed, ed., *Autobiography*, 614; Seward to Lincoln, Jan. 4, 8, 1861, Weed to Lincoln, Jan. 14, 1861, all in Lincoln Papers.

29. Gilmer to Seward, Jan. 3, 1861, Seward Papers; Seward to Lincoln, Jan. 4, 8, 15, 1861, Lincoln Papers; Lincoln to Seward, Jan. 12, 1861, *CWAL*, 4:173; Weed, ed., *Autobiography*, 614; Jerome Dowd, *Sketches of Prominent Living North Carolinians* (Raleigh: Edwards and Broughton, 1888), 96.

30. Henry Winter Davis to David Davis, Jan. 5, 1861, photocopy, David Davis Papers.

31. The fullest and most satisfactory account of the internal struggle within the Republican party is in William E. Baringer, *A House Dividing: Lincoln as President Elect* (Springfield: Abraham Lincoln Association, 1945). See also John G. Nicolay and John Hay, *Abraham Lincoln, A History*, 10 vols. (New York: Century, 1890), 3:345–74; Allan Nevins, *The Emergence of Lincoln*, 2 vols. (New York: Charles Scribner's Sons, 1950), 2:436–47, 452–55; John Niven, *Gideon Welles: Lincoln's Secretary of the Navy* (New York: Oxford

University Press, 1973), 303–23; Willard L. King, *Lincoln's Manager: David Davis* (Cambridge, Mass.: Harvard University Press, 1960), 162–80; Henry J. Carman and Reinhard H. Luthin, *Lincoln and the Patronage* (New York: Columbia University Press, 1943), 11–52; James G. Randall, *Lincoln the President,* 4 vols. (New York: Dodd, Mead, 1945–55), 1:256–72; Potter, *Lincoln and His Party,* 20–44; Sowle, "Conciliatory Republicans," 422–29. The published and unpublished Lincoln Papers are full of material on the cabinet struggle, as are the Simon Cameron Papers, the Horace Greeley Papers, and the Salmon P. Chase Papers, all in LC, and the Salmon P. Chase Papers, HSP. For a shrewd analysis of Greeley's role in the secession crisis, see Bernard A. Weisberger, "Horace Greeley: Reformer as Republican," *Civil War History* 23 (March 1977): 5–25. For important recent assessments of how the corruption issue weakened Weed, Seward, and Cameron, see Mark W. Summers, "'A Band of Brigands': Albany Lawmakers and Republican National Politics, 1860," ibid. 30 (June 1984): 101–19; and Mark W. Summers, *The Plundering Generation: Corruption and the Crisis of the Union, 1849–1861* (New York: Oxford University Press, 1987), 261–80, 293–95.

32. A widely reprinted and accurate short summary of the cabinet struggle first appeared in the *New York Evening Post,* Feb. 22, 1861. For an incisive unpublished account, see Charles Francis Adams, Jr., to Richard H. Dana, Jr., Feb. 21, 1861, Dana Papers.

33. The issues of cabinet making and southern policy, too often treated in a compartmentalized manner in the existing histories of the secession period, were, in fact, "inextricably intertangled" (Nevins, *Emergence of Lincoln,* 2:438). Of the available accounts, Baringer, *House Dividing,* 118–23, 145, 163–64, 321–22, 326–29, is the most illuminating, albeit incomplete. See also Nicolay and Hay, *Lincoln,* 3:361–67; Potter, *Lincoln and His Party,* 146–55; Randall, *Lincoln the President,* 1:267–70; Bancroft, *Seward,* 2:39–40. As if to illustrate the danger of rigidly applying supposed historical "lessons," the Blairs managed to blur the profound differences between the crises of 1832–33 and 1860–61. Instead of a single disaffected state, as in 1832–33, Lincoln confronted a situation in which seven states together defied federal authority and several more hung precariously in the balance. The Blairs also tended to forget that a carrot of compromise as well as a stick of threatened force had aided Andrew Jackson in quashing nullification in South Carolina. See William W. Freehling, *Prelude to Civil War: The Nullification Controversy in South Carolina, 1816–1836* (New York: Harper & Row, 1966), 265–95; Merrill D. Peterson, *Olive Branch and Sword—The Compromise of 1833* (Baton Rouge: Louisiana State University Press, 1982). The statement by Francis P. Blair, Sr., is from an article entitled "The Political Troubles: Their Cause and Their Remedy," *New York Evening Post,* Feb. 15, 1861, enclosed in John A. Briggs to Abraham Lincoln, Feb. 16, 1861, Lincoln Papers. See also William Ernest Smith, *The Francis Preston Blair Family in Politics,* 2 vols. (New York: Macmillan, 1933), 2:7–9.

34. Seward to Lincoln, Jan. 15, 1861, Lincoln Papers; Lincoln to Seward, Jan. 12, 1861, *CWAL,* 4:173; Isaac Newton to William A. Graham, Feb. 8,

1861, Graham Papers, SHC-UNC, in Hamilton and Williams, eds., *Graham Papers*, 5:230–31; W. W. Gitt to William P. Fessenden, Feb. 17, 1861, William P. Fessenden Papers, LC, quoted in Randall, *Lincoln the President*, 1:268. Nicolay and Hay, *Lincoln*, 3:364, state incorrectly that Gilmer definitely refused the cabinet offer by late January. Their error originated from misdating Gilmer's letter to Lincoln of December 29, 1860, as January 29, 1861, and from assuming that Gilmer's disinterest in traveling to Springfield closed the issue. In fact, Gilmer was not yet aware of his potential nomination to the cabinet when he wrote to Lincoln on December 29. Nicolay and Hay misled Potter, *Lincoln and His Party*, 152–53, 305; Nevins, *Emergence of Lincoln*, 2:447; and Roy Franklin Nichols, *The Disruption of American Democracy* (New York: Macmillan, 1948), 449, among others. On Seward's inability to find another non-Republican southerner suitable to Lincoln, see Seward to Lincoln, Dec. 25, 28, 1860, Jan. 1, 4, 8, 15, 1861, Lincoln Papers, substantially summarized and excerpted in Seward, *Seward*, 2:487–93, and in Nicolay and Hay, *Lincoln*, 3:361–64; Lincoln to Seward, Dec. 29, 1860, Jan. 3, 12, 1861, *CWAL*, 4:164, 170–71, 173.

35. Weed, ed., *Autobiography*, 607, 611; Henry Winter Davis to Samuel F. Du Pont, Mar. 12, 20, 1861, transcriptions, Du Pont Papers.

36. Julian M. Sturtevant to Lyman Trumball, Jan. 30, 1861, B. W. Lewis and E. Lewis to Trumbull, Feb. 4, 1861, Lyman Trumbull Papers, LC.

37. Carl Schurz to Abraham Lincoln, Dec. 18, 1860, Lincoln Papers; William Herndon to Lyman Trumbull, Dec. 21, 1860, Feb. 9, 1861, William T. Barron to Trumbull, Feb. 2, 1861, all in Trumbull Papers; George Metcalfe to Charles Francis Adams, Dec. 7, 1860, Adams Papers.

38. J. S. P. (James Shepherd Pike), Jan. 7, 1861, in *New York Tribune*, Jan. 9, 1861; Salmon P. Chase to Norman B. Judd, Jan. 20, 1861, Lincoln Papers; Charles Sumner to Salmon P. Chase, Jan. 19, 1861, Chase Papers, LC.

39. John D. Defrees to Lincoln, Jan. 8, 1861, Richard W. Thompson to Lincoln, Dec. 25, 1860, Lincoln Papers.

40. "B." to the Republican Members of Congress, in the *National Intelligencer*, Jan. 16, 1861. Quotations in the following paragraph are from the same source.

41. *New York Times*, Jan. 10, 1861 (Washington dispatch of Jan. 9); *New York Tribune*, Jan. 9, 1861 ("J. S. P.," Jan. 7); *National Intelligencer*, Jan. 19, 21, 1861; Leonard Swett to Abraham Lincoln, "Friday" (Jan. 4 or 11, 1861), unsent letter misfiled in Dec. 1860 folder of David Davis Papers; Elihu B. Washburne to Abraham Lincoln, Jan. 7, 1861, Lincoln Papers, in Mearns, ed., *Lincoln Papers*, 2:390; *Albany Evening Journal*, Jan. 9, 17, 1861.

42. On the Border State plan, see *New York Tribune*, Jan. 7, 8, 1861; *Philadelphia North American*, Jan. 7, 1861 ("Independent"—James E. Harvey—Jan. 6, 1861), Jan. 8, 16, 1861 ("Independent"—James E. Harvey—Jan. 15, 1861); *New York Times*, Jan. 7, 8, 1861; *Albany Evening Journal*, Jan. 5, 7, 9, 1861; *National Intelligencer*, Jan. 8, 1861; *CG*, 36:2, 279–82; Sowle, "Conciliatory Republicans," 221–27; Crofts, "Harvey and the Secession Crisis," 181–82.

43. Quotations from Roger A. Pryor to Lewis E. Harvie, Jan. 7, 1861, M. R. H. Garnett, Thomas S. Bocock, and Roger A. Pryor to Lewis E. Harvie, Jan. 7, 1861, both in *OR*, I:51:2, p. 3.

44. James R. Hale to Lincoln, Jan. 6, 1861, Elihu B. Washburne to Lincoln, Jan. 7, 1861, Lincoln Papers, the latter printed in Mearns, ed., *Lincoln Papers*, 2:390; Lincoln to Hale, Jan. 11, 1861, *CWAL*, 4:172.

45. Corwin to Lincoln, Dec. 24, 1860, Lincoln Papers; Graebner, "Thomas Corwin and the Sectional Crisis," 229–47; R. Alton Lee, "The Corwin Amendment and the Secession Crisis," *Ohio Historical Quarterly* 70 (Jan. 1961): 1–26.

46. Charles Francis Adams, diary entries of Dec. 20, 21, 24, 25, 26, 1860, Adams Papers, quotation from Dec. 26. Corwin also favored admitting the huge expanse to territory north of 36° 30′ into the Union as a single state. The same idea had been raised before the Senate Committee of Thirteen by Senator Henry M. Rice of Minnesota, but it found little favor (Potter, *Lincoln and His Party*, 186–87).

47. Henry Adams to Charles Francis Adams, Jr., Dec. 9, 29, 1860; Jan. 17, Feb. 13, 1861, in Levenson et al., eds., *Letters of Henry Adams*, 1:204–5, 214–16, 221–24, 230–32.

48. John A. Gilmer to William A. Graham, Jan. 2, 1861, Hamilton and Williams, eds., *Graham Papers*, 5:208–9; Charles Francis Adams, diary entries of Jan. 3, 4, 5, 8, 14, 1861, Adams Papers, quotation from Jan. 4.

49. *CG*, 36:2, 341–44; Bancroft, *Seward*, 2:12–16; Potter, *Lincoln and His Party*, 285–87; Sowle, "Conciliatory Republicans," 277–86.

50. James M. Mason to Lewis E. Harvie, Jan. 13, 1861, in *OR*, I:51:2, p. 5; *Alexandria Gazette*, Jan. 15, 1861; Andrew Johnson to Sam Milligan, Jan. 13, 1861, *Johnson Papers*, 4:160–62; "Independent" (James E. Harvey), Jan. 13, 1861, in *Philadelphia North American*, Jan. 14, 1861; James E. Harvey to Thurlow Weed, Jan. 15, 1861, Seward Papers; Charles Sumner to Salmon P. Chase, Jan. 19, 1861, Chase Papers, LC; *New York Times*, Jan. 22, 1861. For other southern Unionist reactions to Seward's speech, see John A. Gilmer to Thurlow Weed, Jan. 12, 17, 1861, Weed Papers; C. C. Walden to Seward, Jan. 17, 1861, William Thomas Sutherlin to Seward, Jan. 24, 1861, Thomas L. Smith to Seward, Jan. 28, 1861, all in Seward Papers; *Nashville Republican Banner*, Jan. 16, 17, 1861; *Nashville Daily Patriot*, Jan. 16, 18, 1861.

51. Readers will recall Whittier's scathing *Ichabod*: "Of all we loved and honored, naught / Save power remains; . . . All else is gone; from those great eyes / The soul has fled: . . . Walk backward, with averted gaze, / And hide the shame!" (Hyatt H. Waggoner, ed., *The Poetical Works of Whittier* [Boston: Houghton Mifflin, 1975], 186–87).

52. Ibid., 332. "To William H. Seward" was first published in the *New York Evening Post*, Jan. 28, 1861. Whittier intended his poem to be "*admonitory* as well as *commendatory*." He hoped Seward would resist any "compromise" that sanctioned expansion of slavery. "Tell Mr. Seward I have bound him to good behavior in my verse," Whittier wrote to a mutual friend (Whittier to Francis Henry Underwood, Feb. 7, 1861; Whittier to William Sidney Thayer,

Feb. 1, 1861, both in John B. Pickard, ed., *The Letters of John Greenleaf Whittier*, 4 vols. [Cambridge, Mass.: Harvard University Press, 1975], 3:10–13).

53. Adams, "Great Secession Winter," 685.

54. Charles Francis Adams, diary entries of Jan. 13, 14, 1861, Adams Papers; *New York Times*, Jan. 18, 1861.

55. Corwin to Lincoln, Jan. 16, 1861, Lincoln Papers, in Nicolay and Hay, *Lincoln*, 3:218, and in Mearns, ed., *Lincoln Papers*, 2:406 (misdated as Jan. 18); Corwin to Alexander H. H. Stuart, Jan. 17, 1861, Alexander H. H. Stuart Papers, UVA.

56. Charles Francis Adams, diary entries of Jan. 21, 25, 1861, Adams Papers.

57. *CG*, 36:2, A124–27.

58. Henry Adams to Charles Francis Adams, Jr., Feb. 5, 1861, Adams Papers, in Levenson et al., eds., *Letters of Henry Adams*, 1:227–29; *Louisville Daily Journal*, Feb. 9, 1861; *CG*, 36:2, A108, A137, A104; Robert Hatton to his wife, Jan. 30, 1861, in Drake, *Hatton*, 323. See also Joseph C. G. Kennedy to Charles Francis Adams, Feb. 4, 1861, Adams Papers.

59. Charles Francis Adams to F. W. Bird, Feb. 11, 1861, Adams to Alpheus Harding, Feb. 11, 1861, Adams to Richard H. Dana, Jr., Feb. 9, 1861, copies, all in Adams Papers; Charles Francis Adams, diary entry of Jan. 23, 1861, Adams Papers.

60. *Boston Daily Advertiser*, Feb. 13, 15, 16, 1861 ("Carolus," Feb. 13, in edition of Feb. 16); *New York Times*, Feb. 12, 1861; *Nashville Patriot*, Feb. 18, 1861; Sowle, "Conciliatory Republicans," 303–26, 345–66.

61. Henry Adams to Charles Francis Adams, Jr., Feb. 8, 13, 1861, Adams Papers, in Levenson et al., eds., *Letters of Henry Adams*, 1:229–32; Charles Francis Adams, *Charles Francis Adams, 1835–1915: An Autobiography* (Boston: Houghton Mifflin, 1916), 78.

62. Seward to Lincoln, Jan. 27, 1861, Lincoln Papers, in Mearns, ed., *Lincoln Papers*, 2:421–23.

63. Chase to Lincoln, Jan. 28, 1861, Lincoln Papers, in ibid., 2:424–25.

64. Thaddeus Stevens to Salmon P. Chase, Feb. 3, 1861, Chase Papers, HSP; George C. Fogg to Lincoln, Feb. 5, 1861, Cassius M. Clay to Lincoln, Feb. 6, 1861, both in Lincoln Papers.

65. James A. Hamilton and other New York Republicans to Lincoln, Jan. 29, 1861, Lincoln Papers. Seward's close allies Moses H. Grinnell and Richard M. Blatchford were among the group. See also Philip S. Foner, *Business and Slavery: The New York Merchants and the Irrepressible Conflict* (Chapel Hill: University of North Carolina Press, 1941), 248–59.

66. George Sumner to John A. Andrew, Jan. 21, 1861, John A. Andrew Papers, MHS; William Herndon to Lyman Trumbull, Jan. 27, 1861, Trumbull Papers; Lincoln to Seward, Feb. 1, 1861, *CWAL*, 4:183.

67. Charles Francis Adams, diary entries of Feb. 5, 11, 1861, Adams Papers; Charles Sumner to John A. Andrew, Jan. 18, Feb. 8, 10, 1861, Andrew Papers; *Proceedings of the Massachusetts Historical Society* 40 (1927): 227–28; Sowle, "Conciliatory Republicans," 371–75.

68. Lincoln, speeches in Indianapolis and Pittsburgh, *CWAL*, 4:195–96, 211; Potter, *Lincoln and His Party*, 245–47; Sowle, "Conciliatory Republicans," 401–5.

69. Charles Francis Adams, diary entries of Feb. 16, 19, 1861, Adams Papers; Charles Francis Adams, Jr., to Richard H. Dana, Jr., Feb. 21, 1861, Dana Papers; Charles Francis Adams, Jr., to John A. Andrew, Feb. 22, 1861, Andrew Papers, in *Proceedings of the Massachusetts Historical Society* 40 (1927): 233–35. Quotations in the following paragraph are also drawn from the two letters written by Charles Francis Adams, Jr.

70. Charles Francis Adams, Jr., to Richard H. Dana, Jr., Feb. 28, 1861, Dana Papers; Seward to James Watson Webb, Feb. 16, 1861, James Watson Webb Papers, Yale University; Charles Francis Adams, diary entry of Feb. 19, 1861, Adams Papers; Weed to Seward, Feb. 14, 21, Seward Papers.

71. Seward to James Watson Webb, Feb. 16, 1861, Webb Papers; Bancroft, *Seward*, 2:40; Nicolay and Hay, *Lincoln*, 3:311–21; Sowle, "Conciliatory Republicans," 406–13; Baringer, *House Dividing*, 293–310; Charles Francis Adams, Jr., to Richard H. Dana, Jr., Feb. 28, 1861, Dana Papers; Seward to Lincoln, Feb. 24, 1861, Lincoln Papers, in Bancroft, *Seward*, 2:23–25; *Washington Evening Star*, Feb. 23, 25, 26, 1861.

72. Henry Villard, *Memoirs of Henry Villard, Journalist and Financier, 1835–1900*, 2 vols. (Boston: Houghton Mifflin, 1904), 1:156; Charles Hamilton and Lloyd Ostendorf, *Lincoln in Photographs: An Album of Every Known Pose* (Norman: University of Oklahoma Press, 1963), 76–85.

73. Baringer, *House Dividing*, 323, 326–29; Nicolay and Hay, *Lincoln*, 3:366–67; *Washington Evening Star*, Feb. 25, 1861.

74. "Special," Feb. 25, 26, 27, 1861, in *Baltimore American*, Feb. 26, 27, 28, 1861; *New York Tribune*, Feb. 25, 1861; *Washington Evening Star*, Feb. 25, 28, 1861; *New York Herald*, Feb. 28, 1861; *Philadelphia North American*, Feb. 26, 1861. Four North Carolinians had served as secretary of the navy during the preceding several decades: John Branch (1829–31), George E. Badger (1841), William A. Graham (1850–52), and James C. Dobbin (1853–57).

75. Thomas Bragg, diary entry of Feb. 26, 1861, Thomas Bragg Papers, SHC-UNC.

76. Gilmer to Lincoln, probably late Jan. or early Feb. 1861, filed as Feb. 21, 1861 (item 41861), Lincoln Papers.

77. "List of Senators' Preferences for Cabinet Appointment," Mar. 1(?), 1861, *CWAL*, 4:248; Henry Winter Davis to Samuel F. Du Pont, Mar. 12, 20, 1861, transcriptions, Du Pont Papers; John M. Morehead to Thomas Ruffin, Mar. 5, 1861, Ruffin Papers, SHC-UNC, in J. G. deRoulhac Hamilton, ed., *The Papers of Thomas Ruffin*, 4 vols. (Raleigh: Edwards and Broughton, 1918–20), 3:137–38.

78. Henry Adams, "Great Secession Winter," 683. Newspaper reports originally assigned to Blair the cabinet position Gilmer had declined, secretary of the navy (*New York Herald*, Mar. 2, 1861; *New York Times*, Mar. 4, 1861).

79. Gilmer to Lincoln, probably late Jan. or early Feb. 1861, filed as Feb.

21, 1861 (item 41861), Lincoln Papers; "First Inaugural Address—First Edition and Revisions," *CWAL*, 4:248–62; Sowle, "Conciliatory Republicans," 407–10, 448–56. The cryptic account in the *North Carolina Semi-Weekly Standard*, Mar. 9, 1861, suggests that Gilmer saw the earlier version of the address.

80. Seward to Lincoln, Feb. 24, 1861, Lincoln Papers, in Bancroft, *Seward*, 2:24–25.

81. Chittenden, *Report*, 180–89, 256–59, 305–6; statement by Charles S. Morehead, Oct. 9, 1862, in *Mississippi Valley Historical Review* 28 (June 1941): 68; Sowle, "Conciliatory Republicans," 420–21; Alexander R. Boteler, "Mr. Lincoln and the Force Bill," in *The Annals of the War Written by Leading Participants North and South* (Philadelphia: Times Publishing Company, 1879), 225.

82. Chittenden, *Report*, 482–583, includes congressional debates pertinent to this paragraph and the next. Baker's speech, for example, is at 526–32. See also Robert G. Gunderson, *Old Gentlemen's Convention: The Washington Peace Conference of 1861* (Madison: University of Wisconsin Press, 1961), 93–95; *CG*, 36:2, 1333, 1404–5; Sowle, "Conciliatory Republicans," 436–37.

83. Charles Francis Adams, diary entry of Feb. 27, 1861, Adams Papers; "Carolus," Mar. 1, 1861, in *Boston Daily Advertiser*, Mar. 4, 1861; Potter, *Lincoln and His Party*, 301.

84. Statement by Charles S. Morehead, Oct. 9, 1862; *New York Tribune*, Mar. 2, 5, 1861; Lee, "Corwin Amendment," 24; Adams, "Great Secession Winter," 683.

85. "A" (Henry Adams? Charles Francis Adams, Jr.?), Mar. 1, 1861, in *Boston Daily Advertiser*, Mar. 5, 1861; Charles Francis Adams, diary entries of Feb. 28, Mar. 1, 1861, Adams Papers; *Boston Daily Advertiser*, Mar. 8, 1861; Potter, *Lincoln and His Party*, 301–2; *CG*, 36:2, 1326–27.

86. Chittenden, *Report*, 417, 433; Charles Francis Adams, diary entry of Feb. 27, 1861, Adams Papers; Sowle, "Conciliatory Republicans," 375–92.

87. Reese, ed., *Virginia Convention*, 1:671, 2:699, 3:93–94, 122, 255; John J. Jackson to unknown, Mar. 1, 1861, Seward Papers; Shanks, *Secession Movement in Virginia*, 172–74.

88. Sowle, "Conciliatory Republicans," 397–401.

89. Robert Hatton to his wife, Mar. 1, 1861, in Drake, *Hatton*, 344.

90. Sherrard Clemens to unknown, Mar. 1, 1861, William P. Palmer Civil War Collection, Western Reserve Historical Society, Cleveland, Ohio; *Easton* (Pa.) *Argus* in *Wheeling Daily Intelligencer*, Mar. 18, 1861. See also A. W. Campbell et al. to Lincoln, Mar. 16, 1861, and Campbell to Lincoln, Mar. 17, 1861, both in Lincoln Papers. John A. Gilmer had telegraphed the ailing Clemens, still "lame" because of severe injuries suffered in a duel, to come from Richmond to Washington to vote for House ratification of the Adams amendment ("C," [A. W. Campbell] from Richmond, Feb. 25, 27, 1861, in *Wheeling Daily Intelligencer*, Mar. 2, 1861).

91. Morehead to Ruffin, Mar. 5, 1861, in Hamilton, ed., *Ruffin Papers*, 3:137–38. The letter was written during the morning of March 5, because Morehead mentioned plans to catch a two o'clock train later that day. The

text of Lincoln's Inaugural Address, delivered the previous day, clearly had not yet reached Greensboro.

CHAPTER 10

1. Seward to Lincoln, Mar. 2, 1861, Abraham Lincoln Papers, LC (microfilm edition), in John G. Nicolay and John Hay, *Abraham Lincoln: A History*, 10 vols. (New York: Century, 1890), 3:370; Patrick M. Sowle, "The Conciliatory Republicans during the Winter of Secession" (Ph.D. dissertation, Duke University, 1963), 448–49.

2. *Baltimore*(?) *Exchange* in *Wheeling Daily Intelligencer*, Mar. 12, 1861. Parts of the inaugural, referring to actions taken by Congress after midnight in the early hours of March 4, must have been added at the last minute. Compare original and revised versions of the Inaugural Address in *CWAL*, 4:248–71. Seward's hand is especially evident at 250, 254, 258, 261–62, 266, and 271.

3. Seward to Lincoln, Feb. 24, Mar. 5, 1861, Lincoln Papers; Lincoln to Seward, Mar. 4, 1861, *CWAL*, 4:273; Seward to Mrs. William H. Seward, Mar. 8, 1861, in Frederick W. Seward, *Seward at Washington, as Senator and Secretary of State: A Memoir of His Life, with Selections from His Letters*, 2 vols. (New York: Derby and Miller, 1891), 2:518–19; Thurlow Weed to Seward, Mar. 7, 1861, William H. Seward Papers, University of Rochester; Nicolay and Hay, *Lincoln*, 3:319–23, 369–72. Sowle, "Conciliatory Republicans," 448–57, first recognized the well-hidden cause-and-effect relationship between Seward's resignation, the revision of the Inaugural Address, and Seward's change of heart.

4. *CG*, 36:2, 1264, 1284–85, 1364–1403; T. A. R. Nelson to William G. Brownlow, Mar. 13, 1861, in *National Intelligencer*, Mar. 25, 1861; David M. Potter, *Lincoln and His Party in the Secession Crisis* (New Haven: Yale University Press, 1942), 277–78; Roy F. Nichols, *The Disruption of American Democracy* (New York: Macmillan, 1948), 467; Robert W. Johannsen, *Stephen A. Douglas* (New York: Oxford University Press, 1973), 830–31.

5. *CWAL*, 4:270; Potter, *Lincoln and His Party*, 301, 321; Johannsen, *Douglas*, 836–39; Nichols, *Disruption of American Democracy*, 475–81; Albert D. Kirwan, *John J. Crittenden: The Struggle for the Union* (Lexington: University of Kentucky Press, 1962), 411–21; *Harper's Weekly* 9 (Mar. 16, 1861): 162.

6. T. A. R. Nelson to William G. Brownlow, Mar. 13, 1861, in *National Intelligencer*, Mar. 25, 1861; *Baltimore American*, Mar. 6, 1861; Gilmer to Douglas, Mar. 8, 1861, Stephen A. Douglas Papers, University of Chicago; *CG*, 36:2, 763–66; *North Carolina Semi-Weekly Standard*, Apr. 3, 6, 1861; Robert Hatton, speech reported in *Lebanon Herald*, quoted in Drake, *Hatton*, 345.

7. Alfred M. Barbour to William H. Seward, Feb. 21, 1861, Joseph Segar to Seward, Feb. 22, 1861, Frederick W. Lander to Seward, Feb. 22, 1861, Sherrard Clemens to John C. Underwood, Feb. 18, 1861, Underwood to

Seward, Feb. 23, 1861, all in Seward Papers, and all but the last in Frederic Bancroft, *The Life of William H. Seward*, 2 vols. (New York: Harper & Brothers, 1899–1900), 2:536–41; Potter, *Lincoln and His Party*, 275–77; *CG*, 36:2, 1232; Joseph Segar to Alexander R. Boteler, Feb. 25, 1861, Alexander R. Boteler Papers, Duke; Alexander R. Boteler, "Mr. Lincoln and the Force Bill," in *The Annals of the War Written by Leading Participants North and South* (Philadelphia: Times Publishing Company, 1879), 220–27.

8. David M. Potter, "Preface to the 1962 Edition," *Lincoln and His Party in the Secession Crisis*, xxix; ibid., 280–314.

9. *Richmond Whig*, Mar. 5, 1861.

10. Gilmer to Seward, Mar. 7, 8, 12, 1861, Seward Papers, excerpted in Bancroft, *Seward*, 2:545–48; Gilmer to Seward, Mar. 9, 1861, Lincoln Papers; Gilmer to Douglas, Mar. 8, 10, 1861, Douglas Papers. Quotations in this and subsequent paragraphs are from the four letters to Seward.

11. "Independent," Mar. 24, 1861, in *Philadelphia North American and United States Gazette*, Mar. 25, 1861; Alexander H. H. Stuart to Joseph C. G. Kennedy, Apr. 1, 1861, Seward Papers.

12. *New York Times*, Mar. 21, 1861, in Perkins, ed., *Northern Editorials*, 1:365–67; Potter, *Lincoln and His Party*, 329–31.

13. *Richmond Enquirer*, Mar. 5, 1861, in Dumond, ed., *Southern Editorials*, 474–75; John W. Brockenbrough to John C. Rutherfoord, Mar. 5, 1861, John C. Rutherfoord Papers, Duke; James C. Taylor to Stephen A. Douglas, Mar. 18, 1861, Douglas Papers.

14. *North Carolina Standard*, Mar. 9, 1861, *Nashville Republican Banner*, Mar. 14, 1861, both in Dumond, ed., *Southern Editorials*, 476–79, 483–86; *Lynchburg Virginian*, Mar. 11, 1861.

15. William C. Wickham to Winfield Scott, Mar. 11, 1861, Lincoln Papers, in David Mearns, ed., *The Lincoln Papers: The Story of the Collection with Selections to July 4, 1861*, 2 vols. (Garden City, N.Y.: Country Life Press, 1948), 2:481–83; Reese, ed., *Virginia Convention*, 1:582–84.

16. *CG*, 37 Cong., Special Senate Sess., 1436–39, 1442–43, 1445–46; Johannsen, *Douglas*, 845–48.

17. Quentin Busbee to Douglas, Mar. 11, 1861, Alfred M. Barbour to Douglas, Mar. 13, 1861, Henry W. Miller to Douglas, Mar. 31, 1861, George Blow to Douglas, Mar. 13, 1861, James R. Holt et al. to Douglas, Mar. 10, 1861, all in Douglas Papers.

18. T. A. R. Nelson to William G. Brownlow, Mar. 13, 1861, in *National Intelligencer*, Mar. 25, 1861; *Richmond Whig*, Mar. 9, 1861; *Lynchburg Virginian*, Mar. 11, 1861; *Raleigh Semi-Weekly Register*, Mar. 16, 1861.

19. "Special," Mar. 17, 1861, in *Baltimore American*, Mar. 18, 1861; *Lynchburg Virginian*, Mar. 19, 1861; *New York Herald*, Mar. 16, 1861.

20. *Richmond Whig*, Mar. 26, 29, 1861; John Letcher to James D. Davidson, Mar. 24, 1861, James D. Davidson Papers, Wisconsin State Historical Society, copy in the U. B. Phillips Papers, Yale University; Rolfe S. Saunders to Andrew Johnson, Feb. 19, 1861, Andrew Johnson Papers, LC (microfilm edition).

21. *Richmond Whig*, Feb. 13, 1861; "Special," Mar. 19, 1861, in *Baltimore American*, Mar. 20, 1861; Henry Adams, "The Great Secession Winter of 1860–61," *Proceedings of the Massachusetts Historical Society* 43 (1910): 684.

22. *Lynchburg Virginian*, Oct. 22, 1860.

23. James M. Callahan, "George William Summers," *DAB*, 18:206–7; A. Clinton Loy, "George W. Summers and His Relation to the Formation of the State of West Virginia" (M.A. thesis, West Virginia University, 1937); Francis Pendleton Gaines, Jr., "The Virginia Constitutional Convention of 1850–51: A Study in Sectionalism" (Ph.D. dissertation, University of Virginia, 1950), 190–94; Clement Eaton, *The Mind of the Old South*, rev. ed. (Baton Rouge: Louisiana State University Press, 1967), 3–23, esp. 19. The Lewis Summers and George W. Summers Papers at the University of West Virginia contain little of interest after 1843.

24. *Richmond Semi-Weekly Enquirer*, Mar. 16, 1861; Reese, ed., *Virginia Convention*, 3:699.

25. V. M. Brown to Alexander R. Boteler, Apr. 2, 1861, Boteler Papers; *Richmond Whig*, Mar. 29, 1861.

26. Henry Dering to Waitman T. Willey, Apr. 10, 12, 1861, Waitman T. Willey Papers, West Virginia University.

27. *Nashville Republican Banner*, Mar. 31, 1861; A. A. Kyle to T. A. R. Nelson, Feb. 19, 1861, T. A. R. Nelson Papers, McClung Collection, Lawson McGhee Library, Knoxville, Tenn.; Elkenah D. Rader to Andrew Johnson, Mar. 20, 1861, *Johnson Papers*, 4:417–18.

28. Jeptha Fowlkes to Andrew Johnson, Mar. 10, 1861, *Johnson Papers*, 4:378–80.

29. David F. Caldwell to Andrew Johnson, Feb. 28, 1861, Johnson Papers; George E. Badger to Salmon P. Chase, Mar. 20, 1861, enclosed in Chase to Edward Bates, Apr. 5, 1861, General Records of the Department of Justice, RG 60, NA; Robert C. Kenzer, "Portrait of a Southern Community, 1849–1881: Family, Kinship, and Neighborhood in Orange County, North Carolina" (Ph.D. dissertation, Harvard University, 1982), 94; *Raleigh Semi-Weekly Register*, Apr. 10, 1861; *North Carolina Semi-Weekly Standard*, Apr. 6, 1861.

30. *Lynchburg Virginian*, Mar. 11, 1861; Reese, ed., *Virginia Convention*, 1:603, 608; Marc W. Kruman, *Parties and Politics in North Carolina, 1836–1865* (Baton Rouge: Louisiana State University Press, 1983), 216–17.

31. Gilmer to Lincoln, Dec. 29, 1860, Lincoln Papers; Gilmer to Weed, Jan. 12, 1861, Thurlow Weed Papers, University of Rochester; Gilmer to Seward, Mar. 7, 8, 9, 12, 25, Apr. 7, 11, 21, 1861, all in Seward Papers except Mar. 9 and Apr. 7, which are in the Lincoln Papers, with the latter addressed also to Lincoln. For excerpts from the Gilmer letters in Seward Papers, see Bancroft, *Seward*, 2:545–49. See also Kruman, *Parties and Politics in North Carolina*, 218; *New York Times*, Mar. 6, 1861; "Special," Mar. 12, 1861, in *Baltimore American*, Mar. 13, 1861; *Richmond Whig*, Mar. 8, 22, 1861; "Reconstruction," *Harper's Weekly* 9 (Mar. 9, 1861): 146.

32. Barbour to Seward, Feb. 8, 1861, Seward Papers, printed with minor inaccuracies in Bancroft, *Seward*, 2:534–36; Barbour to Douglas, Feb. 6,

1861, Douglas Papers. Barbour, however, as noted above in Chapters 5 and 9, was a fast ultimatumist. Republican rejection of territorial compromise undermined his conditional Unionism.

33. "L. A. W.," Feb. 8, 1861, in *Louisville Daily Journal*, Feb. 12, 1861; Hamilton Jones to Stephen A. Douglas, Mar. 10, 1861, Douglas Papers; *Richmond Whig*, Feb. 13, 1861, see also Mar. 22, 1861.

34. *National Intelligencer*, Mar. 2, 1861; "Independent" (James E. Harvey), Feb. 18, 1861, in *Philadelphia North American and United States Gazette*, Feb. 19, 1861; *New York Herald*, Feb. 28, 1861; *Richmond Whig*, Feb. 28, 1861; *Louisville Daily Journal*, Feb. 18, 1861.

35. *New York Times*, Feb. 26, 1861 (Washington report of Feb. 25, 1861). The article may have been reprinted from a different source.

36. *Louisville Daily Journal*, Mar. 6, 1861; Charles Arnold to Andrew Johnson, Mar. 14, 1861, *Johnson Papers*, 4:391–94; Nichols, *Disruption of American Democracy*, 484; *Richmond Semi-Weekly Enquirer*, Mar. 2, 1861, quoting John W. Forney's *Philadelphia Press*.

37. *New York Herald*, Feb. 28, Mar. 1, 1861.

38. Henry G. Connor, *John Archibald Campbell, Associate Justice of the United States Supreme Court, 1853–1861* (Boston: Houghton Mifflin, 1920), 116; Daniel B. Carroll, *Henri Mercier and the American Civil War* (Princeton: Princeton University Press, 1971), 34–36; Alexander R. Boteler, "A Table Talk with Seward," clipping from the *Philadelphia Times*, Scrapbook I, Boteler Papers.

39. Potter, *Lincoln and His Party*, 258–60, 306–10, 343–49; Benjamin P. Thomas and Harold M. Hyman, *Stanton: The Life and Times of Lincoln's Secretary of War* (New York: Knopf, 1962), 99–100.

40. James Barbour to Seward, Feb. 8, 1861, Seward Papers, in Bancroft, *Seward*, 2:534–36; James Barbour to William C. Rives, Feb. 7, 1861, William C. Rives Papers, LC; James Barbour to Stephen A. Douglas, Feb. 6, 1861, Douglas Papers; James C. Welling to the Editor, Nov. 21, 1879, *Nation* 29 (1879): 383–84; George W. Summers to James C. Welling, Mar. 19, 1861, in ibid.; Seward to Lincoln, Mar. 19, 1861, Lincoln Papers; *Richmond Whig*, Mar. 14, 1861; *North Carolina Weekly Standard*, Mar. 20, 1861.

41. James E. Harvey to Henry C. Carey, undated (early 1861), Henry C. Carey Papers, Edward Carey Gardiner Collection, HSP; George C. Fogg to Lincoln, Feb. 5, 1861, Lincoln Papers; Edward Chalfant, *Both Sides of the Ocean: A Biography of Henry Adams, His First Life, 1838–1862* (Hamden, Conn.: Shoe String Press, 1982), 218–25; Henry Adams, "Great Secession Winter," 685.

42. Scott to Seward, Mar. 3, 1861, Seward to Lincoln, Mar. 4, 1861, both in Lincoln Papers, in Mearns, ed., *Lincoln Papers*, 2:456–57, 461; Charles W. Elliott, *Winfield Scott, the Soldier and the Man* (New York: Macmillan, 1937), 697–700; Bancroft, *Seward*, 2:95–96.

43. Martin J. Crawford to Robert Toombs, Mar. 6, 1861, Crawford, John Forsyth, and A. B. Roman to Toombs, Mar. 8, 1861, both quoted in Bancroft, *Seward*, 2:108–10; Lyons to Lord John Russell, Feb. 4, 1861, quoted in

Allan Nevins, *The Emergence of Lincoln,* 2 vols. (New York: Charles Scribner's Sons, 1950), 2:401.

44. Sherrard Clemens to Lincoln, Mar. 4, 1861, Clemens to Reverdy Johnson, Mar. 22, 1861, Reverdy Johnson to Seward, Mar. 24, 1861, Edwin M. Stanton to Lincoln, Mar. 6, 1861, Seward to Lincoln, Mar. 9, 1861, Thomas H. Hicks to Lincoln, Mar. 11, 1861, William G. Brown and James C. McGrew to Lincoln, Mar. 10, 1861, all in Lincoln Papers; *Baltimore American,* Mar. 14, 18, 1861; *Philadelphia North American,* Apr. 2, 1861.

45. Information in this paragraph summarizes a large number of letters regarding federal patronage in the upper South, preserved in the General Records of the Department of Justice, RG 60, NA. See, particularly, George E. Badger to Salmon P. Chase, Mar. 20, 1861, enclosed in Chase to Edward Bates, Apr. 5, 1861, George E. Badger to Seward, Mar. 25, 1861, T. A. R. Nelson to Lincoln, Mar. 7, 1861, Robert Hatton to Lincoln, Mar. 18, 1861, memo of agreement between Andrew Johnson and Emerson Etheridge, Mar. 19, 1861, Andrew Johnson to Edward Bates, Mar. 25, 1861, the last also in *Johnson Papers,* 4:431–32. See also John A. Gilmer to Lincoln and Seward, Apr. 7, 1861, Lincoln Papers; Gilmer to Seward, Mar. 27, 1861, Seward Papers; John A. Kasson to Andrew Johnson, Mar. 11, 1861, Salmon P. Chase to Johnson, Mar. 13, 1861, George Harrington to Johnson, Mar. 14, 1861, a note dated Mar. 25, 1861, on the reverse side of Harvey M. Watterson to Johnson, Mar. 18, 1861, T. A. R. Nelson to Johnson, Apr. 5, 1861, all in Johnson Papers, with the Chase letter printed in *Johnson Papers,* 4:386; John Millson to Salmon P. Chase, Mar. 18, 1861, Treasury Department Records, RG 56, NA. Professor David E. Meerse of the State University of New York at Fredonia kindly brought the Millson letter to my attention.

46. Robert Anderson to Samuel Cooper, Feb. 28, 1861, Joseph Holt to Abraham Lincoln, Mar. 5, 1861, Winfield Scott to Lincoln, Mar. 5, 11, 12, 1861, all in Lincoln Papers, and all but the last in Mearns, ed., *Lincoln Papers,* 2:450–51, 461–65, 476–78. Most useful on the Sumter dilemma are James G. Randall, *Lincoln the President,* 4 vols. (New York: Dodd, Mead, 1945–55), 1:311–50; Richard N. Current, *Lincoln and the First Shot* (Philadelphia: J. B. Lippincott, 1963).

47. Bancroft, *Seward,* 2:124, 97–101; Seward to Lincoln, Mar. 15, 1861, Lincoln Papers.

48. See J. H. Plumb, *Chatham* (Hamden, Conn.: Archon Books, 1965), 147–53.

49. Secretary of War Simon Cameron, Secretary of the Navy Gideon Welles, and Attorney General Edward Bates wrote opinions opposing the effort to hold Sumter, and Secretary of the Interior Caleb Smith tentatively opposed it. Secretary of the Treasury Salmon Chase guardedly supported Blair on the assumption that no general war would follow a federal effort to resupply Sumter. All the opinions are in John G. Nicolay and John Hay, eds., *Complete Works of Abraham Lincoln,* 12 vols. (New York: Francis D. Tandy, 1905), 4:192–220. See Randall, *Lincoln the President,* 1:320–21; Ban-

croft, *Seward,* 2:105–6; Current, *Lincoln and the First Shot,* 65–67; *CWAL,* 4:284–85.

50. *CWAL,* 4:266; *New York Express* quoted in *Richmond Semi-Weekly Enquirer,* Mar. 16, 1861.

51. "Memorandum on Fort Sumter," Mar. 18(?), 1861, *CWAL,* 4:288–90.

52. James C. Welling to the Editor, Nov. 21, 1879, *Nation* 29 (1879): 383–84; George W. Summers to James C. Welling, Mar. 19, 1861, ibid.; Seward to Lincoln, Mar. 19, 1861, Lincoln Papers; Reese, ed., *Virginia Convention,* 1:626.

53. Connor, *Campbell,* 122–48; Potter, *Lincoln and His Party,* 342–49. Seward's communications with the Confederates regarding Sumter have received far more careful scholarly scrutiny than his simultaneous signals to upper South Unionists. Here is a fine example of the more general problem discussed in the Preface to this book—the tendency among historians of the secession crisis to overlook the upper South.

54. James C. Welling to the Editor, Nov. 21, 1879, *Nation* 29 (1879): 383–84; George W. Summers to Welling, Mar. 19, 1861, ibid., copy in Blair Family Papers, LC; Seward to Lincoln, Mar. 19, 1861, Lincoln Papers.

55. *Richmond Whig,* Mar. 26, 1861.

56. *Lynchburg Virginian,* Mar. 14, 1861; *Alexandria Gazette,* Mar. 18, 1861 ("Aliquis," in Loudoun County, Mar. 15, 1861).

57. Samuel McD. Moore to James D. Davidson, Mar. 29, Apr. 6, 1861, Davidson Papers, copies in Phillips Papers; *Richmond Semi-Weekly Enquirer,* Mar. 16, 19, 1861; Reese, ed., *Virginia Convention,* 3:725–26.

58. *Washington Evening Star,* quoted in *Wheeling Intelligencer,* Apr. 6, 1861; *Louisville Daily Journal,* Mar. 20, 1861; Jeptha Fowlkes to Andrew Johnson, Mar. 10, 1861, *Johnson Papers,* 4:378–80.

59. John Monroe to David Pugh, Mar. 24, 1861, John Monroe Papers, Duke; Ralph L. Berkshire to Waitman T. Willey, Mar. 12, 1861, Henry Dering to Willey, Mar. 26, 1861, both in Willey Papers.

60. *Baltimore American,* Mar. 20, 1861; *New York Times,* Mar. 11, 18, 1861; Letcher to James D. Davidson, Mar. 17, 1861, Davidson Papers, copy in Phillips Papers; *Richmond Whig,* Mar. 26, 1861.

61. Joseph Segar to Simon Cameron, Mar. 26, 1861, J. M. McCue to Cameron, Mar. 26, 1861, both in *OR,* I:51:1, pp. 318–19; *Richmond Semi-Weekly Enquirer,* Feb. 19, 1861; Roger A. Pryor, speech of Apr. 10, 1861, quoted from the *Charleston Mercury* by Potter, *Lincoln and His Party,* 213.

62. William B. Campbell to A. C. Beard, Mar. 15, 1861, Campbell Family Papers, Duke; *Baltimore American,* Mar. 18, 1861; Robert Hatton to T. A. R. Nelson, Mar. 27, 1861, Nelson Papers; *Gallatin Courier,* Mar. 27, 1861. See also Robert Hatton to Abraham Lincoln, Mar. 18, 1861, General Records of the Department of Justice, RG 60, NA.

63. Samuel Williams to Andrew Johnson, Mar. 25, 1861, Jeptha Fowlkes to Johnson, Mar. 17, 1861, both in *Johnson Papers,* 4:430–31, 401–2; *Wheeling Intelligencer,* Mar. 23, 1861 (Washington correspondence, Mar. 20, 1861).

64. Jonathan Worth to D. G. Worth, Mar. 16, 1861, Worth Family Papers, Duke; Jonathan Worth to T. C. Worth, Mar. 16, 1861, Worth letterbook,

NCDAH (a printed version in J. G. deRoulhac Hamilton, ed., *The Correspondence of Jonathan Worth,* 2 vols. [Raleigh: Broughton, 1909], 1:133–35, contains misleading inaccuracies); Quentin Busbee to Stephen A. Douglas, Mar. 11, 1861, Douglas Papers; W. C. Kerr to B. S. Hedrick, Apr. 6, 1861, Benjamin Sherwood Hedrick Papers, Duke; Kruman, *Parties and Politics in North Carolina,* 214–20, quotations on 220, 216.

65. William A. Graham, "Speech upon the Political Situation," Apr. 27, 1861, *Hillsborough Recorder,* May 1, 1861, in J. G.deRoulhac Hamilton and Max R. Williams, eds., *The Papers of William Alexander Graham,* 7 vols. to date (Raleigh: North Carolina State Department of Archives and History, 1957–), 5:245; Jonathan Worth to Dr. C. W. Woolen, May 17, 1861, Worth letterbook, in Hamilton, ed., *Worth Correspondence,* 1:145–48.

66. *Salisbury Carolina Watchman,* Mar. 26, 1861; Jonathan Worth to T. C. Worth, Mar. 16, 1861, Worth letterbook; *Richmond Whig,* Mar. 11, 16, 20, 25, 1861; John Letcher to James D. Davidson, Mar. 24, 1861, Davidson Papers, copy in Phillips Papers.

67. David Schenck Diary, Feb. 1, Mar. 18, May 15, 1861, SHC-UNC.

68. *Richmond Semi-Weekly Enquirer,* Feb. 19, 1861; John D. Imboden to John S. McCue, Feb. 24, 1861, McCue Family Papers, UVA; G. D. Gray to Angus R. Blakey, Dec. 31, 1860, Feb. 22, 1861, Angus R. Blakey Papers, Duke.

69. Alfred M. Barbour to Captain William Maynadier, Jan. 21, 1861, in *OR,* I:51:1, p. 308; Donald B. Webster, Jr., "The Last Days of the Harpers Ferry Armory," *Civil War History* 5 (1959): 31; John A. Harman and John D. Imboden to Alexander H. H. Stuart, Feb. 18, 1861, John D. Imboden Papers, UVA; John D. Imboden to John McCue, Feb. 24, 1861, McCue Family Papers; Reese, ed., *Virginia Convention,* 1:30–38; James D. Davidson to James B. Dorman, Mar. 4, 1861, Davidson Papers, copy in Phillips Papers; *Louisville Daily Journal,* Mar. 22, 1861.

70. *Charlottesville Review* in *Alexandria Gazette,* Mar. 16, 1861; Davidson to John Letcher, Apr. 2, 1861, Davidson Papers, copy in Phillips Papers.

71. Alfred M. Barbour to Stephen A. Douglas, Apr. 2, 1861, Douglas Papers; Robert Young Conrad to his wife, Mar. 24, 30, 1861, Robert Young Conrad Papers, VHS; John Letcher to James D. Davidson, Mar. 9, 1861, James B. Dorman to Davidson, Mar. 31, 1861, both in Davidson Papers, copies in Phillips Papers; John Janney to his wife, Apr. 2, 1861, Janney Papers, in possession of Lucas Phillips, Leesburg, Va.; three letters from unidentified Unionist leaders in Virginia, one of whom was almost certainly George W. Summers, to Maryland Congressman J. Morrison Harris, Mar. 26, 1861, in *Baltimore American,* Apr. 1, 1861.

72. Quentin Busbee to Stephen A. Douglas, Mar. 11, 1861, Douglas Papers; Kenneth M. Stampp, *And the War Came: The North and the Secession Crisis, 1860–61* (Baton Rouge: Louisiana State University Press, 1950), 205–8, 231–38, 265–70, 276, 286. "Memorandum on Fort Sumter," Mar. 18(?), 1861, *CWAL,* 4:288–90, thought to reflect Lincoln's weighing of the pros and cons on withdrawing from Sumter, lists as the most important obstacle "the danger of demoralizing the Republican party by a measure which

might seem to many to indicate timidity or in common parlance, 'want of pluck.'" See Current, *Lincoln and the First Shot*, 67–73; Allan Nevins, *The War for the Union*, 4 vols. (New York: Charles Scribner's Sons, 1959–71), 1:46–49.

73. Richard Hofstadter, "The Tariff Issue on the Eve of the Civil War," *American Historical Review* 44 (1938): 50–55; Arthur M. Lee, "Henry C. Carey and the Republican Tariff," *Pennsylvania Magazine of History and Biography* 81 (1957): 280–302, *Philadelphia North American*, Feb. 28, 1861.

74. Philip S. Foner, *Business and Slavery: The New York Merchants and the Irrepressible Conflict* (Chapel Hill: University of North Carolina Press, 1941), 261–66, 275–84, 297–305; Stampp, *And the War Came*, 231–38; Randall, *Lincoln the President*, 1:314–15; *Philadelphia North American*, Mar. 23, 25, 29, Apr. 3, 1861; Edwin M. Stanton to James Buchanan, Mar. 16, 1861, James Buchanan Papers, HSP.

75. *New York Times*, Mar. 22, 23, 27, 30, 1861; compare with the optimistic economic assessments in ibid., Jan. 19, 26, Feb. 2, 7, 1861. See Alfred D. Chandler, Jr., *Henry Varnum Poor: Business Editor, Analyst, and Reformer* (Cambridge, Mass.: Harvard University Press, 1956), 199–204, 233–35, 331–32 (nn. 58–71), 338–39 (nn. 31–33); [Henry Varnum Poor], *The Effects of Secession upon the Commercial Relations between the North and the South and upon Each Other* (1861; rpt. New York: Johnson Reprint Corporation, 1966).

76. Lincoln to Edward Bates, Mar. 18, 1861, Lincoln to Salmon Chase, Mar. 18, 1861, Lincoln to Gideon Welles, Mar. 18, 1861, *CWAL*, 4:290–93; Reese, ed., *Virginia Convention*, 1:625; William C. Wickham to Winfield Scott, Mar. 11, 1861, Lincoln Papers, in Mearns, ed., *Lincoln Papers*, 2:481–83; Current, *Lincoln and the First Shot*, 69–70.

77. *Cincinnati Commercial*, Mar. 23, 1861, in Perkins, ed., *Northern Editorials*, 1:371–75; Nicolay and Hay, *Lincoln*, 3:382; Abraham Lincoln, "Message to Congress in Special Session," July 4, 1861, *CWAL*, 4:424.

78. Stephen A. Hurlbut to Lincoln, Mar. 27, 1861, Lincoln Papers; Nicolay and Hay, *Lincoln*, 3:390–92; Current, *Lincoln and the First Shot*, 73–74; Jeptha Fowlkes to Andrew Johnson, Mar. 10, 17, 21, 23, 1861, *Johnson Papers*, 4:379, 401, 423, 425–26.

79. *National Intelligencer*, Mar. 21, 1861; *Louisville Daily Journal*, Mar. 22, 23, 26, 1861; *Alexandria Gazette*, Mar. 22, 1861 ("Homo," Mar. 21, 1861); *Lynchburg Virginian*, Mar. 27, 1861; *Nashville Daily Patriot*, Mar. 22, 24, 26, Apr. 2, 1861; *Cincinnati Commercial*, Mar. 29, 1861.

80. *New York Times*, Mar. 21, 1861, in Perkins, ed., *Northern Editorials*, 1:365–66; Bancroft, *Seward*, 2:121; "Independent," Mar. 25, 28, 1861, in *Philadelphia North American*, Mar. 26, 29, 1861; Stephen A. Hurlbut to Lincoln, Mar. 27, 1861, Lincoln Papers.

81. *Gallatin Courier*, Apr. 10, 1861; *Lynchburg Virginian*, Apr. 4, 1861; John M. Botts to Jonas C. Hewett, Feb. 21, 1861, in *Wheeling Intelligencer*, Feb. 27, 1861. See also Botts to Edward Bates, Apr. 19, 1861, in *Brownlow's Weekly Knoxville Whig*, May 4, 1861; Zebulon B. Vance to C. C. Jones, Feb. 11, 1861, Zebulon B. Vance Papers, SHC-UNC; A. Waldo Putnam to Andrew

Johnson, Feb. 14, 18, 1861, Johnson Papers, the latter in *Johnson Papers*, 4:310–12.

82. John Bell's speech of Apr. 23, 1861, in *Nashville Republican Banner*, May 10, 1861; William A. Graham to Alfred M. Waddell, Feb. 5, 1861, in *North Carolina Weekly Standard*, Feb. 13, 1861, in Hamilton and Williams, eds., *Graham Papers*, 5:222–24.

83. *Richmond Enquirer*, Mar. 2, 1861; *CG*, 37th Cong., Special Senate Session, 1444.

84. Foote to Crittenden, in *Nashville Union and American*, Apr. 2, 1861.

CHAPTER 11

1. George W. Summers to James C. Welling, Mar. 19, 1861, in *Nation* 29 (1879): 383–84, copy in Blair Family Papers, LC.

2. *Lynchburg Virginian*, Mar. 29, 1861; Henry W. Miller to Stephen A. Douglas, Mar. 31, 1861, Stephen A. Douglas Papers, University of Chicago; Alexander H. H. Stuart to Joseph C. G. Kennedy, Apr. 1, 1861, William H. Seward Papers, University of Rochester; Jeptha Fowlkes to Andrew Johnson, Mar. 21, 23, 1861, *Johnson Papers*, 4:422–23, 425–26.

3. Kenneth M. Stampp, *And the War Came: The North and the Secession Crisis, 1860–61* (Baton Rouge: Louisiana State University Press, 1950), 204–38; Bernard Weisberger, "Horace Greeley: Reformer as Republican," *Civil War History* 23 (Mar. 1977): 22–23; *New York Tribune*, Feb. 27, 1861 ("Shall We Have a Federal Union?").

4. *New York Tribune*, Apr. 10, 1861.

5. Weisberger, "Horace Greeley," 5–25.

6. *New York Tribune*, Feb. 13 ("Where We Are"), Mar. 16 ("The Future"), Apr. 9, 1861 ("Border-State Politics").

7. Ibid., Feb. 13 ("Where We Are"), Feb. 16 ("Southern Unionists"), Feb. 26 (Washington Report of Feb. 25 by James S. Pike), Mar. 15 ("John Cochrane in Virginia"), Mar. 16 ("The Future"), Apr. 9, 1861 ("Border-State Politics").

8. James Buchanan to James Gordon Bennett, Mar. 11, 1861, in George Ticknor Curtis, *The Life of James Buchanan, Fifteenth President of the United States*, 2 vols. (New York: Harper & Brothers, 1883), 2:530; *New York Herald*, Apr. 9, 1861 (Richmond correspondent, Apr. 2, 1861).

9. *New York Herald*, Jan.–Apr. 1861, quotations from Apr. 3, 4, 1861; Reese, ed., *Virginia Convention*, 3:375. Historians, notably Allan Nevins, have likewise used the *Herald* to document the "common knowledge" that Virginia "teetered on the edge of secession" by late March and early April (Nevins, *The War for the Union*, 4 vols. [New York: Charles Scribner's Sons, 1959–71], 1:59, 64).

10. *New York Tribune*, Apr. 9, 1861 ("Border-State Politics").

11. Ibid., Feb. 8 ("Buying Off Rebellion"), Mar. 16, 1861 ("The Future").

12. *Boston Advertiser*, Apr. 11, 1861; see also issues of Mar. 16 and Apr. 4,

6, and 9, 1861, for increasingly critical comments about Virginia Unionists. *New York Times*, Apr. 3, 1861 ("Wanted—A Policy!"), *Newburyport* (Mass.) *Daily Herald*, Mar. 25, 1861 ("The State of the Country"), *Philadelphia Daily Evening Bulletin*, Apr. 8, 1861 ("War"), all in Perkins, ed., *Northern Editorials*, 2:660–64, 654–58, 671–74.

13. William P. Mellen to Salmon P. Chase, Apr. 6, 1861, Salmon P. Chase Papers, HSP.

14. Federal control of two island installations in the Gulf of Mexico off the south coast of Florida did not threaten a collision with Confederate forces. See Chapter 12, n. 8.

15. Grady McWhiney, "The Confederacy's First Shot," *Civil War History* 14 (Mar. 1968): 5–14; McWhiney, *Braxton Bragg and Confederate Defeat*, Vol. 1: *Field Command* (New York: Columbia University Press, 1969), 157–73.

16. *Philadelphia North American*, Mar. 27, 1861 (James E. Harvey—"Independent"—Mar. 26, 1861); Reese, ed., *Virginia Convention*, 3:454–83; *Nashville Patriot*, Mar. 16, 1861.

17. David M. Potter, *Lincoln and His Party in the Secession Crisis* (New Haven: Yale University Press, 1942), 358–59.

18. Winfield Scott memorandum, undated (Mar. 28, 1861?), *OR*, I:1, pp. 200–201; Frederic Bancroft, *The Life of William H. Seward*, 2 vols. (New York: Harper & Brothers, 1899–1900), 2:124; Potter, *Lincoln and His Party*, 361; John G. Nicolay and John Hay, *Abraham Lincoln: A History*, 10 vols. (New York: Century, 1890), 3:394. On the problem of dating Scott's memorandum, see Ari Hoogenboom, "Gustavus Fox and the Relief of Fort Sumter," *Civil War History* 9 (1963): 387, n. 14.

19. Nicolay and Hay, *Lincoln*, 3:394–95; Samuel Ward to S. L. M. Barlow, Mar. 31, 1861, S. L. M. Barlow Papers, Huntington Library, San Marino, Calif.; Richard N. Current, *Lincoln and the First Shot* (Philadelphia: J. B. Lippincott, 1963), 75–79, 83–84.

20. Robert Means Thompson and Richard Wainwright, eds., *Confidential Correspondence of Gustavus Vasa Fox*, 2 vols. (New York: DeVinne Press, 1918–20), 1:16–38; Hoogenboom, "Gustavus Fox and the Relief of Fort Sumter," 383–87; Nevins, *War for the Union*, 1:44, 48–49, 53; Nicolay and Hay, *Lincoln*, 3:383–85, 389–90; Current, *Lincoln and the First Shot*, 57–62, 71–72, 79–81; Howard K. Beale, ed., *The Diary of Edward Bates, 1859–1866, American Historical Association, Annual Report, 1930*, 4 vols. (Washington, D.C.: U.S. Government Printing Office, 1933), 4:177–78 ("Note added after March 16").

21. Nevins, *War for the Union*, 1:55.

22. Lincoln to Gideon Welles, Mar. 29, 1861, Lincoln to Simon Cameron, Mar. 29, 1861, both in *CWAL*, 4:301–2; Nicolay and Hay, *Lincoln*, 3:429–34 (includes written opinions of cabinet members).

My account deliberately excludes the frequently repeated story about a dramatic meeting on the night of the twenty-ninth between Lincoln and Francis Preston Blair, Sr., the elderly former Jacksonian and father of Montgomery Blair. The senior Blair allegedly told Lincoln that "it would be treason to surrender Sumter" and that if Lincoln did so, he might be impeached. Available manuscript evidence strongly suggests that the meeting in fact occurred on March 11, weeks before the fateful moment of decision, that Blair worried he had left "a bad impression," and that he wanted afterward to apologize. Allan Nevins has correctly charged Gideon Welles with "gross overstatement" for writing that the Blair interview made Lincoln decide to resupply Sumter. See Francis P. Blair, Sr., to Montgomery Blair, Mar. 12, 1861, Montgomery Blair to Lincoln, Mar. 12, 1861, both in Abraham Lincoln Papers, LC (microfilm edition); Nevins, *War for the Union*, 1:46–48; Elbert B. Smith, *Francis Preston Blair* (New York: Free Press, 1980), 275–76. For sources of the apocryphal tradition, see John T. Morse, Jr., ed., *The Diary of Gideon Welles*, 3 vols. (Boston: Houghton Mifflin, 1911), 1:13–14 (entry is a memoir, not a true diary); William Ernest Smith, *The Francis Preston Blair Family in Politics*, 2 vols. (New York: Macmillan, 1933), 2:9–10.

23. Bancroft, *Seward*, 2:127–28; Seward's written opinion, Mar. 29, 1861, in Nicolay and Hay, *Lincoln*, 3:430.

24. Bancroft, *Seward*, 2:128–30; Nicolay and Hay, *Lincoln*, 3:434–41.

25. Seward's "Thoughts" were first printed in Nicolay and Hay, *Lincoln*, 3:445–47. Quotations in the next two paragraphs are also from the "Thoughts."

26. Kinley J. Brauer, "Seward's 'Foreign War Panacea': An Interpretation," *New York History* 55 (Apr. 1974): 132–57, quotations on 136, 154.

27. Potter, *Lincoln and His Party*, 367–71; Bancroft, *Seward*, 2:134–35.

28. Brauer, "Seward's 'Foreign War Panacea,'" 154–57. Brauer too criticized Seward's plan, primarily on grounds that he exaggerated the strength of southern Unionism. Seward, however, had no immediate hopes for Unionism in the deep South. He relied instead on upper South Unionists, whose power was more formidable than Brauer recognized.

29. Lincoln to Seward, Apr. 1, 1861, *CWAL*, 4:316–18; Patrick Sowle, "A Reappraisal of Seward's Memorandum of April 1, 1861, to Lincoln," *Journal of Southern History* 33 (May 1967): 234–39; *New York Times*, Apr. 3, 1861, in Perkins, ed., *Northern Editorials*, 2:660–64; *Albany Evening Journal*, Apr. 4, 1861; Nicolay and Hay, *Lincoln*, 3:448–49.

30. George W. Summers to William H. Seward, Apr. 1, 1861, Seward Papers. The letter is addressed to Seward, but it was sent "under cover to a mutual friend in Washington, Mr. Seaton." William W. Seaton edited the *National Intelligencer*, the traditionalist Whig newspaper in Washington. James C. Welling, the go-between earlier used by Seward to communicate with Summers, was associate editor of the *Intelligencer*. See William E. Ames, *A History of the National Intelligencer* (Chapel Hill: University of North Carolina Press, 1972), 324–25.

This highly important document has not before been properly used by historians of the secession crisis. Summers's letter establishes that neither he nor any other leading Unionist in the Virginia convention spurned an overture from Lincoln during March. It thus demolishes the influential account in Nicolay and Hay, *Lincoln*, 3:427–28, which accused Virginia Unionists of ignoring an invitation to consult that Lincoln had extended sometime during March. The Summers letter is mentioned, but misdated as April 7,

1861, and therefore out of context, in Patrick M. Sowle, "The Conciliatory Republicans during the Winter of Secession" (Ph.D. dissertation, Duke University, 1963), 497–99.

31. Allan B. Magruder, "A Piece of Secret History: President Lincoln and the Virginia Convention of 1861," *Atlantic Monthly* 35 (1875): 438–45, quotations on 439; John B. Baldwin, *Interview between President Lincoln and Col. John B. Baldwin, April 4th, 1861: Statements and Evidence* (Staunton, Va.: Spectator Job Office, 1866), 10, 22–27. Baldwin's pamphlet includes his testimony of Feb. 10, 1866, before the Joint Committee on Reconstruction, plus letters corroborating his testimony.

Allan Nevins observed, and other historians of the secession period would probably agree, that "no episode of the time is murkier than this interview arranged by Seward" (*War for the Union*, 1:64, n. 57). The account that follows should make the Baldwin-Lincoln encounter more comprehensible.

On Baldwin, see H. W. Howard Knott, "John Brown Baldwin," *DAB*, 1:536; J. Lewis Peyton, *History of Augusta County, Virginia* (Staunton, Va.: S. M. Yost & Son, 1882), 379–85.

32. Baldwin, *Interview*; John Minor Botts, *The Great Rebellion: Its Secret History, Rise, Progress, and Disastrous Failure* (New York: Harper & Brothers, 1866), 194–202; Jack P. Maddex, Jr., *The Virginia Conservatives, 1867–1879: A Study in Reconstruction Politics* (Chapel Hill: University of North Carolina Press, 1970), 39–42; U.S. Congress, Joint Committee on Reconstruction, *Report of the Joint Committee on Reconstruction at the First Session Thirty-ninth Congress* (Washington, D.C.: U.S. Government Printing Office, 1866), pt. 2, 102–9, 114–23, see also 69–73 and 146.

33. Magruder, "Secret History," 439.

34. U.S. Congress, Joint Committee on Reconstruction, *Report of the Joint Committee on Reconstruction*, pt. 2, 102–9; Baldwin, *Interview*, 1–15.

35. Baldwin, *Interview*, 13–14, 23.

36. Samuel M. Price to John B. Baldwin, May 29, 1866, George W. Summers to Baldwin, May 18, 1866, Alexander H. H. Stuart to Baldwin, May 29, 1866, all in Baldwin, *Interview*, 24–27.

37. Baldwin, *Interview*, 6, 8, 15. Baldwin's movements are fully verified by contemporary evidence. He did not vote in the convention on April 4 or in the morning session on April 5, but he did return to vote by late afternoon, April 5. He made a Union speech before a large audience in Alexandria the night of April 4. The speech, announced in the *Alexandria Gazette* on April 4, and briefly summarized on April 5, gave Baldwin the "cover" to travel to Washington. Reese, ed., *Virginia Convention*, 3:137–38, 161, 203, 205, 209; *Alexandria Gazette*, Apr. 4, 5, 1861.

38. Botts, *Great Rebellion*, 195; U.S. Congress, Joint Committee on Reconstruction, *Report of the Joint Committee on Reconstruction*, pt. 2, 114–23, esp. 114; Wilmer L. Hall, "Lincoln's Interview with John B. Baldwin," *South Atlantic Quarterly* 13 (1914): 268–69; Baldwin, *Interview*, 3–5.

39. *New York Express*, quoted in *Richmond Semi-Weekly Enquirer*, Mar. 16, 1861; Baldwin, *Interview*, 13–14. Botts certainly did talk with Lincoln. He and several members of the Virginia legislature saw Lincoln on Friday

night, April 5. In all likelihood, Botts remembered correctly that he subsequently had a private meeting with Lincoln at the White House on Sunday night, April 7. There is a letter in the Lincoln Papers from Botts, dated April 7, asking for an interview that same evening. Botts was definitely in the Washington area as late as April 11, when he was reported urging distribution of federal patronage in Virginia to Douglas Democrats as well as to Union Whigs. There is no reason to discredit Botts's recollection that he did not return to Richmond until Monday the fifteenth. See *Cincinnati Commercial*, Apr. 8, 1861 (Washington report of Apr. 6, 1861), in *Louisville Daily Journal*, Apr. 9, 1861; *Alexandria Gazette*, Apr. 6, 8, 12, 1861 ("Homo" in Washington, Apr. 5, 7, 1861); *New York Herald*, Apr. 6, 7, 1861; Botts to Lincoln, Apr. 7, 1861, Lincoln Papers, LC (microfilm edition); Botts, *Great Rebellion*, 206. See also George Plumer Smith to John Hay, Jan. 9, 1863, Lincoln Papers, a document considered by some historians to provide corroboration for Botts from Lincoln himself; Benjamin P. Thomas, *Abraham Lincoln: A Biography* (New York: Knopf, 1952), 252, 540.

40. Alexander H. H. Stuart to John B. Baldwin, May 29, 1866, in Baldwin, *Interview*, 25–26.

41. Ibid., 10, 13.

42. Ibid., 11–12. By another account, Baldwin told Lincoln that an explicit administration promise not to coerce the seceded states would reduce the territorial controversy to "harmless and manageable dimensions" (Rev. R. L. Dabney, "Memoir of a Narrative Received of Colonel John B. Baldwin, of Staunton, Touching the Origin of the War," *Southern Historical Society Papers*, 44 vols. [Richmond: Southern Historical Society, 1876–1923], 1:448–49).

43. Baldwin, *Interview*, 11–13.

44. Samuel M. Price to John B. Baldwin, May 29, 1866, in Baldwin, *Interview*, 26–27.

45. Ibid.

46. Simon Cameron to Robert Anderson, Apr. 4, 1861, Abraham Lincoln to Andrew Curtin, Apr. 8, 1861, both in *CWAL*, 4:321–22, 324; Current, *Lincoln and the First Shot*, 96–102, 114, 196–99, 218–19; *New York Herald*, Apr. 5, 8, 1861.

47. The *Powhatan* episode has been a source of controversy ever since it occurred. Seward's commandeering of the ship impressed Navy Secretary Gideon Welles and others as a deliberate attempt to sabotage the Sumter resupply mission. Welles certainly had reason to feel indignant at Seward's high-handed meddling in naval business, but Potter sensibly concluded that Welles's accusations "do not seem justified" (Potter, *Lincoln and His Party*, 365–67; see also Bancroft, *Seward*, 2:129–30, 138–39, 144; Current, *Lincoln and the First Shot*, 103–6). For a good recapitulation of the *Powhatan* episode, see John Niven, *Gideon Welles: Lincoln's Secretary of the Navy* (New York: Oxford University Press, 1973), 332–36.

48. Simon Cameron to Robert S. Chew, Apr. 6, 1861, *CWAL*, 4:323–24; Current, *Lincoln and the First Shot*, 108–10, 116–17; Bancroft, *Seward*, 2:142–44; Nevins, *War for the Union*, 1:65. The attempt to reprovision Sumter also led to the rupture of communications between Seward and the

three Confederate commissioners in Washington, which had continued informally for a month through the agency of Supreme Court Justice John A. Campbell and was based on the assumption that Sumter would be evacuated (Bancroft, *Seward*, 2:140–42; Potter, *Lincoln and His Party*, 342–49; Henry G. Connor, *John Archibald Campbell, Associate Justice of the United States Supreme Court, 1853–1861* [Boston: Houghton Mifflin, 1920], 122–48).

My account does not address the much-debated question of just when Lincoln made an irrevocable decision to proceed with the Sumter resupply expedition. Lincoln himself retrospectively fixed the date as Saturday, April 6, when, upon learning that federal control over Fort Pickens was more precarious than he had earlier thought, he dispatched the messenger to South Carolina (*CWAL* 4:323–24, 424–25). Historians who emphasize his pacific inclinations find Lincoln's account persuasive: Potter, *Lincoln and His Party*, 362–63, and the introduction to the 1962 paperback edition, xxvi–xxvii; James G. Randall, *Lincoln the President*, 4 vols. (New York: Dodd, Mead, 1945–55), 1:333–35. Historians who depict Lincoln as having already concluded that force would be necessary to challenge the Confederacy tend, however, to place the date earlier, either on March 29, when he met with the cabinet, or on April 4, when he instructed both Captain Fox and Major Anderson about the resupply mission (Stampp, *And the War Came*, 282–84; Current, *Lincoln and the First Shot*, 96–102, 194–99). I have elsewhere introduced one new fragment of evidence that raises doubts about the Potter-Randall interpretation: Daniel W. Crofts, "James E. Harvey and the Secession Crisis," *Pennsylvania Magazine of History and Biography* 103 (Apr. 1979): 189–90. But see also the sophisticated reassessment by John Niven, which substantially corroborates Potter and Randall, *Gideon Welles*, 331–38.

49. Samuel Ward to S. L. M. Barlow, Apr. 8, 1861, Barlow Papers. Exceptionally accurate accounts may be found in the *New York Tribune*, Apr. 5, 6, 8, 10, 1861 (Washington reports dated Apr. 4, 5, 7, 9, 1861). *Tribune* reporter James E. Harvey, who had unique access to privileged information, probably filed the articles. See Crofts, "James E. Harvey and the Secession Crisis," 177–95.

CHAPTER 12

1. George W. Summers to James C. Welling, Mar. 19, 1861, in *Nation* 29 (1879): 383–84, copy in Blair Family Papers, LC; Robert Young Conrad to his wife, Mar. 24, 26, 29, 30, 1861, Robert Young Conrad Papers, VHS; Shanks, *Secession Movement in Virginia*, 183.

2. Alfred M. Barbour to Stephen A. Douglas, Apr. 2, 1861, Stephen A. Douglas Papers, University of Chicago; Reese, ed., *Virginia Convention*, 3:163, 311; Robert Young Conrad to his wife, Apr. 3, 4, 1861, Conrad Papers; John Janney to his wife, Apr. 4, 7, 1861, John Janney Papers, in possession of Lucas Phillips, Leesburg, Va.

3. Reese, ed., *Virginia Convention*, 3:203, 205, 209, 325–26, 333–34, 343–45; *Baltimore American*, Mar. 18, 1861 ("Special," Mar. 17, 1861); *Lynchburg*

Virginian, Mar. 19, 1861; *Cincinnati Commercial*, Apr. 8, 1861 (Washington report of Apr. 6, 1861), in *Louisville Daily Journal*, Apr. 9, 1861; *Alexandria Gazette*, Apr. 6, 8, 1861 ("Homo" in Washington, Apr. 5, 7, 1861); *New York Herald*, Apr. 6, 7, 1861.

4. Reese, ed., *Virginia Convention*, 3:271, 282–87, 290–91, 317.

5. Ibid., 304, 312, 317–20, 322, 328, 349–51; James B. Dorman to James D. Davidson, Apr. 9, 1861, James D. Davidson Papers, Wisconsin State Historical Society, copy in the U. B. Phillips Papers, Yale University; John Janney to his wife, Apr. 9, 1861, Janney Papers.

6. J. Everett to William H. Seward, Apr. 4, 1861, W. Dunn to John A. Gilmer, Apr. 11, 1861, Gilmer to Seward, Apr. 12, 1861, all in William H. Seward Papers, University of Rochester; James B. Dorman to James D. Davidson, Apr. 9, 1861, Davidson Papers, copy in Phillips Papers.

7. Reese, ed., *Virginia Convention*, 3:432; Robert Young Conrad to his wife, Apr. 11, 13, 1861, Conrad Papers.

8. Reese, ed., *Virginia Convention*, 3:454–56, 463–72. Fort Taylor at Key West and Fort Jefferson on Dry Tortugas Island (further beyond Key West in the Gulf of Mexico) were so remote from settled parts of Florida that they did not pose any threat of a collision between federal and Confederate forces. See *National Intelligencer*, Mar. 21, 1861.

9. George W. Summers to William C. Rives, Apr. 12, 1861, William C. Rives Papers, LC; Robert Young Conrad to his wife, Apr. 10, 11, 13, 1861, Conrad Papers.

10. W. A. Swanberg, *First Blood: The Story of Fort Sumter* (New York: Charles Scribner's Sons, 1957), 299–332; Robert Young Conrad to his wife, Apr. 13, 14, 1861, Conrad Papers; Reese, ed., *Virginia Convention*, 3:722–23, 725–29.

11. William C. Rives to George W. Summers, Apr. 15, 1861, copy, Rives Papers; James B. Dorman to James D. Davidson, Apr. 14, 1861, Davidson Papers, copy in Phillips Papers; Robert Young Conrad to his wife, Apr. 14, 1861, Conrad Papers; John Janney to his wife, Apr. 15, 1861, Janney Papers.

12. *Alexandria Gazette*, Apr. 12, 1861; Abraham Lincoln, "Reply to a Committee from the Virginia Convention," Apr. 13, 1861, in *CWAL*, 4:329–31; Shanks, *Secession Movement in Virginia*, 195–99; Reese, ed., *Virginia Convention*, 3:733–35, 4:12–13; James B. Dorman to James D. Davidson, Apr. 14, 1861, Davidson Papers, copy in Phillips Papers; Robert Young Conrad to his wife, Apr. 14, 1861, Conrad Papers. The Virginia commissioners sailed from Norfolk to Baltimore on the same ship, coincidentally, as Lincoln's messenger, R. S. Chew, who was returning to Washington after notifying South Carolina authorities that an attempt would be made to reprovision Fort Sumter (*Alexandria Gazette*, Apr. 12, 1861).

13. "Proclamation Calling Militia and Convening Congress," Apr. 15, 1861, *CWAL*, 4:331–33.

14. John Strother Pendleton to William H. Seward, Apr. 13, 1861, Alexander H. H. Stuart to Seward, Apr. 15, 1861 (telegram), both in Seward Papers; Robert Young Conrad to his wife, Apr. 14, 1861, Conrad Papers; John

Janney to his wife, Apr. 15, 1861, Janney Papers; Reese, ed., *Virginia Convention,* 4:12–13.

15. Reese, ed., *Virginia Convention,* 3:749–50, 759–64.

16. Ibid., 4:12–13.

17. Ibid., 3, 12–13, 26–28, 38–47, 75–76; F. N. Boney, *John Letcher of Virginia: The Story of Virginia's Civil War Governor* (University, Ala.: University of Alabama Press, 1966), 112.

18. James B. Dorman to James D. Davidson, Apr. 16, 1861, Davidson Papers, copy in Phillips Papers; Reese, ed., *Virginia Convention,* 4:21–23, 70, 122–23, 144–45. Baldwin and Summers voted with the minority of unconditional Unionists against secession.

19. Robert Young Conrad to his wife, Apr. 20, 1861, Conrad Papers; *Richmond Semi-Weekly Enquirer,* Apr. 20, 1861; Shanks, *Secession Movement in Virginia,* 208.

20. *Wheeling Intelligencer,* Mar. 2, 1861 (A. W. Campbell in Richmond, Feb. 26, 1861); *Baltimore Clipper,* in *Louisville Daily Journal,* Mar. 15, 1861; Mrs. William C. Rives to William C. Rives, Jr., Mar. 15, 1861, Rives Papers.

21. Samuel McD. Moore to James D. Davidson, Apr. 6, 1861, Davidson Papers, copy in Phillips Papers; *Alexandria Gazette,* Apr. 11, 1861; Frederic Bancroft, *Slave-Trading in the Old South* (1931; rpt. New York: Ungar, 1959), 94–119.

22. Samuel McD. Moore to James D. Davidson, Mar. 29, Apr. 6, 1861, James B. Dorman to Davidson, Mar. 29, 31, 1861, Davidson to Dorman, Apr. 2, 1861, all in Davidson Papers, copies in Phillips Papers; *Wheeling Intelligencer,* Feb. 27, 1861 (report by Alexander Campbell in Richmond, Feb. 24, 1861); *Nashville Weekly Patriot,* Apr. 8, 1861; *New York Tribune,* Mar. 20, 1861 (report from Richmond, Mar. 17, 1861); Shanks, *Secession Movement in Virginia,* 184, 188.

23. William K. Scarborough, ed., *The Diary of Edmund Ruffin,* 2 vols. to date (Baton Rouge: Louisiana State University Press, 1972–), 2:568–71 (entry of Feb. 7, 1863). On Willoughby Newton, see ibid., 1:10 n., 199–200, 203, 221–25 (entries of June 5, 23, Aug. 12, 13, 14, 17, 1858); Shanks, *Secession Movement in Virginia,* 34, 71–73. On Ruffin's departure from Virginia before Lincoln's inauguration, see Scarborough, ed., *Ruffin Diary,* 1:557–59 (entries of Feb. 27, 28, Mar. 2, 3, 1861).

24. Scarborough, ed., *Ruffin Diary,* 2:568–71 (entry of Feb. 7, 1863); *Wheeling Intelligencer,* Apr. 1, 1861; *Alexandria Gazette,* Apr. 1, 1861; *New York Herald,* Apr. 3, 1861. Several collections of secessionist manuscripts contain correspondence about the proposed April 16 meeting. See James W. Walker to Angus R. Blakey, Mar. 30, 1861, Angus R. Blakey Papers, Duke; James S. Grigsby to John Warren Grigsby, Apr. 14, 1861, John Warren Grigsby Papers, Filson Club, Louisville, Ky.; Richard L. Ellis to Charles Ellis, Apr. 13, 1861, and William A. Perkins to Charles Ellis, Apr. 1861, both in Munford-Ellis Family Papers, Duke.

25. Alice Janney to John Janney, Apr. 4, 5, 1861, Janney Papers; *Wheeling Intelligencer,* Apr. 3, 1861; *Wellsburg Herald* and *Grafton Virginian* in *Wheeling Intelligencer,* Apr. 6, 13, 1861.

26. Scarborough, ed., *Ruffin Diary*, 2:568–71 (entry of Feb. 7, 1863).

27. The indispensable new biography of Wise by Craig M. Simpson, *A Good Southerner: The Life of Henry A. Wise of Virginia* (Chapel Hill: University of North Carolina Press, 1985), includes a fine chapter on the crisis of 1860–61: "Failed Hope and the Choice of War," pp. 219–51. The quotation is on 220; physical descriptions are on 19, 95, 110–11.

28. Henry A. Wise to Andrew Hunter, Apr. 2, 1861, in *Proceedings of the Massachusetts Historical Society* 46 (Dec. 1912): 248; Wise to George Booker, Jan. 14, 20, 1861, George Booker Papers, Duke; Wise to Angus R. Blakey, Feb. 3, 1861, Blakey Papers; Reese, ed., *Virginia Convention*, 3:460–62.

29. Henry A. Wise to Andrew Hunter, Apr. 2, 1861, in *Proceedings of the Massachusetts Historical Society* 46 (Dec. 1912): 248; John Janney to Alice Janney, Mar. 26, 1861, Janney Papers; George P. Tayloe to B. O. Tayloe, April 20(?), 1861, quoted in B. O. Tayloe to William H. Seward, Apr. 23, 1861, Seward Papers.

30. *Lynchburg Virginian*, Apr. 9, 10, 1861; Reese, ed., *Virginia Convention*, 3:474–75.

31. Scarborough, ed., *Ruffin Diary*, 2:568–71 (entry of Feb. 7, 1863).

32. Robert Young Conrad to his wife, Apr. 14, 1861, Conrad Papers.

33. Ibid., Apr. 15, 1861.

34. James B. Dorman to James D. Davidson, Apr. 16, 1861, Davidson Papers, copy in Phillips Papers; Reese, ed., *Virginia Convention*, 4:50, 58; John Beauchamp Jones, *A Rebel War Clerk's Diary, at the Confederate States Capital*, 2 vols. (Philadelphia: J. B. Lippincott, 1866), 1:20–21 (entry of Apr. 16, 1861).

35. Henry A. Wise, *Seven Decades of the Union* (Philadelphia: J. B. Lippincott, 1872), 278; Barton H. Wise, *The Life of Henry A. Wise of Virginia, 1806–1876* (New York: Macmillan, 1899), 274–80; Boney, *Letcher*, 112–16; John Niven, *Gideon Welles: Lincoln's Secretary of the Navy* (New York: Oxford University Press, 1973), 340–45; John Sherman Long, "The Gosport Affair, 1861," *Journal of Southern History* 23 (1957): 155–72, esp. 159–60; Donald B. Webster, Jr., "The Last Days of the Harpers Ferry Armory," *Civil War History* 5 (1959): 30–44. Federal forces abandoned both Harpers Ferry, on the night of April 18, and Gosport, on April 20.

36. Reese, ed., *Virginia Convention*, 4:124, 160–62, 171–78.

37. Sitterson, *Secession in North Carolina*, 203.

38. John Minor Botts, *The Great Rebellion: Its Secret History, Rise, Progress, and Disastrous Failure* (New York: Harper & Brothers, 1866), 206.

39. Francis H. Pierpont to William H. Seward, Apr. 8, 1861, William A. Harrison to Seward, Apr. 2, 1861, both in Seward Papers.

40. Felix Zollicoffer to Stephen A. Douglas, Dec. 31, 1860, Douglas Papers; *Nashville Union and American*, Dec. 25, 1860; William R. Hurley to Andrew Johnson, Dec. 23, 1860, *Johnson Papers*, 4:74–75.

41. Robert Johnson to Andrew Johnson, Jan. 13, 1861, *Johnson Papers*, 4:157–60; *Nashville Union and American*, Jan. 3, 19, 1861; William S. Flippin in *Nashville Weekly Patriot*, Jan. 28, 1861.

42. John Lellyett to Andrew Johnson, Jan. 23, 1861, William R. Hurley to

Johnson, Jan. 14, Mar. 4, 1861, all in *Johnson Papers*, 4:167–68, 184–86, 365–66; *Nashville Democrat* quoted in *Wheeling Intelligencer*, Jan. 19, Mar. 14, 1861.

43. John Bell to A. Burwell, Dec. 6, 1860, Neill S. Brown to A. Milan et al., Dec. 10, 1860, both in *Nashville Weekly Patriot*, Dec. 10, 17, 1860; Robert Johnson to Andrew Johnson, Jan. 17, 1861, Jesse B. Clements to Johnson, Mar. 1, 1861, both in *Johnson Papers*, 4:178–79, 348–50.

44. John Edmond Gonzales, "The Public Career of Henry Stuart Foote, 1804–1880" (Ph.D. dissertation, University of North Carolina, 1957); Gonzales, "Henry Stuart Foote: A Forgotten Unionist of the Fifties," *Southern Quarterly* 1 (1963): 129–39.

45. Jeremiah Clemens to Henry S. Foote, Feb. 10, 1861, Foote to Clemens, Feb. 20, 1861, both in *Nashville Union and American*, Feb. 21, 1861; Foote to John J. Crittenden in ibid., Apr. 2, 1861. Foote obscured his secession crisis role in two postwar books, written from a markedly more pro-Republican and antisecessionist perspective than his actual view in early 1861: *War of the Rebellion; or, Scylla and Charybdis. Consisting of Observations upon the Causes, Course, and Consequences of the Late Civil War in the United States* (New York: Harper & Brothers, 1866), 264–334; and *Casket of Reminiscences* (Washington, D.C.: Chronicle Publishing Co., 1874), 133–42. Foote's books were a lame effort, disguised as memoirs, to ally himself with the victors of the Civil War. But *War of the Rebellion* and *Casket of Reminiscences* prevented John E. Gonzales, Foote's biographer, from recognizing how totally he had renounced his traditional Unionism by late January 1861.

46. *Nashville Union and American*, Jan. 27–Feb. 10, 1861, passim; abortive withdrawal offer on Feb. 2; election results on Feb. 10, 12.

47. Ibid., Mar. 9, 22, 1861; *Memphis Appeal*, Mar. 17, 20, 23, 1861; *Memphis Avalanche*, Mar. 13, 1861.

48. "W." in *Nashville Patriot*, Mar. 10, 1861; John Bell in *Nashville Republican Banner*, May 10, 1861; Jeptha Fowlkes to Andrew Johnson, Mar. 10, 1861, *Johnson Papers*, 4:378–80.

49. *Nashville Union and American*, Oct. 12, 1860, in Dumond, ed., *Southern Editorials*, 183; Jesse B. Clements to Andrew Johnson, Feb. 18, Mar. 1, 1861, *Johnson Papers*, 4:308, 348–50. On the "Post Office Clique," see ibid., 337–38 (n. 3), 343, 350, 432. Embracing the Bank of Tennessee and the *Nashville Union and American* in addition to the Nashville Post Office, the "clique" made up a powerful interest in the Tennessee Democratic party.

50. Herman Cox to Edward Bates, Mar. 11, 1861, General Records of the Department of Justice, RG 60, NA; Andrew Johnson to Edward Bates, Mar. 25, 1861, William R. Hurley to Johnson, Mar. 14, 25, 1861, Hu Douglas to Johnson, Feb. 28, 1861, Jeptha Fowlkes to Johnson, Mar. 13, 1861, Cave Johnson to Andrew Johnson, Mar. 21, 1861, all in *Johnson Papers*, 4:342–44, 388–89, 394–95, 424–25, 427–28, 431–32; John Lellyett to T. A. R. Nelson, Mar. 27, 1861, T. A. R. Nelson Papers, McClung Collection, Lawson McGhee Library, Knoxville, Tenn.; *Nashville Republican Banner*, Mar. 26, 1861; *Nashville Patriot*, Mar. 28, 1861. Former postmaster Samuel R. Anderson be-

came president of the Bank of Tennessee in March 1861 (*Johnson Papers*, 4:343, n. 4; Samuel R. Anderson to Johnson, Mar. 26, 1861, ibid., 432).

51. Felix A. Reeve to William H. Seward, Apr. 6, 1861, T. A. R. Nelson to Abraham Lincoln, Apr. 14, 1861, both in General Records of the Department of Justice, RG 60, NA; James M. Quarles to Andrew Johnson, Mar. 27, 1861, William McNish to Johnson, Mar. 28, Apr. 3, 1861, all in Andrew Johnson Papers, LC (microfilm edition); John Lellyett to T. A. R. Nelson, Mar. 27, 1861, Nelson Papers; *Johnson Papers*, 4:337–38 (n. 3); *Brownlow's Weekly Knoxville Whig*, Mar. 30, Apr. 6, 1861.

52. Jeptha Fowlkes to Andrew Johnson, Mar. 10, 1861, *Johnson Papers*, 4:378–80; *Brownlow's Weekly Knoxville Whig*, Mar. 23, Apr. 6, 13, 1861. Brownlow, a skilled political infighter, did not allow consistency to stand in his way. He attacked the Johnson-Etheridge combination from both directions simultaneously. Brownlow thus accused Johnson of sponsoring the appointment to federal office of several secessionist Democrats. Etheridge's sins were different, according to Brownlow. The congressman was a Republican in disguise, who was therefore responsible for Lincoln's appointment to diplomatic posts of abolitionists such as Joshua Giddings.

53. William S. Cheatham to T. A. R. Nelson, Apr. 3, 1861, Nelson Papers; *Nashville Union and American*, Apr. 2, 1861; *Nashville Republican Banner*, Apr. 5, 1861.

54. *Nashville Republican Banner*, Apr. 9, 1861.

55. Henry Clay Yeatman to his wife, Apr. 17, 1861, Polk-Yeatman Collection, TSLA; Alexander J. D. Thurston to Andrew Johnson, Apr. 20, 1861, *Johnson Papers*, 4:472–73; *Nashville Republican Banner*, Apr. 17, 18, 1861; A. Himan to William B. Campbell, Apr. 21, 1861, Campbell Family Papers, Duke; William V. Mathews to George B. Boyles, Apr. 15, 17, 1861, Eliza H. Gordon Papers, Duke.

56. A. Himan to William B. Campbell, Apr. 21, 1861, Campbell Papers; *Nashville Union and American*, Apr. 21, 1861; Joseph H. Parks, "John Bell and Secession," *East Tennessee Historical Society Publications* 16 (1944): 30–47; Joseph H. Parks, *John Bell of Tennessee* (Baton Rouge: Louisiana State University Press, 1950), 395–401.

57. A most inaccurate explanation for the collapse of Unionist strength in Tennessee must be addressed here. Historian J. Milton Henry, relying heavily on evidence about the renewed feud between William G. Brownlow and Andrew Johnson in March 1861, developed the farfetched thesis that "Bell Unionists," indignant about the Johnson-Etheridge monopoly of Tennessee patronage, decided to support secession and give up "their lengthy battle to save the Union." In Henry's view, patronage quarrels were thus the true reason for Tennessee's dramatic shift from Unionism to secession in April. Lincoln's rejection of a "pacific policy" in calling for troops "was conveniently seized upon by the disgruntled Conservatives in order to defend their action and give it the appearance of a plausible consistency" (Henry, "The Revolution in Tennessee, February, 1861, to June, 1861," *Tennessee Historical Quarterly* 18 [1959]: 99–119, quotations on 113, 117).

Such an analysis obscures the truth and distorts the historical record. The reason for the collapse of Unionism in Middle and West Tennessee could hardly be more obvious: Lincoln's proclamation for seventy-five thousand troops forced Tennesseans to make the dreaded choice of allegiance in a war between the North and the South, and most chose the South. Until that stark choice was forced upon them—and the shock was intensified because Lincoln's course in March had appeared "pacific"—Tennesseans overwhelmingly favored the delusive option of peaceable reunion.

It makes no sense to argue that the sudden revolution of public sentiment occurring in Tennessee in mid-April 1861 resulted from patronage disagreements. Henry's essay utterly failed to document that Brownlow spoke for Bell or other Unionist leaders, or that Brownlow's obviously self-serving course had any serious influence on the Unionist electorate. What the Brownlow-Johnson rupture of late March 1861 showed was just the opposite of what Henry thought. Looking ahead a month and knowing that the Union party had by then almost shrunk from sight, Henry identified factional disagreement as its fatal weakness. In fact, however, factional disagreements during March demonstrated that Unionists considered their majority secure enough to quarrel among themselves. Two months before, they would not have dared, and a month later, such Unionists as were left in the state, Brownlow and Johnson prominent among them, earnestly subordinated any hint of rivalry.

It is regrettable that the editors of *The Papers of Andrew Johnson* have partially accepted J. Milton Henry's unsound scholarship and thereby given it undeserved permanence (4:xii, 470, 5:xxxii). See also James L. Baumgardner, "Abraham Lincoln, Andrew Johnson, and the Federal Patronage: An Attempt to Save Tennessee for the Union," *East Tennessee Historical Society Publications* 45 (1973): 51–60. Baumgardner echoes Henry.

58. Robert Johnson to Andrew Johnson, Apr. 29, 1861, *Johnson Papers*, 4:474–75; S. B. Moore to William B. Campbell, May 5, 1861, Campbell Papers.

59. C. B. Harrison to Lawrence O'B. Branch, Dec. 2, 1860, Lawrence O'B. Branch Papers, Duke; *Raleigh Daily Ad Valorem Banner*, Feb. 21, Apr. 5, 1861; *North Carolina Tri-Weekly Standard*, Feb. 5, 1861; *North Carolina Semi-Weekly Standard*, Mar. 2, 23, 27, 1861; *Raleigh Semi-Weekly Register*, Mar. 27, Apr. 6, 1861.

60. *Raleigh Semi-Weekly Register*, Mar. 2, 1861; George E. Badger to Salmon P. Chase, Mar. 20, 1861, in Chase to Edward Bates, Apr. 5, 1861, in General Records of the Department of Justice, RG 60, NA.

61. *North Carolina Weekly State Journal*, Mar. 6, 1861 ("Oriens," Mar. 1, 1861).

62. Lawrence O'B. Branch to his wife, Dec. 11, 1860, Mrs. Lawrence O'B. Branch Papers, NCDAH; Branch to A. M. Lewis, Feb. 20, 1861, in *North Carolina Semi-Weekly Standard*, Mar. 30, 1861; *Raleigh Daily Ad Valorem Banner* in *North Carolina Semi-Weekly Standard*, Apr. 6, 1861; William W. Pierson, Jr., "Lawrence O'Bryan Branch," *DAB*, 2:597–98.

63. Beth G. Crabtree and James W. Patton, eds., "*Journal of a Secesh Lady*":

The Diary of Catherine Ann Devereux Edmondston, 1860–1866 (Raleigh: North Carolina Department of Cultural Resources, Division of Archives and History, 1979), 16–17 (diary entry of Nov. 25, 1860); Henry W. Miller to Stephen A. Douglas, Mar. 31, 1861, Nov. 28, 1860, Douglas Papers. See also Henry W. Miller to Lawrence O'B. Branch, May 22, 1860, Mrs. L. O'B. Branch Papers; Henry W. Miller to William A. Graham, Dec. 29, 1860, Graham Papers, SHC-UNC, in Max R. Williams and J. G. deRoulhac Hamilton, eds., *The Papers of William Alexander Graham*, 7 vols. to date (Raleigh: North Carolina State Department of Archives and History, 1957–), 5:203–5.

64. *Raleigh Semi-Weekly Register*, Mar. 23, 27, Apr. 6, 1861; *North Carolina Semi-Weekly Standard*, Apr. 13, 1861. Southern Rights organizers had met in Goldsborough on March 22–23: see Sitterson, *Secession Movement in North Carolina*, 234–37.

65. *North Carolina Semi-Weekly Standard*, Apr. 24, May 8, 1861.

CHAPTER 13

1. Horace Maynard to Edward Bates, Apr. 18(?), 1861, General Records of the Department of Justice, RG 60, NA.

2. John Bell, speech of Apr. 23, 1861, in *Nashville Republican Banner*, May 10, 1861; *North Carolina Semi-Weekly Standard*, Apr. 20, 1861.

3. John Minor Botts, *The Great Rebellion: Its Secret History, Rise, Progress, and Disastrous Failure* (New York: Harper & Brothers, 1866), 205–6.

4. Josiah Cowles to Calvin J. Cowles, June 3, 1861, Calvin J. Cowles Papers, NCDAH, quoted in John C. Inscoe, "Slavery, Sectionalism, and Secession in Western North Carolina" (Ph.D. dissertation, University of North Carolina at Chapel Hill, 1985), 261; Conway D. Whittle to Lewis N. Whittle, May 10, June 13, 1861, Lewis N. Whittle Papers, SHC-UNC; Jonathan Worth to Springs, Oak, & Co., May 13, 1861, Worth to Dr. C. W. Woolen, May 17, 1861, in J. G. deRoulhac Hamilton, ed., *The Correspondence of Jonathan Worth*, 2 vols. (Raleigh: Broughton, 1909), 1:143, 145–48; Callaway Campbell to Mildred Walker Campbell, May 6, 1861, Charles Campbell Papers, College of William and Mary.

5. W. N. H. Smith to Zebulon Vance, Apr. 26, 1861, in Frontis W. Johnston, ed., *The Papers of Zebulon Baird Vance*, 1 vol. to date (Raleigh: North Carolina State Department of Archives and History, 1963), 99–100; Benjamin O. Tayloe to William H. Seward, Apr. 23, 1861 (including extracts from George P. Tayloe to Benjamin O. Tayloe, Apr. 20?, 1861), John A. Gilmer to Seward, Apr. 21, 1861, both in William H. Seward Papers, University of Rochester; Jonathan Worth to Springs, Oak, & Co., May 13, 1861, Hamilton, ed., *Worth Correspondence*, 1:143.

6. Bruce S. Greenawalt, ed., "Unionists in Rockbridge County: The Correspondence of James Dorman Davidson Concerning the Virginia Secession Convention of 1861," *Virginia Magazine of History and Biography* 73 (1965): 100–101 (n. 32); James D. Davidson to James B. Dorman, Apr. 16, 1861, James D. Davidson Papers, Wisconsin State Historical Society, copy in U. B.

Phillips Papers, Yale University, in ibid., 100–101; *Richmond Semi-Weekly Enquirer*, June 18, 1861.

7. William C. Rives to George W. Summers, Apr. 15, 19, 1861, copies, William C. Rives to William C. Rives, Jr., Apr. 20, May 6, 1861, all in William C. Rives Papers, LC.

8. *Louisville Daily Journal*, Apr. 15, 1861.

9. James B. Dorman to James D. Davidson, Apr. 16, 1861, Davidson Papers, copy in Phillips Papers; William S. Pettigrew's notes for a speech at Cool Spring, North Carolina, Apr. 26, 1861, Pettigrew Family Papers, SHC-UNC; John H. Bills Diary, entries of Feb. 8, Apr. 16, June 8, 1861, SHC-UNC.

10. Jonathan Worth to T. C. Worth and B. G. Worth, May 13, 1861, Worth to Springs, Oak & Co., May 13, 1861, Worth to Dr. C. W. Woolen, May 17, 1861, all in Hamilton, ed., *Worth Correspondence*, 1:141–43, 145–48.

11. *Salisbury Carolina Watchman*, Apr. 16, 23, 1861; *Alexandria Gazette*, Apr. 16, 23, 1861; Jonathan Worth to Dr. C. W. Woolen, May 17, 1861, in Hamilton, ed., *Worth Correspondence*, 1:148.

12. J. H. Gilmer to Stephen A. Douglas, Apr. 17, 1861, Samuel A. Gordon to Douglas, Apr. 17, 1861, both in Stephen A. Douglas Papers, University of Chicago; *Alexandria Gazette*, Apr. 19, 1861 ("Aliquis," Apr. 17, 1861).

13. John H. Bills Diary, Apr. 16, 1861, SHC-UNC; Thomas Macon to Jonathan Worth, May 6, 1861, Worth to H. L. Myrover, May 6, 1861, Worth to David G. Worth, May 15, 1861, Worth to Dr. C. W. Woolen, May 17, 1861, all in Hamilton, ed., *Worth Correspondence*, 1:138–40, 144–48; Jonathan Worth to David G. Worth, Apr. 26, 1861, Worth Family Papers, Duke.

14. John A. Gilmer to William H. Seward, Apr. 21, 1861, Seward Papers.

15. Shanks, *Secession Movement in Virginia*, 204–13; Campbell, *Attitude of Tennesseans*, 194–212; Sitterson, *Secession Movement in North Carolina*, 240–49.

16. The above paragraph is reconstructed from the vote totals (and indications of voting patterns in counties not officially reported) issued by Virginia Governor John Letcher, June 14, 1861, in *Richmond Semi-Weekly Enquirer*, June 18, 1861, supplemented by vote totals and approximations of totals for missing counties in Richard Orr Curry, *A House Divided: A Study of Statehood Politics and the Copperhead Movement in West Virginia* (Pittsburgh: University of Pittsburgh Press, 1964), Appendix I, 141–47. I have made inferences about unreported totals for a few eastern counties.

17. Sitterson, *Secession Movement in North Carolina*, 244–49; Marc W. Kruman, *Parties and Politics in North Carolina, 1836–1865* (Baton Rouge: Louisiana State University Press, 1983), 219–20. On persistent wartime Unionism in North Carolina, see the following works by William T. Auman: "North Carolina's Inner Civil War: Randolph County" (M.A. thesis, University of North Carolina at Greensboro, 1978), plus three important articles from the *North Carolina Historical Review*, the first of which was coauthored by David D. Scarboro: "The Heroes of America in Civil War North Carolina," 58 (Autumn 1981): 327–63; "Neighbor against Neighbor: The Inner Civil War in the Randolph County Area of Confederate North Carolina," 61 (Jan. 1984):

59–92; "Bryan Tyson: Southern Unionist and American Patriot," 62 (July 1985): 257–92. See also Philip Shaw Paludan, *Victims: A True Story of the Civil War* (Knoxville: University of Tennessee Press, 1981).

18. Appendix I, which introduces the reader to multiple regression, contains additional information about voting behavior in Tennessee during the secession crisis.

19. Oliver P. Temple, *Notable Men of Tennessee, from 1833 to 1875, Their Times and Their Contemporaries* (New York: Cosmopolitan Press, 1912), 243.

20. Southern Claims Commission Records for George W. Eastham, De Kalb County, Tennessee, and Edward L. Jourdan, Rutherford County, Tennessee, RG 217, NA.

21. Southern Claims Commission Records for Henry C. Sinclair, Williamson County, Tennessee, Samuel B. Watkins and Edward L. Jourdan, Rutherford County, Tennessee, and William H. Krantz, Loudoun County, Virginia, RG 217, NA.

22. Southern Claims Commission Records for James M. Haynes and John J. Neely, Rutherford County, Tennessee, and Henry L. Rhodes, Rockingham County, Virginia, RG 217, NA, the latter cited in Samuel Horst, *Mennonites in the Confederacy: A Study in Civil War Pacifism* (Scottdale, Pa.: Herald Press, 1967), 26–27.

23. Southern Claims Commission Records for Starling Proctor, Orange County, North Carolina, Joseph R. Thompson, Rutherford County, Tennessee, and Amasa Hough, Loudoun County, Virginia, RG 217, NA.

24. June 1861 returns by voting district for Bedford County are filed in the TSLA. Southern Claims Commission reports for the following Bedford County individuals are illuminating: Benjamin F. Wiggins, Mary Atkinson, William H. H. Baxter, and Thomas W. Buchanan, RG 217, NA.

25. Voting returns for Liberty and Alexandria, Tennessee, are in the *Nashville Republican Banner*, Feb. 12, June 11, 1861. Southern Claims Commission reports for the following De Kalb County individuals tell much about local unconditional Unionism and Stokes's regiment: George W. Eastham, Ruth Hathaway, John Jones, and John Davis, Sr., RG 217, NA.

26. Gary Blankinship, "Colonel Fielding Hurst and the Hurst Nation," *West Tennessee Historical Society Papers* 34 (1980): 71–87; Weston A. Goodspeed, ed., *History of Tennessee from the Earliest Times to the Present: Together with an Historical and Biographical Sketch of Maury, Williamson, Rutherford, Wilson, Bedford, and Marshall Counties* (Nashville: Goodspeed Publishing Co., 1886), 823.

27. Southern Claims Commission records for Jane Read and William A. Read, Henderson County, Tennessee, and for Caleb Cox, Kindred Dodds, Thomas J. Fariss, and Henry C. Harris, McNairy County, Tennessee, RG 217, NA.

28. February 1861 voting returns for Smith County are filed at TSLA. The slave population percentage is derived from ICPSR data. See Prologue, n. 2.

29. F. H. Gordon to William B. Campbell, Apr. 21, 1861, Campbell Family Papers, Duke.

30. Ibid.

31. Ibid., May 24, 1861. Quotations in the next paragraph draw from the same source.

32. Ibid., Emerson Etheridge to Campbell, May 9, 1861, both in ibid. Etheridge's own influence helped to turn out a substantial Union vote in his congressional district (Campbell, *Attitudes of Tennesseans*, 206).

33. B. C. Smith to William B. Campbell, June 2, 1861, Campbell Papers; William B. Stokes and William B. Campbell to Andrew Johnson, May 8, 1862, F. H. Gordon to Johnson, May 27, 1862, James M. Thomas to Johnson, June 15, 1862, all in *Johnson Papers*, 5:370–71, 423–25, 482–83.

34. A. O. P. Nicholson to "Dear Greene" (unidentified), May 5, 1861, in Joseph H. Parks, ed., "Some Tennessee Letters, 1849 to 1864," *Tennessee Historical Quarterly* 4 (1945): 251–53.

35. *Nashville Republican Banner*, May 3, 4, 1861, parts of which are preserved in the William B. Campbell scrapbooks, Campbell Papers.

36. *Lebanon Herald*, in *Nashville Republican Banner*, May 3, 1861.

EPILOGUE

1. Henry Adams, "The Great Secession Winter of 1860–61," *Proceedings of the Massachusetts Historical Society* 43 (1910): 683–84.

2. *Richmond Whig*, Mar. 19, 21, 1861. The Arkansas convention, which met between March 4 and 21, appointed delegates to the Border State Conference and instructed them to work for agreement on an ultimatum of constitutional amendments that would be submitted to the northern states for approval. The convention then adjourned to await the action of the conference. See James M. Woods, *Rebellion and Realignment: Arkansas's Road to Secession* (Fayetteville: University of Arkansas Press, 1987), 133–52; Jack B. Scroggs, "Arkansas in the Secession Crisis," *Arkansas Historical Quarterly* 12 (1953): 208–15. Virginia Unionists had similar plans. See Reese, ed., *Virginia Convention*, 1:527–28.

3. U. B. Phillips, *The Course of the South to Secession*, ed. E. Merton Coulter (1939; rpt. New York: Hill and Wang, 1964), 134–40; Stephen A. Channing, *Crisis of Fear: Secession in South Carolina* (New York: Simon and Schuster, 1970), 94–130; William H. Harrison to Edmund Ruffin, Apr. 7, 1861, Edmund Ruffin Papers, VHS; James S. Grigsby to John Warren Grigsby, Apr. 14, 1861, John Warren Grigsby Papers, Filson Club, Louisville, Ky.

4. Bertram Wyatt-Brown, *Yankee Saints and Southern Sinners* (Baton Rouge: Louisiana State University Press, 1985), 205.

5. Harry A. Volz III, "Party, State, and Nation: Kentucky and the Coming of the American Civil War" (Ph.D. dissertation, University of Virginia, 1982), 439–68.

6. Glyndon G. Van Deusen, *William Henry Seward* (New York: Oxford University Press, 1967), 249, 283; Kenneth M. Stampp, *And the War Came: The North and the Secession Crisis, 1860–61* (Baton Rouge: Louisiana State Uni-

versity Press, 1950), 271–72; Frederic Bancroft, *The Life of William H. Seward*, 2 vols. (New York: Harper & Brothers, 1899–1900), 2:120–21; Allan Nevins, *The War for the Union*, 4 vols. (New York: Charles Scribner's Sons, 1959–71), 1:39, 72, 74.

7. Seward to Lincoln, Mar. 15, 1861, Abraham Lincoln Papers, LC (microfilm edition), in Bancroft, *Seward*, 2:99.

8. Montgomery Blair to Lincoln, Mar. 15, 1861, Lincoln Papers.

9. Seward to Lincoln, Mar. 15, 1861, Lincoln Papers, in Bancroft, *Seward*, 2:100.

10. Lincoln contributed the famous phrase but disavowed the policy ("Annual Message to Congress," Dec. 3, 1861, *CWAL*, 5:49).

11. David M. Potter, *The South and the Sectional Conflict* (Baton Rouge: Louisiana State University Press, 1968), 245–46.

12. Adams, "Great Secession Winter," 684.

APPENDIX I

1. For explanations about the use of multiple regressions to study voting behavior, see William H. Flanigan and Nancy H. Zingale, "Relationships among Variables," in Jerome H. Clubb, William H. Flanigan, and Nancy H. Zingale, *Analyzing Electoral History: A Guide to the Study of American Voter Behavior* (Beverly Hills: Sage, 1981), 235–66, esp. 249–58; Allan J. Lichtman, "Critical Election Theory and the Reality of American Presidential Politics, 1916–1940," *American Historical Review* 81 (Apr. 1976): 324–26; Peyton McCrary, Clark Miller, and Dale Baum, "Class and Party in the Secession Crisis: Voting Behavior in the Deep South," *Journal of Interdisciplinary History* 8 (Winter 1978): 449–50; William E. Gienapp, "Nebraska, Nativism, and Rum: The Failure of Fusion in Pennsylvania, 1854," *Pennsylvania Magazine of History and Biography* 109 (Oct. 1985): 464; William E. Gienapp, *The Origins of the Republican Party, 1852–1856* (New York: Oxford University Press, 1987), 478–80.

All multiple regression calculations in Appendix I are weighted proportionate to the number of eligible voters in each county in 1860.

2. The "beta weight," or standardized regression coefficient, measures the relative influence of each of two or more explanatory variables on the vote received by a particular party. Explanatory variables that are themselves highly intercorrelated (*r* value above .7) will prevent a multiple regression analysis from yielding useful results. So long, however, as the explanatory variables are not highly intercorrelated, and so long as each displays significant coefficients of multiple determination (an R^2 change of .02 or .03 is a frequently used cutoff), the respective beta weights, when compared with each other, will provide a relative measurement of influence of each explanatory variable on the dependent variable, that is, the voting pattern being studied.

APPENDIX II

1. Ecological regression is a procedure designed to estimate the voting behavior of individuals. Like the multiple regression analysis in Appendix I, ecological regression uses aggregate data (county-level, in this instance) and a linear regression equation. But whereas multiple regression analyzes the behavior of voting units, or counties, ecological regression allows the researcher to estimate voters' transitions between two elections or to estimate the distribution of votes by measurable groups at a particular election.

The results of ecological regression analysis are usually displayed in a contingency table. Each number in a contingency table is a percentage of the entire eligible electorate. The total figures, or marginals, are known, and taken together add up to 100 percent. The cell entries are estimates.

As in the multiple regression calculations in Appendix I, all calculations here are weighted proportionate to the number of eligible voters in each county in 1860.

For explanations about the use of ecological regressions to study voting behavior, see J. Morgan Kousser, "Ecological Regression and the Analysis of Past Politics," *Journal of Interdisciplinary History* 4 (Autumn 1973): 237–62; Peyton McCrary, Clark Miller, and Dale Baum, "Class and Party in the Secession Crisis: Voting Behavior in the Deep South," *Journal of Interdisciplinary History* 8 (Winter 1978): 431–35; William E. Gienapp, "Nebraska, Nativism, and Rum: The Failure of Fusion in Pennsylvania, 1854," *Pennsylvania Magazine of History and Biography* 109 (Oct. 1985): 456–57; William E. Gienapp, *The Origins of the Republican Party, 1852–1856* (New York: Oxford University Press, 1987), 478, 480–81.

For a specific rejoinder to Kousser and other proponents of ecological regression, see Lee Benson, "The Mistransference Fallacy in Explanations of Human Behavior," *Historical Methods* 17 (Summer 1984): 118–31, esp. 122–27. Benson believes that ecological regression estimates are unsuitable for analysis of voting behavior; I disagree.

It is important to recognize that ecological regression has limitations and that the procedure may generate inaccurate estimates. Its greatest potential pitfall, as Benson properly notes, is the assumption of behavioral consistency (for example, that nonslaveowners will vote similarly in both low-slaveowning and high-slaveowning counties). Obviously, neither behavioral consistency nor merely random inconsistency should be taken for granted. A certain amount of inaccuracy is almost inevitable, and the researcher must be alert to situations in which behavior is too inconsistent to generate reasonable estimates. Nobody, therefore, should ever view figures generated by ecological regression as more than approximations.

More temperate worries about ecological regression are presented by William H. Flanigan and Nancy H. Zingale, "Alchemist's Gold: Inferring Individual Relationships from Aggregate Data," *Social Science History* 9 (Winter 1985): 71–91, which draws considerably upon Gudmund R. Iversen, "Group Data and Individual Behavior," in Jerome H. Clubb, William H. Flanigan, and Nancy H. Zingale, *Analyzing Electoral History: A Guide to the*

Study of American Voter Behavior (Beverly Hills: Sage, 1981), 267–302. Sharing Benson's concern about the difficulties inherent in assuming behavioral consistency, Flanigan and Zingale suggest that a "range estimate" would be more honest than a "point estimate," because any point estimate simply suggests that "the real value is somewhere close to this." They use survey research data from the 1968 and 1972 presidential elections, in which the true cell entries are known, to verify the accuracy of ecological regression procedures. They conclude that the estimates are "not too far off" but "not correct either" ("Alchemist's Gold," 87–88). A stronger endorsement for regression estimation, based on access to individual-level data, appears in Paul F. Bourke and Donald A. DeBats, "Individuals and Aggregates: A Note in Historical Data and Assumptions," *Social Science History* 4 (Spring 1980): 241–45.

When ecological regression is used in tandem with multiple regression, the historian of voting behavior should be able to get a clearer picture of what actually happened. The utility of such an approach has been impressively demonstrated. Notable recent examples include Dale Baum, *The Civil War Party System: The Case of Massachusetts, 1848–1876* (Chapel Hill: University of North Carolina Press, 1984), and Gienapp, *Origins of the Republican Party*, two methodologically sophisticated studies that, ironically, reach sharply divergent conclusions.

Historians of voting behavior attempt to study the interior of dark caves. They traditionally have worked with matches and candles. Given sufficient skill and patience, the researcher may thus produce a good description of his particular cave. Ecological regression offers the researcher a flashlight, enabling him to see things that might never be visible by candlelight. The cave, of course, is large and complex; the flashlight can distort as well as illuminate. If the researcher with the flashlight fails to invest sufficient time and effort, he may well produce a description inferior to what could be achieved with matches and candles. But should we therefore abandon flashlights?

2. Ecological regression estimates occasionally produce logically impossible values (greater than 100 percent or less than zero). Such estimates tend to occur when "a group overwhelmingly supports or opposes a candidate or referendum proposal." Logically impossible estimates suggest that "the assumption of behavioral consistency across all the counties may have been violated." For example, nonslaveholders may have voted more strongly against secession in those areas where they formed greater percentages of the eligible electorate (all three states displayed such a pattern, especially North Carolina). So also, 1860 nonvoters and Democrats were more likely to vote against secession in low-slaveowning counties. Logically impossible values may also indicate a relationship between two variables that is not linear, which may be checked by plotting the values on a scattergram (Kousser, "Ecological Regression," 250–52, quotations on 252, 250; see also, McCrary, Miller, and Baum, "Class and Party in the Secession Crisis," 433).

In choosing to replace negative values with zero, or with a small positive number if that seems consistent with available evidence, I employ a procedure explained in L. G. Telser, "Least-Square Estimation of Transition Probabilities," in Carl F. Christ et al., *Measurements in Economics* (Stanford: Stanford University Press, 1963), 280–82; and Theodore W. Meckstroth, "Some Problems of Cross-Level Inference," *American Journal of Political Science* 18 (1974): 45–66.

Here, for example, a negative number of North Carolinians who voted Democratic in 1860 were initially calculated to have voted pro-Union in February 1861. Because the evidence is quite conclusive that some North Carolina Democrats in the piedmont and mountain areas followed William Holden's lead and voted pro-Union, I have made a county-by-county estimate of antisecession voting by Democrats and recalculated the other values accordingly (see Table A-9). The recalculation of logically impossible values thus tends to produce more plausible estimates.

The regression estimates presented here differ slightly from an earlier version delivered as a paper to the Southern Historical Association in November 1984. I thank Professor Thomas Jeffrey of Rutgers University for his criticisms of the original paper and his suggestions about measuring Union voting among North Carolina Democrats.

There is good reason to believe that the number of 1860 North Carolina nonvoters who voted pro-Union in 1861 was initially exaggerated by the same regression procedure that undercounted, so to speak, Democratic Unionists. All modifications of regression estimates in Appendix II are indicated in parentheses.

APPENDIX III

1. Jerry C. Oldshue, "A Study of the Influence of Economic, Social, and Partisan Characteristics on Secession Sentiment in the South, 1860–1861: A Multiple and Partial Correlation Analysis Employing the County as a Unit of Observation" (Ph.D. dissertation, University of Alabama, 1975), quotation on 185.

2. Peyton McCrary, Clark Miller, and Dale Baum, "Class and Party in the Secession Crisis: Voting Behavior in the Deep South," *Journal of Interdisciplinary History* 8 (Winter 1978): 429–57, esp. 450–55.

3. A recent statistical study of secession in Texas, coauthored by Baum, finds that 63 percent of support for secession there may be explained by the combination of slaveowning and Breckinridge voting and an additional 15 percent by a combination of socioeconomic variables (Robin E. Baker and Dale Baum, "The Texas Voter and the Crisis of the Union, 1859–1861," *Journal of Southern History* 53 [Aug. 1987]: 395–420, esp. Table 5 on p. 408).

4. J. Mills Thornton III, *Politics and Power in a Slave Society: Alabama, 1800–1860* (Baton Rouge: Louisiana State University Press, 1978), 414–18, 427–30; McCrary, Miller, and Baum, "Class and Party in the Secession Crisis," 450–55. Baker and Baum's recent article on Texas finds that opposition to secession bore scant relationship to slaveowning or previous party affilia-

tion, although a combination of religious and agricultural variables did have considerable explanatory value ("Texas Voter," 408).

5. Michael P. Johnson, *Toward a Patriarchal Republic: The Secession of Georgia* (Baton Rouge: Louisiana State University Press, 1977), xxi, 87.

6. Steven Hahn, *The Roots of Southern Populism: Yeoman Farmers and the Transformation of the Georgia Upcountry, 1850–1890* (New York: Oxford University Press, 1983), chap. 3, esp. 90–91, 105–16; Fred Siegel, "Artisans and Immigrants in the Politics of Late Antebellum Georgia," *Civil War History* 27 (Sept. 1981): 221–30; J. William Harris, *Plain Folk and Gentry in a Slave Society: White Liberty and Black Slavery in Augusta's Hinterlands* (Middletown, Conn.: Wesleyan University Press, 1985), 64–93.

7. Johnson, *Patriarchal Republic*, 198, 203, 210, 213.

8. Ibid., 73–78, 198, 201, 223–25.

9. An important recent study of the secession crisis in Kentucky, Harry A. Volz III, "Party, State, and Nation: Kentucky and the Coming of the American Civil War" (Ph.D. dissertation, University of Virginia, 1982), complements my work on Virginia, North Carolina, and Tennessee. Indeed, Kentucky spawned a Union party strong enough to survive the sectional polarization of April 1861. On Arkansas, the one state not included in this study that rejected secession in February and March, only to reverse its position after April 15, see James M. Woods, *Rebellion and Realignment: Arkansas's Road to Secession* (Fayetteville: University of Arkansas Press, 1987).

10. Paul D. Escott, "Secession and the Irrepressible Conflict within the South," unpublished revision of a paper presented at the 1979 meeting of the Organization of American Historians. The paper, which uses county-level data, properly discriminates between voters and nonvoters, so as to estimate turnout patterns.

11. Escott has recently contributed a superb analysis of class tensions in North Carolina, emphasizing how the wrenching experience of war "exposed lines of division" rooted in earlier social arrangements, producing chronic class conflict during the postwar era. Nowhere in the lower South did the tendencies emphasized by Escott prove so salient. See Paul D. Escott, *Many Excellent People: Power and Privilege in North Carolina, 1850–1900* (Chapel Hill: University of North Carolina Press, 1985), quotation on 83.

BIBLIOGRAPHICAL ESSAY

PRIMARY SOURCES

Manuscripts

This study makes frequent use of manuscript collections pertaining to Unionism in the Upper South. Most collections focus on developments in one state or locality.

Manuscript collections are available for several major Virginia Unionists. The William C. Rives Papers, Library of Congress, fully depict the outlook and activities of the elder statesman among the Whiggish conditional Unionists of eastern Virginia, who represented his state at the Peace Conference. The Rives Papers include a wealth of material on political developments in Virginia during the secession winter, as well as numerous letters between Rives, his wife, his sons, and his brother, Virginia state senator Alexander Rives. The collection is supplemented by the Alfred Landon Rives Papers at Duke University and by the Rives Family Papers at the University of Virginia. Two leading Whig Unionists at the Virginia convention, John Janney, president of the convention, and Robert Young Conrad, chairman of the Committee on Federal Relations, both wrote regularly to their wives while the convention was in session, and those important letters have survived. The Janney Papers are held by Lucas Phillips of Leesburg, Virginia. The Conrad Papers are in the Virginia Historical Society. A good deal of material about Alexander H. H. Stuart, Virginia state senator from Augusta County and prominent convention delegate, may be found in the Alexander H. H. Stuart Papers at the University of Virginia and the Stuart Family Papers at the Virginia Historical Society. The James D. Davidson Papers in the Wisconsin State Historical Society contain key letters during the secession crisis from two leading Douglas Democrats, Virginia Governor John Letcher and convention delegate James B. Dorman. Davidson, Letcher, and Dorman were all residents of Lexington in Rockbridge County. I have used copies of the Davidson Papers in the U. B. Phillips Papers, Yale University. Some letters from the Davidson Papers appear in Bruce S. Greenawalt, ed., "Unionists in Rockbridge County: The Correspondence of James Dorman Davidson Concerning the Virginia Secession Convention of 1861," *Virginia Magazine of History and Biography* 73 (1965): 78–102. A vitally important letter from George W. Summers to James C. Welling, Mar. 19, 1861, may be found in the *Nation* 29 (1879): 383–84, with a copy in the Blair Family Papers, Library of Congress. The Alexander R. Boteler Papers at Duke provide significant insights about events in Washington during the secession winter, as well as information about the 1860 campaign of the Constitutional Union party. Boteler, from Jefferson County in the Shenandoah Valley, was the state's only Whig or Opposition congressman in 1860–61. The most important collection for a major unconditional northwestern Virginia Unionist is the Waitman T. Willey Papers, University of West Virginia, which proved especially helpful in writing the last section of Chapter 6.

Many other collections shed light on Virginia Unionism. At Duke, the following proved useful. The John Monroe Papers include letters from a Hampshire County Unionist who communicated with Union convention delegate David Pugh. The Charles Wesley Andrews Papers include correspondence between a Shepherdstown Unionist and his secessionist son in Hardy County. The Edward C. Turner Papers were written by a Fauquier County Unionist. The Jasper Davis Papers include a useful letter from L. G. Reichert, Dec. 7, 1860, to Davis, a Halifax County Unionist. The diary of William C. Adams provides insights about an Albemarle County Unionist. The Edmund Jennings Lee Papers include revealing pro-Union letters from C. F. Lee and C. H. Lee. Two collections in the Southern Historical Collection at the University of North Carolina illuminated the history of Virginia Unionism. The Lewis N. Whittle Papers include letters from Conway D. Whittle, a Mecklenberg County Unionist, and his mother, Mary Ann Whittle of Petersburg. Interesting letters from L. M. Whitlock of Augusta County appear in the Lewis Thompson Papers. The Elliott L. Story Diary at the Virginia Historical Society provides the valuable perspective of a Southampton County Unionist. Callaway Campbell, a young Virginia Unionist attempting to build up a farm in North Georgia, wrote letters that appear in the Charles Campbell Papers, Earl Gregg Swem Library, College of William and Mary. The Wyndham Robertson Papers at the University of Chicago contain useful letters written by an influential Union Whig state legislator.

Many Virginia secessionists and Southern Rights supporters left manuscript collections. The Edmund Ruffin Papers at the Library of Congress and Virginia Historical Society are especially valuable. Ruffin's unique diary for the late antebellum and early war period has been published: William K. Scarborough, ed., *The Diary of Edmund Ruffin*, 2 vols. to date (Baton Rouge: Louisiana State University Press, 1972–). There are several significant collections at the University of Virginia. The R. M. T. Hunter Papers shed light on the activities of the prominent U.S. senator. See also the McCue Family Papers from a Nelson County family with important correspondents, the Burwell Family Papers, which include an important letter from former Secretary of War John B. Floyd, dated February 7, 1861, and the John D. Imboden Papers, revealing the frustrations of a Southern Rights man and future Confederate general in strongly pro-Union Augusta County in the Shenandoah Valley. Duke University has a number of helpful Virginia secession collections. Important letters from Henry A. Wise appear in the George W. Booker Papers and the Angus R. Blakey Papers; letters from R. M. T. Hunter appear in the Booker Papers and in the J. R. Tucker Papers in the Southern Historical Collection, University of North Carolina. Also at Duke may be found the Munford-Ellis Family Papers, including the incoming mail of Richmond secessionist Charles Ellis, a promoter of Henry A. Wise's spontaneous Southern Rights convention in April 1861. See especially the letters to Charles Ellis from his brother Richard L. Ellis in Buckingham County. The John Coles Rutherfoord Papers at Duke complement the Rutherfoord Family Papers at the Virginia Historical Society, which include the diary of John Coles Rutherfoord, a Southern Rights state legislator. The Francis H. Hill Papers at Duke include an interesting letter written by Hill, of Madison County, on March 8, 1861. The James M. Schreckhise Papers include a revealing letter from G. T. Tifer in Augusta County, April 20, 1861. Other useful collections at Duke on Virginia secession include the Charles H. Hunton Papers, the William Patterson Smith Papers, the Isaac H. Carrington Papers, and the Richard I. Cocke Papers. In the Southern Historical Collection see the Hubard Family Papers, Buckingham County secessionists. The John Warren Grigsby Papers, in the Filson Club, Louisville, Kentucky, contain a revealing letter, dated April 14, 1861, from James S. Grigsby. Both brothers, one from Danville in Pittsylvania County, the other from Mercer County in the far southwest, were ardent Southern Rights supporters who corresponded about the spontaneous Southern Rights gathering of April 1861. Letters from a secessionist Bedford County state legislator, Edward C. Burks, appear in James E. Walmsley, ed., "The Change of Secession Sentiment in Virginia in 1861," *American Historical Review* 31 (1925): 82–98.

North Carolina Unionists left a substantial trail, some of which appears in print. J. G. deRoulhac Hamilton and Max R. Williams, eds., *The Papers of William Alexander Graham*, 7 vols. to date (Raleigh: North Carolina State Department of Archives and History, 1957–), contains secession crisis material in Volume 5 from the Graham Papers, Southern Historical Collection. Former Governor Graham was a prominent Whig Unionist with national stature. J. G. deRoulhac Hamilton, ed., *The Correspondence of Jonathan Worth*, 2 vols. (Raleigh: Broughton, 1909), includes valuable letters in Volume 1 from the Unionist state senator and future governor. Some printed transcriptions from the Worth letterbook, North Carolina Department of Archives and History, are unfortunately marred by inaccuracies, notably the key letter from Jonathan Worth to T. C. Worth, March 16, 1861. Important unpublished Worth material is also in the Worth Family Papers, Duke, and the Charles Beatty Mallett papers, Southern Historical Collection. Frontis W. Johnston, ed., *The Papers of Zebulon Baird Vance*, 1 vol. to date (Raleigh: North Carolina State Department of Archives and History, 1963), contains a good deal of important secession crisis correspondence to and from the Union Whig congressman and future governor. Originals of the Vance Papers are located primarily in the Southern Historical Collection and North Carolina Department of Archives and History. The printed collection should be supplemented by material from the William T. Lenoir Papers, Southern Historical Collection, and the W. Vance Brown Papers, North Carolina Department of Archives and History. The latter collection, covering a Buncombe County Unionist and relative of Vance's, includes revealing full letters from Brown to his son John Evans Brown, March 21 and April 15–26, 1861. J. G. deRoulhac Hamilton, ed., *The Papers of Thomas Ruffin*, 4 vols. (Raleigh: Edwards and Broughton, 1918–20), contains several useful letters from 1860 and the secession crisis, to be supplemented by unpublished letters in the Thomas Ruffin Papers, Southern Historical Collection. Judge Ruffin was a Union Democrat and Peace Conference delegate.

Many valuable unpublished collections help to trace the course of North Carolina Unionism. At the North Carolina Department of Archives and History see the following. The Bartholomew F. Moore Papers contain typescripts of secession crisis letters from the eminent North Carolina legal scholar to his daughter in Mississippi, Mrs. B. A. Capehart. The Edward Jones Hale Papers include a few useful items sent to the editor of the pro-Union *Fayetteville Observer*. The Calvin J. Cowles letterbook fully documents the views of a politically active Wilkes County Unionist. A lone but extremely valuable letter in the John A. Gilmer Papers, to Dr. D. H. Albright, January 8, 1861, is quoted at length in Chapter 5. At the Southern Historical Collection, see the Allen Turner Davidson Papers, letters from an Asheville Unionist to his wife, written during a trip to the deep South in April 1861; the Thomas Settle Papers, which provide glimpses of the Douglas Democrat and postwar Republican congressman from Rockingham County; the James Graham Ramsey Papers, which include letters from the Unionist state senator from Rowan County to his wife; and the Platt K. Dickinson Papers, letters from a Wilmington Unionist to his sister in Rochester, New York. Also in the Southern Historical Collection are the Lewis Thompson Papers, incoming correspondence to a wealthy Bertie County planter and future Republican, including a fascinating letter from William M. Clark of Alabama, January 10, 1861, mentioned in my Preface. The Pettigrew Family Papers and the Hayes Collection, both in the Southern Historical Collection, read in conjunction with the Pettigrew Papers, North Carolina Department of Archives and History, provide many revealing documents about a prominent Washington County family that included outspoken Unionists, conditional Unionists, and South Carolina secessionists. A diary by Mrs. John A. Gilmer is in the Addison Gorgas Brenizer Papers, Southern Historical Collection, and the Zeb Vance Walser Papers there include a file on John A. Gilmer, compiled by the historian of Confederate congressmen and senators from North Carolina. At Duke, researchers will find a number of collections pertinent to North Carolina Unionism. The Benjamin Sherwood Hedrick Papers give the perspective of a North Carolina exile who supported the Republican party. The Bedford Brown Papers include an interesting letter from J. Spear Smith, January 25, 1861, to Brown, the pro-Union Democratic state senator from Caswell County. The William Horton Pease Jenkins Papers contain an important letter from W. S. Joyner, March 7, 1861, to Jenkins, a Franklinton Unionist. In the Daniel S. Hall Papers, see a letter from William P. Williams, February 23, 1861, to Hill, a Franklin County Unionist. The Jacob Sheeh and Jonathan Smith Papers include letters from state legislator H. B. Howard to Davie County Democratic Unionists. The John McLean Harrington Papers contain letters from state legislator J. S. Harrington, a Harnett County Unionist. The Alexander McMillan Papers are from a Robeson County state legislator.

Several collections provided insight into North Carolina secessionists or quasi-secessionists. The Lawrence O'Bryan Branch Papers, Duke, complement the Mrs. Lawrence O'Bryan Branch Papers, North Carolina Department of Archives and History. Branch was the prominent congressman from the Raleigh area whose difficulties during the secession crisis are explored at the end of Chapter 12 in this study. The Southern Historical Collection contains a variety of useful material. The diary kept by U.S. Senator Thomas Bragg in January and February 1861 recorded the impressions of a Southern Rights sympathizer, who observed with dismay the Unionist surge of early 1861. Bragg also was well informed about the offer to John A. Gilmer of a seat in Lincoln's cabinet. The Burgwyn Family Papers include letters from prominent Northampton County planter Henry K. Burgwyn while on a visit to Washington in February 1861, plus letters from his son Henry K. Burgwyn, Jr., a Virginia Military Institute cadet, who viewed the Unionism of upcountry Virginia with revulsion. The Daniel M. Barringer Papers include frequent letters from a Southern Rights supporter and Peace Conference delegate to his wife. The Eli W. Hall Papers have information on the state senator from Wilmington, a rare Whig secessionist. In the Thomas David Smith McDowell Papers, see a letter to the Bladen County planter from state legislator N. L. Williamson, January 16, 1861. The John Lancaster Bailey Papers have letters from the secession-tending judge from Swannanoa to his wife in April 1861. The public pronouncements and private correspondence of Governor John W. Ellis, a Southern Rights Democrat, appear in Noble J. Tolbert, ed., *The Papers of John Willis Ellis*, 2 vols. (Raleigh: North Carolina State Department of Archives and History, 1964). The revealing diary kept by Catherine Edmondston views her substantially Unionist family from a secessionist perspective: Beth G. Crabtree and James W. Patton, eds, *"Journal of a Secesh Lady": The Diary of Catherine Ann Devereux Edmondston, 1860–1866* (Raleigh: North Carolina Department of Cultural Resources, Division of Archives and History, 1979).

Tennessee Unionism must be approached through the invaluable Andrew Johnson Papers, Library of Congress, for which there is a microfilm edition. The majority of significant Johnson Papers for the secession crisis are published in Volume 4 of LeRoy P. Graf and Ralph W. Haskins, eds., *The Papers of Andrew Johnson*, 7 vols. to date (Knoxville: University of Tennessee Press, 1967–). Though few of Johnson's own letters survive, the voluminous incoming correspondence, scrupulously annotated by Graf and Haskins, testifies to the Unionist groundswell in Tennessee in early 1861. There are manuscript collections for several other key Tennessee Unionists. The Campbell Family Papers, Duke, illuminate the role of former Governor William B. Campbell and include important letters from Congressman Robert Hatton, like Campbell a Union Whig from Wilson County. An extremely valuable collection of letters from Hatton to his wife is preserved in James Vaulx Drake, *Life of General Robert Hatton, Including His Most Important Public Speeches; Together with Much of his Army and Washington Correspondence* (Nashville: Marshall and Bruce, 1867). Letters to Union Whig Congressman T. A. R. Nelson are preserved in his papers in the McClung Collection of the Lawson McGhee Library, Knoxville. The Oliver P. Temple Papers at the University of Tennessee,

Knoxville, contain some primary secession crisis material and a good deal of retrospective information compiled in the 1890s, while Temple prepared to write a book about East Tennessee during the Civil War. See especially the letters to Temple between 1890 and 1894 from John Bell Brownlow, son of William G. Brownlow. There are secession crisis letters to John Bell in the Polk-Yeatman Papers, Southern Historical Collection; and the Yeatman-Polk Papers at the Tennessee State Library and Archives feature letters from Henry Clay Yeatman, son of John Bell's wife by her first marriage. Two other Tennessee State Library and Archives collections have important material. The Cooper Papers contain letters from Henry Cooper, former Whig state legislator from Bedford County, who became an unconditional Unionist. The Robertson Topp Papers depict the efforts by a prominent Memphis conditional Unionist, who edited the *Memphis Bulletin* and was president of the Memphis and Ohio Railroad, to reconcile East Tennessee to secession in August 1861. Union Democrat William H. Polk, brother of the former president and Union party candidate for governor in July 1861, is represented by a collection in the North Carolina Department of Archives and History. At Duke, see the Samuel Powel III Papers, especially a letter from Sam Milligan, dated January 25, 1861, to the Rogersville Unionist. Former Democratic Congressman George Washington Jones of Fayetteville made Unionist professions early in the secession crisis, which are preserved in his papers in the Southern Historical Collection. The Gustavus A. Henry Papers, Southern Historical Collection, show that the 1853 Whig candidate for governor was judged to be excessively Unionist by his sons, who saw little prospect for a peaceful resolution to the secession crisis. The William Henry King Memoirs, Southern Historical Collection, were written in 1925 by the son of James Moore King, an ardent Whig Unionist and large slaveholder from Rutherford County, who very reluctantly became a Confederate. Episcopal Bishop James T. Otey of Memphis wrote strongly pro-Union letters before the proclamation, which are printed in James E. Walmsley, ed., "The Change of Secession Sentiment in Virginia in 1861," *American Historical Review* 31 (1925): 98–101.

Tennessee secessionists, badly outnumbered before April 15, left proportionately fewer manuscript collections. Of greatest importance are the papers of Governor Isham G. Harris at the Tennessee State Library and Archives. His incoming mail shows that Harris, a quasi-secessionist Southern Rights supporter, tried without success to hold Democratic ranks together in face of the pro-Union tidal wave in early 1861. The Eliza H. Gordon Papers at Duke contain useful letters to George W. Boyles of Fayetteville from secessionists in Lincoln and Bedford counties. The Yandell Family Letters, at the Filson Club in Louisville, Kentucky, contain letters from Lunsford P. Yandell, Jr., an ardent Memphis secessionist, to his father, a Louisville Unionist.

Several manuscript collections pertaining to Kentucky and Maryland Unionists proved important. The papers of Kentucky Senator John J. Crittenden are divided between the Library of Congress and Duke. Both collections contain valuable Unionist material from correspondents North and South. Vitally important letters and copies of letters from Maryland Congressman Henry Winter Davis are preserved in the Samuel F. Du Pont Papers, Eleutherian Mills Historical Library, Greenville, Delaware. The Henry Page Papers, Southern Historical Collection, contain letters from John W. Crisfield, a Maryland delegate to the Peace Conference. A few useful items from or to James Guthrie, prominent Kentucky Union Democrat and Peace Conference delegate, may be found in his papers in the Southern Historical Collection and the Filson Club, Louisville, Kentucky. The Tayloe Family Papers, University of Virginia, contain useful material about a prominent family with branches in Maryland, Virginia, and Washington, D.C.

The three most important northern conciliators, William H. Seward, Thurlow Weed, and Stephen A. Douglas, received abundant correspondence during the secession crisis from southern Unionists. The Seward Papers and the Weed Papers, at the Rush Rhees Library, University of Rochester, and the Douglas Papers, at the University of Chicago, thus constitute vital sources for this study. Many Virginia Unionists wrote to Seward. Douglas Democrats throughout the upper South and some from the lower South reported to the Illinois senator. Essential letters from John A. Gilmer appear in all three collections. Frederic Bancroft, *The Life of William H. Seward*, 2 vols. (New York: Harper & Brothers, 1899–1900), 2:532–49, includes selections from some of the most important letters sent to Seward by Gilmer and other southern Unionists.

To understand the efforts of northern conciliators, several collections in addition to the Seward, Weed, and Douglas Papers must be consulted. A variety of uniquely revealing material may be found in the Adams Family Papers, Massachusetts Historical Society, including the unpublished diary of Charles Francis Adams and letters written by his precocious sons, Henry Adams and Charles Francis Adams, Jr. For published versions of Henry Adams's letters during the secession crisis, consult Worthington C. Ford, ed., *Letters of Henry Adams*, 2 vols. (Boston: Houghton Mifflin, 1930–38), 1:62–89; and J. C. Levenson et al., *The Letters of Henry Adams*, 3 vols. (Cambridge, Mass.: Belknap Press of Harvard University Press, 1982), 1:203–34. Seward's closeness to the Adams family magnifies the significance of the collection, which is available on microfilm. Additional Adams material appears in the John Andrew Papers and the Richard H. Dana, Jr., Papers, also both in the Massachusetts Historical Society. Henry Adams, "The Great Secession Winter of 1860–61," *Proceedings of the Massachusetts Historical Society* 43 (1910): 656–87, written in April 1861, is in effect a primary source, and one of great value. A less well-remembered conciliatory ally of Seward's and Weed's was James E. Harvey, crack reporter and columnist for the *Philadelphia North American* and for the *New York Tribune*. Several of Harvey's letters may be found in the Henry C. Carey Papers of the Edward Carey Gardiner Collection, Historical Society of Pennsylvania.

Various Republican manuscript collections contain a great deal of material about the interparty struggle over southern policy and occasional letters from southern Unionists or reports about developments in the South. The Abraham Lincoln Papers, Library of Congress (microfilm edition), are, of course, uniquely valuable. All of Lincoln's outgoing letters during the secession crisis appear in Volume 4 of Roy P. Basler, ed., *The Collected Works of Abraham Lincoln*, 8 vols. plus index (New Brunswick: Rutgers University Press, 1953–55). Although some of the incoming correspondence during the secession crisis appears in David Mearns, ed., *The Lincoln Papers: The Story of the Collection with Selections to July 4, 1861*, 2 vols. (Garden City, N.Y.: Country Life Press, 1948), and in Volumes 3 and 4 of John G. Nicolay and John Hay, *Abraham Lincoln: A History*, 10 vols. (New York: Century, 1890), much essential material remains unpublished. Other Republican collections yielding useful sources for this study included the David Davis Papers, Chicago Historical Society, which contain valuable letters from Thurlow Weed and Henry Winter Davis; the two collections of Salmon P. Chase Papers, Library of Congress and Historical Society of Pennsylvania; the Lyman P. Trumbull Papers, Library of Congress (microfilm edition); the Simon Cameron Papers, Library of Congress (microfilm edition); the Horace Greeley Papers, Library of Congress; the Blair Family Papers, Library of Congress; the Charles Sumner Papers, Houghton Library, Harvard University; and the James Watson Webb Papers, Yale University. An interesting series of private letters written by an assistant editor of the *New York Evening Post* is reprinted from the Bancroft Davis Papers, Library of Congress, in Martin Crawford, ed., "Politicians in Crisis: The Washington Letters of William S. Thayer, December 1860–March 1861," *Civil War History* 27 (Sept. 1981): 231–47.

Although the Douglas Papers are the paramount nonsouthern Democratic collection for studying the secession crisis in the upper South, useful nuggets also appear in the James Buchanan Papers, Historical Society of Pennsylvania, and in the S. L. M. Barlow Papers, Huntington Library, San Marino, California. Sam Ward, one of Seward's several secret agents during the secession crisis, corresponded freely with Barlow.

Several different sources of manuscript material in the National Archives proved very helpful. Many patronage requests and endorsements from the upper South appear in the General Records of the Department of Justice, Record Group 60. Material from March and April 1861 is of special value. When applying for a presidential pardon in 1865, prominent conditional Unionists who later supported the Confederacy recounted their activities before the proclamation and often included corroboration. See the Applications for Pardon in Record Group 94 (microfilm series M1003), which are filed alphabetically by state. Reports filed with the Southern Claims Commission frequently provided compelling insights about events in 1861 because any claimant had to prove unconditional Unionist allegiance. Record Group 217, the successful claims, are organized by county, thereby facilitating research on a particular region or locality.

Newspapers

Contemporary newspapers provided a great deal of important information for this study. Major dailies gave more thorough coverage to developments in Washington than could be found in any but a handful of modern American newspapers. The principal newspapers published in the state capitals likewise printed a wealth of material about state politics, elections, legislatures, and conventions. Smaller weeklies often provided valuable insights into local sentiment and affairs.

The Virginia Union papers that proved most useful in this study included the *Alexandria Gazette*, the *Lynchburg Virginian*, the *Charlottesville Review*, the *Wheeling Intelligencer*, and the *Wellsburg Herald*. The *Richmond Whig*, the most important Virginia Union paper, was bought out by secessionists in late March to secure a change of editors and editorial policy. I have consulted the *Richmond Enquirer* and the *Norfolk Southern Argus* for a secessionist perspective.

Any listing of North Carolina Union newspapers must begin with William W. Holden's *North Carolina Standard*, the Democratic party's newspaper of record until the secession crisis. Two other Union newspapers also were printed at the state capital: the *Raleigh Register*, the Whig-Opposition newspaper of record, and the *Raleigh Ad Valorem Banner*. I have also used the pro-Union *Greensboro Patriot*, the *Greensboro Times*, the *Fayetteville Observer*, the *Salem People's Press*, and the *Salisbury Carolina Watchman*. Southern Rights and secessionist viewpoints got full airing in the *Raleigh State Journal* and the *Wilmington Journal*.

Tennessee Unionists had the support of the two influential Whiggish Nashville newspapers, the *Patriot* and the *Republican Banner*. The pro-Douglas *Nashville Democrat* was an outspoken Union journal, but copies of it apparently survive only in selections reprinted in other newspapers. William G. Brownlow's *Knoxville Whig* played a pivotal role in coordinating the Unionist insurgency in East Tennessee. Two firmly pro-Union newspapers from outlying parts of Middle Tennessee were the *Gallatin Courier* and the *Clarksville Jeffersonian*. Two equivocally pro-Union newspapers from West Tennessee proved interesting: the (Jackson) *West Tennessee Whig*, and the *Trenton Star Spangled Banner*. Tennessee newspaper support for Southern Rights and secession received strongest expression in the *Nashville Union and American*, the *Memphis Avalanche*, and the *Memphis Appeal*. The latter was pro-Douglas but completed a rapid prosecession somersault by mid-December. Less widely circulating Southern Rights viewpoints appeared in the *Fayetteville Observer* and the *Paris Sentinel*.

Newspapers from adjacent border regions proved very important, notably George D. Prentice's *Louisville Journal* and the *Baltimore American*, each of which printed regular letters from a Washington correspondent ("L. A. W." and "Special," respectively). The *Cincinnati Commercial*, widely read in Kentucky and Tennessee, contained reports from an apparent series of Washington correspondents ("Omega," "Sigma," and "Special"). The *National Intelligencer*, published in Washington, D.C., had faithful Whiggish readers throughout the upper South and editors who provided secret channels by which William H. Seward could communicate with Virginia Unionists. The *Washington Evening Star* covered day-to-day events in the capital more fully than the *Intelligencer*.

A variety of northern newspapers proved centrally important to the research for this study. Thurlow Weed's *Albany Evening Journal* and Henry J. Raymond's *New York Times* articulated conciliatory Republican policy. Weed and Seward had been on extremely close terms for decades; Raymond moved into the Seward-conciliatory orbit in January. The *Boston Daily Advertiser*, which provided a forum for Henry Adams's anonymous contributions, took a conciliatory stance. James E. Harvey wrote a daily column from Washington, signed "Independent," in the *Philadelphia North American*. Insiders properly regarded the conciliatory Harvey as exceptionally well informed. The Democratic-leaning *New York Herald*, edited by James Gordon Bennett, had the largest daily circulation of any newspaper in the United States. It reached many southern readers. Bennett's great rival, Horace Greeley, edited the *New York Tribune*, the bible of northern antislavery Republicans. Greeley estimated that a million persons read his weekly edition, which had a press run of more than a quarter of a million copies. Though the *Tribune* tried to report on southern developments, its southern correspondents and its few southern readers had to remain anonymous, and southern postal officials tried to suppress it. At the beginning of Chapter 11, I have addressed the problems inherent in using either the *Herald* or the *Tribune* as a source of information about the upper South during the secession crisis.

No discussion of newspapers during the secession crisis would dare to omit two essential anthologies. Dwight Lowell Dumond, ed., *Southern Editorials on Secession* (New York: Century, 1931), contains well-chosen selections of editorial opinion during the 1860 presidential campaign and the secession crisis in both the upper and lower South. A more recent monograph complements Dumond's effort: Donald E. Reynolds, *Editors Make War: Southern Newspapers in the Secession Crisis* (Nashville: Vanderbilt University Press, 1970). The northern counterpart to Dumond's volume, Howard Cecil Perkins, ed., *Northern Editorials on Secession*, 2 vols. (New York: D. Appleton-Century, 1942), presents an even larger sample, organized topically. Northwestern Virginia is included in Perkins's "North."

Government Documents

Research for this study required extensive knowledge of three deliberative gatherings: Congress, the Virginia convention, and the Peace Conference. The *Congressional Globe* was therefore an indispensable source. The second session of the Thirty-sixth Congress met during the fateful secession winter. Its proceedings include the special Senate session of the Thirty-seventh Congress that met for several weeks in March 1861. The *Globe* contains verbatim accounts of the many speeches made by southern Unionists in late January and early February 1861 as part of the campaign to prevent secession in the upper South. Equally full records of the Virginia convention have also been compiled from newspaper transcripts: George H. Reese, ed., *Proceedings of the Virginia State Convention of 1861*, 4 vols. (Richmond: Virginia State Library, 1965). Reese's four thick volumes, along with Volume 4 of the *Papers of Andrew Johnson*, are the two modern editorial enterprises of greatest value for historians of secession in the upper South. Two invaluable sources illuminate the history of the Peace Conference. A Vermont delegate, Lucius E. Chittenden, recorded and later published a full journal of the secret proceedings: Lucius E. Chittenden, *A Report of the Debates and Proceedings in the Secret Sessions of the Conference Convention, for Proposing Amendments to the Constitution of the United States, Held at Washington, D.C., in February, A.D., 1861* (1864; rpt. New York: Da Capo Press, 1971). Chittenden's *Report* should be used in conjunction with a splendidly researched modern monograph: Robert Gray Gunderson, *Old Gentlemen's Convention: The Washington Peace Conference of 1861* (Madison: University of Wisconsin Press, 1961).

Several other collections of government documents proved useful. Significant items on the months before the war were printed in *The War of the Rebellion: A Compilation of the Official Records of the Union and Confederate Armies*, 70 vols. in 128 (Washington, D.C.: U.S. Government Printing Office, 1880–1901). The records of the several state legislatures that met during the secession crisis provided important information. For Virginia, see *Journal of the House of Delegates of the State of Virginia for the Extra Session 1861* (Richmond: William F. Ritchie, 1861); *Journal of the Senate of the Commonwealth of Virginia: Begun and Held at the Capitol in the City of Richmond January 7, 1861, Extra Session* (Richmond: James E. Goode, 1861); and *Acts of the General Assembly of the State of Virginia Passed in 1861* (Richmond: William F. Ritchie, 1861). For North Carolina, see *Journal of the House of Commons of the General Assembly of the State of North Carolina at the Session of 1860–61* (Raleigh: John Spelman, 1861); *Journal of the Senate of the General Assembly of the State of North Carolina at the Session of 1860–61* (Raleigh: John Spelman, 1861); and *Public Laws of the State of North Carolina, Passed by the General Assembly at Its Session of 1860–61* (Raleigh: John Spelman, 1861). For Tennessee, see *House Journal of the State of Tennessee, Extra Session, January 1861* (Nashville: J. O. Griffith, 1861); *Senate Journal of the State of Tennessee, Extra Session, January 1861* (Nashville: J. O. Griffith, 1861); and *Public Acts of the State of Tennessee, Extra Session, January, 1861, and Extra Session, April, 1861* (Nashville: E. G. Eastman, 1861). In ascertaining the actual procedures for holding elections, the various state codes proved illuminating: George W. Munford, ed., *The Code of Virginia*, 2d ed. (Richmond: Ritchie, Dunnavant, 1860); Bartholomew F. Moore and Asa Biggs, eds., *Revised Code of North Carolina* (Boston: Little, Brown, 1855); and Return J. Meigs and William F. Cooper, eds., *The Code of Tennessee* (Nashville: E. G. Eastman, State Printers, 1858).

SECONDARY SOURCES

State Studies: Virginia

Published over fifty years ago, a competent, thoroughly researched monograph deservedly remains the standard study of secession in Virginia: Henry T. Shanks, *The Secession Movement in Virginia, 1847–1861* (1934; rpt. New York: Da Capo Press, 1970). Significant secondary supplements to Shanks on the immediate 1860–61 period include Robert Gray Gunderson, "William C. Rives and the 'Old Gentlemen's Convention,'" *Journal of Southern History* 22 (1956): 459–76; Patrick Sowle, "The Trials of a Virginia Unionist: William Cabell Rives and the Secession Crisis, 1860–1861," *Virginia Magazine of History and Biography* 80 (Jan. 1972): 3–20; William S. Hitchcock, "Southern Moderates and Secession: Senator Robert M. T. Hunter's Call for Union," *Journal of American History* 59 (Mar. 1973): 871–84; William W. Freehling, "The Editorial Revolution, Virginia, and the Coming of the Civil War: A Review Essay," *Civil War History* 16 (Mar. 1970): 64–72; David F. Riggs, "Robert Young Conrad and the Ordeal of Secession," *Virginia Magazine of History and Biography* 86 (July 1978): 259–74; and Shearer Davis Bowman, "Conditional Unionism and Slavery in Virginia, 1860–61: The Case of Dr. Richard Eppes," *Virginia Magazine of History and Biography* 96 (Jan. 1988): 31–54.

The impact of the secession crisis in trans-Allegheny Virginia, which led directly to the founding of the state of West Virginia, is a subject unto itself. By far the most reliable and well-researched study of events in the northwest is Richard O. Curry, *A House Divided: Statehood Politics and the Copperhead Movement in West Virginia* (Pittsburgh: University of Pittsburgh Press, 1964). Several older sources also remain useful: Granville D. Hall, *The Rending of Virginia* (Chicago: Mayer & Miller, 1901); Charles H. Ambler, *Sectionalism in Virginia from 1776 to 1861* (1910; rpt. New York: Russell and Russell, 1964); James C. McGregor, *The Disruption of Virginia* (New York: Macmillan, 1922); and James Morton Callahan, *A History of West Virginia, Old and New*, 3 vols. (Chicago: American Historical Society, 1923).

A variety of important studies about antebellum Virginia politics and society aided in the research for this study. On political developments, see Lynwood M. Dent, Jr., "The Virginia Democratic Party, 1824–1847" (Ph.D. dissertation, Louisiana State University, 1974); William G. Shade, "Political Culture and Party Development in Virginia, 1828–1852" (paper delivered at the American Historical Association Convention, Washington, D.C., Dec. 1982); Alison Goodyear Freehling, *Drift toward Dissolution: The Virginia Slavery Debate of 1831–1832* (Baton Rouge: Louisiana State University Press, 1982); and Francis P. Gaines, Jr., "The Virginia Constitutional Convention of 1850–1851: A Study in Sectionalism" (Ph.D. dissertation, University of Virginia, 1950). Two important articles focused on Prince Edward County draw on an 1840 list of voter partisanship: Paul F. Bourke and Donald A. DeBats, "Identifiable Voting in Nineteenth-Century America: Toward a Comparison of Britain and the United States before the Secret Ballot," *Perspectives in American History* 11 (1977–78): 259–88; and William G. Shade, "Society and Politics in Antebellum Virginia's Southside," *Journal of Southern History* 53 (May 1987): 163–93. The politically marginal antecedents of secessionism in Virginia are persuasively analyzed in Robert J. Brugger, *Beverley Tucker: Heart over Head in the Old South* (Baltimore: Johns Hopkins University Press, 1978). Craig M. Simpson, *A Good Southerner: The Life of Henry A. Wise of Virginia* (Chapel Hill: University of North Carolina Press, 1985), which appeared as this manuscript neared completion, should win recognition as the most important book ever written about late antebellum Virginia politics. Simpson's

Chapter 12, pages 219–51, covers events during 1860 and the secession crisis.

On Virginia politics in the 1859–60 period, see William S. Hitchcock, "The Limits of Southern Unionism: Virginia Conservatives and the Gubernatorial Election of 1859," *Journal of Southern History* 47 (Feb. 1981): 57–72; William G. Bean, "John Letcher and the Slavery Issue in Virginia's Gubernatorial Contest of 1858–59," *Journal of Southern History* 20 (1954): 22–49; William G. Bean, "The Ruffner Pamphlet of 1847: An Antislavery Aspect of Virginia Sectionalism," *Virginia Magazine of History and Biography* 61 (1953): 260–82; F. N. Boney, *John Letcher of Virginia: The Story of Virginia's Civil War Governor* (University, Ala.: University of Alabama Press, 1966). See also John V. Mering, "The Slave-State Constitutional Unionists and the Politics of Consensus," *Journal of Southern History* 43 (Aug. 1977): 395–410.

A Ph.D. dissertation by John T. Schlotterbeck, "Plantation and Farm: Social and Economic Change in Orange and Greene Counties, Virginia, 1716 to 1860" (Johns Hopkins University, 1980), is the finest study of the antebellum Virginia economic and social order currently available. It is summarized in John T. Schlotterbeck, "The 'Social Economy' of an Upper South Community: Orange and Greene Counties, Virginia, 1815–1860," in Orville Vernon Burton and Robert C. McMath, Jr., eds., *Class, Conflict and Consensus: Antebellum Southern Community Studies* (Westport, Conn.: Greenwood Press, 1982), 3–28. Also very useful is Frederick Fein Siegel, "A New South in the Old: Sotweed and Soil in the Development of Danville, Virginia" (Ph.D. dissertation, University of Pittsburgh, 1978). (The book based on the dissertation appeared after completion of this manuscript: *The Roots of Southern Distinctiveness: Tobacco and Society in Danville, Virginia, 1780–1865* [Chapel Hill: University of North Carolina Press, 1987].) Siegel has persuasively criticized the applicability to Virginia of Eugene Genovese's "paternalist" paradigm: "The Paternalist Thesis: Virginia as a Test Case," *Civil War History* 25 (Sept. 1979): 246–61. A splendid Ph.D. dissertation by Patricia Hickin, "Antislavery in Virginia, 1831–1861" (University of Virginia, 1968), traces the persistent antislavery undercurrent in Virginia during the era when slavery officially became a "positive good." See also her prizewinning essay "Gentle Agitator: Samuel M. Janney and the Antislavery Movement in Virginia, 1842–1851," *Journal of Southern History* 37 (May 1971): 159–90.

State Studies: North Carolina

Joseph Carlyle Sitterson, *The Secession Movement in North Carolina* (Chapel Hill: University of North Carolina Press, 1939), remains as solid and reliable a study of its topic as the Shanks monograph on Virginia. It must be supplemented, however, by Marc W. Kruman, *Parties and Politics in North Carolina, 1836–1865* (Baton Rouge: Louisiana State University Press, 1983), a work of broader scope and greater interpretive strength. Kruman's eighth chapter, pages 180–221, is the best modern summary of developments in 1860–61 in North Carolina. Important articles by Kruman include: "Dissent in the Confederacy: The North Carolina Experience," *Civil War History* 27 (Dec. 1981): 293–313; and "Thomas L. Clingman and the Whig Party: A Reconsideration," *North Carolina Historical Review* 64 (Jan. 1987): 1–18.

Several useful studies of antebellum North Carolina politics complement Sitterson and Kruman. The most important analysis to date of party development in any American locality is focused on Fayetteville: Harry L. Watson, *Jacksonian Politics and Community Conflict: The Emergence of the Second American Party System in Cumberland County, North Carolina* (Baton Rouge: Louisiana State University Press, 1981). Watson's insights, as suggested in Chapter 2 above, make many aspects of both southern and national politics more comprehensible. Thomas E. Jeffrey, author of "The Second Party System in North Carolina" (Ph.D. dissertation, Catholic University of America, 1976), has prepared several well-researched articles for the *North Carolina Historical Review*: "'Free Suffrage' Revisited: Party Politics and Constitutional Reform in Antebellum North Carolina," 59 (Winter 1982): 24–48; "Internal Improvements and Political Parties in Antebellum North Carolina, 1836–1860," 55 (Spring 1978): 111–56; "'Thunder from the Mountains': Thomas Lanier Clingman and the End of Whig Supremacy in North Carolina," 56 (Autumn 1979): 366–95; "Beyond 'Free Suffrage': North Carolina Parties and the Convention Movement of the 1850s," 62 (Oct. 1985): 387–419. See also Thomas E. Jeffrey, "National Issues, Local Interests, and the Transformation of Antebellum North Carolina Politics," *Journal of Southern History* 50 (Feb. 1984): 43–74.

Several new investigations of North Carolina social and economic history directly address the links between society and politics. Robert Charles Kenzer, "Portrait of a Southern Community, 1849–1881: Family, Kinship, and Neighborhood in Orange County, North Carolina" (Ph.D. dissertation, Harvard University, 1982), shows how ties of kinship and locality mitigated class conflict. (The book based on the dissertation appeared after completion of this manuscript: *Kinship and Neighborhood in a Southern Community: Orange County, North Carolina, 1849–1881* [Knoxville: University of Tennessee Press, 1987].) Antebellum party affiliation in Orange County likewise was neighborhood-based rather than class-based. John C. Inscoe, "Slavery, Sectionalism, and Secession in Western North Carolina" (Ph.D. dissertation, University of North Carolina at Chapel Hill, 1985), identifies a slaveholding elite that promoted economic development, thereby gaining both political power and the loyalty and support of western nonslaveholders. (The book based on Inscoe's dissertation is forthcoming from the University of Tennessee Press.) Paul D. Escott, *Many Excellent People: Power and Privilege in North Carolina, 1850–1900* (Chapel Hill: University of North Carolina Press, 1985), diverges from Kenzer and Inscoe to emphasize persistent democratic challenges to elite dominance. Escott suggests that latent class resentments became increasingly salient in late antebellum North Carolina.

For studies of the immediate prewar period in North Carolina, see Victor B. Howard, "John Brown's Raid at Harpers Ferry and the Sectional Crisis in North Carolina," *North Carolina Historical Review* 55 (Autumn 1978): 396–420; Kent Blaser, "North Carolina and John Brown's Raid," *Civil War History*

24 (Sept. 1978): 197–212; Clifton H. Johnson, "Abolitionist Missionary Activities in North Carolina," *North Carolina Historical Review* 40 (1963): 295–320; Noble J. Tolbert, "Daniel Worth: Tarheel Abolitionist," *North Carolina Historical Review* 39 (1962): 284–304; Donald C. Butts, "A Challenge to Planter Rule: The Controversy over Ad Valorem Taxation of Slaves in North Carolina, 1858–1862" (Ph.D. dissertation, Duke University, 1978); Donald C. Butts, "The 'Irrepressible Conflict': Slave Taxation and North Carolina's Gubernatorial Election of 1860," *North Carolina Historical Review* 58 (Winter 1981): 44–66.

William T. Auman has written extensively about persistent wartime Unionism in North Carolina. See his "North Carolina's Inner Civil War: Randolph County" (M.A. thesis, University of North Carolina at Greensboro, 1978), plus three important articles from the *North Carolina Historical Review*, the first of which was coauthored by David D. Scarboro: "The Heroes of America in Civil War North Carolina," 58 (Autumn 1981): 327–63; "Neighbor against Neighbor: The Inner Civil War in the Randolph County Area of Confederate North Carolina," 61 (Jan. 1984): 59–92; "Bryan Tyson: Southern Unionist and American Patriot," 62 (July 1985): 257–92. See also Philip Shaw Paludan, *Victims: A True Story of the Civil War* (Knoxville: University of Tennessee Press, 1981).

William W. Holden, whose eventful public career spanned from the 1840s into Reconstruction, has attracted two recent biographers: Horace W. Raper, *William W. Holden: North Carolina's Political Enigma* (Chapel Hill: University of North Carolina Press, 1985), and William C. Harris, *William Woods Holden: Firebrand of North Carolina Politics* (Baton Rouge: Louisiana State University Press, 1987).

State Studies: Tennessee

The standard monograph on secession in Tennessee, comparable in many respects to the volumes by Shanks on Virginia and Sitterson on North Carolina, is Mary Emily Robertson Campbell, *The Attitude of Tennesseans toward the Union, 1847–1861* (New York: Vantage Press, 1961). Also very useful is Joseph H. Parks, *John Bell of Tennessee* (Baton Rouge: Louisiana State University Press, 1950), supplemented by Parks's two articles: "John Bell and Secession," *East Tennessee Historical Society Publications* 16 (1944): 30–47; "The Tennessee Whigs and the Kansas-Nebraska Bill," *Journal of Southern History* 10 (1944): 308–30. For political developments through the presidential election of 1860, but not the secession crisis, see Paul H. Bergeron, *Antebellum Politics in Tennessee* (Lexington: University Press of Kentucky, 1982).

Several Ph.D. dissertations on antebellum Tennessee politics deserve mention. John Edgar Tricamo, "Tennessee Politics, 1845–1861" (Columbia University, 1965), is a useful source that complements and anticipates Bergeron's *Antebellum Politics in Tennessee*. But Tricamo's analysis of secession, in chapters 15–17, should not be relied upon. Tricamo gives too much weight to the unsatisfactory interpretation presented in J. Milton Henry, "The Revolution in Tennessee, February, 1861, to June, 1861," *Tennessee Historical Quarterly* 18 (1959): 99–119. See my critique of Henry in note 57 to Chapter 12. Frank Mitchell Lowrey III, "Tennessee Voters during the Second Two-Party System, 1836–1860: A Study in Voter Constancy and in Socio-Economic and Demographic Distinctions" (Ph.D. dissertation, University of Alabama, 1973), employs sophisticated techniques of data analysis. Lowrey concluded that the Tennessee electorate "exhibited an extremely high degree of voter consistency and that party lines were very tightly drawn during the 1840–1860 period" (p. 38). He also demonstrated that larger commercial towns, especially in Middle Tennessee, displayed a slight Whiggish tendency and that Democrats tended to run slightly more strongly in "rural areas characterized by a lower level of economic development" (p. 218). Carroll Van West, " 'The Money Our Fathers Were Accustomed To': Banks and Political Culture in Rutherford County, Tennessee, 1800–1850" (Ph.D. dissertation, College of William and Mary, 1982), shows that the second party system crystallized in 1839 in this important Middle Tennessee County, amid state and national controversy about banking. West's thesis that Whigs were strongest in fertile "garden" districts, with Democrats doing best in the "barren" hills, is overstated.

The unconditional Unionists of Tennessee wrote several important memoirs and histories and have attracted a good deal of modern scholarly scrutiny. The most notable participant-historian among East Tennessee Unionists was Oliver P. Temple of Knoxville, elected as a delegate in February 1861 to the convention that never met. See his two important books: *East Tennessee in the Civil War* (1899; rpt. Freeport, N.Y.: Books for Libraries Press, 1971); and *Notable Men of Tennessee from 1833 to 1875: Their Times and Their Contemporaries* (New York: Cosmopolitan Press, 1912). Modern studies include E. Merton Coulter, *William G. Brownlow: Fighting Parson of the Southern Highlands* (1937; rpt. with introduction by James W. Patton, Knoxville: University of Tennessee Press, 1971); Thomas B. Alexander, *Thomas A. R. Nelson of East Tennessee* (Nashville: Tennessee Historical Commission, 1956); Steve Humphrey, "*That D——d Brownlow*" (Boone, N.C.: Appalachian Consortium Press, 1978); Charles Faulkner Bryan, Jr., "The Civil War in East Tennessee: A Social, Political, and Economic Study" (Ph.D. dissertation, University of Tennessee-Knoxville, 1978). The following articles from the *East Tennessee Historical Society Publications* are significant: Verton M. Queener, "Origins of the Republican Party in East Tennessee to 1867," 13 (1941): 66–90; Verton M. Queener, "East Tennessee Sentiment and the Secession Movement, November, 1860–June, 1861," 20 (1948): 59–83; Ralph W. Haskins, "Andrew Johnson and the Preservation of the Union," 33 (1961): 43–60. LeRoy P. Graf, coeditor with Haskins of the monumentally important *Johnson Papers*, also wrote "Andrew Johnson and the Coming of the Civil War," *Tennessee Historical Quarterly* 19 (Sept. 1960): 208–21.

The unconditional Unionists of Middle and West Tennessee have received less attention from historians than their more numerous counterparts in the East. Volumes 5, 6, and 7 of the *Johnson Papers* are brimming with pertinent information. Samuel M. Arnell, a wealthy slaveowner and future postwar

Republican congressman, was one of seven voters in Maury County to vote against secession in June 1861. A typed transcript of Arnell's unpublished memoirs, "The Southern Unionist," completed and revised by his son Samuel M. Arnell, Jr., may be found in the Special Collections of the University of Tennessee–Knoxville Library. The following articles are also valuable. Albert W. Schroeder, Jr., ed., "Writings of a Tennessee Unionist," *Tennessee Historical Quarterly* 9 (1950): 244–72, 344–61, consists of a graphic memoir by Mary Katherine Sproul [Bowden] of Livingston, Overton County. Mary Jean DeLozier, "The Civil War and Its Aftermath in Putnam County," *Tennessee Historical Quarterly* 38 (1979): 436–61, is a well-researched excerpt from the author's *Putnam County Tennessee, 1850–1970* (Nashville: McQuiddy Printing Co., 1979). Unionists lived in western Putnam County adjacent to DeKalb County, home of Colonel William B. Stokes of the Fifth Tennessee Cavalry Regiment (USA). The violent world of McNairy County Unionists is the subject of Gary Blankinship, "Colonel Fielding Hurst and the Hurst Nation," *West Tennessee Historical Society Papers* 34 (1980): 71–87. A case study of the wartime dangers facing Unionists in Weakley County, home of Emerson Etheridge, is examined in Paul R. Coppock, "The Killgore Killing," *West Tennessee Historical Society Papers* 15 (1961): 40–54. Ronnie W. Faulkner, "Return Jonathan Meigs: Tennessee's First State Librarian," *Tennessee Historical Quarterly* 42 (Summer 1983): 151–64, introduces an eminent unconditional Unionist who fled north from wartime Nashville.

Two important studies of Tennessee social history have just appeared. Stephen V. Ash, *Middle Tennessee Society Transformed, 1860–1870: War and Peace in the Upper South* (Baton Rouge: Louisiana State University Press, 1988), is an elegantly written and deeply researched monograph that illuminates the experiences of whites and blacks in the Tennessee heartland—before, during, and after the war. Fred Arthur Bailey, *Class and Tennessee's Confederate Generation* (Chapel Hill: University of North Carolina Press, 1987), places greater emphasis on class conflict than Ash.

Studies of the Secession Crisis and the Late Antebellum South

Historians have written a great deal about the secession crisis but have had surprisingly little to say about southern Unionism. Broadly focused studies of the crisis, or of key participants in it, almost inevitably emphasize the dramatic action of the deep South and the response to it by the Buchanan and Lincoln administrations. Southern "fire-eaters" and "stiff-backed" Republicans tend to become the major actors in most accounts. When the secession crisis is viewed in this way, the men in the middle disappear from view. Because a majority of Virginians, North Carolinians, and Tennesseans ended up on the Confederate side, it is tempting to project post–April 15 allegiances into the pre–April 15 period and to dismiss southern Unionism as a deceptive phantom.

Only a relative handful of the major biographies or studies of the secession period have therefore attempted to explain developments in the upper

South during the secession crisis or to give adequate attention to the Union-saving efforts of southern Unionists and conciliatory northerners. Rather than attempt a full-scale evaluation of secession historiography, I shall therefore comment here on those works of most immediate value to the historian of the upper South in the secession crisis.

My interest in the subject was originally stirred by reading David M. Potter, *Lincoln and His Party in the Secession Crisis* (New Haven: Yale University Press, 1942, rpt. with a new introduction, 1962), an exquisitely written monograph. Even though Potter's principal concern was to explain the Republican party's response to the secession crisis, he captured the drama and significance of the upper South's rejection of secession in January and February 1861 (chapters 10 and 11, pages 249–314). The would-be conciliator of the upper South, William H. Seward, is easily the most arresting personality in the book. Potter's account has certain limitations, as I have indicated above in Chapter 9, note 1. But no student of secession in the upper South should overlook this first book by one of the greatest of American historians.

In exploring the effort by conciliatory Republicans to hold the upper South in the Union, Potter depended heavily on published material written by the Adams family, especially young Henry Adams, and on Seward material then in print. Potter alerted me to the correspondence in the Seward Papers from John A. Gilmer and other southern Unionists, parts of which were published by Frederic Bancroft, in an appendix to his discerning biography of Seward. Those sources remain vital and may now be supplemented by additional unpublished material described above, which was unavailable to Potter.

The general stance and tone of Potter's volume was echoed in James G. Randall, *Lincoln the President*, 4 vols. (New York: Dodd, Mead, 1945–55), 1:207–350. Randall, like Potter, emphasized Lincoln's pacific instincts. Both, in my judgment, therefore understated the extent to which the decision to resupply Sumter was, under the circumstances, a decision for war. The concluding chapters of Roy Franklin Nichols's masterful analysis of the Democratic party between 1856 and 1861, *The Disruption of American Democracy* (New York: Macmillan, 1948), 348–506, surveyed the response to secession by the losers of the 1860 presidential election. Doing for the Democrats somewhat what Potter had done for the Republicans, Nichols illuminated the struggle between Union savers and secessionists that wracked an already bitterly divided party. Neither Potter, Randall, nor Nichols ever wrote in detail about southern Unionists. By focusing on national political developments and on the internal histories of the two major parties, they tended to overlook the emergence in the upper South of a self-proclaimed Union party, led for the most part by former Whigs who had no ties to either dominant national party.

Mainstream American historiography since 1950 has reestablished an interpretation of the Civil War—and the secession crisis that preceded it—very similar to that held by patriotic northerners in the late nineteenth century. Kenneth Stampp and Allan Nevins present the two most striking examples. They considered the quest for peaceable reunion to have been both improbable and morally tainted. Plainly influenced by the experience of World War II, Nevins and Stampp condemned the "appeasement" contemplated by conciliatory Republicans and deplored the pursuit of peace "at any price." Efforts to arrange a Union-saving compromise impressed Stampp as "superficial" or "fraudulent" and "doomed from the start." He thought Seward guilty of "incredible blindness" in relying on "the kind of qualified Unionism" that prevailed in the upper South. See Stampp, *And the War Came: The North and the Secession Crisis, 1860–61* (Baton Rouge: Louisiana State University Press, 1950), esp. 18–21, 131–32, 157–59, 161, 172, 174, 271–72; Nevins, *The War for the Union*, 4 vols. (New York: Charles Scribner's Sons, 1959–71), esp. 1:39, 72, 74.

Several historians, however, have swum against the dominant interpretive current in the profession to reexamine the efforts of southern Unionists and their northern sympathizers. Patrick M. Sowle, "The Conciliatory Republicans during the Winter of Secession" (Ph.D. dissertation, Duke University, 1963), shared Bancroft's and Potter's view that the effort to hold the upper South in the Union deserved serious study. As explained in Chapter 9, note 1, Sowle showed that the question of southern policy divided the Republican party more severely than Potter acknowledged, and he correctly identified Lincoln as an ally of the unyielding faction. Sowle also showed conclusively how proponents of a conciliatory policy won temporary support from the heretofore inflexible Lincoln at the very beginning of his term in office, only to have the rapprochement disintegrate a few weeks later over the question of Fort Sumter. Better known than the Sowle dissertation are authoritative modern biographies of two of the most important conciliators. Substantial sections on the secession crisis may be found in both Albert D. Kirwan, *John J. Crittenden: The Struggle for the Union* (Lexington: University of Kentucky Press, 1962), esp. 366–434, and Robert W. Johannsen, *Stephen A. Douglas* (New York: Oxford University Press, 1973), esp. 808–62.

Two key border states that did not secede have been the topic of modern studies. For Maryland, see especially William J. Evitts, *A Matter of Allegiances: Maryland, 1850–1861* (Baltimore: Johns Hopkins University Press, 1974). Also useful is Jean H. Baker, *The Politics of Continuity: Maryland Political Parties from 1858 to 1870* (Baltimore: Johns Hopkins University Press, 1973). The secession crisis in Kentucky is the topic of a fine recent assessment: Harry A. Volz III, "Party, State, and Nation: Kentucky and the Coming of the American Civil War" (Ph.D. dissertation, University of Virginia, 1982). The formation of Kentucky's Union party in early 1861 closely paralleled developments in Virginia, North Carolina, and Tennessee. Yet Kentucky's course after April 15 was very different. The ability of Kentucky Unionists to prevent secession led me to venture some perhaps farfetched hypothetical speculation in the Epilogue.

To understand the one seceding state from the upper South not included in this book, one should consult Jack B. Scroggs, "Arkansas in the Secession Crisis," *Arkansas Historical Quarterly* 12 (1953): 179–224; and especially James M. Woods, *Rebellion and Realignment: Arkansas's Road to Secession* (Fayetteville: University of Arkansas Press, 1987). Woods's able monograph establishes that a Union party could arise in a state that lacked a tradition of effective two-party competition. Upcountry nonslaveowners in Arkansas seized the political initiative in early 1861, just as their counterparts did in the three states I studied.

For a discerning analysis of the prominent roles played by prewar Unionists in the postwar state governments established by Andrew Johnson, see Dan T. Carter, *When the War Was Over: The Failure of Self-Reconstruction in the South* (Baton Rouge: Louisiana State University Press, 1985). James Alex Baggett, "Origins of Upper South Scalawag Leadership," *Civil War History* 29 (Mar. 1983): 53–73, demonstrates that the great majority of native white Republicans in Virginia, West Virginia, North Carolina, and Tennessee during Reconstruction had Whiggish or Douglas antecedents and that 95 percent opposed secession. Baggett's systematic study of relationships between prewar and postwar politial loyalties adds a significant dimension to my analysis of voting behavior during the secession crisis.

My debt to Michael F. Holt's *The Political Crisis of the 1850s* (New York: Wiley, 1978) should be especially apparent in Chapters 2 and 4. Holt insists that the sectional crisis had more to do with symbol than substance—that the territorial issue revolved primarily around powerful intangibles such as equality, right, and honor. Because almost all upper South Unionists as well as many secessionists saw the matter similarly, I find Holt's interpretation very persuasive. J. Mills Thornton and Kenneth Greenberg, in books discussed below, provide similar interpretations of southern grievances.

Several influential studies advance the opposite view—that southerners both wanted and required new slave territory. See Eugene D. Genovese, *The Political Economy of Slavery: Studies in the Economy and Society of the Slave South* (New York: Pantheon, 1965); William L. Barney, *The Road to Secession: A New Perspective on the Old South* (New York: Praeger, 1972); and Robert E. May, *The Southern Dream of a Caribbean Empire, 1854–1861* (Baton Rouge: Louisiana State University Press, 1973). A new study by May, *John A. Quitman: Old South Crusader* (Baton Rouge: Louisiana State University Press, 1985), suggests, however, that both southern expansionism and secession were desperate tactical responses to growing northern power, rather than objectives of intrinsic value.

Holt has also formulated a fresh way to explain why only the lower South embraced immediate secession. His *Political Crisis of the 1850s* shows that the upper and lower South had increasingly divergent political arrangements during the last decade of the antebellum era, with a competitive two-party system surviving only in the upper South. Extreme Southern Rights spokesmen could gain more leverage within the dominant Democratic parties of the lower South, Holt suggests, because the Whiggish Opposition was more or less moribund. But the resilient Opposition parties of the upper South provided a rallying point around which antisecession sentiment could mobilize. This fruitful insight seems to me to explain a great deal about the vitality of upper South Unionism, a judgment shared both by Marc Kruman in his book about North Carolina politics and by Harry Volz in his dissertation on Kentucky. I contend, however, in the first part of Chapter 6, that Virginia, North Carolina, and Tennessee rejected immediate secession not only because they had competitive Opposition parties but also because they had relatively smaller concentrations of plantation slavery than did the states of the lower South. Unlike Holt, I stress the interaction between these two distinguishing upper South characteristics. It is very important to recognize that Opposition parties in the upper South, especially in North Carolina and Tennessee, had substantial support in the low-slaveowning upcountry.

The most original interpretation of late antebellum southern politics has been presented by J. Mills Thornton III. His *Politics and Power in a Slave Society: Alabama, 1800–1860* (Baton Rouge: Louisiana State University Press, 1978) enables the reader to see the world of the mid-nineteenth century through the eyes of the average white Alabamian. Thornton contends that the state was engulfed in a severe crisis long before 1860. Cherished principles of freedom, equality, and autonomy appeared threatened, especially during the 1850s, by the relentless expansion of market relations and commercial agriculture. Alabamians were thus, he judged, prepared to believe the worst once Lincoln was elected. I would ask Thornton, Why was the sense of crisis far less acute in the upper South, even though the pace of economic and social change there was more rapid than in Alabama? Thornton also makes a dubious effort to put the small farmers from the Jacksonian hill counties of northern Alabama at the head of the state's secession bandwagon. He would have been on more solid ground and would not seriously have impaired his main argument had he said that the upcountry acquiesced in secession once it happened, rather than led it.

The relationship between political behavior and the expansion of a market economy in the late antebellum South is also explored in Steven Hahn's book *The Roots of Southern Populism: Yeoman Farmers and the Transformation of the Georgia Backcountry, 1850–1890* (New York: Oxford University Press, 1983), 15–116. Harry L. Watson, author of the already cited *Jacksonian Politics and Community Conflict*, has made a pioneering effort to integrate recent work on antebellum southern social, economic, and political history: "Conflict and Collaboration: Yeomen, Slaveholders, and Politics in the Antebellum South," *Social History* 10 (Oct. 1985): 273–98. Self-sufficient yeomen, in Watson's view, "collaborated in their own transformation" by allowing promoters of a market economy to gain political influence. Resultant "doubts and frustrations" provided fertile soil for the argument that southern rights and liberties were menaced by Black Republicanism (p. 297).

Modern studies of secession in the lower South have repeatedly forced me to think about the differences between the upper and lower South. Contrasting perceptions of reality and increasingly dissimilar political systems clearly divided the two Souths. William L. Barney, *The Secessionist Impulse: Alabama and Mississippi in 1860* (Princeton: Princeton University Press, 1974), focuses on developments in 1860 and 1861. Barney's Alabamians and Mississippians were gripped by fears of racial upheaval amid a Republican-engineered slow strangulation of the slave system. An almost hysterical mob psychology enabled secessionists to carry their cause with a minimum of opposition. Stephen A. Channing, *Crisis of Fear: Secession in South Carolina* (New York: Simon and Schuster, 1970), examines the most estranged southern state, which of course led the secession movement. The runaway racial fears emphasized by Channing flourished in a political environment that so valued consensus and unanimity that it had never produced competing political parties.

Despite my criticisms of it in Appendix III, Michael Johnson's book *Toward a Patriarchal Republic: The Secession of Georgia* (Baton Rouge: Louisiana State University Press, 1977), is an illuminating and gracefully written monograph. The actual building of a potentially antiplanter political party during the secession crisis was, however, much more clearly manifested in the upper South than in Georgia. Walter L. Buenger, *Secession and the Union in Texas* (Austin: University of Texas Press, 1984), shows that regions of Texas settled from the upper South behaved very differently during the secession crisis than regions settled from the lower South. Kenneth S. Greenberg, *Masters and Statesmen: The Political Culture of American Slavery* (Baltimore: Johns Hopkins University Press, 1985), has presented a lucid and original study of secessionist thought, especially on pages 107–46. Greenberg's work, which draws especially on South Carolina sources, leaves unanswered the question of why so many people in the slave states opposed secession before mid-April and instead favored compromise. He hints that the political culture of the upper South was subtly different from that of the lower South (pp. 45–51). An especially persuasive brief analysis of deep South secessionism, emphasizing the interaction of racial and class fears at a moment when control of the federal government appeared to have fallen into hostile hands, may be found in J. William Harris, *Plain Folk and Gentry in a Slave Society: White Liberty and Black Slavery in Augusta's Hinterlands* (Middletown, Conn.: Wesleyan University Press, 1985), 132–39.

Several other modern studies of antebellum southern history have sharpened my awareness of important issues. The significance of honor is explored in Bertram Wyatt-Brown's fascinating book *Southern Honor: Ethics and Behavior in the Old South* (New York: Oxford University Press, 1982). See also Bertram Wyatt-Brown, "Honor and Secession," (paper delivered at the Southern Historical Association Convention, Memphis, Nov. 1982), a revised version of which appears in Bertram Wyatt-Brown, *Yankee Saints and Southern Sinners* (Baton Rouge: Louisiana State University Press, 1985), 183–213. On honor, see also Edward L. Ayers, *Vengeance and Justice: Crime and Punishment in the Nineteenth-Century American South* (New York: Oxford University Press, 1984), 9–33.

William J. Cooper, Jr., has written two complementary studies. In *The South and the Politics of Slavery, 1828–1856* (Baton Rouge: Louisiana State University Press, 1978), he contends that slavery was the paramount issue in antebellum southern politics. Although Cooper minimizes other potent sources of party rivalry, there can be no doubt that antebellum southern politicians did habitually accuse their opponents of unsoundness on the slave issue. The concluding chapter in Cooper's sequel, *Liberty and Slavery: Southern Politics to 1860* (New York: Knopf, 1983), emphasizes the catalytic role of fire-eaters in building support for secession. Of the three states here studied, Virginia had the largest concentration of fire-eaters, Tennessee had the fewest, and pre–

April 15 secession sentiment was strongest in Virginia and weakest in Tennessee. But secessionists were outnumbered even in Virginia. The dramatic reversal in April, when majorities in all three states suddenly embraced secession, occurred because conditional Unionists suddenly discovered that they had to choose sides in a war. They made their decision, even though continuing to regard fire-eaters as deluded fanatics who bore heavy responsibility for the disastrous turn of events.

Three gifted analysts of northern politics have helped me to identify the distinctive characteristics of partisan competition in the late antebellum upper South. As noted in Chapter 2, Ronald P. Formisano's study *The Transformation of Political Culture: Massachusetts Parties, 1790s–1840s* (New York: Oxford University Press, 1983), masterfully describes the evolution from a consensual political order, in which local elites wielded great influence and voting was a "social act," to one in which increasing religious, cultural, and economic diversity provided a basis for greater partisan competition at the local level. Few parts of the antebellum upper South experienced similarly intense changes. Nor did the upper South experience the political convulsion that shook the North during the 1850s, a topic expertly analyzed in William E. Gienapp's prize-winning *The Origins of the Republican Party, 1852–1856* (New York: Oxford University Press, 1987). While a major party realignment took place in the North, political allegiances in the upper South remained frozen in place. But the secession issue, as emphasized especially in Chapter 7 above, had the potential to inaugurate party realignment in the upper South. Walter Dean Burnham's brilliant synthesis, *Critical Elections and the Mainsprings of American Politics* (New York: Norton, 1970), emphasizes the centrality of partisan realignment in American political history.

Methodological Studies

An explanation of statistical techniques employed in Chapter 7 may be found in Appendixes I and II. Key sources regarding the historical analysis of election data include J. Morgan Kousser, "Ecological Regression and the Analysis of Past Politics," *Journal of Interdisciplinary History* 4 (Autumn 1973): 237–62; William H. Flanigan and Nancy H. Zingale, "Relationships among Variables," in Jerome H. Clubb, William H. Flanigan, and Nancy H. Zingale, *Analyzing Electoral History: A Guide to the Study of American Voter Behavior* (Beverly Hills: Sage, 1981), 235–66; William E. Gienapp, "Nebraska, Nativism, and Rum: The Failure of Fusion in Pennsylvania, 1854," *Pennsylvania Magazine of History and Biography* 109 (Oct. 1985): 425–71, esp. 456–57, 464; Gienapp, *Origins of the Republican Party*, 478–81; Allan J. Lichtman, "Critical Election Theory and the Reality of American Presidential Politics, 1916–1940," *American Historical Review* 81 (Apr. 1976): 317–51, esp. 324–26; Peyton McCrary, Clark Miller, and Dale Baum, "Class and Party in the Secession Crisis: Voting Behavior in the Deep South," *Journal of Interdisciplinary History* 8 (Winter 1978): 429–57, esp. 431–35, 449–50. The McCrary team's work, focused on Alabama, Mississippi, and Louisiana, with supplementary information about Texas, provided a constructive model and many helpful hints for analyzing data on the upper South. See the comparisons in Appendix III between my findings on the upper South and McCrary's on the lower South. That appendix contains an assessment of how historians of the secession crisis have used statistical evidence.

Author's Earlier Efforts

At the risk of seeming to conclude on a shameless note of self-aggrandizement, I wish to list the articles from which this book was in part constructed. Segments from all four of the following articles reappear here in revised form, but the originals contain more sustained discussion about certain aspects of the story: Daniel W. Crofts, "The Union Party of 1861 and the Secession Crisis," *Perspectives in American History* 11 (1977–78): 327–76; "A Reluctant Unionist: John A. Gilmer and Lincoln's Cabinet," *Civil War History* 24 (Sept. 1978): 225–49; "James E. Harvey and the Secession Crisis," *Pennsylvania Magazine of History and Biography* 103 (Apr. 1979): 177–95; "Secession Winter: William Henry Seward and the Decision for War," *New York History* 65 (July 1984): 229–56. The article on Seward contains additional comments on historiography of the secession crisis, pages 230–37.

INDEX